Systems Analysis and Design:

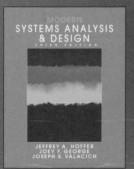

MODERN
SYSTEMS ANALYSIS
& DESIGN
THIRD EDITION

JEFFREY A. HOFFER
JOEY F. GEORGE
JOSEPH S. VALACICH

Hoffer/George/Valacich, *Modern Systems Analysis and Design 3/e*

Marakas, *Systems Analysis and Design: An Active Approach*

Valacich/George/ Hoffer, *Essentials of Systems Analysis & Design 2/e*

Kendall & Kendall, *Systems Analysis an Design 5/e*

Telecomm
Networkin
Business D
Communic

Business Data
Communications Sixth Edition

David A. Stamper • Thomas L. Case

Security:

Panko, *Corporate Computer and Network Security*

Other Titles:

Awad, *Knowledge Management*

Marakas, *Decision Support Systems*

Corporate
Computer and
Network Security

Raymond R. Panko

Decision Support Systems
In the 21st Century
Second Edition

George M. Marakas

ies for
gh your
ll
representative or by email at
CIS Service@prenhall.com

Corporate
Computer and
Network
Security

Raymond R. Panko

University of Hawaii

Prentice Hall
Upper Saddle River,
New Jersey 07458

Library of Congress Cataloging-in-Publication Data

Panko, R. R.
   Corporate computer and network security / Raymond Panko.
      p.   cm.
   Includes bibliographical references and index.
   ISBN 0-13-038471-2
   1. Computer security.   2. Computer networks—Security measures.   3. Electronic data
processing departments—Security measures.   I.Title.

   QA76.9.A25P36 2003
   005.8—dc21

                                                    2002193119

Executive Editor, MIS: David Alexander
Executive Editor, MIS: Bob Horan
Editorial Project Manager: Lori Cerreto
Editorial Assistant: Maat Van Uitert
Publisher: Natalie E. Anderson
Media Project Manager: Joan Waxman
Senior Marketing Manager: Sharon K. Turkovich
Marketing Assistant: Danielle Torio
Managing Editor (Production): Gail Steier de Acevedo
Production Editor: Vanessa Nuttry
Permissions Coordinator: Suzanne Grappi
Associate Director, Manufacturing: Vincent Scelta
Manufacturing Buyer: Natacha St. Hill Moore
Cover Design: Bruce Kenselaar
Composition and Full-Service Project Management: BookMasters, Inc.
Project Manager: Sharon Anderson, BookMasters, Inc.
Printer/Binder: The Maple Vail Book Manufacturing Group

Pearson Education LTD
Pearson Education of Australia Pty. Limited
Pearson Education Singapore, Pte. Ltd.
Pearson Education North Asia Ltd.
Pearson Education Canada, Ltd.
Pearson Educación de Mexico, S.A. de C.V.
Pearson Education—Japan
Pearson Education Malaysia, Pte. Ltd.

PEARSON
Prentice
Hall

10 9 8 7 6 5
ISBN 0-13-038471-2

To Michael Cress
and Hazel Beh

Brief Contents

Contents

Preface for Teachers

TOPICS

Why a security course?
Why this security book?
Teaching this book
Certifications

WHY A SECURITY COURSE?

OK, that's an easy question. Let's face it; security is one area in which businesses today are clamoring for trained graduates. Quite simply, there are not enough information technology (IT) professionals out there who understand the issues involved in bringing computer and network security into corporations. One course won't make students security experts, but it will give them a leg up when it comes to getting hired.

WHY THIS SECURITY BOOK?

If you have decided to teach a security course, which book should you select? Of course, I'd advise you to select this one. Here is why.

Focused on Corporate Information Systems Security

Many textbooks on IT security focus on what computer scientists need to know to develop new security algorithms and products. However, information systems (IS) graduates will not go out and invent new encryption algorithms or firewall-filtering processes. IS graduates will have to go out and purchase the right equipment, install it, configure it, and keep it working. More importantly, graduates have to know how to create security plans and architectures that will reflect their specific companies' needs and that leave their companies without weak links in their security. They also have to know how to manage security on a daily basis and what to do when security breaches occur. Although computer science security information would be nice to know, knowledge of algorithms and firewall design skills is not enough for corporate IS security professionals.

Comprehensive Coverage

Another problem with a lot of security books is that they tend to focus on one security area, such as management, firewalls, or encryption—or on only a few areas. In an introductory course, students need a comprehensive understanding of security issues. This book attempts to give them this broad understanding.

Up-to-Date, Market-Focused Coverage

As discussed later, some security certifications, such as CompTIA's Security+, pride themselves in being vendor neutral. Although this has some theoretical benefits, it is pretty useless in practice. In corporations today, over 90 percent of all computers are Windows based. Any security course that fails to reflect that fact of life is pretty unrealistic. In discussing security algorithms, in turn, we focus on the very few that are widely used instead of deluging the students with vast numbers of algorithms and saying almost nothing about each. In all areas, this book attempts to focus on the state of the market in technology today.

Strong Teacher Support, Including Full PowerPoint Lectures

Security is a tough subject to teach. Most teachers will not have extremely strong backgrounds in security. To help teach the course, there are PowerPoint presentations available for each chapter. These are not just "a few selected figures," these are full lectures you can use in class. Check them out at the book's website, www.prenhall.com/panko or pankosecurity.com.

You can have your students print out the presentations and follow them in class. This will considerably reduce note-taking burdens on students. You are welcome to mirror the presentations on your computer's servers for easier student access.

The website will provide other support for you and for your students in the forms of new information, errata lists, links to open-source and shareware security software that you can demonstrate in class or have your students use, and so forth. In addition, text art, chapter teaching hints, answer keys to text questions, and a test bank in Microsoft Word will be available in a secure, password-protected area of the text's website, www.prenhall.com/panko.

TEACHING THIS BOOK

Graduates and Undergraduates

You can use this book with both undergraduates and graduate students (MS/MIS students and MBA students). For undergraduates, this is a book for a junior/senior elective course, and a networking prerequisite is a really good idea. For MS/MIS and MBA students, you might want to focus somewhat more on technology and management, respectively.

Using the PowerPoint Lectures

As just noted, you can use the PowerPoint presentations for lectures. If you also want to demonstrate some software in class, you might want to open both the software and the PowerPoint presentation. Then, during your PowerPoint presentation, you can alt-tab to the demonstration software at an appropriate point in the presentation. The website has links to some open-source and shareware security software.

Twelve Chapters to Fit Your Term

In a three-credit semester course, each of the 12 chapters is designed to take 1 week (2-1/2 classroom hours) to cover. Given start-up time, a last class wrap-up, and a couple of exams, the book should fit the course fully but comfortably. For a quarter course, you may need to make some adjustments depending on the number of credits in the course.

Prior Networking Knowledge?

Should networking be a prerequisite? I'd suggest it. However, if making a security course a prerequisite is not feasible, you might spend an extra week or so on Chapter 3 and talk more about Ethernet in Chapter 2. I personally require networking as a co-requisite.

In-Chapter Review Questions

The chapters have several types of review questions you can assign as homework.

- ➤ Test-your-understanding questions spread throughout the chapters help students review facts and concepts immediately after reading a section.
- ➤ At the end of the chapter, there are thought questions and sometimes design and troubleshooting questions to help students get a deeper understanding of the material. (In Chapter 5, for example, thought questions have students modify a firewall access control list for a new threat, and in Chapter 10, students examine an integrated log file to analyze an incident.)

I have my students do the review questions for homework (there is a Word for Windows questions file for each chapter at the website.) In class, I have students bring up things they aren't sure of and spend some time on the meaty end-of-chapter questions.

Ethics

Chapter 1 has a dismal fact: Many break-ins, sabotage attacks, and other attacks are done by IT professionals, including security professionals. It is critical to emphasize ethics in dealing with security knowledge.

I personally limit my students' use of hacker software and countermeasure software to my network technologies laboratory, which has an air gap separating it from our main network when dangerous software is in use. Quite simply, there is little way to use such software in general network environments without violating acceptable use policies and often the law. I tell my students that if they are caught "playing with" security software in the open network, I will fail them.

You might even have students sign an ethics statement before having them use security software in a closed environment to emphasize the importance of ethical behavior.

CERTIFICATIONS

One question is whether the book follows a particular certification program so that students can take certification tests after the course. The simple answer is no. However, I did try to cover most areas of the Certified Information Systems

Security Professional (CISSP) exam described later, and the book probably has 90 percent or more of what students would need for a Security+ certification. Focusing completely on a specific certification, however, would mean teaching to the test's idiosyncrasies, and that doesn't seem wise for a general textbook.

CompTIA's Security+

The Computing Technology Industry Association (CompTIA) offers a number of entry-level certifications. It began its Security+ certification about the time this book went to press. The organization's website is CompTIA.com.

Like most CompTIA certifications, Security+ is an entry-level certification that does not have a requirement for prior work experience in the field. At the CompTIA website, you can get a list of the topics that will be covered in the exam. My textbook covers nearly all of them. However, I generally do not cover some of the more-than-obsolete network technologies they include.

That said, is this book a good preparation for Security+? The experiences of my students who have taken the Network+ certification after studying my networking book have indicated that CompTIA certifications generally are reasonable. However, Network+ has a number of idiosyncrasies. For instance, one student, when asked to select a protocol in a multiple-choice question, selected the Internet Protocol. Wrong answer. It was the Transmission Control Protocol. (Hello! Internet *Protocol*!) Although I realize that some UNIX people reserve the word protocol for transport-layer features, that is hardly fair. I'd advise students to pick up a Security+ book and scan through it for specifics they haven't seen in my book.

In addition, Security+ prides itself on being vendor neutral. I have a real problem with that because I don't think you can ignore market realities. I believe that you need to teach both general principles and some vendor-specific information. For instance, Chapter 6 discusses host hardening for Windows and UNIX. The moderate level of vendor-specific detail in the chapter helps students understand what the general concepts mean.

CISSP and SSCP

The most widely recognized security certification is the CISSP certification of the International Information Systems Security Certification Consortium (ISC^2). The consortium also has an entry-level certification, the Systems Security Certified Practitioner (SSCP) certification. Both are described at the (ISC^2) website, isc2.org.

A major problem in getting these certifications is that both require *prior security work experience*. SSCP only requires a year of prior security work, while the CISSP requires 4 years of prior security work (3 if you are a college graduate). These certifications, then, are not for students who have only taken a security course.

Both certifications have common bodies of knowledge (CBKs). In designing this book, I kept the CISSP CBK in mind, and I cover most topics in the CBK.

However, the CISSP CBK is heavily influenced by military security. It has a good deal of material that is specific to military security with its multilevel security, which classifies information as secret, top secret, and so forth. This approach simply does not work in corporations, and I treat military-specific security topics only lightly.

Another set of topics I downplayed was fire safety and equipment redundancy because the IT security professionals I know are not responsible for this area. Finally, I did not go into the details of the systems development life cycle or database technology because IS students get this in other courses.

SANS' GIAC

The gold standard in security certification today is the Global Information Assurance Certification (GIAC) of the SANS (SysAdm, Audit, Network, and Security) Institute. This certification requires multiple in-depth courses. Each course is followed by an exam and typically by a practicum that requires the student to apply knowledge gained during the training. Details of the certification can be found at www.giac.org.

Achieving this gold standard certification, unfortunately, takes a lot of gold. This certification requires students to take a fairly large number of courses at about $2,500 per course, so it is for a security professional working for a company with deep training pockets. The GIAC courses are offered across the United States and selectively in a limited number of other countries.

Although GIAC is a great program, there are some things about it that I feel are modest weaknesses. One is that I believe it is a bit too strongly focused on TCP/IP, UNIX and firewalls, reflecting the strengths of its staff. The material on encryption and LAN security is good but not as strong.

At these prices, hands-on training should be a big part of things. Quite a few GIAC courses now include bring-your-own-notebook training sessions. This notebook should be a dual-boot system with Windows and LINUX.

CISCO's CCSP

Cisco offers the Cisco Certified Security Professional (CCSP®) program for its products.

REVIEWERS

We wish to thank the following faculty for their participation in reviews of this text:

Manish Agrawal, University of South Florida
Michael Allyn Fratto, Syracuse University
Sunil Hazari, University of Maryland
Vincent LeVeque, University of California at Los Angeles
Richard McCarthy, Central Connecticut State University
Gregory B. Newby, University of North Carolina at Chapel Hill
Harry L Reif, James Madison University
Ram Sriram, Georgia State University
Wayne Summers, New Mexico Highlands University
George Wright, Loyola College

About the Author

Dr. Raymond R. Panko is a professor of information technology management in the College of Business Administration at the University of Hawaii. He received his doctorate from Stanford University, graduating with a 4.0 GPA. He received his B.S. in physics summa cum laude and his M.B.A. from Seattle University. His doctoral dissertation was conducted under contract to the Office of the President of the United States.

Before coming to the University of Hawaii, he was a project manager at Stanford Research Institute (now SRI International), where he did extensive research on e-mail and videoconferencing, and where he worked with Doug Engelbart, inventor of the mouse and many groupwork innovations.

Among his consulting and research clients have been the Defense Advanced Research Projects Agency (DARPA); NSF; National Institutes of Standards and Technology; AT&T; the Xerox Palo Alto Research Center; Western Union Telegraph Company; British Post Office; Bell Canada; Trans-Canada Telephone System; Fujitsu; Hughes Aircraft Space Division; RCA; Royal Dutch Shell; The Council of European Post and Telecommunications Administrations (CEPT); RCA; 20th Century-Fox; ABC; CBS; NBC; HBO; NASA; NSF; Congressional Office of Technology Assessment; Secretary of Health, Education, and Welfare; U.S. Army Development and Readiness Command; U.S. Army Ballistics Research Laboratory; Naval Electronics Laboratory Command; A.C. Nielson DATAQUEST; and Communications Studies and Planning (United Kingdom).

In addition to publishing in such research journals as *MIS Quarterly*, the *Communications of the ACM*, the *IS Audit and Control Journal*, the *Journal of Management Information Systems*, the *Journal of the Association of Information Systems*, and *Decision Support Systems*, he has written several book chapters and encyclopedia articles (including three on security in the forthcoming *Internet Encyclopedia*), and he has written two earlier textbooks in end user computing and in networking and telecommunications, including *Business Data Networks and Telecommunications*, Fourth edition (Prentice Hall, 2003).

Ray is an avid racer and surfer in six-place Hawaiian outrigger canoes.

CHAPTER 1

A FRAMEWORK

Learning Objectives

By the end of this chapter, you should be able to discuss:

- Trends in security incidents.
- Types of attackers.
- Types of attacks and defenses.
- Why security is primarily a management issue, not a technology issue.
- The importance of top-to-bottom commitment and comprehensive security.
- The core security goals: confidentiality, integrity, and availability (CIA).
- The Plan-Protect-Respond (PPR) cycle.
- How corporate IT security is distinguished from military security.

CORPORATIONS AT RISK

As its title suggests, this chapter presents a framework for thinking about security threats and security management in corporations. We will flesh out this framework in the rest of the book. We will begin by looking at the growing severity of threats facing corporations.

CSI/FBI Computer Crime and Security Surveys

Figure 1-1 shows some key 1997 and 2002 findings from the annual *CSI/FBI Computer Crime and Security Survey,* which receives questionnaires from about 500 U.S. security professionals each year. The survey is conducted by the Computer Security Institute (www.gocsi.com).

Although the survey methodology is imperfect, this is the best data we have on the relative frequencies and severities of various security threats. The best data in the study probably are the prevalence data, which report whether the respondent's company suffered at least one successful attack in the threat category. Unfortunately, this does not indicate whether the respondent's firm suffered from one successful attack in the category or many.

More caution has to be used with loss estimates; only a fraction of the respondents who said that their firms experienced a successful attack in a category were willing to estimate losses, and loss estimation is notoriously difficult to do. Still, the broad patterns in this data are so important that they cannot be ignored.

The Overall Picture

The two most important trends in the figure are that security incidents in which attackers are successful are almost universal and that corporations face a broad spectrum of threats.

Ninety percent of the 2002 respondents cited at least one incident, and although the table does not show it, many listed multiple incidents, sometimes ten or more.

The CSI/FBI survey does not rate attacks by severity, but a survey of 148 U.K. firms by the Confederation of British Industry found that two-thirds had experienced a "serious" cybercrime in the previous year.[1]

Also, corporations face a broad spectrum of threats. The threat environment resembles multiple poisons, any of which can make a corporation seriously sick.

High-Prevalence Threats

Two incident categories are experienced by a majority of companies each year: virus attacks and laptop thefts.

Virus Attacks   Eighty-five percent of the respondents reported at least one *virus* incident in 2002, a figure that has remained more or less constant since the survey began. At the time of this writing, one e-mail message in every 200 to 400 contains a virus, and

---

[1]   Laura Rohde, "Study: Many U.K. Businesses Prey to Cybercrime," CNN.com, August 30, 2001. www.cnn.com/2001/TECH/internet/08/30/uk.cybercrime.idg/.

Had at Least One Security Incident in This Category (May have had several)	Percent Reporting an Incident 1997	Percent Reporting an Incident 2002	Number Reporting Quantified Losses 2002	Average Reported Annual Loss per Firm (Thousands) 1997	Average Reported Annual Loss per Firm (Thousands) 2002
Any Incident		90%			
Viruses	82%	85%	178	$ 76	$ 283
Laptop Theft	58%	65%	134	$ 38	$ 89
Denial of Service	24%	40%	62	$ 77	$ 297
System Penetration	20%	40%	59	$132	$ 226
Unauthorized Access by Insiders	40%	38%	15	NA	NA
Theft of Intellectual Property	20%	20%	26	$954	$6,571
Financial Fraud	12%	12%	25	$958	$4,632
Sabotage	14%	8%	28	$164	$ 541
Telecom Fraud	27%	9%	16	NA	NA
Telecom Eavesdropping	11%	6%	5	NA	NA
Active Wiretap	3%	1%	0	NA	NA

Survey conducted by the Computer Security Institute (www.gocsi.com).
Based on replies from 503 U.S. Computer Security Professionals.
If fewer than 20 firms reported quantified dollar losses for a threat, loss data for the threat are not shown.

Figure 1-1   CSI/FBI Computer Crime and Security Survey Results

this fraction is rising fairly rapidly.[2] These figures are even more alarming when you realize that 90 percent of all firms implement antivirus software.[3]

Almost 40 new viruses and worms are found each day, but only three or four become prevalent "in the wild."[4] Even fewer viruses and worms become widespread, but those that do can cause billions of dollars in damages. Code Red in 2001 was estimated to do $2.5 billion in damages, and the earlier Melissa virus produced an astounding $6.7 billion in damages.

[2] MessageLabs. www.messagelabs.com. MessageLabs screens e-mail for many client organizations. The company forecasts that one e-mail in ten will contain a virus in 2007 if trends continue.
[3] 2002 CSI/FBI Computer Crime and Security Survey, Computer Security Institute, www.gocsi.com.
[4] Laura Rohde, "Security Company Releases 'Top 20' Viruses for 2001," IDG News Service, November 28, 2001. www.idg.net.

Laptop Thefts   *Laptop thefts* are less prevalent than viruses but are still experienced by a majority of firms. In addition, the figures in the table for laptop thefts probably are understated because many firms do not have a central way to report laptop losses.[5]

Perspectives   Although prevalence data in these two categories has been static or growing only moderately, average reported losses per firm have been growing rapidly. This indicates that many firms are now experiencing multiple incidents in these categories each year.

Clearly, firms need to have strong security programs for virus attacks and laptop theft. As just noted, most already have virus defense programs, but these obviously are not working perfectly. Laptop security programs are unfortunately much less common.

Traditional Hacker Attacks

Systems Penetration (Hacking)   Hollywood movies often show hackers breaking into corporate computers to steal information or to do other damage. Hacking is also called **systems penetration**.

Figure 1-1 shows that systems penetration (hacking) attacks have roughly doubled in both prevalence and losses in the seven years the survey has been active. These trends are disturbing because 89 percent of the respondents said that their firms have firewalls, which are designed to prevent system penetration. In addition, deliberate penetration tests have shown for many years that most successful system penetrations go unnoticed, so the system penetration percentages shown in the table probably are considerably understated.

Denial-of-Service Attacks   When hackers cannot break into a system, they may vandalize it with a *denial-of-service (DoS)* attack designed to prevent legitimate users from using the system. A growing number of attackers do not even attempt system penetration. Instead, a denial-of-service attack is their main goal. Since denial-of-service estimates were first collected in 1998, prevalence has doubled, and average loss per firm has quadrupled. One website hosting company received about one major DoS attack monthly in 2002.[6]

In February of 2000, a number of major firms were subjected to devastatingly effective DoS attacks that blocked each of their e-commerce systems for hours at a time. Victims of this series of attacks included CNN.com, eBay, Yahoo.com, Amazon.com, Dell.com, eTrade, and other major firms. At first thought to be the work of an elite hacker, the attack was instead found to be the work of a 15-year-old hacker in Canada, who received a sentence of only a few months in a juvenile detention center.

---

[5]   Corroborating the survey's data, Safeware (www.safeware.com), an insurance company, paid claims on 591,000 notebook computers stolen in 2001, an increase from the 387,000 stolen the previous year and 208,000 in 1995. Note that these are only claims paid by a single insurance company. Note that this high figure does *not* include stolen computers that were uninsured or insured by other companies. In addition, between 1997 and 2001, the British Defense Ministry officers lost an average of 51 notebooks per year. *Most* contained classified information. Michelle Delio, "The Spy Who Lost Me," *Wired Magazine*, April 17, 2001. www.wired.com/news/politics/0,1283,43088,00.html.

[6]   Deborah Radcliff, "Denying Network Service," *Computerworld*, July 15, 2002. computerworld.com/securitytopics/security/story/0,10801,72649,00.html.

One company has even been put out of business by DoS attacks. This was Cloud Nine, a small Internet service provider in England. Anonymous attackers repeatedly hit the company with denial-of-service attacks. Cloud Nine ceased business when it realized that the cost of repairs would bankrupt the company.

Unauthorized Access by Insiders   The *unauthorized access by insiders* category is difficult to discuss because it represents a very broad spectrum of transgressions, from the trivial to the devastating. In addition, very large attacks in this category may be reported in other threat categories. However, it is clear that unauthorized insider access to computer systems is fairly common and a credible threat.

Overall, traditional hacker attacks and related attacks by both insiders and outsiders are important threats that need to be taken seriously. As just discussed, firms are erecting firewall and intrusion detection system defenses, but these are only partially effective.

Low-Prevalence, High-Impact Attacks

Three attacks—*financial fraud, theft of proprietary information (trade secrets),* and *sabotage*—are relatively uncommon and so may tend to be overlooked in security planning. However, these attacks do have significant probabilities of occurring. More importantly, losses from these attacks can be devastating. Average losses per firm reporting losses in these categories ranged from a half million dollars to over six million dollars in 2002. Such threats cannot be overlooked.

Financial Fraud   When financial fraud hits, the damage can be very large. For example, two accountants at Cisco Systems used computer access to issue themselves $8 million worth of Cisco stock.[7]

Theft of Trade Secrets   The theft of trade secrets (proprietary information) can also be damaging. In one case, a paralegal employee in a law firm copied the company's plans for a plaintiff in an important court case.[8] These plans cost several million dollars to develop. He attempted to sell the plans to one of the firms representing the defendants.

Sabotage   In sabotage, the attacker deletes files or damages hardware. In one case,[9] Patrick McKenna, a former employee, broke into his company's database and deleted hundreds of computer files and altered billing records. He then sent a damaging e-mail in the name of the firm to over one hundred of his firm's customers.

---

[7]   U.S. Department of Justice, "Former Cisco Systems Accountants Sentenced for Unauthorized Access to Computer Systems to Illegally Issue $8 Million in Cisco Stock to Themselves," November 26, 2001. www.cybercrime.gov/Osowski_TangSent.htm.

[8]   U.S. Department of Justice, "Manhattan Paralegal Sentenced for Theft of Litigation Trial Plan," January 30, 2002. www.cybercrime.gov/farrajSentence.htm.

[9]   U.S. Department of Justice, "Hampton Man Convicted and Sentenced for Hacking into Former Employer's Computer Server," June 18, 2001. www.cybercrime.gov/McKennaSent.htm.

Uncommon, Low-Impact Attacks

Although Hollywood often portrays eavesdropping through wiretaps or the capture of messages as they pass over telecommunications facilities, these threats are extremely uncommon. So is telecommunications fraud. While due diligence is needed in these areas, existing protections generally are working—although it is likely that most attackers are simply focusing on easier ways to attack corporations instead of using these more difficult attacks.

Website Attacks

The 2002 survey asked more in-depth questions about attacks on websites. Thirty-eight percent of respondents reported at least one unauthorized use or misuse of a corporate website. Thirty-nine percent who reported an incident reported 10 or more incidents. Of the respondents who reported a website incident, 70 percent experienced vandalism (usually, webpage defacement), 55 percent experienced denial-of-service attacks, 12 percent experienced the theft of transfer information, and 6 percent experienced financial fraud. These numbers are extremely disturbing.[10]

Comprehensive Security Programs

In general, the media tend to focus on flashy threats, such as hacking into servers. However, Figure 1-1 shows that companies need to take a much broader view of the many diverse threats facing them.[11] A broad security program is needed if firms are to be reasonably safe from heavy attacks.

Media Myopia

Another danger in reading the popular and trade media is that the media normally only report *new* threats. Once an attack becomes commonplace, the press typically stops talking about it—even when it continues to grow as a threat. You must realize that neither the popular press nor the trade press is giving you a good picture of the security threats facing corporations.

TEST YOUR UNDERSTANDING

1. a) In the CSI/FBI Survey, what percentage of corporations experienced at least one security incident? b) Name the two highest-prevalence threats, which are experienced by a majority of firms. c) Describe trends for the three traditional hacker attacks. d) Describe trends in the three low-prevalence, high-impact attacks. e) Why do you think companies may have a difficult time planning for low-prevalence, high-impact attacks? f) Describe trends for wiretapping, telecommunications eavesdropping, and telecommunications fraud. g) Describe data on website attacks. h) Does media coverage typically mirror the importance of threats?

---

[10] Data on website defacements are maintained online by Alldas (defaced.alldas.org), which noted that website defacements jumped from four thousand to twenty-three thousand from 2000 to 2001. Current (2002) data indicate that although 50 percent to 60 percent of all defaced sites run Windows, UNIX (including LINUX) sites are frequently defaced.

[11] The survey also asks about insider abuse of network access, such as wasting time surfing the Web or sending inappropriate e-mails. However, this is not a normal security concern. We will look at such matters in Chapter 12, however.

Other Empirical Attack Data

Although the CSI/FBI surveys give the most comprehensive picture of security threats, the survey methodology limits their accuracy. Many attacks are not detected in the average firm, and respondents must have answered quite a few questions by estimation. Fortunately, there are several empirical sources of attack data, as Figure 1-2 shows. Although each covers only some attacks, they offer more reliable data than the CSI/FBI survey because they deal with objective data.

Riptech Analysis of Firewall Logs

Firewalls screen incoming packets, dropping attack packets. When firewalls drop packets, they note the details of each dropped packet in a log file. Riptech (www.riptech.com) analyzed 5.5 billion firewall log entries from 300 firms between July and December 2001. They identified 128,678 attacks—an annual rate of 1,000 per firm.

Riptech then *excluded* Code Red and Nimda virus/worm attacks, which accounted for 63 percent of all attacks before the exclusion. Of the remaining attacks, 39 percent appeared to target the victim firm deliberately, while the rest appeared to be random attacks based on the firm's IP address range. With Code Red and Nimda attacks added back in, an overwhelming majority of all attacks were random.

In July 2002, Riptech examined data from 400 of its customers in detail. It noted that only about 1 percent of attacks were sophisticated aggressive attacks. However, when sophisticated aggressive attacks did appear, they were 26 times more likely to do severe damage than moderately sophisticated aggressive attacks. Twenty-three percent of all firms experienced at least one sophisticated aggressive attack in the first 6 months of 2002. Consequently, companies need to be alert for sophisticated aggressive attacks.

SecurityFocus Data

SecurityFocus is a managed security firm. In 2001, it collected data from 10,000 customers.[12] These companies experienced a staggering 129 million network scanning probe packets (13,000 per firm). They also experienced 29 million website attack packets (3,000 per firm) and 6 million denial-of-service attack packets (600 per firm).

Microsoft Windows accounted for 31 million operating system–specific attack packets, followed by 22 million UNIX (including LINUX) attack packets and 7 million attack packets on Cisco's IOS (Cisco's operating system for routers and switches). All popular operating systems, in other words, are attacked frequently.

U.K. Department of Trade and Industry

In early 2002, the U.K. Department of Trade and Industry had PriceWaterhouseCoopers survey firms in the United Kingdom. They found that two-thirds of most firms' most serious incident cost less than $15,000 to resolve. However, 4 percent cost more than $725,000.

---

[12] Sam Costello, "RSA: Security in 2002 Worse Than 2001, Exec Says," CNN.com, February 25, 2002. www.cnn.com/2002/TECH/internet/02/25/2002.security.idg/index.html.

RIPTECH

Analyzed 5.5 billion firewall log entries in 300 firms in 5-month period
Detected 128,678 attacks—an annual rate of 1,000 per firm
23 percent of all firms experienced a highly aggressive attack in a 6-month period
Only 39 percent of attacks *after* viruses were removed were directed at individual firms
Only 1 percent of all attacks are sophisticated aggressive attacks
However, sophisticated aggressive attacks are 26 times more likely to do severe damage
   than even moderately sophisticated aggressive attacks.

SECURITYFOCUS

Data from 10,000 firms in 2001
Attack Frequency
   129 million network scanning packets (13,000 per firm)
   29 million website attack packets (3,000 per firm)
   6 million denial-of-service attack packets (600 per firm)
Attack Targets
   31 million Windows-specific attacks
   22 million UNIX/LINUX attacks
   7 million Cisco IOS attacks
   All operating systems are attacked!

U.K. DEPARTMENT OF TRADE AND INDUSTRY

Two-thirds of U.K. firms surveyed lost less than $15,000 from their worst incident
However, 4 percent lost more than $725,000

MESSAGELABS

One in every 200 to 400 e-mail messages is infected
Most e-mail users are sent infected e-mail several times each year
The percentage of e-mails that are infected is rising

HONEYNET PROJECT

Networks set up for adversaries to attack
Windows 98 PC with open shares and no password compromised five times in 4 days
LINUX PCs took 3 days on average to compromise

Figure 1-2 Other Empirical Attack Data

MessageLabs

MessageLabs is an antivirus outsourcing firm, which filters e-mail for viruses before its customers receive the mail. The company presents data on the rate of virus infections at its website, MessageLabs.com. As noted earlier, the infection rate varies daily from about one in 200 messages to one in 400, as noted earlier. This means that most users can expect to be hit by mail containing viruses several times each year. Furthermore, the percentage of e-mails that are infected is rising steadily.

The Honeynet Project

The Honeynet Project (project.honeynet.org) sets up real computer systems, then watches as hackers attack them. The goal is to understand hacker activity and methods.

When the Honeynet Project set up a Windows 98 PC with shares enabled and without passwords, the PC was compromised five times in 4 days. Although this was not the default configuration, it is a common configuration when people set up home networks.

When the project set up several Red Hat 6.2 LINUX PC servers *with default configurations,* in turn, it took only 3 days on average to compromise each computer. So LINUX is not the magical cure for security that some have claimed.

TEST YOUR UNDERSTANDING

2. a) In the Riptech data, how many times is the average firm attacked each year? b) What percent of all firms experienced a highly aggressive attack in the first half of 2002? c) Are most attacks targeted at specific firms? d) Why are sophisticated aggressive attacks especially dangerous? e) In the SecurityFocus data, how many times is the average firm probed each year? f) How many times is the average firm's website attacked each year? g) How many times is the average firm subjected to denial-of-service attack packets? h) Which operating systems are attacked frequently? i) In the Honeynet Project data, how quickly were Windows 98 PCs with open shares and without passwords attacked? j) Were LINUX PC servers safe from attack?

Tomorrow Will Be Worse

Although the situation today is bad, today's threat environment should not be the basis for planning. Planning must look 2 to 5 years into the future because of the lead time needed to install protection and train personnel. In 2 to 5 years, threats are likely to be far worse.

Growing Attack Frequency

Most obviously, attacks will increase in frequency. Figure 1-3 shows the number of **security incidents** reported to the CERT Coordination Center (www.cert.org). A CERT is a computer emergency response team whose job is to deal with security incidents.

Obviously, the number of incidents has been rising rapidly. In recent years, we have seen roughly a doubling in incidents each year. This means that in 2 years, we can expect four times as many incidents. In 5 years, we can expect about *thirty* times as many incidents as we see today. Planning for the future must assume a threat model with far higher incident frequency than we see today.

GROWING INCIDENT FREQUENCY

Incidents reported to the Computer Emergency Response Team/Coordination Center
  1997: 2,134
  1998: 3,474 (75% growth from the year before)
  1999: 9,859 (164% growth)
  2000: 21,756 (121% growth)
  2001: 52,658 (142% growth)
  Tomorrow?

GROWING RANDOMNESS IN VICTIM SELECTION

In the past, large firms were targeted
Now, targeting is increasingly random
No more security through obscurity for small firms and individuals

GROWING MALEVOLENCE

Most early attacks were not malicious
Malicious attacks are becoming the norm

GROWING ATTACK AUTOMATION

Attacks are increasingly automated, rather than humanly directed
Essentially, viruses and worms are attack robots that travel among computers
Attack many computers in minutes or hours

Figure 1-3   Attack Trends (Study Figure)

Growing Randomness in Victim Selection

Most early attacks were aimed at specific firms, usually large firms. Although smaller firms sometimes were attacked, especially by disgruntled employees or ex-employees, most small firms could depend somewhat on "**security through obscurity**."

However, the majority of attacks today are the equivalent of shooting guns into crowds. Every computer attached to the Internet must have an IP address. A large and rapidly growing number of attackers now scan large numbers of randomly selected IP addresses and attack the computers they find at these addresses indiscriminately. This practice of random attacks has turned the threat distribution on its head. Poorly protected home computers probably are at greatest risk, followed by small firms with minimal security protection.

Today, IT threats are equal-opportunity menaces.

Growing Malevolence

Until recently, most Internet attacks were not strongly malicious. Many attackers who broke into corporate computers consciously attempted to avoid doing harm during break-ins, although what they regarded as "not harm" was often unsettling.

More recently, however, we have seen rapidly growing readiness and even eagerness to do damage during attacks. Viruses and their kin increasingly carry **malicious payloads** that damage the data and software on computers they infect. We also have seen rapid growth in denial-of-service attacks that vandalize networks by making them unavailable to users. Remote network attacks seem to give many attackers a sense of disassociation from the victim that makes them heedless to the economic and personal harm they inflict.

Today, many companies have a false sense of security created by the relatively benign nature of many of today's attacks. This Pollyanna view of attacks must not be allowed to dominate planning for tomorrow's ever more malevolent attacks.

Growing Attack Automation

Viruses and related attacks are not merely a category of attack. They represent a trend toward **attack automation**—the creation of software robots that spread rapidly using exploits and approaches formerly used by individual attackers. While individual attackers can only do limited damage, these new mass automation robots can do billions of dollars in damages in a few hours. Today's rather simple viruses and worms are not representative of the sophisticated software attack robots we will see in the next few years.

TEST YOUR UNDERSTANDING

3. a) Describe the four ways in which tomorrow's security threats will be worse than today's. b) Should we plan based upon current experiences? Explain.

ATTACKERS

When we think of human crime, we think of low-life burglars or white-collar criminals. When we think of computer crime, we tend to think of hackers with super-human knowledge of networks. However, the universe of attackers is much broader than this.

Elite Hackers

Hacking

Hacking is intentionally accessing (using) a computer without authorization or beyond authorized permission. Note that even if someone has an account and password, they may not use it in an unauthorized way. In the Washington Leung case described in Chapter 1a (Example 2), Leung was given passwords by his employer but certainly was not authorized to use these passwords to attempt to frame a fellow co-worker.

Hacking is intentionally accessing (using) a computer without authorization or beyond authorized permission.

Once a hacker gets into a computer, he or she can read sensitive files, delete or modify files, and change the system to make it easier to attack in the future. If the

ELITE HACKERS

Hacking: intentional access without authorization or in excess of authorization

Cracking versus hacking

Technical expertise and dogged persistence

Use attack scripts to automate actions, but this is not the essence of what they do

Ethical hackers or white hat hackers

   Invited hackers

   Hack but report weaknesses

   Hack but with code of ethics

      Codes of conduct are often amoral

      "Do no harm," but delete log files, destroy security settings, etc.

      Distrust of evil businesses and government

Deviants and hacker groups

VIRUS WRITERS AND RELEASERS

Virus writers versus virus releasers

Only releasing viruses is punishable

SCRIPT KIDDIES

Use prewritten attack scripts (kiddie scripts)

Viewed as "lamers" and "script kiddies"

Large numbers make dangerous

Noise of kiddie script attacks masks more sophisticated attacks

CRIMINALS

Many attackers are ordinary garden-variety criminals

Credit card and identity theft

Stealing trade secrets (intellectual property)

Extortion

CORPORATE EMPLOYEES

Have access and knowledge

Financial theft

Theft of trade secrets (intellectual property)

Sabotage

Consultants and contractors

IT and security staffs are biggest danger

CYBERTERRORISM AND CYBERWAR

New level of danger

Infrastructure destruction

   Attacks on IT infrastructure

   Use of IT to attack physical infrastructure (energy, banks, etc.)

Simultaneous multi-pronged attacks

Cyberterrorists by terrorist groups versus cyberwar by national governments

Amateur information warfare may be highly effective

Figure 1-4 Framework for Attackers (Study Figure)

hacking is intentional, and if a sufficient amount of damage is done, hacking is a crime in the United States and in many other countries.

Hacking Versus Cracking

Many hackers prefer to distinguish between hacking and cracking. In this distinction, hacking is performing any difficult computer task with exceptional expertise, as in, "Last night, I hacked out a solution to that e-mail problem we haven't been able to solve all week." **Cracking** in this distinction is what we have defined as hacking—illegal access. However, the broad usage of the term *hacking* seems to favor the terminology we introduced in the last paragraph.

There is one context, however, in which we will use the term cracking. This is *password cracking*—the guessing of passwords using password cracking software. We will see password cracking in Chapter 2.

Technical Excellence and Dogged Persistence

In movies and on television, we often see elite hackers break into highly secure computers on well-protected networks. It often takes them only a few seconds to do, and sometimes they break in by guessing only two or three passwords.

As an example of Hollywood hype, the movie *Swordfish* begins with a rant against the lack of realism in Hollywood movies. Later, a hacker breaks into a highly secure military site protected by "128-bit DES encryption." This attack takes only a minute despite a gun being held to the hacker's head and other distractions. When asked how he performed this miracle, the hacker eventually said that he was just working on the basis of intuition.

Nonsense. Although elite hackers do exist, they rarely break into well-protected systems quickly or easily. Attacking a well-defended system often takes days, weeks, or even months of hard work. By the time a hack is made—if it can be made at all—the hacker may know as much about the network and victim computer as the network administrator does.

Some students in security courses ask to play with packaged hacker software to "get a feel" for how hackers work. In addition to almost certainly being illegal,[13] using hacking tools this way would completely miss the point that hacking is about skill and dogged persistence, not just tools.

"White Hat" Hackers

Some hackers call themselves "**white hat hackers**." They break into corporate networks but tell network administrators or the vendor of the security system they compromised how they broke into the network and, preferably, how to prevent this attack in the future. They avoid doing damage if possible and never extort the company buy telling it that they will hack again unless they are paid.

---

[13]   It is nearly impossible to use these tools in a public or university network without breaking the law. They should only be used in isolated laboratories with prior written permission and an approved contract describing exactly what will be done.

Hackers who hack but then report vulnerabilities argue that they perform a valuable function by finding new vulnerabilities and alerting companies who are vulnerable. However, the companies who are hacked in the process point out that they can never tell what else the hacker has done in their systems.

In contrast, black hat hackers hack to do damage or just to look around; in either case, they do not report vulnerabilities they find. In the middle, gray hat hackers switch back and forth between white hat hacking and black hat hacking.

Hacking With a Code of Ethics   In some cases, people calling themselves ethical hackers say that it is all right to break into a network if they follow certain ethical principles. A number of books have reported on studies of elite hackers and personal experiences with elite hackers.[14] In many cases, these books leave a relatively positive impression of elite hackers as being motivated primarily for the love of learning and as subscribing to strict **hacker codes of ethics**.

In many cases, elite hackers actually do subscribe to codes of ethics, one tenet of which often is, "Do no harm." However, if you look closely at published codes, you see that even the most benign codes approve changing security logs and disabling corporate security protections as a way of protecting the hacker's identity.

They also argue that it is ethical to read sensitive corporate information, despite the fact that if a corporation knows that a critical plan or product design is compromised, it may have to take expensive actions.

Many of these codes, furthermore, are rife with diatribes about the evil nature of corporations, which supposedly have perverted computer technology in the name of profit, and about the corruptness of governments. Businesses and governments are also viewed as open to legitimate attack because their security is "lame." It is as if someone with a "mere deadbolt lock" on each door is just asking to have people break into his or her house.

Overall, many of these hackers with codes of ethics at best have questionable ethics. And, of course, criminal codes of conduct are often violated.

White Hat Hacking, Ethical Hacking, and Criminality

In any case, the laws that deal with hacking typically do not ask about the motivation for hacking. The U.S. Federal criminal code, for instance, makes hacking illegal if the hacker intended to break in and does substantial damage. It does not even specify the damage was intentional, and there is nothing regarding the hacker's motivation in breaking in.

Deviants and Hacker Groups

Psychologically, most elite hackers are what psychologists call **deviants**. They have different values and beliefs than society as a whole. Many genuinely believe that what they are doing is perfectly fine and even beneficial to society because it keeps stupid corporations on their toes. In addition, hackers tend to communicate with one another

---

[14]   The following are examples. Michelle Slatalla and Joshua Quittner, *Masters of Deception: The Gang That Ruled Cyberspace*, HarperPerennial: New York, 1995. Bruce Stirling, *The Hacker Crackdown*, Bantam: New York, 1992. Paul A. Taylor, *Hackers*, Routledge: London, 1999.

extensively online. This allows them to brag about exploits to increase their social standing, exchange information, and reinforce their deviant beliefs.

Tenuous Grasps on Reality

The deviant nature of many hackers sometimes makes them believe absurd things. For example, one young hacker defaced a firm's website and later notified the administrator of the exploit. In exchange for a notebook computer, he said, he would tell the administrator how to fix the problem. Amazingly, when the firm told him that he would have to sign a consultant's agreement, he agreed, supplying large amounts of personal information. When the UPS truck arrived, the men in brown really were FBI agents. The hacker was surprised.

TEST YOUR UNDERSTANDING

4. a) What is hacking? b) Are hackers distinguished from other attackers by their skill or by their use of attack software? c) Describe the motivations of elite hackers. d) Distinguish between white hat hackers, black hat hackers, and gray hat hackers. e) What are ethical hackers? f) Are white hat hackers and ethical hacking defenses against criminal prosecution?

Virus Writers and Releasers

A special place in hell is reserved for virus writers who write viruses they intend to release or do release "in the wild." However, simply writing a virus is not a crime in most countries. To commit a crime, you must *release* the virus into the world. Many virus writers post their viruses on the Internet but disingenuously add notes warning people not to release them.[15] Tracking the spread of a virus to determine who released it usually is impossible, and even when virus releasers are tracked down or suspected, a paucity of legal sanctions often prevents their prosecution or gives them only a slap on the wrist. For example, although the creator and releaser of the devastating Melissa virus of 1999 was caught and pleaded guilty, he only received a sentence of 20 months in prison and was fined only $5,000.[16] Part of this light sentence was due to his cooperation with authorities after capture.

TEST YOUR UNDERSTANDING

5. a) What do you think are the motivations of virus writers? b) Virus releasers? (You will need to draw your own conclusions to answer these questions.)

Script Kiddies

To make their lives easier, elite hackers often develop software tools to help them automate repetitive aspects of hacking. They call these programs **scripts**. They tend to exchange these scripts among themselves.

---

[15] To their credit, some virus writers merely describe a virus they created and do not give enough detail for non-expert virus writers to exploit.

[16] U.S. Department of Justice, "Creator of Melissa Computer Virus Sentenced to 20 Months in Federal Prison," May 1, 2001. www.cybercrime.gov/melissaSent.htm.

Low Status, High Threat

Unfortunately, they also tend to make attack scripts available to large numbers of relatively unskilled hackers. Although elite hackers dismiss these people as **lamers** and **script kiddies**, attack scripts allow millions of attackers around the world to initiate attacks against corporations. As the saying goes, "Never underestimate the power of stupid people in large numbers"—especially if they are armed with automated attack scripts. For example, as noted earlier the DoS attacks on CNN.com, eBay, Yahoo.com, Amazon.com, Dell.com, eTrade, and other major firms in 2000 were carried out by a 15-year-old script kiddie.

Creating a Smoke Screen

Having scripts does not guarantee penetration, but it at least creates a high volume of attacks that makes it difficult for firms to know when serious attacks by more skilled attackers are underway.

Growing Lethality

In addition, these scripts are growing in lethality. While hacking into a server is difficult, vandalizing a server or network is comparatively easy. Script kiddies with modest skills conduct many of the denial-of-service attacks discussed later in this chapter.

Difficulty of Prosecution

Many script kiddies are under legal age and so face only juvenile prosecution if the authorities are willing to prosecute them at all. Consequently, many corporations are reluctant to press legal charges and expose themselves to embarrassing publicity with little hope of punishing the perpetrator.

Virus Kiddie Scripts

Scripts are also available for virus writing. While script-based hacking attacks are only occasionally fruitful, virus-writing scripts give millions of people the ability to create tools of mass destruction.

TEST YOUR UNDERSTANDING

      6.   a) Who are script kiddies? b) What makes them dangerous? c) Why are corporations often unwilling to prosecute script kiddies?

With Criminal Intent

Garden-Variety Criminals

While many hackers may be driven by curiosity rather than criminal intent, the lure of money is strong. Many attackers are simply garden-variety criminals motivated by nothing more than greed.

Credit Card and Identity Theft

Perhaps the most common IT-based crime is the theft of credit card numbers and other personal identity information. There is a thriving online market for valid credit card numbers, and criminal **carders** can rack up thousands of dollars in charges with a single credit card number. Often, online merchants do a poor job protecting the credit card numbers in their data files.

Credit card number thefts can be massive. Near the beginning of 1999, the hacker "Maxim" allegedly broke into CD Universe and stole 300,000 credit card numbers.[17] While most credit card number thefts are smaller, they typically number in the thousands.

If the attacker can gather even more information about people, he or she can perform **identity theft**—using personal information to set up new credit card numbers, buy a car, or do many other things. By the time the victims discover that their identities have been stolen, their credit ratings may be in shambles, and repair may take several painful months.

Stealing Trade Secrets (Intellectual Property)

Corporations have many **trade secrets** (also called **intellectual property**)[18], ranging from formulas for products to strategic corporate plans. As noted earlier, thieves love to steal trade secrets because they can profit from them.

In other cases, **spies** employed by competitors or (increasingly) national governments steal trade secrets for competitive purposes. Corporate and governmental **espionage** is especially dangerous because corporations and governments can hire extremely skilled criminals and spies. Robert Gates, director of the CIA from 1991 to 1993, has said that government economic espionage is widespread.[19] Although he cited the French intelligence services as probably the most egregious offender, he identified several other countries whose espionage services spy on foreign companies for competitive advantage, including Russia, China, South Korea, Germany, Israel, India, and Pakistan.

A distinct danger is that foreign governments will recruit hackers to hack for them. In 1997 and 1998, a young Israeli hacker, Ehud Tenenbaum (the Analyzer) recruited U.S. students to break into U.S. government computers, including defense computers. Although it appears that Tenenbaum was not working for a government, he could have been. Even in the 1980s, governments used hackers. In 1989, Cliff Stoll tracked down hackers working for the Russian KGB.[20] By working through hackers instead of hacking directly, governments get deniability if the hackers are caught.

Extortion

Selling credit card numbers or trade secrets after they are stolen can be difficult. Some thieves instead use **extortion**, giving their victims the choice of paying hush money or seeing their security lapses published widely. For fear of losing customers or watching their stock prices slide because of falling investor confidence, some firms choose to pay the extortionist. In other cases, there is a real or implied threat to break in again unless the firm pays the hacker to "help" them close the attack vector. For example, as noted earlier, "Maxim" stole 300,000 credit card numbers from CD Universe. He threatened to

---

[17] "Hijacked Web Site Regroups After Infamouse Attack," February 29, 2000. www.fan590.com/HackerAttackfeb29_apreshack.html.

[18] In the book, we will primarily use the term *trade secrets* for this type of information. The term *intellectual property* is increasingly being used to describe the products of music producers and other producers who wish to protect online property.

[19] Margret Johnson, "Business Spy Threat Is Real, Former CIA Chief Says," NetworkWorldFusion, October 17, 2000. www.nwfusion.com/news.1017spythreat.html.

[20] Clifford Stoll, *The Cuckoo's Egg*, Doubleday, 1989.

post the credit card numbers online unless he was paid $100,000. When CD Universe balked, he posted 25,000 of the stolen credit card numbers online.

TEST YOUR UNDERSTANDING

7. a) List the major types of criminal attacks. b) Distinguish between stealing credit cards and identity theft.

Corporate Employees

Although Internet-based attacks receive the most publicity, dishonest and disgruntled corporate employees still represent an extremely large security danger to firms. In fact, the site, www.cybercrime.gov, which is the best source of examples of U.S. federal crimes, illustrates that a larger fraction of all convictions for cybercrime involve employees or ex-employees.

The Danger of Employees: Access and Knowledge

Employees are especially dangerous because most corporate defenses lie at the boundary between the company's private network and the Internet. Operating *within* the company's private network, employees have relatively easy access to internal computers. In fact, they may already have the required access permissions needed to commit crimes on key hosts.

In addition to their high level of access, their knowledge of the company's private network and computers often allows them to engage in attacks that would be very difficult or impossible to implement from outside the firm.

Financial Theft

Thanks to their access and knowledge, employees and sometimes ex-employees can engage in financial theft (stealing money) or can steal information that allows them to profit.

In too many cases, the procedural security checks and balances that firms put in for manual systems are missing in the design of computer-based systems. This allows a single person to execute financial theft instead of requiring **collusion** by two or more people when there are proper checks and balances.

Sabotage

A major concern is that employees who are angry with the firm or who have been laid off or fired will **sabotage** (damage) the IT system. They may delete key files under their control. They may plant backdoor programs that allow them to get access later even if their account is terminated. They may write **logic bombs** that wipe out large amounts of data under specific conditions or on a certain date and time.

It is no accident that many firms now lay off or fire employees abruptly, allowing them only to go to their office to pick up personal effects. Even then, a guard accompanies them. These firms also cancel all accounts used by the terminated person.

Consultants and Contractors

A firm has control over its own employees, but when a firm delegates work to a consultant or contractor, it is also delegating security, sometimes with painful results. The Justice Department's cybercrime website, www.cybercrime.com, describes numerous attacks by employees of contracting firms.

Sometimes, these attacks were undertaken in retaliation for how the contracting firm treated the employee and had nothing to do with the victim. For example,[21] an employee of a firm managing servers for the U.S. Internal Revenue Service planted a logic bomb on the servers when he learned he was about to be fired. Although he was seeking vengeance on his own company, the IRS would have been the real victim had his logic bomb succeeded.

IT and Security Staffs

Paradoxically, by far the largest internal danger is the company's own IT and security staff. IT staff members have very wide knowledge and access permissions. In fact, server administrators (called **systems administrators**) can read every file on a server and make whatever changes they wish. Often, each server has several IT staff members with systems administrator access. In Example 15 in Chapter 1a, Timothy Lloyd used his status as systems administrator to plant a logic bomb in the server. The gaping security risk posed by IT staffs is the dirty little secret of IT security.

An even more dangerous group is the company's security staff. Security personnel are especially dangerous because they know the flaws in corporate systems. As the old saying goes in military and government security circles, "Who will watch the watchers?"

TEST YOUR UNDERSTANDING

8. a) Why are corporate employees especially dangerous? b) What kinds of attacks do they perpetrate? c) Why are corporate IT and security staffs especially dangerous?

Cyberterrorism and Cyberwar

A New Level of Danger

Until now, attackers have been loners or members of small loosely organized groups. Today, however, both organized terrorist organizations and national governments are capable of implementing damage on an unprecedented scale. Companies accustomed to "normal" attacks may find themselves overwhelmed by cyberterrorism and cyberwar that go far beyond their current and planned defenses.

Infrastructure Destruction

Cyberwar and **cyberterror** are massive attacks by governments or nongovernmental groups respectively that focus on a country's IT infrastructure and its physical infrastructure; in the latter case, attackers may use computers to assist in the physical attack.

Cyberterror and cyberwar are attacks by governments or nongovernmental groups respectively that focus on a country's IT infrastructure and its physical infrastructure; in the latter case, attackers may use computers to assist in the physical attack.

---

[21] U.S. Department of Justice, "Lusby, Maryland Man Pleads Guilty to Sabotaging IRS Computers," July 24, 2001. www.cybercrime.gov/carpenterPlea.htm.

Multi-Pronged Attacks

Most directly, attackers may focus on the country's **IT infrastructure** (networks, computers, databases, and so forth). Both types of attackers will use **multi-pronged attacks**—the simultaneous implementation of multiple IT attacks, each using a different attack method, to maximize destruction and to confuse defenders. They will release worms, actively hack, conduct DoS attacks on antivirus companies, attack Internet routers, and do many other things.

Using Computers in Physical Infrastructure Attacks

In attacks on physical infrastructure, cyberterrorists and cyberwarriors can use computers and networks to plan and coordinate attacks. They can also disable communication during physical crises to make response difficult. They can also attack IT infrastructure and physical infrastructure simultaneously to overload a country's ability to respond.

Cyberterrorists Versus National Governments

Although it is often assumed that cyberwar will appear on a much larger scale than cyberterrorism because of the larger budgets of governments, the events of September 11, 2001, showed that well-funded terrorists are capable of implementing large and complex attacks.

On a more limited basis, we are beginning to see **hacktivism**, in which the attacker hacks for political motivation. On at least two occasions, hackers in the United States and China have engaged in private but widespread hacking against the other country. This type of individual and small-group attack based on political reasons is perhaps the most rapidly growing aspect of hacking today.

Amateur Cyberterrorism and Information Warfare

In fact, there is considerable danger that **information warfare** (another name for cyberwar) will first be waged by individual amateur attackers or by small groups of amateurs. In recent years, we have seen individual amateurs create billions of dollars in damage through IT attacks on corporations and individuals. Putting together even a small number of attack tools and executing them simultaneously could create an unprecedented level of damage. Some would argue that releasing worms or viruses, which sometimes create a billion dollars or more in damage, should be viewed as cyberterror.

TEST YOUR UNDERSTANDING

9. a) What are the goals of both cyberwar and cyberterror? b) Distinguish between cyberwar, cyberterrorism, and amateur information warfare. c) What implications do cyberterror and cyberwar have for corporate IT security planning?

ATTACKS

Having looked at attackers, we will look at the way adversaries attack targets in the next few sections. Figure 1-5 gives a broad taxonomy of the most important attacks. We have already seen some of these attacks in this chapter; we will now look at these attacks in the context of a systematic framework.

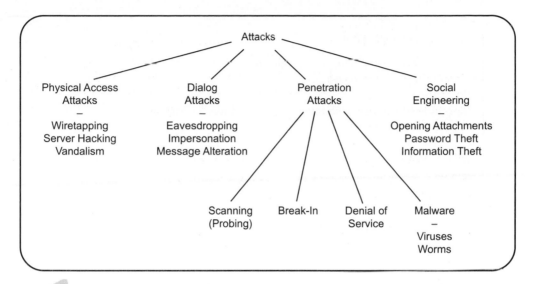

Figure 1-5   Framework for Attacks (Study Figure)

Access Control

Most attacks, although not all, attempt to give the attacker access to corporate computers or access to dialogs between communicating parties. **Access control** is the body of strategies and practices that a company uses to prevent improper access.

> Access control is the body of strategies and practices that a company uses to prevent improper access.

Prioritizing Assets

An essential step in access control is understanding the firm and prioritizing the most important targets that must be protected from illicit access. The most sensitive resources need the most access control attention and resources.

Specifying Access Control Technology and Procedures for Each Asset

The next step is to design and implement access control technology and appropriate access control procedures for each important asset.

Testing Access Control Protection

A major theme of this book is that unless protections are tested, they cannot be trusted. It is too easy to make errors, and it is too easy for faithful performance to lapse or for protections to be actively circumvented by employees.

ACCESS CONTROL

Access control is the body of strategies and practices that a company uses to
    prevent improper access
Prioritize assets
Specify access control technology and procedures for each asset
Test the protection

SITE ACCESS ATTACKS AND DEFENSES

Wiretaps (including wireless LANs intrusions)
Hacking servers with physical access

SOCIAL ENGINEERING

Tricking an employee into giving out information or taking an action that reduces
    security or harms a system
Opening an e-mail attachment that may contain a virus
Asking for a password claiming to be someone with rights to know it
Asking for a file to be sent to you

SOCIAL ENGINEERING DEFENSES

Training
Enforcement through sanctions (punishment)

DIALOG ATTACKS AND DEFENSES

Eavesdropping
Encryption for confidentiality
Impostors and authentication
Cryptographic systems

Figure 1-6   Attacks and Defenses (Study Figure)

Site Access Attacks and Defenses

When most people think about security, they think about attackers who use the
Internet to allow them to strike from a distance and with comparative anonymity.
However, the most devastating attacks occur when an attacker has physical access to
equipment on corporate sites.

Wiretaps

Attackers with physical access can tap into LAN wires to read signals and insert their
own signals. The growing number of wireless networks allows hackers to tap into networks even from just outside the site's premises—a tactic known as drive-by hacking.

Hacking Servers with Physical Access

When we think of attackers hacking servers, we tend to think of them working over the Internet, say by guessing passwords. Yet most servers will lock out accounts after a few failed login attempts, so password-guessing attacks over a network are very difficult to accomplish.

However, a user with sufficient authority and physical access can install **password-cracking software** on a server and quickly learn the passwords of many users. They can also install other software on the victim server to facilitate its downfall.

TEST YOUR UNDERSTANDING

10. What are the main types of attacks?
11. a) What is the purpose of wiretaps? b) How have wireless LANs made wiretapping easier? c) Why is password cracking difficult if you do not have physical access to the computer?

Social Engineering Attacks and Defenses

Social Engineering Attacks

When we think of data theft or hacking, we often think of technology. However, exploiting employee gullibility often is a far more effective approach. For example, a social engineering attacker might call a secretary to ask for the boss's password, ostensibly because the attacker is working on a project with the boss. This is much easier than guessing the boss' password. Tricking an employee into giving out information or taking an action that reduces security or harms a system is called **social engineering**.

Social engineering is tricking an employee into giving out information or taking an action that reduces security or harms a system

---

Kevin Mitnick, a famous hacker of the 1990s, often used social engineering to get what he wanted instead of relying on his technical skills. Once, for instance, he persuaded an employee to send him the detailed schematics of a sensitive new product.[22] The U.S. General Accounting Office (GAO), which has an auditing responsibility within the Federal government, conducted social engineering tests on more than 20 other Federal agencies.[23] The GAO reported widespread success even from the simple expedient of calling up and asking for passwords.

Of course, most e-mail viruses are spread by social engineering. The receiver is enticed into opening an attachment that turns out to be a virus instead of a promised photograph or—ironically—a promised antivirus program. Often, the virus then sends many copies of the message that appear to come from the victim.

---

[22] Tsutomu Shimomura with contributions by John Markoff, *Take-Down; The Pursuit and Capture of Kevin Mitnick, America's Most Wanted Computer Outlaw—By the Man Who Did It,* Hyperion Press, 1996.

[23] Diane Frank, "Training the Security Troops," *Federal Computer Week,* April 10, 2000. www.civic.com/fcw/articles/2000/0410/sec-train-04–10–00.asp.

Social Engineering Defenses: Training and Enforcement

What are the defenses against social engineering? There are two: training staff in how to recognize social engineering ploys and enforcing company rules by punishing employees who ignore their training and take actions that allow social engineering attacks to be successful.

TEST YOUR UNDERSTANDING

    12.   a) What is social engineering? b) How can it be stopped?

Dialog Attacks and Defenses

When we send letters, we expect to have secure **dialogs** (bi-directional message exchanges between two parties), meaning that we expect our messages to get through without being opened or changed. We also want to have secure electronic dialogs. With messages sent over a network, it is often relatively easy to intercept messages.

Eavesdropping

Figure 1-7 illustrates that an attacker can intercept messages going between two victims. This is **eavesdropping**. Historically, security writers have called the two victims Bob and Alice and have called the attacker Eve (perhaps short for "eavesdropper" or "evil"). As a consequence of Eve's position, her attacks are called **attacker-in-the-middle attacks**.[24]

    The most obvious danger is that the attacker will intercept and read the messages. If the content is sensitive, this eavesdropping attack can produce considerable damage.

Encryption for Confidentiality

As Figure 1-8 shows, Bob and Alice can thwart eavesdropping by **encrypting** their messages before transmission. Encryption takes the message and effectively "scrambles" it so that the message looks like a random string of bits to Eve. However, the receiver will be able to decrypt the message, unscrambling it back to the original message. Bob and Alice will have **confidentiality**—freedom from the fear that their messages are being read.[25]

Impostors and Authentication

If the communication takes place over a network, how can Alice be sure that the person claiming to be Bob really is Bob? As Figure 1-9 illustrates, the person claiming to be Bob actually may be Eve. If the **impostor** can fool Alice into talking with her, Eve may gain a great deal of sensitive information. If Alice is a server rather than a person, the impostor may be able to log in as Bob and use his account.

    In light of this danger, Alice should **authenticate** people trying to talk to her, that is, require them to prove their identity. In the human world, Alice might ask someone for information that only Bob would know. Network authentication is a more complex matter because computers are not humanly intelligent and so cannot answer open-ended questions.

---

[24]   These were called man-in-the-middle attacks before gender-neutral language.
[25]   Confidentiality is also called privacy. However, the term privacy is increasingly being used primarily to describe the protection of personal information.

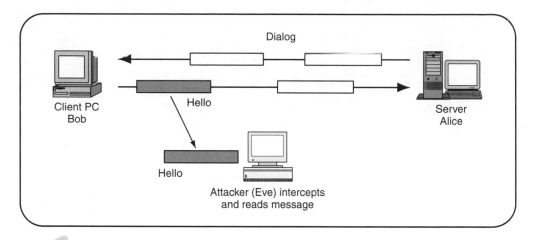

Figure 1-7   Eavesdropping on a Dialog

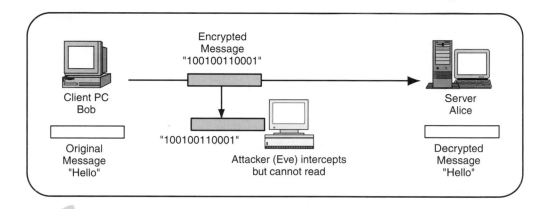

Figure 1-8   Encryption for Confidentiality

Message Alteration

As Figure 1-10 shows, one danger of Eve's attacker-in-the-middle attack is that the attacker will alter a message en route. Secure dialog provides **message integrity**—the assurance that the receiver will be able to detect any changes made en route.

Cryptographic Systems

Many other types of message attacks on message streams are possible. We will look at them (and at defenses to thwart them) in Chapter 7. In general, companies adopt **cryptographic systems** (see Figure 1-11) that automatically implement confidentiality, authentication, integrity, and other safeguards as a package. Some cryptographic systems that we will see in Chapter 8 are SSL/TLS, IPsec, PPTP, and L2TP.

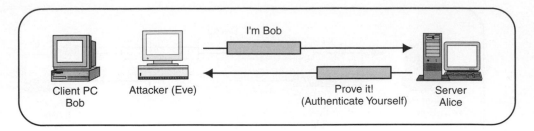

Figure 1-9   Impersonation and Authentication

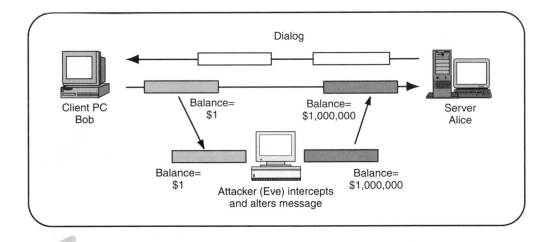

Figure 1-10   Message Alteration

TEST YOUR UNDERSTANDING

13.   a) What is an attacker-in-the-middle attack? b) What is eavesdropping? c) How is eaves-dropping thwarted? d) What is confidentiality? e) What is impersonation? f) What is authentication? g) What is message integrity? h) What is a cryptographic system?

PENETRATION ATTACKS AND DEFENSES

Although corporations are concerned with the security of communication exchanges, they are literally being deluged today by **penetration attacks**, in which one or many messages (packets) are sent to them via a network to probe their defenses or do actual damage, as Figure 1-12 illustrates. Here, the packets are coming into a company's internal private network from the Internet.

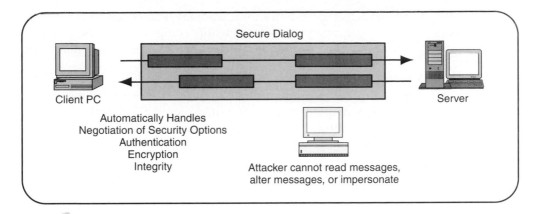

Figure 1-11   Cryptographic System

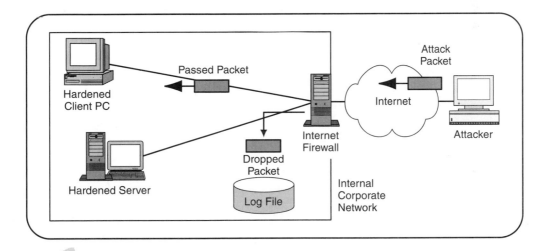

Figure 1-12   Network Penetration Attacks and Firewalls

Penetration Attack Dangers

There are four general types of penetration attacks: scanning (probing) attacks, break-in attacks, denial-of-service attacks, and malware (virus and worm) attacks. We will look at them briefly here. We will look at these attacks in more detail in Chapters 4 and 9.

Scanning (Probing) Attacks

The most common penetration attacks are designed to scan a network for weaknesses. When a thief is studying a neighborhood, he will notice which houses are there, when people are likely to be home, who has weak locks on their doors, and other **surveillance** information. Similarly, as Figure 1-13 shows, **scanning attacks** send a large number of **probing** packets to a corporate network to identify computer addresses, what services computers are running, and various other fingerprints of potential vulnerability.

Break-In Attacks

In some cases, an attacker can send a single message that will take over control of a computer or force the computer to execute a single command that the attacker wishes to run, as Figure 1-14 shows. These **single-message break-in** attacks are possible because of weaknesses in the designs or coding of computer operating systems or application programs running on the computer. Often, the single command the attacker can execute will allow the attacker to log into the computer and continue working. Other break-in attacks will require many actions of various types to succeed.

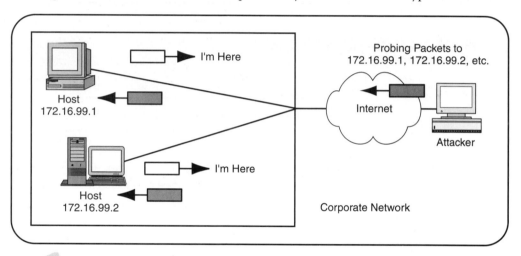

Figure 1-13   Scanning (Probing) Attacks

Figure 1-14   Single-Message Break-In Attack

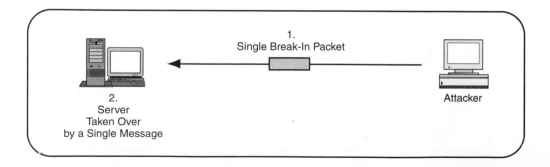

Denial-of-Service Attacks

In **denial-of-service (DoS)** attacks, the attacker usually sends a long stream of attack packets to a target, overwhelming the target's ability to handle the traffic load. Figure 1-15 illustrates such a "flooding" DoS attack. DoS attacks are devastating because the overloaded system cannot serve its customers. As noted earlier, eBay, CNN, Yahoo, Dell, Amazon.com, and other large Internet sites were victimized in February 2000 for hours or days by a teen-aged Canadian attacker, "Mafiaboy." Although newspapers today rarely report DoS attacks because they are not new, the volume of DoS attacks is far greater today than it was in 2000.

Malware: Viruses and Worms

In the types of penetration attacks we have discussed so far, the attacker actively directs the attack. In contrast, **malware**—a category that consists of viruses, worms, and other tools we will see in Chapter 4—are "fire and forget" weapons. The attacker merely releases them, and they spread to victims without further attacker action.

> ➤ **Viruses** are spread primarily through human ignorance, most commonly through the opening of malicious e-mail attachments. When a file infected with a virus is executed it infects other files.

> ➤ **Worms**, in contrast, spread on their own, using scanning, break-in, and even denial-of-service attacks much as a human attacker would, but, of course, far more rapidly.

> ➤ New **blended attacks** spread both virally and as worms to maximize their probability of success. In essence, malware tools are robotic attack agents. As we noted earlier in this chapter, the sophistication of these attacks is increasing.

TEST YOUR UNDERSTANDING

14. Briefly describe the four types of penetration attacks.

Penetration Defenses

Firewalls

As Figure 1-12 shows, the first line of defense against penetration attacks is a special computer called a **firewall**, which is designed to keep attacker messages out of the company's internal private network while still allowing messages from authorized

Figure 1-15   Denial-of-Service (DoS) Flooding Attack

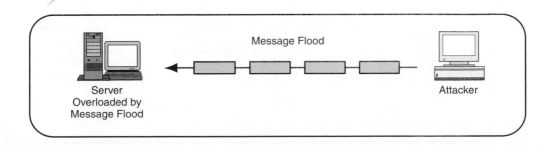

users to get through. Firewalls do this by examining every packet that arrives or leaves. If the firewall detects the **signature** (pattern) of an attack message, it drops the packet. Otherwise, it passes the packet through to the internal network.

Intrusion Detection Systems (IDSs)

When firewalls drop attack packets, they usually do so silently, without telling anyone. A more sophisticated defensive tool is the **intrusion detection system (IDS)**. An IDS is like a burglar alarm. It warns administrators if it detects a possible attack underway. This can allow the network administrator to take appropriate action quickly, preventing the attacker from leisurely trying many different attacks until he or she finds one that succeeds. Like a firewall, an IDS reads each arriving or outgoing packet looking for attack signatures, as Figure 1-16 illustrates. However, it takes no actions on the packets it examines beyond storing copies of packets for later forensic analysis and warning the network administrator of problems. We will look at IDSs in some detail in Chapter 10, which deals with incident response; IDSs are critical to the handling of incidents.

Firewalls Versus IDSs

Why don't we have one device to both deny access and warn of dangers? The answer is that dropping packets should only be done if there are violations of specific clear-cut rules. Otherwise, legitimate packets may be dropped. However, IDSs also need to identify packets that are merely suspicious; such packets cannot be dropped arbitrarily.

At the same time, quite a few firewalls are beginning to act more like IDSs. They use heuristic rules to recognize certain specific types of penetration attacks and take the initiative in dropping attack packets related to these attacks. They may also alert administrators if certain types of attacks appear. Even so, IDSs identify a much broader range of suspicious activity too uncertain to allow machine-only decisions about dropping packets. Firewalls and IDSs have complementary but not identical roles.

Figure 1-16   Intrusion Detection System (IDS)

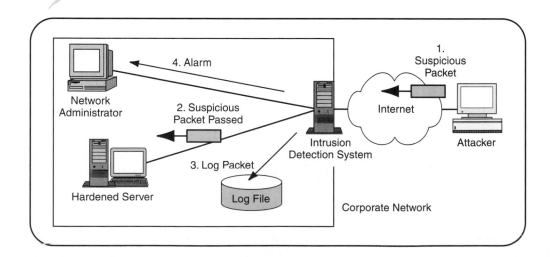

Hardening Servers: Patches and Other Measures

Firewalls are first lines of defense, but some attack packets inevitably get through them to the company's internal servers and clients. Consequently, it is important to **harden** servers and clients, making them more difficult to exploit.

Most servers and clients installed with typical default settings are filled with **known vulnerabilities** that attackers know how to exploit. Over time, in addition, new security vulnerabilities are found. It is critical to keep installing vendor **security patches** that fix these known weaknesses. Server hardening goes well beyond patching known vulnerabilities, but if patches are not installed rapidly when they come out, nothing else matters.

Patching host software is probably the single most important thing companies can do to improve their security. A large majority of attacks today exploit known vulnerabilities because there are so many and because so many companies fail to apply the needed patches.

Patching host software is probably the single most important thing companies can do to improve their security.

TEST YOUR UNDERSTANDING

15. a) What do firewalls do? b) What do IDSs do? c) Why must servers be hardened? d) What are known vulnerabilities? e) How are they addressed? f) What probably is the single most important thing that companies can do to improve their security?

SECURITY MANAGEMENT

Primarily a Management Issue, Not a Technology Issue

There is a strong tendency for upper management and even IT professionals to think of security in terms of firewalls, antivirus programs, and other technology protections. This is extremely dangerous because without excellent management, operational procedures, and implementation diligence, the best technology will make no difference. In fact, we noted earlier that although a large majority of all firms implement firewalls and antivirus programs, successful attacks are very frequent, as Figure 1-1 indicates.

All corporate security books point out that security is primarily a management issue, not a technology issue. Without a deep change in a corporation's security culture and practices, buying technology will bring little safety.

Security is primarily a management issue, not a technology issue.

TEST YOUR UNDERSTANDING

16. Why is security primarily a management issue, not a technology issue?

Top-To-Bottom Commitment

The most important thing in security management is having *top-to-bottom commitment* to security. A breakdown in "buy in" at any level of a corporation can cripple security.

Top Management Commitment

Unless top corporate management is strongly committed to security, there almost certainly will not be sufficient resources or direction to make security work.

Top IT management also needs to be strongly committed to security. Security often is the unwanted stepchild of corporate IT departments. For instance, in 2002, respondents to the Network World 500 Survey reported that three of their top five IT concerns were security concerns—securing the corporate network, improving disaster-recovery systems, and building virtual private networks.[26] Yet these same respondents also said that they only planned to increase their security budgets an average of 5 percent.

Operational Execution

It is also critical for IT personnel and other corporate employees to execute their security jobs faithfully and well. Most attacks take advantage of vulnerabilities created by the incorrect configuration of security tools and by the failure of operational employees to patch software with known security weaknesses.

Enforcement

Perhaps most distastefully, it is critical to enforce security rules by sanctioning employees who break them. A basic principle of management is that you get what you enforce. Many operational-level employees and even top managers will break security rules to make their lives easier and for various other reasons. Unless violators are sanctioned, security is not likely to thrive.

In security, you get what you enforce.

Of course, security people need to provide training and be realistic in proposing sanctions. If security becomes viewed as the corporate Gestapo, it will loose its support. In general, first-time offenders of minor infractions should be let off with a warning. However, for repeat offenders with moderately serious infractions or even for first-time offenders with serious infractions, termination should not be ruled out.

TEST YOUR UNDERSTANDING

    17.   a) What is top-to-bottom security? b) Why is the enforcement of security policies through the sanctioning of violators important?

Comprehensive Security

Another critical lesson taught by painful security incidents is that a firm must have **comprehensive security**—it must close out *all* avenues of attack. Otherwise, it will be only show security, such as the strengthening of airline inspection stations while allowing easy ramp access to aircraft.

---

[26]   John Cox, "Survey: Security Remains Job 1," *Network World,* May 20, 2002. www.nwfusion.com/news/ 2002/0520nw500.html.

Asymmetrical Warfare

While the company defending itself must try to close down all vulnerabilities, the attacker only has to find a single weakness. In this **asymmetrical warfare**, the attacker has the advantage.

Defense in Depth

One way to improve defenses it to create **defense in depth**, meaning that the attacker has to break through multiple countermeasures to succeed. For instance, we will see in Chapter 5 that many firms have screening firewalls, main firewalls, and firewalls on individual host computers. An attacker has to break through all three firewalls to hack a host computer.

Security Audits

Security countermeasures are difficult to configure, so it is easy to have vulnerabilities even when a company thinks it has comprehensive security. For comprehensive security, it is important to have **security audits**, in which an attack team hired by the firm attempts to penetrate the system.

TEST YOUR UNDERSTANDING

18. a) What is comprehensive security? b) Why is security an example of asymmetrical warfare? c) Describe defense in depth. d) What are security audits, and why are they crucial for comprehensive security?

General Security Goals

What does it mean to be secure? As Figure 1-17 shows, the core security goals are confidentiality, integrity, and availability (**CIA**).

Confidentiality

If I tell someone something in confidence, other people should not be able to hear it. In IT security, as we saw earlier, confidentiality means that information should not be readable by unauthorized people. For confidentiality, companies must manage **access control** to their computers and databases. They also must encrypt messages so that attackers who intercept them en route cannot read them.

Integrity

As we also saw earlier, integrity means that information has not been added to, altered, or deleted—except with authorization. No one has broken into a bank's database and changed his or her account balance. No one has intercepted a financial transaction en route and changed it in his or her favor.

Availability

If users cannot reach a computer, it does not matter if the computer has the information they need. **Availability** means that authorized users can get access to IT resources. If an attacker mounts a denial-of-service attack against your network—by flooding your network with messages, for example—users will not be able to reach critical resources even if the computer and database are working. Of course, crashing a computer or an application program also will make information unavailable.

SECURITY IS PRIMARILY A MANAGEMENT ISSUE, NOT A
TECHNOLOGY ISSUE

TOP-TO-BOTTOM COMMITMENT

Top-management commitment
Operational execution
Enforcement

COMPREHENSIVE SECURITY

Closing all avenues of attack
Asymmetrical warfare
Defense in depth
Security audits

GENERAL SECURITY GOALS (CIA)

Confidentiality
Integrity
Availability

Figure 1-17   Security Management (Study Figure)

TEST YOUR UNDERSTANDING

19.   a) In security, for what does the acronym "CIA" stand? b) Describe the three concepts
in this acronym.

THE PLAN-PROTECT-RESPOND (PPR) CYCLE

Companies that are serious about providing comprehensive security must go through
a process called the **plan-protect-respond (PPR)** cycle.

Planning

Comprehensive Security Planning

As noted, the main objective in security management is **comprehensive security**, which
closes all doors to attackers. If you have elaborate security at the main entrance to a
building but no protection at fire doors or other possible entrances, you do not have
comprehensive security. Attackers only have to find a single weakness to succeed.
Comprehensive security planning keeps asking, "What have we missed?"

Risk Analysis

Although businesses want to ensure security, they also must be careful how they spend
money. It makes no sense to spend a million dollars to counter a five thousand dollar
threat. Companies need to conduct **risk analyses**, in which they weigh the costs of

PLANNING

Need for comprehensive security (no gaps)
Risk analysis (see Figure 1-19)
    Enumerating threats
    Threat severity = estimated cost of attack $\times$ probability of attack
    Value of protection = threat severity − cost of countermeasure
    Prioritize countermeasures by value of protection
Security policies drive subsequent specific actions (see Figure 1-20)
    Selecting technology
    Procedures to make technology effective
    The testing of technology and procedures

PROTECTING

Installing protections: firewalls, IDSs, host hardening, etc.
Updating protections as the threat environment changes
Testing protections: security audits

RESPONDING

Planning for response (Computer Emergency Response Team)
Incident detection and determination
    Procedures for reporting suspicious situations
    Determination that an attack really is occurring
    Description of the attack
Containment and recovery
    Containment: stop the attack
    Repair the damage
Punishment
    Forensics
    Prosecution
    Employee punishment
Fixing the vulnerability that allowed the attack

Figure 1-18   The Plan-Protect-Respond Cycle (Study Figure)

threats against the costs of defenses. Although threats are damaging, security itself is expensive in terms of both applying countermeasures and lost productivity because of inconveniences due to higher security. (For example, on business trips, several hours are lost because of higher security since the September 11, 2001, disaster.)

In risk analysis, firms must weigh the costs of threats against the costs of defenses.

Enumerating Threats   Figure 1-19 illustrates a simplistic threat severity analysis. It shows that the first job is **threat enumeration**. This is the identification of all threats. This can be a daunting problem in itself. In the figure, only four threats are shown, but corporations face numerous threats that must be assessed.

Threat Severity Analysis   Next, the cost of each threat must be estimated and a probability of occurrence assigned. The **threat severity** for the threat is the estimated cost of the attack—the cost of a successful attack times the probability of a successful attack.

In the figure, Threat A has a high probability of occurrence and a high amount of damage if the attack succeeds. Threat A therefore has a high threat severity and must be considered very carefully. Threat B is low on both probability and damage and so represents a small threat. The other two threats shown are high on one dimension but low on the other and therefore are not severe threats.

Apply Countermeasures?   Although a threat may be significant, the cost of a countermeasure to stop the attack may be prohibitive. In this case, the company should accept the risk or, if possible, insure against the threat if the cost of insurance is not prohibitive. The **value of protection** is the cost of the threat severity minus the countermeasure cost.

In Figure 1-19, only Threats A and C have countermeasures inexpensive enough to be worth applying. For Threats B and D, countermeasures exceed the threat severity, so a company should not apply the countermeasures and should accept the risks.

Prioritization   The last step in the risk analysis is to prioritize the application of countermeasures. In Figure 1-19, this is easy to do. Threat A has the highest value of protection by far, and there is only one other threat (Threat C) that has a positive value of protection. Companies need to implement their highest-priority countermea-

Figure 1-19   Threat Severity Analysis

STEP	THREAT	A	B	C	D
1	Cost if attack succeeds	$500,000	$10,000	$100,000	$10,000
2	Probability of occurrence	80%	20%	5%	70%
3	Threat severity	$400,000	$2,000	$5,000	$7,000
4	Countermeasure cost	$100,000	$3,000	$2,000	$20,000
5	Value of protection	$300,000	($1,000)	$3,000	($13,000)
6	Apply countermeasure?	Yes	No	Yes	No
7	Priority	1	NA	2	NA

sures first, then work down to less important countermeasures. In this case, the firm would implement the countermeasure for Threat A first.

Security Policies

The next job is to define **security policies**, which specify at a broad level what should be done in terms of security. For instance, the company should have a policy that everyone must take a 2-week vacation each year, with at least 1 week being taken in consecutive days. This will stop many internal scams because the employee attacker's method may become apparent when he or she is not around. Another policy may be to require centrally managed antivirus protection on all employee home and mobile computers that access the firm's internal network.

In Chapter 2, we will see an important class of security policies, access control policies. These policies list, for each resource, who should have access to the resource, what they may do to the resource, and how access control is to be protected and audited.

Policies Guide Technology, Procedures and Testing

A strong and comprehensive set of security policies is critical for guiding all lower-level actions. When specific questions arise, the first question people should always ask is "What's the policy?" A strong set of security policies drives everything else, as Figure 1-20 illustrates.

Policies Drive Technology   First, policies drive technology. To support a policy requiring access control between the Internet and site networks, you will need firewalls, and you will need them in certain places.

Figure 1-20   Policy-Driven Technology, Procedures, and Testing

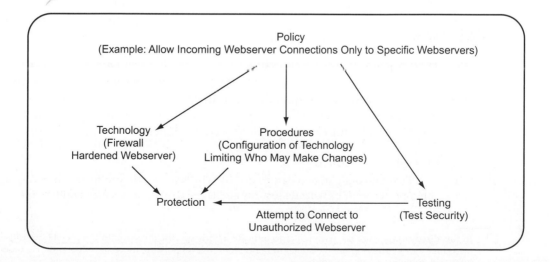

Policies Drive Procedures   Second, policies drive procedures.[27] If a policy states that it is vital to protect social security numbers stored on an e-commerce server, then numerous actions will need to be taken, for instance, keeping software patched with security updates to ensure that attackers cannot break in and read the file easily. In addition, even systems administrators should have limited access to a sensitive social security number file.

Policies Drive Testing   Finally, policies should drive testing. Technology is difficult to set up, and procedures may be overlooked or deliberately bypassed. Companies need to test their systems frequently, using testing suites based on the same corporate security policies used to select technology and create procedures. If a test attack succeeds, then technology, procedures, or both will have to be changed.

TEST YOUR UNDERSTANDING

20.   a) What costs do firms weigh in risk analysis? b) How is threat severity computed? c) How is the value of protection computed? d) Why is prioritization important, and how is it done? e) Why are security policies important? f) What do they drive?

Protecting

Most of a firm's security effort is spent in the protecting phase, during which most attacks are successfully thwarted, although some attacks will inevitably succeed.

Selection, Installation, and Protections

Protections such as firewalls must be selected, purchased, and installed. Configuring a firewall is extremely tricky, and misconfiguration will cause a firewall to leak bad packets like a sieve. Installation and configuration are critical (and difficult) for almost all security tools. Security policies should guide security personnel all the way down to the configuration of firewall rules.

Updating Protections

Threats change constantly, so antivirus tools, firewalls, and most other security tools need to be updated frequently. A security system that is set up and left alone becomes useless over time.

Testing Protections: Security Audits

One consequence of the difficulty of configuring security tools is the need to test them to see if they are working. Consequently, it is critical to use security audits to test firewalls after they are configured. These attacks invariably encounter a large number of misconfigurations and failures to implement security policies.

TEST YOUR UNDERSTANDING

21.   a) Why is misconfiguration easy to do? b) Why is it necessary to update firewalls and other protections? c) What do security audits do? d) Why are security audits necessary?

---

[27]   In this discussion, we use the term policy to indicate a fairly specific directive. In Chapter 11, we will introduce a more finely grained distinction between high-level policies; more specific standards, baselines and guidelines; and procedures.

Responding

Even with strong protection, an attacker will sometimes break through, creating a security incident.

Planning for Response

During a security incident, tension is high and there is intensive time pressure to recover quickly. Appropriate and rapid response is impossible without prior planning and rehearsals.

Companies need strong procedures for reporting and formally declaring security incidents, analyzing attacks, stopping the attacker, repairing damage, and (in some cases) punishing attackers. For substantial incidents, companies need **computer emergency response teams (CERTs)** that are well-trained and that frequently engage in drills to assess their readiness and approaches.

Incident Detection and Determination

When an incident occurs, the situation usually is ambiguous. Often, a vague symptom alerts someone that something is wrong. There must be a well-defined process for anyone to report suspicious activity.[28]

Once a potential incident is reported, someone in the firm needs to study the situation quickly to determine if it really is a security incident or whether it is a "normal problem," such as inefficient application software or a router crash.

If the problem is a real security incident, the analyst or the CERT will then have to analyze the situation in depth to develop a good understanding of the situation.

Containing the Attack and Recovery

The first priorities have to be containing (stopping) the attack and recovery (repairing damage). Viruses and other malware have to be removed from attacked computers. Modified or possibly modified data have to be restored. Many other recovery steps need to be taken. This recovery phase must be done quickly under strong time pressure yet done well. Again, rehearsal is critical for performance during a time of attack.

Punishment

In some cases, a firm may wish to prosecute an outside attacker. This is a difficult decision because publicizing an attack can be harmful to the firm. More commonly, companies use **forensics** (the application of science to legal problems) to detect and punish internal violators. It is much easier to fire an employee than to prosecute a teenage hacker in a foreign country even if you can identify the external attacker, which is unlikely.[29]

---

[28] In many firms, employees do not even know what telephone number to call if they suspect a security incident.

[29] In the 2001 CSI/FBI survey, only 36 percent of companies with intrusions reported intrusions to law enforcement agencies. Reasons for not reporting intrusions included concerns about negative publicity (90 percent), concern that competitors would take advantage of the disclosure (75 percent), a lack of awareness that the incident could be reported (54 percent), and a belief that civil remedies seemed best (64 percent). Computer Security Institute, "2001 CSI/FBI Computer Crime and Security Survey," *Computer Security Issues and Trends*, Vol. VII, No. 1, 2001.

Fixing Vulnerabilities

The last important step in incident response is to fix the vulnerability that allowed the attacker into the system so that other attackers cannot exploit it.

TEST YOUR UNDERSTANDING

22. a) Why is prior planning critical for incident response? b) What is a CERT? c) What do containment and recovery involve? d) What is forensics? e) Are you more likely to be able to punish employees or external hackers? Explain.

THE BOOK

As noted at the beginning of this chapter, the rest of the book fleshes out the framework you saw in this chapter.

Chapter 2: Access Control and Site Security

The next chapter provides a deeper framework on the issue of access control. It then discusses site security, including server exploits that require physical access, passwords, biometrics, and wiretapping, including the drive-by hacking of wireless LANs.

Chapter 3: Review of TCP/IP Internetworking

This book assumes basic knowledge of networks. Chapter 2 introduces some common LAN attacks on Ethernet and wireless networks. However, most attacks come in via the Internet, which uses TCP/IP protocols. Chapter 3 discusses TCP/IP protocols in more depth than a typical networking class, reflecting the fact that a strong knowledge of TCP/IP is needed by security professionals.

Chapters 4–5: Penetration Attacks and Firewalls

Chapters 4 and 5 deal with penetration attacks and firewall defenses. Chapter 4 begins with a discussion of the steps taken by attackers in hacking and denial-of-service attacks. Chapter 4 then discusses virus attacks and antivirus defenses. Chapter 5 then discusses packet filter firewalls, stateful firewalls, NAT, application firewalls, and firewall architectures.

Chapter 6: Host Security

The next chapter discusses host security. Some packet attacks will get through firewalls, so host operating systems must be protected. Chapter 6 discusses how to protect hosts that undergo attacks.

Chapter 7: The Elements of Cryptography

Cryptographic systems require encryption for confidentiality, integrity, and authentication. Chapter 7 discusses the complex and sometimes confusing world of **cryptography**—the use of encryption to support these goals. It looks at the elements of cryptographic systems.

Chapter 8: Cryptographic Systems

Chapter 8, in turn, brings the elements of cryptography together to see how they are implemented in cryptographic systems. The chapter focuses on the most important cryptographic systems in organizations today, including SSL/TLS, IPsec, PPTP, L2TP, and Kerberos. Several of these cryptographic systems are used to create **virtual private networks (VPNs)**: the use of the Internet with added security for protected dialogs.

Chapter 9: Application Security

Most hacking attacks on servers take place through applications running on hosts rather than through the host operating system. Chapter 9 discusses security problems and countermeasures for a number of key applications, including the World Wide Web and e-mail.

Chapter 10: Incident and Disaster Response

Chapter 10 discusses incident response organization and processes, as well as how intrusion detection systems (IDSs) work and are used during incident response. This chapter also discusses business continuity planning and disaster recovery.

Chapter 11: Managing the Security Function

Chapter 11 discusses the broad process of security management. Although management is more fundamental than the technologies discussed in Chapters 3 through 10, it is only possible to discuss security management in depth after the technology is understood.

Chapter 12: The Broader Perspective

Corporate IT managers understandably focus on internal firm issues. However, society in general is wrestling with many broad security-related social policy issues, most notably personal and customer privacy. Chapter 12 also discusses cyberterrorism and cyberwar—two wild cards that may require fundamental changes in corporate IT security management.

CONCLUSION

Corporate IT security is driven by the plan-protect-respond (PPR) cycle. In this chapter we looked at these three phases briefly. The rest of the book will look at the PPR cycle in some depth. We will start with and spend most of our time on the protecting phase because this takes up most of the corporate security professional's time. With the technical and procedural base we learn in this part of the book, we will move on to planning and responding.

Risk Management, Not Risk Elimination

A key theme of security is risk management. Risks can never be completely eliminated, and the company must carefully balance the potential damage of various risks with the costs of addressing these risks, including the cost of disrupted workflow and the costs of purchasing, installing, and managing countermeasure technologies.

CORPORATE VERSUS MILITARY SECURITY

This is a book about *corporate* IT security rather than *military* IT security. Although the two have much in common, and although we will cover some key aspects of military security in sidebars, military security has a number of features not found in corporate security.

Multilevel Security

Most notably, the military uses **multilevel security**, in which documents and data are **classified** according to sensitivity levels, such as unclassified, secret, top secret, eyes only, and the apocryphal burn before reading. This classification system then drives security processes. For instance, only people with top-secret clearance may read top-secret documents, and documents with certain security levels must be stored in specific ways.

Although businesses may label some information as confidential or company-private, the strict multilevel classification system of the military has not proven workable in corporations.

Extreme Measures

In addition, the military often has to take extreme measures, such as building a **black** (secret) computer system on a small local area network that is not connected at all to the outside world. (This is called "having an **air gap**.")

The military also has entirely separate networks for highly secure and non-secure information. Such extreme measures are rarely appropriate in business.

National Security Versus Cost-Effective Risk Management

Most importantly, the military has a very different approach to risk than corporations do. In the military, national survival itself can be at stake, so the military seeks enormous funding even against extremely rare threats. Such expenditures would bankrupt corporations. Corporations, on the other hand, must engage in risk management, as we note in the body of this chapter. Security is extremely expensive, in terms of both dollars and productivity loss due to the restrictions of working in a more secure environment. Only security actions that are cost-justified can be taken by corporations.

TEST YOUR UNDERSTANDING

23. a) Describe multilevel security. b) Why would the extreme security measures used by the military not work in business? c) Contrast military and business approaches to setting security spending limits.

Security Is Primarily a Management Issue, Not a Technology Issue

Another key theme is that security is primarily a management issue, not a technology issue. Although we will look at various security technologies, security is about management, from strategic management down to the fine processes of configuring firewalls and other equipment. Unless there are fundamental changes in corporate security procedures and the company's security culture, even the best technology will fail miserably.

Testing

A fourth theme we will see repeatedly is the importance of testing. Even with intensive planning, implementation, and maintenance, error will be inevitable. Just because you implemented your firewall to stop a particular attack does not mean it actually will stop the attack. Security audits are critical to ensuring that planned protections actually are working.

THOUGHT QUESTIONS

1. Why do you think most people focus on security technology rather than on corporate security management?
2. The Riptech and SecurityFocus data indicate that the average firm is attacked thousands of times per year. Yet only a moderate percentage of people who responded to the CSI/FBI survey reported incidents. Explain this apparent inconsistency.
3. Create three corporate security policies. These policies should be specific. Otherwise, there would be ambiguity in their application.
4. After the September 11, 2001, disaster, National Guard troops were stationed at U.S. airport checkpoints. In Pennsylvania, at least, the troops were not allowed to load their weapons, and loading them would take several seconds.[30] What were the risks involved in loading weapons versus leaving weapons unloaded?
5. During the height of the September 11, 2001, crisis, a hacker group called Yihat (Youth Intelligent Hackers Against Terrorism) broke into a Saudi Arabian bank and hacked a server to seek evidence that terrorists were using the bank. They copied at least a spreadsheet file. The group's goal was not to harm the bank but to look for terrorists. The bank used no firewall and configured the server for easy outside access. Comment on this.

TROUBLESHOOTING QUESTION

1. You put a firewall between your company and the Internet. a) Argue for putting the IDS on the *Internet side* of the firewall. b) Argue for putting the IDS on the side of your firewall going to the *internal network*.

---

[30] "Guard Troops Had Unloaded Guns at Airports," CNN.com. May 26, 2002. www.cnn.com/2002/US/05/26/rec.national.guard.ap/index.html.

EXAMPLES OF SECURITY PROBLEMS

INTRODUCTION

If you like horror stories, this is the chapter for you. It brings together two things:

➤ First, it brings together a number of cases in which attackers have been arrested, prosecuted, convicted or sentenced. Most cases deal with U.S. Justice Department prosecution. The full text of press releases for these and other cases can be found at www.cybercrime.gov.

➤ Second, the September 11, 2001, disaster was unfortunately a model example of why security is primarily a management problem, not a technology problem. The chapter looks at some of the major security weaknesses in the air transport system prior to September 11, 2001. Many of the weaknesses that lead to the September 11 disaster have been only somewhat reduced.

These examples and the September 11, 2001, discussion are relevant to many topics throughout this book, so they are brought together in one place for easier reference.

EXAMPLES

1. Herbert Pierre-Louis: Sabotage by a Disgruntled Employee

An employee, Herbert Pierre-Louis, was convicted of placing a virus in many places within servers at Purity Wholesale Grocers, one of the largest companies in Florida. He put the company out of operation for several days, causing $75,000 in damages. Pierre-Louis, a computer hardware technician, had been reprimanded by his supervisor 10 days earlier for work-related behavior.[1]

2. Washington Leung: Cyberframing a Female Employee Who Spurned Him

A male employee, Washington Leung, was spurned by a female employee. He left the firm and later logged into his ex-firm's servers using passwords given to him while employed there. He deleted over 900 files related to employee compensation. To frame the female employee, he gave her a $40,000 annual raise and a $100,000 bonus. In addition, he created a Hotmail account in her name and used the account to send senior managers at the company an e-mail containing some information from the deleted files. However, the frame failed. On his computer at his new place of employment, authorities found evidence of the e-mail he sent to senior managers. He was convicted and sentenced to 18 months in prison.[2]

3. Two Programmers: A Denial-of-Service Attack by IT Employees

Two programmers at Internet Trading Technologies, Inc., threatened to quit an important project unless given a large pay increase. They demanded an immediate payment of $70,000 plus $50,000 in stock options and pay raises. They reached a tentative settlement but backed out on the agreement and demanded more money. The company refused.

One of the programmers allegedly launched a denial-of-service attack against the company in retaliation. These attacks went on for 3 days, causing the company to be concerned with its very survival. It ended when federal monitoring equipment traced the attack to a public computer at Queens College where the attacker was a student. Arriving shortly after the attack, authorities found witnesses who placed the programmer at the computer when the attack was being made.[3]

4. Two Accountants: Financial Theft Through Procedure Exploitation

Two accountants at Cisco Systems used computer access to issue themselves $8 million worth of Cisco stock. In fact, they issued themselves stocks three times before being caught. They committed the crime by exploiting the company's procedures for issuing stock to employees. They were sentenced to 34 months in prison, followed by 3 years of supervised release. They were also ordered to repay $8 million to Cisco. Goods and stocks valued at over $5 million that were seized by the government were credited toward the $8 million.[4]

---

[1]   U.S. Department of Justice, "Jury Convicts Herbert Pierre-Louis of Sending Computer Virus to Destroy Purity Wholesale Grocers Inc's [sic] Computer Systems," September 6, 2001. www.cybercrime.gov/pierre-louis_Convict.htm.

[2]   U.S [sic] Department of Justice, "U.S. Sentences Computer Operator for Breaking into Ex-Employer's Database," March 27, 2002. www.cybercrime.gov/leungSent.htm.

[3]   Ann Harrison, "Database Programmer Arrested for Attack on Wall St. Employer's Systems," *Computerworld*, March 17, 2000. www.computerworld.com/news/2000/story/0,11280,41869,00.html.

[4]   U.S. Department of Justice, "Former Cisco Systems Accountants Sentenced for Unauthorized Access to Computer Systems to Illegally Issue $8 Million in Cisco Stock to Themselves," November 26, 2001. www.cybercrime.gov/Osowski_TangSent.htm.

5. Cisco Systems Employee: Theft of Trade Secrets by Employee for Personal Benefit

A Cisco Systems employee copied many trade secret files to CD-ROM and took the disks to his new employer, Calix Networks, which cooperated with the investigation.[5]

6. Paralegal Employee: Theft of Trade Secrets to Sell Them

A paralegal employee in a law firm copied the company's plans for a plaintiff in a large court case. These plans cost several million dollars to develop. He attempted to sell the plans to one of the firms representing the defendants.[6]

7. Patrick McKenna: Computer Sabotage and Damage of Reputation

Patrick McKenna, a former employee, broke into his company's database and deleted hundreds of computer files and altered billing records. He then sent a damaging e-mail in the name of the firm to over one hundred of the firm's customers. McKenna was sentenced to 6 months in federal prison, followed by 2 years of supervised release. He also had to pay $13,614.11 in restitution.[7]

8. Eric Burns: Website Hacking and Defacement

A hacker named Eric Burns, who went by the handle ZYKLON, developed an exploit program to attack websites, "Web Bandit." He was arrested and eventually pleaded guilty to using the exploit against many websites and defacing them. On one occasion, he made thousands of pages of information at a website unavailable. Web Bandit was used to hack the White House website, but the hacker, Eric Burns, only admitted that he helped with the planning. Burns was sentenced to 15 months in prison and 3 years of supervised release. He was ordered to pay $36,240 in compensation.[8]

9. Raymond Torricelli: Hacking to Make Money from Stolen Computer Resources

Raymond Torricelli, known as "Rolex," hacked into computers and ran chat room discussions on the hacked computers, using up processor time, memory, and disk resources. A member of the hacking group #Conflict, Torricelli's goal was to get participants to go to a pornographic website. He admitted to being paid $0.18 for each participant who went to the website. This earned him $300 to $400 per week. Upon conviction, Torricelli was sentenced to 4 months in prison and 4 months of home confinement. He was ordered to pay $4,400 in restitution. This case illustrates how the

---

[5] U.S. Department of Justice, March 21, 2001. www.cybercrime.gov/MorchPlea.htm.
[6] U.S. Department of Justice, "Manhattan Paralegal Sentenced for Theft of Litigation Trial Plan," January 30, 2002. www.cybercrime.gov/farrajSentence.htm.
[7] U.S. Department of Justice, "Hampton Man Convicted and Sentenced for Hacking into Former Employer's Computer Server," June 18, 2001. www.cybercrime.gov/McKennaSent.htm.
[8] U.S. Department of Justice, "'Web Bandit' Hacker Sentenced to 15 Months Imprisonment, 3 Years of Supervised Release, for Hacking USIA, NATO, Websites." November 19, 1999. www.cybercrime.gov/burns.htm.

dividing line between traditional break-in hacking and criminal activity has blurred in recent years.[9]

10. Vasiliy Gorshkov: Credit Card Theft by Hacker

A Russian hacker, Vasiliy Gorshkov, stole credit card numbers and other personal information from numerous computers in the United States. He received a job offer from a U.S. recruiting firm, Invita. He was required to demonstrate hacking skills against a test network before coming to the United States. At a job interview with Invita in Seattle, he discussed hacking freely. When asked about his concerns with the FBI, he said that the FBI was no problem because the FBI could not get him in Russia. Yes, you guessed it. Invita was an FBI front. Gorshkov was tried and convicted.[10]

11. Three NEC Toshiba Space Systems Workers: Industrial Espionage on Third-Party Computer

Company employees may spy without permission, often with embarrassing results. In 2001, three workers at NEC Toshiba Space Systems allegedly stole data on Mitsubishi's antenna design for a high-speed Internet access satellite. The data was stored on the computers of the Japanese National Space Development Agency. The three workers were subsequently arrested. Both NEC and Toshiba were banned from bidding on National Space Development Agency projects for a month.[11]

12. Two Kazakhstan Employees of a Business Partner Use Extortion to Reveal a Vulnerability

Two employees in a company in Kazakhstan allegedly got access to a Bloomberg financial information database because their company was an affiliate of Bloomberg. They allegedly demanded $200,000 from Bloomberg to reveal how they got access to the database. Bloomberg opened a numbered offshore account with $200,000 and invited the pair to London, where they personally met with Michael Bloomberg, who is currently the mayor of New York City. Also at the meeting were police officials who arrested the two alleged extortionists. Note that finding a vulnerability and requiring payment to learn about it may be considered extortion.[12]

---

[9]   U.S. Department of Justice, "Hacker Sentenced in New York City for Hacking into Two NASA Jet Propulsion Lab Computers Located in Pasadena, California," September 5, 2001. www.cybercrime.gov/torricellisent.htm.

[10]   U.S. Department of Justice, "Russian Computer Hacker Convicted by Jury," October 10, 2001. www.cybercrime.gov/gorshkovconvict.htm.

[11]   CNN.com, "Aerospace Workers Arrested for Hacking," May 31, 2002. www.cnn.com/2002/TECH/internet/05/31/japan.space.hackers.ap/index.html. CNN.com, "Aerospace Workers Arrested for Hacking," May 31, 2002. europe.cnn.com/2002/WORLD/asiapcf/east/05/30/japan.spacehackers.ap/index.html.

[12]   U.S. Department of Justice, "Two Kazakhstan Citizens Accused of Breaking into Bloomberg L.P.'s Computer and Extortion Are Extradited," May 21, 2002. www.cybercrime.gov/bloombergIndict.htm.

13. Financial Brokerage Firm: Extortion to Avoid a Denial-of-Service Attack

At a mid-size financial services firm, an executive received a call on Sunday night threatening to take the system down the next day unless the company paid the attacker one million dollars. The IT staff worked furiously to find a problem but could not. Early the next morning, the system crashed. The attacker called again and threatened to crash the system during its busiest period unless the extortion money was paid. This company paid the extortionist.[13]

14. Patrice Williams and Makeebrah Turner: Theft of Credit Card Numbers by an Employee

Patrice Williams and Makeebrah Turner, employees at Chase Financial Corporation, were able to obtain customer information, including credit card numbers, for a number of accounts. They gave this information to outside conspirators. They were each sentenced to a year and a day in federal prison.[14]

15. Tim Lloyd: Computer Sabotage by Terminated Systems Administrator

In 1996, a systems administrator fired for being threatening and disruptive, Tim Lloyd, attacked his company's computer network using a logic bomb that he planted on a critical server.

The logic bomb, under pre-set conditions, destroyed the programs that ran the company's manufacturing machines, resulting in $10 million in business losses and $2 million in reprogramming costs. To prevent recovery, Lloyd also erased the firm's backup tapes.

This attack led to 80 layoffs. It also led to a permanent loss of the company's competitive status in the high-tech instruments and measurements market because the company could not recover the proprietary design software it had been using. "We will never recover," said the plant manager in court.

Lloyd was sentenced to 41 months in federal prison and ordered to pay $2 million in restitution, but this was a hollow victory for the company.[15]

16. Claude Carpenter: Sabotage by an IT Contractor Employee

A 19-year-old employee of a firm managing servers for the U.S. Internal Revenue Service, Claude Carpenter, planted a logic bomb on the servers when he learned he was about to be fired. Although he was seeking vengeance on his own company, the

---

[13] Sandeep Junnarkar, "Online Banks: Prime Target for Attacks," Znet.com, May 1, 2002. techupdate. zdnet.com/techupdate/stories/main/0,14179,2863266-1,00.html.

[14] U.S. Department of Justice, "Former Chase Financial Corp. Employees Sentenced for Scheme to Defraud Chase Manhattan Bank and Chase Financial Corporation," February 19, 2002.

[15] Sharon Gaudin, "Computer Saboteur Sentenced to Federal Prison," *Computerworld*, February 26, 2002. www.computerworld.com/itresources/rcstory/0,4167,STO68624_KEY73,00.html.

IRS would have been the real victim had his logic bomb succeeded. He also planted the code in his supervisor's computer to frame the supervisor.

The logic bombs did not go off as scheduled. When he repeatedly called in to ask how the servers were doing, his former employer became suspicious. It successfully defused the time bomb, but other firms in similar situations have not been so lucky.[16]

17. Pakistani Hacktivist: Website Defacement and the Posting of Identity Theft Information

In one case, a Pakistani was indicted for attacking the computers of the American-Israel Public Affairs Committee, a pro-Israel public affairs group in the United States. The attack allegedly defaced the website and, more seriously, posted confidential credit card and other personal information of AIPAC on public websites to encourage identity thieves to attack them.[17] This was just one of a growing number of "hacktivist" attacks based on political motivations.

18. Mafiaboy: Distributed Denial-of-Service Attacks Against E-Commerce Sites

In February of 2000, a number of major firms were subjected to devastatingly effective distributed denial-of-service (DDoS) attacks that blocked each of their e-commerce systems for hours at a time. Victims of this series of attacks included CNN.com, eBay, Yahoo.com, Amazon.com, Dell.com, eTrade, ZDNet, and other major firms.

The Yankee Group estimated that these attacks cost $1.2 billion in 48 hours—$100 million in lost revenue, $100 million from the need to create tighter security, and $1 billion in combined market capitalization loss.

At first the attack was thought to be the work of an elite hacker, but the culprit was found to be a 15-year-old hacker in Canada, who was caught only because he bragged online about the attack. The attacker, who went by the screen name Mafiaboy, received a sentence of only a few months in a juvenile detention center.

19. Kevin Mitnick: Many Hacking Infractions

Kevin Mitnick, who spent many years hacking, had been on the FBI's Most Wanted list before his arrest in 1995. Among his victims were Motorola, Nokia, Sun Microsystems, and the University of Southern California. In 1999, he reached a plea agreement with the federal government and was sentenced to 3 years and 10 months in prison. He was also required not to use computers and many other electronic devices for 3 years after his release.[18] Finally, he was given a modest $4,125 restitution requirement because it was unlikely he would be highly paid after his release.

---

16   U.S. Department of Justice, "Lusby, Maryland Man Pleads Guilty to Sabotaging IRS Computers," July 24, 2001. www.cybercrime.gov/carpenterPlea.htm.

17   U.S. Department of Justice, "Computer Hacker Intentionally Damages Protected Computer," October 22, 2001. www.cybercrime.gov/khanindict.htm.

18   CNN.com, "Mitnick Ordered to Pay $4,125 in Restitution for Hacking Crimes," August 9, 1999. cnn.com/TECH/computing/9908/09/mitnick.sentence.ap/index/html.

20. Jason Diekman: Hacking While out on Bail

Jason Diekman, 21 years old, admitted hacking into "hundreds, maybe thousands" of computers. He admitted to having hacked into computers at the Jet Propulsion Laboratory, NASA, Harvard, Cornell, UCLA, and many other organizations. He also used stolen credit card numbers and used them to make purchases over the Internet. He was arrested but continued to hack while out on bail. When finally convicted, he was sentenced to 21 months in federal prison and barred from using computers without the permission of his probation officer for 3 years after his release. He was also ordered to pay $88,000 in restitution.[19]

21. Matthew Kroker: Extortion to Explain a Hack

A 16-year-old Kansas teenager allegedly hacked a California city's website using a kiddie script. This probably was part of a long string of attacks.

Shortly afterward, he allegedly sent an e-mail to the webmaster taking credit for the defacement and offering to tell her how to secure the site. In return, she had to send him a notebook computer.

The webmaster, Cathy Sloan, immediately called the local police, who called in the FBI when they realized that Kroker was in another state. She exchanged over 90 e-mails with Kroker over the course of several weeks. She told him that he would have to fill out an application form, which he did, including a great deal of personal information.

When the UPS truck arrived with his computer, the deliverymen were FBI agents. The agents took a statement from him and confiscated his computer. Later, the State of Kansas charged Kroker with 11 felony counts of computer crime.[20]

22. Stephan Puffer: Demonstrating Break-Ins Results in Prosecution

Stephan Puffer, a Houston computer security analyst, demonstrated to a county official and to a reporter from the *Houston Chronicle* how easy it was to break into the district clerk's wireless system.[21] Puffer had done war driving earlier and discovered the open wireless LAN. In the demonstration, he used the wireless LAN to break into the court's host computers. The county eventually closed the new wireless LAN it had set up.

Although Puffer had broken into the host computer as a demonstration, he had broken in. The county prosecutor took his case to the grand jury, which indicted Puffer. This case demonstrates that breaking into a computer system is never a safe activity.

---

[19]   David Eosenzweig, "Computer Hacker Sentenced to 21 Months," *Los Angeles Times*, February 5, 2002. www.latimes.com/news/local/la-000009016feb05.story.

[20]   Bryan McWilliams, "Teen Hacker's Offer to Help Leads to Felony Charges," SecurityFocus, March 13, 2002. online.securityfocus.com/news/352.

[21]   John Leyden, "Ethical Hacker Faces War Driving Charges," *The Register*, July 26, 2002. www.theregister.co.uk/content/55/26397.html.

23. Princeton Director of Admissions Hacks Yale[22]

Yale University's admissions program decided to make it easier for applicants to determine their status. Consequently, Yale created a web-based system to provide this status information. Candidates used their browsers to access the system.

This information was very personal, so applicants had to prove their identity before accessing the system. This was done by having them respond to questions based on data in their application, including last names, birth dates, and social security numbers.

Many of these students also applied to other top universities. At Princeton, associate dean and director of admissions Stephen LeMenager knew that the private information that Yale used to control access was also in the applications that candidates submitted to Princeton. He used this information to log into the Yale system several times as applicants.

When word of the break-in got out, LeMenager admitted doing the break-ins but said that he was merely testing the security of the Yale system. Princeton put him on administrative leave.

This case emphasizes that information used to control access must not be generally available. Even if LeMenager had not broken in, using last names, birth dates, and social security numbers is terrible security. Similarly, the case shows the danger of consumers dealing with multiple companies that use similar information to govern access.

TEST YOUR UNDERSTANDING

1. List which of the attacks just described might have been stopped by a firewall.
2. Describe how each of the attacks described could have been stopped.
3. What fraction of the attacks listed were conducted by employees or ex-employees? (Also list the attacks in this category.)
4. What fraction of the attacks listed were conducted by IT or security employees? (Also list the attacks in this category.)

THE SEPTEMBER 11 DISASTER

On September 11, 2001, 19 hijackers walked through airport security and boarded four jet aircraft, which they quickly turned into weapons of mass destruction. Although the terrorists prepared meticulously for the attack, they were aided by massive air transport security weaknesses at all levels.

Managerial Deficiencies

At the managerial level, both the Federal Aviation Administration (FAA) and the major airlines knew that airport security was only show security. Penetration testers regularly got through checkpoints with handguns and other weapons. It often was pos-

---

[22]   Pamela Ferdinand and Michael Barbaro, "Yale Tells FBI of Rival's Breach of Web Site," www.washington post.com/wp-dyn/articles/A2983–2002Jul25.html. MSNBC.com, "Princeton President Blasts Snooping," July 30, 2002. www.msnbc.com/news/787772.asp. Elsie Jordan and Arielle Levin Becker, "FBI to Investigate Princeton Admissions Hacking Incident," July 26, 2002. www.yaledailynews.com/article.aps?AID=19455. CNN.com, "Princeton Accused of Ivy League Hacking," July 25, 2002. www.cnn.com/2002/US/07/25/yale.princeton/index.html.

sible for people to walk up to aircraft waiting on ramps. Quite a few security employees were later found to have criminal records. Yet before September 11, 2001, the FAA and the airlines did little to improve airport security.

Operational Deficiencies

Staffing

At the operational level, people who staffed airport inspection stations were low-wage workers with no hope of job advancement. Turnover rates were extremely high, leading to a crisis in experience level. In addition, because these security guards worked for the airlines, they may have felt pressure not to slow down boarding with rigorous inspections.

Furthermore, quite a few airport employees were themselves criminals or illegal aliens. A sweep at 15 airports by authorities several months after September 11 led to the arrest of 450 workers. Many of these workers were security personnel. Although Argenbright Security had been fined $1 million in 2000 for failing to check the backgrounds of its security employees, there appears to have been little interest in checking on security personnel until well after the September 11, 2001, disaster.[23]

Known Vulnerabilities

For several years, penetration tests routinely found that a large fraction of test weapons passing through airport security checkpoints were not found. Even well after the September 11 disaster, 26 percent of all weapons went undetected in a checkpoint audit. In some airports, the failure rate was 50 percent.[24] Despite a long history of poor detection performance, airlines made few changes in their checkpoint staffing or procedures.

Nonsensical Procedures

However, even if security employees were extremely diligent, they would not have been able to stop the hijackers. FAA security rules then in effect inexplicably allowed box cutters to be brought aboard aircraft! The hijackers used these as their weapons.

Clutching Defeat from the Jaws of Victory

Perhaps most sadly of all, 9 of the 19 hijackers actually were singled out for special attention—two because of irregularities in their documentation—but all of them were subsequently permitted to board their aircraft.[25]

Government Breakdowns

At the national level, the breakdown continued. In July, an FBI field agent, Kenneth Williams, warned of Arabs with suspicious backgrounds taking flying lessons.[26] His memo was ignored. On August 16, Zacarias Moussaoui, who police believe was the

---

23 CNN.com, "Big Net Makes Big Haul at Airports," April 28, 2002. www.cnn.com/2002/TRAVEL/
    NEWS/04/28/airport.crackdown/index.html.
24 MSNBC.com, "Airports Miss 26% of Weapons in Test," June 17, 2002.
25 Dan Eggen, "Airports Screened 9 of Hijackers," WashingtonPost.com, March 2, 2002.
26 James Poniewozik, "The Man Behind the Memo: How an FBI Agent's Prescient Warning Was Lost in
    the Bureau's 'Black Hole,'" Time.com, May 27, 2002. www.time.com/time/covers/1101020527/
    phoenix.html.

20th terrorist in the plot, was arrested after officials at a Minnesota flight school noti-fied authorities that Moussaoui was acting strangely.[27] (Actually, the company had to call the FBI repeatedly before anybody would listen to them.) Moussaoui wanted to learn how to fly a jumbo jet but was uninterested in learning how to take off and land. He paid his $6,300 tuition in cash, was belligerent, and could not speak French, which he said was his native language. In addition, the French government gave field opera-tives working on the case large amounts of incriminating information about Moussaoui. Agent Coleen Rowley passed this information to FBI headquarters, which ignored this information, refused to request a search warrant of Moussaoui's apart-ment and computer, and impeded the investigation in other ways.[28]

TEST YOUR UNDERSTANDING

    5. Describe the managerial, operational, and national deficiencies that made the September 11, 2001, hijackings possible.

    6. Why do you think there were so many weaknesses in the air transport system?

---

[27] Dana Bash and Terry Frieden, "Mueller: Justice Department to Launch FBI Probe," CNN.com, May 24, 2002. www.cnn.com/2002/US/05/24/fbi.minnesota.memo/index.html.

[28] Romesh Ratnesar and Michael Weisskopf, "How the FBI Blew the Case," Time.com, May 25, 2002. www.time.com/time/nation/article/0,8599,249994,00.html.

ACCESS CONTROL AND SITE SECURITY

Learning Objectives

By the end of this chapter, you should be able to discuss:

- Access control.
- Reusable passwords.
- Building security, including data wiring.
- Access cards.
- Biometric authentication, including verification and identification.
- 802.11 Wireless LAN security.

INTRODUCTION

Access Control

One of the most important principles in security is **access control**, which is the policy-driven limitation of access to systems, data, and dialogs. Quite simply, if attackers can't get to sensitive resources, they can't harm them.

Access control is the policy-driven limitation of access to systems, data, and dialogs.

Enumeration of Resources

The first step in creating an access control policy is to enumerate all of a firm's sensitive systems, such as human resources databases, file servers containing important trade secrets, and consoles in the server room.

Sensitivity of Each Resource

The next step is to determine how sensitive each resource is for the firm. Some resources will be mission-critical, meaning that if they are damaged, the firm could go out of business. Others are not sensitive at all.

Who Should Have Access?

The next step is to determine who should have access to each resource. Normally, this is done by **roles**. For instance, certain files on a file server should be accessible to all logged-in users, while others should be accessible to the server's systems administrators or to a certain application program. Permitting access on the basis of role instead of to each individual is attractive because organizations have many fewer roles than individual people.

What Access Permissions (Authorizations) Should They Have?

For each role (or individual), the next step is to determine the specific access permissions, also called authorizations, that the role or user should have for the resource. **Access permissions (authorizations)** define whether a role or individual should have any access at all and, if so, exactly what they should be allowed to do to the resource. This creates an **access control policy** for the resource.

Access permissions (authorizations) define whether a role or individual should have any access at all and, if so, exactly what the role or individual should be allowed to do to the resource.

For instance, only logged-in users might be allowed any access to a certain file, and they might be limited to reading the file. Systems administrators, however, probably will need to be able to do anything to the file.

Access permissions or authorizations normally are specified by a list of possibilities. For instance, UNIX allows only three possibilities: read-only, write (create, change, delete), and execute (for program files). An individual user or group may have none of these permissions, all of them, or only one or two.

ACCESS CONTROL

Access control is the policy-driven limitation of access to systems, data, and dialogs
Prevent attackers from gaining access, stopping them if they do

ENUMERATION OF RESOURCES

Each important resource must be listed

SENSITIVITY OF EACH RESOURCE

The sensitivity of each resource must be assessed

WHO SHOULD HAVE ACCESS?

A decision must be made over who should have access to each resource
Can be set by individual
More efficient to define by roles (logged-in users, systems administrators, project team
   members, etc.)

WHAT ACCESS PERMISSIONS (AUTHORIZATIONS) SHOULD THEY HAVE?

Access permissions (authorizations) define whether a role or individual should have
   any access at all and, if so, exactly what the role or individual should be allowed to do
   to the resource
Usually presented as a list (read-only, change, execute program, etc.)
Each resource should have an access control policy

HOW SHOULD ACCESS CONTROL BE IMPLEMENTED?

For each resource, need an access protection plan for how to implement protection in
keeping with the selected control policy
For a file on a server, limit authorizations to a small group, harden the server against
   attack, use a firewall to thwart external attackers, etc.

POLICY-BASED ACCESS CONTROL AND PROTECTION

Have a specific access control policy and an access protection policy for each resource
Focuses attention on each resource
Guides the selection and configuration of firewalls and other protections
Guides the periodic auditing and testing of protection plans

Figure 2-1   Access Control (Study Figure)

How Should Access Control Be Implemented?

The last step in access control is to determine how access control protection will be provided to each resource. For instance, a file on a sensitive server may be protected by making the file unreadable except to a small and well-defined group of people, by hardening the host to reduce the likelihood of compromise, and by limiting access to the server via firewalls. These decisions should be documented in an **access protection policy** for each resource.

Policy-Based Control and Protection

Requiring the creation of an access control policy and an access protection policy for each important resource has many benefits.

➤ First, it ensures that the firm will spend at least some time thinking about the security implications of each resource and how these implications can be addressed. It has been said that the main benefit of any plan is to focus attention.

➤ Second, when the server is configured, when firewalls are installed, and when other protections are put into place, each can be selected and configured with respect to its roles in the overall environment of protection for important resources.

➤ Third, it allows for auditing and testing. Periodically, the access protection policy for each resource should be compared to the protection it actually is receiving.

Site Security

Most attacks come into a firm from the Internet. However, some of the most devastating attacks take place within sites, where attackers can put their hands on a target computer or on the site's LAN wiring and switches. Thanks to wireless LANs, eavesdroppers can even lurk just outside the company's premises and attack the firm.

In this chapter, we will look at access control and protection mechanisms needed to defend against attackers who have physical access to sites. (Some of these mechanisms, such as reusable passwords, are also of interest even for remote users.) In the next four chapters, we will look at attacks coming in from the Internet and how to defend against these attacks with firewalls and host hardening.

REUSABLE PASSWORDS

Hands-On Software Cracking

To log onto a server, you need to know an account name and its password. This password normally is a **reusable password** that the account user can use for weeks or months at a time.

Over a network, an attacker could try to log in repeatedly with different possible account names and passwords, but unless the systems administrator is stupid or careless, such an attacker will be locked out after a few attempts. This might constitute a denial-of-service attack against users who cannot get into their locked-out accounts, but it will not give attackers access to the machine.

With physical access, however, an attacker may be able to install a password-cracking program that will try thousands of possible account name/password combinations, or the attacker may be able to copy the password file and crack it at leisure on another machine.

REUSABLE PASSWORDS

DIFFICULTY OF CRACKING PASSWORDS BY GUESSING REMOTELY

HACKING ROOT

Super accounts
Hacking root in UNIX
Super accounts in Windows and NetWare
Elevating privileges
The rarity of hacking root

PHYSICAL ACCESS PASSWORD CRACKING

L0phtcrack
Brute-force password guessing
    Alphabet, no case
    Alphabet, case
    Alphanumeric (letters and digits)
    Keyboard characters
Importance of password length (Figure 2-3)
Dictionary attacks
Hybrid attacks

PASSWORD POLICIES

Good passwords
    At least 6 to 8 characters long
    Change of case, not at beginning
    Digit (0 through 9), not at end
    Other keyboard character, not at end
    Example: tri6#Vial
Testing and enforcing passwords
Password duration policies
Password sharing policies: Generally, forbid shared passwords
Disabling passwords that are no longer valid
Lost passwords (password resets)
    Opportunities for social engineering attacks
    Leave changed password on answering machine
    Automated password resets (problem of easily guessed questions)
Encrypted password files
UNIX passwords
    Ordinary password files
    Shadow password files
Windows passwords
    Obsolete LAN manager passwords (7 characters maximum) should not be used
    Windows NT passwords are better
    Option (not default) to enforce strong passwords

(continued)

Figure 2-2 Server Password Cracking (Study Figure)

SHOULDER SURFING

KEYSTROKE CAPTURE SOFTWARE

Professional versions of Windows protect RAM during password typing
Trojan horse throws up a fake login screen later, reports its finding to attackers

WINDOWS CLIENT PC SOFTWARE

Consumer version login screen is not for security
BIOS passwords allow boot-up security
Screensavers with passwords allow away-from-desk security
Windows professional provides good security

Figure 2-2   (Continued)

TEST YOUR UNDERSTANDING

1.   a) What are reusable passwords? b) Why is password cracking over a network diffi-
     cult to do?

Hacking Root

Super Accounts

Every server has a **super account** that has the access privileges to do anything its owner
wishes in any directory on the server. If attackers get access to this account, they essentially own the computer and can read files, delete files, install software to let the attackers back in later, and do other mischief.

Hacking Root in UNIX

In UNIX, the super account is the **root** account, and being able to log into the root
account is called "**hacking root**." Hacking root is the ultimate prize for UNIX attackers.

Super Accounts in Windows and NetWare

"Hacking root" is commonly, although inaccurately, used to describe hacking the
super account in any operating system. In Microsoft Windows, the super account is
administrator. In Novell NetWare, it is *supervisor*.

Elevating Privileges

Sometimes, even if an attacker can only get access to an account with normal limited
privileges, he or she may be able to **elevate privileges** to gain super account privileges.
For instance, in 2002, there were many attacks on Microsoft SQL server programs,
which by default installed the crucial SA administrative account without a password. A
worm called SQL snake exploited this vulnerability. It created a Guest account with

limited privileges, then elevated this account to administrator status by placing it in the Administrators group.

The Rarity of Hacking Root

Although hacking root is very desirable, it is very difficult to do because only fools give weak passwords to super accounts. Most of the time, password guessing can crack only the passwords of individual user accounts with limited privileges. However, this still can allow attackers to do a great deal of damage. Although hacking root through password guessing is uncommon, a number of the application software attacks we will see in Chapter 9 can give root access without the need for password guessing.

TEST YOUR UNDERSTANDING

2. a) What are super accounts? b) What are the super accounts in UNIX, LINUX, Windows, and NetWare? c) What is hacking root? d) Why is hacking root by password cracking uncommon? e) What is elevating privileges?

Physical Access Password Cracking

Just getting physical access to a server is not enough. It usually is necessary for the systems administrator to have logged in as the super account and to have walked away. Although this is a poor security practice, it is not uncommon.

L0phtcrack

On Windows servers, the password-cracking program of choice is l0phtcrack.[1] This program, like other password-cracking programs, can attempt to crack password files in multiple ways.

Brute-Force Guessing

The obvious approach to password guessing is to try all possible passwords on all (or selected) accounts. This **brute-force** approach tries all possible single-character passwords, then all possible two-character passwords, and so forth.

Forms of Brute-Force Guessing   The attacker can limit **brute-force guessing** to the 26 letters of the alphabet, to uppercase and lowercase letters, to alphanumeric characters (letters and the digits from 0 to 9), or to all possible characters that can be typed on a keyboard. The broader the character set is, the larger the number of combinations that must be tried becomes

Possible Combinations   If a password is N characters long, there are 26^N possible combinations to be tried if simple letters are used. Using uppercase and lowercase increases this to 52^N, using alphanumeric characters increases this to 62^N, and using all keyboard characters increases the number of possible combinations to about 80^N.

Password Length   Secure passwords must be long passwords. Figure 2-3 shows how password length is related to the number of possible passwords a password cracker

---

[1]   L0phtcrack is spelled "l0phtcrack." The second character is a zero. The *L* is capitalized in titles or at the beginnings of sentences.

Password Length in Characters	Alphabetic, No Case (N = 26)	Alphabetic, Case Sensitive (N = 52)	Alphanumeric: Letters and Digits (N = 62)	All Keyboard Characters (N = 80)
1	26	52	62	80
2	676	2,704	3,844	6,400
4	456,976	7,311,616	14,776,336	40,960,000
6	308,915,776	19,770,609,664	56,800,235,584	2.62144E+11
8	2.08827E+11	5.34597E+13	2.1834E+14	1.67772E+15
10	1.41167E+14	1.44555E+17	8.39299E+17	1.07374E+19

Figure 2-3   Password Length

has to search through. Even in the simple situation of case-insensitive alphabetic passwords, the number of possibilities grows rapidly with password length. For two-character passwords, 676 possibilities exist. Increasing password length to four characters increases the number of possibilities to more than 400,000. With six characters, more than 300 million possibilities exist. Given the speed of the computers that can be used in password cracking, however, rather long passwords are needed for safety.

Number of Guesses   On average, an attacker will have to try half of the possible combinations before finding the correct one. Due to the way probability works, however, brute-force guessing sometimes will find a password after only a small number of attempts.

Dictionary Attacks on Common Word Passwords

Few people have passwords that are random combinations of letters, digits, and other keyboard characters. Instead, many users create **common word passwords**, such as *gasoline*. They may even use the names of relatives, pets, or, the lamest password of all, *password*.

A 2002 Pentasafe Security Technologies survey of 15,000 staff members in 600 organizations in the United States and Europe found that 25 percent used common dictionary words like "banana." Fifty percent base their passwords on the names of family members, friends, or pets. Thirty percent use the names of pop idols or sports heroes. Ten percent base their passwords on fantasies. Only 10 percent use complex passwords that are difficult to break.[2]

Although there are millions of random combinations of characters that are six to eight characters long, there are only a few thousand common words in any language. **Dictionary attacks** compare passwords to dictionary lists of common words, with the

---

[2]   Andrew Brown, "UK Study: Passwords Often Easy to Crack," CNN.com, March 13, 2002. www.cnn.com/2002/TECH/ptech/03/13/dangerous.passwords/index.html.

most common words first. If a user creates a common word password, cracking it usually will take only a few seconds. Adding dictionaries with names of sports teams or celebrities will catch many other simple passwords.

Some users create long passwords by using phrases, such as "Nowisthetime." Dictionary attacks also can be used to search for common phrases.

Hybrid Attacks

Many users try to modify common word passwords in simple ways, such as putting a single digit at the end of the word. **Hybrid attacks** try such simple modifications of common passwords.

Effectiveness of Password Cracking

How effective are password-cracking programs? Long, nonword passwords are still quite difficult to crack on ordinary computers, but many users create easily guessed passwords. Several studies reported by Smith[3] indicate that about one fifth to one third of all passwords are fairly easily cracked.

For industrial-strength password cracking, crackers can use specially built password-cracking machines or grids of many PCs. However, most corporate attacks would not merit this.

TEST YOUR UNDERSTANDING

3. a) What is brute-force password guessing? b) Why is password length important? c) What is a dictionary attack? d) Why are dictionary attacks fast compared to brute-force guessing? e) What are hybrid attacks?

Password Policies

Good Passwords

It is important for corporations to have policies that require strong passwords. For example, a corporate policy might require that passwords have the following characteristics.

➤ Be at least six to eight characters long.
➤ Have at least one change of case, not at the start of the word.
➤ Have at least one digit, not at the end of the password.
➤ Perhaps have at least one nonalphanumeric character, not at the end of the password.

A good example of a password that fits all of these rules is tri6#Vial. Although modifying a common word is not ideal, passwords that cannot be memorized almost always are written down, and attackers may be able to find the written version.

Testing and Enforcing for Passwords

Systems administrators can run l0phtcrack against their own servers to check for policy violations. In addition, most operating systems can now be set up to enforce the selection of strong passwords by users, making them less vulnerable.

---

3   Richard E. Smith, *Authentication: From Passwords to Public Keys*, Boston: Addison-Wesley, 2002.

Password Duration Policies

Password policies also should require the frequent changing of passwords. For instance, user passwords should be changed perhaps every 90 days. This reduces the time that each password can be exposed and used by attackers. Crucial passwords should be changed even more frequently.

Shared Password Policies

One especially dangerous password practice is having several people share a password. This is bad for two reasons. First, shared passwords are rarely changed because of the number of people who must be coordinated. The longer a password goes unchanged, the better the odds that an attacker will find it.

Second, and more importantly, if the account is used in an attack, it will be impossible to tell from audit logs who committed the attack. Companies should have clear policies to prohibit shared passwords.

It often is important to avoid shared passwords by assigning access rights to groups. This way, people can all do the same things while maintaining their auditable identity. Unfortunately, some application programs, such as recent versions of Microsoft Exchange, require shared passwords.

Disabling Invalid Accounts

Many accounts and passwords in corporations are invalid because the owner has left the firm, because the account was a temporary one for a contractor, and for other reasons. International Data Corporation has estimated that 30 percent to 60 percent of all accounts in large corporations are invalid. Strong policies and effective procedures should be in place for disabling accounts that become invalid.

Lost Passwords

Roughly a quarter to a third[4] of all calls to help desks are placed because of lost passwords. Therefore, handling lost passwords cannot be ignored. At the same time, dealing with lost passwords is dangerous.

Password Resets   Help desk employees cannot read existing passwords, but they normally have the ability to create a new password for the account. This action is called, not entirely accurately, a **password reset**. One insurance company, Wellpoint, receives 14,000 calls monthly from employees who have lost their passwords.[5] At Wellpoint, the cost of a reset is at least $25 and can range up to $200 if the employee has access to multiple systems.

The Danger of "Lost Password" Social Engineering Attacks   A major social engineering danger is that an attacker will call the help desk claiming to be the owner of an account and request a password reset, usually expressing extreme urgency and

---

4   These are widely quoted percentages. For specific data, see David Lewis, "Bank Cuts Help Desk Costs, *Internetweek*, October 22, 2001. www.internetweek.com/netresults01/net102201.htm.

5   Alexander Salkever, "Software That Asks 'Who Goes There?'" SecurityFocus, February 26, 2002. online.security.focus.com/news/339.

authority. A harried help desk employee might yield to pressure and reset the account password. Afterward, the attacker effectively would own the account, and the proper account owner would be locked out.

Using Answering Machines   The most common recommendation for avoiding this danger is for the help desk employee to reset the password but leave the changed password on the employee's office voice mailbox instead of giving it out directly over the telephone. This is somewhat dangerous, but it is better than giving out reset passwords directly.

Automating Password Resets   Some firms now have automated password reset systems. Employees log into the password reset system and type in their account names. Each employee is then asked a prepared question, such as "Where were you born?" Unfortunately, someone who knows the account holder well or does modest research on the person often can guess many prepared questions.

TEST YOUR UNDERSTANDING

4.   a) What is a good policy for passwords? b) How can programs like l0phtcrack be used to enforce policy? c) Why are password resets for lost passwords dangerous? d) Why are they necessary? e) How can the danger be reduced?

Encrypted Password Files

To make things harder for password crackers, modern operating systems encrypt their password files. This encryption is a modification of the DES algorithm discussed in Chapter 7. It uses the password plus a two-letter "salt" to make cracting even more difficult.

UNIX password encryption is a one-way function, meaning that you cannot compute the password if you only know its encrypted string.

Figure 2-4   Password Encryption

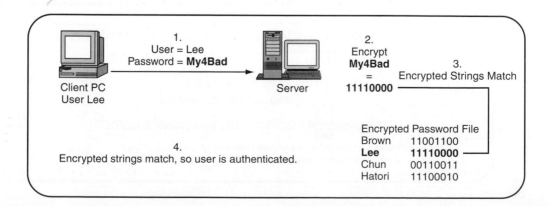

When the user types a password, the server must encrypt the transmitted password. This encryption is replicable, so when a user sends a password to the computer and the computer encrypts it, the encrypted string will match the encrypted string stored in the password file.

Encrypted password files offer considerable security. Systems administrators cannot be tricked into giving out passwords because they cannot retrieve them. Only the password's encrypted string is stored, and it cannot be converted into the original password.

At the same time, if attackers can steal the encrypted password file, they can crack passwords if given sufficient time. An attacker can simply generate many possible passwords, encrypt them, and compare the result with the encrypted strings stored in the encrypted password file.

TEST YOUR UNDERSTANDING

5. a) What threat do encrypted password files reduce? b) When a user submits a password, how is it compared against the encrypted password file? c) If an encrypted password file is stolen, how can it be cracked?

UNIX Passwords

The /etc/passwd File

Almost all versions of UNIX have an **/etc/passwd** file, meaning that the filename is *passwd* and that this file is in the *etc* directory directly under the top-level (root) directory. This file contains essential information for each account. Figure 2-5 illustrates a line from the /etc/passwd file for user Pat Lee's account, *plee*. This record has several fields separated by colons.

Figure 2-5   UNIX /etc/passwd File Entry Without and with Password Shadowing

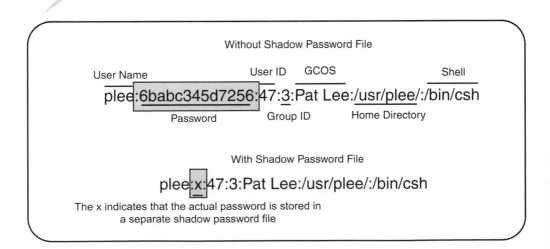

Without Shadow Password File

User Name   User ID   GCOS   Shell

plee:6babc345d7256:47:3:Pat Lee:/usr/plee/:/bin/csh

Password   Group ID   Home Directory

With Shadow Password File

plee:x:47:3:Pat Lee:/usr/plee/:/bin/csh

The x indicates that the actual password is stored in a separate shadow password file

➤ **User Name** (*plee*). This is the account name.

➤ **Password** (*6babc345d7256*). This is the encrypted password (abc . . .) preceded by a *salt value* (6b) to be used with the password. Salts make the encrypted string more difficult to compute.

➤ **User ID** (UID) (*47*). This is a number assigned to this user name for system use in identifying the account.

➤ **Group ID** (GID) (*3*). This is the ID for the user's group. A user is assigned to only one group at a time, although some versions of UNIX relax this constraint.

➤ **GCOS** (*Pat Lee*). Named after an early operating system, the GCOS field holds humanly-readable information about the account owner. Different versions of UNIX put different information in the GCOS field. In this example, only the account owner's name is included.

➤ **Home Directory** (*/usr/plee*). This is the user's home directory. A user normally has full access rights in his or her home directory.

➤ **Shell** (*/bin/csh*). This is the user's default shell program, which provides the user interface. UNIX allows different users to have different shell programs.

Shadow Password Files

The /etc/passwd file must be readable by all processes, so the top design in Figure 2-5 would allow anyone to copy the password file to crack its contents at his or her leisure.

Consequently, almost all UNIX implementations today have **shadow password files** that store the real passwords in an area accessible only to the root account. Where the password entry would be in the original design, there is an x or some other placeholder instead, as the bottom design in Figure 2-5 shows.

Unfortunately, many software processes run with root privileges and so can read the password file. If the attacker can take over such a program, the attacker will have access to the shadow password file.

TEST YOUR UNDERSTANDING

6. a) Why are traditional UNIX /etc/passwd files dangerous? b) How is this danger reduced?

Windows Server Passwords

When Microsoft first created network operating system (NOS) software for servers, its first product was **LAN Manager**. More recently, Microsoft NOS server software has been **Microsoft Windows Server** (NT, 2000, and .NET).

LAN Manager Passwords

LAN Manager had many security weaknesses, including its **LAN Manager password system**. Passwords were effectively limited to only seven characters.

Although passwords of up to 14 characters could be created, they would be divided into two 7-character parts. For instance, the password *Headquarters* would be stored as the encrypted strings for "Headqua" and "rters".

The second part, which has only four characters, would be easy to crack. From this second part and from general context, the attacker may be able to guess that the password is "Headquarters".

Windows NT Passwords

For Windows NT Server and later versions of Windows Server, Microsoft created a new password system, generally called the **Windows NT LAN Manager (NTLM)** system. Version 1 of NTLM allowed longer passwords and with dividing into two strings and was case sensitive. NTLMv2 was even stronger. NTLM can even impose requirements that passwords be strong, although this is not the default.

Disabling LAN Manager Passwords

However, most versions of Windows Server allow LAN Manager passwords for backward compatibility. When installing Windows Server, it is important to disable LAN Manager passwords.

Even then, NTLM is not entirely secure because even NTLMv2 is susceptible to replay attacks in which a login is retransmitted rapidly.

TEST YOUR UNDERSTANDING

     7. a) Compare LAN Manager passwords and Windows NT passwords. b) Why should LAN Manager passwords be disabled on Windows servers?

Shoulder Surfing

One method that attackers with physical access can use to learn passwords is to watch someone while he or she types a password. This is called **shoulder surfing**. Attackers sometimes even talk to the person typing the password to slow the typing rate. Even if an attacker can get only a few characters, this might help the attacker guess the correct password.

TEST YOUR UNDERSTANDING

     8. What is shoulder surfing?

Keystroke Capture Software

One way to get passwords is to capture them as the user types them in, say by planting a **keystroke capture program** on the user's client PC or server. This method also can be used to capture the encryption keys we will see in Chapter 7.

Protected RAM Buffers

When the user types his or her password, the characters are stored in a special RAM buffer. The simplest way to capture passwords is to read this RAM buffer. However, in UNIX and Microsoft Windows Server, this buffer is protected so that only the operating system itself can read the password. Although Microsoft Windows 2000 and XP professional provide such protection on the client side, Windows 98, ME, and XP home do not.

Trojan Horse Password Capture Software

If the attacker can plant a **Trojan horse**[6] **password capture program** on the client PC, the program may pop up a standard-looking login screen and ask the user to retype his

---

[6]   A Trojan horse is a program that appears to be one thing but is really another. Chapter 4 describes various types of Trojan horses.

or her user name and password. If the user complies, the program transmits the information to the attacker.

TEST YOUR UNDERSTANDING

9.   a) Why is it difficult to write a program that captures passwords as users type them in?
b) How do Trojan horse password capture programs get around this problem?

Windows Client PC Passwords

If an attacker can walk up to a client PC in an office, he or she may be able to use the computer to log into a server with the user's access permissions.

Login Passwords

When a consumer Windows client operating system (95, 98, ME, XP home) first boots up, users may be asked for a login name and password. However, anyone can bypass this **login password** by hitting escape, so this does not function as a security feature. It is used in personalizing Windows and in peer-to-peer file sharing and printing.

BIOS Passwords

Almost all client PCs, however, have a BIOS (Basic Input/Output System) boot-up password that takes effect when the computer is booted and before Windows is loaded. This **BIOS password** does control access. Each PC's BIOS password setup is different, so users must consult their manuals.

However, if the attacker has time and privacy, he or she can open the computer's case and remove the small battery (about the size of a dime) that supplies power to BIOS memory. This will erase the contents of BIOS memory, changing everything back to the initial factory specification—including the absence of a BIOS password.

Screensaver with Passwords

BIOS passwords protect you when you boot up. However, if a user steps away from his or her PC and leaves it on, an attacker can still use the system. Fortunately, Windows allows users to add passwords to their screensavers so that people walking by cannot use their unattended systems. Screensavers should come on quickly in order for this to be useful. Again, losing the **screensaver password** is a serious problem.

Saving Passwords

Windows typically asks users if they wish to save passwords. This is dangerous because it means that if attackers gain access to their PCs, the attackers will be able to log in as the users.

Windows Professional

Windows 2000 professional and XP professional actually do have logon passwords that provide strong security. You cannot simply bypass them by hitting escape as you can with Windows 95, 98, ME, and XP home.

TEST YOUR UNDERSTANDING

10.   a) Do logon passwords for consumer versions of Windows provide security? b) How can users of consumer versions of Windows protect their computers from people

walking by and using them? c) Why are lost passwords a serious problem? d) Why is saving passwords dangerous? e) Do logon passwords provide security for professional versions of Windows?

BUILDING SECURITY

To thwart physical access attacks, it is important to prevent people from touching wires and equipment to which they do not have legitimate access. This requires controlling access to and within buildings.

In most firms, physical building security is under a different department than network security. However, this may change in the future, and it is important for IT security professionals to understand physical access control.

More directly, building access control is moving increasingly to biometric security and security cards, which are likely to be used heavily in IT security, as well. We will spend most of this section looking at biometrics.

Figure 2-6 Building Security (Study Figure)

BUILDING SECURITY BASICS

    Single point of (normal) entry to building
    Fire doors, etc.: Use closed-circuit television (CCTV) and alarms
    Security centers
        Monitors for CCTV
        Videotapes that must be retained
        Alarms
    Interior doors
    Piggybacking
    Enforcing policies
    Training security personnel
    Training all employees
    Phone stickers with security center phone number
    Thwarting piggybacking
    Dumpster diving

DATA WIRING SECURITY

    Telecommunications closets
    Wiring conduits
    Server rooms

Building Security Basics

Building Access Control: Single Entry Points

The most basic element in building security is controlling access from the outside. A building should have only a single normal entry point, and a guard station should be located at the entry point for identifying employees and checking the credentials of visitors.

Other Building Entry Points

Fire regulations almost always require fire exits. All fire exit doors should have alarms, and fire exit doors should be monitored by **closed-circuit television (CCTV)**.

Security Centers

Building security personnel normally operate out of a **security center**. There, a bank of **TV monitors** shows various CCTV views of critical corridors and doors. These camera feeds should be captured on **video recorders** for later playback if questions arise or for evidence in legal prosecution or employee disciplining. The videotapes must be retained in the center for a prescribed period of time. Alarms on fire exits and windows also should ring in this room.

Interior Doors

In secure buildings, there often are locked **interior doors** between parts of the building. This reduces the ability of employees and visitors to move to parts of the building to which they have no legitimate access. Interior doors are difficult to control because there are so many of them and because they are geographically distributed.

If possible, each door access should be **logged** (reported) for later analysis. If several incidents occur, an analysis of the door logs might be able to narrow the number of possible perpetrators to only a few. Those logs are maintained in the security center.

Piggybacking

A major problem with security at interior doors is that attackers often can wait until someone else opens a door. They then follow the legitimate employee through the open door. Often, the employee will even hold the door open for the attacker. This process, called **piggybacking**, tends to be extremely effective because most people feel that not letting a person follow you through a door is rude and confrontational.

Enforcing Policies

Entry control and locked interior doors do little good if strong training and policy enforcement are not put in place. Piggybacking, entry without IDs, and other physical penetration techniques are successful far too often. In discussions with the author, physical penetration testers, who test corporate security at the request of the corporations being penetrated, report that they are almost never stopped. One penetration tester even drove into a military base holding up a dollar bill instead of a green military ID card.

Training Security Personnel

As in everything else, training is a serious issue. Building entry guards must be trained in the need to check all employee badges and ensure that contractors and maintenance personnel are from the companies they claim to represent. Security center personnel must be trained on both equipment and procedures.

Training All Employees

All employees should be trained in the importance of reporting suspicious people in secure areas. The training should attempt to foster an atmosphere of watchfulness in which reporting unusual people in an area is a normal aspect of business.

Phone Stickers

Physically, every telephone should have a sticker with the security room's extension. It is amazing how few people in typical organizations even know how to report suspicious activity.

Thwarting Piggybacking

Piggybacking is a particularly difficult problem to address. A different culture is needed, and scenario discussions and role playing may be needed to change employee culture.

In addition, piggybacking prohibitions must be enforced. One approach is to monitor some security doors and issue warnings to employees who allow piggybacking.

Dumpster Diving

A final common, building-related threat is **Dumpster diving**, in which an attacker goes through a firm's garbage looking for documents, backup tapes, floppy disks, and other information-carrying media. Building Dumpsters should be located in a secure and lighted area, perhaps under CCTV surveillance.

TEST YOUR UNDERSTANDING

11. a) Describe the elements of building security. b) What is piggybacking? c) How can piggybacking and similar problems be controlled? d) What is Dumpster diving?

Data Wiring Security

Data networks and telephony require running thousands of cords through buildings. It is important to secure this wiring from access by wiretappers. Figure 2-7 shows data wiring in a typical large building.

Telecommunications Closets

Switches, routers, and other devices concentrate many transmission cords in single places. Normally, firms put such devices in locked **telecommunications closets**, along with telephone wiring concentrators such as hubs, switches, and routers. It is important to control access to these closets because attackers can plant stand-alone sniffers in such rooms easily if they are not locked. Access should be limited, and each access should be logged. These rooms are rarely visited and contain a great

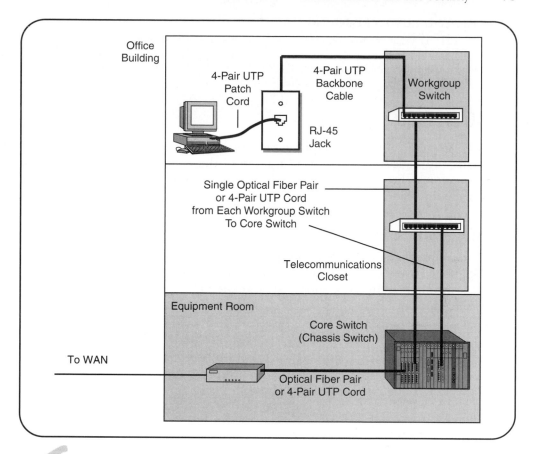

Figure 2-7   Physical Building Wiring

deal of equipment, making the detection of sniffers placed there unlikely for weeks or even months.

Wiring Conduits

Wires traveling between telecommunications closets and equipment rooms must be protected. Often, running them through false ceilings provides decent security because working on such wiring is highly visible. In other cases, wiring paths with many cords between floors and on floors can be placed in hard **conduits** that make interception en route more difficult.

Server Rooms

Normally, servers are located in central **server rooms**. Unfortunately, many people pass through these server rooms, including employees from many areas in the firm, contractors, and maintenance personnel. A higher-than-average level of vigilance is important in such rooms.

TEST YOUR UNDERSTANDING

12. a) What are telecommunications closets, and why should they be protected? b) How do conduits provide security against wiretapping? c) What are server rooms, and why do they need special protection?

ACCESS CARDS

Many companies require employees to carry **identity badges** or **identity cards**. These cards and badges normally have a photo of the employee for authentication. In a growing number of cases, these cards and badges also are being used as **access cards** for interior doors and building entry. Some are used for computer account access.

Magnetic Stripe Cards

The simplest access cards use magnetic stripes like the ones on your credit cards. Magnetic stripes can store authentication information about the individual. If you have traveled recently, you know that **magnetic stripe (mag stripe)** cards are often used for hotel room access.

Figure 2-8   Access Cards (Study Figure)

MAGNETIC STRIPE CARDS

SMART CARDS

   Have a microprocessor and RAM
   More sophisticated than mag stripe cards

TOKENS

   Constantly changing passwords

CARD CANCELLATION

   Requires a central system

PINs

   Personal Identification Numbers
   Short: About 4 digits
   Can be short because attempts are manual
   Should not choose obvious combinations (1111, 1234) or important dates
   Provide two-factor authentication

Smart Cards

Smart cards look like magnetic stripe cards but have built-in microprocessors and memory. This allows smart cards to do processing for more sophisticated authentication.

Tokens

A **token** is an access card or other small device that has a number that changes frequently and is visible on its screen. Users must type this number into key locks (or into their computers).[7] This **one-time password** avoids the need for reusable passwords, which, we saw earlier, are often easy to defeat.

Card Cancellation

If an employee loses a mag stripe card, smart card, or token, it is important to be able to disable access. For instance, in hotels, if you lose your card, a front desk employee will disable the old card's access to all locks. The employee will then give you a new card for your room.

Of course, this requires installing wiring from the security center to individual access doors and also requires the purchase of fairly expensive locks. However, card loss is so common that not dealing actively with lost access devices would make such systems useless. These wiring connections also are needed for access logging.

TEST YOUR UNDERSTANDING

13.   a) Distinguish among mag stripe, smart, and token access cards. b) Why is disabling lost access cards important?

PINs: Two-Factor Authentication

PINs

Even with systems that can disable cards, a window of opportunity will exist for attackers who steal cards or find lost cards. Some firms require employees to type **personal identification numbers (PINs)** when they use access cards.

Short PINs

Passwords need to be long because attackers can try millions of comparisons per second. However, PINs must be entered manually, so attackers can try only a single PIN every second or two. In addition, someone standing over an access door trying many PIN codes would be highly visible and therefore vulnerable to detection. Still, the company should ban easily guessed PINs such as 1111, 2222, 1234, the last four digits of the user's social security number, or an important personal date in month/day format.

Two-Factor Authentication

The combination of information on access cards and PINs is called **two-factor authentication** because it uses two forms of identification. Two-factor authentication is an important principle for physical and computer access control.

---

[7]   In the movie *A Beautiful Mind*, John Nash believes that he has been given an implant that does something similar.

14. a) What is a PIN? b) Why can PINs be short—only about four digits—but passwords must be much longer? c) What is two-factor authentication?

BIOMETRIC AUTHENTICATION

Biometric Identification

We forget passwords. We lose access cards. Yet despite jokes about forgetting our heads, we always take our bodies with us. This permits **biometric authentication** based on physical and motion (bio) measurements (metrics). Biometric authentication is based on something you are (your fingerprint, iris pattern, face, hand geometry, and so forth) or something you do (write, type, and so forth). A major promise of biometrics is to make reusable passwords obsolete.

TEST YOUR UNDERSTANDING
15. a) What is biometric authentication? b) What is the major promise of biometrics?

Biometric Systems

Enrollment
Figure 2-10 shows how biometric authentication is done. Each user must first be **enrolled** in the system. This means that each person's biometric data must be **scanned** by a reader, **processed** to extract a few **key features**, and then stored as the user's **template** in the database.

Later Access Attempts
Later, when users wish authentication, they are scanned again. This **access data** is processed and then matched against the database.

Acceptance or Rejection
A **match index** is computed to determine the goodness of fit. If the match index meets **decision criteria**, the applicant is accepted. Otherwise, the applicant is rejected.

TEST YOUR UNDERSTANDING
16. a) Describe the enrollment process. b) Distinguish between scanning and processing. c) What are key features? d) What is a template? e) What is access data? f) What are match indices, and how are they related to decision criteria?

Authentication and Identification

Verification
Biometric authentication can be done in two ways. In **verification**, an applicant claims to be a particular person, and the challenge is to measure the applicant's biometric sample data against that of the person he or she claims to be.

In verification, there is a one-to-one comparison between the applicant and a single profile. The system makes the access decision based on the probability that an applicant is the person he or she claims to be.

BIOMETRIC AUTHENTICATION

BIOMETRIC SYSTEMS (Figure 2-10)

Enrollment (scan, process for key features, store template)
Later access attempts
Acceptance or rejection

VERIFICATION VERSUS IDENTIFICATION

Verification: Are applicants who they claim to be? (compare with single template)
Identification: Who is the applicant? (compare with all templates)
Verification is good to replace passwords in logins
Identification is good for door access and other situations where entering a name
   would be difficult

PRECISION

False acceptance rates (FARs): Percentage of unauthorized people allowed in
False rejection rates (FRRs): Percentage of authorized people rejected
   Can be reduced by allowing multiple access attempts
   Can harm user acceptance
Vendor claims tend to be exaggerated through tests under ideal conditions

USER ACCEPTANCE IS CRUCIAL

Fingerprint recognition has a criminal connotation
Some methods are difficult to use, require a disciplined group

BIOMETRIC METHODS

Fingerprint recognition
   Simple, inexpensive, well proven
   Can be defeated with copies
Iris recognition
   Pattern in colored part of eye
   Very low FARs
   High FRR rate can harm acceptance
   Somewhat difficult to use: Must line up eye exactly
Face recognition (surreptitious identification is possible)
Hand geometry
Voice recognition
   High error rates
Keystroke recognition
   Normally restricted to passwords
   Ongoing during session could allow continuous authentication
Signature recognition
   Pattern and writing dynamics

BIOMETRIC STANDARDS

Poor standards situation
Missing standards, competing standards
Worst for user data (fingerprint feature databases)

Figure 2-9   Biometric Authentication (Study Figure)

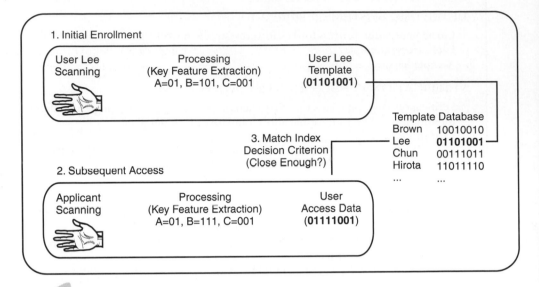

Figure 2-10 Biometric Authentication System

Identification

In **identification**, in contrast, the applicant does not claim to be a particular person. It is the job of the system to identify the applicant, that is, to determine who he or she is. In identification, the applicant's biometric sample data must be matched against the data for *everyone whose profile is stored in the system.* The system makes the access decision based on the most probable acceptable match.

Verification Versus Identification

Verification is easier than identification because the access data has to be matched only against a single user's template. However, although identification requires many matches, it frees users from the need to type their names or account names. Verification is good for replacing computer account passwords. Identification is good for door access control.

TEST YOUR UNDERSTANDING

17. a) Distinguish between verification and identification. b) What is the advantage of verification compared to identification? c) When would you use verification? d) What is the advantage of identification compared to verification? e) Under what circumstances would you use identification?

Precision

Some biometric methods make fewer errors than others, but precision (freedom from errors in making access decisions) also depends on how a method is implemented and on environmental conditions as the data is collected.

False Acceptance Rate (FAR)

Accepting an applicant when the person should be rejected is called a false acceptance. The **false acceptance rate (FAR)** is the percentage of applicants who should be rejected but are instead accepted. False acceptances are very bad for security.

False Rejection Rate (FRR)

False rejections occur when a legitimate user is locked out. Although not necessarily bad from a security viewpoint, a significant **false rejection rate (FRR)** can lead to a great deal of user dissatisfaction and is likely to kill the system. Most systems allow users to attempt access several times to improve their probability of access.

Vendor Claims

Unfortunately, vendor claims for FARs and FRRs often are misleading. They usually are based on highly idealized situations not representative of real-world conditions.

TEST YOUR UNDERSTANDING

18. a) Distinguish between FARs and FRRs. b) Why are FARs important? c) Do FARs and FRRs vary by method? d) Why are FRRs important? e) What does allowing multiple access attempts do? f) Are vendor claims about FARs and FRRs accurate?

User Acceptance

Nanavati, Thieme, and Nanavati[8] have noted that some techniques are more acceptable to users. Some, like fingerprint recognition, have unfortunate associations because they are used to identify criminals. In addition, some techniques are difficult to use and require precise positioning; these are likely to be useful only in disciplined communities.

TEST YOUR UNDERSTANDING

19. a) Why is user acceptance important? b) What factors influence user acceptance?

Biometric Methods

Fingerprint Recognition

From crime movies, almost everyone is familiar with fingerprint identification. **Fingerprint recognition** technology is well developed and inexpensive. Unfortunately, fingerprint recognition can have precision problems.

The cheapest fingerprint readers are dangerous because they are not based on 3D imaging and may be fooled by a photo of a fingerprint. However, most fingerprint readers read 3D images that would require a fake finger to be built. This usually requires the true party's cooperation, but researchers in 2002 were able to defeat 80 percent of fingerprint recognition systems by creating a 3D finger from a **latent print** (that is, a print left on a glass or other object).[9]

---

[8] Samir Nanavati, Michael Thieme, and Raj Nanavati. *Biometrics, Identity: Verification in a Networked World,* New York: Wiley Computer Publishing, John Wiley & Sons, 2002.

[9] "Doubt Cast on Fingerprint Security," BBC News, May 17, 2002. news.bbc.co.uk/hi/english/sci/tech/newsid_1991000/1991517.stm.

Iris Recognition

The iris is the colored part of the eye. Irises are far more complex and individual than fingerprints. In fact, **iris recognition** probably is the most precise form of biometric authentication. In general, iris scanning is the gold standard in biometric authentication. Unfortunately, like gold, it is expensive.

Iris scanners can read iris patterns from several centimeters away to a meter or so away.[10] Unfortunately, iris scanning requires user training and care in eye positioning. This limits the communities of users in which iris recognition can be used.[11]

Face Recognition

Facial features can be read from several meters away. This makes **face recognition** useful for door access control. However, face recognition has environmental problems.[12] It is highly sensitive to lighting differences between the scanned image stored on the computer and the situation in which the scan is taken. It also is moderately sensitive to changes in facial features such as facial hair, head position, and even changes in expression.

Hand Geometry

Human **hand geometry**, including finger lengths, finger widths, palm widths, and other matters, is fairly easy to measure and is used mostly in door access control because of its large physical form factor.

Voice Recognition

Fingerprint, iris, face, and hand geometry recognition are examples of something you *are*. **Voice recognition**, in contrast, is based on something you *do*, namely speak. Unfortunately, voice recognition is difficult and can sometimes be fooled by recordings. High FRRs make voice recognition frustrating to users.

Keystroke Recognition

When people type, they tend to have distinctive rhythms in the timing between keystrokes for certain pairs of characters. The simplest **keystroke recognition** systems check only login passwords. Ideally, however, keystroke recognition could be done during an entire session to ensure that someone else has not walked up to the person's keyboard during the real user's absence.

Signature Recognition

Using handwriting for identification is an old technique. Signature recognition goes well beyond the final image that appears on paper. With **signature recognition**, the timing and pressure of the signature process are captured, as well as character shapes. However, signature recognition does not fit naturally into the worlds of either PCs or access doors. It is most likely to be used in retail stores, which sometimes already capture signatures.

---

[10]   In contrast, retinal scanning, which is based on patterns in the retina at the back of the eyeball, requires users to press their eye sockets against a reader; many users will not do this. *Biometrics, Identity*.
[11]   *Biometrics, Identity*.
[12]   *Biometrics, Identity*.

20. a) What is the advantage of fingerprint recognition? b)What are the disadvantages? c) What is the advantage of iris recognition? d) What are the disadvantages? e) What is the advantage of face recognition? f) Where is hand geometry recognition used? g) What is the advantage of voiceprint recognition? h) What are the disadvantages? i) Compare keystroke and signature recognition.

Biometric Standards

The General Situation

Without interoperability among vendors, companies are understandably reluctant to install biometric systems. Unfortunately, biometric standards are just beginning to appear. Although some standards exist, they are collectively inadequate, and in several cases they compete.

User Data

The most difficult standards problem is creating standards for specifying user data, for instance, how to represent fingerprint data or iris data. Here, little progress is being made, although the ANSI NCTIS standards are making some progress, most notably in the B10.8 standards for drivers' licenses and ID cards.

21. a) What is the status of biometric standards in general? b) Why is this bad? c) What is the most difficult biometric standards problem?

Can Biometrics Be Duped?

The Importance of Biometrics

Companies already are investing a great deal in biometrics. Several airports are installing biometric face scanners to catch criminals. Some countries are even developing national ID cards that use biometrics.

Concerns

All of this is being undertaken despite little research on normal false positives and false negatives. An even bigger concern is whether attackers who deliberately try to dupe biometrics systems can succeed.

Airport Security Systems

A special concern of privacy advocates are airport systems designed to use face identification to catch criminals. As people walk through airports, they are compared to pictures of known criminals and terrorists. Travelers are stopped for questioning if a match is indicated.

Inherently, this is a bad idea. It is likely that few of the thousands of people passing through airports each day are criminals, and far fewer are likely to be terrorists. Even a tiny false identification rate will mark dozens of innocent people each day.

In addition, evidence is growing that face scanners can be easily fooled. For instance, the American Civil Liberties Union (ACLU) recently examined results from an 8-week trial of a face detection system at the Palm Beach International Airport. The face recognition system was loaded with data on a small number of volunteers. Data collected during the test found that when volunteers walked through the airport, only 455 out of 958 were identified—a false rejection rate of more than 50 percent. In other words, the system was almost but not quite as good as a coin flip.

The recognition rate went down if a person wore glasses, especially with tinted lenses. The recognition rate also went down if the person looked away from the camera. In addition, the system used high-quality photographs that were likely to be much better than the photos that would be fed into a real system. Poorer photos would further reduce the detection rate.

The false acceptance rate—declaring a match incorrectly—was also disturbing. False acceptances occurred at a rate of 250 per week over a 4-week recording period. Although this was less than a 1 percent false acceptance rate, inconveniencing 250 passengers and employees each week is a problem.

In addition, the system had a database of only 250 photographs. Any realistic database would include thousands of criminals and terrorists. This would generate a much higher incorrect match rate because there would be many more chances for false matches.

DOD Tests

In 2002, the U.S. Department of Defense conducted a 270-person pilot study with a face recognition system and an iris recognition system. It found that the face recognition system identified the correct person only 51 percent of the time. The iris recognition system was better, identifying the correct person 94 percent of the time. Yet even for the iris recognition system, a 6 percent identification failure rate is completely unacceptable. Also, note that there were only 270 people in the database. With thousands or millions of people, the recognition rates would have been far worse.

Deliberate Duping

As discouraging as the Palm Beach and DOD data are, the subjects were not deliberately trying to evade the system. What if an attacker set out to beat a fingerprint identification system by spoofing fingerprints?

The German magazine *c't* had bad news when it set out to fool 11 face and fingerprint security systems.[13] Some fingerprint systems could be fooled if the tester simply breathed on the sensor. This brought up the previous person's fingerprint. Other fingerprint systems would call up previous fingerprints if a small bag of water was placed on the sensor. Some face recognition systems could be fooled by a movie of a legitimate user on a laptop screen.

Professor Matsumoto's Experiments

Engineering Professor Tsutomo Matsumoto's research team at Yokohama National University in Japan tested a commercial fingerprint system. He first created a gelatin mold of a copy of a fingerprint and fooled the sensors of 11 commercial fingerprint systems 80 percent of the time. He then created another gelatin finger—this time with a latent fingerprint lifted off a glass. He again had an 80 percent success rate.[14]

13   BBC News, "High-Tech Security Flaws Exposed," May 31, 2002. news.bbc.co.uk/hi/english/sci/tech/newsid_2016000/2016788.stm.
14   Tsutomo Matsumoto, "Importance of Open Discussion on Adversarial Analyses for Mobile Security Technologies: A Case Study for User Investigation," ITU-T Workshop on Security, Seoul, May 14, 2002. www.itu.int/itudoc/itu-t/workshop/security/present/s5p4.pdf.

The Revocation Problem

Another concern is the **revocation problem**—what to do if the biometric signature in the database is stolen through hacking or some other means. Then it would be easy for attackers to impersonate the person whose identity information was stolen.

With passwords, the revocation problem is trivial. The user is given a new password and told not to use the old one. For biometric access control, the situation is not as simple. Obviously, users cannot be told to cut off their fingers and grow new ones or poke out their right eye and grow another one. Given the permanence of biometric signatures, the revocation problem is crucial, but little progress seems to have been made in addressing it.

TEST YOUR UNDERSTANDING

22.   a) Describe the key results of the Palm Beach International Airport study. b) Describe some key results of the *c't* research. c) How effective were efforts to fool fingerprint scanners in Professor Matsumoto's study? d) What is the revocation problem? e) Why is the revocation problem especially dangerous in biometric access?

802.11 WIRELESS LAN (WLAN) SECURITY

Ethernet uses physical transmission media—copper wire and optical fiber. Wireless LANs (WLANs), in contrast, use radio for transmission. Unlike wires and fiber, which largely contain signals within the medium, WLANs spread their signals widely, allowing attackers to read messages easily. In addition, in **drive-by hacking**, an attacker reads frames and can even send attack frames without entering the premises.

TEST YOUR UNDERSTANDING

23.   What is drive-by hacking?

802.11

The main standard for wireless LANs is the **802.11** family of standards. Although Bluetooth is also becoming popular, Bluetooth is used mostly for connecting devices within a few meters of each other, making Bluetooth useful primarily for eliminating cabling among devices. In contrast, 802.11 signals travel a few tens of meters, and 802.11 WLANs can be extended to cover entire sites by placing multiple access points around the premises. These distances, unfortunately, also give attackers easy access.

Basic Operation

Figure 2-12 illustrates a portion of a typical 802.11 WLAN. This figure shows a number of key elements.

Main Wired Network

First, the figure shows that the wireless LAN is connected to the site's main wired LAN. We will assume in this example that it is an Ethernet LAN. The main Ethernet LAN is needed because most wireless devices are client machines, and the servers they need to access are located on the Ethernet LAN.

802.11 WIRELESS LAN FAMILY OF STANDARDS

BASIC OPERATION (Figure 2-12)

Main wired network for servers
Wireless stations with wireless NICs
Access points
Access points are bridges
Propagation distance: Farther for attackers than users
Handoffs as wireless stations move from one access point to another

MULTIPLE 802.11 STANDARDS (Figure 2-13)

APPARENT 802.11 SECURITY

Spread spectrum transmission does not provide security
SSIDs are broadcast, so no security

WIRED EQUIVALENT PRIVACY (WEP)

Not enabled by default
40-bit encryption keys are too small
  Nonstandard 128-bit (really 104-bit) keys are reasonably interoperable
Shared passwords
  Access points and all stations use the same password
  Difficult to change, so rarely changed
  People tend to share shared passwords too widely
Flawed security algorithms

802.1x AND 802.11i (Figure 2-14)

Authentication server
User data server
Individual keys given out at access point
Multiple authentication options
  TLS
    In strongest option, both client and access point must have digital certificates
    Difficult to create public key infrastructure for digital certificates
    Option for only access point to have a digital certificate; no authentication for station
  TTLS
    Access point must have digital certificate
    Station authenticated with password or other weak approach
  MD5 CHAP authenticates only wireless station, with reusable password
Apparent security weaknesses in 802.11i; severity or ease of exploitation is not known
Temporal Key Integrity Protocol (TKIP)
  Temporary stopgap method; many older systems can be upgraded
  Key changed every 10,000 frames to foil data collection for key guessing

Figure 2-11 802.11 Wireless LAN (WLAN) Security (Study Figure)

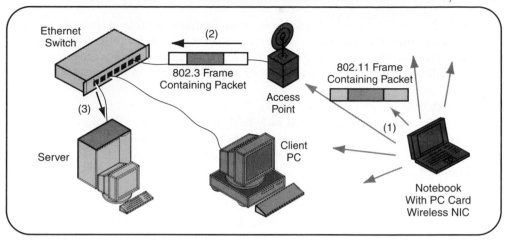

Figure 2-12   802.11 Wireless LANs

Access Points

The **access point** (or wireless access point) serves a number of functions. First, it is a bridge between the main wired LAN and the wireless LAN. **Bridges** are devices that connect two LANs of different technology—in this case 802.3 and 802.11 technologies.

Second, the access point controls the wireless stations. For instance, it tells stations what signal power to use when they transmit. The access point also engages in several other types of supervisory communication with them during operation.

Wireless Stations

Wireless stations normally need an add-in card called a **wireless NIC** (network interface card). Typically, wireless NICs are credit card–size push-in boards that simply snap into the station using the PC Card standard. In some cases, however, NICs are external boxes that connect via USB ports. Wireless NICs have built-in radios and antennas.

Normal Operation

When a wireless station has a message to send, it places a packet in an 802.11 frame and transmits the frame to the access point. The access point removes the packet from the 802.11 frame, places the packet in an Ethernet frame, and sends the Ethernet frame to the server.

When the server replies, its reply packet contained in an Ethernet frame goes to the access point. The access point removes the packet from the Ethernet frame, places the packet in the 802.11 frame, and transmits the 802.11 frame.

Propagation Distance

Radio signals propagate only a few tens of meters. As distance increases, propagation difficulties grow. Wireless stations and access points cope with these difficulties by reducing the transmission speed for distant stations.

However, extremely sensitive equipment might be able to pick up at least parts of conversations at considerably longer distances. Quoted distances in vendor brochures and reviews refer to distances over which propagation will be *good*. This is not a good guideline for distances over which your signals are vulnerable.

Handoffs

A single access point can reach only fairly nearby devices. To cover a larger site, it is necessary to have several access points whose signal ranges overlap. When stations move between access points, they are handed off from one access point to another. Handoff allows companies to build large, sitewide WLANs.

TEST YOUR UNDERSTANDING

24. a) What is the main family of wireless LAN standards? b) Why is a wired LAN still necessary? c) What do access points do? d) Compare maximum distances for normal users and drive-by hackers. e) What are handoffs?

Multiple 802.11 Standards

Figure 2-13 shows that several 802.11 standards exist. These standards vary in rated speed, the unlicensed radio band used, and propagation distance. Actual data throughput often is only half of the rated speed near the access point and falls off rapidly with distance. The 5-GHz unlicensed band has about three times the capacity of the 2.4-GHz unlicensed band and so can support many more users.

Apparent 802.11 Security

Spread Spectrum Operation and Security

All 802.11 versions use spread spectrum transmission, in which the signal is spread over a wide range of frequencies. Spread spectrum transmission is used in the military for security. However, the types of spread spectrum transmission used in 802.11 transmission offer no security; they were designed to make it easy for stations to find and hear one another.[15]

SSIDs

To work with an access point, your station must know the access point's **Service Set Identifier (SSID)**.[16] (All access points in a WLAN have the same SSID.) This requirement for stations to know the SSID might seem to give security. However, SSIDs in frame headers are transmitted in the clear, so sniffer programs can find SSIDs easily.

TEST YOUR UNDERSTANDING

25. a) Does spread spectrum transmission in 802.11 create security? b) What are SSIDs, and do they offer security?

---

[15] Spread spectrum transmission is mandated for unlicensed radio bands to improve propagation. Many propagation difficulties are frequency dependent, and using a broad spectrum of frequencies reduces the damage of frequency-specific problems.

[16] Extended SSIDs (ESSIDs) are used instead of SSIDs by some access points but are essentially the same thing.

Standard	Rated Speed (a)	Unlicensed Radio Band	Effective Distance (b)
802.11b	11 Mbps	2.4 GHz	~30–50 meters
802.11a	54 Mbps	5 GHz	~10–30 meters
802.11g	54 Mbps	2.4 GHz	?

Notes: (a) Actual speeds are much lower and decline with distance. (b) These are distances for good communication; attackers can read some signals and send attack frames from longer distances.

Figure 2-13   802.11 Wireless LAN Standards

Wired Equivalent Privacy (WEP)

The 802.11 Working Group's initial solution for WLAN security was **wired equivalent privacy (WEP)**. This approach, unfortunately, is full of security holes.

Off by Default
Although WEP is inherently weak, as we will soon see, the biggest problem with WEP is that it is not turned on by default. As a consequence, many users fail to turn on WEP. In the spring of 2002, netstumbler.com had a list of more than 25,000 unprotected access points in the United States.

40-Bit Passwords
Another major weakness in WEP is that the basic specification calls for an access point and all of its users to share a single 40-bit-long password. Forty bits is too short for good security, as we will see in Chapter 7. However, many vendors now offer optional 128-bit passwords (really 104-bit passwords with 24-bit initialization vectors). Interoperability among these nonstandard 128-bit password implementations is fairly good.

Shared Passwords
More importantly, having **shared passwords**—in which the access point and all stations using it use the same reusable password—is a bad idea. It is difficult to change shared passwords because the change must be coordinated on the access point and every mobile device that uses the access point. Consequently, shared passwords are rarely changed. Given enough time, attackers can crack the password.[17]

Flawed Algorithms
A major tenet of encryption is that you should always use well-tested algorithms because most new algorithms are quickly broken by cryptoanalysts. The 802.11 Working Group violated this principle and then proved its truth as cryptoanalysts soon

---

17   In addition, because "everybody knows" the password, people share the password freely even when they should not.

found a number of serious weaknesses in the WEP security algorithms that allowed anyone listening to traffic to break the encryption in a reasonable period of time.[18]

TEST YOUR UNDERSTANDING

26.   a) What is the biggest problem with WEP? b) What key lengths are used with WEP? c) How does WEP use shared passwords? d) Why is this bad? e) Are the fundamental security algorithms used in WEP safe?

802.1x and 802.11i

The 802.11 Working Group is now working to strengthen security through the 802.11i option, which is based on the 802.1x authentication algorithm developed by another 802 working group, 802.1. Figure 2-14 illustrates how this approach works.

Authentication Server

The heart of the system is the authentication server, which makes access decisions about individual wireless devices seeking to connect to the access point. This authentication normally follows the RADIUS standard, which, as we will see in Chapter 8, is popular in organizations. The WLAN access point's basic job is to connect the wireless device and the RADIUS server during the authentication process.

User Data Server

The authentication server can call upon another server that holds data about individual users, most commonly a directory server or a Kerberos server (see Chapter 8). Many corporations store most of their important information in such servers to ensure central control.

Keying at the Access Point

Once the user is authenticated, the access point can send an individual key to the wireless station. This avoids shared keys. It also allows the access point to re-key the wireless station automatically, with a frequency appropriate for the threat level.

Multiple Authentication Options

Authentication in 802.1x uses the **Extensible Authentication Protocol (EAP)**, which gives the organization many options for authentication.

➤   For instance, the **MD5 CHAP** option only requires the wireless station to have a password and does not authenticate the access point at all. This is weak authentication, but it avoids the need for the company to create and manage a public key infrastructure (PKI) to manage digital certificates (see Chapter 7). PKIs are expensive and cumbersome to use.

➤   The **TLS** (Transport Layer Security) option uses digital certificates and so requires a PKI. The access point *must* have a digital certificate. Wireless stations *may* have digital certificates but are not *required* in the standard to have digital certificates. If clients do not have digital certificates, however, they are not authenticated at all.

---

[18]   A good summary of problems with WEP algorithms is found in Nikita Borisov, Ian Goldberg, and David Wagner, "Security of the WEP Algorithm" (undated). www.isaac.cs.berkeley.edu/isaac/wepfaq.html.

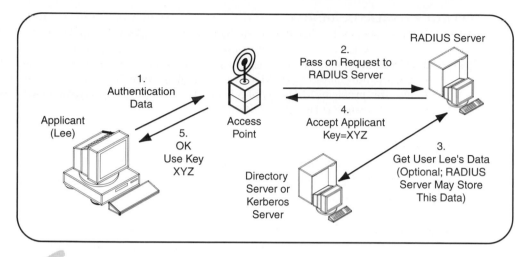

Figure 2-14   802.1x Authentication for 802.11i WLANs

➤   The emerging **TTLS** (Tunneled TLS) option requires the access point to use digital certificates but allows weaker wireless station authentication, for instance, password authentication. This is not as good as TLS with certificates on both sides, but it is better than TLS without client certificates.

Other options are also possible. For instance, Cisco offers its proprietary LEAP protocol. The problem with having so many options, of course, is ensuring that the organization selects an option that makes sense given its threat environment. Furthermore, the selection of an EAP authentication method is broader than 802.11 WLAN security because 802.1x is likely to be used on the company's main wired LAN, as well. It might be desirable to use a single EAP method for WLANs and wired LANs.

Is 802.11i Safe?
Although 802.11i promises to be a major improvement over WEP, it has some weaknesses of its own according to some cryptanalysts.[19] It is not clear at this time how serious these weaknesses are or how easy they would be to exploit.

TKIP
It will take some time for 802.11i to be widely adopted. As a stopgap method, the 802.11 Working Group has created the **Temporal Key Integrity Protocol (TKIP)**, which can be added to many existing wireless access points and NICs through software upgrades. TKIP uses a 128-bit key and changes this key every 10,000 frames, making many key guessing attacks impossible.

---

[19]   William A. Arbaugh, Narender Shankar, and Y.C. Justin, Wan, "Your 802.11 Wireless Network Has No Clothes," Department of Computer Science, University of Maryland, March 30, 2001. www.cs.umd. edu/~waa/wireless.pdf.

TEST YOUR UNDERSTANDING

27. a) How are 802.1x and 802.11i related? b) Describe 802.1x authentication with an 802.11 WLAN. c) Does 802.1x use shared keys? d) What is the weakest EAP authentication method? e) What does it authenticate? f) What is the strongest EAP authentication method? g) What is the problem with TLS, and how does TTLS reduce this problem? h) Has 802.11i been proven to be safe by cryptanalysts? i) Why was TKIP created? j) How does TKIP work?

CONCLUSION

Although most attacks come into a firm through the Internet, security within corporate sites must be strong as well.

Hands-On Password Cracking

Password cracking is difficult over the Internet because most servers will lock out attackers after a few consecutive incorrect login attempts. However, if attackers can put their hands on machines, they might be able to crack passwords. This chapter discussed UNIX and Windows password security. We will see more of this topic in Chapter 6.

Building and Wiring Security

Building security must be implemented by limiting building access; limiting internal access to various parts of a building; and creating a security system of CCTV cameras, videotape machines, and alarms that allows physical security to be managed from a security center. Wiring closets, server rooms, and other important facilities must be especially protected, and wiring is best run through hard conduits between wiring closets.

      Door security is easily overridden through piggybacking. Employees must be well trained on the danger of piggybacking and reprimanded for allowing it.

Smart Cards and Biometric Authentication

For access through internal doors, many firms are beginning to resort to access cards and biometric authentication. Biometric authentication is attractive because there is nothing extra for a person to bring. However, uncertainties about true error rates, the general lack of biometric standards today, and uncertainties about how easy biometric systems are to fool are concerns for firms considering biometric authentication.

802.11 Wireless LAN Eavesdropping and Other Attacks

The 802.11 Working Group, which creates wireless LAN standards, did a poor job on security. Consequently, many wireless LANs are open to eavesdropping, DoS, and other attacks. The working group's wired equivalent privacy (WEP) approach was poorly conceived, leaving many wireless LANs with little or no security. The new 802.1x/802.11i EAP standards will improve matters, but retrofitting existing 802.11 systems might be difficult or impossible. Even if EAP is used, the company must choose wisely among the options offered by EAP. Some of these options provide poor authentication.

As this book went to press, the Wireless Fidelity Alliance, which certifies 802.11 products under the name "Wi-Fi," announced that certification in 2003 and 2004 would have to incorporate an increasing amount of security under the Alliance's **Wireless Protected Access (WPA)** standard. WPA will require the phased implementation of TKIP, selected parts of 802.11i, and having security turned on as a default during installation. Unfortunately, WPA will not require the upgrading of the many systems that will have been installed before WPA takes full effect.

TEST YOUR UNDERSTANDING

28.   a) What will the Wireless Protected Access standard require? b) Will existing 802.11 products have to be upgraded to WPA compliance? c) Who created the WPA standard?

THOUGHT QUESTIONS

1.   The CSI/FBI survey we saw in Chapter 1 suggests that wiretapping is rare. Should companies still be concerned with wiretapping? Explain.

2.   Reusable passwords offer poor security. What do you think is holding back their replacement with other approaches?

3.   What topics would you put in a user awareness program for site security?

4.   Many airports are installing face recognition systems to identify terrorists and criminals. Suppose the FAR is 5 percent. (A false acceptance is accepting an innocent person as being a terrorist.) The FRR is about 30 percent. About one passenger in a million is a terrorist. Is this system likely to be workable? Use calculations to support your answer. Explain using a spreadsheet analysis with reasonable assumptions.

TROUBLESHOOTING QUESTION

1.   Your company installs a face recognition system for door access. a) Its FRR is much worse than the vendor's claims. What problems might be causing this? b) The system's FRR increases over time. What might be causing this? c) Why is this system likely to be discontinued?

CHAPTER

3

REVIEW OF TCP/IP INTERNETWORKING

Learning Objectives

By the end of this chapter, you should be able to discuss:

- The distinction between single networks and internets. The difference between internets and the Internet.
- The TCP/IP standards architecture, including RFCs. The hybrid TCP/IP–OSI standards architecture.
- The vertical cooperation between adjacent layer processes on hosts and routers.
- TCP/IP security.
- The Internet Protocol (IP) and its security implications.
- The Transmission Control Protocol (TCP) and its security implications.
- The User Datagram Protocol (UDP) and its security implications.
- The Internet Control Message Protocol (ICMP) and its security implications.

INTRODUCTION: A REVIEW

This book assumes a working knowledge of networking concepts. However, because so many attacks involve the Internet and internal networks that follow TCP/IP standards, this chapter reviews core TCP/IP principles and standards. Some teachers will skim through the chapter quickly or assign it for student reading.

However, this chapter goes somewhat beyond basic TCP/IP knowledge by discussing the security implications of key TCP/IP standards. The next two chapters will use this information.

SINGLE NETWORKS VERSUS INTERNETS

In Chapter 2, we looked at individual networks within sites. In this chapter, we will look at security involving **internets**, in which several individual networks are connected by routers. Figure 3-1 shows the elements of a simple internet with three networks. Note that a mobile client host on one network (Network 1) can reach server Host B on another network (Network 3) across an intermediate network (Network 2).

The most important internet, of course, is the worldwide **Internet**, which has hundreds of millions of host computers. (All computers attached to the Internet are **host computers**—including large servers, small host PCs, and even personal digital assistants.)

The Internet and **intranets**—private internets within corporations—use TCP/IP standards. Due to the large number of attacks that come into a company through the Internet, it is critical to understand TCP/IP standards.

TEST YOUR UNDERSTANDING

1. a) Distinguish between single networks and internets. b) Distinguish between internets in general and the Internet. c) What are intranets?

TCP/IP STANDARDS

Origins

In the late 1960s and early 1970s, the U.S. Defense Advanced Research Projects Agency (DARPA) funded the creation of the first packet-switched wide area network, the **ARPANET**. This network linked the agency's major research contractor sites in the United States.

During the 1970s, several other research-oriented, packet-switched networks appeared, including CSNET in computer science, BITNET for researchers in business schools and behavioral science departments, and research networks in other countries. Vint Cerf conceived of the creation of a worldwide Internet that would link these and other emerging networks together. DARPA decided to build the Internet, using the ARPANET as the initial backbone for interconnecting other networks.

The standards for the new Internet would be called **TCP/IP standards** for reasons we will soon see. These standards would be created by the **Internet Engineering Task Force (IETF)**, which already existed as the de facto standards agency for the ARPANET.

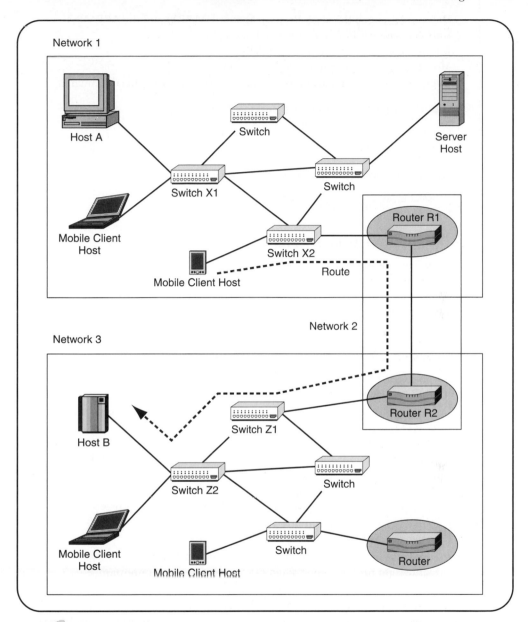

Figure 3-1   A Simple Internet

ORIGINS

Defense Advanced Research Projects Agency (DARPA) and the ARPANET

Internet connects multiple individual networks

Internet Engineering Task Force (IETF)

Most IETF documents are requests for comments (RFCs)

Internet Official Protocol Standards: List of RFCs that are official standards

HYBRID TCP/IP-OSI ARCHITECTURE (Figure 3-3)

Combines TCP/IP standards at layers 3–5 with

OSI standards at layers 1–2

SINGLE-NETWORK STANDARDS (Figure 3-4)

Physical link

Data link

FRAMES AND PACKETS (Figures 3-5 and 3-6)

Frames are messages at the data link layer

Packets are messages at the internet layer

Packets are carried (encapsulated) in frames

There is only a single packet that is delivered from source to destination host

This packet is carried in a separate frame in each network

INTERNET AND TRANSPORT LAYERS (Figure 3-7)

Purposes

   IP is hop-by-hop protocol at the internet layer

   Transport layer is end-to-end (host-to-host) protocol involving only the two hosts

Internet Protocol (IP)

   IP is unreliable—does not correct errors

   This is good: Reduces the work each router along the route must do

   TCP can correct errors not caught by IP

Transmission Control Protocol (TCP)

   Reliable and connection-oriented service at the transport layer

   Catches errors that IP cannot catch

User Datagram Protocol (UDP)

   Unreliable and connectionless service at the transport layer

   Lightweight protocol good when catching errors is not important

APPLICATION LAYER (Figure 3-8)

To govern communication between application programs, which may be written by
   different vendors

Document transfer versus document format standards

   HTTP / HTML for WWW service

   SMTP / RFC 822 (or RFC 2822) in e-mail

Many application standards exist because there are many applications

Figure 3-2   TCP/IP Standards (Study Figure)

IETF documents, for historical reasons, are called **requests for comment (RFCs)**. For example, the Internet Protocol that we will see later was originally standardized as RFC 791. Not all RFCs are standards. About once every two years, an RFC is released that lists currently approved **Internet Official Protocol Standards**.

TEST YOUR UNDERSTANDING

2. a) Who creates TCP/IP standards? b) What are publications by this organization normally called? c) How can you determine which of these publications are official standards?

The Hybrid TCP/IP-OSI Architecture

Standards must be created within a broad framework called a **standards architecture**. Figure 3-3 shows that network standards architectures are created as a series of layers, each of which provides services to the next-higher layer.

The figure compares the relatively simple four-layer **TCP/IP** standards architecture and the more complex seven-layer **OSI**[1] standards architecture. TCP/IP does not define single-network standards, such as Ethernet or 802.11. It expects implementers to use OSI single-network standards for **subnets** (single networks).[2] Single networks use the two lowest layers in the OSI architecture.

Consequently, what the Internet and most corporate internets actually use is a five-layer **hybrid TCP/IP-OSI architecture**. At the bottom two layers, companies use OSI standards. At the internet and transport layers (and typically at the application layer, as well), companies use TCP/IP standards.

TEST YOUR UNDERSTANDING

3. a) In the hybrid TCP/IP-OSI standards architecture, which layers come from OSI? b) Which layers come from TCP/IP?

Single-Network Standards

Figure 3-4 shows the links for standards at the three lowest layers—the physical, data link, and internet layers. The lowest two layers govern communication within a single network. The internet layer governs communication through an internet.

Physical Layer Links

Physical layer standards govern each connection within a single network between a station and a switch, between two switches, or between a switch and a router. One **physical link** exists between Host A and Switch X1 in Network X. The next exists between Switch X1 and Switch X2. The third exists between Switch X2 and Router R1. Four more physical links lead to Host B. Physical link standards govern physical connectors; transmission media; and electrical, optical, or radio signaling.

---

[1] Reference Model of Open Systems Interconnection.
[2] Sometimes the IETF does create lower-layer standards, such as PPP at the data link layer (Layer 2). However, when it does, it develops them within the OSI framework.

TCP/IP	OSI	Hybrid TCP/IP–OSI
Application	Application	Application
	Presentation	
	Session	
Transport	Transport	Transport
Internet	Network	Internet
Use OSI Standards Here for Single Networks	Data Link	Data Link
	Physical	Physical

Note: The Hybrid TCP/IP-OSI Architecture is used on the Internet and dominates internal corporate networks.

Figure 3-3   TCP/IP and OSI Architectures

Data Link Layer Links (Data Links)

Within single networks, it is important for there to be effective end-to-end communication across the network. Links that span a single network are called **data links**. **Data link layer** standards govern how switches forward arriving single-network messages called **frames**.

In Network X, there is an end-to-end data link between Host A and Router R1. In Network Y, there is a data link between Router R1 and Router R2. In Network Z, there is a data link between Router R2 and Host B.

Internet Layer Links (Routes)

To internetwork multiple single networks (three in Figure 3-4), the IETF had to create a third type of link, namely a route. A **route** is an end-to-end link between the source host (Host A) and the destination host (Host B), across multiple networks. Only a single route is shown in Figure 3-4. The **internet layer** governs how routers receive internet layer messages, called **packets**.

TEST YOUR UNDERSTANDING

4. a) In an internet, will you have more physical links or data links? Explain. b) How many data links will a frame travel through in a single network? c) How many routes will a packet travel through in an internet?

Frames and Packets

We have noted that messages in single networks are called *frames* while messages in internets are called *packets*.

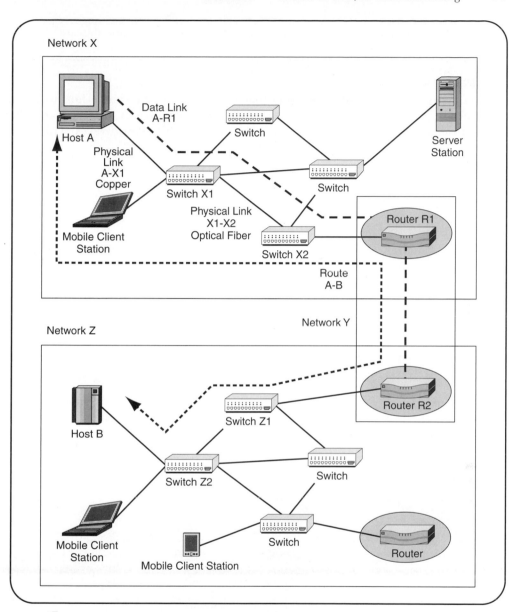

Figure 3-4 Physical, Data Link, and Internet Links

Messages in single networks are called *frames;* messages in internets are
called *packets.*

Packets

Packets are internet layer messages that are created by the source host to be read by
the destination host. Figure 3-5 illustrates the structure of an IP packet, showing
32 bits on each line. All host computers have 32-bit IP addresses. The source IP

Figure 3-5 IP Packet

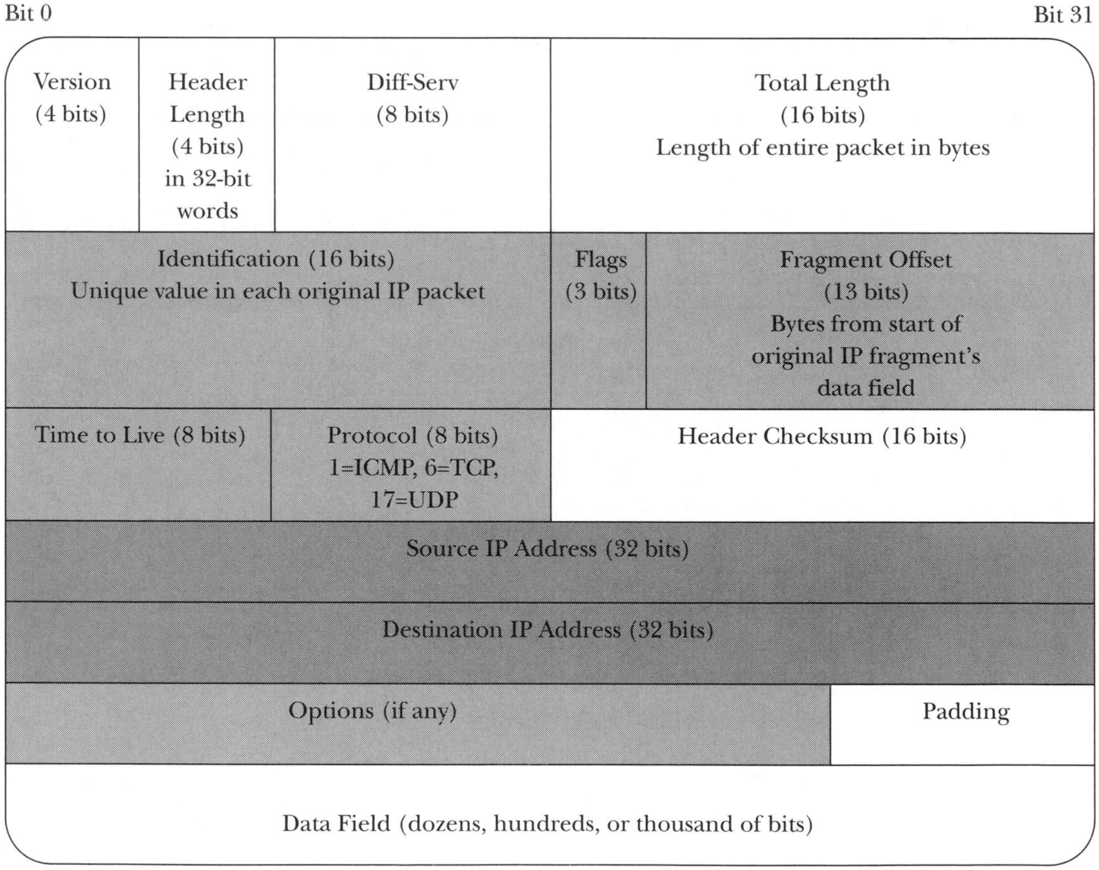

Bit 0   Bit 31

Version (4 bits)	Header Length (4 bits) in 32-bit words	Diff-Serv (8 bits)	Total Length (16 bits) Length of entire packet in bytes	
Identification (16 bits) Unique value in each original IP packet			Flags (3 bits)	Fragment Offset (13 bits) Bytes from start of original IP fragment's data field
Time to Live (8 bits)	Protocol (8 bits) 1=ICMP, 6=TCP, 17=UDP		Header Checksum (16 bits)	
Source IP Address (32 bits)				
Destination IP Address (32 bits)				
Options (if any)				Padding
Data Field (dozens, hundreds, or thousand of bits)				

Notes:
  Bits 0–3 hold the version number.
  Bits 4–7 hold the header length.
  Bits 8–15 hold the Diff-Serv information.
  Bits 16–31 hold the total length value.
  Bits 32–47 hold the Identification value.

address field gives the IP address of the sending host. The destination IP address field gives the IP address of the intended receiver. Routers along the way read the destination IP addresses of arriving packets; based on these destination IP addresses, routers forward packets toward the destination host like a post office.

Frames

Like postal letters, data link layer frames contain destination addresses, and switches use these destination addresses to deliver each frame to its destination station or router in the network. In Ethernet and 802.11 LANs, these addresses are 48-bit **Media Access Control (MAC)** addresses.

The Relationship Between Frames and Packets

Figure 3-6 shows how frames and packets are related.

Packet Creation and Transmission Within a Frame   The figure shows that the client PC creates a packet intended for a server. The client PC places the packet in the data field of a frame appropriate for its network (Network 1). The client sends the frame to Router A via intermediate switches (only one switch is shown).

Encapsulation   Placing a message in the data field of another message is called **encapsulation**. As we will see later in this chapter, encapsulation is a very common and important process.

Figure 3-6   Frames and Packets

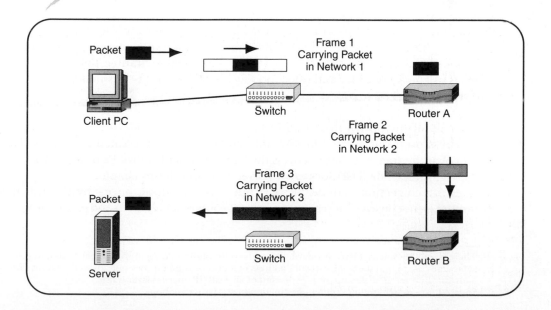

On the First Router: Decapsulation and Reencapsulation   The first router (Router A) pulls the packet out of Frame 1 and discards the frame. The router decides what to do with the packet and sends it on to the second router in a new frame (Frame 2)—a frame appropriate for Network 2.

On the Second Router   The second router does the same thing, decapsulating the packet from Frame 2 and encapsulating it in a third frame (Frame 3), which is appropriate for Network 3.

One Packet But Many Frames   Overall, a single packet is sent through an internet, but it is carried in a different frame in each network along the way. If there are fifteen networks along the way, there will be one packet but fifteen different frames.

TEST YOUR UNDERSTANDING

5.   a) At what layer would you find frames? b) At what layer would you find packets? c) Which is encapsulated in the other—frames or packets? d) In a transmission between two hosts separated by five networks, how many packets will there be? e) How many frames?

Internet and Transport Layers

Figure 3-7 shows that the internet and transport layers work together in the delivery of messages.

IP and the Internet Layer

At the internet layer, TCP/IP normally uses the **Internet Protocol (IP)**.[3] IP governs what happens on each hop between routers and between the source and destination hosts and their routers. If three routers separate the two hosts, there will be four hops[4] governed by IP.

The IETF decided to keep IP simple. For instance, IP does not do error correction on each hop between routers. (Consequently, IP is an **unreliable** protocol.)

To do error correction on each hop would create a great deal of additional work for each router because error correction is processing intensive. Not doing error correction reduces the cost of routers. Unreliability is good in routers (and in switches) because of this ability to save money. IP does not even guarantee that successive IP packets will arrive in order and offers no way for routers or the destination host to put incoming IP packets in order.

Transmission Control Protocol (TCP)

To address problems created by IP's unreliability, the IETF created a highly **reliable** protocol at the **transport layer**. This is the **Transmission Control Protocol (TCP)** standard. We will see how TCP does error correction later in this chapter.

Error correction is done in TCP, but it is only done once—by the two host computers—not on every hop between pairs of routers. This end-to-end error correction

---

[3]   There is another internet layer standard, the Address Resolution Protocol (ARP) that hosts and routers sometimes use to find the single-network address of a host or router if they only know the target's IP address. However, IP makes up over 99 percent of all TCP/IP internet layer traffic.

[4]   Source host - router - router - router - destination host. Dashes are hops.

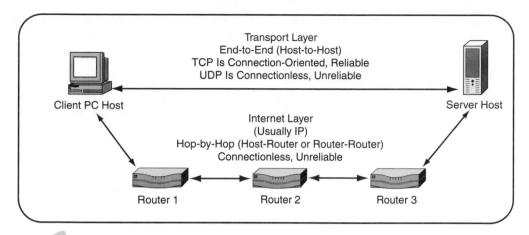

Figure 3-7 Internet and Transport Layers

creates additional work for the hosts, but the overall amount of work is far less than it would be with hop-by-hop error correction conducted by many routers along the route.

Effectively, TCP and IP work together to provide efficient and reliable message delivery between the source and destination hosts.

User Datagram Protocol (UDP)

Some applications do not need reliability. For instance, in IP telephony, which uses an intranet or the Internet to allow two people to talk to one another, the application cannot wait for the retransmission of lost or damaged packets. Telephony has to work in real time, and error correction would create delays of a quarter of a second to half a second. During that delay, the flow of sound would have to stop.

Network management programs, in turn, ask each managed device for its status every few seconds. Unreliable service greatly reduces processing cost and network traffic (by not transmitting acknowledgements), and a lost packet merely means that information about one device in a network is a few seconds old.

For applications that do not require reliability, the IETF defined a second transport layer standard, the **User Datagram Protocol (UDP)**, which we will see later.

TEST YOUR UNDERSTANDING

6. a) Why was IP created as an unreliable protocol? b) Why is IP's unreliability actually good? c) How does TCP make up for the limitations of IP? d) In what way is UDP superior to TCP?

The Application Layer

The bottom four layers provide a link between a particular application on the source host and a particular application on the destination host. **Application layer** standards are needed to allow the two application programs to work together even if they are written by different software vendors. For example, the HTTP standard we will see next allows a Microsoft Internet Explorer browser on a client PC to work with a SUN ONE webserver program on a webserver.

Document Format Standards

Most application standards come in pairs. One member of the pair governs the format of the particular application file being delivered. In webservice, for example, the Hypertext Markup Language (HTML) governs the formatting of webpages, as Figure 3-8 illustrates. In e-mail, the original standard for text-only mail messages was RFC 822 (replaced later by RFC 2822). Other applications have different **document format standards**.

Document Transfer Standards

HTML governs the formatting of webpages, but it does not specify how a client can ask a webserver for a webpage or how the webserver can send back the webpage. That is the job of a separate but related standard, the Hypertext Transfer Protocol (HTTP). In e-mail, the transfer protocol for sending messages is the Simple Mail Transfer Protocol (SMTP), as shown in Figure 3-8. The transfer protocol for retrieving messages from a user's server mailbox is the Post Office Protocol (POP). Other applications have different **document transfer standards**.

Many Application Standards

There is a dominant internet layer standard in TCP/IP (IP), and there are two transport layer standards (TCP and UDP), but there are many application layer standards in TCP/IP because there are so many different applications. The vast majority of all TCP/IP standards are application layer standards.

TEST YOUR UNDERSTANDING

> 7. a) At the application layer, what two types of standards do you usually find for an application? b) Why are there many application layer standards?

Figure 3-8   HTML and HTTP

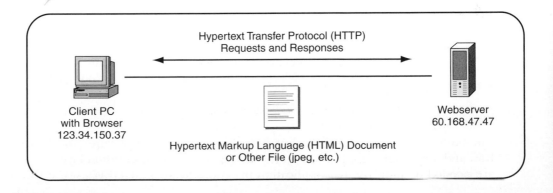

Client PC
with Browser
123.34.150.37

Hypertext Transfer Protocol (HTTP)
Requests and Responses

Webserver
60.168.47.47

Hypertext Markup Language (HTML) Document
or Other File (jpeg, etc.)

LAYER COOPERATION

Although layer processes each have their own roles, they must work together on the source host, on the destination host, and on each router along the way.

On the Source Host

On the source host, adjacent layer processes work together, as Figure 3-9 illustrates. Each layer process, after creating its message, passes the message down to the next-lower layer. The receiving layer creates its own message, encapsulating the next-higher layer message in the data field of its own message.

Figure 3-9   Layer Cooperation Through Encapsulation on the Source Host

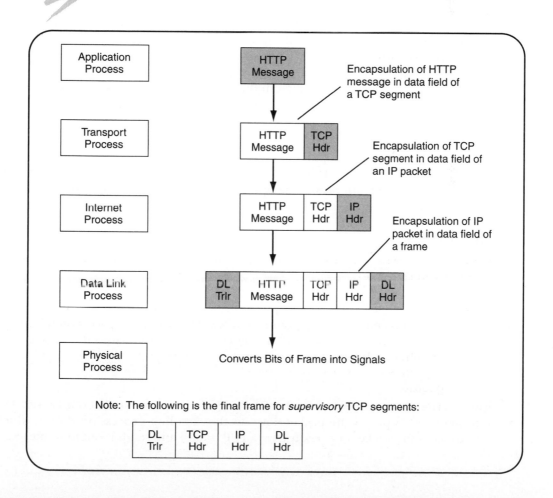

Encapsulation

In the figure, an HTTP message is encapsulated within a TCP segment. (The transport process uses the HTTP message as the segment data field and adds a TCP header.) The TCP segment is then encapsulated within an IP packet (by adding an IP header). The IP packet is then encapsulated in a data link layer frame, usually by adding a data link layer header and data link layer trailer. (Not all data link layer standards have trailers.)

The Physical Layer

The physical layer is different. The physical layer transmits bits rather than messages. When the frame comes down to the physical layer process from the data link process, the physical process converts the bits into signals and sends them on.

The Final Frame

As Figure 3-9 shows, the final frame delivered to the physical layer consists of a data link header, an IP header, a TCP header, the HTTP message, and a data link trailer. The physical layer converts the bits of the frame into physical signals.

Other Final Frames

Figure 3-9 shows the transmission of an application layer HTTP message. However, not all messages begin at the application layer. For instance, TCP processes on the source and destination hosts often talk to each other even when they are not sending application messages. At the bottom, the figure shows that TCP supervisory messages (which carry supervisory information in the TCP header) have a data link header, an IP header, a TCP header, *no application message*, and (usually) a data link trailer.

On the Destination Host

On the destination host, the process is reversed, as Figure 3-10 illustrates. The physical layer receives signals, converts them into bits, and passes the frame up to the data link process. Each subsequent process decapsulates the message for the next-higher layer and passes the message up to that layer.

On Routers

Figure 3-11 shows what happens on routers. It specifically shows what happens on Router R1 in Figure 3-1.

Reception

The router first receives a frame from Switch X2. The data link process on the receiving port (Port 1) decapsulates the IP packet in the frame and passes the packet up to Router R1's internet layer process.

Transmission

The internet layer process on Router R1 decides to send the packet out Port 4. The internet process passes the packet down to the data link process on Port 4, which encapsulates the packet in a new frame (a PPP frame) and sends it out to Router R2.

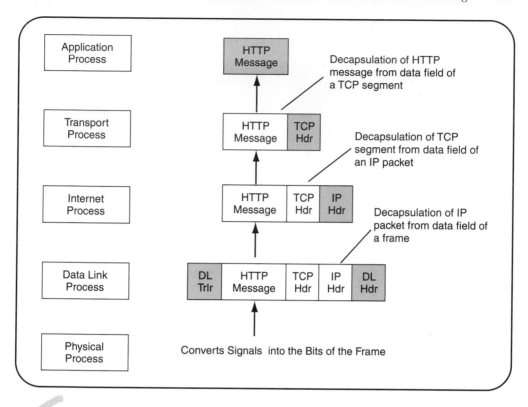

Figure 3-10   Layer Cooperation Through Decapsulation on the Destination Host

TEST YOUR UNDERSTANDING

8.   a) What is encapsulation? b) If Layer N creates a message, does Layer N or Layer N-1 (the next lower layer) encapsulate the message? c) Do destination hosts decapsulate or encapsulate messages? d) Do routers first encapsulate or decapsulate?

TCP/IP and Border Security

Figure 3-12 shows that companies typically add a firewall between their internal network and the Internet. More specifically, they place the firewall at their end of the data link between their premises and their Internet service provider (ISP). Typically, this data link is a point-to-point leased line running PPP at the data link layer.

   This physical/data link connection is very difficult for attackers to exploit. Consequently, most firewalls only look at the internet, transport, and application layer data in incoming packets, ignoring the data link header and trailer. This simplifies filtering, thus reducing firewall processing and cost.

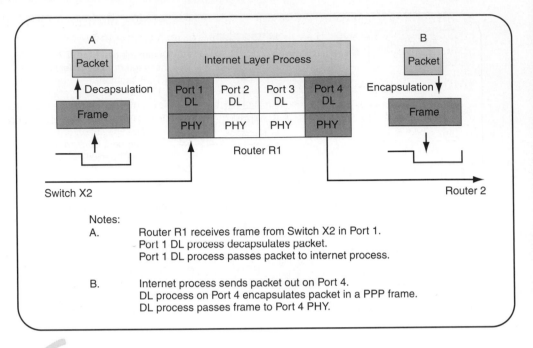

Figure 3-11 Vertical Communication on a Router

Figure 3-12 Site Connection to an ISP

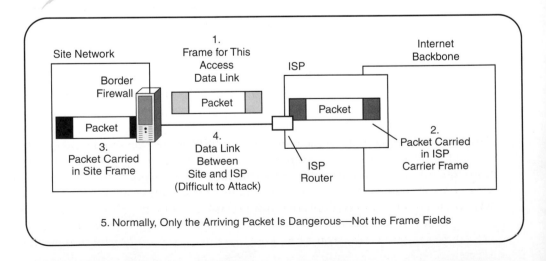

Within internal networks, however, data links and even physical links are highly exploitable, as we saw in the last chapter. So although a strong focus on TCP/IP is justified, single network security is also important within sites.

TEST YOUR UNDERSTANDING

9. a) Why do companies focus on security at the border to the Internet? b) Why is a focus on TCP/IP acceptable for border firewalls? c) Where are physical and data links exploitable?

THE INTERNET PROTOCOL (IP)

We looked at the Internet Protocol (IP) earlier at a general level. Now we will look at IP in more detail.

Basic Characteristics

IP's designers could not make many assumptions about underlying networks. Consequently, the IETF made the Internet Protocol simple. This would allow IP to run over any current or future single network. As Vint Cerf has often proclaimed, "IP over everything."

Connection-Oriented Service and Connectionless Service

There are two types of service in standards—connection-oriented service and connectionless service.

Connection-Oriented Service

In a telephone call, you talk within a structured communication session. At the start, there is at least implicit agreement that the two parties are free to communicate. At the end of the session, you do not simply hang up on the other party but end the conversation by mutual agreement. This is **connection-oriented** service.

Connectionless Service

However, when you send a letter, no overall connection exists. You can send the letter any time you wish. This is **connectionless service**.

IP Is Connectionless

IP is a connectionless service. As Figure 3-14 shows, the sending internet process transmits IP packets any time it wishes, without setting up a prior connection.

TEST YOUR UNDERSTANDING

10. a) Distinguish between connection-oriented service and connectionless service. b) Is IP connection-oriented or connectionless?

IP Is Unreliable

As noted earlier in this chapter, IP is unreliable. Note in Figure 3-14 that the IP packet is not acknowledged. There is no way the sender can know whether the IP packet was received, so there is no way for it to know whether it should or should not retransmit

BASIC CHARACTERISTICS

CONNECTION-ORIENTED SERVICE AND CONNECTIONLESS SERVICE

Connection-oriented services have distinct opens and closes (telephone calls)
Connectionless services merely send messages (postal letters)
IP is connectionless

IP IS UNRELIABLE (CHECKS FOR ERRORS BUT DOES NOT CORRECT ERRORS)

HIERARCHICAL IP ADDRESSES

Postal addresses are hierarchical (state, city, postal zone, specific address)
  Most post offices have to look only at state and city
  Only the final post offices have to be concerned with specific addresses
32-bit IP addresses are hierarchical
  Network part tells what network the host is on
  Subnet part tells what subnet the host is on within the network
  Host part specifies the host on its subnet
  Routers along the way have to look only at network or subnet parts, except for the
    router that delivers the packet to the destination host
  Total is 32 bits; part sizes vary
  Network mask tells you the size of the network part
  Subnet mask tells you the length of the network plus subnet parts combined

IP ADDRESSES AND SECURITY

IP address spoofing: Sending a message with a false IP address
Gives sender anonymity so that attacker cannot be identified
Can exploit trust between hosts if spoofed IP address is that of a host the victim host
  trusts
LAND Attack: Send victim a packet with victim's IP address in both source and
  destination address fields and the same port number for the source and destination.
  In 1997, many computers, switches, routers, and even printers crashed when they
  received such a packet.

(continued)

Figure 3-13   Internet Protocol (IP) (Study Figure)

OTHER IP HEADER FIELDS

Protocol field: Identifies content of IP data field
    Firewalls need this information to know how to process the packet's data field
Time-to-Live field
    Each router decrements the TTL value by one
    Router decrementing TTL field to zero discards the packet
    Router also sends an error advisement message to the sender
    The packet containing this message reveals the sender's IP address to the attacker
    Traceroute uses TTL to map the route to a host
        Tracert on Windows machines
Header Length field and Options
    Options are dangerous
Fragmentation
    Routers may fragment IP packets (really, packet data fields) en route
    All fragments have same Identification field value
    Fragment offset values allows fragments to be ordered
    More fragments bit is 0 in the last fragment
Harms packet inspection: TCP header, etc., only in first packet in series
    Cannot filter on TCP header, etc., in subsequent packets
Teardrop attack: Crafted fragmented packet does not make sense when reassembled
Some firewalls drop all fragmented packets, which are rare today

Figure 3-13   (Continued)

the packet. As noted earlier in the chapter, not doing error correction on a hop-by-hop basis reduces router costs.

Hierarchical IP Addresses

Hierarchical Postal Addresses

Postal addresses are **hierarchical**. The receiver's address has a country (often implicit), a city, a postal zone, a street, a house address, and perhaps an apartment or suite number.

Hierarchical addressing simplifies delivery. The post office that first receives your letter sorts arriving letters into those destined for other countries, those for the same city, and those for other cities within the country. This first post office does not worry about streets or other local details. Only the last post office along the route to the receiver has to worry about local details. This greatly simplifies sorting at each post office along the way and therefore reduces sorting costs.

Hierarchical IP Addresses

IP addresses also are hierarchical, as Figure 3-15 illustrates.

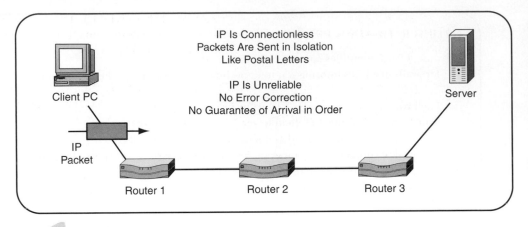

Figure 3-14   Connectionless IP Service

Figure 3-15   Hierarchical IP Address

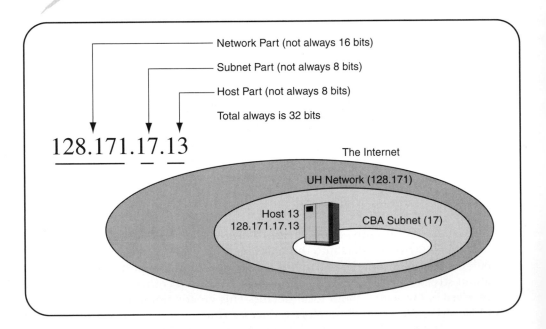

Network Part   The figure shows an IP address, 128.171.17.13. In this address, 128.171 is the **network part**. These 16 bits tell us that the host is on the University of Hawaii network. All hosts on this network begin with 128.171.

Subnet Part   Next, 17 is the **subnet part**. These 8 bits identify the host as being on the College of Business Administration subnet of the University of Hawaii Network. All hosts on this subnet begin with 128.171.17.

Host Part   Finally, the **host part** is 13. This 8-bit number identifies a particular host on the College of Business Administration subnet of the University of Hawaii.

Hierarchical IP Addresses and Smaller Routing Table

Routing on the Internet exploits the hierarchical nature of IP addresses. The first router and other routers along the way look only at the network part of the IP address or perhaps the network and subnet parts combined to make their routing (packet forwarding) decisions.

Although hundreds of millions of hosts are on the Internet, most routers have only a few hundred thousand decision rules for forwarding incoming packets.

Each rule is based on either a network part or a network part plus a subnet part. Each rule is used to forward all packets going to a particular network or to a particular subnet on a particular network.

For example, a rule on a particular router might state that all packets going to network 60 should be sent out Port 3, to next-hop router 123.17.22.101. It is not necessary to have a separate rule on this router for each of the thousands of IP addresses that might be on the 60 network.

Only the final router, which delivers the packet to the destination host, must look at the host part of the IP address.

IP Address Masks

Part Lengths Vary   For the IP address shown in Figure 3-15, the network part was 16 bits long, the subnet part was 8 bits long, and the host part was 8 bits long. However, different IP addresses may not have the same part lengths. Although the total IP address length always is 32 bits, the individual part sizes vary. Network parts, for instance, vary from 8 to 24 bits.

Masks Tell the Sizes of Address Parts   When routers consider IP addresses, they also have address **masks** that tell the size of either the network part (indicating what network it is on) or the network plus subnet parts (indicating a particular subnet on a particular network).

Network Mask

A mask is a 32-bit number. **Network masks** have ones in the network part and zeros in the subnet and host parts. For the IP address in Figure 3-15, the network mask would be 255.255.0.0 (8 ones correspond to 255 in decimal, and 8 zeros correspond to 0 in decimal).

Applying Network Mask 255.255.0.0 to 128.171.17.13   Figure 3-16 shows how an IP network mask is used. First, there is an IP address, 128.171.17.13. You already have been told that 128.171 is the 16-bit address part. However, the figure shows how a router determines this.

The network mask for 128.171.17.13 is 255.255.0.0. If you apply any mask to an IP address, you get the address bits back where there are ones, and you get zeros where there are zeros. So masking 128.171.17.13 with 255.255.0.0 gives 128.171.0.0. The 16-bit network part is 128.171, as we already knew.

Figure 3-16   IP Address Masking with Network and Subnet Masks

	NETWORK MASKING	SUBNET MASKING
Mask Represents	Tells the size of the network part	Tells the size of the network and subnet parts combined
Eight ones give the decimal value	255	255
Eight zeros give the decimal value	0	0
Masking gives	IP address bit where mask value is 1; 0 where mask bit is 0	IP address bit where mask value is 1; 0 where mask bit is 0
EXAMPLE 1		
IP Address	128.171.17.13	128.171.17.13
Mask	255.255.0. 0	255.255.255.0
Result	128.171.0.0	128.171.17.0
Meaning	16-bit network part is 128.171	Combined 24-bit network plus subnet part are 128.171.17
EXAMPLE 2		
IP Address	60.47.123.7	60.47.123.7
Mask	255.0.0.0	255.255.0.0
Result	60.0.0.0	60.47.0.0
Meaning	8-bit network part is 60	Combined 16-bit network plus subnet parts are 60.47

Applying Network Mask 255.0.0.0 to 60.47.123.7   Now we will look at a new IP address, 60.47.123.7, and a new network mask, 255.0.0.0. Applying this 8-bit network mask to this IP address yields 60.0.0.0. The network part is 60.

Subnet Masks

A **subnet mask** has ones in both the network *and* subnet parts. It tells you the combined length of the network and subnet parts, not their individual lengths. It is used to create a rule to route all packets going to a particular subnet on a particular network.

Applying Subnet Mask 255.255.255.0 to 128.171.17.13   For the IP address in Figure 3-15, the subnet mask would be 255.255.255.0. Applying this mask to 128.171.17.13 yields 128.171.17 as the combined 24-bit network and subnet part. Note again that the subnet mask does not tell which bits are the network bits and which bits are the subnet bits—only their combined length.

Applying Subnet Mask 255.255.0.0 to 60.47.123.7   Figure 3-16 shows another subnet mask, 255.255.0.0, which is applied to IP address 60.47.123.7. Here, the result is 60.47.0.0. Therefore, the 16-bit combined network and subnet part are 60.47.

TEST YOUR UNDERSTANDING

> 11. a) What are the three parts of a hierarchical IP address? b) Describe what each part tells you. c) What parts do routers in the main part of the Internet consider? d) If you apply the network mask 255.0.0.0 to the IP address 123.12.203.6, what do you learn? e) If you apply the subnet mask 255.255.255.0 to the IP address 123.12.203.6, what do you learn?

IP Addressing and Security

IP Address Spoofing

IP address spoofing is replacing the sender's source IP address with another IP address. IP address spoofing is extremely easy to do. There are two main reasons for doing IP address spoofing.

Sender Anonymity   One reason for IP source address spoofing is to hide the identity of an attacker. The victim cannot read the spoofed packet's source IP address field and determine the identity of the true attacker, as Figure 3-17 illustrates. Here, the attacker's real IP address is 1.34.150.37. However, the attacker places 60.168.4.6 in the source IP address of the attack packet. The victim will think that the attacker is 60.168.4.6. However, this is the IP address of an innocent host.

Exploiting Trust   Another reason for address spoofing is to exploit trust between hosts. In Figure 3-17, Host 60.168.47.47 trusts Host 60.168.4.6. This means that Host 60.168.47.47 will accept packets from Host 60.168.4.6 without security checking or at least without extensive security checking. By placing 60.168.4.6 in the source IP address field of attack packets, the attacker may be able to get Host 60.168.47.47 to accept the packet.

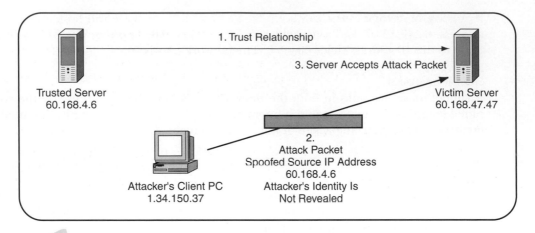

Figure 3-17   IP Address Spoofing

LAND Attack

One attack that exploits IP address spoofing is the **LAND** attack, which is illustrated in Figure 3-18. The attacker sends a packet with the target host's IP address in both the source and destination IP address fields. The source and destination port number are also made the same (we will see port numbers in the section on TCP).

It makes no sense for the source and destination IP addresses and port numbers to be the same, and many hosts crashed when they tried to process LAND attack messages. When the LAND attack first appeared in 1997, all Windows clients and servers and a large number of UNIX servers, switches, routers, and even printers were vulnerable to it. Newer systems are resistant to it, but LAND showed how unexpected combinations of parameters can create problems.

Figure 3-18   LAND Attack Based on IP Address Spoofing

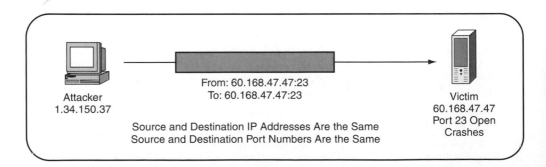

TEST YOUR UNDERSTANDING

12. a) What is IP address spoofing? b) For what two reasons do hackers do IP address spoofing? c) In a LAND attack, the attacker is 3.34.150.37 and the intended victim is 80.168.47.47. When the attacker sends the attack packet, what will be in the source IP address field? In the destination IP address field? d) In this LAND attack, if the destination port number is 80, what will the source port number be?

Other IP Header Fields

Figure 3-5 shows that IP packets have two parts. First, there is the **header**, which is a collection of smaller units called **fields**. Second, there is the **data field**, which usually contains an encapsulated TCP segment, a UDP datagram, or an ICMP supervisory message. (We will see ICMP later in this chapter.)

Protocol Field

The 8-bit **protocol field** tells which type of message is present in the data field. The value 1 indicates that an ICMP message is encapsulated in the data field, while 6 indicates a TCP segment, and 17 indicates a UDP datagram. In filtering a packet, it is important to read the protocol field to be able to know how to filter the next header.

Time-to-Live (TTL) Field

The 8-bit **time-to-live (TTL)** field prevents packets with bad headers from circulating endlessly around the Internet. The sending host puts a value of up to 65,535 in this field. Each router along the way reduces the TTL field value by one.[5] If a router reduces the TTL field to zero, that router discards the packet.

The TTL field allows attackers to learn about your network. They begin by sending a few packets with the TTL set to one. The first router the packet encounters sets the TTL value to zero, discards the packet, and sends back an ICMP error message (as discussed later). This response gives the IP address of the router. Packets are sent with TTL values of 2, then 3, and so forth. The replies identify successive routers along the way to whatever destination IP address is used in the probe messages. If probe packets are sent intelligently, the attacker can get a good map of your routers.

In fact, the **Traceroute** program in UNIX uses TTL time-outs (discards after decrementing to zero) to trace the routers along the route to a destination host. Traceroute is a good management tool and also a good hacker tool for mapping a victim network. In Windows, the **Tracert** program is used instead of Traceroute.[6]

Figure 3-19 shows a Tracert trace for www.hawaii.edu. Note that Tracert shows latency and sometimes host names for the first routers along the way. For the last few routers, however, Tracert fails to provide information. This suggests that routers beyond those that give information are protected by a firewall or refuse to respond to the Tracert program themselves.

---

[5] Originally, it was planned that TTL would give a time-to-live in seconds; however, the TTL value is now treated as the number of hops between routers the packet makes.
[6] Go to the command prompt. Then type "tracert *hostname*" or "tracert *IP address*."

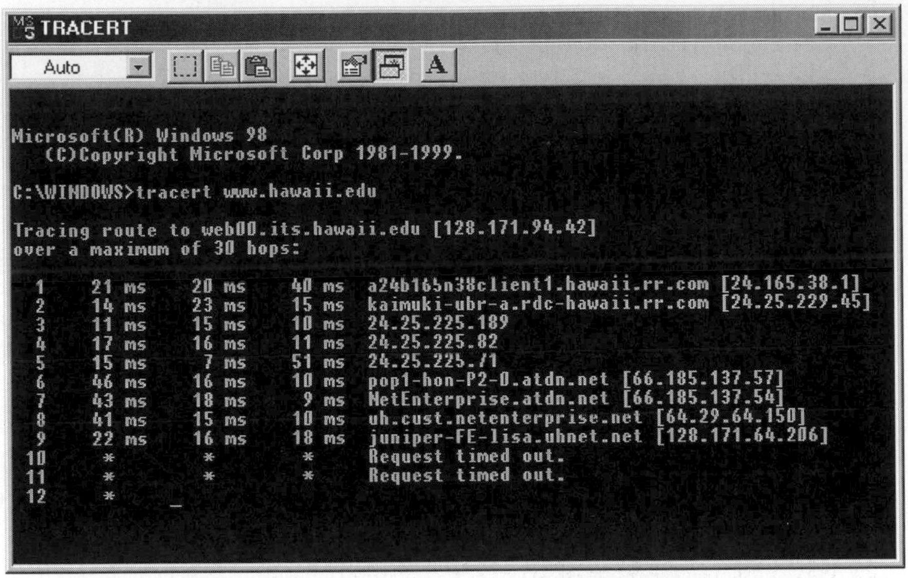

```
MS
 5 TRACERT                                                              _ □ X
 Auto        ▼   [:]  ▤ ▤   ⊞   ☞ ▤   A

Microsoft(R) Windows 98
     (C)Copyright Microsoft Corp 1981-1999.

C:\WINDOWS>tracert www.hawaii.edu

Tracing route to web00.its.hawaii.edu [128.171.94.42]
over a maximum of 30 hops:

  1     21 ms     20 ms     40 ms   a24b165n38client1.hawaii.rr.com [24.165.38.1]
  2     14 ms     23 ms     15 ms   kaimuki-ubr-a.rdc-hawaii.rr.com [24.25.229.45]
  3     11 ms     15 ms     10 ms   24.25.225.189
  4     17 ms     16 ms     11 ms   24.25.225.82
  5     15 ms      7 ms     51 ms   24.25.225.71
  6     46 ms     16 ms     10 ms   pop1-hon-P2-0.atdn.net [66.185.137.57]
  7     43 ms     18 ms      9 ms   NetEnterprise.atdn.net [66.185.137.54]
  8     41 ms     15 ms     10 ms   uh.cust.netenterprise.net [64.29.64.150]
  9     22 ms     16 ms     18 ms   juniper-FE-lisa.uhnet.net [128.171.64.206]
 10      *         *         *      Request timed out.
 11      *         *         *      Request timed out.
 12      *        _
```

Figure 3-19   Tracert Program in Windows

Header Length Field and Options

The **header length** field gives the length of the IP header in 4-byte chunks. The normal header length value is five, indicating that the header has no options field and therefore has a length of 20 bytes. If there are **options**, the header length field value will be more than five. Some firms have their firewalls block all IP packets that contain options (which are rare) because options can be used in attacks.[7]

Total Length Field

The **total length** field gives the length of the entire IP packet in bytes. This is a 16-bit field, so the maximum length is 65,535 bytes. An early DoS attack, the **Ping-of-Death** attack, used a ping packet (described later in the chapter) whose length was greater than 65,535. Figure 3-20 shows that this attack caused many early TCP/IP programs to crash. Most operating systems now reject such packets automatically.

Header Checksum Field

The **header checksum field** contains a value that allows the receiving internet process to check for errors in the header. The sender computes a value based on the IP header field values and places the result in the header checksum field. The receiver does the

---

[7] In source routing options, the packet can declare what routers it should pass through along its route to the destination host. This can be used in network mapping.

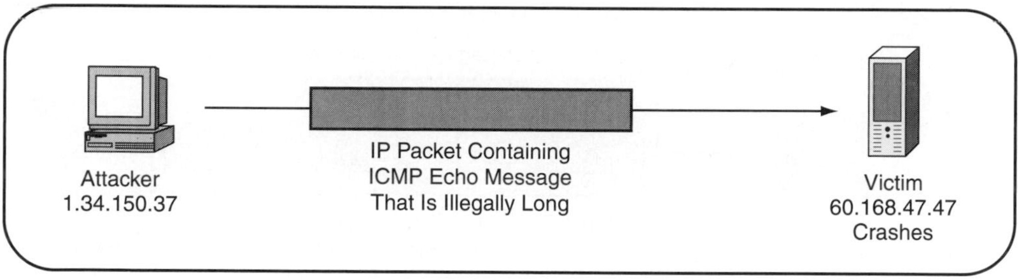

Figure 3-20   Ping-of-Death Attack

same calculation and compares its value with the number in the header checksum field. If they match, there have been no transmission errors.

Some people find error checking confusing because they know that IP is unreliable. However, if the receiving internet process finds a header error, it merely discards the packet. There is no error correction, which requires retransmission. Discarding is done because of the potential damage that bad headers can cause. However, the next IP standard (IP Version 6) will not provide this protection because the consensus now is that header protection is unnecessary.

Fragmentation

Suppose a large IP packet arrives at a router. The router selects a subnet to send the packet back out to, but the router realizes that the IP packet is too large for the subnet. (Different network standards have different maximum packet sizes.)

Fragmentation   In this situation, the router fragments the IP packet, dividing the packet's data field into several pieces and sending each piece in a separate IP packet.

Reassembly   To allow the destination host to reassemble the packet data fields, all fragments are given the same **identification field** value that the original packet had. This allows the receiver to recognize the fragments as belonging to the same initial packet.

The router gives the first fragment a **fragment offset** value of zero. Subsequent fragments get fragment offset values consistent with their data's place in the data field of the original packet. The destination host orders pieces of the original data field according to their fragment offset values.

Finally, all fragments have their **more fragments** bit set except the last fragment; its more fragments bit is made zero, indicating that it is the last fragment. When the destination host comes to this IP packet, it knows that reassembly is finished.

Teardrop Denial-of-Service Attack   One early denial-of-service attack that exploited fragmentation was the **Teardrop** attack, which created a series of packets that had the form of fragments. However, their lengths and fragment offset values were not consistent. Figure 3-21 shows that the data field that was defragmented had gaps and

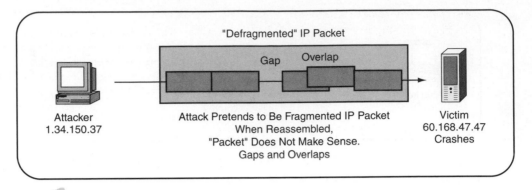

Figure 3-21   Teardrop Denial-of-Service Attack

overlaps among the data groups in the "fragments." Many operating systems crashed when Teardrop streams arrived because of their inability to make sense of the results when they tried to defragment the packet.

Fragmented Packets and Firewalls   Fragmentation also is dangerous because it makes it hard for firewalls to examine the contents of individual packets. For instance, the TCP, UDP, or ICMP header appears only in the first fragment, as Figure 3-22 shows. If the header has dangerous content, the firewall may drop the first fragment. However, it might not drop subsequent fragments because they do not contain objectionable headers. Some firewalls drop all fragmented packets because of the danger and because fragmented packets are rare in practice today.

Figure 3-22   TCP Header Is Only in the First Fragment of an IP Packet

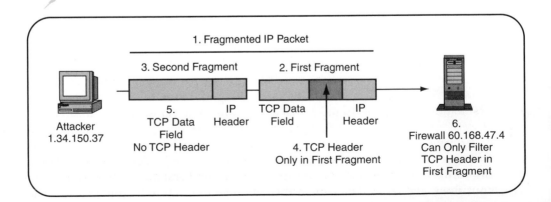

TEST YOUR UNDERSTANDING

13. a) What does the IP protocol field tell you? b) Why do firewalls need this information? c) What is the purpose of the TTL field? d) How do hackers exploit it? e) Why are IP options dangerous? f) What vulnerability did the Ping-of-Death exploit? g) What is fragmentation? h) Why is it dangerous from a security point of view? i) Which single-message denial-of-service attack abuses fragmentation?

TRANSMISSION CONTROL PROTOCOL (TCP)

Probably the most common data field in IP packets is the **Transmission Control Protocol (TCP)** message, called a **TCP segment**. Figure 3-24 shows an IP packet with a TCP segment as its data field. We will look especially at the **flags** field, which has several one-bit flags.

Reliable Service

Figure 3-25 shows communication between two transport layer processes during a TCP connection. Note that every correct TCP segment that a transport process receives is acknowledged with an **ACK** segment (a segment with the ACK bit set).

What if a particular segment is not acknowledged, for instance, Segment 8 in Figure 3-25? Then the transport process that originally sent the segment will assume that it was lost or damaged in transmission. The original sending transport process will retransmit the lost or damaged segment (Segment 9).

Connections

IP is connectionless, but TCP is connection oriented. TCP has distinct openings and closings.

Three-Way Opens

Connection openings use three TCP segments, so they are called **three-way opens**.

First, the transport process initiating the opening sends a TCP **SYN** segment (1)—a segment with the SYN bit set (made equal to one).

Second, the other process, if it is willing, will send back a **SYN/ACK** segment (2) with both the SYN bit set to indicate that it is willing to open the connection and the ACK bit set to acknowledge the original SYN segment.

Third, the originating side then sends an ACK segment (3) to acknowledge the SYN/ACK segment.

At this point, both sides have indicated their willingness to communicate and have had this willingness acknowledged by the other side. The connection is open.

Normal Four-Way Closes

Normal closes take four TCP segments. In this **four-way close**, one side sends a **FIN** segment (13), indicating that it is finished transmitting (except for acknowledgements). The other side sends an acknowledgement (14) of the FIN segment. Later, when the other side is finished sending, it sends a FIN segment (15) and receives back an ACK segment (16). The connection is closed.

MESSAGES ARE TCP SEGMENTS (Figure 3-24)

Flags field has several one-bit flags: ACK, SYN, FIN, RST, etc.

RELIABLE (Figure 3-25)

Receiving process sends ACK to sending process if segment is correctly received
ACK bit is set (1)
If sending process does not get ACK, resends the segment

CONNECTIONS (Figure 3-25)

Formal open and close
Three-way open: SYN, SYN/ACK, ACK
Four-way close: FIN, ACK, FIN, ACK
Abrupt close: RST
Will send RST segment in packet that contains host's IP address
Useful for hackers because it reveals which IP addresses are live (Figure 3-26)

SEQUENCE AND ACKNOWLEDGEMENT NUMBER

Sequence numbers identify segment's place in the sequence
Acknowledgement number identifies which segment is being acknowledged

PORT NUMBER (Figure 3-27)

Well-known ports (1–1023) used by applications that run as root
HTTP=80, Telnet=23, FTP=21 for supervision, 20 for data transfer, SMTP=25
Registered ports (1024–49152) for any application
Ephemeral/dynamic/private ports (49153–65355) used by client (16,384 in total)
Socket format is IP address: Port, for instance, 128.171.17.13:80
Designates a specific program on a specific machine
Port spoofing (Figure 3-28)
Incorrect application uses a well-known port
Especially 80, which often is allowed through firewalls

Figure 3-23   Transmission Control Protocol (TCP) (Study Figure)

Abrupt RST Closes

A second way to close a TCP connection is like hanging up on the other party in a human telephone conversation.

In an **abrupt close**, a single TCP segment closes the connection. At any time, either transport process can send a TCP **RST** (reset) segment with the RST bit set. This means that the RST sender will no longer talk to the other transport process.

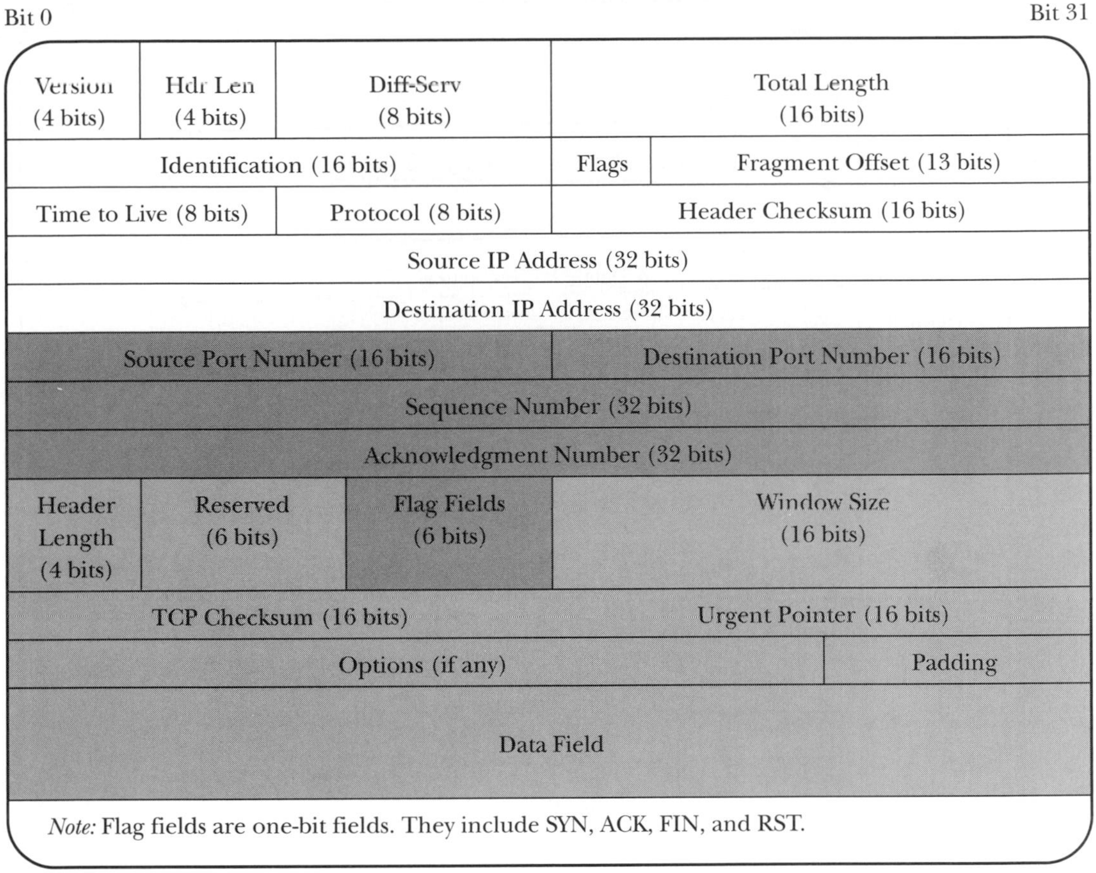

Bit 0   Bit 31

Version (4 bits)	Hdr Len (4 bits)	Diff-Serv (8 bits)	Total Length (16 bits)		
Identification (16 bits)			Flags	Fragment Offset (13 bits)	
Time to Live (8 bits)		Protocol (8 bits)	Header Checksum (16 bits)		
Source IP Address (32 bits)					
Destination IP Address (32 bits)					
Source Port Number (16 bits)			Destination Port Number (16 bits)		
Sequence Number (32 bits)					
Acknowledgment Number (32 bits)					
Header Length (4 bits)	Reserved (6 bits)	Flag Fields (6 bits)	Window Size (16 bits)		
TCP Checksum (16 bits)			Urgent Pointer (16 bits)		
Options (if any)				Padding	
Data Field					

Note: Flag fields are one-bit fields. They include SYN, ACK, FIN, and RST.

Figure 3-24   IP Packet with a TCP Segment Data Field

SYN/ACK Probing Attacks   For example, suppose one transport process sends an illegal TCP SYN/ACK segment to a transport process that did not earlier send it a SYN segment to the attacker, as shown in Figure 3-26. The victim receiving the SYN/ACK segment will send back an RST segment. This is a **SYN/ACK probing attack**.

The IP packet that carries the RST segment has the source IP address of the host sending the RST segment. This gives valuable information to an attacker because it identifies the IP address as operational and therefore a potential victim. Sending SYN/ACK packets to all IP addresses in a range is a good way of identifying possible victims.

Sequence and Acknowledgement Numbers

Each TCP segment is given a sequence number to indicate the segment's place in the sequence of segments being sent by one side within a connection. Although sequence numbers are somewhat complex, it is generally true that the sequence numbers of

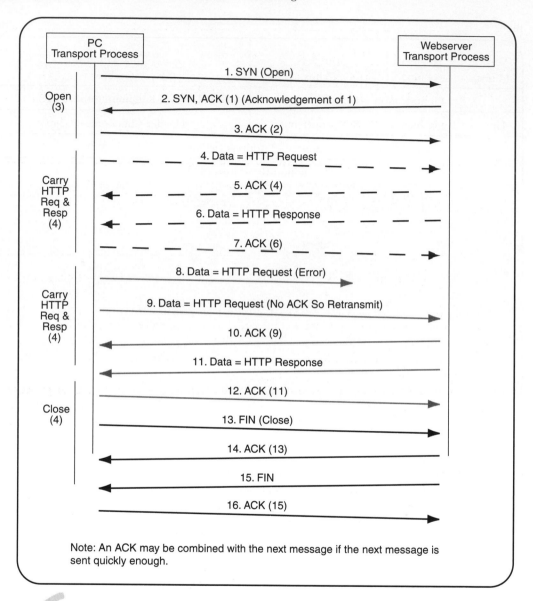

Figure 3-25   Communication During a Normal TCP Session

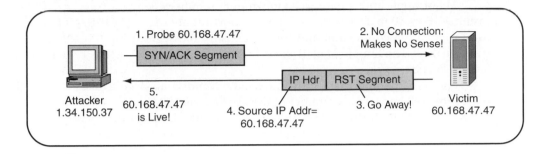

Figure 3-26   SYN/ACK Probing Attack Using TCP Reset (RST)

succeeding segments always get higher.[8] Each side uses its own sequence numbering during the session.

Sequence numbers allow TCP segments delivered by out-of-sequence IP packets to be put in proper sequence. In addition, if an acknowledgement is lost and a segment is resent in error, the resent segment will have the same sequence number as the original segment. The receiving transport process, recognizing the duplicate sequence number, will discard the duplicate segment.

Acknowledgement numbers, in turn, allow the receiving transport process to indicate which segment it is acknowledging with the ACK segment. One might think that the acknowledgement number of a segment would equal the segment's sequence number, but that is not the case.

TEST YOUR UNDERSTANDING

14.   a) How does TCP implement reliability? b) What messages are exchanged in a three-way opening? c) What messages are exchanged in a normal four-way closing? d) What is an RST close? e) What is a SYN/ACK probing attack, and why is it done? f) How can a receiving process put TCP segments that have arrived out of order in their proper order? g) Can error correction sometimes cause the receiver to receive the same message twice? Explain. h) If so, why would this not cause problems?

Port Numbers

Each TCP segment begins with 16-bit source and destination **port numbers**. So do UDP datagrams. Clients and servers use these fields differently.

Servers and Well-Known Port Numbers

For servers, port numbers indicate which application program on the server should receive the data field of the TCP segment or UDP datagram. (The server may be operating several application services simultaneously.)

---

[8]   The only exception is if the sequence number wraps—gets to its maximum value. The sender then starts over at zero or another small sequence number.

Major applications have **well-known port numbers** between zero and 1023. For instance, Port 80 in TCP is the well-known port number for HTTP. In FTP, Port 21 is used to set up a connection and for supervisory messages, while Port 20 is used to transfer data. The Simple Mail Transfer Protocol uses Port 25, while Telnet uses well-known Port 23.

Figure 3-27 shows that every time a client sends a message to a server, the client places the well-known port number of the application (80 for the webserver and 25 for the SMTP server) in the *destination* port number field. When the server responds, it places its well-known port number in the *source* port address field.

Registered Port Numbers

Well-known port numbers should be used only by privileged applications running at root authority. Other application services can run at lower authority. Instead of using well-known port numbers, these should use **registered port numbers** between 1024 and 49152.

Clients

Clients do something different. Whenever a client connects to an application program on a server, it creates an **ephemeral port number** between 49153 and 65535. These 16,383 port numbers also are called **private port numbers** or **dynamic port numbers**.

The port number ranges we have shown are those recommended by the IETF. However, although all operating systems respect the well-known port number range of 0 to 1023, many use nonstandard ranges for ephemeral port numbers.

Figure 3-27   Use of TCP and UDP Port Numbers

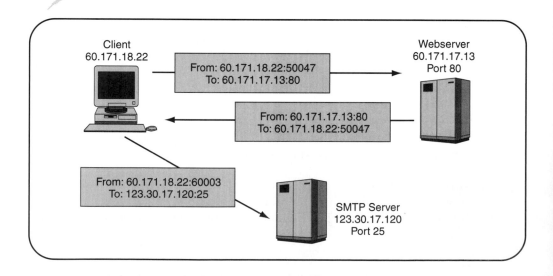

For transmission to the webserver, the port number is 50047. For a session with an SMTP mail server, the ephemeral port number is 60003. The client places the ephemeral port number in the source port number field of all outgoing segments to the server. The server places the ephemeral port number in all destination port number fields going back to the client.

Sockets
The figure uses **socket** notation, which is an IP address, a colon, and then a port number—for instance, 60.171.18.22:50047. A socket is a particular application on a particular host.

Port Spoofing
In **port spoofing**, an application uses a well-known port number despite not being the service that normally uses that well-known port number, as illustrated in Figure 3-28. For instance, because of the popularity of HTTP, many firms allow communication to and from Port 80 to pass through their firewalls. A number of applications ranging from hacker-installed programs to commercial programs, however, also may use Port 80. In the Firewalls chapter (Chapter 5), we will see how applications that spoof Port 80 and other commonly passed port numbers can be detected and stopped by application firewalls.

TEST YOUR UNDERSTANDING

15. a) What kind of port numbers do major services, such as e-mail, use to designate themselves? b) What kind of port numbers do clients use to designate themselves? c) What is a socket? d) What does a socket designate? e) What is port spoofing? f) Why would attackers use port spoofing on Port 80?

Figure 3-28 Port Spoofing

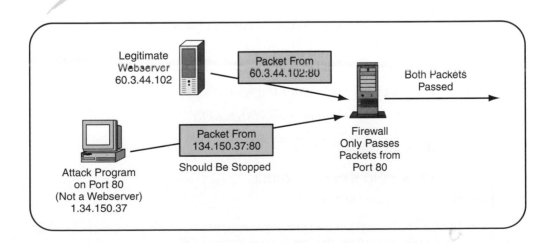

USER DATAGRAM PROTOCOL (UDP)

UDP Datagrams

Figure 3-30 shows an IP packet with a **UDP datagram** in its data field. Note that the UDP datagram is far simpler than the TCP segment because UDP is connectionless and unreliable. There is no need for acknowledgements, sequence numbers, flags, and the other complexities of TCP.

The UDP datagram has only source and destination port numbers, a UDP length field to indicate the size of the datagram, and a UDP checksum field to check for errors. If an error is found, the datagram is simply discarded. There is no retransmission.

UDP Port Spoofing

Due to its simplicity, UDP gives attackers fewer opportunities than TCP. Attackers have fewer fields in which to try unusual values. However, like TCP, UDP is susceptible to port number spoofing.

UDP Datagram Insertion

With TCP, it is difficult to insert crafted TCP segments into an ongoing dialog maliciously because sequence numbers are used. The crafted segment would have to have the next expected sequence number. Although sequence number guessing is not impossible, it tends to be difficult. With UDP, inserting a UDP datagram into an ongoing UDP dialog is easier because no sequence numbers exist to help the receiver detect the insertion.

TEST YOUR UNDERSTANDING

16.   a) How many fields does UDP have? b) Is UDP susceptible to port spoofing? c) Is message insertion easier with TCP or UDP? Explain. d) Otherwise, why is UDP generally safer than TCP?

Figure 3-29   User Datagram Protocol (UDP) (Study Figure)

UDP DATAGRAMS ARE SIMPLE (Figure 3-30)

Source and destination port numbers (16 bits each)
UDP length (16 bits)
UDP checksum (16 bits)

PORT SPOOFING STILL POSSIBLE

UDP DATAGRAM INSERTION

Insert UDP datagram into an ongoing dialog stream
Hard to detect because no sequence numbers in UDP

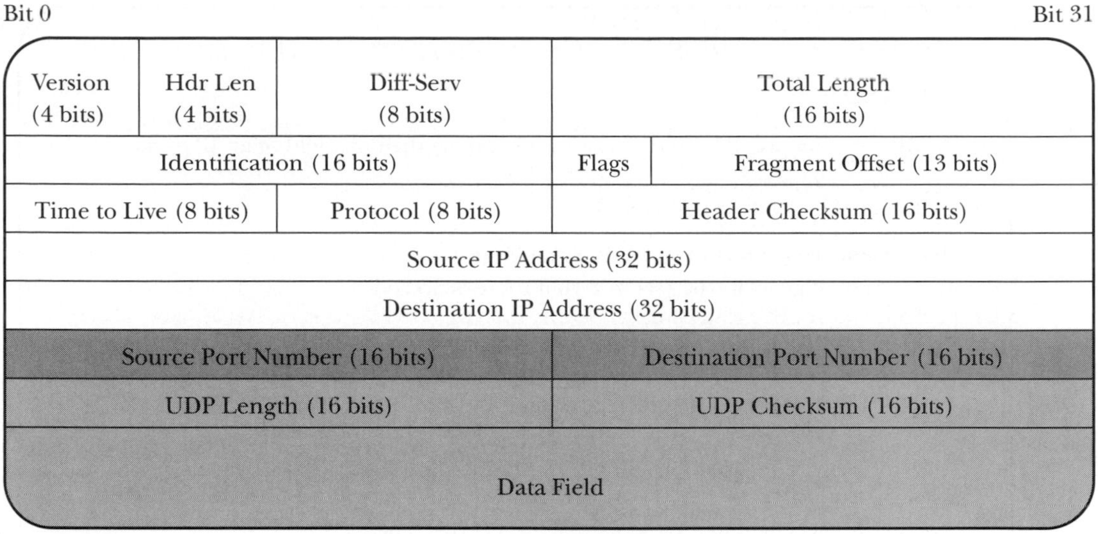

Bit 0   Bit 31

Version (4 bits)	Hdr Len (4 bits)	Diff-Serv (8 bits)	Total Length (16 bits)	
Identification (16 bits)			Flags	Fragment Offset (13 bits)
Time to Live (8 bits)		Protocol (8 bits)	Header Checksum (16 bits)	
Source IP Address (32 bits)				
Destination IP Address (32 bits)				
Source Port Number (16 bits)			Destination Port Number (16 bits)	
UDP Length (16 bits)			UDP Checksum (16 bits)	
Data Field				

Figure 3-30   IP Packet with a UDP Datagram in the Data Field

INTERNET CONTROL MESSAGE PROTOCOL (ICMP) FOR SUPERVISORY INFORMATION

The Internet Protocol (IP) merely provides message *delivery*. Its packets contain almost no *supervisory* information. To make up for this gap, the IETF created the **Internet Control Message Protocol (ICMP)** standard for internet layer supervisory information.

ICMP and IP

ICMP and IP are closely related. As Figure 3-32 shows, ICMP messages are carried in the data fields of IP packets. To further indicate the closeness of the two standards, IP was first published as RFC 791 and ICMP was first published as RFC 792. Also, all IP implementations are required to support ICMP.

ICMP Message Types

ICMP has a number of message types, each carrying a different type of supervisory communication. Figure 3-31 illustrates some common ICMP message types. In general, there are three major categories of ICMP messages: error advisement messages, control messages, and network analysis messages.

Types and Codes

Different ICMP messages have different syntaxes. However, all begin with two 8-bit fields: type and code. The **type** field identifies the general kind of ICMP message being

ICMP IS FOR SUPERVISORY MESSAGES AT THE INTERNET LAYER

ICMP AND IP

  ICMP messages are delivered in (encapsulated in) the data field of an IP packet

TYPES AND CODES (Figure 3-32)

  Type: General category of supervisory message
  Code: Subcategory of type (set to zero if there is no code)

NETWORK ANALYSIS MESSAGES

  Echo (Type 8, no code) asks target host if it is operational and available
  Echo reply (Type 0, no code). Target host responds to echo sender
  Ping program implements Echo. Like submarine pinging a target
  Useful for network managers to diagnose problems based on failures to reply
  Useful for hackers to identify potential targets (live ones reply)

ERROR ADVISEMENT MESSAGES

  Advise sender of error but there is no error correction
  Host Unreachable (Type 3, multiple codes)
    Many codes for specific reasons for host being unreachable
    Target sends back IP packet whose source address reveals the target's IP address
      to attackers
  Time Exceeded (Type 11, no codes)
    Each router decrements time-to-live (TTL) field by one
    Router decrementing TTL to 0 discards packet, sends time exceeded message
    Message reveals router's IP address
    By progressively incrementing TTL values by 1 in successive packets, attacker can
      scan progressively deeper into the network, mapping the network

CONTROL CODES

  Control network/host operation
  Source Quench (Type=4, no code)
    Tells other host to slow down its transmission rate
    Legitimate use: Flow control if host sending source quench is overloaded
    Attackers can use for denial-of-service attack
  Redirect (Type 5, multiple codes)
    Tells host or router to send packets in different way than they have
    Attackers can disrupt network operations, for example, by sending packets down
      black holes

MANY OTHER ICMP MESSAGES

Figure 3-31 Internet Control Message Protocol (ICMP) (Study Figure)

Bit 0   Bit 31

Version (4 bits)	Hdr Len (4 bits)	Diff-Serv (8 bits)	Total Length (16 bits)	
Identification (16 bits)			Flags	Fragment Offset (13 bits)
Time to Live (8 bits)		Protocol (8 bits)	Header Checksum (16 bits)	
Source IP Address (32 bits)				
Destination IP Address (32 bits)				
Type (8 bits)		Code (8 bits)	Depends on Type and Code	
Depends on Type and Code				

Figure 3-32   IP Packet with an ICMP Message Data Field

sent. The **code** field, which is used only with some types, specifies the message's specific function. If a code is not used by a message type, the code field value is set to zero.

TEST YOUR UNDERSTANDING

17. a) Why is ICMP needed? b) In what message is an ICMP message encapsulated? c) What are the three major categories of ICMP messages? d) Distinguish between ICMP types and codes.

ICMP Network Analysis Messages

The first category of ICMP messages are **network analysis** messages, which allow a network administrator (or, unfortunately, a hacker) to learn about the status of the network.

Echo and Echo Reply (Ping)

When a submarine commander wishes to be certain about the location of a target, he or she sends an acoustical ping, which bounces back to reveal the target's precise location.

Similarly, when a network administrator wants to know if a particular host is operational, the administrator can send the host an **echo** message (Type 8, no code). If it is able, the target host should send back an **echo reply** message (Type 0, no code). Not surprisingly, the most popular program for sending echo messages and analyzing echo reply messages is called **Ping** (Packet INternet Groper). Echo and echo reply are ICMP network analysis protocols.

Network administrators love Ping. If a problem arises, troubleshooters ping many of their routers and hosts to see which ones are reachable. The pattern of responses helps pinpoint the source of the trouble.

Sadly, hackers also love Ping. It is a great way for them to learn about your network. In fact, some hackers send so many pings into a network that it constitutes a de facto denial-of-service attack because of increased network traffic and the time it takes each host to respond to echo requests.

TEST YOUR UNDERSTANDING

18.   a) Why is Ping popular with network administrators? b) What two ICMP message types does it use? c) Why is Ping dangerous?

ICMP Error Advisement Messages

Error advisement messages tell a host or router that a problem has occurred in delivery. This does not give rise to the retransmission of messages, so it is not an error correction mechanism. It is merely an **error advisement** mechanism.

Destination Unreachable

The main family of ICMP error advisement messages is the **destination unreachable** (Type 3) message. It is sent by a router to indicate that a packet could not be delivered. Different codes indicate different reasons for delivery failure. To give examples, Code 1 indicates that the host itself is unreachable, while Code 2 tells the sender that the port specified was unreachable.

Unfortunately, attackers often send packets that they know are undeliverable, hoping that the host or router at a particular IP address will send an ICMP error advisement message. The source IP address of the packet delivering this response message will confirm that the address is "live," allowing the hacker to map the network.

Why would hackers do this instead of simply pinging hosts? The answer is that firewalls almost always filter out ping messages arriving from outside the network because only hackers are likely to send such messages. Hackers then use error advisement messages to attempt to get network mapping information.

Time Exceeded

As noted earlier in this chapter, each router along the route decrements the time-to-live (TTL) value by one. If a router decrements the TTL value to zero, it drops the packet and sends an ICMP **time exceeded** error advisement message (Type 11, no code). This also allows the hacker to map the network by noting the source IP address of the packet delivering the message.

TEST YOUR UNDERSTANDING

19.   a) What is error advisement? b) Why do hackers use ICMP error advisement messages to scan for host IP addresses? c) Why don't they simply use Ping?

ICMP Control Messages

ICMP **control messages** can actually change how a network operates. These are extremely dangerous because they allow a hacker to modify important aspects of network operation.

Source Quench

Some ICMP message types are control messages used to modify host and router operation. The ICMP **source quench** message is designed for **flow control**, in which one host needs the other host to slow down.

ICMP source quench messages (Type 4, no code) tell the receiver of the message to transmit more slowly. Each time a host receives a source quench message, it should slow its transmission rate. Source quench is a good example of an ICMP control message.

Unfortunately, attackers can send source quench messages in a denial-of-service attack, causing hosts to slow their transmission rates so much that they cannot serve their user bases.

Redirect

Other types of control messages also exist. Especially dangerous are **redirect** messages (Type 5, multiple codes) that tell a host or router that there is a better way to send an IP packet to a particular destination. This has infinite potential for mischief. For example, the redirect message might tell routers to send all traffic for a particular network to the wrong network or to send the traffic into a black hole where it is simply deleted.

Other ICMP Messages

Many other types of ICMP messages exist. Almost all of them are dangerous to allow into a network from the outside. For a list of ICMP messages, go to the Internet Assigned Number Authority (IANA) at www.iana.com.

TEST YOUR UNDERSTANDING

20.   a) Why are ICMP control messages especially dangerous? b) What do source quench messages do? c) How can hackers abuse them? d) What do ICMP redirect messages do? e) How can hackers abuse them?

CONCLUSION

This chapter had two purposes. The first was to review TCP/IP concepts rather than to teach TCP/IP. It is assumed that the reader already understands TCP/IP reasonably well and mainly needs to "get the rust out."

The second was to discuss aspects of TCP/IP related to security, especially vulnerabilities. To do this, we sometimes did have to introduce TCP/IP concepts that probably were new to most readers or explain how TCP/IP standards can be used by attackers.

THOUGHT QUESTIONS

1. Why do Ping-of-Death, Teardrop, LAND, and other attacks require new approaches to software testing beyond those needed for error detection?
2. Discuss prospects for redesigning the Internet from scratch to make it more secure. This is a highly complex question.
3. How do you think attackers send crafted packets if they work on Windows PCs?
4. Why do you think network mapping is important to attackers?
5. In an ICMP echo message, what is the value in the code field?

TROUBLESHOOTING QUESTIONS

1. In your intrusion detection system log, you notice a number of packets with both the TCP FIN and SYN bits set. Is this likely to be an attack packet? Explain. What is the attacker probably trying to do?

2. In your IDS log, you notice many outgoing packets coming from Port 80 (HTTP). These packets are coming from client PCs. What may be happening?

CHAPTER 4

ATTACK METHODS

Learning Objectives

By the end of this chapter, you should be able to discuss:

- The difference between targeted attacks and target-of-opportunity attacks.
- Typical steps in break-in (hacking/penetration) attacks.
- Denial-of-service (DoS) attacks.
- Target-of-opportunity malware attacks.

INTRODUCTION

In Chapter 3, we looked at TCP/IP-based communication. In this chapter, we will examine how adversaries use TCP/IP packets to attack corporate systems. We will look at three major types of attacks, including targeted break-in attacks (which typically require a number of consecutive actions), targeted denial-of-service attacks, and target-of-opportunity malware attacks.

Targeted Attacks

There is a fundamental difference between targeted attacks and target-of-opportunity attacks. **Targeted attacks** aim at a specific organization. The goal is either to break into an internal system or to conduct a denial-of-service attack against the organization. As we saw in Chapter 1, targeted attacks are no longer the most common type of attack, but they still are widespread. In addition, they are especially dangerous because they often are carried out with hostile intent. At the same time, targeted attacks often fail if a firm is well defended.

Target-of-Opportunity Attacks

In turn, **target-of-opportunity attacks** do not aim at specific firms. Rather, they attack firms randomly. The classic example is an e-mail–based virus that is released into the wild. It hits whatever firms have employees who receive the e-mail and open the attachment. Target-of-opportunity attacks are dominant today and are dangerous because of their ability to do massive damage—sometimes costing billions of dollars.

Targeted attacks are aimed at a specific organization.
Target-of-opportunity attacks strike firms randomly.

TEST YOUR UNDERSTANDING

1. a) Distinguish between targeted attacks and target-of-opportunity attacks. b) Which of these types of attack is more common?

TARGETED HACKING ATTACKS (SYSTEM PENETRATION/BREAK-INs)

A common reason for targeted attacks is to **hack** computers; that is, to access computers intentionally without authorization or in excess of authorized permission. Hacking also is called **system penetration** or a **break-in**. If the hack is successful, the attacker can read information, change information, and install unauthorized software on the computer.

Unobtrusive Information Collection

Sending attack packets into a network is a noisy process that is likely to set off intrusion detection alarms. Consequently, before attackers begin sending packets into a network, they usually first engage in unobtrusive information gathering.

UNOBTRUSIVE INFORMATION COLLECTION

Corporate website
Trade press (often online)
Securities and Exchange Commission (SEC) web-enabled Edgar service (Figure 4-2)
Whois database (Figure 4-3)
 Information about responsible person
 Information about IP addresses of DNS servers, to find firm's IP address block
 Easy if assigned a classful address block (Figure 4-4)
 Difficult if CIDR address block or a block of ISP addresses

IP ADDRESS SPOOFING (Figure 3-17)

Put false IP addresses in outgoing attack packets
Attacker is blind to replies
Use series of attack platforms (Figure 4-5)

HOST SCANNING

To identify IP addresses of potential victims
Ping all IP addresses in block for live IP addresses (Figures 4-6 and 4-7)
Send TCP SYN/ACK to generate RST segments (Figure 4-8)
 These are carried in IP packets that reveal the potential victim's IP address
Other RST-generating attacks (SYN/FIN segments)

NETWORK SCANNING

To learn about router organization in a network
Send Traceroute messages (Tracert in Windows systems)

PORT SCANNING

Most break-ins exploit specific services
Scan servers for open ports (Figure 4-9)
 Send SYN segments to a particular port number
 Observe SYN/ACK or reset (RST) responses
May scan for all well-known TCP ports and all well-known UDP ports (0 to 1023)
Or may scan more selectively
Scan clients for Windows file sharing ports (135–139)

(continued)

Figure 4-1   Targeted System Penetration (Break-In Attacks) (Study Figure)

FINGERPRINTING

Identify a particular operating system or application program and (if possible) version
Useful because most exploits are specific to particular programs and versions
Active fingerprinting
    Send odd messages and observe replies
    Different operating systems and application programs respond differently
Passive fingerprinting
    Read packets and look at parameters (TTL, window size, etc.)
    Different operating systems and application programs respond differently
Stealth scanning
    Scan fewer systems and ports and/or scan more slowly to avoid detection

THE BREAK-IN

Password Guessing
    Seldom works because attacker is locked out after a few guesses
Exploits that take advantage of known vulnerabilities that have not been patched
    Exploits are easy to use
    Frequently effective
    The most common break-in approach today
Session Hijacking (Figure 4-10)
    Take over an existing communication session
    Difficult to do so not commonly done

AFTER THE BREAK-IN

Install rootkit
    Usually downloaded through trivial file transfer protocol (TFTP)
Erase audit logs
Create backdoors for reentry if original hacking vulnerability is fixed
    Backdoor accounts
    Trojanized programs that permit reentry
Weaken security
Unfettered access
Install victimization software
    Keystroke capture programs
    Spyware
    Remote Administration Trojans (RATs)
    Attack software

Figure 4-1   (Continued)

Corporate Websites

An obvious source of information about a company is its corporate website. Often, corporate websites tell a great deal about current activities, officers, work locations, products, and important aspects of internal operation.

Social Engineering   Sometimes this information can be used in social engineering. If an attacker knows that Pat Lee is the manager of a particular product, the attacker might place a call claiming to be Pat Lee's assistant. Bolstered by knowledge about the product, the attacker might be able to trick the called party into giving out crucial information, perhaps even a password or a crucial design document.

Background Information to Guide Later Steps   In other cases, the knowledge gained by this search might provide background that helps later in the attack process. For instance, suppose hackers learn that "Wichita" is the code name for a new product under development at the Barclough site. Then if hackers discover that the Barclough site network has a server named "Wichita" or "NewProds," they might select this server as their main target.

Many corporations give their servers descriptive names to make information easier for users to find and to make maintenance easier for the systems administration staff. However, using descriptive server names also makes the information easier for attackers to find.

Trade Press

Although websites provide extensive information, they are not likely to say anything negative about the firm, and they might not discuss products under development. On the other hand, the trade press in the target firm's industry might provide extensive information about the firm's financial prospects and leaks about products under development. The trade press also tends to publish the names of people responsible for key activities and new products. In many cases, trade periodicals are online and offer search capabilities that make it easy to find information about the target firm.

Securities and Exchange Commission's (SEC's) Edgar System

In the United States, all publicly traded firms must provide certain information to the **Securities and Exchange Commission (SEC)**. These documents reveal a great deal of information about each firm's operation and finances. The SEC makes all of these reports available online through its web-based **Edgar** service. Figure 4-2 shows the initial screen for Edgar.

Whois

Corporations typically have second-level domain names, such as pukanui.com. The **Whois** database contains important information about second-level domains. For example, Figure 4-3 shows Whois data for pukanui.com. Here, the Whois database was accessed via www.netsol.com, but many other ways exist to search the Whois database.

Responsible Administrator   Note that Whois lists the person responsible for the domain name, along with contact information for this firm. Social engineers can use this information to attempt to get more information about the firm. A number of

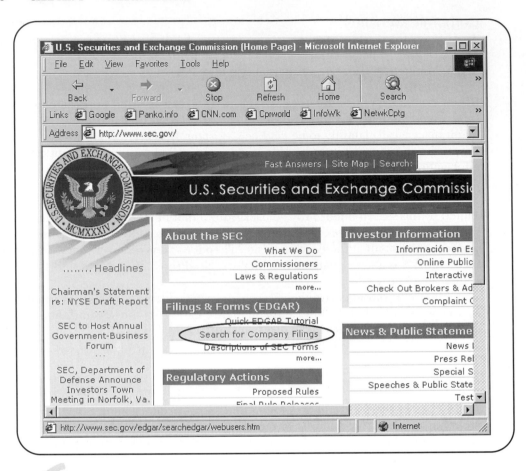

Figure 4-2 Securities and Exchange Commission's Edgar Service

firms put false contact information in their applications to fool attackers so that any-one calling the fictitious person listed in the Whois database is transferred to the secu-rity department.

DNS Server Information   An even more important piece of information in the Whois database is information about the DNS servers that store information about a company's servers. If these DNS servers can be compromised, the attacker will learn a great deal about the firm. If these DNS servers cannot be compromised, they may be brought down by DoS attacks—effectively knocking the firm off the Internet.

IP Address Blocks

Even the IP addresses of these servers can be enlightening. For instance, many firms are given blocks of IP addresses. Companies also tend to give their DNS hosts IP addresses near the bottom of their assigned block. This information may allow the

Registrant:
Panko, Ray (PUKANUI-DOM)
   1000 Pukanui Ave.
   Honolulu, HI 96820
   US
   Domain Name: PUKANUI.COM
   Administrative Contact:
      Panko, S. (RP17477)   S@Panko.com
      1000 Pukanui
      Honolulu, HI 96820
      US
      (808) 372-6721
   Technical Contact:
      VeriSign, Inc. (HOST-ORG)   namehost@WORLDNIC.NET
      VeriSign, Inc.
      21355 Ridgetop Circle
      Dulles, VA 20166
      US
      1-888-642-9675 fax: - namehost@worldnic.net
   Record expires on 07-Jul-2003.
   Record created on 07-Jul-2001.
   Database last updated on 7-Jun-2002 15:07:22 EDT.
   Domain servers in listed order:
   NS76.WORLDNIC.COM   216.168.225.216
   NS75.WORLDNIC.COM   216.168.225.215

Figure 4-3 Whois Data for Pukanui.com

attacker to guess the firm's IP address range—information an attacker needs for the next phase in the break-in attack, namely the sending of scanning (probing) packets.

Classful Addressing   Until recently, firms were given blocks of IP addresses according to the **classful addressing** scheme that gave each firm a block of Class A, Class B, or Class C addresses. Although this classful addressing scheme has been replaced by a new allocation scheme, many firms have IP address blocks based on the classful system. Figure 4-4 illustrates classful addressing.

Class B Addresses   For example, larger firms normally were given Class B blocks of addresses, which contain 65,534 contiguous IP addresses.[1] This is enough for even

---

[1]   Not 65,536 (2^{16}) because network, subnet, and host parts may not consist entirely of zeros or ones. All-zeros address parts are used by hosts when they boot up but before they are given an IP address by a DHCP server. All-ones address parts are used for broadcasting. This exclusion of all zeros or all ones in an address part applies to all IP address ranges in this section.

CLASS	INITIAL IP ADDRESS IN CLASS	LAST IP ADDRESS IN CLASS	SIZE OF NETWORK PART	ADDRESSES IN BLOCK ALLOCATED TO FIRM
A	0.0.0.1	127.255.255.254	8	16,777,214
B	128.0.0.1	191.255.255.254	16	65,534
C	192.0.0.1	223.255.255.254	24	254

Example
    Suppose DNS server is 128.171.17.1
    Must be a Class B address block (from table)
    Therefore, the network part is 16 bits: 128.171
    Address block must be 128.171.0.1 to 128.171.255.254

Figure 4-4   Classful IP Address Allocations

large firms. As Figure 4-4 shows, **Class B** IP addresses lie between 128.0.0.1 and 191.255.255.254. If attackers learn that a corporate DNS server has an IP address in this range, they will know that the firm was assigned a Class B address range.

Next, the hacker must know the firm's specific IP address range within the Class B address space. Class B addresses begin with 16 bits that lie between 128.0 and 191.255. The firm assigns the last 16 bits to individual hosts. So, if a firm has host 190.44.3.3, its IP address range will run from 190.44.0.1 to 190.44.255.254.

Class C Addresses   Smaller firms might be given Class C addresses, which contain a mere 254 contiguous IP addresses. **Class C** addresses lie between 192.0.0.1 and 223.255.255.254.

Class C addresses begin with 24 bits that lie between 192.0.0 and 223.255.255. The firm assigns the last 8 bits to individual hosts. Therefore, if enemies see that a firm has a host with the IP address 200.10.6.3, they know that the IP address range will run from 200.10.6.1 to 200.10.6.254 if a classful address was assigned.

CIDR   More recently, blocks of addresses have been assigned to firms through the **CIDR** (Classless InterDomain Routing) process, in which firms are given blocks of between 254 and 65,534 IP addresses.

Class A Addresses   Finally, Class A address blocks contain 16,777,214 contiguous IP addresses apiece. **Class A** addresses lie between 0.0.0.1 and 127.255.255.254. These addresses begin with 8 bits between 1 and 127. Together, they account for half of all possible IP addresses.

Class A addresses normally are given to large ISPs, which then give out individual addresses or blocks of addresses from this range to their residential and organizational customers. This practice makes it more difficult for attackers to identify a target firm's IP address range, but it is still possible for them to do so because assignments usually are given in blocks of contiguous addresses.

TEST YOUR UNDERSTANDING

2. Why do attackers do unobtrusive observation instead of just sending scanning packets at the target organization?

3. a) An organization has a host with an IP address of 128.171.17.13. What is its address class? b) How many IP addresses can the firm have in total? Explain. c) A firm has a host with IP address 60.34.231.3. How did it probably get this IP address? d) A firm needs 300 IP addresses. What type of classful range is it likely to get? (This requires some thought, and the answer is not explicitly in the book.) e) An organization has a DNS server with IP address 128.171.3.1. What IP address range would an attacker search to find hosts to attack?

IP Address Spoofing and Attack Chaining

IP Address Spoofing: Recap

As discussed in the last chapter, many attacks use **IP address spoofing**; that is, they replace source IP addresses in packets with different IP addresses. This hides the attacker's identity and may assist the attacker's hacking effort if the spoofed source IP address is that of a host trusted by the target host.

Blind to Replies

A drawback to IP source address spoofing is that reply packets will go back to the spoofed IP address rather than to the attacker. This is fine for many types of attack packets. However, in the scanning attacks we will see next, the attacker may need to see replies. In such cases, the attacker cannot use IP address spoofing.[2]

Serial Attack Platforms

However, the attacker can still maintain anonymity by taking over a chain of attack hosts, as Figure 4-5 illustrates. The attacker attacks the target victim using a point host—the last host in the attack chain. Even if authorities learn the point host's identity, they might not be able to track the attack through the chain of attack hosts all the way back to the attacker's base host.

TEST YOUR UNDERSTANDING

4. a) What is IP address spoofing? b) Why don't all attack packets use IP address spoofing to maintain anonymity? c) How does using a chain of attack hosts maintain anonymity?

Scanning Attacks

A typical hacking attack has several phases.

➤ In early phases, hackers send probing packets to scan the network in order to get information about the network.

➤ After this surveillance phase identifies targets, additional probes seek ways to exploit weaknesses on these targets.

➤ Finally, the hacker sends attack packets to break into specific victims. If these attack packets succeed, the system will be wide open to exploitation.

---

[2] They can, however, compromise another computer and send scanning packets from the compromised computer. By the time the victim traces the attack to the compromised computer, the attacker will have left after covering his or her traces.

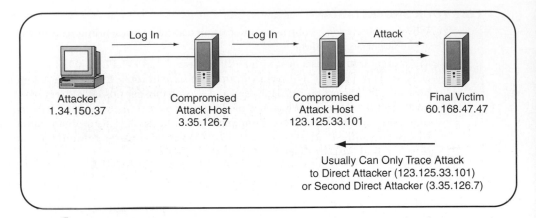

Figure 4-5   Using a Chain of Attack Hosts to Maintain Anonymity

Host Scanning Attacks

To send a break-in packet to a host, the attacker must know the host's IP address. Host scanning attacks attempt to identify which IP addresses in a firm have active hosts using them.

Ping Scanning   Chapter 3 introduced pinging, which uses ICMP echo and echo reply messages to see if there is an active host at a particular IP address. Figure 4-6 shows how to use Ping at the Microsoft Windows Command Prompt. The user simply types "Ping" followed by the IP address of the target host. (The user also can type a host name instead of an IP address.) Ping sends several echo requests and displays time delays in echo responses.

In **ping scanning**, the attacker pings a wide range of IP addresses likely to be found within the target firm. If a firewall does not block these ping scans, the attacker is likely to end the exercise with a list of active IP addresses. Figure 4-7 shows how *Ping Sweep* from Solarwinds.net can be used to ping a range of IP addresses. For each responding host, Ping Sweep reports the IP address and latency (in milliseconds). It also does a reverse DNS lookup if possible to get the host name for the IP address. Only hosts that respond are listed.

TCP SYN/ACK Attacks   Many firms use border firewalls to block ICMP echo messages arriving from outside the organization, so ping scanning only works against poorly-defended firms. If pinging is blocked, attackers still might be able to use other tools to scan for host IP addresses. As companies block each new attack method, attackers tend to find newer and more difficult-to-block tools.

A popular tool for scanning when pings are blocked is the TCP SYN/ACK host scanning attack shown in Figure 4-8. Here, the attacking host sends a TCP SYN/ACK segment. This appears to be a reply to a TCP SYN segment from the target host whose

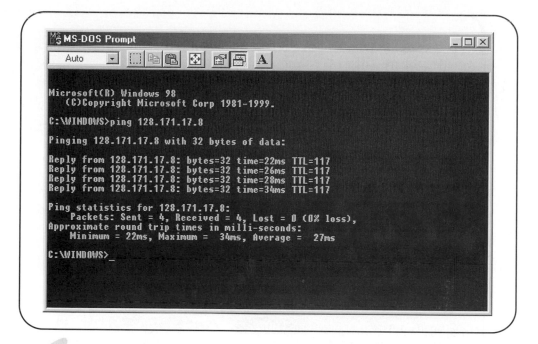

Figure 4-6   Ping at the Windows Command Prompt

IP address is in the destination IP address field. Many firewalls pass on the TCP SYN/ACK segment, not realizing that it is not a reply.

As we saw in Chapter 3, the target host receiving this segment will realize that it had not tried to initiate a connection to the attacking host. It will send back a TCP RST segment to tell the attacker to break off the attempted connection.

Unfortunately, this TCP RST segment will be carried inside an IP packet whose source IP address is that of the target host. When the packet reaches the attacker, the attacker will learn that the IP address is a live host.

Other RST-Generating Attacks   The SYN/ACK scanning attack, as just noted, attempts to generate RST segments from potential victims. Many other types of attacks also generate RST responses. For instance, it makes no sense for the SYN and FIN bits to be set in a segment. Why would a transport process want to both open and close a connection at the same time? A confused transport process receiving a SYN/FIN segment might generate an RST segment in reply.

TEST YOUR UNDERSTANDING

5. a) What is the purpose of host scanning? b) How does ping scanning work? c) Why are ping scans often not effective? d) Why are SYN/ACK scans done? e) How may hosts respond to SYN/FIN messages?

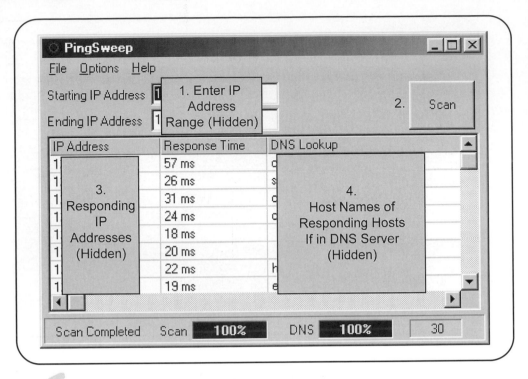

Figure 4-7   Ping Scanning with Ping Sweep

Figure 4-8   TCP SYN/ACK Host Scanning Attack

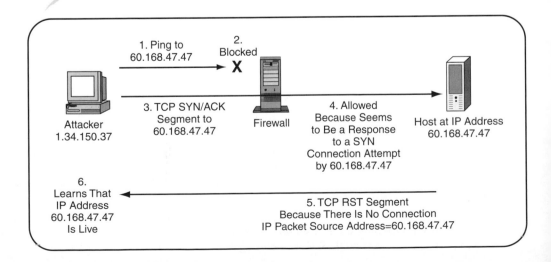

Network Scanning

Sometimes hackers attempt to go beyond identifying host IP addresses to understanding the internal structure of the network they are attempting to attack.

As discussed in Chapter 3, once attackers identify an IP address, they can use Traceroute (Tracert in Windows) to identify the routers along the way to the target host. By employing Traceroute against many IP addresses, the attackers may be able to develop a fairly complete map of a network, including how a company subnets its IP address space. We saw in Chapter 3 how Traceroute (Tracert in Windows) can do detailed network scans.

TEST YOUR UNDERSTANDING

6. a) How does Traceroute work? b) Why do attackers use it? c) What is the comparable program on Windows computers?

Port Scanning

Now that hosts have been enumerated (and, perhaps, the network mapped), the attacker begins to select specific victims to be attacked. The first step is to identify services running on the victim host. Most takeover attacks are service specific, so just knowing a target victim's IP address is not enough.

Server Port Scanning   As Chapter 3 discussed, most major applications use well-known TCP or UDP port addresses. Once an attacker identifies a target victim, an obvious first question is whether the victim is a server and what services it is running.

The simplest way to tell is to send a series of TCP SYN segments to the victim host, each to a different well-known TCP port number. This is called **TCP port scanning**. In most cases, a server will not be running the application and so will send back RST segments or will not reply at all if security is good on the host. However, if a service is active, such as HTTP on Port 80, then a SYN segment sent to Port 80 will receive a SYN/ACK reply from Port 80. The attacker now knows that the victim host is a server and knows which services it is running.

UDP port scanning is more difficult and less reliable. The attacker sends login requests or other messages to well-known UDP ports, hoping that the response will be illuminating. Sometimes it is, but often it is not.

Identifying services is important because most break-ins are service specific. Until services running on the server are identified, the attacker cannot begin planning the break-in.

Figure 4-9 shows output from a graphical front end to the popular NMAP network mapping program from insecure.org. (NMAP is inherently a command-line program.) The figure shows results from port scanning on a target server. It shows that a number of ports are active. This list may suggest possible attack vectors to the attacker.

Client Port Scanning   Although servers are important, taking over clients can be a fruitful way of getting into a network. Using remote control Trojans discussed later, an attacker can use a compromised client to attack other systems. In addition, clients increasingly have data that is valuable to attackers.

To see if a target host is a Windows client with shares enabled, attackers typically scan Ports 135 through 139. These are NetBIOS ports used in file and print sharing. If

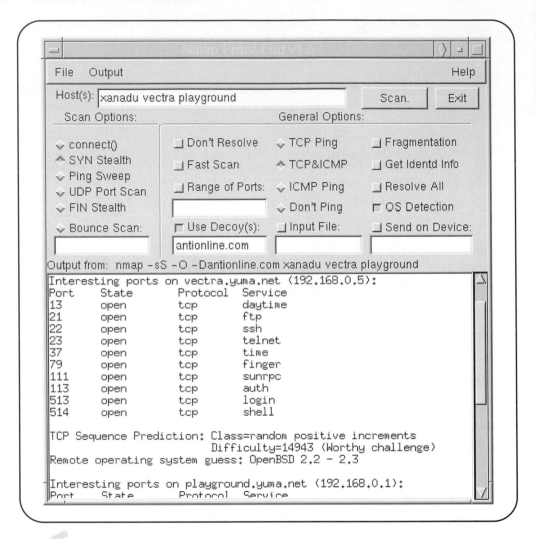

Figure 4-9 NMAP Port Scanning and Operating System Fingerprinting

a Windows client has shares and has weak or no password protection, the attacker might be able to read information on shared directories. NMAP and other port scanners can scan clients, as well as servers.

In fact, GRC (grc.com) offers an online service called ShieldsUp! If you go to the website and select ShieldsUp!, you will be scanned to see which of your ports are open to attackers on the Internet. The results can be rather alarming.

TEST YOUR UNDERSTANDING

7. a) Why is port scanning done? b) Is port scanning done on servers, clients, or both? c) How does TCP port scanning work? d) How does UDP port scanning work? e) If

both TCP and UDP port scanning are done against a host, how many ports need to be scanned to test all well-known ports? f) What ports tend to be scanned on clients?

Fingerprinting

Once the hacker has identified a potential victim host running a particular application service, the next step may be to **fingerprint** the software; that is, to determine the specific software the host is running.

For instance, a webserver application may be Microsoft's Internet Information Server (IIS), Apache, Sun ONE, or another webserver program from another vendor. It is also important, if possible, to identify the version of the software the host is running, because some vulnerabilities are fixed in later versions of most programs, although some new ones are introduced. Learning the specific product and version are important because many exploits are specific to particular programs and even to specific versions of these programs.

Active Fingerprinting   **Active fingerprinting** attacks send messages whose responses fingerprint (identify) a particular vendor's program and perhaps version, much like human fingerprints can be used to identify individual people. If active fingerprinting works, the attacker can prepare a takeover attack tailored to the particular vendor program running on the target host. Figure 4-9 illustrates that NMAP offers active fingerprinting.

NMAP and other active fingerprinting programs send a series of packets to a potential victim. These packets usually contain TCP segments or ICMP messages. Some of these packets usually contain malformed or at least unusual IP, TCP, or ICMP headers. Different operating systems will respond differently to these odd packets. For instance, a particular packet will be accepted by some operating systems, rejected by others with no reply sent, and rejected by others, with particular replies sent.

Passive Fingerprinting by Examining Received Packets   Active fingerprinting is noisy and may set off intrusion detection alarms. Consequently, many attacks use **passive fingerprinting** in which the attacker merely looks at IP packets and their contents to fingerprint a system. For instance, different operating systems place different values in a number of key IP and TCP fields, including time-to-live, sequence numbers, and identification. They also tend to differ in how they implement some fields in a series of packets, including how they increment the identification field. Application programs also tend to place specific values in important fields in the application message.

For example, suppose that the time-to-live field in a packet is 113 and that its windows size field has the value 18,000.[3] This host clearly is not using the size TTL value of 64 recommended in RFC 1700. Most packets take 10 to 20 hops to reach their destination, so the initial TTL value must have been 128, which is the only value used within this range. A TTL value of 128 says that we are receiving packets from a newer Windows 9X machine, a Windows NT 4.0 or 2000 machine, or a Novell NetWare server.

However, the windows size field is 18,000. Windows 2000 uses window sizes in the range of 17,000 to 18,000, Windows 9X/NT 4.0 uses values in the 5,000 to 9,000 range,

---

[3]   Data in this example are taken from Lance Spitzner, "Lists of Fingerprints for Passive Fingerprint Monitoring," version of May 23, 2000. project.honeynet.org/papers/finger/traces.txt.

and Netware uses values in the 32,000 to 32,768 range. Therefore, this must be a Windows 2000 server.

Passive fingerprinting is difficult because many values are not constant over a connection or vary by the application or transport layer protocol being implemented. In addition, users can change their default implementation values to confuse hackers, say by changing the TTL value on a Windows machine to 64, to make it look like a LINUX or other type of operating system.

Passive Fingerprinting by Reading Banners In many cases, sophisticated passive fingerprinting is unnecessary. Many application programs and operating systems present a **banner** to communication partners as part of the initial connection process. (Most simply, try using telnet or FTP to connect to the host.) This banner often names the software, including its version number. Even failed login attempts often present the banner to potential attackers. In most cases, these banners can be modified to avoid presenting software and version information. They can even be modified to present false information to attackers.

TEST YOUR UNDERSTANDING

8. a) What is fingerprinting? b) Distinguish between active and passive fingerprinting. c) Why is reading banners attractive compared to more complex passive fingerprinting?

Stealth Scanning

The Noisiness of Attacks The fact that most firms have intrusion detection systems (IDSs) makes scanning attacks somewhat dangerous. Scanning all hosts within a range means that hundreds or thousands of pings or other host scanning messages must be sent. In addition, once hosts are identified, just over 2,000 packets must be sent to each if all well-known ports in TCP and UDP are scanned. Active fingerprinting adds to the rain of attack packets going into the network.

The Exposure of the Attacker's IP Address In addition, in scanning attacks, it is necessary to hear the replies, so attackers usually have to put their real IP addresses in the source IP address fields of attack packets. Even weak IDSs will begin setting off alarms if high volumes of scanning attacks begin to come from a single IP source address.

Reducing the Rate of Attacks Below IDS Thresholds One way to minimize the probability of detection is to reduce the rate of attack packets, say to a few per hour. Many IDSs have volume thresholds and only set off alarms if a large number of attacks come from a single IP address in a certain time period.

Scanning Selective Ports In addition, in service scanning, the attacker may reduce packet volume by scanning only a few ports on each host—the ports of services for which the attacker has exploits. This also will reduce traffic and, therefore, the likelihood of setting off an IDS alarm.

TEST YOUR UNDERSTANDING

9. a) Why is sending a long stream of scanning messages dangerous for attackers? b) How do attackers use stealth scanning to reduce this danger?

The Break-In

Now that a victim host has been identified and services running on the victim have been identified and perhaps fingerprinted, attackers can reach into their bags of dirty tricks and attempt to take over the victim.

Password Guessing

Most servers have account names and passwords to protect them. After the attacker connects to an application, he or she will be asked for an account name and a password.

To hack these computers, the attacker must know or guess both account names and passwords for these accounts. This can be difficult to do. In addition, most operating systems and applications limit password guessing to a few tries. After a few tries, the account usually is locked for a period of time, making further guessing impossible. The hacker cannot simply keep trying thousands of possible account names and passwords.

However, if hackers can somehow download the computer's password file, they can crack passwords at leisure.

Exploiting Known Vulnerabilities

Known Vulnerabilities   Most break-in attacks today exploit **known vulnerabilities** in operating systems, utilities, and application programs. Thousands of vulnerabilities are discovered each year. Vendors often are slow to create software patches, leaving a window of vulnerability to attackers. In addition, many firms do not install all security patches for a variety of reasons, leaving their systems eternally open to attack via the known vulnerabilities they fail to patch. Attackers turn to exploits for known vulnerability for most break-ins today because using such exploits is easy and frequently effective.

Exploits   To take advantage of known vulnerabilities, attackers often can rely on **exploits**, which are programs created to exploit known vulnerabilities. These exploits can be used directly or can be incorporated within broader attack programs. Exploits give the attacker point-and-click power to take over vulnerable systems.

Host Hardening   By installing patches and taking other measures, firms can harden at least some of their hosts. (Host hardening is mentioned in Chapter 1, but due to the complexity of host hardening, it will be discussed in greater depth in Chapter 6 rather than here.)

Session Hijacking

Another way to compromise a host computer is session hijacking, in which the attacker takes over a TCP communication session between the victim and another host. Figure 4-10 illustrates session hijacking.

Impersonation and DoS   Here, the attacker impersonates one of the two parties. To be successful, the attacker must prevent the impersonated party from continuing to take part in the conversation. The attacker usually does this by mounting a denial-of-service attack against the impersonated party.

IP Address Spoofing   The attacker then sends packets to the victim host using source IP addresses that spoof those of the impersonated party. This way, the destination host

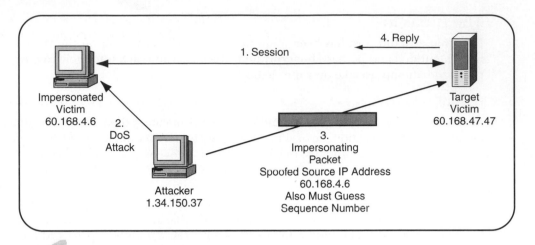

Figure 4-10   Session Hijacking

will think that these packets come from the impersonated party and will accept them as legitimate.

Sequence Number Guessing   Of course, if the application uses TCP, the attacker must have correct sequence numbers. However, sequence number guessing often is possible, especially in the opening stages of a connection when the messages are the most predictable.

Some operating systems create easily-guessable sequence numbers, for instance, adding 64K to the initial sequence number of succeeding connections. Others are semi-random, but if randomization is poor, a small number of attempts might be all that is needed to take over a connection.

One-Way Communication   Session hijacking is not perfect. For example, the victim host will send replies to the impersonated party, and the attacker normally will not be able to read these packets. Session hijacking is not good for maintaining long conversations.

Instead, the attacker typically sends a single attack packet to the victim host. That packet will do something of value to the attacker, perhaps even taking over the victim computer.

It should be noted that when the impersonated host receives TCP reply segments from the victim host, it will recognize that it did not send the original messages. It will send reset (RST) segments back to the victim host, and this will kill the connection.

Relay Session Hijacking   Blind session hijacking attacks, in which the attacker cannot see responses to the victim, are the most common session hijacking attacks. However, if attackers can stand in the middle of a conversation, say with a sniffer, they can more easily predict sequence numbers for both the victim and impersonated computers. They can then knock out the impersonated computer and carry on a continuing conversation with the victim computer after the hijacking, relaying messages between them.

TEST YOUR UNDERSTANDING

10. a) What three general approaches for breaking in (hacking) were discussed in this section? b) Why is password guessing not likely to work in most cases? c) Which approach is used most often? d) Why is it used most often? e) Distinguish among known vulnerabilities, exploits, and patches. f) Briefly describe session hijacking.

After the Compromise

Rootkits

Once hackers take over a computer, they can do whatever they wish. In practice, the first thing they usually do is download a **rootkit**, which is a set of programs designed for posthack activities. They download the rootkit to the target computer from their personal site (dangerous), from another computer they have compromised, or from a public site

Typically, the attacker downloads the rootkit using the **Trivial File Transfer Protocol (TFTP)**, which is simpler than FTP and does not require a user name or password. It generally is a good idea for a firewall to block TFTP commands in which an internal computer tries to retrieve files from an external host.

Deleting Audit Logs

Most operating systems and many application programs maintain **audit logs** that record who took what actions and when they were taken. To avoid detection and to stop the victim firm from learning in detail what the attacker did, hackers normally attempt to delete the computer's audit logs. This is like burglars wiping their fingerprints off a lock after picking it.

Creating Backdoors

Next, attackers make sure they can get back in by creating a **backdoor**, which permits access later even if the vulnerability that allowed the initial break-in is fixed.

Backdoor Accounts Most simply, the attacker can create a new account with an easy password or, preferably, no password at all. The attacker gives this **backdoor account** full privileges in all directories on the computer. Later, the attacker simply logs into this account. This means that even if the vulnerability that allowed the original break-in is fixed, the attacker will still be able to get back in.

Trojan Horse Backdoor Programs The problem with backdoor accounts is that the systems administrator who manages the server may see the new account and realize that it is illegitimate. More sophisticated attackers replace an existing system file with a **Trojan horse backdoor program** with the same filename and extension. Trojan horse programs are programs that pretend to be one thing (such as a game or a systems program) but really are something else. The attacker later logs into this Trojan.

Weakening Security

After ensuring that they have removed audit traces and can get back in, attackers might next weaken security on the compromised program. They might change the operating system configuration files to a lower level of security parameters than the systems administrator previously set. They also might turn off intrusion detection programs, block the downloading of antivirus updates, or do other things to reduce security.

Unfettered Access

The attacker now "owns" the computer. If attackers have achieved root access, they can read any files on the system, delete important files, or do other types of mischief. Even if the attackers have taken over an account with only limited privileges, they might be able to do a great deal of damage.

Victimization Software

Finally, the attacker can install one or more **victimization software** programs. These programs continue to harm the computer's true owner long after the attack.

Keystroke Capture Programs As noted in Chapter 2, installing a **keystroke capture program** on a computer allows the attacker to record encryption keys and other important information. Periodically or when prompted, the keystroke capture program sends its information to the attacker.

Spyware **Spyware** programs "phone home" to the attacker, sending back potentially sensitive information from the compromised computer, including social security numbers, passwords, and other information.

Remote Administration Trojans (RATs) **Remote Administration Trojans (RATs)** allow the attacker to control all aspects of the victim computer remotely, almost as if the attacker were sitting at the keyboard. The attacker can cause the computer to send e-mail as if it came from the computer's true user; transfer files via FTP, IRC, or instant messaging; and do many other things. At a prankish level, the attacker can open and close CD-ROM drives and can do other things that will confuse and alarm a person working at the victim computer. Back Orifice, NetBus, SubSeven, and several other RATs infest many client PCs and even servers across the Internet.

Attack Software Attackers often download attack software in order to use the compromised host to attack other hosts, as illustrated in Figure 4-5.

TEST YOUR UNDERSTANDING

11. a) List the main things a hacker is likely to do after a break-in. b) What is a rootkit? c) Why do hackers delete audit logs? d) What are backdoors? e) Distinguish between the two types of backdoors listed in this section. f) Distinguish among the types of victimization software listed in this section.

DENIAL-OF-SERVICE ATTACKS

An application is worthless if it is not *available* to users. Denial-of-service (DoS) attacks make a particular computer or network unavailable to users or available with only a poor degree of service.

Vandalism

Elite Internet hackers often look down on DoS attackers, viewing their "work" as mere vandalism by "lamers" not good enough to be real hackers. Just as a thief who cannot break into a house might damage something in frustration, DoS attacks are done strictly to damage a firm.

Figure 4-11   Denial-of-Service (DoS) Attacks (Study Figure)

INTRODUCTION

    Attack on availability
    Act of vandalism

SINGLE-MESSAGE DoS ATTACKS

    Crash a host with a single attack packet
    Examples: Ping-of-Death, Teardrop, and LAND
    Send unusual combinations that developers did not test for

FLOODING DENIAL-OF-SERVICE ATTACKS

    SYN flooding (Figure 4-12)
       Try to open many connections with SYN segments
       Victim must prepare to work with many connections
       Victim crashes if runs out of resources; at least slows down
       More expensive for the victim than the attacker
    Smurf attack (Figure 4-13)
    Distributed denial-of-service (DDoS) attack (Figure 4-14)

STOPPING DoS ATTACKS (Figure 4-14)

    Ingress filtering to stop attack packets
    Limited ability of ingress filtering because link to ISP might become overloaded
    Egress filtering by attacker's company or ISP
    Requires cooperating from attacker's company or ISP
    Requires a community response; victim cannot do it alone

TEST YOUR UNDERSTANDING

12. a) Do DoS attacks focus primarily on confidentiality, integrity, or availability? b) Why do hackers tend to despise DoS attackers?

Single-Message DoS Attacks

The earliest DoS attacks used a single malformed message to crash a victim host. Programmers write their programs assuming correct input on the part of users. Consequently, attackers often try incorrect input to see if this unexpected input will crash the system or leave it vulnerable in other ways. The more outrageous the bogus input, the more likely it is to crash or otherwise harm the target software.

In Chapter 3, we saw three single-message DoS attacks: Ping-of-Death, Teardrop, and LAND. These are older attack methods that rarely work today. However, new single-message DoS attacks that crash systems keep appearing because developers rarely test their software for the kind of absurd input patterns in IP, TCP, UDP, ICMP, and other protocols that classic single-message DoS attacks exploit.

TEST YOUR UNDERSTANDING

13. a) What is a single-message DoS attack? b) What do these attacks have in common?

Flooding Denial-of-Service (DoS) Attacks

SYN Flooding

Other DoS attacks flood a host with a long series of messages. **Flooding DoS attacks** either make the target host so busy that it cannot respond to legitimate users, or they cause the overloaded victim to crash when it runs out of resources.

The most famous flooding DoS attack is the SYN flooding attack, which Figure 4-12 illustrates. In this attack, the sender transmits a long series of SYN TCP segments to the victim host. Each time the host receives a SYN segment, it sets aside some room in memory and engages in a good deal of other preparatory work. It then sends back a SYN/ACK message indicating its willingness to open the connection. Afterwards, it waits for an ACK message to indicate the completion of the connection.

Figure 4-12   SYN Flooding DoS Attack

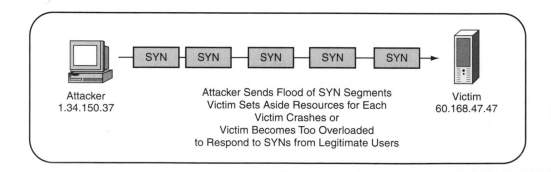

If the sender sends many SYN segments, the server host might run out of memory or might spend so much time processing connection openings that it fails or is too busy to respond to connection openings from legitimate users. Whether the host fails completely or limps along in a barely functional state, users will be denied service.

SYN flooding, like other flooding DoS attacks, operates on the basis of **work asymmetry**. Little processing power is required to create and transmit SYN segments, especially if the sender does not intend to open a connection and so does not set aside resources for the connection. However, the SYN receiver, believing the connection to be legitimate, must set aside RAM and other resources to handle the new connection. Even a few SYN messages will overload a victim machine with expensive work.

Smurf Flooding Attacks

Another flooding attack is the **Smurf**[4] attack, shown in Figure 4-13. Here, the attacker sends a long stream of pings (ICMP echo messages) to a third party. The attacker uses IP address spoofing, making the source IP address in these pings the IP address of the victim. Consequently, pinged hosts send their ICMP echo replies *to the victim host*, overwhelming it.

For this attack to be successful, the third party being pinged must have a router that will broadcast the ping message to all hosts in the router's attached networks. This way, a single echo request can give rise to dozens or even hundreds of echo response packets that will flood the victim host.

Figure 4-13   Smurf Flooding DoS Attack

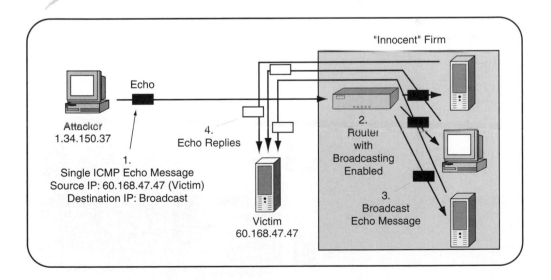

---

[4]   Smurfs are small, blue, German cartoon characters. Although they are small, there are many of them. The name "Smurf attack" is ironic because almost all Smurfs in the cartoons were good.

Most routers today will no longer broadcast messages to all of their attached hosts because of this attack. However, it took several years for enough routers to turn off broadcasting to make this type of attack difficult to implement, and even today not all routers have turned off broadcasting. This slow response demonstrates why even old attack methods often work surprisingly well.

Distributed DoS Attacks

Sending DoS attack packets from a single attack computer leaves the attacker vulnerable to identification even if IP address spoofing is used. In addition, DoS attacks from a single source all pass through the same routers along the way, making them (relatively) easy to stop.

Consequently, many DoS attackers now use **distributed DoS (DDoS)** attacks in which they attack the victim with messages from multiple hosts. Figure 4-14 illustrates a DDoS attack.

Phase 1: Installing Handler and Zombie Computers

Before initiating the denial-of-service attack, the attacker first installs attack programs on other computers. **Zombie programs** actually carry out the attack on the victim. **Handler programs** tell the zombie programs when to carry out attacks.

Phase 2: Implementing the Attack

Once the handler and zombie programs are in place, the attacker sends messages to the handler computers, telling them to carry out the attack. The handlers in turn tell the zombie programs under their control to carry out the attack.

Figure 4-14 Distributed Denial-of-Service (DDoS) Attacks

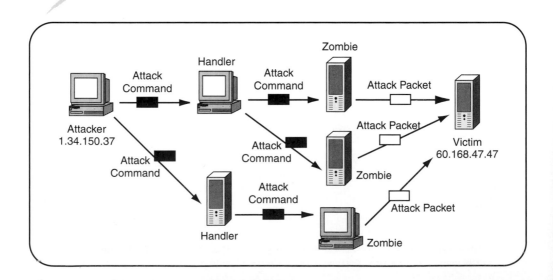

Difficulty in Identification

The attacker's computer, which is two steps removed from the attack, is very difficult to identify. In addition, because zombies can be spread all over the Internet, the attack messages come from many different sources, making them difficult to filter out at border firewalls.

Case Study: Mafiaboy

In late 1999, law enforcement personnel realized that DDoS zombies were being installed on large numbers of Internet computers. Then, in February 2000, devastating DDoS attacks using the DDoS program Stacheldraht were carried out against CNN.com, eBay, Yahoo.com, Amazon.com, Dell.com, eTrade, and other major Internet sites. Victims could do little to stop the attacks when they were occurring. Attacks on their firms ended only when the attacker switched to another victim or eventually stopped. When the dust settled, damages ranged somewhere between hundreds of millions of dollars to a few billion dollars.

After the attacks, authorities had no clue regarding who made the attacks until someone with the screen name Mafiaboy bragged about his exploits in a chat room. If not for that bragging, it is questionable whether the attacker ever would have been caught.

Although many analysts initially believed that the attacks were carried out by a sophisticated attacker, the perpetrator turned out to be a 15-year-old Canadian hacker who used a DDoS attack script. He subsequently confessed and received a trivial sentence of eight months in a detention center and was given a nominal fine of $250.

This pattern of victim impotence coupled with extreme difficulty in identifying DDoS attackers has been characteristic of the many subsequent DDoS attacks that have occurred since Mafiaboy's siege of major websites. Many of these attacks have been bigger than his, but the media have given little attention to these later attacks because they were not "news."

TEST YOUR UNDERSTANDING

14.   a) Describe SYN flooding. b) Why is it effective in terms of relative costs for attackers and victims? c) Describe the Smurf attack. d) Describe DDoS attacks. e) Why do attackers use DDoS attacks instead of simpler attacks?

The Difficulty of Stopping DoS Attacks

DoS attacks are difficult to stop. Attack traffic tends to look like legitimate traffic, making it difficult to filter incoming packets. For example, TCP SYN segments from legitimate customers coming into a webserver look exactly like TCP SYN segments sent as part of a SYN flood.

Ingress Filtering

In addition, it is difficult to stop attacks at the victim's firewall, as Figure 4-15 illustrates. Even if the firewall is able to use ingress filtering to stop incoming attack packets, the level of traffic coming into the site tends to be so large that both the site's router and access line are likely to be overloaded. Legitimate traffic will have little chance of getting into the corporate network.

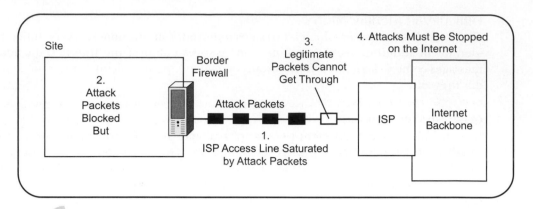

Figure 4-15   The Difficulty of Stopping DoS Attacks

The Limitations of Ingress Filtering

Although ingress filtering at a boundary firewall can reduce DoS attacks, these attacks need to be stopped at their source. Otherwise, the receiver's router and access line may be overloaded by DoS packets. Although the DoS packets will not get into the firm, the firm's Internet access may be so overloaded that no one will be able to send in legitimate packets. This would be devastating to e-commerce sites and many other sites.

The Need for Egress Filtering

The only effective way to stop flooding attacks is for ISPs, universities, and corporations to perform **egress filtering** on outbound data to stop DoS attack packets before these packets enter the Internet. It is extremely important for routers to have proper egress rules that detect when one of a firm's computers is being used in DoS attacks and to discard DoS-related packets.

The Need for Cooperation

In many cases, victim firms can trace the source of attack packets. Victim firms can then contact the ISP or organization whose computers are being used in the attack. However, convincing the organization to take action to stop an attack can be difficult. For instance, in Smurf attacks, the firm whose routers are used to broadcast DoS messages will observe a flood of IP packets whose source IP addresses are those of the victim firm, indicating that the victim firm is attacking them. It might be difficult to convince the firm whose routers are doing the broadcasting to help the victim firm.

Community Responsibility

Overall, DoS attacks require community responses in which all parties behave reasonably. In addition to egress packet filtering, companies must update security on all their computers, as discussed in Chapters 6 and 9, to prevent their networks from being used in attacks.

TEST YOUR UNDERSTANDING

15.   Why is stopping DoS attacks an issue for the Internet community?

MALWARE ATTACKS

Malware (malicious software) is a general term for a variety of programs, including viruses, worms, remote administration Trojans, and other forms of attack software that act in an **autonomous** or semi-autonomous fashion. The danger of autonomous action is that attacks can be carried out on vast scales.

Types of Malware

Viruses

The most widely known type of malware is the **virus**, which is a piece of code that attaches itself to a file (file-infector) or, infrequently, to a sensitive system sector[5] of the victim computer's hard disk. Viruses propagate when infected files are passed to another computer and executed there or, in the case of system sector viruses, when a floppy disk is placed in an infected machine's disk drive. The virus then infects the system sectors on that disk.

Worms

Often confused with viruses, **worms** do not infect other program files or system sectors. Rather, they spread by sending themselves to other computers. For instance, a worm might scan hosts for webserver programs with known weaknesses. When it finds one, it might execute a single-message break-in attack. That single message might transfer the worm to that machine.

In 1988, the Robert Morris worm infested approximately 6,000 hosts on the Internet—what was then a substantial fraction of Internet hosts. Propagating in several ways that exploited fairly well known vulnerabilities, the worm reproduced far more rapidly than Morris had anticipated and effectively took the young Internet "offline." It did approximately $10 million in damage in a few days. Morris tried to contact systems administrators to tell them about a fix to stop his program, but he could not get through because Internet e-mail was inoperable.

In 2001, a rash of worm attacks (e.g., Code Red, Nimda, etc.) occurred based on known vulnerabilities in the Microsoft IIS webserver program. According to Computer Economics, Code Red alone infested more than 500,000 servers and caused $2.6 billion in damage. Viruses in total cause $13 billion in damage.

Payloads

Viruses and worms usually contain **payloads**, which are sections of code that are executed some time after a virus or worm propagates to a new system.

Malicious Payloads   Many payloads are **malicious payloads** designed to do damage, for instance, reformatting a computer's hard disk drive.

---

[5]   A hard disk drive is divided into regions called sectors. The boot sector contains code that is executed when a computer is first booted up. Partition sectors mark divisions between partitions on a disk. Boot sectors and partition sectors are collectively called system sectors. Neither type of system sector virus is common today.

MALWARE: MALICIOUS SOFTWARE
Essentially an Automated Attack Robot Capable of Doing Much Damage

TYPES OF MALWARE

  Viruses: infect files or system sectors on disk
    Attach themselves to executable programs or to disk system sectors (mostly the former)
  Worms: propagate by themselves between hosts
  Payloads
    Malicious
    "Benign" may do damage accidentally
  Active Content
    HTML scripts or small programs (applets)
    Attack directly or download a malicious program
    User can turn off active content execution, but webpage functionality will be reduced
  Non-mobile malware
    Trojan horses, etc.
  Blended threats
    Propagate as viruses, worms, and active content
    Do damage directly and download non-mobile attack programs

VIRUSES

  Executable versus macro viruses
    Executable viruses attach to executable programs (traditional)
    Macroviruses attach as macros to data files; executed when file is opened
  Propagation vectors
    Exchange floppy disks
    E-mail attachments
      E-mail offers easy attachment delivery
      90% of viruses spread via e-mail attachments today
      An epidemic: virus in every 200 to 400 e-mail messages
      Users open attachments from people they trust
      But good people get viruses
      Viruses send e-mail pretending to be coming from victim
      Should open e-mail attachments only if specifically expected and still scan with updated antivirus program
      HTML bodies may execute malware automatically
    IRC and instant messaging (IM)
    FTP and website downloads

(continued)

Figure 4-16   Malicious Software (Malware) (Study Figure)

ANTIVIRUS PROTECTION

Location
  On clients (often disabled by users)
  On mail servers (does not require user compliance)
  Outsourced e-mail scanning outside the firm (advantages of scale and experience)
Scanning method
  Signatures
  Behaviors
Two nightmares for antivirus professionals
  Flash viruses that spread too rapidly for signatures to be developed
    Behavioral scanning and outsourcing firms that see many instances quickly will become important
  Metamorphic viruses
    Instead of placing their code at the end of the infected file, they place it throughout the file
    Might make signature detection inaccurate and too slow to be practical
Recovery
  Detection and identification
  Repair
    Go to the antivirus vendor's website
    Malware-specific repair program or manual procedure
    Often, infected programs must be reinstalled—sometimes the entire operating system
    Some or all data since the last backup might be lost
    If damage to data files takes place over a period of time, a company might not know when its last clean backup was
    Extremely time consuming

NIMDA WORM

Spread by sending through e-mail
Spread by open file shares on client
Spread by clients infecting webservers
    Client scanning for IIS webservers almost constitutes a DoS attack
    Client infects IIS webserver through backdoors left by previous viruses and worm
    Client infects IIS webserver through unpatched directory traversal vulnerability
Spread by IIS webserver infecting clients with downloads, often executed automatically
Trojanizes various files so they are difficult to find and clean out

Figure 4-16   (Continued)

Benign Payloads   Other payloads are **benign payloads** designed not to do damage beyond some prank such as putting up a message on a user's screen. However, poor design often causes payloads intended to be benign to do damage. An early virus, Stoned, did damage because it was designed when 720 KB floppy disk drives were popular. During its spread, 1.44 MB floppy drives became popular. Unintentionally but effectively, Stoned damaged data on these disks.

In the Eyes of the Beholder   In some cases, attackers consider their payloads to be benign when they really are not. For instance, it is common for the payload code to weaken a computer's security defenses, leaving it open for further attack. Firms would consider this to be malicious regardless of what the attacker believes.

Active Content

Adding Code to HTML   To make webpages and e-mail more "lively," browsers were given the capability to execute **active content**, which attaches either a small script or a small program (called an applet) to an HTML webpage. Javascript and VBscript are common scripting languages. Java and Active X are common programming languages. Unfortunately, attackers use active content to damage the reader's system—either directly or by causing the user's browser or e-mail program to download a malicious program.

Similar to Viruses   Active content is similar to viruses in that attackers often add malicious active content to an existing webpage document, much as they would add a macro virus (discussed later) to a word processing or spreadsheet document. For historical reasons, however, active content attacks are treated as separate from virus attacks.

Users Can Turn Off Active Content   Browsers and e-mail programs have options that cause scripting languages and program applets in HTML documents to be ignored. This will eliminate most active content infections. However, it may also reduce the functionality of legitimate webpages.

Nonmobile Malware

Nonmobile attack programs are not designed for propagation. Rather, they are designed to be installed on a victim host and then to remain there without propagating. Remote Administration Trojans, keystroke capture programs, and the other post-break-in tools that we saw earlier are examples of non-mobile malware.

Blended Threats

A growing number of new malicious programs are **blended threats** that combine the features of viruses, worms, and non-mobile malware. They propagate in several ways—by infecting files, by adding active content to webpages and e-mail, and by moving between systems as worms. They do direct damage and also deposit non-mobile malware when their payload executes.

TEST YOUR UNDERSTANDING

16.   a) What are the major categories of malware? b) Distinguish between viruses and worms. c) What is a payload? d) Distinguish between "benign" and malicious pay-

loads. e) Why was the term *benign* in quotes in the previous sub-question? f) What is active content? g) In what two ways does active content attack users? h) Can users turn off active content execution? i) What is non-mobile malware? j) What are blended threats?

Viruses

Having looked at the broad spectrum of malware, we will begin to look in more detail at some specific types of malicious programs, beginning with viruses. We will look only at **file-infector viruses**, which attach themselves to files, because system sector viruses are comparatively rare.

Executable Versus Macro Viruses

Executable File Infectors   Many file-infector viruses infect **executable files**, such as those with the .exe extension. Most computers have many executables, giving the virus many choices for file victims. In recent years, many new types of executable programs and script languages have appeared.

Macro Virus Infectors   Other file infectors infect data files. More specifically, a growing number of programs have **macro** capabilities, in which they can record a series of keystrokes and save these in data files. Later, when the data files open, or when the user takes other actions such as typing key groups or saving the file, the macro commands will execute. Macro viruses are extremely common, yet many users still believe that data files cannot be infected by viruses.

Propagation Vectors

How do viruses spread from computer to computer? In general, the answer is social engineering, or to put it less charitably, user gullibility.

Exchanging Floppy Disks   Early viruses were spread by people exchanging floppy disks containing boot sector viruses or file-infector viruses. People often exchanged pirated software or "amusing diversions" that seemed like fun.

Opening E-Mail Attachments   Modern e-mail systems make the sending and reading of e-mail attachments easy. E-mail attachments can contain infected program files and data files with macro viruses. They also can contain worms that are executed when the attachment is opened. Today, about 90 percent of all viruses are spread by e-mail attachments.

An Epidemic

Virus and worm transmission via e-mail are already at epidemic levels and will only get worse. MessageLabs (messagelabs.com) runs a service that scans e-mail for viruses before messages get to users. The company reports that between one in 200 and one in 400 e-mail messages sent each day (the ratio fluctuates day-to-day) contained malicious content as of mid-2002. This is a far higher rate of infection than MessageLabs found just a year earlier.

Trusting People

Many people believe that they can safely open attachments from people they know and trust. However, anyone can get virus infections without knowing it, so believing that someone you trust will not harm you with viruses or worms in e-mail attachments is a bad idea.

In addition, many e-mail viruses and worms send bogus messages to large numbers of people on an infected computer's e-mail mailing list. These messages appear to come from the person owning the computer, but they are merely coming from the person's compromised e-mail program.

Specific Expectations   A better rule is that people should open attachments only from people who they know have strong antivirus programs *and* from whom they are *expecting a specific attachment*. Even then, attachments should be opened only if an antivirus program first checks the attachment.

E-Mail HTML Bodies   Many mail programs now accept messages with HTML bodies. This allows attractive message formatting. However, some mail programs, such as Microsoft Outlook, tend to execute code in HTML documents without first prompting the user. In other words, viruses and worms sometimes can spread *even if the victim does not deliberately open an attachment in a message.*

IRC and Instant Messaging

E-mail is not the only popular human communication tool. Internet users have long used Internet Relay Chat (IRC) to form discussion groups and exchange files. Instant messaging (IM), in turn, allows one-to-one communication and file sharing, is growing explosively, and tends to get through firewalls unfiltered. In addition, IRC and IM usually are not examined by antivirus software installed on user PCs.

FTP and Website Downloads

Another popular way to get viruses is to download files from FTP sites or websites. The increasing popularity of pirated software, which frequently contains viruses, has led to increases in FTP-related infections. Websites are becoming dangerous places because webpages can contain malicious scripts, which are executed automatically when a webpage is viewed unless the receiver has implemented secure browser options.

TEST YOUR UNDERSTANDING

17.   a) What are the two types of file-infector viruses, based on what is infected? b) Name ways that viruses propagate. c) Why is opening attachments only from people you trust not a good policy?

Antivirus Protection

Antivirus programs are designed to prevent viruses from spreading onto user computers and servers. Nearly all firms use antivirus programs, but these programs are not extremely effective, primarily because of poor procedures.

Location of Antivirus Software

Antivirus software can be located on client PCs, on mail servers, and in the offices of external mail inspection firms.

Client Antivirus Software   Many users now install antivirus programs on their client PCs. These programs scan arriving e-mail messages and sometimes certain types of file downloads before they reach the user.

Unfortunately, many users fail to update their antivirus programs frequently by downloading new virus definitions from the antivirus vendor's website. Although most antivirus programs now make updating easy, many users turn off updating because of download time, especially if they are using modems with slow connection speeds. In today's threat environment, daily updating is mandatory.

In fact, users often turn off antivirus programs installed by their companies to speed boot-up and other actions, or at least they turn off periodic full-system virus scans or limit these scans to only certain types of files.

Companies with many office employees and home workers need remotely managed client software on which the user cannot set options. The firm, however, should be able to set options and monitor operations remotely.

Mail Server Software   When mail comes into an organization, it first goes to a mail server or to one of several mail servers. Given end-user laxness and resistance, it is useful to install antivirus software on the mail server itself in order to scan mail for viruses and perhaps other objectionable content, such as pornography or sexual or racial harassing material. Even if users are lax about antivirus protection, **mail server antivirus programs** will protect them.

Outsourced Antivirus Filtering   A growing number of companies use **antivirus outsourcing firms** that do antivirus filtering on each message before the message is sent on to the customer site. These outsourcing companies scan hundreds of thousands or millions of messages each day. These companies often are quick to identify new viruses and may be able to filter these viruses even before the antivirus vendors have developed updates for their programs.

Antivirus Filtering Methods

Antivirus programs work in two general ways: by looking for virus signatures and by observing program behavior.

Virus Signatures   At any moment, 200 to 400 viruses are circulating in the wild. Most of these viruses have well-defined **signatures**, that is, bit patterns that are characteristic of them. Antivirus scanning tools look for these bit patterns in the files they scan.

Newer viruses attempt to hide their signatures by changing what they do on different computers, but antivirus signature scanning has proven to be highly effective to date. However, the general state of virus creation is crude, and future viruses could make signature-based scanning more difficult and less reliable.

In addition, it takes hours or days to create signatures for new viruses. Until those signatures are created, companies have no protection from new viruses. Some viruses spread widely in as little as two hours.

Behavioral Virus Scanning   If a program attempts to reformat your hard disk, you are justified in being rather suspicious. Some antivirus programs do **behavioral scanning** to look for suspicious activities in programs as they run. When these programs find such behavior, they stop the program and notify the user. Behavioral scanning can stop even new viruses.

However, behavioral scanning programs tend to generate many false alarms, and users often do not understand their error messages. If users simply tell the program to ignore a valid warning, they will lose protection. On the other hand, if they frequently have to stop and call the help desk about false alarms, they will waste productivity just as they would with a real virus attack.

Two Nightmares for Antivirus Protection

Up to now, antivirus programs have been quite successful in stopping attacks. However, two disturbing trends could change the balance of power between virus writers and antivirus professionals.

Flash Viruses The first nightmare is the flash virus or instant virus. It used to take two or three years for a virus to become the most widespread virus in the old days of floppy disk infections. Once e-mail infections began, it took the viruses only a few days to reach the top of the virus list. This put more pressure on antivirus companies, but it was still feasible to get out new antivirus definitions before much damage was done.

Now, however, blended threats that combine worm propagation with virus propagation have created **flash viruses** that cut the time for a virus to reach the top of the virus pack to hours and sometimes to minutes. (In 2001, Nimda took only 22 minutes to reach the Number One position.) Under conditions like these, there is no time to analyze viruses, develop new signatures, and distribute them before massive damage is done. Behavioral detection and the detection of new flash viruses by outsourcing firms who will see many instances quickly probably will be much more important in the future.

Metamorphic Viruses Another nightmare is a new type of virus called the metamorphic virus, which could make the use of signature detection impractical. Most viruses today add a Go To statement at the front of the infected file and append their own code to the end of the file. Antivirus programs find the Go To statement, jump to the indicated location, and read the next few bytes of code. This normally is enough to identify the virus.[6]

New **metamorphic viruses**, however, try to radically change the way they appear—including by placing their code at several places within the body of the infected program. To defeat metamorphic viruses, antivirus programs will have to scan a program's entire code. Even then, separating attack code from legitimate code would be difficult. Even if full-program scanning could be done accurately, the time needed to do antivirus sweeps might become impractical. Although metamorphic viruses have been found only in the laboratory at the time of this writing, they could be built by expert virus writers.

---

[6] Even polymorphic viruses that used encryption and other techniques to change their code could be caught this way if they were first forced to run on a virtual machine. To attack this virtual machine, they had to unscramble themselves, making themselves easily detectable.

Recovery

Despite strong efforts to avoid them, firms frequently experience successful virus attacks. Recovery is needed for the affected computers.

Detection and Identification   The first step in recovery is to detect that a system is infected. The second is to identify the specific infection. Often, antivirus programs doing full system scans will be able to do both tasks. In other cases, more detective work is needed.

The **Computer Emergency Response Team/Coordination Center (CERT/CC)** (www.cert.org) publishes advisories when major virus attacks occur. These advisories often tell how to detect and identify specific viruses, worms, and other forms of malware.

Repair   The next step must be to repair the computer. Fortunately, CERT/CC alerts often tell how to do the repair or point to vendor websites that give repair instructions. Often, a repair program has to be downloaded, installed, learned, and finally used. In other cases, instructions are given only for manually repairing the system.

Unfortunately, repair often is far from perfect. Frequently, damaged program files have to be deleted and reinstalled because they cannot be repaired. In many cases, the entire operating system has to be reinstalled.

If data have been damaged, the real nightmare begins. Some or all of the data entered since the last backup might be lost. This can be devastating.

Worse yet, if the virus is subtle, it will make small changes to data files over a long period of time. By the time this kind of virus is discovered, a company might have no idea when its last clean backup was.

Repair usually is time consuming. One program for cleaning the Nimda worm out of systems had to be run repeatedly, over a period of several hours, before it wiped out all traces of the worm. Antivirus protection looks even better after a successful virus or worm outbreak.

TEST YOUR UNDERSTANDING

18.   a) Where can virus scanning be done? b) List advantages and disadvantages of each approach. c) What are the two types of scanning? d) List the advantages and disadvantages of each. e) Why is repair difficult?

Case Study: The Nimda Worm

The year 2001 saw a large number of highly damaging viruses and worms, including Code Red, Code Red II, Sircam, and Nimda. In this rogues' gallery, however, the Nimda worm stood out because of its sophistication. It is the kind of super worm we certainly will see much more of in the future.

Rapid Spread

The Nimda worm was effective because it spread in a number of different ways. If one avenue of propagation was blocked, Nimda simply chose another. This led to Nimda's fantastic infestation rate, allowing it to become the top malware threat in only minutes.

E-Mail

Like many viruses and worms, Nimda spread via e-mail. It harvested a user's computer for e-mail addresses from the user's web cache and e-mail files and mailed itself to a number of these users. It repeated this process every 10 days until it was stopped. Nimda even varied the subject field to make the attack messages more difficult to detect.

Nimda was included in a two-part MIME file. The Nimda part of this file was described in the part header as an audio/x-wav file, indicating that it was an audio data file instead of the executable file it really was, readme.exe. Mail programs running on most then-current versions of Internet Explorer opened the file automatically when the user looked at the message, without further user action to open the attachment.

Open Client File Shares

Nimda also copied itself into shared directories that the computer's owner made available to outsiders. This allowed the worm to spread through unwitting downloads by other client PCs.

Infesting Webservers

In addition, infested clients attacked webservers. First, they sent Port 80 scans to large numbers of IP addresses looking for webservers. This port scanning was so heavy in some firms that Nimda effectively constituted a DoS attack on the network.

When it found a webserver, Nimda attempted to exploit several known directory traversal vulnerabilities in IIS.

In addition, Nimda exploited backdoors in servers that had previously been infested by Code Red II and sadmind/IIS. Note that if recovery is not done well, a system might be more vulnerable to a later round of attacks.

In either case, the client sent a copy of the Nimda worm to the webserver via the trivial file transfer protocol (TFTP) on UDP Port 69. Nimda stored itself in many directories, usually as readme.eml.

In addition, Nimda created a backdoor Guest account and placed it in the Administrators group for later hacking.

It also Trojanized several legitimate programs. When these programs were run, they reinfested the system, even if all readme.eml files had been removed.

Infesting More Clients Using Webservers

When users went to infested webservers, they often found themselves downloading webpages with scripts that download Nimda to their client PCs. In many versions of Internet Explorer with the preview option selected, the Nimda link was executed automatically, infesting the machine.

TEST YOUR UNDERSTANDING

19. a) List ways Nimda used to propagate to other systems. b) Why did this use of multiple propagation vectors make Nimda especially effective?

CONCLUSION

In this chapter, we examined three major categories of attacks that use the TCP/IP standards we reviewed in the last chapter.

Targeted break-ins (hacks) are aimed at particular firms. Break-ins typically require a sequence of steps, including unobtrusive data collection, host scanning to identify potential victims, port scanning to identify services running on potential victims, software fingerprinting, the break-in itself, and actions after the break-in.

Targeted denial-of-service (DOS) attacks, in turn, try to make a particular host or a particular network unavailable through single-message attacks that cause a host to crash or through flooding attacks that overwhelm a victim host or network with messages. Stopping DoS attacks often requires a community response because they are difficult to stop by the victim.

Target-of-opportunity malware attacks release malicious software into a community to do damage to whichever systems are vulnerable to the attack. They are essentially software robots capable of doing mass damage. Viruses infect other files or disk sectors, and worms propagate on their own, moving from host to host, mostly via known vulnerabilities. Patching and proper user training (especially regarding the opening of e-mail attachments) are keys to reducing such attacks.

THOUGHT QUESTIONS

1. a) List types of attacks for which IP address spoofing will be unattractive. b) List types for which it will be attractive.
2. What rules would you add to the firewall to prevent the SYN/ACK attack shown in Figure 4-8?
3. How many packets would be sent by an attacker to port scan 100 hosts for all well-known ports?
4. Why do Ping-of-Death, Teardrop, LAND, and other attacks require new approaches to software testing beyond those needed for error detection?
5. List actions that must be done by Internet community members to stop DoS attacks.
6. Create a policy statement on when a user may open an e-mail attachment.

TROUBLESHOOTING QUESTION

1. You have been infected with the worm Blalah.exe. You believe that you have cleaned out all copies of Blalah.exe from your hard disk. Yet when you turn your computer on again, you find that you are immediately reinfested. What could be the problem?

CHAPTER 5

FIREWALLS

Learning Objectives

By the end of this chapter, you should be able to discuss:

- The basic filtering operation of firewalls, including ingress and egress filtering and the types of protection offered by firewalls.
- Hardware/software packaging for firewalls, including routers, computer-based firewalls, firewall appliances, and host firewalls.
- Static packet filter firewall operation, including access control lists (ACLs).
- Stateful firewall operation.
- Network address translation (NAT) operation.
- Application firewall operation.
- Firewall architectures, including common firewall architectures for firms of different sizes.
- Firewall configuration, testing, and maintenance, including the importance of policies and reading logs.
- Check Point's FireWall-1 and Cisco's PIX firewall.

INTRODUCTION

In the previous two chapters, we looked at TCP/IP and at how hackers use TCP/IP to attack organizations. In this chapter, we will look at firewalls, which protect against TCP/IP packet attacks.

Firewalls

High-security buildings have entry stations where guards screen people entering the premises from the outside. Similarly, Figure 5-1 shows that most firms have **border firewalls** that screen packets coming into their **private networks** from external, **untrusted networks**, especially the Internet.

Ingress Packet Filtering

Firewalls examine each incoming packet and either **pass** the packet into the internal network or **drop** (deny) the packet. This is **ingress filtering**.

In some cases, the firewall notifies the security administrator if an especially dangerous packet attempts to enter the network or if a suspicious pattern of packets indicates that a major attack is underway. However, the firewall usually drops packets without notification.

Whether or not the firewall notifies the administrator, it always records key fields from each denied packet in a **log file** for later analysis. Firewall administrators should examine these log files daily to understand current attack patterns.

Egress Packet Filtering

The figure also illustrates **egress filtering**, which is done on packets leaving the internal network to enter the Internet. Egress filtering can prevent unauthorized connections to external computers on the untrusted network.

Types of Protection

Several types of firewall protection exist. We will look primarily at three types in this chapter—packet inspection (static and stateful), application inspection, and network address translation—because they are the most well-developed and widely used protections. We will note the final two types of protection—authentication and virtual private network handling—but these concepts are discussed in detail in Chapters 7 and 8.

Packet Inspection

Recall from Chapter 3 that an arriving packet is likely to have an IP header followed by a TCP, UDP, or ICMP header. TCP and UDP headers are likely to be followed by application messages. **Packet inspection** focuses on the contents of IP, TCP, UDP, and ICMP headers.

Initially, packet inspection employed **static packet filtering**, in which each packet was examined in isolation. However, a number of attacks can be stopped only by **stateful filtering**, which accepts or rejects a packet primarily on the basis of whether it is part of an approved conversation or whether it is attempting to establish a legitimate conversation. Most packet filtering firewalls now use stateful inspection.

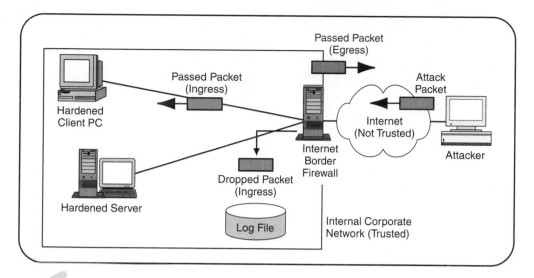

Figure 5-1   Border Firewall

Application Inspection

Packet inspection does not examine application message content. In contrast, application inspection uses programs called proxies to examine the contents of application messages contained in TCP and UDP data fields. Application inspection can stop many types of attacks that packet filtering cannot, such as malicious executable attachments.

Network Address Translation (NAT)

One danger is that an attacker will place a sniffer program outside the firewall and collect packet data. This will allow the attacker, among other things, to learn the IP addresses of internal hosts. Network address translation (NAT) benignly spoofs the IP addresses of outgoing packets so that sniffers will learn only spoofed IP addresses—not the true IP addresses of internal hosts.

Denial-of-Service Inspection

Denial-of-service inspection recognizes the inception of denial-of-service attacks and takes steps to alleviate them. Although the recognition of SYN flooding and a few other common DoS attacks is widespread, denial-of-service inspection generally is fairly rudimentary. We will not look at DoS protection in this chapter beyond giving a single example except to note that some firewalls offer it.

Cisco PIX firewalls typically deal with SYN flooding attacks through a process called TCP intercept. The router responds to incoming SYN messages itself, with SYN/ACK messages. If the external host that attempted to initiate the connection does not respond quickly, the TCP connection will be dropped. The internal host will never see it. However, if the external host completes the connection, the PIX firewall passes the connection to the internal host.

PACKET INSPECTION

Examines IP, TCP, UDP, and ICMP header contents
Static packet filtering looks at individual packets in isolation; misses many attacks
Stateful inspection inspects packets in the context of the packet's role in an ongoing or incipient conversation
Stateful inspection is the preferred packet inspection method today

APPLICATION INSPECTION

Examines application layer messages
Stops some attacks that packet inspection cannot

NETWORK ADDRESS TRANSLATION

Hides the IP addresses of internal hosts to thwart sniffers
Benignly spoofs source IP addresses in outgoing packets

DENIAL-OF-SERVICE INSPECTION

Recognizes incipient DoS attacks and takes steps to stop them
Limited to a few common types of attacks

AUTHENTICATION

Only packets from users who have proven their identity are allowed through
Not commonly used, but can be valuable

VIRTUAL PRIVATE NETWORK HANDLING

Virtual private networks offer message-by-message confidentiality, authentication, message integrity, and anti-replay protection
VPN protection often works in parallel with other types of inspection instead of being integrated with them

INTEGRATED FIREWALLS

Most commercial products combine multiple types of filtering
Some freeware and shareware firewall products offer only one type of filtering

Figure 5-2 Types of Firewall Inspection (Study Figure)

Authentication

Although it does not deal with the inspection of message contents, another way to ensure that only legitimate packets get through a firewall is to have the firewall authenticate users (force users to prove their identity) before their packets are allowed through a firewall. The use of authentication is not common, but where it can be applied, it provides strong insurance that packets are legitimate. We will not look at authentication in this chapter because we will not see the details of how authentication is done until Chapters 7 and 8.

Virtual Private Networks

In Chapter 8, we will look at virtual private networks (VPNs), which provide not only authentication but also confidentiality, message integrity, and anti-replay protection—and which do so for each and every packet.

Most firewalls provide VPN protection, which we will examine in Chapter 8. However, although authentication is integrated with other inspection technologies, VPN protection on firewalls often runs in parallel with other forms of inspection and authentication. Firewalls often handle arriving packets either through normal inspection and authentication or through a VPN handling module.

Integrated Firewalls

Most firewalls offer multiple types of inspection, either directly or through close cooperation between other types of firewalls. For instance, as noted later in this chapter, Check Point FireWall-1 firewalls, which lead the market, primarily offer stateful packet inspection, but they also offer network address translation, authentication, VPN handling, and limited application filtering (which they augment with pass-through standards for sending packets to application-filtering products from third parties).

Although we will talk about static packet filter firewalls, application firewalls, and other single-function firewalls, most commercial vendors look more broadly at firewalls. In the freeware and shareware markets, however, pure firewalls that provide only one type of protection are more common.

TEST YOUR UNDERSTANDING

1. a) What are border firewalls? b) Distinguish between ingress and egress filtering. c) Name the types of firewall inspection. d) Do commercial products normally limit themselves to a single type of inspection?

FIREWALL HARDWARE AND SOFTWARE

Firewall functionality comes packaged in several ways, each with its own strengths and weaknesses.

Types of Firewalls

Screening Router Firewalls

Corporations already have **border routers** that connect their internal networks to the external internet. Cisco and other router vendors offer optional firewall software for their routers. Typically, this software offers only lightweight protection. As we will see,

SCREENING ROUTER FIREWALLS

Add firewall software to router
Usually provide light filtering only
Expensive for the processing power—usually must upgrade hardware, too
Screens out incoming "noise" of simple scanning attacks to make the detection of
  serious attacks easier
Good location for egress filtering—can eliminate scanning responses, even from the
  router

COMPUTER-BASED FIREWALLS

Add firewall software to server with an existing operating system: Windows or UNIX
Can be purchased with power to handle any load
Easy to use because know operating system
Firewall vendor might bundle software with hardened hardware and operating system
General-purpose operating systems result in slower processing
Security: Attackers might be able to hack the operating system
    Change filtering rules to allow attack packets in
    Change filtering rules to drop legitimate packets

FIREWALL APPLIANCES

Boxes with minimal operating systems
Therefore, difficult to hack
Setup is minimal
Not customized to specific firm's situation
Must be able to update

HOST FIREWALLS

Installed on hosts themselves (servers and sometimes clients)
Enhanced security because of host-specific knowledge
    For example, filter out everything but webserver transmissions on a webserver
Defense in depth
    Normally used in conjunction with other firewalls
    Although on single host computers attached to internet, might be only firewall
If not centrally managed, configuration can be a nightmare
    Especially if rule sets change frequently
Client firewalls typically must be configured by ordinary users
    Might misconfigure or reject the firewall
    Need to centrally manage remote employee computers

Figure 5-3 Firewall Hardware and Software (Study Figure)

routers normally are used as screening firewalls to get rid of simple, high-volume, low-complexity scanning (probing) attacks. We saw in the last chapter that hackers send large numbers of packets to probe potential victims for target hosts and ports. For example, in 2001, one bank received an attack packet every 1.5 seconds during one sample week.[1] Most of these were scanning probes. By eliminating such probes, screening reduces the work the main firewall has to do.

Of course, in a small office or home (SOHO) network, the border router may be the only firewall.

High Cost for Sufficient Performance   On the negative side, firewall software for routers is optional and tends to be expensive. Also, the addition of filtering requires more router CPU cycles and memory, so more expensive routers or hardware upgrades are needed if screening is to be done. Prices for router processing power and memory tend to be much higher than those of ordinary computers.

A Place for Egress Filtering   The border router also is a good place for egress filtering. As discussed later in this chapter, many attack packets are designed to elicit replies from potential victims. These replies contain information that attackers can use to plan their attacks. Putting egress filtering on the border router ensures that none of these reply packets escape. It also prevents the router itself from replying to attack probes.

Computer-Based Firewalls

A more general solution is to add firewall software to a host computer, generally a computer running UNIX or Windows Server as its operating system.[2]

Power   Computer-based firewalls can be found to handle any filtering load. If the filtering load becomes too great, a larger, computer-based firewall can always be used.

Ease of Use   In addition, computer-based firewalls normally have attractive graphical user interfaces for configuration.

Packages   Although using an ordinary computer as a firewall is economically attractive, the fact that a firewall has a general-purpose operating system makes it vulnerable to hacking. It is best to purchase computer-based firewalls as hardware-software bundles from firewall vendors.

These packages contain hardened versions of the operating system that have known weaknesses fixed and have the other improvements discussed in Chapter 6. In addition, the computer-based firewall vendor usually replaces the TCP/IP software that comes with the operating system with its own highly secure TCP/IP software.

---

[1]   Tuesday, Vince (pseudonym), "Who's Knocking on My Door? Go Away." *Computerworld*, May 14, 2001. www.computerworld.com/securitytopics/security/story/0,10801,60469,00.html.

[2]   Although it is debatable which operating system theoretically is better for host-based firewalls, it generally is more important to use an operating system with which the firm is experienced. Lack of intimate familiarity almost always leads to misconfiguration, giving hackers an open door.

Performance Concerns with General Operating Systems   One concern with computer-based firewalls is performance. Having an operating system adds a layer of processing, slowing all tasks somewhat. A computer firewall must have sufficient processing power and RAM to handle the volume of work that will be required. Routers also have operating systems, such as Cisco's IOS. However, these are simplified operating systems designed for high performance.

Security   A final concern is with the security of the firewall itself. Unless the general-purpose operating system is hardened well, attackers might be able to hack the firewall itself. This will allow them to change the firewall's filtering rules to allow attack packets in. Attackers can even configure malicious rule sets that drop legitimate traffic.

Firewall Appliances

In your home, an appliance is something you can plug in and use immediately, for instance, a toaster. Similarly, **firewall appliances** are closed boxes that you simply plug into your router at one end and into your network at the other end. You power them up, turn them on, and use them immediately.

Firewall appliances either have no operating systems or minimal operating systems. This makes them fast for a given performance requirement level.

Firewall appliances come pre-packaged with a good set of filtering rules, making them suitable for smaller firms that lack the security staff needed to optimize filtering rules. Of course, as threats grow, rules need to be updated. Most firewall vendors provide rule updates, much as antivirus vendors provide virus signature updates for their software.

Host Firewalls

One approach is to add firewall software to individual client and server hosts. In contrast to other firewalls, these **host firewalls** protect only the hosts on which they operate.

Enhanced Security Because of Host-Specific Knowledge   Host firewalls can be configured with knowledge of the specific host. For instance, if the host is a webserver, only webservice requests should be allowed through.

Defense in Depth   Host firewalls typically are used in conjunction with other firewalls, providing defense in depth. However, on single home computers attached to the Internet, host firewalls are the only firewall protection.

Configuration Difficulty   Unless host firewalls can be configured and managed from a central location, the configuration of many firewalls can be a nightmare, especially if rule sets have to change rapidly to meet new threats.

Client Firewalls   Client firewalls are especially difficult to configure because the work normally has to be done by the users themselves. Client firewalls can present the user with confusing options, resulting in either misconfiguration or total rejection by the user. It is highly desirable for organizations to manage firewalls on employee computers.

TEST YOUR UNDERSTANDING

2. a) What is the purpose of a screening router firewall? b) Why are routers attractive as screening firewalls? c) Why are routers not attractive?

3. a) Why are computer-based firewalls attractive to customers? b) Why are they somewhat unattractive?

4. a) Why are firewall appliances attractive? b) Why are they somewhat unattractive?

5. a) Why are host firewalls attractive? b) Why are they somewhat unattractive?

Firewall Processing Requirements

Performance must be considered for all firewalls. Filtering is a complex process, and if the firewall does not have sufficient processing capacity and RAM, it might not be able to process all packets. For security, packets that do not get processed must be dropped, and this is detrimental to user service.

Traffic Volume and Sophistication of Filtering

Figure 5-4 shows that two factors drive performance requirements for firewalls.

➤ The first driving factor is the volume of traffic to be filtered, measured as the number of **packets per second (PPS)**.

➤ The second is the complexity of filtering, which is proportional to the number and complexity of rules against which each packet must be compared.

Estimating the Complexity of Filtering

Although the traffic volume is relatively easy to compute and so to forecast, filtering complexity is difficult to estimate. Although the complexity of filtering is roughly proportional to the number of filtering rules, some rules require much more processing

Figure 5-4 Drivers of Performance Requirements

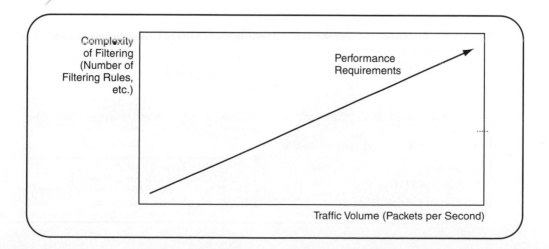

time than others. In addition, some screening router firewalls take a big performance hit if even a single filtering rule is introduced.

In addition, as the number of threats grows and as the sophistication of these threats grows, the firewall will have to handle more rules and more complex rules. Firewalls should be purchased with a lot of room for growth.

Checking Logs Daily

An important practice for ensuring adequate performance is checking statistics in the firewall's log file each day. A crucial statistic is the number of packets dropped because the firewall was too busy to handle them. If this number is not close to zero, the firewall may be starting to run out of capacity.

TEST YOUR UNDERSTANDING

6. a) Why is firewall performance important? b) What determines performance requirements? c) What do firewalls do if they cannot handle the stream of packets they are to filter? d) Why is it important to check firewall logs as a way to understand the sufficiency of current firewall performance?

STATIC PACKET FILTER FIREWALLS

Figure 5-5 shows the simplest kind of firewall, a static packet filter firewall.

Figure 5-5   Static Packet Filter Firewall

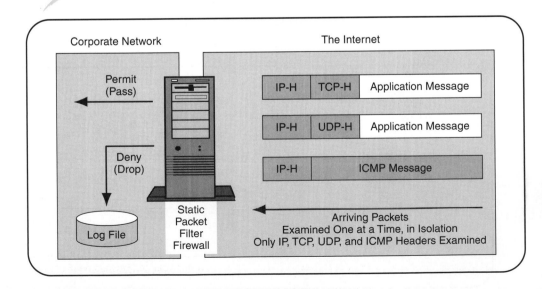

Basic Characteristics

Limited to Examining Headers

The most basic firewalls do static packet filtering. **Static packet filtering** has two main characteristics. First, it only looks at values in selected fields of IP, TCP, UDP, and ICMP headers. It does not look at the contents of the application messages as well.

Filtering Individual Packets in Isolation

Second, and more problematically, static packet filter firewalls look only at individual packets in isolation. In normal communication streams, many packets are flowing back and forth. A packet's place within the broader context might be highly important for understanding whether it is a threat. However, static packet filtering cannot make use of this context.

TEST YOUR UNDERSTANDING

　　7.　What are the two characteristics of static packet filter firewalls?

Access Control Lists (ACLs) for Ingress Filtering

Static packet filtering organizes its filtering rules into **access control lists (ACLs)**. Figure 5-6 illustrates an ACL in a generic format.

If-Then Format

Rules follow **if-then** formats. If certain of the packet's field values match certain criterion values, then we say that the packet matches the rule. Based on the "then" part of the rule, the firewall will either pass or deny the packet. If the packet does not match the rule, the firewall does not take action based on that rule.

Sequential Rule Evaluation

When a packet is evaluated, it is evaluated against the rules in the ACL. This evaluation is **sequential**. The packet is first evaluated against the first rule, then against the second, and so forth.

Action on Matches

This sequential processing continues until a rule results in a pass or deny decision or until the last rule in the ACL is reached.

Deny All

If the packet does not match any specific rule, the last rule usually denies all packets. This **Deny All** rule ensures that attack packets do not accidentally get through because of ACL configuration errors.

Sensitivity to Misordering

The sequential nature of rule evaluation makes ACLs difficult to write because the slightest misordering can pass a packet that should be denied. For example, suppose that rule 190 in a particular ACL (not the one shown in Figure 5-6) denies all packets whose TCP SYN and FIN bit are both set. Such packets make no sense. Why would one

1. If source IP address = 10.*.*.*, DENY *[private IP address range]*
2. If source IP address = 172.16.*.* to 172.31.*.*, DENY *[private IP address range]*
3. If source IP address = 192.168.*.*, DENY *[private IP address range]*
4. If source IP address = 60.47.*.*, DENY *[internal address range]*
5. If source IP address = 1.2.3.4, DENY *[black-holed address of attacker]*
6. If TCP SYN=1 AND FIN=1, DENY *[crafted attack packet]*
7. If destination IP address = 60.47.3.9 AND TCP destination port = 80 OR 443, PASS *[connection to a public webserver]*
8. If TCP SYN=1 AND ACK=0, DENY *[attempt to open a connection from the outside]*
9. If TCP destination port = 20, DENY *[FTP data connection]*
10. If TCP destination port = 21, DENY *[FTP supervisory control connection]*
11. If TCP destination port = 23, DENY *[Telnet data connection]*
12. If TCP destination port = 135 through 139, DENY *[NetBIOS connection for clients]*
13. If TCP destination port = 513, DENY *[UNIX rlogin without password]*
14. If TCP destination port = 514, DENY *[UNIX rsh launch shell without login]*
15. If TCP destination port = 22, DENY *[SSH for secure login, but some versions are insecure]*
16. If UDP destination port = 69, DENY *[Trivial File Transfer Protocol; no login necessary]*
17. If ICMP Type = 0, PASS *[allow incoming echo reply messages]*
18. DENY ALL

Figure 5-6   Access Control List (ACL) for Ingress Filtering at a Border Router

host request an opening and a close to a TCP connection? Such packets are designed to elicit TCP RST segments for reconnaissance. However, if rule 170, which comes earlier, passes all packets to a particular server's IP address, a packet will be passed to that server even if the SYN and FIN bits are set.

TEST YOUR UNDERSTANDING

8. a) What is an ACL? b) Why are so many errors made when ACLs are configured?

Ingress Filtering Based on Source IP Addresses

The first rules in Figure 5-6 deny packets based upon source IP addresses. Each rule identifies a source IP address that cannot possibly be legitimate.

Private IP Addresses   The first three rules deny packets from private IP addresses.[3] As we saw in Chapter 3, these addresses should never appear in packets traveling over the Internet. These packets must be **crafted** (hand-built by an attacker).

---

[3] The private IP address ranges include all IP addresses beginning with 10, all IP addresses beginning with 172.16 through 172.31, and all IP addresses beginning with 192.168.

Internal IP Addresses   The fourth rule in Figure 5-6 filters out incoming packets from the firm's own public IP address range. These are internal addresses that should not be seen in packets arriving from the outside, unless the firm has multiple sites. If a firm has multiple sites, only the IP address range used within the particular site protected by the border firewall should be filtered out.

Black-Holed Addresses   The fifth rule filters out a specific IP address (1.2.3.4) that is to be "black holed" because it has been used recently by a hacker to attack the firm.

TEST YOUR UNDERSTANDING

9.   What types of ingress filtering are done on IP addresses in Figure 5-6?

TCP Flag-Based Ingress Filtering

RST Generation   Rule 6 filters all packets whose SYN and FIN bits are both **set** (have the value "1"). As we saw in the last chapter and as we just noted in this chapter, these are crafted reconnaissance packets. Real-world ACLs typically deny several combinations of TCP flag bits that are designed to elicit RST segments.

FIN Segments   Jumping past Rule 7 temporarily, we see that Rule 8 filters SYN segments whose ACK bits are not set. Such segments are connection-opening attempts from outside hosts. The firm normally limits TCP connections initiated from the outside while allowing most connections initiated from the inside.

Passes to Specific Servers   Returning to Rule 7, however, we see that this rule permits TCP connection attempts to a particular webserver, 60.47.3.9. Note that this rule has to come before Rule 8. If the rules were accidentally reversed, the segment would be filtered out before it reached the pass rule.

TEST YOUR UNDERSTANDING

10.   a) What kind of ingress filtering tends to be done based on TCP connection flags? b) Why does Rule 7 have to come before Rule 8? c) In general, why do exceptions usually have to come before general deny rules?

Rules Based on TCP Port Numbers

Permitting Webserver Access on Port 80   Rule 7, which permits connections to the internal server with IP address 60.47.3.9, also requires the TCP destination Port number to be 80 (HTTP) or 443 (HTTP over SSL/TLS[4]). In other words, only webserver requests are allowed to go to this host by this rule.

Blocking FTP and Telnet   The next four rules in the ACL block a number of incoming connection requests for popular services that the company does not provide. These include connection requests for FTP (TCP Port 20 for data transfers and TCP Port 21 for supervisory information) and Telnet (TCP Port 23). FTP and Telnet are

---

[4]   SSL/TLS, which is described in Chapter 8, is used for secure transactions.

particularly vulnerable to sniffing because they usually send passwords in the clear, without encryption.

Blocking NetBIOS Probes   Next comes Rule 12, which prevents incoming connections to TCP Ports 135 through 139, which are for NetBIOS access to shared directories and printers in Windows peer-to-peer networking.

UNIX r Services and SSH   Then come two rules that block UNIX "r" services, which allow access without logging in if the source IP address in packets matches one of the addresses in an admission list. IP address spoofing is devastatingly effective against such hosts.

These r services include, among others, rlogin on TCP Port 513 and rsh on TCP Port 514. The rlogin command allows logging in without giving a password. The rsh command allows a user to start up a shell (user interface) program on a computer without logging in to the host.

Also blocked is the more robust SSH (secure shell) protocol on TCP Port 22. SSH allows Telnet-like access to servers but with security. Unfortunately, SSH Version 1 had inadequate security, and many servers that support SSH Version 2 access also accept Version 1 connections as a default. In any case, SSH is used legitimately primarily for the external management of internal servers; this is not done in this firm.

TEST YOUR UNDERSTANDING

11.   a) What ports need to be allowed for webservers using SSL/TLS? b) How does this change if SSL/TLS will not be implemented? c) What ports need to be allowed for FTP servers? d) For Telnet access? e) Why are FTP and Telnet dangerous? f) Why are r commands dangerous? g) On what operating system are r commands used? h) What ports need to be blocked to prevent rlogin? i) rsh? j) SSH? k) When might SSH be permitted?

UDP Filtering

For UDP traffic, there is only a single rule (16). It blocks Trivial File Transfer Protocol traffic on Port 69. TFTP allows file downloads without logging in.

ICMP Filtering

As noted in Chapter 3, ICMP headers have two diagnostic fields: type and code. Type defines the general kind of supervisory information the ICMP message contains. Code further specifies the kind of supervisory information in the ICMP message.

ICMP is a dangerous protocol because of its power as a network diagnostic tool. Rule 17 allows a single ICMP type to enter the network—Type 0 (echo reply). This allows internal hosts to ping external hosts and receive replies. The next rule drops all remaining ICMP messages. This practice of allowing only ICMP echo replies is usual practice in the industry.

TEST YOUR UNDERSTANDING

12.   a) What UDP service is denied? Why? b) What usually is the single ICMP message type passed by ingress filtering? Give its name and type value.

Ingress: Deny All

As noted earlier, the last rule denies access to all packets. Anything not specifically permitted by earlier rules will be denied by this rule. If legitimate traffic is blocked, an earlier rule can be added to permit it.

Cisco ACLs have an *implicit* Deny All rule at the end of any ACL, so the Deny All rule is not explicitly required. However, placing an explicit Deny All rule at the end of the ACL makes the intent of this critical rule easier to understand.

TEST YOUR UNDERSTANDING

13. Why is it a good policy to block anything not specifically permitted?

Egress Filtering

Figure 5-6 showed an ingress filtering ACL for packets arriving from the Internet. However, **egress filtering** (outbound filtering) also is important. Figure 5-7 shows an egress filtering ACL for the router we have been discussing.

Source IP Address Filtering

To be a good neighbor, a firm never should allow attack packets to be sent from inside the firm to another firm. Although few firms have internal hackers, compromised hosts often are used to send attack packets.

Most attack packets have spoofed IP source addresses. The first three rules in Figure 5-7 filter out packets with private IP addresses. The fourth rule filters out all packets that do not have the site's particular internal IP address range. Although the

Figure 5-7   Access Control List (ACL) for Egress Filtering at a Border Router

1. If source IP address = 10.*.*.*, DENY *[private IP address range]*
2. If source IP address = 172.16.*.* to 172.31.*.*, DENY *[private IP address range]*
3. If source IP address = 192.168.*.*, DENY *[private IP address range]*
4. If source IP address NOT = 60.47.*.*, DENY *[not in internal address range]*
5. If ICMP Type = 8, PASS *[allow outgoing echo messages]*
6. If Protocol = ICMP, DENY *[drop all other outgoing ICMP messages]*
7. If TCP RST= 1, DENY *[do not allow outgoing resets; used in host scanning]*
8. If source IP address = 60.47.3.9 and TCP source port = 80 OR 443, PASS *[public webserver]*
9. If TCP source port = 0 through 49151, DENY *[well-known and registered ports]*
10. If UDP source port = 0 through 49151, DENY *[well-known and registered ports]*
11. If TCP source port = 49152 through 65536, PASS *[allow outgoing client connections]*
12. If UDP source port = 49152 through 65536, PASS *[allow outgoing client connections]*
13. DENY ALL

first three rules are redundant with the fourth, the ACL builder decided to exclude private IP addresses explicitly for easier reading.

ICMP Filtering

The fifth rule allows ICMP echo messages to leave the firm so that internal hosts can ping external hosts. The sixth rule denies all other outbound ICMP messages. As noted in Chapter 3, many of these are error advisement messages. Their packets contain the IP addresses of hosts or routers sending these error messages. This gives the hacker information about the network, so these messages must be stopped from leaving the site network.

TCP Reset (RST) Filtering

The seventh rule drops TCP reset (RST) segments that are sent when the hacker sends TCP segments that cause the target host to reject the connection. This rejection generates a TCP RST segment (that has the RST bit set). Packets carrying TCP RST segments have the target host's IP address in the source IP address field and so should not be permitted to get back to the attacker.

Server Port Filtering

The eighth rule in Figure 5-7 allows outgoing message transmissions from two specific TCP ports (80 and 443) on a specific server (60.47.3.9). As we saw earlier, this is the firm's public webserver, so access to it is important.

The following two rules drop packets from any other server operating on a well-known or registered TCP or UDP port number (0 to 49151). Outside clients should not be permitted access to these servers, so packets from these servers should not be leaving the network.

Allowing Client Connections

When clients connect to external servers, they normally use TCP or UDP ephemeral port numbers (49152 through 65536). Rules 11 and 12 permit outgoing packets with ephemeral port numbers to allow internal clients to connect to external servers.

Deny All

The final rule is Deny All, which denies all other packets.

TEST YOUR UNDERSTANDING

14.   a) What rules based on IP addresses are included in Figure 5-7? Why? b) What are the two ICMP rules? c) Why were the rules set up in this order? d) What do the ICMP rules allow? e) Why? f) Why are RST segments dropped? g) Explain the rule for the webserver. h) Explain how public webservers are handled in the ACL. i) What general ports are stopped? j) How are client connections to outside servers handled in the ACL? k) What is the last rule in the ACL, and why is it important?

STATEFUL FIREWALLS

Limits of Static Packet Filtering

Although static packet filter firewalls provide good protection, they have some serious limitations because they filter individual packets in isolation.

States

Most communication consists of dialogs in which two hosts exchange a series of packets. Each packet has a role to play in the dialog. At any moment, the packet exchange will be in a particular condition or **state**. In the simplest case, the state of the connection is either open or closed.

Figure 5-8   Stateful Inspection Firewalls (Study Figure)

STATE OF CONNECTION: OPEN OR CLOSED

State: Order of packet within a dialog
Often simply whether the packet is part of an open connection

STATIC PACKET FILTER FIREWALLS ARE STATELESS

Filter one packet at a time, in isolation
If a SYN/ACK segment is sent, cannot tell if there was a previous SYN to open a connection
Cannot deal with port-switching applications (Figure 5-11)

STATEFUL FIREWALL OPERATION (Figures 5-9 and 5-10)

For TCP, record two IP addresses and port numbers in state table as OK (open)
Accept future packets between these hosts and ports with little or no inspection
For UTP, also record two IP addresses and port numbers in the state table
Can handle port-switching applications (Figure 5-11)

STATEFUL INSPECTION ACCESS CONTROL LISTS (ACLs)

Primarily allow or deny applications
Simple because probing attacks that are not part of conversations do not need specific rules because they are dropped automatically
In integrated firewalls, ACL rules can specify that messages using a particular application protocol or server be authenticated or passed to an application firewall for inspection

Static Packet Filter Firewalls Are Stateless

Static packet filter firewalls are *stateless*. When a packet arrives, a static packet filter firewall has no idea whether the packet is part of an ongoing connection. This can lead to problems.

Crafted SYN/ACK Segments

When an internal host wishes to open a TCP connection to an external host, it sends a TCP SYN segment, as we saw in Chapter 3. The external host replies with a TCP SYN/ACK segment. However, hackers also send TCP SYN/ACK segments when connections are not open to elicit TCP RST segments.

Static packet filter firewalls cannot tell whether a particular SYN/ACK segment is part of a legitimate internally initiated connection opening or is an attack segment. Consequently, most static packet filter firewalls pass all TCP SYN/ACK segments, giving attackers a well-known free shot at internal hosts.

Port-Switching Applications

Some applications switch ports. For instance, in passive FTP, when an internal client host opens a control connection to an external server, it selects an ephemeral port number for itself. (See Chapter 3.) However, when the FTP server replies, it gives the initiating host a different ephemeral port number to be used in data transfers. A number of other common applications do port switching. Stateless packet filter firewalls have no way of policing such conversations.

Stateful Firewall Operation: TCP Connections

Stateful firewalls keep track of the states of dialogs between pairs of hosts. Figure 5-9 illustrates how a stateful firewall handles TCP connections.

Initiating Segment

An internal host, 60.55.33.12, initiates a TCP connection to an external webserver, 123.80.5.34. The internal host sends a TCP SYN segment containing its own ephemeral port number (62600) in the source port number field and the server's well-known port number (80) in the destination port number field. The IP packet that carries this TCP segment has the IP addresses of the internal client and external server in the source and destination IP address fields, respectively.

State Table

A stateful firewall will note these four pieces of information in its state table. It will set the state of this connection to "on."

Legitimate and Illegitimate Replies

When a SYN/ACK segment arrives back in a packet, the stateful firewall will compare the incoming packet's two IP addresses and two port numbers with the dialogs in its state table. In this case, the packet will match the dialog just entered in the table. The state is "on," so the stateful firewall passes the packet.

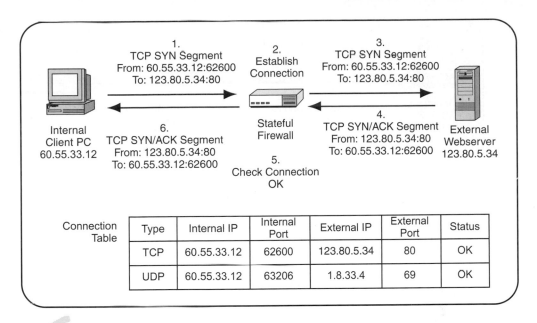

Figure 5-9 Stateful Firewall Operation I

If the attacker sends a crafted TCP SYN/ACK segment, however, in order to elicit a TCP RST reply, the IP addresses and port numbers will not match those of any current connection. The packet will be denied. Figure 5-10 illustrates this situation.

Stateful Firewalls and Connectionless Protocols

How does a stateful firewall handle connectionless protocols such as UDP and ICMP? The answer is that it handles them in the same basic way it handles TCP connections, as Figure 5-9 shows.

Suppose internal host 60.55.33.12 sends a UDP datagram to external host 1.8.33.4. The UDP source port number is 63206, and the UDP destination port number is 69 (Trivial File Transfer Protocol). From the outgoing packet, the firewall will extract the two IP addresses and two port numbers. It will add a session to the state table, as shown in the second row.

Afterward, when UDP datagrams come in from Host 1.8.33.4, the stateful firewall will note that the two IP addresses and two port numbers match those of the session just added to the state table. The firewall will pass these UDP datagrams, as well as further outbound UDP datagrams that match this session.

TEST YOUR UNDERSTANDING

15.   a) What is a state? b) What is a connection (also called a session)? c) How do stateful firewalls work for TCP? d) Can stateful firewalls maintain state information for connectionless protocols like UDP and ICMP? e) If so, how do they do it?

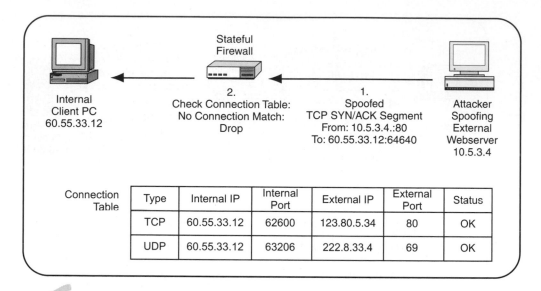

Figure 5-10　Stateful Firewall Operation II

Stateful Firewalls and Port-Switching Applications

Stateful firewalls also can handle port-switching applications such as passive FTP. Figure 5-11 shows how this is done.

The Initial Connection

First, the internal client initiates a connection to an external FTP server, which is listening on Port 21. This message has ephemeral port number 62600. The stateful firewall creates a connection row to indicate this emerging session.

The Second Connection

The external FTP server will send the internal client an IP packet with an FTP message telling the internal client to use ephemeral port number 55336 when it sends and receives data. (The FTP server uses Port 20 on its end for data transfers.)

Recording the Second Connection

The stateful firewall reads the FTP message that tells the internal client which ephemeral port to use for data transfers. It adds this new connection to the state table, and it will allow data transfers belonging to this new session (connection).

　　Note that the stateful firewall reads the application message for specific information. This is an exception to the general rule that static packet firewalls and stateful firewalls only look at IP, TCP, UDP, and ICMP headers.[5]

---

[5]　Streaming media also require port switching. For instance, with RealAudio, a client inside the site connects to an external RealAudio server on TCP Ports 554 and 7070. The response tells the internal client to listen on a UDP port between 6970 and 7100. The data will be streamed on this UDP port.

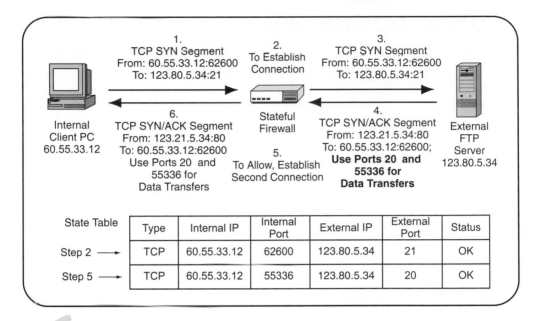

The following state table appears within the figure:

State Table	Type	Internal IP	Internal Port	External IP	External Port	Status
Step 2 ⟶	TCP	60.55.33.12	62600	123.80.5.34	21	OK
Step 5 ⟶	TCP	60.55.33.12	55336	123.80.5.34	20	OK

Figure 5-11 Port-Switching Applications with Stateful Firewalls

Stateful Inspection ACLs

We introduced access control lists in the context of static packet filters. However, stateful inspection firewalls also have ACLs.

Allowing and Denying Applications

Stateful inspection ACLs look a good deal like static packet filter firewall ACLs in that they allow certain applications and deny other applications.

Simpler Than Static Packet Filter ACLs

However, stateful inspection ACLs tend to be simpler than static packet filter ACLs because stateful inspection ACLs do not need to provide rules to do such things as attempting to determine whether a particular packet is being sent in response to a previous packet from the other side of the firewall. Stateful inspection firewalls do these things automatically.

ACLs in Integrated Firewalls

Furthermore, in integrated firewalls ACLs can specify not only add or drop responses but also might specify that conversations using a particular application protocol or server be authenticated. They also can specify that conversations using a particular application protocol or server be passed to an application inspection firewall.

NETWORK ADDRESS TRANSLATION

Both static packet filter firewalls and stateful firewalls often offer a second form of protection called **network address translation (NAT)**.

Sniffers

Hackers sometimes can place sniffers outside of corporation networks. As packets from these corporate networks pass through the sniffer, the sniffer captures them and notes source IP addresses and perhaps port numbers. This information allows a hacker to do host scanning—seeing which hosts are active and therefore are potential victims.

NAT Operation

Figure 5-12 illustrates how network address translation can thwart sniffers.

Packet Creation

First, the internal client sends a packet to an external server. This packet contains the client's real IP address, 192.168.5.7. The UDP datagram or TCP segment it contains has an ephemeral port number created by the client, 61000.

Network and Port Address Translation

The NAT firewall intercepts all outgoing traffic and replaces source IP addresses and source port numbers with stand-in network (IP) addresses and port numbers. In this case, the stand-in IP address is 60.5.9.8, and the stand-in port number is 55380.

Figure 5-12   Network Address Translation (NAT)

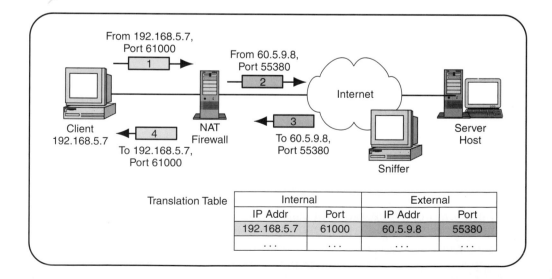

Translation Table

To allow itself to do conversion when replies come in, the NAT firewall places the real IP address, the real port number, the stand-in IP address, and the stand-in port number in a row in the NAT firewall's translation table.

Response Packet

When the server replies, it will send a packet with destination IP address 60.5.9.8 and destination Port 55380. When this packet reaches the firm, the router sends it to the NAT firewall.

Restoration

The NAT firewall notes that the socket 60.5.9.8:55380 is in its translation table. It replaces the destination IP address and destination port number with 192.168.5.7 and 61000. The firewall sends this modified packet to the client PC.

Perspective on NAT

NAT/PAT

Although the kinds of firewalls we have been discussing are called NAT firewalls, they translate both network addresses (IP addresses) and port addresses. Therefore, it would seem appropriate to call them NAT/PAT firewalls. This is seldom done, but it is important to understand that NAT does not only translate network IP addresses.

Transparency

NAT is transparent to both the internal client and the external server. Neither the client nor the server knows that NAT is being done. They do not have to change their way of operating at all.

Problems with Certain Protocols

Certain protocols, including the important IPsec virtual public network protocol discussed in Chapter 8, have problems with network address translation (NAT). We will discuss the IPsec problem in Chapter 8.

Address Multiplication

Even firms that do not use NAT for security often use it to give them more IP addresses. Sometimes, firms are assigned only 254 public IP addresses or even fewer. They might have more computers needing Internet access than they have assigned public IP addresses.

These firms use public IP addresses on the Internet side of the NAT router. Internally, however, they use private IP addresses (see Chapter 3). For each public IP address, more than 16,000 internal-external dialogs can have the same public IP address but different port numbers. Therefore, even if a firm has only 254 IP addresses or even fewer, it can have thousands of internal computers.

TEST YOUR UNDERSTANDING

16. a) Does NAT tend to be used alone or in concert with another type of firewall? b) What danger does NAT address? c) How does a NAT firewall work? d) What problems do NAT firewalls create?

APPLICATION FIREWALLS

Neither static packet filter firewalls nor stateful firewalls examine application messages apart from the limited filtering done by stateful firewalls for port-switching applications. This is unfortunate because application messages contain valuable information for packet pass/deny decisions. Application firewalls make up for this oversight by explicitly looking at application messages.

Application Firewall Operation

Figure 5-13 illustrates how an application firewall works. This is an HTTP application firewall.

Proxy Program

On an application firewall, the program that provides the protection is called a **proxy** program. The proxy on the application firewall in Figure 5-13 is an HTTP proxy. A proxy is someone or something that acts on behalf of another. We will see in the next few paragraphs why these programs are called proxies.

Client Initiation

The client initiates an interaction using an HTTP request message. The client places this HTTP request message within a TCP segment that is delivered within an IP packet.

Figure 5-13   Application Firewall Operation

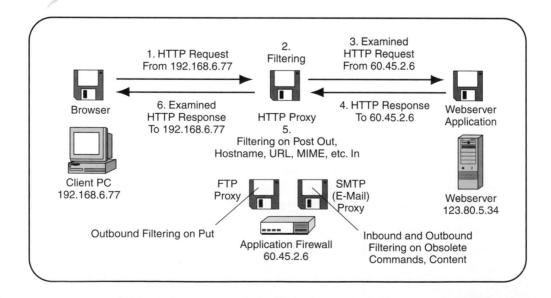

Application Firewall Reception

The HTTP request message does not go directly to the destination HTTP server. Instead, it goes to the application firewall. The HTTP proxy reads the application message and either passes or drops the HTTP request message. We will look at specific pass/deny roles later.

Application Firewall Transmission

The HTTP proxy puts the acceptable HTTP request message in a new TCP segment and new IP packet. It sends this IP packet to the HTTP server.

The Response

The HTTP server finds the file and sends the file back in an HTTP response message. This response goes to the application firewall.

Ingress Filtering

When the application firewall receives the HTTP response message, the HTTP proxy filters the message, either passing or denying it. Again, we will look at specific filtering issues later.

Client Receipt

Finally, the HTTP proxy puts the HTTP response message in a new TCP segment in a new IP packet and sends the packet on to the requesting client.

Client/Server Relaying

In effect, the application firewall relays messages between the client and the server.

To the Client

To the client, the application firewall acts as a server. The client sends the firewall HTTP request messages and gets back HTTP response messages, just as if the application firewall were an HTTP server.

To the Server

To the HTTP server, in turn, the application firewall appears to be a client. The firewall sends the server HTTP request messages, and the server sends back HTTP response messages.

Full Protocol Support

Clients and servers can send many different types of application messages in any complex protocol such as HTTP. The HTTP proxy on the application firewall can handle all HTTP request messages a client can send and all HTTP response messages the server can send. The proxy supports the full HTTP protocol.

TEST YOUR UNDERSTANDING

17.   a) Explain application firewall operation. b) Distinguish between proxies and application firewalls. c) In what sense is a firewall transparent to the client and server?

Core Protections

Just by the way it operates, an application firewall provides three core protections.

IP Address Hiding

Suppose an attacker has a sniffer that reads all packets passing over the connection between the company and the Internet, as Figure 5-13 illustrates. If there is no application firewall (or NAT firewall) in place, the source IP addresses of outgoing packets will reveal the IP addresses of internal hosts, identifying potential victims to exploit.

However, if there is an application proxy before the router leading to the Internet, the source IP address in every outgoing packet passed through the application firewall will be the *application firewall's own* IP address (in this example, 60.45.2.6). The attacker will learn nothing but the IP address of the application firewall. Like NAT, application firewalls do not reveal the IP addresses of internal hosts.

Header Destruction

Figure 5-14 illustrates another automatic protection that application firewalls provide—the destruction of all headers before the application message. The application firewall decapsulates the application message from the packet in which it arrives. In doing so, it discards the IP and TCP or UDP header.

This stops *all* attacks based on IP, TCP, and UDP headers—the attacks specifically stopped by static packet filter and stateful firewalls. The only header-based attacks possible are those aimed at the application firewall itself. Header-based attacks cannot get through the application firewalls to proxied clients.

Figure 5-14 Header Destruction with Application Firewalls

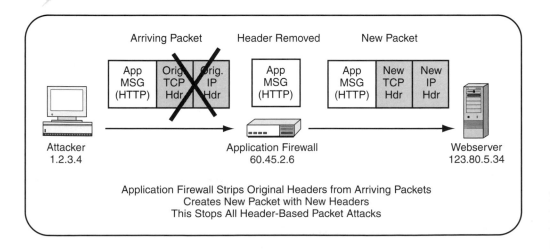

Application Firewall Strips Original Headers from Arriving Packets
Creates New Packet with New Headers
This Stops All Header-Based Packet Attacks

Protocol Enforcement

Many static packet filter and stateful firewalls allow packets to or from Port 80 and other common application ports to pass. Consequently, many attack programs will attempt to communicate with their partners over one of these commonly passed ports, especially Port 80, which is the most seldom blocked. This is called **port spoofing**. It is illustrated in Figure 5-15.

With an application firewall, port spoofing is largely impossible. The application firewall acts like a server to the client, as we have just seen. The HTTP proxy expects the client to be speaking HTTP, and if it tries to speak a different protocol, the HTTP proxy will not understand it and will break the connection. If all Port 80 connections to external hosts must pass through the application firewall, port spoofing will be impossible.

HTTP Filtering

In addition to the three automatic core protections that are always provided by firewalls, application firewalls provide special protection based on the particular application being proxied. We will look at this first with HTTP.

Command-Based Filtering

Application-specific filtering can be used to prevent internal or external hosts from using certain commands. For example, the HTTP *GET* command normally is used to retrieve files and so normally is allowed by an HTTP proxy.

However, the HTTP *POST* command can be used to send files out of firms. These files could contain trade secrets. An HTTP proxy might be configured to reject HTTP request messages using the POST command to thwart attempts to send out trade secrets via HTTP request messages on Port 80.

Figure 5-15   Stopping Port Spoofing with Protocol Enforcement

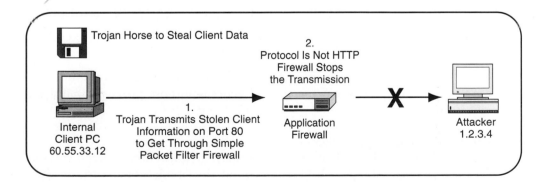

Host or URL Filtering

In addition, the company might want to filter all messages to and from specific hosts and URLs. For instance, lists of hosts and URLs have been developed for pornography sites. Firms might want to black hole HTTP traffic to and from sites on these lists.

MIME Filtering

In HTTP response messages, the header contains a MIME field that specifies the format of the file being delivered in the body. Many HTTP proxies filter out messages containing executable files (.exe, .vbs, etc.) and unspecified binary files that might be executable files. Even word processing and spreadsheet files can be stopped to prevent viruses, but this can block many legitimate attachments.

FTP Filtering

FTP is another application whose commands might be filtered. Many companies allow **FTP Get** commands, which retrieve files from external FTP hosts. However, **FTP Put** commands, which often are used to upload files to external servers, might be filtered to prevent proprietary files from being sent out of the firm this way.

TEST YOUR UNDERSTANDING

18.   a) Briefly explain the core protections offered by all application firewalls. b) How can command filtering provide protection? c) How can content filtering provide protection?

Multiple Proxies

Application proxies filter specific application messages. Not surprisingly, separate application proxies are needed for each application being filtered, as Figure 5-13 illustrates.

A small firm might run all application proxies on a single host computer, as in Figure 5-13. In small firms, traffic volume will not justify the cost of multiple computers.

However, larger firms try to use one computer per application proxy. This way, if a computer is compromised, only one application proxy is compromised.

TEST YOUR UNDERSTANDING

19.   a) If you will proxy four applications, how many proxy programs will you need? b) Can an application firewall operate multiple proxies? c) When is this a good idea? d) Why is it not desirable?

Circuit Firewalls

Not all applications have protocol behaviors that can be filtered usefully. For such applications, companies may use special, general-purpose proxy firewalls called **circuit firewalls**.

Circuit Firewall Applications

Figure 5-16 shows that circuit firewalls establish a connection between specific ports on a pair of hosts. After establishing this circuit, the circuit firewall basically gets out of the way, passing all messages. This might sound like a stateful firewall, but it still provides relaying and so provides the core protections of application firewalls (IP address

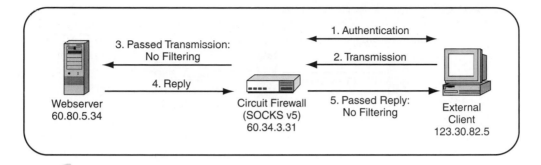

Figure 5-16   Circuit Firewall

hiding and header destruction) but not protocol fidelity. In addition, the circuit fire-wall might do authentication.

SOCKS

The most widely used circuit firewalls follow the SOCKS Version 5 protocol. Although SOCKS offers a standardized way of building application firewalls, SOCKS has a number of limitations. Most seriously, SOCKS software must be added to client computers.

TEST YOUR UNDERSTANDING

20. a) Why are circuit firewalls needed? b) How do they operate? c) What protection do they provide? d) What is the most important circuit firewall standard?

FIREWALL ARCHITECTURES

We have discussed static packet filter firewalls, stateful firewalls, and application fire-walls, as well as network address translation, which can be used by both static packet filter firewalls and stateful firewalls.

We might have made these different firewalls sound like competitors by compar-ing and contrasting them. However, this is not the case. Larger firms and larger sites within firms typically employ several types of firewalls together, using their different strengths to complement one another (and to make up for the weaknesses in indi-vidual types of firewalls).

The way a firm selects and organizes its firewalls is called its **firewall architecture**. Figure 5-17 shows a typical firewall architecture for a larger firm with a single site. We will work through this architecture, then look at architectures for individual PCs in homes, smaller firms, and multisite firms.

TEST YOUR UNDERSTANDING

21. What is a firewall architecture?

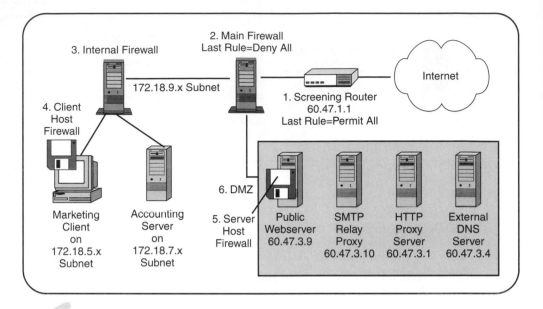

Figure 5-17   Single-Site Firewall Architecture for a Larger Firm with a Single Site

Screening Static Packet Filtering with a Router

Roles for Screening Routers

As shown in Figure 5-17, it is common to use a screening router to do static packet filtering to eliminate common high-volume, low-complexity attacks in order to reduce the work the internal firewall must do.

The site's screening router (60.47.1.1) also does egress filtering to prevent reconnaissance replies from getting back to attackers, to prevent attack packets created inside the network from escaping to the outside, and to do other work. This means that even reconnaissance attacks against the router will fail to elicit useful replies.

Permit All

In normal firewalls, the philosophy is to Deny All packets not specifically permitted. Consequently, the last rule always is Deny All, whether explicitly (as in Figure 5-6) or implicitly, as in Cisco's Deny All default.

However, screening firewalls have a different role. Their job is to screen out many attacks but not to make a full firewall analysis of each and every packet. It is like an airport security guard who checks your boarding pass and your photo ID card before allowing you to go through the full metal detector.

Consequently, the last rule in a screening firewall's ACL must be **Permit All**, in order to pass all packets not specifically denied by earlier rules.

Performance

As noted earlier, adding firewall software to routers tends to be expensive. As a general rule, there is a big performance hit whenever *any* ACL is added to a router, even if it has only two or three rules. The performance hit is relatively constant over the range of a few rules to perhaps a couple of dozen rules, then increases as the number of rules is increased further. (The specific number of rules where performance problems begin depends on the particular router.) Consequently, whether to do firewall filtering on the border router leading to the Internet is a serious decision.

TEST YOUR UNDERSTANDING

22. a) Why are screening routers good? b) Should the last rule of a screening firewall be Deny All or Permit All? Explain. c) Why is performance a concern?

Main Firewall

The main firewall in Figure 5-17 is a stateful firewall, such as a Check Point firewall. This is the main line of defense in the firewall architecture. Computer-based firewalls also have ACLs, but these ACLs tend to be much easier to create and modify than router ACLs. Typically, computer-based ACLs have graphical user interfaces, and routers tend to have command line interfaces and little editing beyond deleting an entire ACL and creating a new one. Finally, computer firewalls can be purchased in a wide range of sizes, so firewall size (and cost) can be matched to corporate needs.

TEST YOUR UNDERSTANDING

23. Why are computer-based main firewalls better to work with than router-based firewalls?

Demilitarized Zones

The main firewall in Figure 5-17 is **tri-homed**, meaning that it connects to three subnets.

The Screening Router

A subnet leads to the screening router. (This is the 60.47.1.x subnet.) This typically is a direct connection, but the connection is given its own subnet address range with only the router within this range. This allows the main firewall to totally control access to the screening router.

The Internal Network

Another subnet (172.18.9.x) connects the main firewall to the hosts and routers of the internal network. Of course, there is nothing preventing several internal subnets from connecting to ports on the main router if enough ports are available. This way, the firewall can control packets passing between different subnets within the firm.

The DMZ

A final subnet (60.47.3.x) is called the **demilitarized zone (DMZ)**. In effect, it is an intermediate area between the internal trusted network and the external Internet. This is where public webservers and other public servers reside.

The main firewall ensures that all connections to public servers go only to a machine in the DMZ. For example, the site's public webserver is 60.47.3.9. The main firewall also ensures that connections between computers in the DMZ and internal computers are strictly limited. This way, if attackers take over a computer in the DMZ, they will not be able to attack many internal computers.

TEST YOUR UNDERSTANDING

24.   a) What is a tri-homed router? b) What is a DMZ? c) Why are DMZs good?

Hosts in the DMZ

In addition to being a good place for public servers, the DMZ is a good place for application firewalls, which also must be connected to the outside world. Application firewalls placed in the DMZ can be used to enforce a policy that all communication with the outside world must pass through the DMZ.

Bastion Hosts

Computers in the DMZ often are called **bastion hosts**. In castles, the bastion is a structure that extends outward. This is the point where attackers will be encountered first, so the bastion is given arrow slits and other protections. Similarly, bastion hosts are especially hardened against attacks, as discussed in the next chapter.

External DNS Server

The DMZ in Figure 5-17 contains an **external DNS server**, 60.47.3.4, which is created to be accessed by the outside world. This external DNS server knows only the host names and IP addresses of bastion hosts in the DMZ. This way, outside attackers cannot use the DNS server in the DMZ to learn about hosts on the internal protected network.

HTTP Proxy Server

The DMZ is the obvious place to put the HTTP proxy server (60.47.3.1), which must connect to the outside world. Note that this host provides only HTTP protection, so if it is compromised, other application proxies will not be compromised, as well.

SMTP Relay Server

The figure also shows an SMTP relay proxy server (60.47.3.10), which connects internally only to the firm's main SMTP mail server (not shown). The SMTP relay server uses a different mail program than the internal mail host. This way, an attacker would have to take over both hosts to do damage. This would require two different exploits to be used within the attack. This would at least slow attackers, if not stop them entirely.

TEST YOUR UNDERSTANDING

25.   a) Why are public servers put in DMZs? b) What are bastion hosts? c) Why is an external DNS host often put in the DMZ? d) What IP addresses does the DNS server know? e) Why are application firewalls usually placed in the DMZ?

Internal Firewalls

Figure 5-17 shows an internal firewall between two subnets—marketing (172.18.5.x) and accounting (172.18.7.x). This way, access to sensitive accounting servers by marketing personnel will be sharply limited. The goal is to make insider attacks more difficult—something that border routers simply do not do.

Host Firewalls

Finally, internal computers can be given **host firewalls** that protect only single client or server computers.

Server Host Firewalls
As noted earlier, server host firewalls can be tailored to specific servers. For instance, a webserver host would reject anything but TCP Port 80 and TCP Port 443 connection requests. This way, even if other services were accidentally left open on the webserver, an attacker could not exploit these misconfigurations.

Client Host Firewalls
In turn, client host firewalls should reject virtually all external connections. In typical client firewalls, the initial setting is to stop all connections to and from the computer. At each subsequent attempt to connect to or from the outside, the user is asked whether to allow the connection once, to allow it always, or to prevent it.

Defense in Depth

A basic principle in this complex architecture is defense in depth. For example, even if an attacker can break through the screening router, the attack is likely to be stalled at the main firewall, at an internal firewall, or at a host firewall. Completing a series of exploits on a succession of servers tends to be difficult.

TEST YOUR UNDERSTANDING

26.   a) Why are internal and host firewalls good? b) How do they provide defense in depth?

Other Firewall Architectures

Although the firewall architecture shown in Figure 5-17 illustrates important architectural issues, both simpler and more complex architectures are often encountered in organizations.

Individual Home Computer Firewalls
Figure 5-18 shows a home PC with a broadband connection to the Internet (cable or DSL service). This is an always-on connection, giving hackers the time and bandwidth needed to execute attacks.

The user PC connects directly to the cable or DSL modem via a UTP cord. This modem offers no firewall protection at all.

The user in the figure has purchased and installed a PC firewall program, such as Zone Alarm. This PC firewall detects and stops more than two dozen attack packets each day. Almost all are scanning (probing) packets, but some are break-in attempts.

SOHO Firewall Architectures
Figure 5-19 shows a slightly more complex situation—a **small office or home (SOHO)** environment with several PCs. This network uses a SOHO router that connects to the shared broadband modem via a UTP cord.

The figure also shows a switch to connect the router to the PCs, but many SOHO routers today have a built-in switch to which the individual PCs connect via UTP cords.

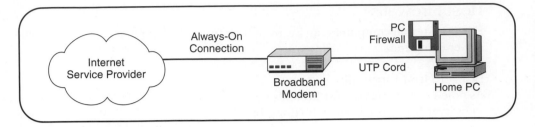

Figure 5-18 Home Firewall

The router has a built-in DHCP server, which gives each PC a private IP address. The router then uses NAT to make use of the single IP address the ISP provides to the premises. The NAT firewall provides a good deal of protection itself.

SOHO routers usually also do lightweight application content filtering by dropping certain types of files likely to be attacks. However, this protection is fairly weak. It is still a good idea to put PC firewalls on the individual PCs for more protection.

TEST YOUR UNDERSTANDING

27. Compare and contrast individual home computer firewall architectures and SOHO firewall architectures.

Figure 5-19 SOHO Firewall Router

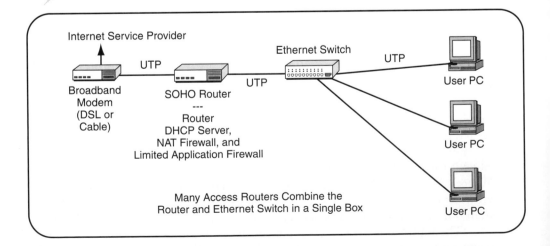

Distributed Firewall Architectures

Figure 5-20 takes us to the other size extreme—a large firm with multiple sites, each with a local firewall system. A major goal of a **distributed firewall architecture** is to provide central management to all of the site firewalls so that attackers cannot simply try different sites until they find a misconfigured firewall.

Unfortunately, remote management is dangerous because if hackers can take over the control channel, they can take over all of the firm's firewalls. Also, remote management has to open at least one port on each site's firewalls, creating a potential hole in protection. It also gives attackers a potential opportunity to take over the firewalls.

Note that one of the sites in Figure 5-20 is an individual home. Distributed firewall architectures must provide protection for employees working at home. Otherwise, attackers can compromise a home computer and use this computer's stored passwords to break into site networks. Microsoft suffered a major break-in in this way in 2000.

TEST YOUR UNDERSTANDING

28.   a) Why are distributed firewall architectures good? b) Why are they dangerous?

Related Architectural Issues

Firewalls only represent part of the technological infrastructure that corporations need to be safe. A full security architecture must include other methods of protection, as well.

Figure 5-20   Distributed Firewall Architecture

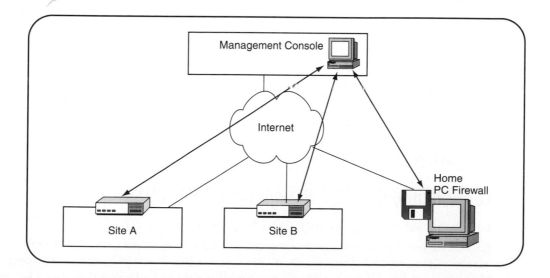

HOST AND APPLICATION SECURITY (CHAPTERS 6 AND 9)

ANTIVIRUS PROTECTION (CHAPTER 5)

INTRUSION DETECTION SYSTEMS (CHAPTER 10)

VIRTUAL PRIVATE NETWORKS (CHAPTER 8)

POLICY ENFORCEMENT SYSTEM

Figure 5-21   Other Security Architecture Issues (Study Figure)

Host and Application Security

In Chapters 6 and 9, we will see how host and application hardening protect the firm when firewalls fail, as they sometimes do.

Antivirus Protection

Firewalls rarely provide antivirus protection, and when they do, they usually provide only limited antivirus protection.

Intrusion Detection Systems

In Chapter 10, we will see how intrusion detection systems (IDSs) provide security administrators with good information about the threat environment, including which new attacks require new firewall policies.

Virtual Private Networks (VPNs)

To communicate over the Internet, many firms build virtual private networks (VPNs), in which they create secure point-to-point connections over the Internet. As we will see in Chapter 8, VPNs are sometimes incompatible with firewalls, so many firewalls combine firewall and VPN capabilities to ensure that every connection to the outside world is protected.

Policy Enforcement Systems

As noted in Chapter 1, policies should drive everything else. Companies need to have policy enforcement systems that control all elements of the security architecture, including firewalls, antivirus protection, intrusion detection systems, and individual client and server hosts.

CONFIGURING, TESTING, AND MAINTAINING FIREWALLS

Firewall Misconfiguration Is a Serious Problem

Earlier, we saw the complexity of access control list configuration, but the firewall ACL we saw earlier was a rather simple access control list. Most ACLs are much longer. Misordered rules will cause breakdowns, and it is easy to make syntax errors. Overall,

FIREWALL MISCONFIGURATION IS A SERIOUS PROBLEM

ACL rules must be executed in series
Easy to make misordering problems
Easy to make syntax errors

CREATE POLICIES BEFORE ACLs

Policies are easier to read than ACLs
Can be reviewed by others more easily than ACLs
Policies drive ACL development
Policies also drive testing

MUST TEST FIREWALLS WITH SECURITY AUDITS

Only way to tell if policies are being supported
Must be driven by policies

MAINTAINING FIREWALLS

New threats appear constantly
ACLs must be updated constantly if firewall is to be effective

Figure 5-22   Configuring, Testing, and Maintaining Firewalls (Study Figure)

misconfiguration is extremely common in firewalls, so firms must exert a great deal of effort configuring, testing, and maintaining firewalls.

Policies

Before creating firewall configurations, it is important for a firm to create firewall policies. For instance, one policy element might be that packets with private source IP addresses should not be allowed to enter from the Internet. Each policy element can then be expressed in one or more ACLs. Policies are much easier to read than ACLs, allowing others to comment on them.

Testing with Security Audits

Creating individual ACL rules is complex and subject to high error rates. In addition, as noted earlier in this chapter, the sequential nature of rule execution can easily cause critical rules to be bypassed.

Security Audits

It is critical to use security audits to test firewalls. In security audits, an employee or trusted outside security auditor transmits a series of attack packets to the firewall. A sniffer at the other side measures which attack packets get through.

Policy-Based Audits

The attacks in the security audit are created based on exactly the policies used to create the firewall ACL rules. By driving both attacks and ACL rules, policies ensure that higher-level thinking will drive firewall protection.

Updating Firewalls

Attackers and firewall administrators are engaged in a constantly escalating arms race, and new threats appear constantly. It is important to update ACLs frequently to meet new threats. Firewalls that are set up and simply left running become fairly useless after just a few weeks.

TEST YOUR UNDERSTANDING

29.   a) Why are configuring, testing, and maintaining firewalls critically important? b) Why is configuration difficult? c) Why are policies crucial? d) Why is audit testing necessary? e) How is audit testing done? f) Do policies drive configuration, testing, or both? g) Why is it important to read firewall logs?

CHECK POINT AND CISCO SYSTEMS FIREWALLS

We will close our discussion of firewalls with a brief look at firewalls from the two companies that dominate the enterprise firewall market today—Check Point and Cisco Systems.

Check Point's FireWall-1

Check Point's main product is FireWall-1. This product pioneered stateful packet analysis (which Check Point calls stateful inspection).

Modules

As Figure 5-23 shows, FireWall-1 has a modular management architecture with three types of modules. These three types of modules can all be on a single machine, in which case you have a stand-alone firewall. Alternatively, as shown in the figure, they can be on separate machines to give a distributed firewall architecture.

The most important module is the firewall module, which enforces the policy given to it and sends log entries to the management module. This firewall module is installed on all firewalls.

Second, a central management module stores security policies and passes these security policies to firewall modules. It also stores and manages the log files from multiple firewalls.

Third, there are the application modules, sometimes called the GUIs. These application modules provide management tools to the security administrator. These tools allow the security administrator to create, delete, and modify security policies on the management modules. These tools also allow the network administrator to study the log files on the management modules. Having graphical user interfaces, these management applications tend to be fairly simple to use.

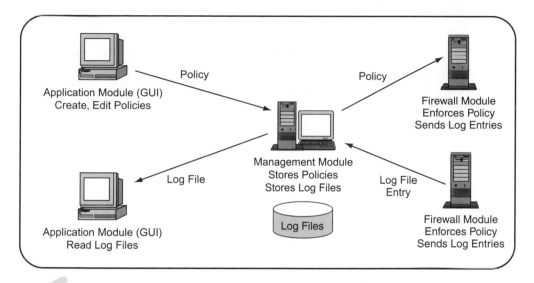

Figure 5-23   FireWall-1 Modular Management Architecture

Service Architecture

In turn, Figure 5-24 shows how a FireWall-1 firewall provides services to users. Note that it mainly provides stateful inspection, although it also provides denial-of-service protection and VPN protection and can provide authentication as another tool to decide whether or not to permit a connection.

It also provides application message inspection. As shown in the figure, it normally handles application inspection by offloading this work to a separate Security Server. The Content Vectoring Protocol (CVP) standard for passing work to and from security servers allows third-party products to be used for application inspection. (For HTTP, FireWall-1 has a second standard method for passing work—the URL Filtering Protocol, UFP.)

Cisco's PIX and Router Capabilities

Cisco Systems dominates the router market and, increasingly, the switch market. It also has a strong presence in firewalls. For historical reasons, Cisco has two product lines that differ somewhat in capabilities and considerably in command structure.

Cisco Routers

First, Cisco routers natively provide static packet filtering and somewhat more advanced firewall tools. With the addition of Cisco Secure Integrated Software, routers become limited firewalls with rudimentary stateful inspection (called Content-Based Access Control), limited application inspection, DoS protection, logging, and even rudimentary IDS functionality.

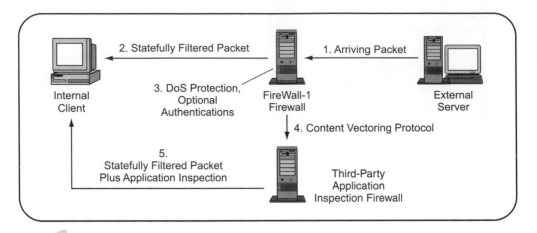

Figure 5-24   FireWall-1 Service Architecture

PIX Firewalls

Second, PIX firewalls offer fuller stateful packet analysis, application filtering, denial-of-service protection, authentication, VPN support, logging, and moderate IDS support.

Security Level-Based Stateful Filtering

Figure 5-25 illustrates that PIX firewall connection permissions depend on something called security levels. Every firewall has at least two ports. An Inside port attaches to the site network, which should be highly secure and by definition has a security level of 100. The other port is the Outside port, which has a security level of 0 to indicate that the external network (usually the Internet) is not secure. The figure also shows a DMZ with a security level of 60 assigned by the security manager.

PIX firewalls follow a simple rule: Connections from a more secure to a less secure network (for instance, from the site to the Internet) are automatically allowed. Conversely, connections from a less secure network to a more secure network (for instance, from the DMZ to the Inside network) are automatically prohibited.

Access control lists modify this basic behavior by telling the firewall specifically to deny or permit certain applications and protocols. So, an access control list rule would be needed to permit external clients (on unsecure networks) to get access to a web-server in the DMZ (more secure).

Fixup Rules

Even with access lists, it might be necessary to give certain applications or protocols more specific support. Cisco PIX firewalls provide "fixup rules" to add capabilities to handle connections for various protocols such as HTTP (URL filtering), RealAudio (dealing with dual connections), and other services. These fixup rules get their name from the fact that they extend (fix up) the basic protocol.

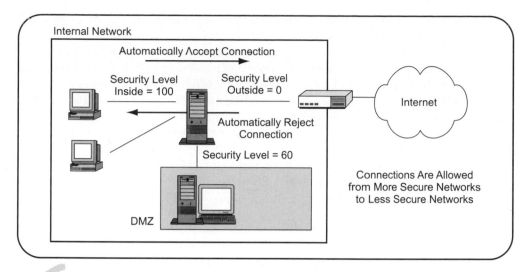

Figure 5-25   Security Level-Based Stateful Filtering in PIX Firewalls

TEST YOUR UNDERSTANDING

30. a) Who produces FireWall-1? b) What protections does FireWall-1 provide? c) Describe FireWall-1's three management modules. d) If you want only a single management machine to manage three firewalls, where would you place the modules? e) How does FireWall-1 integrate with third-party products for application inspection? f) What two products for firewall protection does Cisco offer? g) Which is a better firewall? h) What protections does PIX offer? i) What is the basic PIX rule for creating connections, based on security levels? j) How is this rule modified?

CONCLUSION

In this chapter, we have looked at one of the most important technologies for corporate protection—firewalls. We saw the four types of firewall hardware and software configurations: routers, computer-based firewalls, firewall appliances, and host firewalls.

We also saw that firewalls filter in one of three ways: static packet filtering, stateful analysis, and application proxy filtering. In addition, the firewalls using the first two filtering methods often also use network address translation (NAT). These methods are not mutually exclusive. As Figure 5-17 shows, companies typically use a mixture of hardware/software approaches and filtering types to build firewall architectures that give defense in depth. Many firewalls also offer at least limited denial-of-service (DoS) protection and authentication.

THOUGHT QUESTIONS

1. In Figure 5-6 and Figure 5-7, some statements are redundant given the final Deny All rule in each ACL. List the numbers of rules that can be deleted without reducing protection.

2. Create policy statements that would be used to guide the ACLs shown in Figure 5-6 and Figure 5-7.

3. Change the ACLs in Figure 5-6 and Figure 5-7 to add policies that incoming DNS requests should be permitted at a particular DNS host, 60.47.3.4., and that SSH traffic should be allowed because it is needed to manage firewalls.

4. Change the ACLs in Figure 5-6 and Figure 5-7 to add a policy that all SMTP traffic (TCP Port 25) should pass through an SMTP application proxy, 60.47.3.10.

5. Create a simple ACL for a packet filter firewall that serves a single Windows client PC at home.

6. Change the ACLs in Figure 5-6 and Figure 5-7 to drop rules that would not be needed for stateful inspection firewalls.

7. In the firewall architecture shown in Figure 5-17, what hosts should *not* be protected by NAT?

8. In Figure 5-25, what would have to be done to create a connection a) from an Inside client to an Outside server on the Internet? b) from an Outside server on the Internet to an Internal client PC? c) from an Inside client to a DMZ server? d) from a DMZ server to an Inside server? e) from a DMZ server to a back-end database in the main site LAN?

TROUBLESHOOTING QUESTIONS

1. You have a rule in your ACL to block a particular type of traffic. However, when you do an audit, you find that the firewall is not blocking this traffic. What is the problem likely to be?

2. The port ranges in the egress ACL (Figure 5-7) are based upon IETF recommendations. However, not all operating systems follow this range. Modify the ACL if you have only Microsoft Windows NT and 2000 servers. You will need to go to www.ncftpd.com/ncftpd/doc/misc/ephemeral_ports.html for a list of port ranges.

CHAPTER 6

HOST SECURITY

Learning Objectives

By the end of this chapter, you should be able to discuss:

- The elements of host hardening.
- Types of hosts.
- Security baselines.
- Installation and patching.
- Turning off unnecessary services.
- Managing users and groups.
- Managing permissions.
- Advanced server hardening techniques: logging, backup, file encryption, file integrity checkers, and host firewalls.
- Testing for vulnerabilities.
- Hardening clients.

INTRODUCTION

Although firewalls stop most Internet-based attacks, they cannot stop *all* outside attacks, and they are even less effective for attacks from within a corporation. The bottom line is that some attacks inevitably will reach victim hosts within the firm.

Host Hardening

If you install a server "out of the box," that is, using the operating system's installation media and installation defaults, then connect it to the Internet without protection, a hacker is likely to "own" it within a day or two. Firewalls improve the situation, but only somewhat. Protecting servers, then, is not optional. It is critical.

The Elements of Hardening

The solution is **hardening**—a term used to describe a series of actions corporations should take to make all of their hosts more difficult to attack. This chapter focuses on the steps needed to harden a host. Among these steps are the following:

➤ Provide physical security for the host (discussed in Chapter 2).
➤ Install the operating system with secure configuration options.
➤ Download and install patches for known vulnerabilities.
➤ Turn off unnecessary services.
➤ Harden all remaining applications. (This is the focus of Chapter 9.)
➤ Manage users and groups.
➤ Manage access permissions.
➤ Back up the server regularly.
➤ Employ advanced protections.
➤ Test for vulnerabilities.

Security Baselines for Individual Products

Hardening is a complex and long set of actions, and it is easy to overlook something. Consequently, it is extremely desirable for a firm to have a standard **security baseline**—a set of specific actions to be taken to harden all hosts of a particular type, such as Windows 2000.

Larger companies are likely to develop their own security baselines. Smaller firms are best advised to adopt a security baseline provided by the host operating system vendor or by a standards agency.

Systems Administrators

IT employees who manage individual hosts are called, for historical reasons, **systems administrators**. Consequently, hosts are sometimes referred to as **systems**. Typically, it is the job of the systems administrator for a particular server to conduct the hardening effort. Larger firms have many systems administrators, and security baselines help ensure uniformity across the hardening efforts of systems administrators.

IT employees who manage individual hosts are called, for historical reasons, systems administrators.

THE PROBLEM

Computers installed out of the box have known vulnerabilities
Hackers can take them over easily
They must be hardened—a complex process that involves many actions

ELEMENTS OF HARDENING

Provide physical security for the host (discussed in Chapter 2).
Install the operating system with secure configuration options.
Download and install patches for known vulnerabilities.
Turn off unnecessary services.
Harden all remaining applications. (This is the focus of Chapter 9.)
Manage users and groups.
Manage access permissions.
Back up the server regularly.
Employ advanced protections.
Test for vulnerabilities.

SECURITY BASELINES GUIDE THE HARDENING EFFORT

Specifications for how hardening should be done
Different for different operating systems and versions
Different for different types of servers (webservers, mail servers, etc.)
Needed because it is easy to forget a step

SERVER ADMINISTRATORS ARE CALLED SYSTEMS ADMINISTRATORS

WINDOWS COMPUTERS

Microsoft Network Operating Systems (NOSs)
    LAN Manager (LANMAN), NT, 2000, .NET
Graphical user interface looks like client versions to ease learning (Figure 6-2)
Administrative Tools Group under Programs has Microsoft Management Consoles
    (MMCs) (Figure 6-3)
    Used to conduct most administrative actions
    Can add snap-ins for specific functionality
Windows 2000 introduced hierarchical domain structure with Active Directory
    Domain is a collection of resources
    Domain contains one or more domain controllers, member servers, client PCs
    Group policy objects (GPOs) can implement policies throughout a domain

(continued)

Figure 6-1   Hardening Host Computers (Study Figure)

UNIX

Many versions of UNIX
LINUX is a set of versions for PCs—there are several different distributions
User can select the user interface—GUI or command-line interface (CLI)
CLIs are called shells (Bourne, BASH, etc.)
Picky syntax and spacing

INTERNET OPERATING SYSTEM (IOS) FOR CISCO ROUTERS, SOME SWITCHES, FIREWALLS

OTHER HOST OPERATING SYSTEMS

Macintosh
Novell NetWare
Firewalls
Even cable modems with web-based management interfaces

Figure 6-1   (Continued)

TEST YOUR UNDERSTANDING

1. a) Why is host hardening needed? b) What are the elements of host hardening? c) What is a security baseline, and why is it important? d) What type of device does a systems administrator manage?

Windows Computers

Microsoft has created a number of versions of Windows for both clients and servers. Windows is dominant on corporate clients, and it is widespread on servers. Companies need good security baselines for both Windows clients and servers.

History

LAN Manager   Windows network operating systems began with **LAN Manager** in the early 1980s. As one might expect by its date of origin, **LANMAN**, as it usually was called, was extremely primitive. As discussed in Chapter 2, the LANMAN password system was deeply flawed, although many firms continue to use it as an option on newer versions of Windows server for backward compatibility.

Windows NT Server   Next came **Windows Server NT** (New Technology). NT versions 3.5 and 4.0 were adopted by a considerable number of organizations. NT password authentication was much improved over LANMAN, as Chapter 2 discussed.

Windows 2000 and .NET Server   **Windows 2000** created a new authentication structure based on Active Directory and Kerberos. We will discuss Active Directory in this chapter and Kerberos in Chapter 8. Using Active Directory allows the centralization of many policies, but it also has led to difficulties in implementation that have limited Windows 2000 installations to date. Beyond Windows 2000, **Windows .NET Server** brings new capabilities but largely uses Windows 2000 security features.

The Windows User Interface

One good thing about Windows Server is that all versions of Windows Server tend to look a great deal like client versions of Windows. So learning Windows Server is relatively easy. As Figure 6-2 shows, Windows 2000 Server uses Internet Explorer for downloads and other Internet operations, My Computer for file management, and a Start menu with the choices familiar to desktop users. You can even use standard client software on Windows Server.[1]

Microsoft Management Consoles (MMCs)

As Figure 6-2 shows, most Windows Server management tools are provided through the **Administrative Tools** choice on the Programs menu of the Start menu. This makes it easier for systems administrators to guess where to find the tools they will need.

Figure 6-2   Windows 2000 Server User Interface

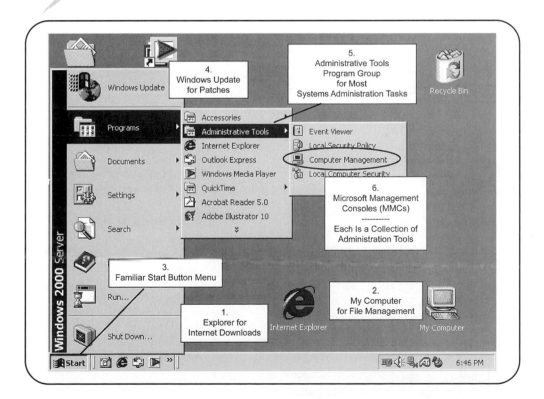

---

[1]   To do the screenshots for the Windows figures in this chapter, I installed Adobe Illustrator—a popular drawing program for Windows client machines—on the server. I couldn't find anything on capturing screen images in the Windows 2000 help system, so I simply tried Alt-PrintScreen, which captures window images in client versions of Windows. It worked. I pasted the PrintScreen images into Adobe Illustrator documents for annotation.

Most administrative tools come in the same general format, called the **Microsoft Management Console (MMC)**. Figure 6-3 shows a typical MMC, Computer Management. Note the tree of tools in the lower-left pane. More choices for the selected tool are shown in the lower-right pane. At the top of the MMC is a menu of choices, including **Action**, which provides actions specific to the selected item on the left or right pane. Other MMCs all have this same general organization, making learning easier.

The individual tools on the tree are called **snap-ins** because they can be added or dropped from the tree list easily. This allows systems administrators to create MMCs easily for their own use or for assistants who each might need to use only a few specific tools.

Stand-Alone Servers and Domains

The **Computer Management** MMC is the tool used to take most security actions on stand-alone Windows servers that are not part of a domain. We will focus on such computers in our Windows examples because they are the simplest to describe.

Figure 6-3   Computer Management Microsoft Management Console (MMC)

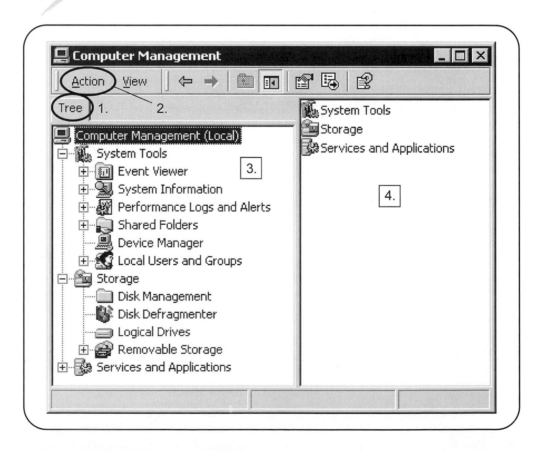

However, companies with many Windows servers are likely to organize their human and computer resources into collections called **domains**. Each domain has one or more **domain controllers** that centralize administration for the domain, including security administration.

Beginning with Windows 2000, the Windows domain structure is integrated tightly into Active Directory (Microsoft's directory server product). All domain controllers have copies of the domain's directory. Active Directory allows a company to build a hierarchical domain structure that can include all of its Windows servers and even all of its Windows clients. On a domain controller in Windows 2000, most security management actions are implemented using the **Active Directory Users and Computers** MMC.

Domains have three types of computers. We already have discussed domain controllers. In addition, **member servers** provide services to users but have a subordinate role to the domain controllers, including not being able to authenticate users themselves. Third are **client PCs**.

The biggest benefit of central management is the ability to create policies that are applied uniformly to all servers or clients within a domain. This ensures that attackers cannot simply try servers until they find one that is misconfigured—a common situation when a firm's servers are not under the control of a policy server.

Although the use of domains can bring great benefits, the migration to an Active Directory–focused domain structure (as opposed to Windows NT's simpler domain structure) is difficult, as noted earlier. Consequently, many Windows servers in organizations today are NT servers, Windows 2000 servers implementing older NT domain structure, or stand-alone Windows servers that are not part of any domain.

Group Policy Objects (GPOs)

One advantage of the use of Active Directory in Windows 2000 is that a systems administrator can associate policies with categories of host computers through a mechanism called **group policy objects (GPOs)**. A GPO can enforce access permissions. It can determine what software can (mandatory) and may (available from a list) be on a computer. It can even determine what the desktop will look like to users.

TEST YOUR UNDERSTANDING

2. a) Comment on the vulnerability of Microsoft Windows servers. b) List the main generations of Windows Server NOSs. c) Why is Microsoft Windows Server easy to learn to use? d) Why are MMCs important? e) How does the systems administrator get to them? f) What are snap-ins? g) What is the role of active directory in Windows systems administration? h) What is a domain? i) Distinguish between domain controllers and member servers. j) What are GPOs? k) Why are they important?

UNIX (Including LINUX)

Many Versions

UNIX is the operating system of choice for large workstation servers. Unfortunately, it is difficult to talk about UNIX installation security in general because many versions of UNIX exist. The major vendors, including IBM, SUN, and Hewlett-Packard, all have their own versions of UNIX. They tend to be interoperable at the kernel level, so they can run the same applications. However, they tend to have different management tools, including security tools. A company does not purchase UNIX; it purchases specific versions of UNIX.

LINUX

For UNIX on PCs, the situation is even more chaotic. The most popular version of UNIX for PCs is **LINUX**. However, LINUX is only the operating system kernel. LINUX vendors offer **distributions** that combine this kernel with other software—usually software from the GNU project. For most functions, GNU offers several alternative programs. Consequently, LINUX distributions tend to be rather different. In addition, besides LINUX, there are other versions of UNIX for PCs, including **FreeBSD** and **OpenBSD**. In many cases, departments purchase PC versions of UNIX without overall coordination by the firm.

LINUX is a version of UNIX that runs on ordinary PCs. Actually, LINUX is only the kernel of the operating system. Actual LINUX packages are distributions that contain the kernel and many other programs—mostly programs from the GNU project.

The fact that many different distributions of LINUX exist makes hardening a LINUX system difficult. It is important to have a good security baseline for the particular LINUX distribution you are using. On the positive side, the lack of a standard distribution means that it is possible to create LINUX distributions that are designed specifically to offer high security. The U.S. National Security Agency, in fact, has been developing such a distribution under the name **Security-Enhanced LINUX**. This distribution's goal is to have strong access control to the major subsystems of the kernel.

UNIX User Interfaces

Shells   Even within a specific version of UNIX, the operating system software may come with several alternative user interfaces. Some of these interfaces will be graphical user interfaces. Others will be **command-line interfaces (CLIs)**, which UNIX calls **shells**.

The Importance of Shells   Many security tools only work at command-line interfaces, so UNIX security specialists tend to find themselves typing complex, syntax-picky shell commands to do security work. The **Bourne shell** was the original popular shell. The current market leader is the **Bourne Again Shell (BASH)**.

The All-Lowercase Horror   UNIX CLIs are almost always case-sensitive. Nearly all UNIX commands are in lowercase, except for file names, which can have mixed case. UNIX CLI shells are also extremely picky about spaces. In this chapter, we will follow the standard UNIX practice of showing program names in lowercase, even in titles.

TEST YOUR UNDERSTANDING

3.   a) Why is UNIX systems administration difficult to describe specifically? b) Distinguish between UNIX and LINUX. c) What is a LINUX distribution? d) What is Security-Enhanced LINUX? e) Does a particular version of UNIX have a single user interface? f) What are UNIX CLIs called? g) Why are CLIs difficult to use?

Cisco's Internetwork Operating System (IOS)

Cisco Systems dominates the market for routers and, to a lesser extent, the market for switches. Its **IOS** software is the operating system it developed for routers and is now making available for many of its switches. To reduce CPU processing burdens, IOS generally uses a command-line interface. On the positive side, once the IOS CLI is mastered, it can be used, with some relearning, on other Cisco products—even Cisco firewalls.

Although we do not ordinarily think of routers and switches as hosts, most routers are full host computers that have their own IP addresses for administrative purposes. This is becoming increasingly true of switches.

If a hacker could take over one or several of your routers or switches, the results could be disastrous. Router and switch hardening are critical in organizations when these products are hosts.

TEST YOUR UNDERSTANDING

4.   a) Are routers hosts? b) Why is protecting routers crucial? c) What is the name of Cisco's operating system? d) On what types of devices does it run?

Other Host Operating Systems

Macintosh

Apple Macintosh computers also are host computers and come in both client and server versions. We will not look at Macintosh host hardening in this chapter because of Macintosh's small market share in organizations. However, a company does have to harden its Macintoshes or they can be taken over and used to attack other hosts.

Novell NetWare

In the 1980s and early 1990s, Novell NetWare was the dominant server operating system for PCs. A series of technological missteps and high pricing have devastated NetWare's market share, but NetWare is still widely used for file and print servers. Due to NetWare's small market share, we will not look at it further in this chapter, but Novell NetWare hosts also have to be hardened.

Firewall Operating Systems

Most firewalls are hosts with operating systems—sometimes even firewall appliances. Most major firewall vendors have reported at least one extremely serious vulnerability. If attackers can take over your firewalls, the potential damage is enormous. For example, in August 2002, a flaw was found in Symantec Raptor, Velociraptor, and Enterprise firewalls that would allow a hacker to hijack supervisory connections and take over firewalls.

Cable Modems

Many other devices can have IP addresses and act as hosts. For instance, cable modems on customer premises often have web-based setup routines. In some cases, cable modems come with no password as a default or have a standard default. Attackers from the outside have been able to log into user cable modems, steal information, and make unauthorized changes to the cable modem's setup profile.

INSTALLATION AND PATCHING

Installation

When installing an operating system on a new machine, the systems administrator must go through a fairly complex installation process. Most installations today use graphical user interfaces, making the installation job fairly straightforward. However, during installation, the installer will be given a number of choices. Some of these have important security implications.

For example, in Microsoft Windows NT, 2000, and later versions, the installer can choose the older FAT32 file system or the newer NTFS file system. Although FAT32 has some advantages, many hardening actions *require* the use of NTFS. Consequently, it is important to choose NTFS. Having a security baseline is crucial to ensure that the correct installation choices are made from a security standpoint.

It is difficult to talk in any depth about security for UNIX. In UNIX (including LINUX), the variability between different vendors' versions of UNIX and of different LINUX distributions makes the transfer of installation expertise across "Unices" somewhat limited. Fortunately, security baselines are available for most versions of UNIX and for many LINUX distributions.

TEST YOUR UNDERSTANDING

5.   a) Do security choices need to be made during installation? b) Why is using a security baseline important during installation?

Known Vulnerabilities and Exploits

The arms race between operating system vendors and hackers is an endless battle. Hackers constantly find new **vulnerabilities**—ways that computers can be attacked. Once they find one, they quickly develop an **exploit**—a piece of software to take advantage of the vulnerability. They typically publish their exploits in hacker newsgroups, hacker websites, and other forums. Known vulnerabilities must be fixed quickly after they are discovered.

Known vulnerabilities may be discovered by the operating system vendors, but they often are discovered by **vulnerability reporters**. Although vendors value vulnerability reporters somewhat, they often complain that vulnerability reporters do not give them enough time to develop fixes before publishing disclosure information and that the disclosure information is too detailed, thereby helping hackers. Vulnerability reporters, in turn, often complain that vendors are too slow to develop patches.

TEST YOUR UNDERSTANDING

6.   a) What is a known vulnerability? b) What is an exploit? c) Why does tension exist between vulnerability reporters and vendors?

Fixes: Patches and Work-Arounds

What do vendors do when a vulnerability is discovered? They create **fixes**.

INSTALLATION OFFERS MANY OPTIONS, SOME OF WHICH AFFECT SECURITY

In Windows, NTFS file system is better for security than FAT32

Need a security baseline to guide installation

KNOWN VULNERABILITIES

Known vulnerabilities

Exploits are programs that take advantage of a known vulnerability

Vulnerability reporters send vulnerability reports to vendors

Vulnerability reporters often say that vendors take too long to fix vulnerabilities

Vendors say that vulnerability reports do not give them enough time, report too much detail to the press

FIXES

Work-around: A series of manual actions to be taken; no new software

Patches: New software to be added to the operating system

Upgrading to a new version of the program

Often, security vulnerabilities are fixed in new versions

If a version is too old, the vendor might stop offering fixes

It might be good to wait to upgrade until after the first round of bug and security fixes

MECHANICS OF PATCHING

Microsoft Windows: Apply Patches on Start menu (Figure 6-2)

LINUX distributions often use rpm

PATCHES OFTEN ARE NOT APPLIED

Companies get overwhelmed by number of patches

Use many products, vendors release many patches per product

Especially a problem for application programs

Cost of Patch installation

Mitigated by patch servers that distribute patches to general servers

More easy-to-use vendor tools are needed

Might simply lack the resources to apply all; might be selective

Risks of Patch installation

Reduced functionality

Freeze machines, do other damage—sometimes with no Uninstall possible

Should test on a patch testing system before deployment in firm

Special problem for mission-critical production systems that must work

Figure 6-4   Installation and Patching (Study Figure)

Work-Arounds

The least satisfactory fix is a **work-around**, which is a series of steps the firm must take to ameliorate the problem. No new software is involved. Unfortunately, work-arounds tend to be highly labor intensive. In addition, they often provide only partial protection.

Patches

It is better when vendors create **patches**, which are new pieces of software that, when added to the operating system, fix the problem on the operating system (or other software). This requires the systems administrator to download the patch and then install it.

Version Upgrades

Usually, the best fix is to **upgrade** the software to its newest version or at least to a newer version. Often, security problems are corrected in newer versions. In addition, if a version is too old, the vendor is likely to stop creating fixes for it when vulnerabilities are discovered.

At the same time, it may be useful to wait on the upgrade decision for a new version until the first release of bug fixes, including security fixes, is available. For example, when Windows XP was released, it had a massive security vulnerability.

TEST YOUR UNDERSTANDING

7.   Distinguish between work-arounds, patches, and upgrades.

The Mechanics of Patch Installation

Microsoft Windows 2000's "Windows Update" Start Menu Option   Most patches are fairly easy to install. First, the systems administrator must go to the vendor's download website. As Figure 6-2 shows, this is easy to do in Microsoft Windows 2000 Server. On the Start menu, the top choice is Windows Update. This will open Internet Explorer and take the user to the Microsoft patch download website. Patches come with installation programs.

LINUX rpm Program   Each UNIX vendor has its own patch download approach. LINUX vendors also use different approaches, although some LINUX vendors follow the **rpm** method created by Red Hat, which is the leading LINUX vendor. This method is named after the rpm command used to initiate a download.

TEST YOUR UNDERSTANDING

8.   a) How do you apply patches in Windows 2000? b) What patch downloading method is commonly used in LINUX?

Failures to Patch

Although patching is critical, many firms fail to patch some of their servers, and patching clients is far less common. A survey of IT professionals in mid-2002 found that only 57 percent even checked security bulletins at least weekly.[2]

---

[2]   IPSOS, *U.S. Business Cyber Security Study,* July 24, 2002.

The Number of Patches

One problem is the sheer number of patches generated annually by vendors. Companies typically use several different operating system vendors, each of which releases many vulnerability reports and patches each year. In addition, companies use many application program vendors, and if these application programs are not patched, attackers often can use application program exploits to take over the computer, as Chapter 9 discusses.

To put numbers on these matters, the Computer Emergency Response Team/ Coordination Center (CERT/CC) counted 2,148 vulnerabilities in the first half of 2002. In recent years, the number of vulnerabilities has doubled each year. In November 2001, Activis estimated that a security manager in a company with only eight firewalls and nine servers would have to apply an average of five patches per day.[3]

Cost of Patch Installation

Although patches are almost always free, the labor needed to learn of their existence, download them, and install them is anything but free. Given the overwhelming number of patches released each year, firms often are selective about installing patches to stay within their budgets.

Vendors are attempting to reduce the cost of patch distribution and installation. They are beginning to provide vulnerability assessment tools that allow firms to scan hosts using a company's operating system in order to detect unpatched vulnerabilities. They are also beginning to provide more automatic ways to apply patches.

The Risks of Patch Installation

In addition, installing patches is not without risks. First, added security often comes at the cost of reduced functionality, which might not be justified given the degree of added safety offered by a patch.

Second, some patches have been known to freeze machines or do other damage; this is particularly bad when patches are offered that have no uninstall option. In 2001, for instance, Microsoft had to withdraw or update patches when the original versions caused problems when installed.

Firms are well advised to download a patch on a patch testing server and examine the effects of a patch thoroughly before rolling the patch out to all servers or clients. If a company has a standard security baseline, chances are good that experiences on the test system will mirror those on other hosts.

Testing is especially crucial for mission-critical production servers that the firm cannot allow to fail because of patch problems. Some firms never patch mission-critical production servers despite the fact that leaving them unpatched could allow a hacker to damage them.

TEST YOUR UNDERSTANDING

    9.   a) Why do many companies not install patches? b) What is a patch testing server?

---

[3] Dan Vernon, "Study: Constant Security Fixes Overwhelming IT Managers," Computerworld.com, November 30, 2001. www.computerworld.com/securitytopics/security/story/0,10801,66215,00.html.

TURNING OFF UNNECESSARY SERVICES

Unnecessary Services

Traditionally, installation turned on many services that few firms needed. Turning on a broad spectrum of services by default was considered to be a good idea because this makes it easy for firms to use them later. However, security experts now agree that a firm should turn off all unnecessary services because a large number of exploits take advantage of vulnerabilities in obscure and little-used services that are turned on automatically during installation.

Figure 6-5   Turning Off Unnecessary Services (Study Figure)

UNNECESSARY SERVICES

    Operating system vendors used to install many services by default

    This made them easier to use

    Attackers found flaws in many of these rare services

    Vendors now install fewer services by default—lock down mode

    Turn to security baseline to know what services to install

    Better to install too few and add than to install too many and remove unwanted services

TURNING OFF SERVICES IN WINDOWS

    Go to the Computer Management MMC

    On the tree, select Services and Applications (Figure 6-6)

    Right click on a service or choose Action to stop a service, etc.

TURNING OFF SERVICES IN UNIX

    Three ways to start services

        inetd to start services when requests come in from users (Figure 6-7)

        rc scripts to start services automatically at boot up (Figure 6-8)

        Start a service manually by typing its name or executing a batch file that does so

    Identifying services that are running at any moment

        ps (processor status), usually with -aux parameters, lists running programs

            Shows process name and process ID (PID)

        netstat tells what services are running on what ports

    Kill PID to kill a particular process

        Add parameters -SIGTERM, -SIGHUP, -SIGKILL in order of increasing urgency

        Only kills for now

        Must search inetd.config, rc scripts, batch files to see where it is being started automatically

Vendors are beginning to offer more of their application programs and even their operating systems in **lock down** mode, which makes noninstallation the default for most services. This practice will help considerably in the future, but for now it is not an option for most operating systems and other commercial software. In addition, lock down mode can make a system more difficult to use.

For the time being, most firms have to turn to their security baseline's list of necessary services for particular types of hosts (webservers, mail servers, and so forth). They then need to compare the security baseline list with the services they are running and turn off unnecessary services. Using a security baseline list is important because accidentally turning off a necessary service can make a server unable to perform its role.

In general, the security baseline should specify the minimum set of services needed to run the computer if it is a webserver, a mail server, or some other type of server. Everything else should be turned off. This is much better than having a list of services that can be turned off safely, because this list could accidentally exclude some unnecessary services that are exploitable.

TEST YOUR UNDERSTANDING

10.   a) Why is turning off unnecessary services important? b) How are operating system vendors beginning to change their approaches to installing services by default? c) What is lock down? d) How can a firm know what services need to be installed?

Turning Off Services in Windows

Figure 6-6 shows the Computer Management MMC. As noted earlier, this MMC is used to manage stand-alone computers. The **Services and Applications** snap-in has been selected in the lower-left pane.

The lower-right pane shows services that currently are running, including each service's name, a brief description of the service, its current status (running, etc.), and how it is started up (automatically, manually, and so forth). Right clicking on a service or clicking on it and selecting Action allows the user to turn off the service.

Note that few of the names are revealing. The descriptions are not much more help. It is crucial to follow a security baseline that will list necessary services to ensure that the computer still will run properly after services are turned off.

TEST YOUR UNDERSTANDING

11.   a) How can a Windows systems administrator learn what services are running? b) How can the Windows systems administrator stop services that are running?

Turning Off Services in UNIX

Turning off services in UNIX is more difficult, because services can be started in three ways.

➤   Some services are started automatically when a computer boots up or takes some other action.

➤   Others are started only when a request for the service arrives from a client.

➤   And, of course, services can be started manually by users (or programs).

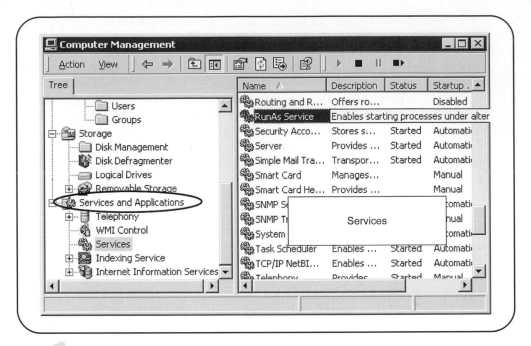

Figure 6-6   Services and Applications in Windows

Services Initiated When Clients Make Requests in UNIX

Some services lie dormant until a client makes a request. As Figure 6-7 shows, client requests coming from the network do not go directly to individual service. Rather, they are sent to the **inetd** daemon (program), which answers for all services. The inetd program is started automatically when the server boots up.

When a request comes in, the inetd program examines the service requested, based on port number. The inetd program then checks its configuration file, **/etc/inetd.config**, to see which service program is associated with that port number. The inetd program starts the service program listed in the inetd.config file and passes the client request to the service.

One problem with this approach is that many versions of UNIX place entries for many unnecessary service programs by default in the inetd.config file. For safety, the systems administrator needs to delete all of the entries not in the security baseline list.

Automatically Starting Services in UNIX with rc Scripts

Turning on services only when needed with inetd makes sense for infrequently used services. However, on a webserver, we would not want to have to relaunch the webservice application each time a client request arrived. UNIX provides a way to start frequently used service applications automatically.

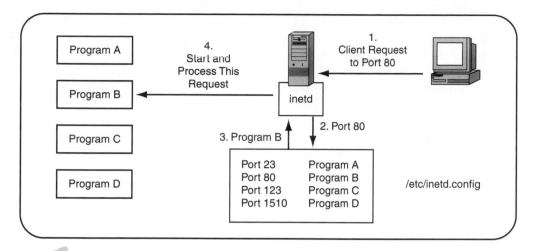

Figure 6-7 UNIX inetd Daemon for Responding to Client Requests

Run Modes   This approach makes use of the fact that UNIX is always on one of several numbered **run modes** (operating conditions). Unfortunately, different versions of UNIX assign different numbers to different run modes. Typically, however, Run Mode 0 is halt (shutdown), Run Mode 6 is system reboot, and Run Mode s is single-user mode.

The /etc/rc.d Directory   In the **/etc/rc.d** directory, UNIX keeps a system of start scripts or kill scripts that respectively start or kill a specific service. These are called **rc scripts**. Figure 6-8 illustrates the contents of the rc directory, including its subdirectories.

The /etc/rc.d/rc#.d Directories   Under the /etc/rc.d directory are several subdirectories of the form **rc#.d**, where # is a run mode number. For example, rc1.d is the directory for scripts to be executed in Run Mode 1 (shutdown). The rc6.d directory, in turn, contains scripts to be executed during a reboot. Finally, rcs.d contains scripts to be executed in single-user mode.

> The brief scripts in each rc#.d directory launch the more sophisticated rc scripts in the /etc/rc.d directory. This way, the systems administrator has to create only one detailed script for each service instead of having to create a detailed script in each rc#.d directory that needs to start or kill a service.

Starting Programs Manually

Both inetd and the rc scripts start programs automatically. In addition, users can do a **manual launch** by typing the program's directory and name (simply the program's name if the program is listed in the system's path command).

> In addition, UNIX allows users to create **batch scripts** that describe a series of individual commands to be executed in order. Program names can be placed in batch scripts. Then, any time the script is executed, the programs in the script will be run.

/etc/rc.d
1. Script to start Service A
2. Script to start Service B
3. Script to start Service F
4. Script to start Service H

rc0.d [scripts to run during System Mode 0-shutdown]
   K2 . . . *[Run the Kill portion of Script 2: Kills Service B]*
   K3 . . . *[Run the Kill portion of Script 3: Kills Service F]*
   . . .

rc1.d
rc2.d
rc3.d
rc4.d
rc5.d

rc6.d [scripts to run during System Mode 6-startup]
   S1 . . . *[Run the Start portion of Script 1: Starts Service A]*
   S2 . . . *[Run the Start portion of Script 2: Starts Service B]*
   . . .

rcs.d [scripts to run during System Mode s—single-user mode]

Figure 6-8   The UNIX rc.d Method of Automatically Starting Services

Identifying All Running Programs

ps   Programs can be started in several ways, so the only way to know which programs are running at a particular moment is to ask the system. Typically, this is done in UNIX by giving the **ps** command, which identifies currently-running program services. A common version of the command is "ps –aux".

One service will be shown per line of output. Each line contains the name of the service and a process identifier (PID) for the service. For instance, the owner might be root, and the PID of a service might be 725. The line also will give other information about the service, depending on the version of UNIX or LINUX.

Netstat   In addition, the UNIX **netstat** command lists current user connections, including the two hosts that are communicating and the service they are using. A common version of the command is **netstat --inet –a**.

Stopping Running Programs

If ps and netstat indicate that a service is running that should not be running, the systems administrator can stop the service with the UNIX **kill *PID*** command. This kills the particular numbered service. For instance, to kill service 725, the systems administrator with root privileges would type "kill 725". Users without the required privileges would not be allowed to kill the service.

The command kill can be followed by an optional parameter indicating the urgency of the termination. In increasing order of urgency, common parameters include -SIGTERM, -SIGHUP, and -SIGKILL, where SIG indicates that the parameter is a signal. It is wise to use the lowest level of signal that will work.

It also is good to know how the service was started so that it can be stopped the next time. This involves searching through inetd.config, rc scripts, and batch files.

TEST YOUR UNDERSTANDING

12. a) What are the three ways to start services in UNIX? b) How can a UNIX systems administrator learn which services are running currently? c) Distinguish between ps and netstat. d) How can a UNIX systems administrator turn off a particular service? e) Killing services stops them only temporarily. How can a UNIXsystems administrator stop them from automatically restarting?

MANAGING USERS AND GROUPS

The next aspect of host hardening we will discuss is creating and managing user accounts and groups. Every user must have an account. In addition, it is common to create groups and add individual users to these groups. When security measures are applied to groups, the users in each group will inherit these measures.

Creating and Managing Users and Groups in Windows

For stand-alone machines, the systems administrator can turn to the Computer Management MMC. As Figure 6-10 shows, there is a **Local Users and Groups** snap-in with two subcategories—Users and Groups. The Users category is selected.

In the right pane, a list of users is shown. The Administrator user is selected. If the administrator selects the Action menu choice or right clicks on Administrator, he or she will be able to delete the Administrator account, rename it, or take other actions. The Actions choice also allows new users to be created and the password for the selected user to be changed.

The Administrator and Guest Accounts

Rename Administrator Administrator is the super user account in Windows and will be the first target of any attacker. It is good practice to rename the Administrator account and then to create a new account called Administrator that has no powers. This is likely to cause attackers to focus on the dummy Administrator account rather than on the real super account.

RunAs It also is considered poor practice to log in as the Administrator. First, if the administrator leaves the computer, anyone can walk up and use it. Second, if the Administrator account is used, several people are likely to share it, and no accountability will be possible if the account is used to take improper actions.

It is best for administrators to log into their own, more limited accounts and for these accounts to have limited power. To give an Administrator command, the systems administrator can log into an account with limited privileges and give the **RunAs** command. This will allow the systems administrator to give a single command with super-user privileges. The systems administrator will have to know the Administrator password to do so.

INTRODUCTION

Every user must have an account
Create groups: Assign security measures to groups, apply to their individual members

CREATING AND MANAGING GROUPS IN WINDOWS

Computer Management: Local Users and Groups snap-in (Figure 6-10)
Select Users
Select user from list
  Right click on user and select Properties: password restrictions, disable box
  Or select Action: change password, etc. (Figure 6-11)
  Add, delete users
  Administrator is the super account
    Change its name and create a new Administrator account with no permissions
    Administrators should not log in as Administrators; log in as their own accounts,
      use RunAs to get temporary Administrator status when needed
  Guest account should be disabled (the default during installation)
Select Groups
  Assign permission to groups
  Standard groups: Administrators, Power Users, Backup Operators, etc.
    Have appropriate permissions by default for their tasks

MANAGING USERS AND GROUPS IN UNIX

Different versions of UNIX do this differently, so it is difficult to talk in general terms
The super account is root
  su (switch user) allows administrators to log in as regular accounts, su to get root
    privileges when desired
Guest account should be disabled

Figure 6-9   Managing Users and Groups (Study Figure)

Disabling the Guest Account   It is also good practice to disable the Guest account. This is done by default during installation; the account is shown in the right pane of Figure 6-10 as being disabled. It is good practice to check that it really is disabled because the Guest account should be used only in low-security environments.

Managing Accounts

Figure 6-11 shows what happens if the systems administrator right clicks on the Administrator account and selects Properties. This action will take the user to the dialog box shown in the figure. The General tab (shown) allows the systems administrator to place password restrictions on the user. Other tabs allow the user to be placed in groups and control dial-in access from the outside.

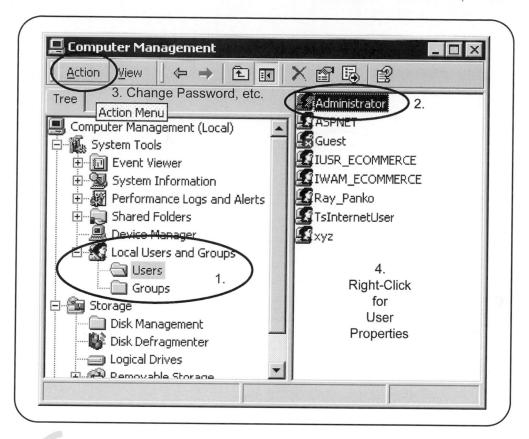

Figure 6-10   Users and Groups in Windows

Note in Item 4 that the account can be **disabled**. This allows the account to be rendered inactive if the user is on vacation. If the user is terminated, disabling the account instead of deleting it immediately will preserve its information.

Creating Users

The Action menu for users allows new user accounts to be created. If a new account is created, the systems administrator will be required to enter an account name, a password, and other information about the account. Figure 6-12 illustrates the information that must be entered. Notice that the account can be created in disabled mode and can be activated later by selecting the account, selecting properties, and unclicking the disabled box.

Windows Groups

In Figure 6-10, selecting the Groups choice instead of Users will show a list of groups. The systems administrator will be able to look at each group to see its members and to add or delete members from the group. Accounts for new employees can be created before they start and enabled when they start.

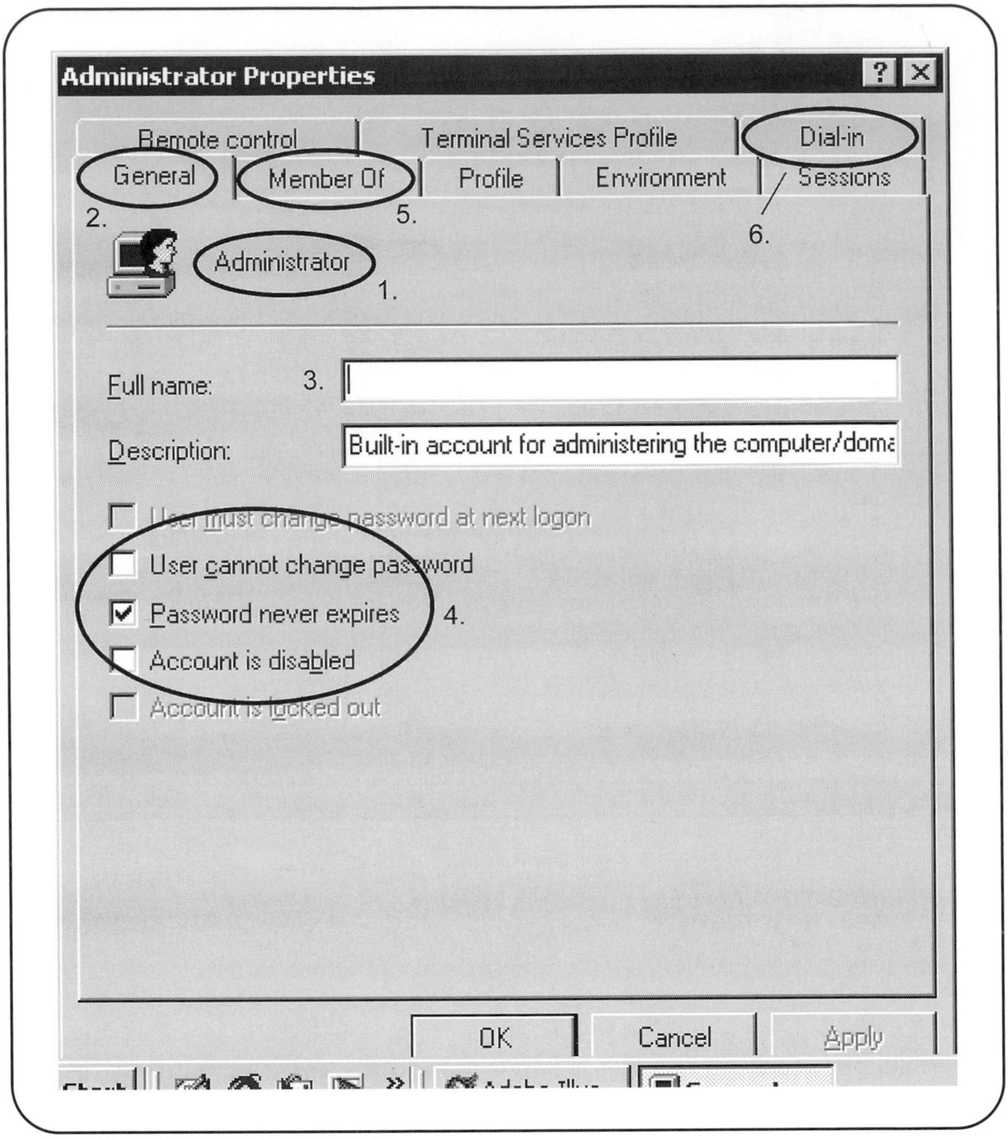

Figure 6-11   Windows User Account Properties

Windows is installed with a number of standard groups. For instance, the **Power Users** group is assigned fewer permissions by default than the Administrators group but far more permissions than the Everyone group. There is even a group for **Backup Operators** with appropriate permissions for someone engaging in that activity.

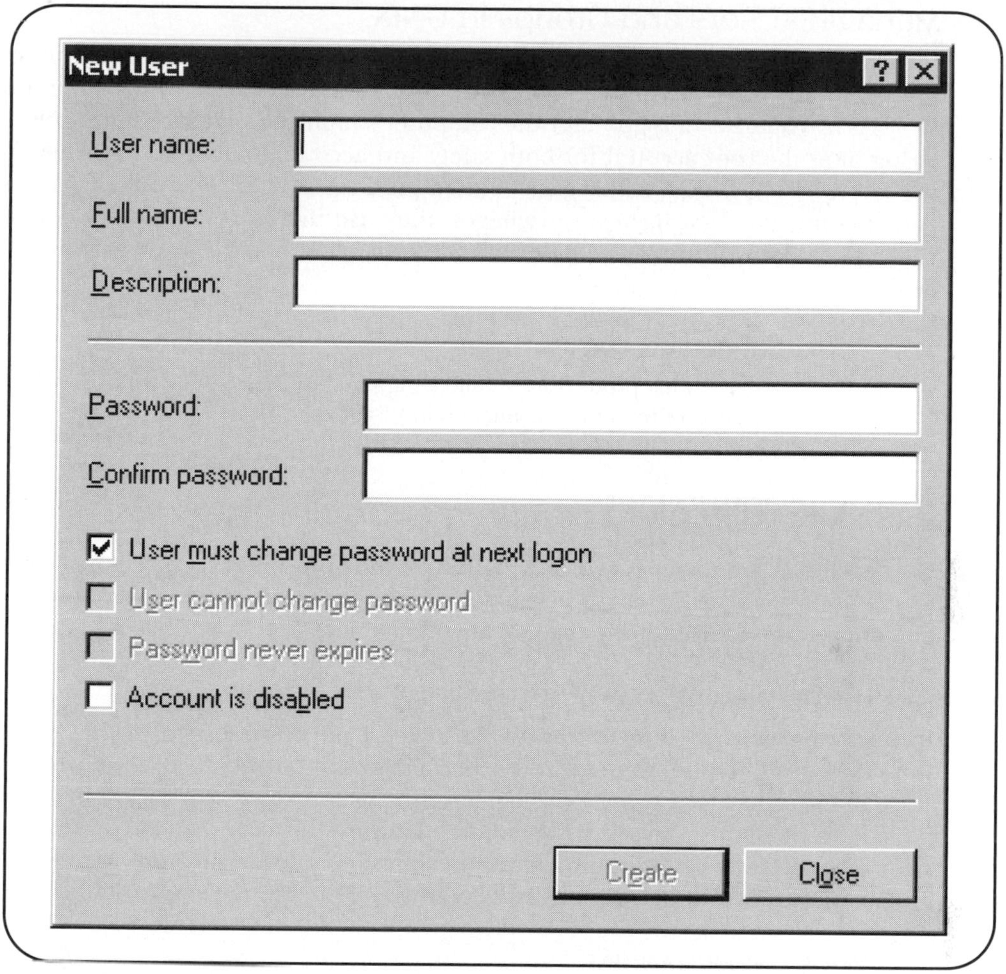

Figure 6-12 Creating a New User in Windows

Creating Users and Groups in Domains

We have been focusing on creating users and groups on stand-alone computers. However, many companies use a Windows domain strategy. Users and groups that are recognized at the domain level can log into multiple servers in the domain. The Active Directory Users and Computers MMC creates domain-wide users and groups.

TEST YOUR UNDERSTANDING

13. a) How are users and groups created on stand-alone Windows servers? b) In domains? c) What protections should be applied to the Administrator account? d) To the Guest account? e) What restrictions can be made during account setup? f) Why are standard groups that are established automatically important in Windows?

Managing Users and Groups in UNIX

It is difficult to discuss managing users and groups in UNIX because different versions of UNIX and even different LINUX distributions add users and groups differently.

As in Windows, it is good for the computer's multiple systems administrators not to log in as the root account for both safety and accountability reasons. They should log into working accounts that have limited privileges. Then, when they wish to execute a command that has root privileges, they use the **su** (switch user) command, which is similar to RunAs in Windows. And, as in Windows, the guest account should be disabled.

TEST YOUR UNDERSTANDING

14.   a) In UNIX, what protections should be applied to the root account? b) What is the UNIX analog of the RunAs command in Windows?

MANAGING PERMISSIONS

User accounts and groups must be assigned permissions for every directory or file with which users must work. These **permissions** define what the user or group can do to files and subdirectories, if they can do anything at all.

The Principle of Least Permissions

In assigning permissions, the **principle of least permissions** states that each user should be given the minimum possible permissions to be able to do their work.

If one starts at the other extreme, by giving users extensive permissions, users will be able to do almost anything they want, creating a security nightmare. It is also far safer to start with a set of minimum permissions and add permissions as needed than to start with extensive permissions and know which ones to remove to achieve security.

TEST YOUR UNDERSTANDING

15.   a) What is the principle of least permissions? b) Why is it important from a security viewpoint?

Assigning Permissions in Windows

In Windows, the systems administrator can right click on a directory or file. In Figure 6-14, the systems administrator has done this for the My Music directory and has selected Properties from the pop-up menu. The systems administrator has then selected the Security tab.

Note that the top pane shows all of the users and groups that have been assigned permissions for this directory. The Power Users group has been selected.

The lower pane shows the six **standard permissions** in Windows and shows which of these permissions have been assigned to the Power Users group. If another group or user were selected, different permissions would appear.

➤   Members of the Power Users group can see the contents of the directory (List Folder Contents),

➤   Can read files (Read),

PRINCIPLE OF LEAST PERMISSIONS: GIVE USERS THE MINIMUM
PERMISSIONS NEEDED FOR THEIR JOB

Easier to add permissions selectively than to start with many, reduce for security

ASSIGNING PERMISSIONS IN WINDOWS (FIGURE 6-14)

Right click on file or directory in My Computer
Select Properties, then Security tab
Select a user or group
Click on or off the 6 standard policies (permit or deny)
List Folder Contents
Read
Read and Execute
Write (change files)
Modify (Write plus delete)
Full Control: all permissions
For more fine-grained control, 13 special permissions collectively give the standard 6

ASSIGNING PERMISSIONS IN UNIX

ls -l shows files in a directory in long format (Figure 6-15)
first character is a - for a file, d for a directory
Only three permissions: read (only), write (change), and execute (run program)
Format is rwx for all or various combinations (r-x is read and execute but not write)
Next three characters are permissions (rwx possible) for the file owner
Next three are permissions (rwx possible) for a single group
Next three are permissions for the rest of the world
Next number is the number of links (irrelevant for our purposes)
Next comes the name of the owner
Last comes the name of the file or directory
Group might be shown, but command parameters to see the group vary
Changing permissions
umask (user mask) command sets the default permissions for future assignments
chmod (change mode) changes permissions for the file
chown (change owner) changes the ownership of a file

Figure 6-13   Managing Permissions (Study Figure)

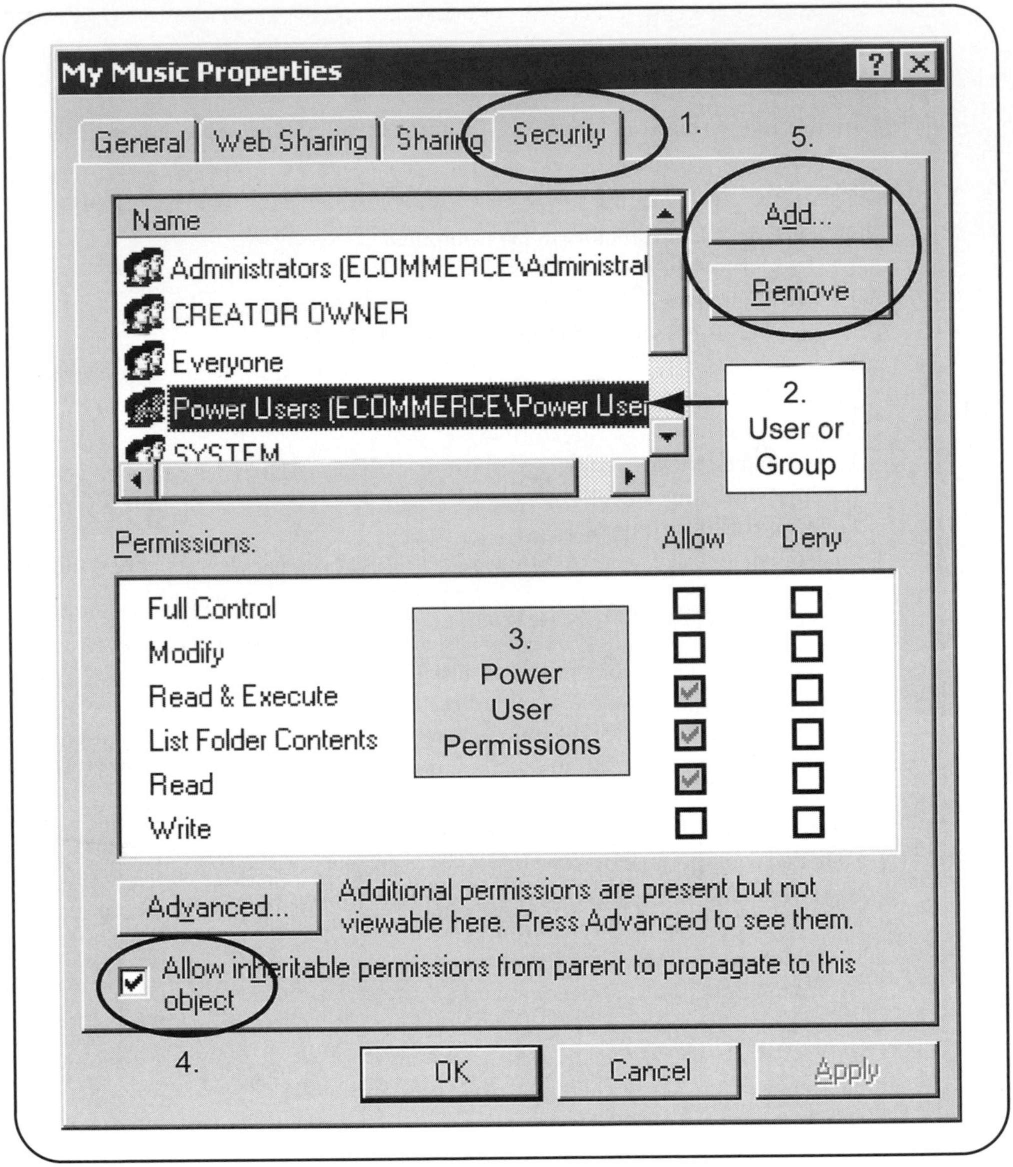

Figure 6-14 Assigning Permissions in Windows

➤ And can read and execute programs (Read and Execute).

➤ However, they may not change files (Write)

➤ Or delete files (Modify).

➤ The Full permission would give all of these permissions.

Although these standard permissions give a good range of options, sometimes more detailed permissions are needed. The advanced button on the Security tab allows permissions to be assigned in more detail if necessary. This button leads to 13 **specialized permissions** that collectively equal the 6 standard permissions.

Note that there are buttons for adding new users or groups and for removing users and groups that have been assigned permissions.

Finally, note that the box has been checked to allow permissions to be inherited from the My Music parent directory.

TEST YOUR UNDERSTANDING

16. a) How are permissions applied in Windows? b) How many permissions does Windows have?

Assigning Permissions in UNIX

Compared to access permissions in Windows, access permissions in UNIX are extremely crude. This is one of the most serious problems associated with security in UNIX computers.

The UNIX ls -l Command

UNIX is very limited in its ability to assign permissions to files and directories. To see the contents of a directory, the systems administrator (or user) can give the command "ls –l" (-L in lowercase). What the systems administrator or user sees varies among versions of UNIX, but he or she will see something like the output in Figure 6-15.

File or Directory

Each line gives information about a single file or subdirectory. The first character is a dash for a file and a "d" for a subdirectory. The end of the line gives the name of the file or the subdirectory. The first row in Figure 6-15 shows a file (purple.exe), the second a directory (reports).

Figure 6-15   Output of the UNIX ls -l Command

```
-rwxr-x---1 root  . . .  purple.exe
drw-r---- 1 brows  . . .  reports
-rw-rw-r--1 lighter  . . .  bronze.txt
```

Link and Owner

The "1" following each set of permissions indicates that the file or directory has one link, which we will not discuss because links have no direct bearing on our security concerns. Following the number of links is the account name of the directory's or file's owner.

Only Three UNIX Permissions: Read, Write, and Execute

After the first character, the next nine characters give the access permissions for the file. UNIX offers only three permissions—read, write, and execute.

> ➤ The **read** permission allows a user or group member to read a file but not change it.
> ➤ The **write** permission allows file creation, file modification, and file deletion.
> ➤ The **execute** permission is for program files; it allows the user or group member to execute the program.

Having only three permissions makes it difficult to apply appropriate protection to files and directories. In contrast, the 6 standard Windows permissions offer substantially greater granularity, and the 13 specialized Windows permissions offer all of the granularity a systems administrator would want.

Owner, Group, and World

In addition, these three permissions can be assigned to only three entities—the user owner, a single group, and the rest of the world. It is impossible to assign appropriate permissions to multiple users and to multiple groups. When this limitation is combined with the three permissions possible in UNIX, you can see that UNIX systems administrators are extremely circumscribed in their ability to assign access permissions.

Owner Permissions   Characters two, three, and four on each line generated by the ls -l command tell whether the owner has read, write, and/or execute permissions. In the first row of Figure 6-15, the bits are "rwx", meaning that the owner has all 3 permissions. In the second row, these bits are "rw-", meaning that the owner has read and write permissions but not execute permissions.

Group Permissions   The next three characters (5 through 7) give the permissions of a single group, again in rwx format. Normally, this group is the group associated with the owner in the /etc/passwd file, as discussed in Chapter 2.

On the first line in Figure 6-15, the group has the permissions "r-x," which means that members of the group can read the file and execute it (it is a program). However, they cannot change the file.

On the second line, the group has permissions "r--," which means that members of the group can read the file but cannot modify it. This is common for data files.

Rest-of-World Permissions   The next three characters (8 through 10) give permissions for the rest of the world—that is, everyone except the owner and group. For the first two files, the permissions are "---", meaning that people other than the owner and members of the group have no access permissions for the file.

Assigning Permissions

umask (User Mask)   When a user creates a file, UNIX sets the owner, group, and world permissions automatically according to the operating system default or according to the default created by the user using the **umask** command.

chmod (Change Mode)   The file owner or a root systems administrator can use the **chmod** (change mode) command to change the owner, group, or world permissions.

chown (Change Owner)   The **chown** command, in turn, is used by the file owner or systems administrator to transfer ownership of the file to another user account. The syntax is "chown *newowner filename*," so the command "chown xyz huskies.doc" transfers ownership of the file huskies.doc to the xyz account.

TEST YOUR UNDERSTANDING

    17. a) What are the 3 UNIX permissions? b) To which three individuals or groups are permissions assigned for a particular file? c) How does the specificity of UNIX file permissions compare with that of Windows? d) Is the third line in Figure 6-15 a file or a directory? e) Who is the owner? f) What is the name of the file? g) What are the owner, group, and rest-of-world permissions? h) What is the purpose of the umask command? i) What command is used to change file or directory permissions? j) What command would you give to change the ownership of the file *wall.doc* to the user *galumpke*?

ADVANCED SERVER HARDENING TECHNIQUES

Logging

Logging is the collection of data on security events in a log file. Typical security-related system events are unsuccessful logins, the changing of file permissions, the starting of programs, and computer reboots. If a security incident occurs, the systems administrator can look through the log file to understand it. More generally, systems administrators should look at the security logs daily for indications that their hardening efforts have weaknesses. Logging is a core issue for host hardening, but it will be discussed in Chapter 10 in the context of intrusion detection.

Windows Security Logging

In Windows 2000, security logging is controlled from the Computer Management MMC, through the **Event Viewer** under System Tools. This is illustrated in Figure 6-17. The default for Windows 2000 is not to log any security activities. Setting up Windows 2000 security involves adding activities to be logged and to set severity levels for each activity. However, once these log activities are selected, all are accessible centrally through the Event Viewer.

UNIX Security Logging

UNIX has a rich set of logging features, including logging for authentication (successful and unsuccessful logins); commands to change permissions; commands to start programs; commands from the kernel; and commands from the World Wide Web, e-mail, and other applications.

READING EVENT LOGS (CHAPTER 10)

The importance of logging to diagnose problems
  Failed logins, changing permissions, starting programs, kernel messages, etc.
Windows 2000 Event Viewer (Figure 6-17)
UNIX has many logging facilities controlled by syslog program (Figure 6-18)
  Syslog program sends log entries of different types to specific directories or other
    hosts
  Syslog.config specifies which log entries and which severity levels should go to which
    directories

BACKUP (CHAPTER 10)

UNIX backup
  tar command (tape archive)
  Create tape archive of a file, group of files, directory tree in a .tar file
  Can use tar to look at table of contents of files in .tar file
  Can use tar to restore one, some, or all files
Windows backup
  Start, Programs, Accessories, System Tools, Backup
  GUI to create backups, restore backups

FILE ENCRYPTION

Protects files even if attacker breaks in
Key escrow: Copy of encryption key is kept elsewhere for retrieval in case of key loss
Windows Encrypting File System (EFS)
  Select file in Windows Explorer, select Properties
  Click on General tab's Advanced button
  Click on the box Encrypt contents to secure data
  Encryption is transparent: Save, retrieve, copy files as usual
  Generally cannot be sent over the network
  Recovery agent (usually on the domain controller) for key escrow

FILE INTEGRITY CHECKER

Creates snapshot of files: hashed signatures
After an attack, compares post-hack signature with snapshot
Determines which files were changed
Tripwire is the usual file integrity checker for UNIX (Figure 6-19)
If applied to too many files, too many false alarms will occur
Must be selective—core programs likely to be Trojanized during attacks

SERVER HOST FIREWALLS

Rules can be specific to the server's role (e-mail, etc.)

Figure 6-16 Advanced Server Hardening Techniques (Study Figure)

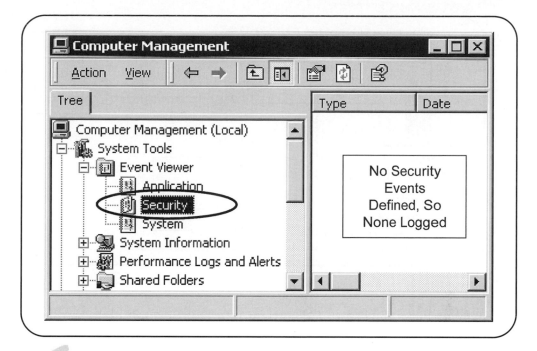

Figure 6-17   Windows 2000 Event Viewer for Logging

As Figure 6-18 shows, the **syslog** program sends log entries to various directories or even to other computers running the syslog program. (Sending log entries to another computer ensures that hackers cannot delete the log files after taking over the computer, although they can stop further logging.)

The syslog program is controlled by the **syslog.config** file, which specifies what to do with different log entries. Each line has a log service, a dot, and a severity level, followed by a space and the directory or computer to which entries of that security level for that log service should be sent.

TEST YOUR UNDERSTANDING

18. a) List some security-related system logging events. b) What snap-in is used to manage logging in Windows? c) Which program is used to manage where logging events are stored in UNIX? d) Does this program store log files locally or on other machines?

Backup

Backup also is a core host hardening issue, not an advanced one. However, backup will be covered in Chapter 10 in the context of disaster recovery. In this chapter, we will merely discuss some of the mechanics of backup.

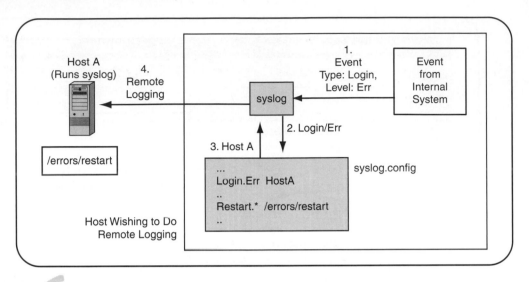

Figure 6-18 Syslog in UNIX

UNIX Backup: tar

Different UNIX systems offer different advanced backup methods, but the core UNIX backup command is **tar** (tape archive). This command creates archives of individual files, groups of files, or entire trees of directories and subdirectories. The tar command places all of this information into a single large file with the .tar file extension.

After a tar file is created, the systems administrator can use the tar command to look at its table of contents to determine what files are there. The systems administrator also can use the tar command to restore all files or selected files.

Windows Backup

Windows, of course, has a GUI backup wizard. The systems administrator goes to the Start button, then Programs, selects Accessories, then Systems Tools (not Administrative Tools), and then Backup. This wizard can be used to back up files or to restore files from backups.

TEST YOUR UNDERSTANDING

19.   a) What is the backup command in UNIX? b) What does it allow a systems administrator to do? c) How does a systems administrator archive and restore files in Windows?

File Encryption

The Need for File Encryption

From time to time, attackers will be able to break through all protections and take over the computer. In such cases, they will be able to read every file in every directory—unless the files are encrypted, and unless they cannot find the decryption key somewhere on the system.

Key Escrow

Although encryption provides a last line of defense, even owners cannot decrypt encrypted files without the decryption key. Given the frequency at which users forget their passwords, one could expect the frequent loss of decryption keys. In addition, disgruntled employees who are terminated might refuse to give the firm their decryption key. If encryption is used, it is important to implement **key escrow**, in which a copy of the decryption key is stored on the computer of a trusted party so that files still can be decrypted if the key is lost.

The Windows Encrypting File System (EFS)

Microsoft Windows 2000 offers the **Encrypting File System (EFS)**, which automates file and directory encryption.

Encrypting a Directory or File   To apply EFS, a user selects a directory or file in Windows Explorer, right clicks on it, and chooses Properties. The user selects the General tab's Advanced Button. The user then clicks on the box labeled "Encrypt contents to secure data."

Transparent During Saves and Retrievals   Afterward, the operating system will work with the file or directory seamlessly. When the user opens an encrypted file, Windows will decrypt it automatically. When a user saves an encrypted file or saves a new file to an encrypted directory, the file will be encrypted automatically. EFS even encrypts temporary copies of encrypted files that application programs create during the editing process.

Different Keys for Different Files in Each Directory   If a directory is selected, each file gets a different encryption key so that individual encrypted files can be copied to other directories, even unencrypted directories. However, encryption and decryption are local to the computer. Encrypted files cannot be sent to other computers and decrypted there, except in the special case of recovery agents, which are described next.

Key Escrow Through Recovery Agents   EFS has built-in key escrow. A copy of each decryption key is sent to a **recovery agent**, which usually is located on a domain controller but can be located on a client. If the key is lost and file encryption needs to be broken, the file can be sent to the recovery agent, which would be able to decrypt it.

TEST YOUR UNDERSTANDING

20. a) Why is file encryption dangerous? b) Why is key escrow needed? c) What actions are needed to encrypt files or directories in Windows? d) Explain how the Windows EFS is transparent to users. e) How is key escrow administered in EFS?

File Integrity Checkers

When attackers take over systems, they are likely to replace some files with Trojan horses or add viruses to these files. Defenders need to be able to look at a system that has been attacked and determine quickly and accurately which files have been changed. **File integrity checkers** make this possible.

Tripwire Operation

On UNIX systems, the dominant file integrity checker is **Tripwire**. Figure 6-19 shows how Tripwire works. The process is similar in other file integrity checkers.

First, the Tripwire is run against a trusted **reference base**, that is, against the computer's files at a time when the files are trusted. It does no good to run a file integrity checker only after an attack.

Next, Tripwire creates **signatures** for the files, most typically using the MD5 algorithm that will be discussed in Chapter 7. Signatures are relatively short bit strings—often only 128 bits per file. The signatures are stored in a **signature base**.

After an attack, the systems administrator recomputes the signatures of the files and looks for any changes in signatures from those in the reference base. Signature computation is sensitive. Even if only a few bits are changed and if the length of a file is left constant by the change, the signature of a changed file will be different than its original signature. The systems administrator can develop a list of changed files quickly.

Intrusion Detection and File Policies to Reduce False Positives

Tripwire and other file integrity checkers also can act as intrusion detection systems, periodically recomputing the signatures of the files and sending alarms if changes are detected. However, there are legitimate reasons for some files to change, so if all files are placed in the reference base, the systems administrator will be deluged with false alarms.

In general, it is important for the systems administrator to plan carefully before using Tripwire, selecting only files that should not change except under attack. This list of files is called the **file policy**. Often, only the system files needed to run the operating system are included, but this allows attackers to Trojanize application program files.

Figure 6-19   Tripwire File Integrity Checker

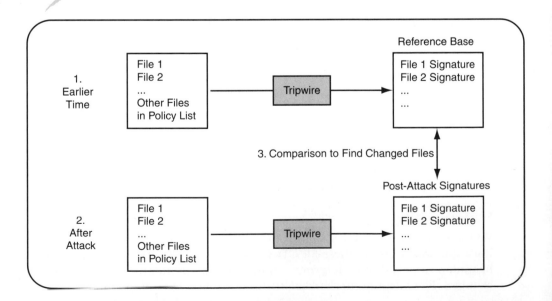

If application program files are placed in the file policy list, then the base signatures must be recomputed each time applications are added. This increases safety, but it also adds work.

Not Good for Data Files

File integrity checkers are not good protectors for data files, which change frequently. Signatures for data files would have to be recomputed constantly, and it would be difficult to know which data file changes were legitimate and which were made during attacks.

Signatures Are Targets for Intruders

Another consideration is that attackers often will look for and attempt to destroy the signature base on the computer. This signature base must be protected, perhaps even by saving it on another machine or at least copying it to another machine.

TEST YOUR UNDERSTANDING

21.   a) What is the purpose of file integrity checkers? b) What is the most popular file integrity checker in UNIX? c) Briefly, how does a systems administrator use Tripwire? d) What are some problems with using Tripwire? e) How do attackers attempt to thwart Tripwire?

Server Host Firewalls

As we saw in Chapter 5, firewalls intercept incoming packets and outgoing packets to detect and drop attack packets. We also saw that border firewalls have a difficult job because they must have rules that reflect dozens to hundreds of internal computers. In contrast, host firewalls on individual hosts need to reflect only the characteristics of the host they are guarding. Consequently, they can be extremely precise.

TESTING FOR VULNERABILITIES

Even if companies attempt to be diligent about implementing protections, they might make mistakes due to the complexities of many protections. **Vulnerability assessment tools** attempt to find weaknesses in a firm's protection suite, giving the systems administrator an understanding of what work still needs to be done.

UNIX

We will begin with UNIX because UNIX developers have created many vulnerability assessment tools, many of which are free. We will consider three classes of vulnerability assessment tools: external auditing tools, host assessment tools, and network monitoring tools. Figure 6-20 shows how these tools are related.

External Auditing Tools

The first class of tools, **external auditing tools**, run on another machine—the **auditing computer**. The auditing computer sends a series of attack probes at the target system, noting which attacks succeeded. After the audit, the auditing computer prepares a

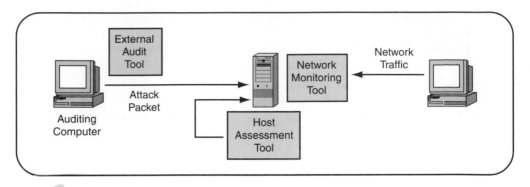

Figure 6-20 Types of UNIX Vulnerability Assessment Tools

report documenting actions that need to be taken to remove the weaknesses discovered during the audit. In UNIX, *Nessus* is the most popular external auditing tool.

Of course, attackers also like to use external auditing tools to find weaknesses in the system. It is important for firms to run auditing tools before attackers do, so that they can see what attackers would see and fix deficiencies before attackers can exploit them.

Host Assessment Tools

In turn, **host assessment tools** sit on the computer being studied. These tools look at the computer's registry and internal settings to find elements that do not fit a security baseline. After the internal assessment, these tools report deviations and actions that need to be taken to alleviate them. On UNIX systems, *Tara* is a popular host assessment system.

Network Monitoring Tools

Network monitoring tools, in contrast to the first two tools, look outward from the host being studied. They look at arriving packets for indications of external attacks, and they are similar to firewalls in what they consider. *PortSentry* is a popular network monitoring system on UNIX hosts.

The Microsoft Baseline Security Analyzer (MBSA)

To look for host weaknesses, Microsoft has produced a tool called the **Microsoft Baseline Security Analyzer (MBSA)**. MBSA scans one or more systems for a wide range of security weaknesses, including patches that need to be installed, insecure configuration practices, the running of unnecessary services, accounts without passwords or with extremely weak passwords (such as *password*), and many other weaknesses.

In addition to looking at Windows, MBSA looks at the most widely used Microsoft applications, including its IIS webserver product, SQL server, Internet Explorer, Office, and Outlook. As discussed in Chapter 9, it is common to attack computers by taking over applications. MBSA scrutinizes the most commonly compromised applications.

MBSA can be installed on individual hosts for self-analysis or on a central server to scan some or all hosts in a domain. The latter approach greatly simplifies the life of the domain administrator.

Although MBSA is attractive, it is still rather limited. It does not even check all of the products it examines for security patches, and it looks at only some security configuration weaknesses.

In addition, it runs only on Windows NT, 2000, and XP. Most firms still have large numbers of Windows 98, ME, and older clients, and these are not examined.

Perhaps most vexingly, if MBSA identifies missing security patches, it does nothing to download them automatically. MBSA, in the final analysis, is a good first step for Windows analysis.

TEST YOUR UNDERSTANDING

22. a) Why is vulnerability assessment done? b) Distinguish among the three types of vulnerability assessment in UNIX. c) Describe MBSA.

HARDENING CLIENTS

The Importance of Clients

Valuable Information on the Client

As servers become increasingly difficult to attack, hackers are beginning to focus more of their attention on easier prey—"soft and juicy" client PCs. Once considered unimportant because of their limited information, client PCs are now rich repositories of information interesting to hackers, including credit card numbers and other identity information and proprietary corporate information.

Short-Circuiting Corporate Protections

In addition, many clients are connected to their organizational networks via remote access, as Chapter 8 discusses. Often, remote access users have their computers remember their login user names and passwords. If hackers take over such a PC, they have carte blanche access to every file and program the compromised client user has permission to use. The firewall will simply wave them through, and hosts will welcome them with open arms. With a compromised client PC, the attacker can short-circuit almost all corporate protections.

Enforcing Good Practice

Corporations would like to enforce good practice on remote PCs, especially home PCs. However, few users understand the importance of strong security, and many more will circumvent any security their companies ask them to employ because of the inconvenience of security.

Patches

First, it is critical for users to download patches (updates) for Windows itself, for integral Windows software such as Internet Explorer and Outlook, and for all application programs users have on their PCs. These programs are as full of holes as Swiss cheese, and failing to patch them makes them easy to compromise.

Unfortunately, client patching is rarely done. Although it is not overly difficult, it is still somewhat complex. In training programs, employees should be given hands-on training in how to install patches to make the task more familiar.

IMPORTANCE OF CLIENTS

Contain important information
If taken over, can get in as user, passing through firewalls and other protections

ENFORCING GOOD PRACTICE

Patching
Antivirus software
Firewall software
Limiting client software to an approved list (e.g., forbidding P2P file exchange products)
Prohibit saving passwords
File encryption

CENTRAL CONTROL IS NEEDED

For example, Microsoft Group Policy Objects (GPOs) for home clients
Require certain programs (antivirus, etc.); forbid programs not on list
Even lock down desktop
Central vulnerability scanning
Difficult to enforce on personally owned home computers

Figure 6-21   Hardening Clients (Study Figure)

Antivirus Software

Many users still fail to implement antivirus software, although they are getting better about doing so. Furthermore, many who do implement antivirus software fail to update it regularly, fail to scan their systems regularly, and fail to scan all incoming mail and web-page downloads. They turn off scanning because it slows them down when they work.

In addition, antivirus software only works with common programs, such as e-mail and browsers. If users have instant messaging or are using a peer-to-peer file sharing program, the antivirus program usually will not even notice file transfers, much less scan them.

Firewall Software

As noted in Chapter 5, firewall and antivirus software are complementary, not either/or choices. Firewalls stop many types of attacks that antivirus programs do not see. However, client host firewalls tend to be application firewalls that provide protection to some applications but not to others. Many, fortunately, also offer NAT protection, which is surprisingly effective for protecting client PCs if users do not download files through their own actions.

However, few users install personal firewalls, as host client firewalls are commonly called. They often fail to see the need, arguing that they already have antivirus software.

Personal firewalls are easy to use. When an application first tries to send or receive to the outside world, the firewall interrupts the user and asks if the connection should be allowed. Although this is a simple process, many users are disconcerted by alarm interruptions and often do not have the vaguest idea of whether they should allow a particular connection. They often turn off their firewalls in fear and confusion.

Limiting Client Software to an Approved List

Corporations realize that rogue software on remote access PCs is a huge security problem. On company-owned PCs, firms often forbid the installation of anything not on an approved list of software. Users, however, often circumvent these restrictions.

Save Passwords

As just noted, Windows has the ability to save passwords so that users will not have to remember them. However, this means that anyone walking up to their computer can log in as them, including a hacker who takes over the computer. Companies often forbid saving passwords in Windows, but users frequently circumvent this protection.

File Encryption

Finally, although file encryption would make it difficult for attackers to read user information, few users know how to use file encryption, and companies are worried about the key escrow problem if they did.

Central Control

Realizing that users—especially home users—will not be willing to take the steps they need to take, many corporations now implement central control over remote PCs.

For example, in Windows, home computers can be members of a domain. A group policy object (GPO) can be applied to home computers. The GPO can control what software is on the home PC, including ensuring that antivirus software is used on the PC and ensuring that rogue software is not installed. The GPO can even control the user's desktop.

Other central control software can scan the client PC periodically to look for vulnerabilities. Unfortunately, this software can seldom install patches by itself.

Although central control is attractive, it is difficult to enforce, especially if the user is accessing the corporate network through a personally-owned PC. Users understandably tend to reject the idea that their home PC should be controlled.

TEST YOUR UNDERSTANDING

23.   a) Why is it important to protect client PCs? b) What protections should be applied to client PCs? c) Why are these protections difficult to apply to client PCs? d) What tool does Windows use to centralize client security? e) What protections can this tool enforce? f) Why is it problematic for employees to use personally owned PCs to access corporate servers remotely?

CONCLUSION

The host is the last line of defense for thwarting attacks. It is important to harden all hosts. This is especially true for servers and routers, but it is also true for client PCs. An attacker can use a compromised client PC to circumvent firewalls and all other defenses.

We focused on Windows because it is widely used. We focused on Windows 2000 because it is the first version of Windows to offer strong security. Windows 2000 introduced Active Directory's powerful potential for central management, including GPOs. However, the difficulty of deploying Active Directory means that many Windows 2000 servers are stand-alone servers. We looked at many elements of Windows security, which uses GUI tools, especially MMCs.

We also focused on UNIX because of its widespread use. Unfortunately, it is difficult to talk specifically about UNIX because several versions of UNIX exist, and they offer different systems administration tools, including security tools. On PCs, LINUX is a family of UNIX versions; although all versions of LINUX use the same LINUX kernel, they are offered as "distributions" that use many other programs, including security programs, and these programs vary among distributions. Although UNIX offers some graphical user interfaces, many security tools must be run from command-line shells.

A key concept in host hardening is the need to have a security baseline that tells the systems administrator what to do. Host security is much too complex for informal planning and implementation.

One aspect of host hardening that was not considered in this chapter is application security. If attackers can take over an application, they usually can execute commands with the permission of the compromised application—often root privileges. Application hardening is perhaps the most crucial aspect of host hardening today. However, application hardening often uses encryption, so we will discuss it in Chapter 9, after two cryptography chapters.

THOUGHT QUESTIONS

1. Why do you think companies often fail to harden their servers adequately?
2. Why do you think companies often fail to harden their clients adequately?
3. Do you think the diversity of UNIX is good or bad?
4. Why is it better to start with minimal permissions and services and add them as needed rather than to begin with a broad set of permissions and services and remove them to enhance security?
5. Why do you think UNIX has such a limited ability to assign permissions compared to Windows?

TROUBLESHOOTING QUESTION

1. You kill some services but see that they are running again the next day. What did you do wrong?

CHAPTER 7

THE ELEMENTS OF CRYPTOGRAPHY

Learning Objectives

By the end of this chapter, you should be able to discuss:

- Basic cryptography concepts, including the importance of key length.
- Encryption for confidentiality, including symmetric key encryption and public key encryption.
- Encryption (and other processes) for authentication, including applicants versus verifiers, hashing, challenge-response authentication, message-by-message authentication (and integrity), the need for digital certificates, and public key infrastructures (PKIs).
- Replay attacks, in which a message interceptor retransmits an intercepted encrypted message without modification.

CRYPTOGRAPHIC ELEMENTS AND SYSTEMS

Cryptographic Systems

In the last two chapters, we have looked at attack prevention systems. Many times, however, two parties simply wish to communicate securely. Figure 7-1 shows that secure communication often takes place under the protection of a **cryptographic system**, in which software processes used by the two communicating partners implement security automatically, often without the awareness of the communicating parties.

Cryptographic systems provide four types of protection to a conversation's messages.

➤ **Confidentiality:** Protection against eavesdroppers understanding intercepted messages.

➤ **Authentication:** Assurance that senders are who they claim to be.

➤ **Message integrity:** Assurance that the message has not been changed en route.

➤ **Anti-replay protection:** Assurance that if an attacker captures a message and transmits it again later, the receiver will not accept the message.

Cryptographic Elements

In this chapter, we will look at the *elements* of cryptographic systems, including encryption for confidentiality, encryption and other processes for authentication, secure key exchange, and anti-replay protection. In the next chapter, we will look at the most important cryptographic systems and learn how they use the cryptographic elements we will see in this chapter to protect conversations.

TEST YOUR UNDERSTANDING

1. a) What are the four protections offered by cryptographic systems? b) Distinguish between what we will study in this chapter and in the next chapter.

ENCRYPTION FOR CONFIDENTIALITY

The term **cryptography** literally means "secret writing." It originally was created as a way to prevent unauthorized people from reading messages. In other words, it was created for confidentiality. We also will see that encryption can be used for other forms of protection, including authentication and message integrity.

Figure 7-1   Cryptographic System

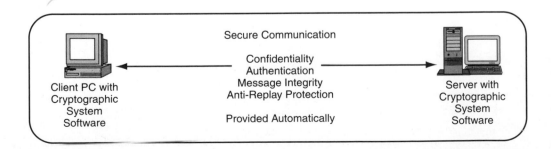

Plaintext, Encryption, Decryption, and Ciphertext

Plaintext

As Figure 7-2 shows, the original message to be sent is called the **plaintext**. This name may seem to imply that only text messages can be protected, but a plaintext message can be graphics, voice, or anything else. The "text" in its name exists for historical reasons—early cryptography actually was limited to text messages. Today that limitation no longer applies.

Encryption and Ciphertext

Figure 7-2 shows that applying **encryption** to the plaintext creates something else called **ciphertext**. Encryption is a mathematical process, and we will look at several popular encryption algorithms later. The ciphertext that encryption produces looks like a random stream of ones and zeros to anyone intercepting the message.

Decryption

When the ciphertext message reaches the authorized receiver, the receiver is able to **decrypt** the message, that is, apply a mathematical process that regenerates the original plaintext. Although unauthorized parties cannot read the ciphertext message en route, the authorized receiver can read the deciphered plaintext.

Keys

Encryption Methods and Keys

Figure 7-2 shows that encryption processes have two parts. One is a mathematical algorithm (the **encryption method**), which is used in the same way on all messages. The

Figure 7-2   Plaintext, Encryption, Ciphertext, and Decryption

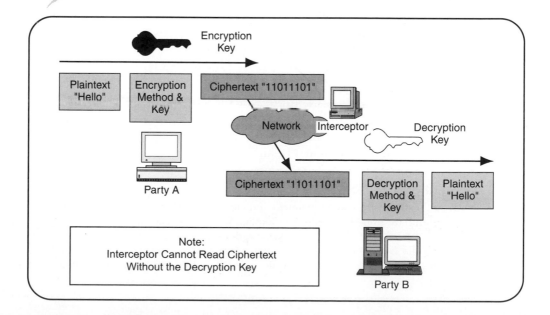

other is a **key**, which is a string of bits. Different keys produce different ciphertexts from the same plaintext even when the same method is used.

Only a few encryption methods have been developed, so it is impossible in practice to keep the encryption method secret. Consequently, communicating partners must keep their encryption keys secret.

Encryption and Decryption Keys

Note the two keys in Figure 7-2: an **encryption key** and a **decryption key**. We will see later in this chapter that sometimes the encryption and decryption keys are the same, but sometimes they are different.

Exhaustive Search

In Chapter 2, we saw that attackers often try to guess passwords by brute force, that is, trying all possible passwords. Similarly, interceptors often try to use **exhaustive search** to guess keys. In an exhaustive search, interceptors try all possible keys to see which one will decrypt the ciphertext. Given enough time, they will succeed.

Key Length

However, just as long passwords make password guessing impractical, long keys make exhaustive searches impractical. *Every additional bit doubles search time*, so adding even a few bits to a key's length greatly increases the time needed to do exhaustive search. Figure 7-3 shows how rapidly the number of possible keys needed in exhaustive searches grows as key length grows.

Changing Keys Frequently

In addition to using long keys, it is important to change keys frequently. **Cryptanalysts** (professionals who specialize in the breaking of encryption) often use attacks that require the capture of a large amount of ciphertext. If keys are changed frequently, such attacks become extremely difficult and perhaps impossible because not enough ciphertext is sent with each key to permit cryptanalysis.

Cryptography for Authentication

Traditionally, encryption was used primarily for confidentiality. However, encryption also is used widely today for authentication. In authentication, a party might try to authenticate itself by proving that it knows something that no one else could possibly know. This secret information may be an encryption key.

TEST YOUR UNDERSTANDING

2. a) Distinguish between plaintext and ciphertext. b) Do encryption methods and keys both have to be kept secret? c) Explain how an attacker uses exhaustive searching to crack keys. d) How does a long key length make cracking difficult? e) What does increasing the key size by one bit do to exhaustive search time? f) What else can be done to thwart key cracking? g) Is encryption used for confidentiality, authentication, or both?

KEY LENGTH IN BITS	NUMBER OF POSSIBLE KEYS
1	2
2	4
4	16
8	256
16	65,536
40	1,099,511,627,776
56	72,057,594,037,927,900
112	5,192,296,858,534,830,000,000,000,000,000,000
112	5.1923E+33
168	3.74144E+50
256	1.15792E+77
512	1.3408E+154

Notes: Shaded keys, with lengths of more than 100 bits, are considered strong symmetric keys today.

Unshaded keys, with lengths of less than 100 bits, are considered weak symmetric keys today.

Public key/private key pairs must be much longer to be strong because of the disastrous consequences of learning someone's private key and because private keys cannot be changed frequently.

Figure 7-3   Key Length and Number of Possible Keys

ENCRYPTION FOR CONFIDENTIALITY WITH SYMMETRIC KEY ENCRYPTION

In general, two types of encryption methods exist: symmetric key encryption methods and public key encryption methods. We will look at how both of them are used to provide confidentiality.

Symmetric Key Encryption: A Single Key

In Figure 7-4, both sides use the same key. A method that uses a single key for both encryption and decryption in both directions is a **symmetric key encryption** method. Each side encrypts with this single key when it sends a message, and each side decrypts with this single key when it receives a message. In other words, the encryption key is the same as the decryption key in both directions.

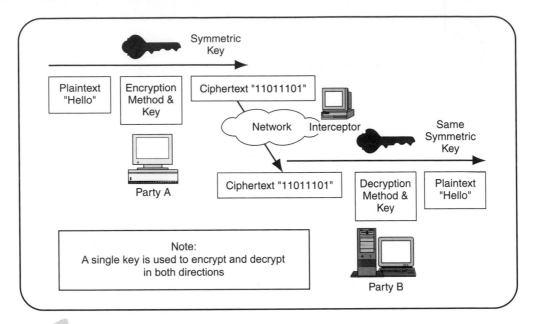

Figure 7-4   Symmetric Key Encryption for Confidentiality

Symmetric Key Encryption Methods

Symmetric key exchange is a family of encryption algorithms. Communication partners always use a *specific* symmetric key method in cryptographic systems. Only a few popular symmetric key encryption methods are in use today.

Data Encryption Standard (DES)

In 1977, the U.S. National Bureau of Standards, which is now the National Institute of Standards and Technology (NIST), created the **Data Encryption Standard (DES)**. DES quickly became the most widely used symmetric key encryption method—a position it is slowly beginning to lose to newer methods.

64-Bit Block Encryption

Figure 7-5 shows that DES is a **block encryption** method that encrypts messages 64 bits at a time. The two inputs for each block are a 64-bit encryption key and 64 bits of plaintext. The output is 64 bits of ciphertext.

56-Bit Key Size

Although the DES key has 64 bits, DES is more properly (and generally) called a 56-bit encryption standard. Eight of the 64 bits are redundant in the sense that they can be computed from the other 56 bits. This is done to detect spurious keys.

Fifty-six bits is a rather small key size for major financial transactions and highly sensitive trade secrets. However, it is sufficient for most consumer applications, and, as noted later, DES has been extended to 3DES for industrial-strength security.

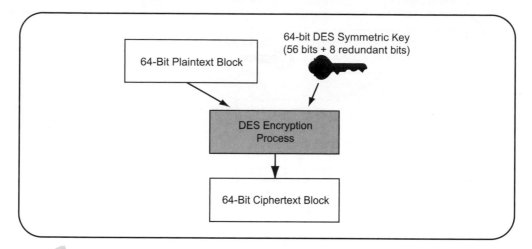

Figure 7-5 Data Encryption Standard (DES)

Attractions of DES

DES currently dominates encryption because it is well developed, has survived everything except painful brute-force exhaustive search attacks, is widely available, and is even supported by hardware accelerators.

DES-CBC (DES-Cipher Block Chaining)

One problem with simple DES is that the same input plaintext always gives the same output ciphertext. This provides opportunities for skilled cryptanalysts to break the DES key. (Recall that cryptanalysts are professionals who attempt to break encryption methods.)

CBC (Cipher Block Chaining)

Consequently, most DES implementations use **DES-CBC**, where CBC stands for **Cipher Block Chaining**. As Figure 7-6 shows, encryption has three inputs. Obviously, it has the key and the plaintext as inputs. In addition, it takes as an input the ciphertext from the *previous block*. This way, the same 64-bit plaintext will not always result in the same 64-bit ciphertext, foiling cryptanalysis (or at least making it much more difficult).

Initialization Vector (IV)

This approach does not work for the first block because there is no prior block of ciphertext to use as an input. As Figure 7-6 shows, the first block receives as its input a 64-bit **initialization vector (IV)** instead of a previous block of ciphertext.

Weak and Strong Symmetric Keys

In symmetric key encryption, keys shorter than 100 bits are considered to be **weak keys** that should not be used beyond consumer e-commerce, and even for that, 56 bits are uncomfortably few.

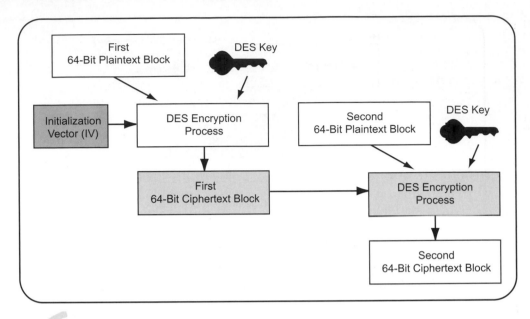

Figure 7-6   DES-CBC (DES-Cipher Block Chaining)

For symmetric keys, **strong keys** today are 100 bits or longer. However, if trans-actions are sensitive, such as major financial transactions, longer keys are needed. Also, as computer processing power improves, 100-bit keys no longer will be strong for any use.

As we will see in this section, newer approaches offer key lengths ranging from 112 to 256 bits in length. Given the fact that strength grows exponentially with key length, this range of key lengths represents an enormous range of encryption strengths.

However, in many computer systems, users only have to type brief passwords and **pass phrases** to generate keys. If these passwords and pass phrases are weak, as they tend to be if users are allowed to select them without complexity requirements, then the keys will not be strong.

Triple DES (3DES)

Where stronger security than DES is needed, many firms turn to **triple DES (3DES)**, which extends the effective key size of DES in a rather simple way, as Figure 7-7 illustrates.

168-Bit 3DES Operation

Normally, the sender and receiver use three DES keys to do the triple encryption. This effectively gives a key length of 168 bits (3 times 56), which is strong enough today even for large bank transactions. More specifically, as Figure 7-7 shows, the sender encrypts the plaintext with the first key, then *decrypts* the output of the first step with the second key, and finally encrypts the output of the second step with the third key. This gives the ciphertext to be sent.

168-BIT ENCRYPTION WITH THREE 56-BIT KEYS

SENDER	RECEIVER
Encrypts plaintext with the 1st key	Decrypts ciphertext with the 3d key
Decrypts output of first step with the 2nd key	Encrypts output of first step with the 2nd key
Encrypts output of second step with the 3d key; gives the ciphertext to be sent	Decrypts output of second step with the 1st key; gives the original plaintext

112-BIT ENCRYPTION WITH TWO 56-BIT KEYS

SENDER	RECEIVER
Encrypts plaintext with the 1st key	Decrypts ciphertext with the 1st key
Decrypts output with the 2nd key	Encrypts output with the 2nd key
Encrypts output with the 1st key	Decrypts output with the 1st key

56-BIT ENCRYPTION WITH ONE 56-BIT KEY (FOR COMPATIBILITY WITH RECEIVERS WHO CAN HANDLE ONLY NORMAL DES)

SENDER	RECEIVER
Encrypts plaintext with the key	Decrypts ciphertext with the key
Decrypts output with the key (undoes first step)	
Encrypts output with the key	

Figure 7-7   Triple DES (3DES)

The receiver, in turn, decrypts the ciphertext with the third key, *encrypts* the output of the first step with the second key, and finally decrypts the output of the second step with the first key. This gives the original plaintext.

Reversibility of Encryption and Decryption

To *decrypt* for confidentiality in the second stage of sending might seem odd. However, in DES and many other algorithms, encryption and decryption work in such a way that you can use decryption to produce ciphertext that can be turned back to plaintext with encryption.

Encrypt-Decrypt-Encrypt

Does the pattern of encrypting, decrypting, and then encrypting again seem odd? The reason is that this method works even if the two parties share only a single DES key. Encrypting plaintext with a DES key and then decrypting the output of the first step with the same key returns the plaintext. The third encryption, then, is equivalent to traditional single DES. This means that the same software can be used to encrypt both 3DES and simple DES. In addition, a receiver that implements only simple DES will be able to work with a 3DES sender and vice versa if a single key is used for 3DES. Of course, the effective key length is still only 56 bits because only a single key is used.

112-Bit 3DES

A variant of 3DES offers 112-bit[1] encryption by using only two keys. In this approach, the third operation of the sender is to encrypt the output of the second step with the *first* key, and the first action of the receiver is to decrypt the ciphertext with the first key.

Perspective on 3DES

From a security standpoint, 3DES gives strong symmetric key encryption. However, from a practical point of view, having to encrypt three times is processing intensive. Although 3DES is safe, it is slow and uses a great deal of RAM. For hand-held devices and even for client PCs, 3DES is not practical.

Advanced Encryption Standard (AES)

In response to the obsolescence of DES and the processing burdens of 3DES, NIST has released a new **Advanced Encryption Standard (AES)**, which is efficient enough in terms of processing power and RAM requirements to use on a wide variety of devices—even cellular telephones and personal digital assistants (PDAs).[2] Figure 7-8 compares AES to other symmetric encryption methods.

In addition, AES offers multiple key lengths that can be tailored to different levels of security threats. Specifically, AES offers three optional key lengths: 128 bits, 192 bits, and 256 bits. Even 128-bit AES is strong. A brute-force code-breaking system that could defeat 56-bit DES in a second would take over 100 trillion years to crack 128-bit AES. Still, for the most secure financial transactions, 192-bit and 256-bit keys are needed. AES is now supported by a number of cryptographic systems.

Other Encryption Methods

IDEA

The Pretty Good Privacy (PGP) cryptographic system, which is used primarily for the protection of e-mail, often uses the IDEA encryption method, which uses 128-bit block encryption.

RC4

The RC4 encryption method uses 40-bit keys. Such keys are far too short for good security. (Hardware exists to crack an RC4 key in about 5 hours.) RC4 is used primarily where laws prohibit the use of longer keys. Unfortunately, 40-bit RC4 is imple-

---

[1]   This is sometimes called 128-bit encryption because each DES key has 64 bits, although only 56 bits are unique. The remaining 8 can be computed from the unique 56 bits.

[2]   3DES requires 48 rounds of processing for encryption. AES only requires 9 to 13 rounds, depending on key size. Although the rounds in 3DES and AES are not completely comparable, this comparison gives you a feeling for why AES is so much faster than 3DES.

	DES	3DES	AES
Key Length (bits)	56	112 or 168	128, 192, 256
Strength	Weak	Strong	Strong
Processing Requirements	Moderate	High	Modest
RAM Requirements	Moderate	High	Modest

Figure 7-8   DES, 3DES, and AES Symmetric Key Encryption Methods

mented on many systems, including 802.11 WEP systems (discussed in Chapter 2). It is easy to use this option by accident.

Efficiency of Symmetric Key Encryption for Long Messages

Symmetric key encryption algorithms in general are fairly efficient, allowing even simple devices to encrypt and decrypt without devoting most of their processing cycles to these processes. Symmetric key encryption is efficient enough to be used even for long messages.

Almost all applications—including e-mail, World Wide Web access, FTP, IM, and database—have long messages and so require symmetric key encryption for confidentiality. In contrast to the public key encryption methods we will see next, symmetric key encryption can be used for **bulk encryption**—encrypting messages and files of normal (long) lengths.

> Almost all applications—including e-mail, World Wide Web access, FTP, IM, and database—have long messages and so require symmetric key encryption for confidentiality. Public key encryption is too processing intensive for confidentiality, although it can be used for authentication and key distribution.

TEST YOUR UNDERSTANDING

3. How many keys are used in symmetric key encryption in two-way conversations between two parties?

4. a) What is the most popular symmetric key encryption method? b) How long is its key? c) How does DES-CBC differ from simple DES?

5. a) Is the DES key strong or weak? Explain. b) How long is a strong symmetric key today? c) Under what circumstances must even longer symmetric key lengths be used? d) Why can the use of passwords and pass phrases make key strength meaningless?

6. Triple DES, like simple DES, uses 56-bit keys. How does 3DES provide longer effective key length? Give a simple answer. Do not go into the detailed process.

7. a) Compare DES and AES in terms of key lengths. b) Compare DES and AES in terms of CPU speed and RAM requirements. c) How strong are the IDEA keys used traditionally in PGP? d) How strong are the RC4 keys used traditionally in WEP?

8. There are two forms of encryption—symmetric key encryption and public key encryption. a) Which is almost always used for confidentiality for e-mail messages? b) For World Wide Web downloads? c) For instant messaging?

ENCRYPTION FOR CONFIDENTIALITY WITH PUBLIC KEY ENCRYPTION

Another class of encryption methods, shown in Figure 7-9, is **public key encryption**. Here, each party has a **private key**, which it keeps secret from the world. In addition, each party has a **public key,** which it shares with everybody because the public key, as its name suggests, does not need to be kept secret.

The Basic Process

Sending
Whenever one party sends, it encrypts the plaintext with the *public key of the receiver.* When A sends to B, A encrypts with *B's* public key. When B sends to A, B encrypts with *A's* public key.

Receiving
Each receiver decrypts with *its own private key.* When A sends to B, B decrypts with *B's* private key. In turn, when B sends to A, A decrypts with *A's* private key.

Once a message is encrypted with the receiver's public key, nobody can decrypt it except the receiver. Even the sender cannot decrypt the message after encrypting it.

Figure 7-9 Public Key Encryption for Confidentiality

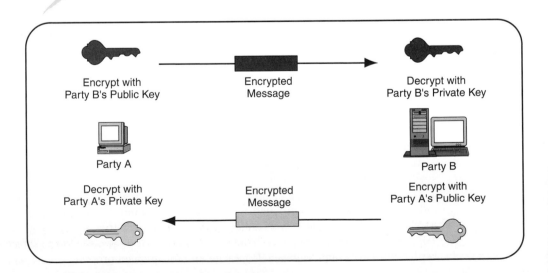

Referring to Public and Private Keys

Note that you should never say "the public key" or "the private key" by itself when describing confidential transmission using public key encryption. Two public keys and two private keys are involved in any two-way exchange. You must always specify something like "A's public key" or "B's private key."

You should never say "the public key" or "the private key" by itself when describing confidential transmission using public key encryption. Always refer to a specific party's public or private key.

Disadvantage and Advantage

Complexity, Processing Intensiveness, and Short Messages

Public key encryption probably strikes you as complex. In fact, it is. It requires many computer processing cycles to do public key encryption and decryption—about 100 times as many cycles as symmetric key encryption requires. The inefficiency of this processing burden is so large that public key encryption can be used only to encrypt small messages.

The Simplicity of Exchanging Public Keys

A major benefit of public key encryption is that public keys are not secret, so there is no need to exchange them securely. Many people post their public keys online for everyone to read. In contrast, with symmetric key encryption, each pair of communication partners needs to have a symmetric key that must be exchanged securely.

Major Public Key Encryption Methods and Key Lengths

RSA

The most widely used public key encryption method is **RSA**, which is named for its creators, Rivest, Shamir, and Adleman.[3] RSA was patented, but its patent expired in 2000. Now that RSA is in the public domain, its domination of public key encryption may grow.

Unfortunately, most commercial implementations use a key length of only 512 bits. This is now considered too small for safety. Companies are now advised to use 1,024 bit keys for normal encryption and 2,048 bit keys for highly sensitive applications.

Elliptic Curve Cryptosystem (ECC)

However, a newer form of public key encryption, the **elliptic curve cryptosystem (ECC)**, promises to provide equal protection with smaller keys and therefore less processing burden. ECC can be implemented on relatively simple devices, such as personal digital assistants. A common key length in ECC is 160 bits, although this is now considered too small. (A strong ECC key is now considered to be at least 512 bits.) On the negative side, ECC is patented.

---

[3] The RSA private key consists of two large primes, p and q. The public key consists of n (which is the product of p and q) and a number e, which shares no factors with p-1 or q-1. To encrypt the message M, the sender computes M^e mod n. Decryption requires knowledge of p and q. Although the sender knows n, which is the product of p and q, determining p and q if the sender knows n is extremely difficult.

STRONG SYMMETRIC KEYS	STRONG PUBLIC AND PRIVATE KEYS
Limited damage if cracked, so can be shorter	Serious damage if cracked, so must be longer
Changed frequently, so can be shorter	Rarely changed, so must be longer
100 bits or more today	1,024 or 2,048 bits for RSA encryption today
Longer for high-value transactions	512 bits for ECC encryption today
Longer tomorrow as cracking power increases	Longer tomorrow as cracking power increases
DES: 56-bits (weak), but 3DES gives 112-bit or 168-bit security	
AES: Key lengths of 128, 192, or 256; yet places a light load on processor and RAM so can be used by mobile devices.	
IDEA: 128 bits	

Figure 7-10   Strong Keys for Symmetric and Public Key Encryption

Strong Key Lengths in Perspective

We saw earlier that 100 bits is the dividing line between weak and strong *symmetric keys* today. However, *public keys* need to be much longer to be considered strong, as Figure 7-10 indicates. First, the consequences of breaking a private key can be disastrous, allowing impersonation. Second, although symmetric keys are changed often—sometimes several times in a session, private keys tend to be used for long periods of time. (Changing one's public key and attendant private key may require notifying many business correspondents.)

TEST YOUR UNDERSTANDING

9. Jason sends a message to Kristin using public key encryption for confidentiality. a) What key will Jason use to encrypt the message? b) What key will Kristin use to decrypt the message? c) What key will Kristin use to encrypt the reply? d) What key will Jason use to decrypt the reply? e) Can the message and reply be long messages? Explain.

10. Does public key encryption have a problem with secure key exchange for the public key? Explain.

11. a) What are the two most popular public key encryption methods? b) Which is in the public domain? c) Which allows smaller keys to be used for a given level of security? d) What is a common key length for RSA? e) What RSA key lengths are recommended? f) What is a common ECC key length? g) What ECC key length is recommended?

ENCRYPTION FOR AUTHENTICATION

So far, we have been discussing encryption as a way to create confidentiality. However, encryption also can be used in **authentication**, that is, verifying the other party's identity.

Applicant and Verifier

In authentication terminology, the **applicant** is the side that tries to prove its identity to the other party, as Figure 7-11 shows. The applicant is sometimes called the **supplicant**. The other party, which tries to authenticate the identity of the applicant, is the **verifier**. In two-way communication, both sides take on both roles because each authenticates the other.

TEST YOUR UNDERSTANDING

12. a) What is authentication? b) In authentication, who is the applicant? c) The supplicant? d) The verifier? e) Can a station be both an applicant and a verifier?

Figure 7-11   MS-CHAP Challenge-Response Authentication Protocol

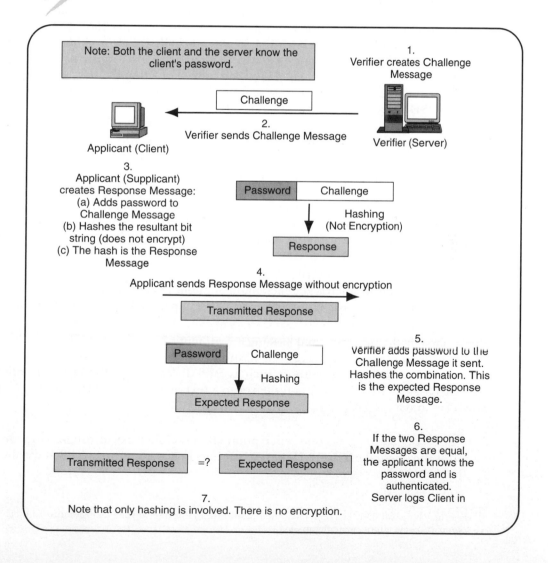

Initial Authentication with MS-CHAP Challenge-Response Authentication

In war movies, when a soldier approaches a sentry, the sentry issues a challenge, and the soldier must respond with the day's correct password. Figure 7-11 shows a form of network **challenge-response authentication** called **MS-CHAP**. It is the Microsoft (MS) version of the IETF **Challenge Handshake Authentication Protocol (CHAP)**.

MS-CHAP Is for Server-Based Authentication

MS-CHAP is used primarily to authenticate a remote user to a server. MS-CHAP relies on the fact that the user has a password that both the user and the server know. This is a very common situation in organizations.

On the Applicant's Machine: Hashing

The server sends the applicant's PC a **challenge message**, which is a random bit string. The applicant's PC then *adds* the user's password to this challenge message.

The applicant's PC next hashes the combined challenge message and password. **Hashing** is a mathematical process that, when applied to a bit string of any length, produces a value of a fixed length called the **hash**. For instance, the **MD5** hashing algorithm always produces a hash of 128 bits, whereas the **Secure Hash Algorithm Version 1 (SHA-1)** always produces a hash of 160 bits.

The hash of the challenge message plus the user's password is the **response message** that the applicant's PC sends back to the server.

On the Verifier's Machine (The Server)

The server itself adds the challenge message to the user's password and applies the same hashing algorithm the applicant used, producing a new hash. If this new hash is identical to the response message, then the person at the client PC must know the account's password.[4] The server then logs in the user.

Perspective: No Encryption!

Does MS-CHAP use symmetric key encryption or public key encryption? Trick question. It does not use either; it uses hashing. Figure 7-12 compares encryption with hashing.

Keys   First, both encryption and hashing for authentication use keys. This is probably why people confuse encryption and hashing. However, encryption uses keys as an input to an encryption method, such as DES. In contrast, MS-CHAP and other hashing-based methods usually add the key to a text message and then hash the combined key and message.

Length of the Result   Second, encryption creates ciphertext of roughly the same length as the original plaintext. However, hashing creates a hash (result) that usually is far shorter than the original message.

---

[4] Users may have had their PCs remember their passwords. In this case, anyone taking control of their computers could impersonate them.

	ENCRYPTION	HASHING
Use of Key	Uses a key as an input to an encryption method	Key (secret) is usually added to text; the two are combined, and the combination is hashed
Length of Result	Output is similar in length to input	Output is of a fixed short length, regardless of input
Reversibility	Reversible; ciphertext can be decrypted back to plaintext	One-way function; hash cannot be "de-hashed" back to the original string

Figure 7-12   Encryption Versus Hashing

Reversible Versus One-Way Processes   Third, encryption is a **reversible (two-way) process**, meaning that something that has been encrypted can be decrypted back to the original plaintext again. In contrast, nothing like "dehashing" is available to turn the hash back to the original message. Hashing is a **one-way process**. You cannot input 10,000 bits into a hashing process, get a 160-bit hash, and expect to regenerate the entire 10,000 original bits from the 160-bit hash. Hashing throws away information, and it is impossible to get it back.

TEST YOUR UNDERSTANDING

13.   a) For what type of authentication is MS-CHAP used? b) How does hashing work? c) What are the two most popular hashing algorithms, and what are the lengths of their hashes? d) How does the applicant create the response message? e) How does the verifier check the response message? f) What type of encryption does MS-CHAP use? (Trick question.) g) What does it mean that hashing is a one-way function?

Message-by-Message Authentication with Digital Signatures

Challenge-response authentication usually is done only at the beginning of a session or at most a few times per session. We would like to be able to authenticate *each message* coming from the other party to ensure that an attacker cannot slip a new or modified message into the message stream.

Digital Signatures

Figure 7-13 shows how to create a **digital signature**, which authenticates each message analogously to the way human signatures authenticate documents.[5]

---

[5]   In the United States, Federal agencies usually use the Digital Signature Standard, which specifies SHA-1 for hashing, and the Digital Signature Algorithm (DSA), which specifies either RSA or the Elliptic Curve Cryptosystem. DSA also includes a random number generator for creating public-private key pairs, but flaws have been found in this algorithm, so another algorithm often is used.

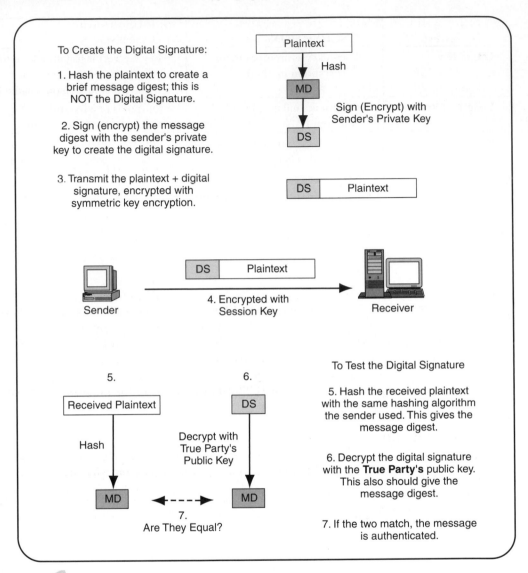

To Create the Digital Signature:

1. Hash the plaintext to create a brief message digest; this is NOT the Digital Signature.

2. Sign (encrypt) the message digest with the sender's private key to create the digital signature.

3. Transmit the plaintext + digital signature, encrypted with symmetric key encryption.

Plaintext

Hash

MD

Sign (Encrypt) with Sender's Private Key

DS

DS   Plaintext

DS   Plaintext

Sender

4. Encrypted with Session Key

Receiver

5.

Received Plaintext

Hash

MD

6.

DS

Decrypt with True Party's Public Key

MD

7.
Are They Equal?

To Test the Digital Signature

5. Hash the received plaintext with the same hashing algorithm the sender used. This gives the message digest.

6. Decrypt the digital signature with the **True Party's** public key. This also should give the message digest.

7. If the two match, the message is authenticated.

Figure 7-13   Digital Signature for Message-by-Message Authentication

Hashing to Produce the Message Digest

To create the digital signature, the sender (who is an applicant) first hashes the plaintext message the sender wishes to transmit securely. This generates a hash called a **message digest**. The hash is generated because digital signatures use public key encryption, which is limited to encrypting short messages, such as hashes.

Signing the Message Digest to Produce the Digital Signature

Next, the sender encrypts the message digest with the sender's own private key. This step creates the **digital signature**. *Note that the message digest is not the digital signature but is only used to produce the digital signature.*

When a party encrypts with its own private key, this is called **signing** a message with its private key. The sender proves his or her identity like a person signing a letter. In this terminology, the sender signs the message digest to create the digital signature.

Sending the Message with Confidentiality

The message that the sender wishes to send, then, consists of the original plaintext message plus the digital signature. If confidentiality is not an issue, the sender can simply send the combined message. However, confidentiality normally *is* important, so the sender normally encrypts the combined original message and digital signature for confidentiality. The combined message is likely to be long, so the sender must use symmetric key encryption.

Verifying the Applicant

The receiver (verifier) decrypts the entire message with the symmetric key used for confidentiality, then decrypts the digital signature with the true party's public key, which is widely known. This will produce the original message digest—if the applicant/sender has signed the message digest with the true party's private key.

Then, the receiver/verifier hashes the original plaintext message with the same hashing algorithm the applicant used. This also should produce the message digest.

If the message digests produced in these two different ways match, then the sender must have the true party's private key, which only the true party should know. The message is authenticated as coming from the true party.

Message Integrity

If someone changes the message en route, or if transmission errors occur, the two message digests will not match. Therefore, digital signatures give **message integrity**—the ability to tell if a message has been modified en route. A message that is changed will not pass the authentication test and so will be discarded.

TEST YOUR UNDERSTANDING

14. a) For what type of authentication is a digital signature used—challenge-response or message-by-message? b) How does the applicant create a message digest? c) How does the applicant create a digital signature? d) What combined message does the applicant send? e) How is the combined message encrypted for confidentiality? f) How does the verifier check the digital signature? g) Besides authentication, what security benefit does a digital signature provide? h) Explain what this benefit means.

DIGITAL CERTIFICATES

In public key-based authentication, the verifier must know the public key of the true party. It should not ask the applicant for the true party's public key, because if the applicant is an **imposter**, the impostor will send his or her *own* public key claiming that this is the true party's public key, as Figure 7-14 illustrates.

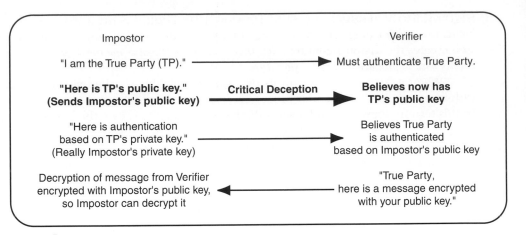

Figure 7-14   Public Key Deception

If the verifier is gullible and accepts the impostor's public key as the true party's public key, the imposter will sign digital signatures with his or her own private key, and the verifier will use the impostor's public key to verify the impostor as the true party.

Certificate Authorities and Digital Certificates

Certificate Authorities
Instead of getting the true party's public key from the applicant, the verifier must contact a **certificate authority (CA)**, which is an independent and trusted source of information about the public keys of true parties.

Digital Certificate
The certificate authority will send the verifier a **digital certificate** containing the *name of the true party* and the *true party's public key*. The verifier then uses this public key to authenticate the applicant claiming to be the true party.

Certificate Authority Regulation
Unfortunately, certificate authorities in most countries are not regulated, so the verifier must accept a digital certificate only from a certificate authority it trusts. In Europe, however, the European Union has mandated the regulation of CAs by national governments. Other countries may also regulate CAs to improve public confidence in these authorities.

What Do CAs Do?
It is a common misconception that certificate authorities vouch for the honesty of the party named in the certificate. They do not. They merely vouch for the named party's public key! Although CA customers who misbehave may have their certificates revoked, CAs rarely give strong warranties about the honesty of their customers. That is not their job. Their job is to associate a public key with a name.

TEST YOUR UNDERSTANDING

15. a) From what kind of organization does a verifier receive digital certificates? b) Are most CAs regulated? c) Does a digital certificate mean that the firm named in the certificate is well-behaved?

X.509 Digital Certificates

The standard for digital certificates is **X.509**. As Figure 7-15 illustrates, X.509 digital certificates have a number of fields. Only the most important fields are shown in the figure.

Version Number

Three versions of X.509 have been created to date. Each has a different *version number* field value. The Version 3 standard is dominant today, and we will focus on its field structure.

Figure 7-15 Important X.509 Digital Certificate Fields

FIELD	DESCRIPTION
Version Number	Version number of the X.509 standard. Most certificates follow Version 3. Different versions have different fields. This figure reflects the Version 3 standard.
Issuer	Name of the Certificate Authority (CA).
Serial Number	Unique serial number for the certificate, set by the CA.
Subject	The name of the person, organization, computer, or program to which the certificate has been issued. This is the true party.
Public Key	The public key of the subject—the public key of the true party.
Public Key Algorithm	The algorithm the subject uses to sign messages with digital signatures.
Valid Period	The period before which and after which the certificate should not be used. *Note:* Certificate may be revoked before the end of this period.
Digital Signature	The digital signature of the certificate, signed by the CA with the CA's own private key. Provides authentication and certificate integrity. User must know the CA's public key independently.
Signature Algorithm Identifier	The digital signature algorithm the CA uses to sign its certificates.

Issuer

The *issuer* field gives the name of the certificate authority.

Serial Number

The CA gives each digital certificate it creates a unique *serial number*. A company may have multiple digital certificates with the same subject field (discussed next), but each will have a different serial number (and public key). Queries to the CA typically use these serial numbers for searches.

Subject

The *subject* field gives the name of the party that the certificate describes. This is one of the two critical fields in digital certificates. This is the name of the true party.

Public Key

The second piece of critical information is the public key, which is stored in the *public key* field. This gives the public key of the party named in the subject field (the true party).

Public Key Algorithm

Several algorithms are available for creating digital signatures. The *public key algorithm* field tells which algorithm the subject uses. Without this knowledge, it is impossible to use the public key.

Valid Period and Revocation

Every digital certificate has a *valid period*, before which and after which it should not be accepted. However, as discussed later in this chapter, the CA may revoke the certificate before the end of its valid period, so a party receiving a digital certificate should check with the CA to see if the certificate's serial number is on the CA's certificate revocation list (CRL).

Digital Signature

It would be bad if an attacker could obtain a true party's digital certificate (an easy task) and put his or her own public key in the public key field. To prevent this, the CA signs the digital certificate, using the *CA's own* private key. The CA places this information in the certificate's *digital signature* field.

As noted earlier, digital signatures provide message integrity, that is, the ability of the receiver to tell whether a certificate has been altered. Most browsers know the public keys of major CAs, so testing a certificate for alterations is easy. Altered digital certificates, of course, are rejected.

Signature Algorithm Identifier

What digital signature algorithm does the CA use to sign the digital certificate? The algorithm is reported in the certificate in the *signature algorithm identifier* field.

Certificate Authority's Public Key

To test the certificate's digital signature, the verifier must know the certificate authority's public key. In light of the public key deception problem, the user could not accept a CA public key contained in the certificate. The verifier needs to learn the CA's public key in a different way. Most browsers today come with the public keys of well-known certificate authorities.

TEST YOUR UNDERSTANDING

16. a) What are the two most critical fields in the certificate? b) What other field is needed to use the information in these two most critical fields? c) What two fields allow the receiver of a certificate to determine if the certificate has been altered? d) What piece of information not included in the certificate is needed to test for alterations? e) Why is this information not put into the digital certificate? f) Why is the version number field important to the receiver? g) Why is the valid period field important? h) What is the standard for digital certificates?

The Role of the Digital Certificate

Note that a digital certificate does not, by itself, authenticate an applicant! As Figure 7-16 shows, certificates merely provide the public key of the true party for the verifier to use to make the authentication. Similarly, without a digital certificate, the verifier has no proven way to know the true party's public key, so a digital signature alone does not authenticate the applicant. *Digital certificates and public key authentication must be used together in public key authentication.* Neither by itself provides authentication. Specifically, the digital certificate provides the public key that authentication methods such as digital signatures use to authenticate the applicant.

The digital certificate provides the public key that authentication methods such as digital signatures use to authenticate the applicant.

TEST YOUR UNDERSTANDING

17. a) Does a digital signature by itself provide authentication? Explain why or why not. b) Does a digital certificate by itself provide authentication? Explain why or why not. c) Explain how they work together in authentication.

Figure 7-16 Digital Signature and Digital Certificate in Authentication

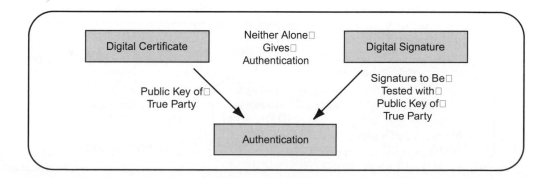

Checking the Certificate Revocation List (CRL)

As noted earlier, the certificate authority may revoke a party's digital certificate before the termination date listed in the digital certificate. Therefore, if the verifier gets the digital certificate from a party other than the certificate authority, the verifier should download the certificate authority's **certificate revocation list (CRL)** to be sure that the digital certificate is still valid.

TEST YOUR UNDERSTANDING

18. Why is it important to check CRLs?

Public Key Infrastructures (PKIs)

Needed Functions

Managing public keys requires several related actions. Public key–private key pairs must be created. The public key will be distributed through digital certificates, but the private key must be distributed securely, often by embedding it in software that is installed on a particular machine. Certificate revocation list checking also must be supported.

PKIs

As Figure 7-17 shows, **public key infrastructures (PKIs)** automate all of these processes. PKIs create a total system (infrastructure) for public key encryption.

Proprietary, Incompatible Products

Unfortunately, all of the PKIs in use today are proprietary products, so interoperability is spotty. They also lack the functionality needed to do all necessary tasks, and they are extremely labor intensive. This has slowed their adoption.

Figure 7-17   Public Key Infrastructure (PKI) with a Certificate Authority

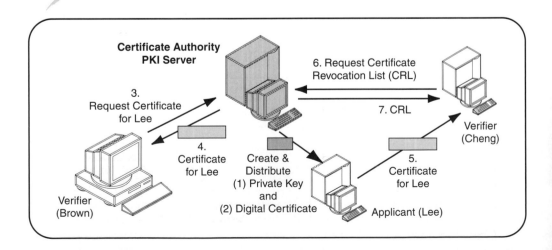

A Critical Mass Problem

More importantly, PKI has a "critical mass" problem. PKI does not work unless a large fraction of the people within a community is using it. Otherwise, some people must be allowed to use weaker authentication, creating holes in the security network. Even for individual firms, it is difficult to implement PKI universally. For consumer products, few merchants require digital signatures for fear of losing customers. In a vicious cycle, few customers bother getting digital certificates.

Issuing Digital Certificates Safely: The Prime Authentication Problem

Most importantly of all, how can digital certificates be issued in a trusted manner nationally and even internationally? There is no regulatory system for certificate authorities. Even if there were, it probably would be fairly easy to use identity theft information to get false digital certificates for individuals and even small companies because CAs usually require only minimum proof for smaller customers. This problem of issuing digital certificates in a trusted manner is the **prime authentication problem**. If it cannot be solved at the level of the entire community a PKI is created to serve, then how can communication partners within the community authenticate other parties safely?

TEST YOUR UNDERSTANDING

19.   a) What are the functions of a PKI? b) What are the three main problems with PKI products today? c) What is the prime authentication problem?

SYMMETRIC KEY EXCHANGE

With symmetric key encryption, both sides must use the same symmetric key. This normally means that a symmetric key must be created and then sent to the two parties. This key exchange must be done securely because any attacker intercepting the key during the exchange transmission will be able to read all subsequent transmissions.

Long-Term Keys Versus Session Keys

Long-Term Symmetric Keys

Some symmetric keys are long-term keys that the two parties will use for days, weeks, months, or even years when they communicate. Some symmetric keys are even permanent keys that are never changed. Using long-term keys reduces the need for key exchange. Unfortunately, if cryptanalysts can get a sufficiently long sample of messages encrypted with the same key, they might be able to break the encryption. Consequently, even long-term keys need to be changed occasionally to maintain security.

Symmetric Session Keys

In contrast, symmetric **session keys** are created and used only when two parties begin to communicate. After the communication, the session key is discarded. The next time the two parties communicate, they will use a different session key. Session keys are attractive because their term of use normally is too brief for cryptanalysts to exploit.

In high-security environments, it even might be necessary to change the symmetric session key several times during a session. The TKIP standard discussed in Chapter 2 does this for 802.11 WLANs.

TEST YOUR UNDERSTANDING

20. a) Distinguish between long-term versus session symmetric keys. b) Why is a long period of use bad?

Symmetric Key Exchange Using Public Key Encryption

Although public key encryption and symmetric key encryption may seem like rivals, they actually are complementary. For example, public key encryption can distribute symmetric session keys securely, as Figure 7-18 illustrates.

➤ First, one side generates a random bit string that will be used as a symmetric key.

➤ Second, that side encrypts this symmetric key with the public key of the other party.

➤ Third, the party that generated the symmetric key sends this encrypted session key to the other party.

➤ Fourth, the other party decrypts the encrypted session key with its own private key.

➤ Fifth, both sides now have the symmetric session key and will use it to send messages confidentially.

This approach reveals a general pattern of using public key encryption for initial stages in cryptographic system transmissions and then switching to symmetric key encryption for ongoing bulk encryption, apart from digital signatures, which are short.

Figure 7-18   Public Key Distribution for Symmetric Session Keys

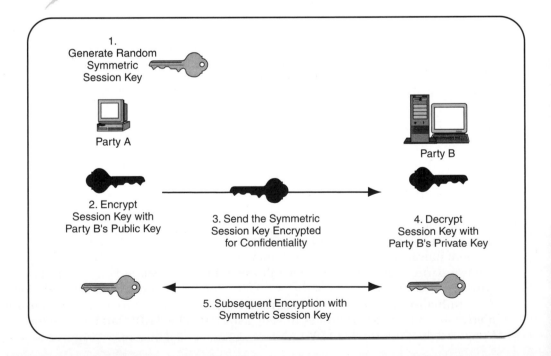

TEST YOUR UNDERSTANDING

21.   Explain how public key encryption can be used to do symmetric key exchange.

Symmetric Key Exchange Using Diffie-Hellman Key Agreement

Although the use of public key encryption to exchange keys is widespread, an increasingly popular way to exchange keys is **Diffie-Hellman key agreement**. This technique was created by the two creators of public key encryption. Although Diffie-Hellman key agreement may seem like magic, it works. Figure 7-19 illustrates Diffie-Hellman key agreement.

Selecting a Diffie-Hellman Group

First, the two sides agree non-securely on a Diffie-Hellman group, which has two parameters, p and g (prime and generator). A number of such groups exist. This agreement is done in the clear, that is, without security.

Computing Numbers

Next, the two sides compute numbers that they will exchange.

➤   First, Party X randomly generates a small string x, then calculates g^x mod p and calls this x'.

➤   At the same time, Party Y randomly generates a small string y, then calculates g^y mod p and calls this y'.

Figure 7-19   Diffie-Hellman Key Agreement

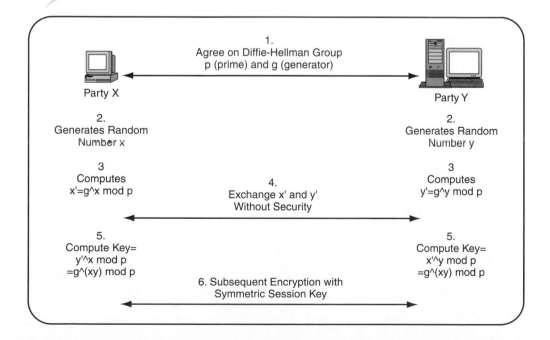

Number Transmission

X sends x' to Y, and Y sends y' to X.

The Key Calculation

X calculates y'^{x} mod p, giving g^{xy} mod p. Y calculates x'^{y} mod p, also getting g^{xy} mod p. The two sides subsequently use this g^{xy} mod p value as their symmetric session key in subsequent transmissions.

Freedom from Interception

These x' and y' values are sent *without security*. Interceptors might read them but will not be able to calculate the session key because they cannot learn x and y from the exchanges.

Agreement, Not Exchange

Note that the two parties *agree* upon a key rather than *exchange* a key. The key never is transmitted explicitly. That is why the process is called "key agreement" rather than "key exchange."

Authenticated Diffie-Hellman Key Agreement

One problem with simple Diffie-Hellman is that unless the two parties authenticate themselves first, an adversary might establish shared session keys in the name of a true partner. Therefore, strong cryptographic systems require the use of authenticated Diffie-Hellman key agreement, in which authentication is an initial part of the process.

TEST YOUR UNDERSTANDING

22. a) What is the role of Diffie-Hellman key agreement? b) In Diffie-Hellman key agreement, is information exchanged with encryption to protect it from eavesdroppers? c) Why is the word *agreement* used instead of *exchange*?

REPLAY ATTACKS AND DEFENSES

Replay Attacks

In this chapter, we have looked at several types of attacks, including:

➤ Intercepting and reading messages, which is thwarted by encryption for confidentiality.

➤ Intercepting and changing messages, then sending them on, which is thwarted by encryption for message integrity.

➤ Impersonating a true party, which is thwarted by encryption and other processes for authentication.

Replay Attacks: Playing Back Encrypted Messages

One type of attack, however, was not discussed. This is the **replay attack**, in which an adversary intercepts an encrypted message and transmits it again later. In the Arabian

Nights tale, the young man overhears robbers giving the password "Open Sesame." Although he does not understand the meaning of the password, he repeats it and is admitted to the treasure cave. Similarly, in poorly designed authentication systems, an attacker can record an encrypted set of commands to log in or do something else, then play them back to institute the same answer.

Thwarting Replay Attacks

Replay attacks can be detected in several ways. In studying them, keep in mind that the message being replayed is encrypted so that the replay attacker cannot read it—merely retransmit it.

Time Stamps

One defense is to ensure "freshness" by including a **time stamp** in each message. If a message is older than a preset cutoff value, the receiver rejects it. If attackers can act quickly, the cutoff value must be kept short.

Sequence Numbers

Another approach is to place a **sequence number** in each encrypted message. By examining sequence numbers, the receiver can detect a retransmitted message, which will contain an earlier sequence number. Initial sequence numbers must be completely randomized so that an attacker cannot predict sequence numbers.

Figure 7-20   Replay Attacks (Study Figure)

REPLAY ATTACKS

Retransmit an intercepted message
Message is encrypted so that replay attacker cannot read it

WHY REPLAY ATTACKS

Repetition might work—for instance, replaying an encrypted user name and password might result in access to a poorly designed system

PREVENTING REPLAY ATTACKS

Insert a time stamp in messages and accept messages only if they are very recent
Insert a sequence number in each message, and do not accept duplicates
Insert a nonce (random number selected for the occasion) in a request message; only accept a reply message with the same nonce. Other party does not accept a request message with a previous nonce

Nonces

A third common approach used in client/server processing is to include a **nonce** (randomly generated number created for the occasion[6]) in each client request. The client never uses the same nonce twice. The response from the server includes the same nonce sent in the request.

By comparing a nonce in a request with previous request nonces, the server can ensure that the request is not a repeat of an earlier one. The client, in turn, can ensure that the response is not a repeat of a previous response.

Nonces work well because even fast attackers cannot exploit them. However, they work only in applications that rely entirely (or almost entirely) on request-response interactions.

TEST YOUR UNDERSTANDING

23. a) What is a replay attack? b) Can the attacker understand the replayed message? c) Why are replay attacks attempted? d) What are the three ways to thwart replay attacks?

ADVANCED TOPICS: QUANTUM COMPUTING AND STEGANOGRAPHY

We will finish the discussion of cryptography with two advanced topics: quantum computing and steganography.

Quantum Computing

To date, cryptography has been based on ordinary digital computers. However, computer scientists are now developing quantum computers, which are based on entirely different principles. These quantum computers, if they can be built with sufficient size, could revolutionize key distribution and public key cracking. Although we cannot discuss quantum computing in any depth because this requires knowledge of quantum mechanics, we will examine these two areas in a cursory way.

Quantum Bits (Q-Bits)

In ordinary computers, each bit is either a zero or a one at any moment. However, in **quantum computing**, each bit may be both a zero and a one simultaneously. Such bits are called **quantum bits (q-bits)**. The process of decoherence causes the q-bit to turn randomly into a classic bit (either one or zero)

Quantum Key Distribution (QKD)

In quantum mechanics, it is possible for two particles to be **entangled**, say in a way that they both must point up or down when read. These two particles can be sent in opposite directions in a quantum state in which they are both up and down simultaneously. At a particular moment, one receiver will read the particle, causing it to decohere. Suppose that he or she receives it in the up state. Due to entanglement, the receiver will know that the other party will see his or her particle in the up state as well. If the up state is taken to be a one and the down state is taken to be a zero, the two sides will both compute the same key bits. Sending a long string of bits this way can deliver the

---

[6] This is related to the Shakespearean expression "for the nonce" (for the present).

QUANTUM COMPUTING

Quantum Bits (Q-Bits)

    In ordinary computers, each bit is either a zero or a one at any time

    In quantum computers, each quantum bit (q-bit) can be both a zero and a one at any moment

    When decohered, the q-bit becomes a classic one or zero randomly

Quantum Key Distributions (QKD) (Simplified)

    Two particles representing q-bits can be entangled so that both will be up or down when read

    The two entangled particles are sent to the two communicating parties

    Both will always read the bit the same way—as a one or a zero

    They will both read the stream of decohered q-bits identically as a key

    Interception of q-bits en route by an eavesdropper is detected easily

    QKD is becoming commercially viable

Quantum Key Cracking

    For determining private keys from public keys

    An array of N q-bits can represent all possible keys of length N

    Operations can be performed on all possible keys *simultaneously*

    Results are put in a results register

    Decoherence gives one result randomly from all possible results

    This single result can be used to compute the private key

    Not instantaneous, but much faster than exhaustive search

    Not practical today

        We can only build quantum computers with a few q-bits

        Quantum computers with 1000 or more q-bits are some time off

STEGANOGRAPHY

Steganography means hidden writing

Hiding a message in an image

    Every image is made of pixels

    There often is about one byte per pixel for each color: red, green, and blue

    One bit in each byte is the least significant—changing it will alter the color by only 1/256

    The process steals the least significant bit from each byte

    The message is written into these bits

    The message may be encrypted before writing it into the bits

    The picture will look unchanged

Digital Watermarking

    Using steganography to hide identifying information in a document

    To prove copyright ownership

    To identify different copies of a document

Figure 7-21   Quantum Computing and Steganography (Study Figure)

same key to both sides. If an attacker intercepts one of the bits, however, the side it was being sent to will not receive it properly and will know that interception has occurred.

This **quantum key distribution (QKD)** technique has moved out of the laboratory and is beginning to be commercialized. Keys have already been distributed over tens of kilometers and adequate transmission rates. However, current key distribution methods tend to be adequate for business use, so the commercial market for QKD may be limited to military uses. Theoretically, however, the only way to create unbreakable encryption is to use one-time keys (used only once) as long as the message being encrypted.

Quantum Key Cracking

Q-bits provide a new way to guess keys. A computer register that has 64 q-bits can represent all possible 64-bit keys. Various operations can act on this register. Each operation can be performed on all possible keys. At the end of the operation, all results are stored in a single register.

Quantum decoherence, which causes the q-bits to become either ones or zeros randomly, can give one result from the many results stored in the results register. However, this result is selected randomly.

A way has been found to act on public keys to generate a set of results in the results register that can *all* be used to find the private key fairly quickly. This means that decoherence will always give a useful result. Although this method is not instantaneous, it is far faster than generating and testing all possible private keys.

Quantum key cracking has the potential to destroy public key encryption, or at least to require the use of far larger keys. However, while QKD is possible today, quantum computers have only been created that have a handful of bits. Quantum key cracking would require building quantum computers with one or two thousand bits. This is likely to take a long time.

Steganography

Although quantum computing generally is a concern for the future, another advanced form of encryption for confidentiality is possible now. This is steganography (hidden writing). The goal of **steganography** is to hide information in images and other documents so that an eavesdropper will not even realize that information has been hidden.

Pixels

A graphic image is made of tiny colored dots called pixels. Each pixel is represented in a computer as a group of bits. For example, there might be eight bits to represent the amount of redness in the pixel, eight bits for greenness, and eight bits for blueness. This can give 256 possible intensity values for each color (2^8), resulting in an enormous range of possibilities when the three colors are combined.

Hiding Information in Pixels

If you have the number 952, the least significant digit is 2. This means that if you change it by 1, the entire number will only change by 1. In contrast, if you increase the 9, which is the most significant digit, even a change of 1 will change the entire number by 100.

Similarly, each byte has a least significant bit. Changing it by 1 will only change the intensity of the color by 1/256, which would not be visible to the human eye.

A simple steganography technique is to steal the least significant bit from every color of every pixel in a picture, replacing it with a bit from the hidden message. In aggregate, this can deliver a large number of bits in even a picture of modest size. Yet the picture will look almost exactly the same. For further security, the bits of the message can be encrypted before being placed in the picture.

Digital Watermarking

Another attraction of steganography is **digital watermarking**—adding information steganographically to identify the image. This can be done to document copyright ownership. It also can be done to secretly number copies of a document sent to different people so that if one of the receivers leaks the document, the leaker can be identified.

TEST YOUR UNDERSTANDING

24. a) What threat do quantum computers create for secure communication? b) How can they aid secure communication?

25. a) What do we call the hiding of messages in graphics images? b) For what two reasons is it done?

CONCLUSION

Major Topics

In this chapter, we looked at the core elements of cryptographic security, including encryption for confidentiality, encryption for authentication, key exchange, and protection from reply attacks.

Cryptographic Systems

In practice, most or all of these protections are provided automatically within cryptographic systems. In the next chapter, we will look at a number of important cryptographic systems, including SSL/TLS, PPP, PPTP, L2TP, IPsec, and Kerberos.

Common Points of Confusion

Two Encryption Methods

This material can be confusing because two types of encryption methods have been developed—symmetric key and public key methods. Symmetric key encryption uses only a *single* key in confidential, two-way dialogs. However, public key encryption uses *four* keys in confidential, two-way dialogs. Each party has a public key and a private key. Therefore, never say "public key" or "private key" without referring to a specific person's key.

Symmetric Keys Are Not Private Keys

Another point of confusion is that although private keys and symmetric keys both must be kept secret, they work in different ways. The secret key in symmetric key encryption is not a private key. Private keys are found only in public key encryption.

Cryptographic Goals and Methods

In addition, two main cryptographic goals exist—confidentiality and authentication. Figure 7-22 shows how encryption methods and hashing can be used for these two goals. Note that not all methods can be used for both goals.

	CONFIDENTIALITY	AUTHENTICATION
Symmetric Key Encryption	Applicable. Sender encrypts with key shared with the receiver.	Not applicable.
Public Key Encryption	Applicable. Sender encrypts with *receiver's public key*.	Applicable. Sender encrypts *with own private key*. Used in digital signatures.
Hashing	Not applicable.	Applicable. Sender adds to the message a key or secret the receiver will know. Hashes the combined key and message. Used in MS-CHAP and HMACs (discussed in the next chapter).

Figure 7-22   Cryptographic Goals and Methods

Also, even if encryption methods can be used for both goals, they may be used differently for confidentiality and authentication. For instance, in public key encryption, the sender encrypts with the receiver's public key for confidentiality but with the sender's private key for authentication.

THOUGHT QUESTIONS

1. If an applicant gives you a digital certificate, what should you do?
2. Did we see symmetric key encryption used for authentication in this chapter? If so, where did we see it?
3. Describe in detail the steps the sender takes when he or she wishes to send a message with a digital signature. Describe in detail the steps the receiver takes.
4. MS-CHAP and digital signatures both are authentication methods. How do they differ?

TROUBLESHOOTING QUESTIONS

1. Party A sends you an order using a digital signature signed by Party A's private key. Later, Party A repudiates (denies sending) the order. a) What defense could Party A offer in court? b) Are they likely to be successful?
2. Party B authenticates itself using MS-CHAP. During this session, Party B sends you an order. Later, they repudiate the order. a) What defense could they offer in court? b) Do you think they are likely to be successful?

CHAPTER 8

CRYPTOGRAPHIC SYSTEMS: SSL/TLS, VPNs, AND KERBEROS

Learning Objectives

By the end of this chapter, you should be able to discuss:

- Cryptographic Systems.
- SSL/TLS.
- Virtual Private Networks (VPNs).
- PPP VPNs.
- PPTP and L2TP VPNs.
- IPsec VPNs.
- Kerberos.

INTRODUCTION

Cryptographic Elements Versus Cryptographic Systems

Major Cryptographic Elements

In the last chapter, we looked at the major elements in cryptographic security. These included the following:

➤ Confidentiality through symmetric key encryption or public key encryption.

➤ Authentication through hashing or public key encryption.

➤ Message integrity through public key encryption. This is also possible through hashing, as we will see in our discussion of IPsec HMACs in this chapter.

➤ Symmetric key exchange using public key encryption or Diffie-Hellman key agreement.

➤ Message replay protection through time stamps, sequence numbers, and nonces.

Complexity of Cryptographic Systems

Each of these matters is complex, and in the last chapter we did not even look at the many options available under each major category. In addition, in any ongoing dialog, the communicating parties need all of these protections, not just one. Consequently, we would not expect average end users (or even average IT professionals) to be able to implement dialog security themselves.

Cryptographic Systems: Multiple Protections

Fortunately, **cryptographic systems**, which are depicted in Figure 8-1, automatically provide confidentiality, authentication, integrity, key exchange, and (usually) protection from replay attacks. These cryptographic systems work with little or no user intervention.

Figure 8-1   Cryptographic System

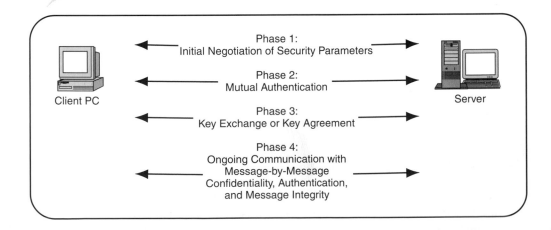

Cryptographic Systems: Automatic Protections

In fact, users often are not even aware that their communication is protected by a cryptographic system. For example, nearly every time you make a purchase over the Internet, that transaction is protected by a cryptographic system, SSL/TLS. There has never been a report of any credit card number being intercepted in transit when protected by SSL/TLS. Yet few users even realize that SSL/TLS is working for them.

TEST YOUR UNDERSTANDING

 1.   Distinguish between cryptographic elements and cryptographic systems.

Cryptographic System Stages

As Figure 8-1 shows, cryptographic systems normally work in a series of four stages. The first three are initial **hand-shaking stages**, in which the cryptographic process is set up. These three stages, in total, take up only a few milliseconds.

The fourth stage—ongoing communication—is everything that comes after these hand-shaking stages. Generally speaking, 99 percent or more of all communication takes place during the ongoing communication stage.

Initial Negotiation

The first step is **initial negotiation**. Many types of symmetric key encryption and public key encryption methods have been created, and most offer users a number of options. The two sides agree upon which methods they will use and which options they will use for each method. Initial negotiation also selects hashing methods and other security methods and options.

This negotiation necessarily takes place in the clear, that is, without cryptographic protection. This naked approach is necessary because the two sides have not yet decided how they will handle encryption. Therefore, there is no way yet for them to implement confidentiality.

Initial Authentication

The next step is **initial authentication**, in which each side authenticates itself to its communication partner. (We will see later that sometimes only one side authenticates itself.) Authentication uses a method and options selected during the negotiation phase. Once authentication is done, subsequent communication can proceed with confidence that the two parties are not communicating with impostors.

Key Exchange

Symmetric key encryption is needed for the long messages that will be sent in the ongoing communication phase. In the **key exchange** phase, the two sides exchange one or more symmetric keys (and perhaps other secrets, as well). As we saw in the previous chapter, they normally use either public key encryption to transfer the key securely or Diffie-Hellman key agreement.

Ongoing Communication

Now that the cryptographic system is initialized, the two parties begin exchanging content messages. In most cryptographic systems, each message is protected for confidentiality, authentication, and integrity in the **ongoing communication** phase.

Re-Authentication and Re-Keying

Although the three hand-shaking stages are done only once, there often is periodic **re-authentication** to ensure that an attacker has not hijacked the connection. Periodic **re-keying** also might be done to reduce the number of messages sent using a single key. Cryptanalysts who intercept messages might be able to decrypt them if they have a large enough sample encrypted with a single key.

TEST YOUR UNDERSTANDING

2. a) How do the first three phases of cryptographic systems differ from the fourth? b) What happens in each of the three hand-shaking stages? c) What protections are provided in the final stage? d) Do some of the hand-shaking stages reappear sometimes during the final stage? If so, explain why.

Major Cryptographic Systems

Figure 8-2 shows a number of major cryptographic systems, including the layer at which each operates. In the rest of this chapter, we will look at these cryptographic systems.

For safety, companies often use two cryptographic systems simultaneously at different layers. This provides defense in depth in case one of the cryptographic systems is compromised, as unfortunately happens with some frequency. Until the broken system is fixed, the other cryptographic system will be able to keep communication safe.

However, using cryptographic systems at two different layers also increases processing time and therefore cost. The added safety of protecting two layers generally is worth the cost, but it rarely would make economic sense to implement cryptographic systems at all layers.

TEST YOUR UNDERSTANDING

3. a) Why is it good to implement cryptographic systems at two layers? b) Why is it rare to implement cryptographic systems at more than two layers?

Figure 8-2 Major Cryptographic Systems

LAYER	CRYPTOGRAPHIC SYSTEM
Application	Kerberos
Transport	SSL/TLS
Internet	IPsec
Data Link	PPTP, L2TP (really only a tunneling system)
Physical	Not applicable. No messages are sent at this layer—only individual bits

Virtual Private Networks (VPNs)
Secure Communication over the Internet
Several of these cryptographic systems—PPTP, L2TP, and IPsec—are used to build **virtual private networks (VPNs)**, which use the Internet for transmission but add security to the dialogs that take place over the unsecure Internet. Figure 8-3 illustrates VPNs.[1]

Remote Access VPNs
In **remote access**, a single PC connects to the protected network. VPNs can be used to provide **remote access** to employees working at home or traveling, to selected customers, to selected suppliers, and to other approved communication partners coming in as individuals.

Site-to-Site VPNs
In contrast, **site-to-site VPNs** carry protected traffic between two sites. These may be two corporate sites or a corporate site and either a customer site or a supplier site. The site-to-site connection cryptographically protects the traffic of many simultaneous conversations taking place between various computers at the two sites.

Figure 8-3   Virtual Private Network (VPN)

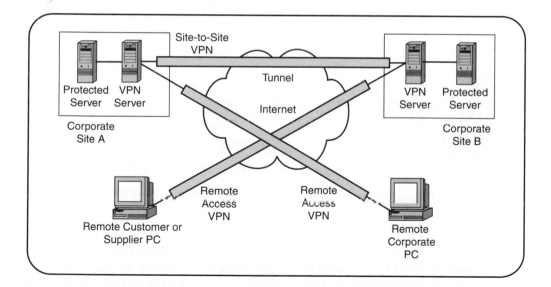

---

[1] Confusingly, the term *virtual private network* (VPN) also is used in another way on the Internet—when a carrier uses MultiProtocol Label Switching (MPLS) to control traffic flow through the Internet. However, MPLS VPNs exist to provide increased quality of service (enhanced speed and reduced latency). MPLS VPNs do not add any real security to these data flows.

TEST YOUR UNDERSTANDING

   4.   a) What is a VPN? b) Distinguish between the two types of VPNs.

SSL/TLS

Origins

When you make a purchase over the Internet, your sensitive traffic usually is protected by a cryptographic system originally called **Secure Sockets Layer (SSL)**. SSL originally was created by Netscape and placed in its Navigator browser.[2] Later, all major browser vendors supported SSL, including Microsoft's Explorer. Later, the standardization effort was passed to the IETF, which renamed the standard **Transport Layer Security (TLS)** to emphasize that it works at the transport layer, as Figure 8-2 shows.[3] We saw SSL/TLS briefly in Chapter 2.

Protection

As Figure 8-4 shows, the fact that SSL/TLS works at the transport layer means that that SSL/TLS can protect all application layer traffic. We will see this pattern of a cryptographic system at a layer protecting all higher-level traffic several times in this chapter.

   However, the protection of higher-layer messages is not **transparent**, meaning that it does not automatically protect higher-layer messages. To be protected, applications have to be SSL/TLS-aware. Although almost all browsers and webserver application programs are SSL/TLS-aware, few other applications have been written to work with SSL/TLS, although some e-mail programs offer SSL/TLS as optional protection. As we saw in Chapter 2, however, SSL/TLS, under the name TLS, is an option in 802.1x authentication and so might increase in popularity.

Operation

Like any cryptographic system, SSL/TLS works in several phases to provide security.

Initial Negotiation

First, the two parties—the customer and the merchant server in e-commerce—engage in a simplified negotiation stage. This stage is brief because SSL/TLS offers few options.

Authentication

Mandatory Server Authentication   Next, the merchant server *must* authenticate itself to the client. This authentication requires the merchant server to send the client a digital certificate. The client must check with the certificate authority to get the certificate revocation list to see if the certificate is still valid. (Many early browsers failed to check the CRL.)

---

[2]   When SSL/TLS is used, the URL begins with https:// instead of http://.
[3]   It also can be viewed as working at a layer above the normal transport layer but below the application layer. Netscape originally called this the Sockets Layer, but the IETF viewed the standard as working in a sublayer of the transport layer and so changed the standard's name.

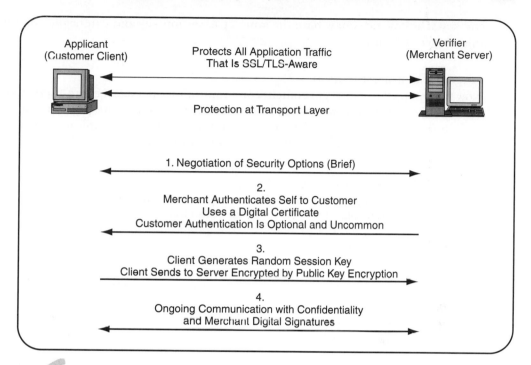

Figure 8-4   SSL/TLS Operation

Optional Client Authentication   The client *may* authenticate itself to the server in this way, but the authentication is optional, as we saw in Chapter 2. The reason for making client authentication optional is pure pragmatism. Few home customers and only some business customers are willing to get digital certificates. To lock out the vast majority of customers to gain higher security usually does not make business sense.

Although not authenticating customers is necessary from a financial standpoint, it has allowed fairly high levels of customer fraud on the Internet. Many websites require customers to use passwords for authentication, but this generally is only a way to collect billing and other data, which customers may spoof. Customer authentication is the Achilles' heel of e-commerce.

Key Exchange

Now that authentication is finished, the two parties must exchange a symmetric key for confidentiality during the ongoing communication phase. In SSL/TLS, this is done using public key encryption. We saw public key encryption for key exchange in the last chapter.

In SSL/TLS, the *customer* (not the merchant) generates a random number to use as a session key for the ongoing communication. The customer then encrypts this session key using the public key of the merchant server. (This public key is contained in the merchant's digital certificate.) The merchant server uses its private key to decrypt the key. The two sides now have the symmetric session key and can begin using it in ongoing communication.

Ongoing Communication

Now the two parties can begin content communication. All messages are encrypted for confidentiality with the symmetric session key exchanged in the previous stage. In addition, each message from the merchant in the ongoing communication phase has a digital signature to ensure that it really was sent by the merchant.

TEST YOUR UNDERSTANDING

5. a) At what layer does SSL/TLS provide protection? b) Describe the authentication weakness in SSL/TLS. c) Why is a widespread lack of client authentication tolerated? d) How is key exchange done? e) What protections are provided during ongoing communication?

Perspective

Moderate Security

SSL/TLS is a flawed cryptographic system. First, and most importantly, only one side of the conversation normally is authenticated. Although this is undesirable, it is pragmatically necessary. SSL also had a number of cryptographic weaknesses. Although most have been fixed by TLS, not all have. However, for household credit card transactions, the cost of potentially breaking an SSL/TLS exchange is too great for attackers to contemplate. It usually is far easier to hack into merchant servers and steal lists of thousands of credit card numbers. As noted earlier, there has not been a single reported case of a credit card number being read en route when protected by SSL/TLS. Overall, SSL/TLS provides moderate security for low-value transactions.

Processing Load

As noted in the last chapter, public key encryption is very processing-intensive compared to symmetric key encryption. SSL/TLS uses public key encryption in key exchange. More importantly, SSL/TLS uses public key encryption to create a digital signature for each message.

Consequently, when merchants turn on SSL/TLS, they often find that they can handle only a few percent of the transactions they could without SSL/TLS.

Despite this high cost, nearly all merchants use it to satisfy customer demands for security. SSL/TLS has long been one of the major security strong points for the Internet.

SSL/TLS and VPNs

As noted earlier, SSL is not transparent to the applications it protects, restricting it primarily to protecting HTTP on webservers. In contrast, we will see that other VPN security protocols are transparent to the layers they protect; it is unnecessary for higher-layer protocols to be modified for protection to work. Although transparency is highly desirable, some VPNs only need HTTP webservice. In these cases, relatively simple SSL/TLS can be a good alternative to implementing a complex VPN protocol.

TEST YOUR UNDERSTANDING

6. a) Comment on the strength of SSL/TLS security. b) Comment on the processing load it creates on servers. c) Why is transparency attractive in full VPNs?

PPP

If you have a dial-up modem connection to the Internet, your frames at the data link layer are almost certainly formatted according to the **Point-to-Point Protocol (PPP)**. As its name suggests, this protocol is limited to a single data link, as Figure 8-5 indicates.

Remote Access

Remote Access Server (RAS)

Early remote users had to dial into sites using a telephone modem and PPP. As Figure 8-5 shows, they connected to a **remote access server (RAS)** at the site. The RAS authenticated them and then gave them access to other computers at the site.

Proprietary RASs

The earliest systems for RAS access control used proprietary protocols that differed among RAS vendors. This technique worked, but if a company used several RAS vendors, it had to learn and maintain multiple remote access server security processes.

Inconsistencies Among Multiple RASs

Another traditional problem with RAS-based security was that a company might have dozens of remote access servers on its site LANs. Unless security was implemented uniformly across RASs, adversaries could simply try different RASs until they found a RAS with improper security. They could then log in and get full access to LAN resources. Individual RAS login security was only as good as the weakest RAS.

Figure 8-5   Using RADIUS for Dial-Up Remote Access

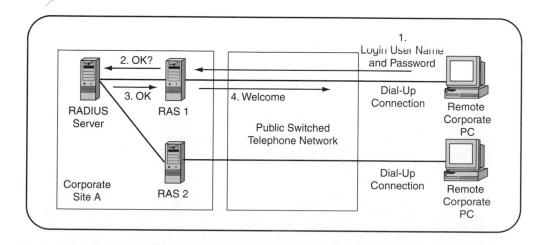

RADIUS

To address the lack of RAS standards and the need to manage multiple RASs, vendors collaborated on a way to implement policy-based authentication on remote access servers. Their standard was the **Remote Authentication Dial-In User Service (RADIUS)**.[4] Figure 8-5 illustrates how RADIUS works.

When a user logs in to the remote access server, the RAS does not do authentication by itself. Instead, it passes the user's login information to the central RADIUS server. The **RADIUS server** then authenticates the user or refuses the user. It passes this information back to the RAS serving the user. The RAS then accepts or rejects the connection.

Although RADIUS works well and is still widely used, we would like to integrate access authentication into our normal Internet protocol suite instead of making it a separate part of network security. We would also like that integration to go beyond authentication to provide confidentiality, as well.

Point-to-Point Protocol Security: The Negotiation Phase

Developed as a basic Layer 2 (data link layer) transmission standard, PPP has added considerable security since its creation.

PPP communication begins with a negotiation phase, during which the two PPP processes can negotiate the transmission and security processes they will use during ongoing communication. Within PPP, the **Link Control Protocol** is used to govern data link layer negotiation.

PPP Authentication

During negotiation, the two sides can agree upon a process to use for authentication. However, as Figure 8-6 notes, authentication is optional in PPP. The two sides can decide not to use it at all. If they do decide to use authentication, they have several options.

Password Authentication Protocol (PAP)

The simplest authentication protocol for PPP is the **Password Authentication Protocol (PAP)**. As Figure 8-6 indicates, the applicant sends the verifier a stream of PAP authentication-request messages until it receives an authenticate-response message (or until the verifier terminates the link).

The PAP authentication-request message contains the user's user name and password. Unfortunately, security specialists cringe at the very name PAP because PAP sends user names and passwords **in the clear** (without encryption). Anyone listening to the traffic can steal passwords!

Another limitation of PAP is that it authenticates the user only once, at the beginning of a session. Afterwards, a third party can send messages in the user's name and no authentication testing will occur.

---

4   Some access systems, instead of using RADIUS servers, use central authentication and authorization servers based on Cisco Systems' TACACS+ (Terminal Access Controller Access Control System) protocol.

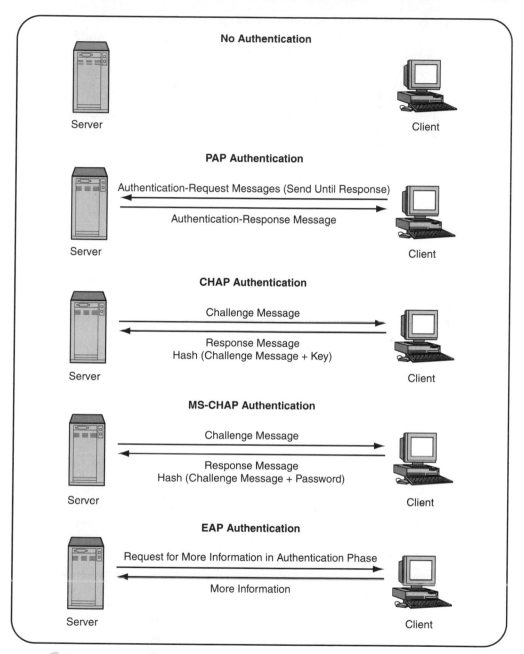

Figure 8-6 PPP Authentication Options

Challenge-Handshake Authentication Protocol (CHAP)

Fortunately, PPP has standardized a much stronger form of authentication, the **Challenge-Handshake Authentication Protocol (CHAP)**. As Figure 8-6 illustrates, the verifier sends a challenge message to the applicant. The applicant sends back a response message that should authenticate the applicant to the verifier.

CHAP works on the basis of a **shared secret**. When the applicant receives the challenge message, it adds the shared secret to the challenge message and then hashes the combined bit stream using MD5 or another agreed-upon hashing algorithm. The applicant sends the resultant hash back to the verifier as its response message.

The verifier also adds the shared secret to the challenge message, hashes the result, and compares the hash with the hash that the applicant sent as its response. If the hashes match, the applicant must know the shared secret and so is authenticated.

Recall that PAP does authentication only once, right after the negotiation phase. CHAP also does authentication then, but it also does so periodically during communication, to thwart an adversary who causes the applicant to crash and then sends a message in the name of the disabled applicant.

Finally, note that CHAP does not use encryption. It uses only hashing. Encryption produces ciphertext that can be decrypted to give back the original plaintext. CHAP merely uses hashing. There is no such thing as dehashing to give back the original hashed string.

Microsoft CHAP (MS-CHAP)

Microsoft has created its own version of CHAP, MS-CHAP, which we saw in the last chapter. We have just seen that CHAP uses a shared secret that must be hashed with the challenge message to create a response message. In **MS-CHAP**, as Figure 8-6 shows, this shared secret is the user's password.

Although the Internet Engineering Task Force (IETF) published an informational RFC (2433) to describe MS-CHAP, it warns at the beginning of the RFC that the "protocol described here has significant vulnerabilities." The basic problem is that, as noted in Chapter 2, users often select passwords that are too easy to guess. MS-CHAP security is only as good as the passwords that users select, and security experts consider this to be insufficient. On the other hand, it does address the fact that passwords often form the basis for authentication in the real world.

Of course, passwords expire and must be renewed. CHAP provides a Change Password message that allows a user to send a new password. A mechanism also is provided for the verifier host to tell the applicant that the old password has expired and that a new password is needed. Unfortunately, the first version of the Change Password process had major security vulnerabilities. Fortunately, a second, stronger version has been released.

Extensible Authentication Protocol (EAP)

The authentication techniques we have seen so far mandate a specific authentication method. However, the **Extensible Authentication Protocol (EAP)** is open-ended. It allows users to select a specific authentication protocol from a list of options.

EAP is the basis for the 802.1x protocol we saw in Chapter 2 for security wireless LANs. We saw that 802.1x offers TLS, MD5-challenge (basically CHAP), and is likely to get the TTLS option soon. Beyond this, EAP is open ended and offers one-time passwords for very high security, Generic Token Card (which works with certain types of security cards), and a growing list of other options. Although only some EAP options are being made available under 802.1x initially, more will be added in future versions of 802.1x.

PPP Confidentiality

We have been focusing on authentication because remote access servers must guard against impostors gaining access to critical internal resources. However, we also would like to have confidentiality in transmissions between users and RASs.

The IETF has provided an **Encryption Control Protocol** for the PPP negotiation phase to allow the parties to agree upon the encryption process. To date, the IETF has specified two encryption algorithms for confidentiality (but will specify additional algorithms in the future). Not surprisingly, given the popularity of DES and 3DES, these are the two algorithms that the IETF has specified. More specifically, DES-CBC and 3DES-CBC were selected.

However, Microsoft's dial-up network (DUN) software uses a non-standard encryption protocol for PPP confidentiality—**Microsoft Point-to-Point Encryption (MPPE)**. Although MPPE is non-standard, it is widely used.

Figure 8-7 shows that the sender encrypts the PPP frame and places it within another PPP frame with a clear text header.

TEST YOUR UNDERSTANDING

7. What is the benefit of RADIUS?
8. Is authentication mandatory in PPP?
9. a) How often is PAP authentication done? b) What is the main problem with PAP?
10. a) In CHAP, what does the applicant do? b) What does the verifier do? c) How often is CHAP authentication done?
11. a) In MS-CHAP, what is the shared secret? b) Why is it attractive to use this type of shared secret? c) Why is using this type of shared secret a potential problem? d) What types of RASs most commonly use MS-CHAP?
12. a) Why is EAP attractive? b) In which 802 standard is EAP used?
13. What encryption algorithms have been defined to date for PPP confidentiality? Be specific.

Figure 8-7   PPP Encryption

PPTP AND L2TP

PPP Tunneling

Although PPP is attractive, it can be used only over a single data link, as Figure 8-8 shows. This is fine for dial-in remote access. However, to be used in VPNs, it would have to travel across multiple networks, each of which would be a single data link. PPP would stop at the end of the first network (data link).

As Figure 8-8 shows, the solution is to tunnel PPP frames within IP packets. **Tunneling** is carrying one message within another message. IP packets, unlike PPP frames, can travel easily through internets. Tunneling allows the end-to-end delivery of PPP frames across an Internet.

It might seem odd to see a frame encapsulated within an IP packet. In Chapter 3, we saw that packets are encapsulated in frames. However, nothing prevents a packet from encapsulating a frame. In any network along the way, the IP packet carrying the PPP frame will be carried within a frame for that network. So within a network, we would see a network frame encapsulating an IP packet that in turn encapsulates a PPP frame. This is hardly elegant, but it works.

In PPP tunneling, the two parties served by the tunnel believe they have a simple PPP connection between them. This means that companies can continue to use the traditional RAS infrastructure they installed for PPP dial-up access. This maintenance of the traditional RAS infrastructure is the main reason for PPP tunneling.

Figure 8-8   PPP on Direct Links and Internets

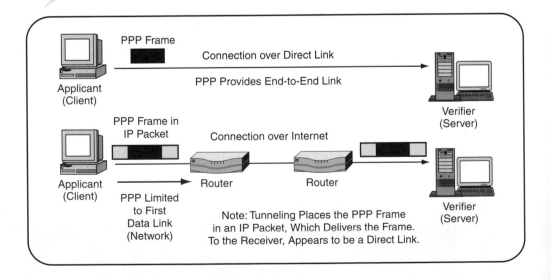

In PPP tunneling, the two parties served by the tunnel believe they have a simple PPP connection between them. This means that companies can continue to use the traditional RAS infrastructure they installed for PPP dial-up access. This maintenance of the traditional RAS infrastructure is the main reason for PPP tunneling.

TEST YOUR UNDERSTANDING

14. a) Why is tunneling needed for PPP? b) How is PPP tunneled across the Internet?

Point-to-Point Tunneling Protocol (PPTP)

For RASs based on Microsoft Windows NT and later versions of Windows, the most widely used PPP tunneling protocol is the **Point-to-Point Tunneling Protocol (PPTP)**. Figure 8-9 illustrates how PPTP usually works.

Client Software

The client must support PPTP. In Windows, this has been the case since Windows 95 (with upgraded dial-up network software). Thanks to this long-time support in Windows and the dominance of Windows on client PCs, many corporations rely on PPTP to implement remote access tunneling. However, PPTP is not an IETF standard,[5] and non-Windows clients do not always implement it.

Connection to the PPTP Access Concentrator

Most commonly, PPTP is supported by ISPs. The PPTP client PC connects to an ISP that has a **PPTP access concentrator** at the ISP point-of-presence. (Not all ISP access servers offer PPTP access concentrator support.) The ISP connects the client PC with

Figure 8-9   Point-to-Point Tunneling Protocol (PPTP)

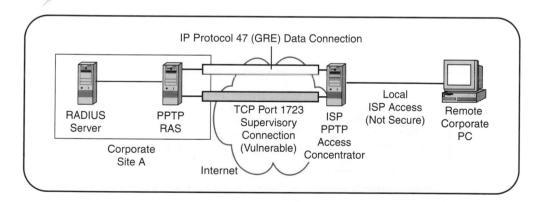

---

[5] There is an IETF RFC describing PPTP, but it is an informational RFC, not a standard.

the concentrator, which then takes over. This connection between the client PC and the access concentrator uses the PPP protocol.

PPTP Connection to the RAS

Next, the PPTP access concentrator establishes a secure connection between itself and the remote access server (RAS)[6] at the corporate site to which the client PC wishes to connect. This connection is set up and maintained via a TCP connection (on TCP Port 1723).

PPTP Data Transmission

Although communication between the access concentrator and the RAS uses a TCP control connection, actual data transfers encapsulate PPP frames directly within IP packets. More specifically, Figure 8-10 shows that the PPP frame is first placed within an **enhanced Generic Routing Encapsulation (GRE)** packet and then within a new IP packet. The new IP header will have 47 in its protocol field to indicate that it carries a GRE packet.

PPTP Authentication

PPTP effectively creates a simple PPP connection between the client PC and the RAS within the PPTP connection. PPTP uses the PPP client authentication methods discussed earlier in this chapter to authenticate the client PC user to the RAS. (Separately, the PPTP access concentrator and the RAS also authenticate themselves to one another.)

PPTP User Data Encryption

When a Windows client is used, PPTP normally uses **Microsoft Point-to-Point Encryption (MPPE)** to encrypt data for confidentiality. This method uses a session key generated from the hashed user password on the server the user hopes to access via the RAS. This use of the hashed password to create an encryption key is a weakness because

Figure 8-10   PPTP Encapsulation for Data Frames

New IP Header; Protocol=47; IP Destination Address Is That of Remote Access Server	Enhanced General Routing Encapsulation (GRE) Header; Information About Encapsulated Packet	Encapsulated Original PPP Packet Frame

---

[6]   Some standards use the term *network access server* (NAS) instead of *remote access server* (RAS). These two terms mean the same thing.

many users have relatively short passwords, resulting in weak encryption keys. On the positive side, data are encrypted all the way from the client PC to the server to which the RAS will give the client access. This prevents data snooping at the access concentrator or RAS.

Security Weaknesses

Although PPTP Version 2 (which is the most widely used version today) fixed most security weaknesses in the first version of PPTP, PPTP still has three serious security weaknesses.

➤ It is possible for sniffers to collect login messages and use a program such as l0pht-crack to crack passwords.

➤ More seriously, the separate TCP connection for control communication is unsecured and open to attacks.

➤ There is no message-by-message authentication—only message-by-message confidentiality.

However, exploiting these weaknesses is fairly difficult, and many firms are willing to give up a moderate amount of security to be able to use a proven tunneling method that most of their remote clients support natively.

TEST YOUR UNDERSTANDING

15.   a) In what versions of Windows has PPTP been implemented? b) Why is this important? c) Explain the purposes of the PPTP access concentrator and the RAS. d) Briefly describe the structure of the PPTP data packet. e) How are user authentication and encryption handled within PPTP? f) What are the main security weaknesses of PPTP?

Layer 2 Tunneling Protocol (L2TP)

PPTP is essentially a Microsoft invention, although it was sponsored by an industry consortium of limited breadth. The IETF has recently created a superior standard for PPP tunneling, the **Layer 2 Tunneling Protocol (L2TP)**. Although L2TP probably will replace PPTP eventually, L2TP is still too underdeveloped for most firms to adopt.

L2TP Operation

As Figure 8-11 indicates, a user typically establishes a DSL connection to a DSL access multiplexer (DSLAM). The DSLAM then establishes an L2TP connection to the RAS. This is similar to the way PPTP works.

Not Tied to IP Internets

PPTP was created to tunnel PPP frames over IP networks only. In contrast, L2TP can tunnel frames over a variety of networks—including IP internets but also including Frame Relay and ATM. L2TP is a more general tunneling protocol.

Security

Relying on IPsec for Security   Rather than reinventing the wheel, L2TP does not provide security itself. Rather, it typically requires the use of IPsec security (discussed later in this chapter) to protect L2TP traffic. In other words, L2TP restricts itself to the tunneling of frames across multiple networks.

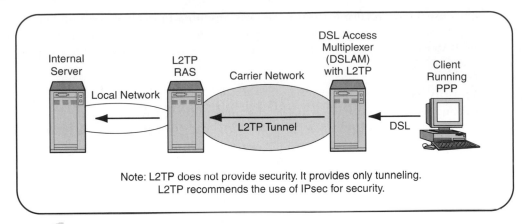

Figure 8-11   Layer 2 Tunneling Protocol (L2TP)

No Unprotected Control Channel   Also, L2TP has no separate unprotected control channel, as there is in PPTP. L2TP tunnels have internal control signaling within their individual encrypted data streams.

Limited Deployment
Although L2TP/IPsec is promising, it has seen only limited deployment to date.

Immature State of Development   Although L2TP is inherently attractive, it is a new standard that is not fully developed. Consequently, few L2TP products are available, and those that are available often are fairly rudimentary and have interoperability issues with the products of different vendors.

IPsec and Certificate Deployment   In addition, deploying L2TP with IPsec requires the deployment of digital certificates to all clients and servers. Deploying certificates is expensive and difficult, and deploying IPsec is expensive, as well.

Only Supported in Recent Versions of Windows   Finally, L2TP is supported only in Windows 2000 and later versions of Windows. This means that the majority of all corporate computers would need to have additional software installed to handle L2TP and IPsec.

TEST YOUR UNDERSTANDING
16.   a) How are PPTP and L2TP broadly similar? b) How is L2TP a more general tunneling approach? c) Does L2TP provide its own security for L2TP frames traveling through the Internet? d) If not, how are L2TP frames usually secured? e) Why has L2TP seen only modest deployment to date?

Voluntary Versus Compulsory Tunneling

Who decides when tunneling should be used? The answer is that there are two options. In **voluntary tunneling**, the remote user decides whether or not to use tunneling. This gives the user maximum freedom, but companies might want to require that tunneling be used so that incoming connections are secure.

In contrast, when corporations tell ISPs to do **compulsory tunneling**, users who attempt to connect to certain IP addresses will simply be tunneled automatically by their ISP, without the user's request and sometimes even without the user's knowledge.

TEST YOUR UNDERSTANDING

17. a) Distinguish between voluntary and mandatory tunneling. b) Why might a company create a policy requiring mandatory tunneling?

IPSEC

For very strong security, some virtual private networks (VPNs) use a family of security standards collectively called **IPsec (IP security)**. IPsec offers much stronger security than PPTP or L2TP. However, IPsec also is more complex and therefore more expensive to introduce than its Layer 2 cousin.

Cryptographic Systems and Internet Layer Protection

SSL/TLS for Non-Transparent Transport Layer Security

Earlier, we looked at SSL/TLS, which operates at the transport layer. This allows it to protect multiple applications, although its lack of transparency limits it primarily to HTTP webservice and some e-mail systems.

IPsec: Transparent Internet Layer Security

In contrast, IPsec operates at the internet layer. This allows it to provide security for the transport layer, including all TCP and UDP traffic, and all other traffic carried in the data field of the IP packet, including ICMP messages. Application layer messages are also protected.

In IPsec, this protection is transparent. There is no need to modify applications or transport layer protocols to work with IPsec. In fact, transport layer protocols and application protocols are not even aware of IPsec's presence when IPsec is used.

IPsec in Both IPv4 and IPv6

IPsec originally was intended for the new version of the Internet Protocol, IP Version 6 (IPv6). However, when it was created, IPsec could be used with IP Version 4 (IPv4) as well. In other words, no matter which version of IP a network uses, IPsec will protect it.

Transport and Tunnel Modes

The most basic concept in IPsec is that there are two **IPsec modes**, that is, ways of operating. As Figure 8-12 indicates, these are the transport mode and the tunnel mode.

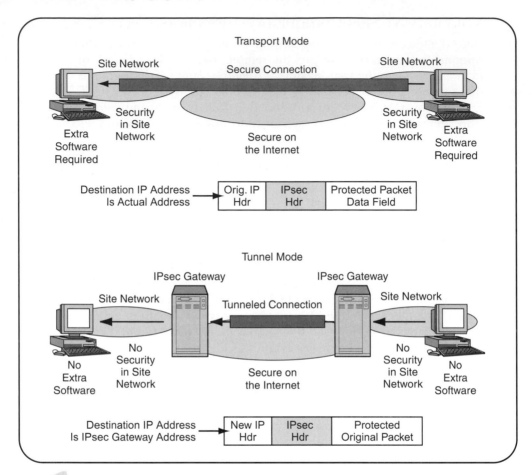

Figure 8-12 IPsec Operation: Tunnel and Transport Modes

Transport Mode

As Figure 8-12 indicates, **transport mode** is used for host-to-host security. Transport mode allows two hosts to communicate securely without regard to what else is happening on the network.

Location of the IPsec Header The figure notes that an **IPsec header** is inserted after the main IP header. As discussed later, this header provides protection for higher-layer protocols, that is, transport and application layer protocols.

Sniffers Can See Stations' IP Addresses In some cases, this header also might provide limited protection for the IP header before it. However, because the IP destination address is needed to route the packet to the destination host, the IP header must be transmitted in the clear, without encryption. This allows a snooper listening to network traffic to understand the distribution of IP addresses, and this can lead to certain types of attacks.

End-to-End Protection   Transport mode is attractive because it provides security when packets travel over internal networks, as well as across the Internet. This end-to-end security can be used even if the internal networks of the sender and receiver are not trusted.

Probable Need to Install IPsec Software on the Two Hosts   On the negative side, transport mode requires that both communication partners have IPsec software on their computers. Microsoft only added IPsec software on its Windows clients and servers beginning with Windows 2000, so transport mode typically requires adding software to the computers instead of using native operating system protocol support.

Tunnel Mode

In contrast, Figure 8-12 shows that **tunnel mode** normally is used to protect communication only between two **IPsec gateways** at different sites. These gateways send traffic securely through the Internet between themselves.

Protection of IP Addresses   In tunnel mode, even the original IP header is fully protected. The transmitting IP gateway encapsulates the original IP packet in a new IP packet by adding a new IP header and an IPsec header.

   The destination IP address in the new IP header is the IP address of the destination IPsec gateway, not the IP address of the ultimate destination host. Therefore, if an adversary snoops on the company's traffic, the only IP addresses it will see will be those of the site's IP gateways. The adversary will learn nothing about other IP addresses.

Protection Is Provided by IPsec Gateways   The source IPsec gateway receives original IP packets and encapsulates them as shown in the figure. The receiving IPsec gateway, in turn, decapsulates the original IP packet and sends it on its way to the destination host within the receiving IPsec gateway's site network.

No Software Is Required on the Two Hosts   On the positive side, tunnel mode operation does not require installing IPsec software on the clients or servers (as noted earlier, native IPsec support in Windows only began with Windows 2000). In fact, the clients and servers do not even know that their packets are being protected as they travel over the Internet.

No Protection at the Two Sites   On the negative side, tunnel mode provides no protection for IP packets passing through the site networks at the two sites. It provides protection only during the packet's passage through the Internet. This leaves packets open to attack within site networks.

Combining Modes

The two IPsec modes can be combined. For instance, two hosts can use transport mode for end-to-end security. At the same time, their packets may be intercepted by IPsec gateways at their sites for tunneling through the Internet to the IPsec gateway at the other site.

This will provide end-to-end protection through transport mode IPsec. It also will hide the IP addresses of the two hosts between the two sites thanks to tunnel mode protection.

TEST YOUR UNDERSTANDING

18. a) Distinguish between transport and tunnel modes in IPsec. b) What are the strengths of each? c) What are the weaknesses of each?

IPsec Headers

The preceding discussion has been deliberately vague about two points. First, it mentioned an "IPsec header" without saying what it was. Second, it talked vaguely about "protection" without specifying whether this was confidentiality, authentication, message integrity, or some combination of these and other protections.

That vagueness was deliberate because in both transport and tunnel modes, IPsec offers two different types of protection. For each type of protection, IPsec uses a different type of IPsec header. Therefore, four mode-header combinations exist.

Figure 8-13 illustrates the placement of these IPsec headers. For IP Version 6, these headers are extension headers. For IP Version 4, these are options.

Encapsulating Security Payload (ESP)

The most commonly used IPsec header is the **Encapsulating Security Payload (ESP)** header. ESP is attractive because it offers full security, including confidentiality, message-by-message authentication, and message integrity. We will see next that another IPsec header type, the Authentication Header, does not offer confidentiality. IP packets carrying ESP headers have the value 50 in their protocol fields.

Figure 8-13 shows that ESP has two parts, a header and a trailer. ESP extends confidentiality to the data following the ESP header and to part of the ESP trailer, as well.

Figure 8-13   IPsec ESP and AH Protection

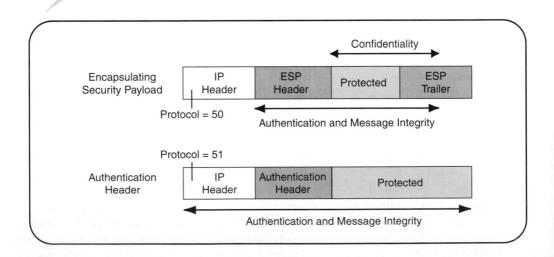

The figure also shows that authentication and message integrity are provided to the entire IPsec header and to part of the ESP trailer.

As a reminder, IPsec headers work in both transport and tunnel modes. In transport mode, the information between the ESP header and ESP trailer is the protected transport header and application message. In tunnel mode, it is the entire original IP packet.

Authentication Header

The other type of IPsec header is the **Authentication Header (AH)**. Like ESP, AH offers authentication and message integrity. However, unlike ESP, AH does not offer confidentiality. Anyone intercepting the message can read it.

Why use a security system that lets anyone read your messages? The answer is that some countries outlaw encryption for confidentiality in certain situations, for instance, in traffic sent to another country. For these situations, AH's authentication and message integrity support still is valuable.

Figure 8-13 shows that AH does offer a bit more authentication and message integrity protection than ESP. AH authenticates and provides message integrity for the entire AH header (there is no AH trailer) and also for the preceding IP header. IP packets carrying AHs have the value 51 in their protocol fields.

TEST YOUR UNDERSTANDING

19.   a) Distinguish between ESP and AH IPsec headers in terms of what protection is given. b) When would you use AH?

Security Associations (SAs)

Before two hosts or IPsec gateways communicate, they have to establish security associations (SAs). The security association is the most fundamental, and perhaps the most confusing, part of IPsec.

How SAs Work

Figure 8-14 illustrates security associations. A **security association (SA)** is an agreement about how two hosts or two IPsec gateways will provide security. The SA specifies what specific algorithms the sending party will use to implement whatever security processes will be used for confidentiality (with ESP), authentication, message integrity, and anti-replay protection. It summarizes the agreement the two parties settle upon for how they will communicate securely.

Separate SAs in the Two Directions

Note that when two parties communicate, *two* security associations must exist—one in each direction. If Party A and Party B communicate, there must be an SA for Party A to use to send to Party B and a separate SA for Party B to use to send to Party A. This use of two security associations allows different levels of protection in the two directions if this is desirable.

Policy-Based SAs

SAs may be governed by policies built into the hosts or IPsec gateways. The company may permit only a few designated combinations of security algorithms to be used as SAs. For instance, certain encryption algorithms might be considered to be too weak to be safe or might be considered to be too processing-intensive to be worthwhile.

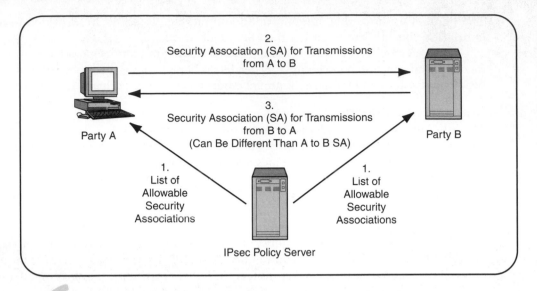

Figure 8-14   IPsec Security Associations

Establishing Security Associations

Establishing security associations is a fairly complex, two-phase process, as Figure 8-15 illustrates.

Establishing Internet Key Exchange (IKE) Security Associations

In the first phase, IPsec relies on the **Internet Key Exchange (IKE)** standard. Although its name suggests that IKE does only key exchange, it handles all of the steps needed to establish a security association. These include the following:

> ➤ Communication to agree upon security algorithms to be used to set up the IKE SA.
> ➤ Authentication.
> ➤ The exchange of symmetric session keys to be used in the IKE session. Different session keys can be used for confidentiality and authentication.

As its name suggests, Internet Key Exchange is not limited to IPsec. It is a general protocol for establishing security associations in cryptographic systems to be used over the Internet.

Establishing IPsec Security Associations Within IKE Protection

However, this generality also means that IKE is not sufficient for IPsec, which has specific security association needs. As Figure 8-15 illustrates, when two parties (in this case IPsec gateways) establish an IKE SA, this forms a blanket of protection within which the two parties can safely negotiate IPsec SAs. For instance, two IPsec gateways may establish different IPsec SAs for traffic types of different sensitivity.

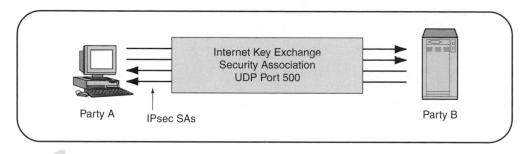

Figure 8-15   Establishing IPsec Security Associations Using IKE

TEST YOUR UNDERSTANDING

20. a) What does an SA specify? b) When two parties want to communicate in both directions with security, how many SAs must be established? c) Why are policies created for SAs?

21. a) Distinguish between IKE SAs and IPsec SAs. b) Is IKE limited to protecting IPsec?

IPsec Mandatory Default Security Protocols

One of the advantages of negotiation is that it permits the two parties to negotiate which specific algorithms they will use for confidentiality and other matters. However, **mandatory default** algorithms *must* be supported and will be used as the **default**, that is, will be used automatically if the two sides do not specify an alternative.

Diffie-Hellman Key Agreement

For IKE and IPsec, the mandatory default algorithm for key exchange is **Diffie-Hellman Key Agreement**, which was discussed in the previous chapter.

DES-CBC

The mandatory default algorithm for bulk encryption (sending long messages) is **DES-CBC**, which also was covered in the previous chapter.

HMAC for Message-by-Message Authentication

In the previous chapter, we saw digital signatures, which use public key encryption to provide message-by-message authentication and integrity.

Although digital signatures are good, the public key encryption used to create digital signatures is slow. An analog of digital signatures, called **key-Hashed Message Authentication Codes (HMACs)**, can be created with hashing.

To create an HMAC, a secret key is added to the original plaintext message, as Figure 8-16 indicates. The combined string of bits is then hashed using MD5 or SHA1. This creates the HMAC. The HMAC is appended to the outgoing messages for authentication.

IKE and IPsec use a slightly more complicated HMAC system described in RFC 2104. Their HMAC method adds a number of refinements to simple hashing in order

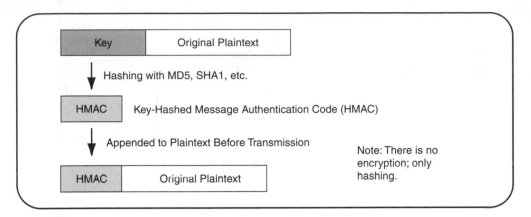

Figure 8-16   Key-Hashed Message Authentication Codes (HMACs) for Message-by-Message Authentication in IPsec

to be more immune to attacks. RFC 2104 defines several HMAC variants that use different hashing algorithms, including HMAC-MD5 and HMAC-SHA1.

Recall from the previous chapter that public key encryption is slow. Consequently, digital signatures, which use public key encryption, place heavy burdens on servers. In contrast, hashing is a fast process, so using HMACs places only a small burden on servers.

HMACs Lack Nonrepudiation

Repudiation means that a sender can deny that he or she sent a message. Digital signatures offer **nonrepudiation** protection, meaning that senders cannot repudiate messages they sent. Digital signatures are signed by the true party's private key, which only the true party should know.

However, HMACs lack nonrepudiation protection. HMACs are created using a key that *both* the sender and receiver know. Consequently, a sender might repudiate a message, pointing out that the receiver also could have created the message and the HMAC. When nonrepudiation is important, HMACs should not be used.

TEST YOUR UNDERSTANDING

22.   a) What is the IPsec mandatory default algorithm for session key exchange? b) What is the default algorithm for confidentiality?

23.   a) In terms of encryption method how does HMAC authentication differ from digital signature authentication? b) In what way is this difference in HMAC authentication superior to digital signature authentication? c) When is HMAC authentication applied: for one-time authentication, occasional authentication, or message-by-message authentication? d) What is nonrepudiation, and do HMACs offer it? e) Do digital signatures?

IPsec Windows Implementation

IPsec is a newcomer to Microsoft Windows. It was only implemented in Windows 2000. Consequently, computers with older versions of Windows must have the software or work in tunnel mode. Therefore, tunnel mode is dominant today.

TEST YOUR UNDERSTANDING

24. In what versions of Windows has IPsec been implemented?

KERBEROS

The default client-server authentication method in Windows 2000 and later versions of Windows is **Kerberos**.[7] As shown in Figure 8-17, three parties are involved in Kerberos authentication: an applicant, a verifier, and a Kerberos server.

Figure 8-17   Kerberos Authentication System

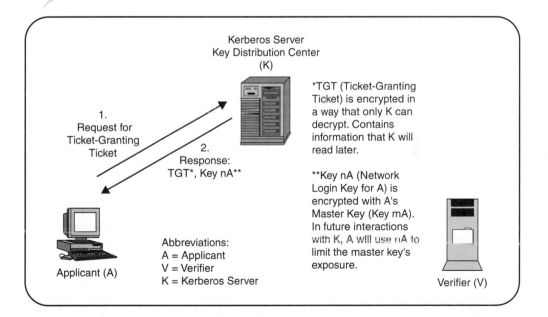

Kerberos Server
Key Distribution Center
(K)

1.
Request for
Ticket-Granting
Ticket

2.
Response:
TGT*, Key nA**

*TGT (Ticket-Granting Ticket) is encrypted in a way that only K can decrypt. Contains information that K will read later.

**Key nA (Network Login Key for A) is encrypted with A's Master Key (Key mA). In future interactions with K, A will use nA to limit the master key's exposure.

Abbreviations:
A = Applicant
V = Verifier
K = Kerberos Server

Applicant (A)

Verifier (V)

---

[7] In mythology, Kerberos (or Cerberus) is a three-headed dog that guards the gates of the underworld, keeping out anyone still living. More precisely, it eats anyone still living, removing that inconvenient "still living" impediment. Kerberos received its name because it has three elements: the two communicating partners and the Kerberos server.

Not shown in the figure, the Kerberos server may access an Active Directory server that stores information about users. The Kerberos server also can store the information itself. We will assume the latter in our discussion.

Authentication

As Figure 8-17 shows, the first phase in a station using Kerberos authentication is for the applicant to be authenticated by the Kerberos server. This is called the **Authentication Service**.

Master Key

Each station has a **master key**, which is created by hashing a password. Both the station and the Kerberos server know this master key. The applicant's master key is Key mA.

Network Login Key

It is undesirable to use the master key extensively because such keys are rarely changed. Using them extensively would make them easy to guess. Yet before Kerberos Version 5 (Kerberos V5), which is the basis for authentication in Windows 2000 and later versions of the operating system, the master key was used frequently.

Kerberos V5 added the authentication service phase to give the station a **network login key** that the station will use only for the duration of its login to the network or for a maximum period of several hours—whichever is shorter. For the applicant, this is Key nA. The station will use this network login key in all dealings with the Kerberos server during this network session. Each time the station logs into the network, it receives a new network login key. This frequent change of keys makes key guessing difficult.

Ticket-Granting Ticket

As Figure 8-17 shows, the applicant station begins by sending a message to the Kerberos server to request a **Ticket-Granting Ticket**. The station will need this Ticket-Granting Ticket after the authentication service phase to request connections to other stations.

The Kerberos server authenticates the user and sends back a response message that contains the network login key, Key nA, and the Ticket-Granting Ticket.

The network login key part of the response is encrypted with the applicant station's master key, Key mA. Other stations cannot decrypt the network login key. If an impostor station sends a Ticket-Granting Ticket request message, the impostor will not be able to decrypt the network login key the Kerberos server sends back because only the true user knows Key mK.

Ticket-Granting Service

The authentication service is used only once in a network login session—usually for a day or less. However, during that network session, the station might want to connect to several other stations. Each time an applicant station wants to make a connection to a verifier server, the applicant station must use the **Ticket-Granting Service**, as Figure 8-18 shows. In the figure, the applicant is a client, and the verifier is a server. This is the normal situation in real organizations.

Ticket-Granting Request Message

The client applicant begins the process. It sends a message to the Kerberos server requesting a Service Ticket for the server verifier. This request message includes the Ticket-Granting Ticket.

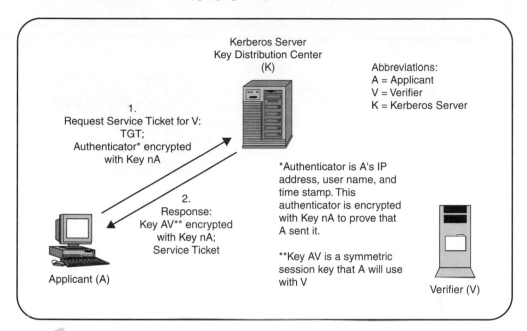

Kerberos Server
Key Distribution Center
(K)

Abbreviations:
A = Applicant
V = Verifier
K = Kerberos Server

1.
Request Service Ticket for V:
TGT;
Authenticator* encrypted
with Key nA

2.
Response:
Key AV** encrypted
with Key nA;
Service Ticket

*Authenticator is A's IP
address, user name, and
time stamp. This
authenticator is encrypted
with Key nA to prove that
A sent it.

**Key AV is a symmetric
session key that A will use
with V

Applicant (A)

Verifier (V)

Figure 8-18   Kerberos Ticket-Granting Service I

Why does the applicant have to send back the Ticket-Granting Ticket? The answer is that the Ticket-Granting Ticket contains the applicant's name and the applicant's network login key encrypted with the master key of the server.

But why does the server need this information? After all, the Kerberos server came up with this information and could have stored it in memory! The answer is that storing this information in memory could use up too much memory if there are many stations in the realm (service area) served by the Kerberos server. Sending the information to the applicant in the Ticket-Granting Ticket and then having the applicant send it back later seems like an odd way to do things, but it saves Kerberos server memory.

This request message also contains an authenticator. This is the applicant's IP address, user name, and time stamp. It is encrypted with Key nA. The Kerberos server decrypts the authenticator and compares it with unencrypted information, such as the source IP address in the client's packet. This allows the Kerberos server to verify that the applicant really did send the request because only A should know Key nA.

The Service Ticket

The Kerberos server sends back a response message that contains two main things. First, it contains a session key, Key AV, that the applicant will use to communicate with the verifier for confidentiality after authentication.

The second main part is the **Service Ticket**. Among other things, the Service Ticket contains the session key, Key AV. However, in the Service Ticket, the key in the

Service Ticket is encrypted with the *verifier's* master key, Key mV. Consequently, the applicant cannot read the Service Ticket it sends to the verifier. Only the verifier can read it.

Sending the Service Ticket

The applicant then sends the Service Ticket to the verifier, as Figure 8-19 shows. As just noted, the Service Ticket is encrypted with the verifier's master key, Key mV. The verifier decrypts the Service Ticket and reads the session key, Key AV, which is encrypted within the Service Ticket.

The message to the verifier also contains an authenticator, this time encrypted with Key AV. The verifier decrypts the authenticator with Key AV and compares the decrypted information with the applicant's IP address and other clear-text information.

The verifier knows that the Kerberos server sent the session key, Kcy AV, because only the verifier and the Kerberos server know Key mV, which was used to encrypt the Service Ticket containing Key AV.

The verifier also knows that the applicant also knows the session key, Key AV. The applicant must have used this key to encrypt the authenticator because when the verifier used Key AV to decrypt the authenticator, it succeeded.

If the Kerberos server sent the verifier the session key, it would only send the session key to a trusted applicant that the Kerberos server had previously authenticated, so the applicant is authenticated.

Figure 8-19 Kerberos Ticket-Granting Service II

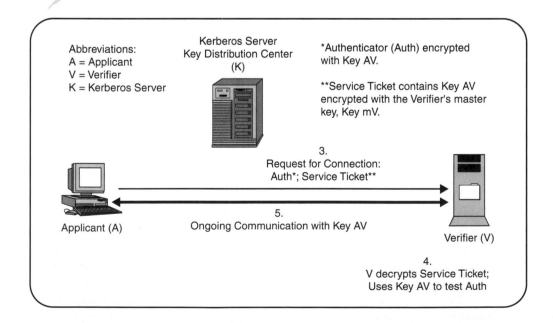

Ongoing Communication

Now that the applicant is authenticated, the applicant and the verifier engage in ongoing communication with symmetric session key, Key AV.

Perspective

A Complete Cryptographic System

Although Kerberos is viewed as an authentication system, it also implements key exchange and ongoing communication. It is a complete cryptographic system.

No Public Key Encryption

Note that Kerberos does not use public key encryption. This makes Kerberos fast. It also means that it is not necessary to distribute digital certificates to all stations on the network. However, because of the advantages of public key encryption, Kerberos can be used with public key encryption during the authentication service phase.

Complexity

It is frustrating to write about Kerberos because it is an extremely complex cryptographic system. RFC 1510, which defines Kerberos Version 5, is good reading for anyone who wants to see the nuts and bolts of how a well-designed cryptographic service faces replay dangers and other threats. However, the RFC is poorly written, for instance using the term "server" with little explanation for both the Kerberos server (there can be separate authentication and ticket-granting Kerberos servers) and verifier servers.

Single Sign-On (SSO)

Kerberos and some other cryptographic systems provide single **sign-on (SSO)** service. This means that a client needs only a single key, namely its master key. Even if it deals with dozens of servers throughout the day, it will not need multiple keys. This is good news for users.

However, it also means that if someone can take over a PC, either physically or remotely, the attacker can then sign on as the user on any computer on the network. SSO might be good news for users, but it is somewhat dangerous unless implemented properly.

Problems

Although Kerberos is promising, it has some important potential problems.

> ➤ One problem with Kerberos is that all applications must be "Kerberosized"; that is, they must be written to work with Kerberos.

> ➤ In addition, Microsoft's implementation of the Kerberos protocol uses some unusual interpretations of the Kerberos protocol. This has led to compatibility problems with Kerberos products from other vendors.

> ➤ Finally, and most importantly, Microsoft only began to offer Kerberos in Windows 2000, so it will take some time for Kerberos to be widely accepted, even among Microsoft users.

TEST YOUR UNDERSTANDING

25.   a) In Kerberos, what two things does the Authentication Service provide to the station? b) In the Ticket-Granting Service, what two things does the applicant receive from the Kerberos server? c) What does the applicant send on to the verifier? d) Is Kerberos a full cryptographic system? e) Why is Kerberos fast? f) What is SSO? g) Why is SSO good? h) Why is SSO dangerous? i) What are the three problems with Kerberos service? j) What three types of key will an applicant use over the course of a typical day?

FIREWALLS AND CRYPTOGRAPHIC SYSTEMS

Firewalls and cryptographic systems are two of the main countermeasures that companies can employ against attackers. Unfortunately, the two countermeasures often do not work well together.

NAT and Cryptographic Systems

In Chapter 5, we saw that NAT firewalls remove source IP addresses and port numbers from outgoing packets and replace them with stand-in source IP addresses and port numbers. The NAT firewall reverses this process for incoming connections.

IPsec, which offers authentication that normally includes the IP addresses and port numbers of internal computers, will reject packets whose IP addresses and port numbers have been changed by NAT. Although the IETF is working on ways to get IPsec (and other security protocols) through NAT firewalls, NAT firewalls today use proprietary approaches that often do not interoperate.[8]

Encryption Versus Inspection

Although the NAT problem is frustrating, there is a much more fundamental problem with using firewalls and cryptographic systems. Firewalls work by examining the contents of packets to detect attack patterns. However, they cannot do this if the information contained in packets is encrypted!

As Figure 8-20 shows, one approach is to place the firewall *after* a site's cryptographic server. This way, the firewall can read packets after they have been decrypted. However, this leaves the cryptographic server open to attack. More fundamentally, IPsec transport mode and other security systems only do encryption and decryption on the end hosts. In such cases, it is not possible for the firewall to do filtering. The cryptographic traffic will have to forego the filtering that firewalls provide. This is highly undesirable.

Consequently, many firms simply punch holes through their firewalls for VPN traffic, giving up on filtering such traffic. To give some examples:

➤   If a firm uses IPsec with ESP, IP Protocol 50 will have to be allowed through the firewall, as well as UDP Port 500 for IKE communication.

➤   If a firm uses IP with AH, IP Protocol 51 and UDP Port 500 will have to be passed.

---

[8]   The simplest approach is static NAT, in which a single external IP address and port number are always used for a single internal IP address and port number.

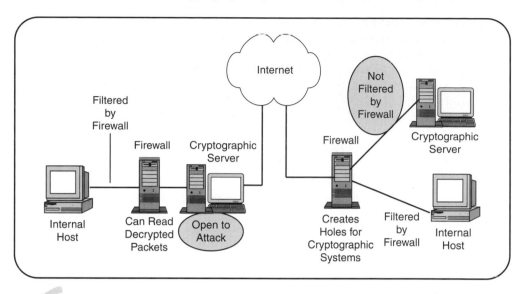

Figure 8-20   Placement of Firewalls and Cryptographic Servers

➤ For PPTP, IP Protocol 47 (GRE) will have to be allowed through for data connections, and packets to TCP Port 1723 will have to be allowed through for the supervisory connection.

➤ L2TP normally uses UDP Port 1701 but can use TCP Port 1701.

➤ For Kerberos, TCP Port 88 and UDP Port 88 will have to be allowed through.

TEST YOUR UNDERSTANDING

26. a) Why does IPsec have a problem with NAT firewalls? b) Is there a general solution to this problem? c) Why are firewalls and cryptographic systems inherently incompatible? d) What are the two approaches to using cryptographic systems with firewalls? e) Evaluate their relative merits.

CONCLUSION

Chapter 7 discussed the elements of cryptography. This chapter discussed how those elements are brought together in cryptographic systems that provide multiple protections automatically, with little or no user intervention.

We began with the simplest cryptographic system, SSL/TLS, which is widely used in electronic commerce. We then looked at the issue of PPP tunneling via PPTP or L2TP to preserve a company's investment in its RAS infrastructure created for dial-up PPP links. Next, we looked at the more general, albeit also more complex, IPsec security. Finally, we looked at Kerberos, which has been Microsoft's strategic focus for user authentication since Windows 2000.

We have seen that the most popular cryptographic systems, including SSL/TLS and PPTP, have some security weaknesses. Although newer security protocols, including

L2TP, IPsec, and Kerberos, have been created, they are new and generally complex. It will take some time for products incorporating them to become fully developed, interoperable with the products of other vendors, and widely used.

Whenever discussing cryptographic systems, it is important to focus on the fact that the overwhelming majority of all corporate client computers use Microsoft Windows and indeed pre-Windows 2000 versions of the operating system. Any cryptographic system that does not reflect this reality is not likely to be successful.

THOUGHT QUESTIONS

1. Although SSL/TLS and PPTP are comparatively weak cryptographic systems, they are still widely used compared to better cryptographic systems. Why do you think that is?
2. a) Why is it important whether Windows supports a security protocol natively? b) Why is it important which versions of Windows support a protocol natively?
3. Modify the firewall ingress and egress ACLs shown in Chapter 5 to allow ESP tunnel-mode connections from the outside. The IPsec gateway is 60.40.3.86. The inside server is 60.2.3.4. The external client is 1.2.3.4. Just give line numbers for where the added statement or statements would go. Put them as close to the top of the list as you can without sacrificing protections.
4. Two hosts communicate via IPsec in transport mode. Between their sites, their communication goes through an ISP tunnel mode connection between IPsec gateways at the two sites. Draw the headers and trailers you would see at the internet layer. (Hint: See Figure 8-12.)

DESIGN QUESTION

1. You want to start an e-commerce site to sell galumpkes. Users can search to find the type of galumpke they wish, read design specifications for it, add items to a shopping cart, and pay by credit card. Which of these actions will you protect with SSL/TLS? Which of these actions would you not protect? Justify your answers.

TROUBLESHOOTING QUESTION

1. You are using IPsec for security. Your firewall is designed to stop a certain type of attack packet, and its configuration has been tested and verified. Yet these attacks continue to get through and hit host computers. What might be the problem?

APPLICATION SECURITY: ELECTRONIC COMMERCE AND E-MAIL

Learning Objectives

By the end of this chapter, you should be able to discuss:

- Why attackers increasingly focus on applications as targets.
- The main steps in securing applications.
- Securing webservice and e-commerce service.
- Securing e-mail.
- Securing other applications, with emphasis on database and instant messaging.

GENERAL APPLICATION SECURITY ISSUES

In Chapter 6, we discussed host security, focusing on the operating system. However, it is equally important to harden applications running on the host. In this chapter, we discuss application security, focusing on the two most important applications today: webservice/e-commerce and electronic mail (e-mail).

Executing Commands with the Privileges of a Compromised Application

Most basically, after attackers take over an application, they usually can execute commands with the access permissions of the compromised application. Many applications run with root (super user privileges), so taking them over gives the attacker total control of the host.

Often, attackers can take over an application with a single message, so gaining root tends to be far easier through application exploits than through password guessing, session hijacking, or other traditionally difficult attacks on the operating system and its network stack. Although hackers still attack operating systems, breaking in by taking over applications is far more popular today.

TEST YOUR UNDERSTANDING

    1. a) What can hackers gain by taking over application programs? b) What is the most popular way for hackers to take over hosts?

Buffer Overflow Attacks

As discussed in Chapter 6, when vulnerabilities are found in application programs, attackers create exploit software. Vendors offer fixes—either software patches or manual work-arounds. It is important to have reasonably up-to-date application software and to apply all patches.

Buffers and Overflows

The most widespread vulnerabilities in application programs are buffer overflow vulnerabilities. Programs often store information temporarily in areas of RAM called **buffers**. If the attacker sends a message with more bytes than the programmer had allocated for a buffer, the attacker's information will spill over into other areas of RAM. This is a **buffer overflow**. The impact of a buffer overflow can range from nothing to the crashing of the server or the ability to execute arbitrary commands on the server.

Stacks

Often, programs run subprograms. When a program must put one subprogram on hold to run another, it writes information about the suspended program in a **stack entry**. Figure 9-2 shows a single stack entry.

Return Address

The stack entry's **return address** points to the location in RAM that holds the address of the next command to be executed in the suspended program. (Programs are stored in RAM when they execute.) When the entry is retrieved from (popped off of) the

EXECUTING COMMANDS WITH THE PRIVILEGES OF A COMPROMISED APPLICATION

If an attacker takes over an application, the attacker can execute commands with the
  privileges of that application
Many applications run with super user (root) privileges

BUFFER OVERFLOW ATTACKS

From Chapter 6: Vulnerabilities, exploits, fixes (patches, manual work-arounds,
  or upgrades)
Buffers are places where data is stored temporarily
If an attacker sends too much data, a buffer might overflow, overwriting an adjacent
  section of RAM
If that section is retrieved, various problems can occur
  Read as data, read as program instructions, illegal values that cause a crash
Stacks are used to hold information temporarily on subprograms
Stack overflows might allow an attacker to execute any command (Figure 9-2)
An example: The IIS IPP Buffer Overflow Attack: Host variable is overflowed

FEW OPERATING SYSTEMS BUT MANY APPLICATIONS

Application hardening is more total work than operating system hardening

APPLICATION SECURITY ACTIONS

Understanding the server's role and threat environment
  If it runs only one or a few services, easy to disallow irrelevant things
Basics: Physical security, backup, harden the operating system
Minimize applications
  Main application
  Subsidiary applications
  Be guided by security baselines
Delete optional learning aids
Install patches
Minimize the permissions of applications
  In UNIX, use chroot to put application in a directory
  Attacks will be limited to this directory and subdirectories
  However, chroot protection can be broken, especially by root applications for which
    it is most critical
Add application layer authentication
Implement cryptographic systems

Figure 9-1   General Application Security Issues (Study Figure)

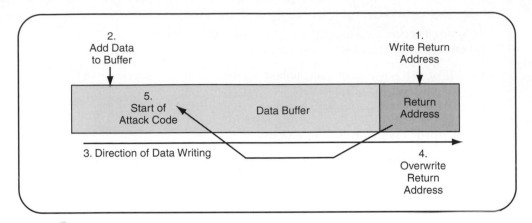

Figure 9-2   Stack Entry and Buffer Overflow

stack, the program that placed the entry there will pass control to the command at the location indicated in the return address. The return address is written into the stack entry before data is written into the buffer.

The Buffer and Buffer Overflow

The program that creates the entry then adds data to the stack's **data buffer**. This information is written from the bottom of the buffer to the top. If too much information is written into the buffer, it will create a **buffer overflow**, overwriting the return address.

Executing Attack Code

When the entry is popped off the stack, the program that called the entry will pass control to the return address for that entry. If the attacker has skillfully overwritten the return address, the return address will point back to "data" in the buffer. If this data really is program code, this attack code will be executed instead of the legitimate program's code.

An Example: The IIS IPP Buffer Overflow Attack

Microsoft's webserver software is the Internet Information Server (IIS). IIS offers a number of services, including an Internet Printing Protocol (IPP) service. Although few users ever use this service, it was turned on by default in early versions of IIS.

Vulnerability reporters discovered that IPP was vulnerable to a buffer overflow attack. Not long after, an attacker created the jill.c program to exploit this vulnerability. This exploit was written in the C programming language.

At its heart, jill.c sends the following HTTP request message to IIS. HTTP requests begin with a line indicating what should be done—in this case, executing a printing request. The next line indicates the host to which the request should go. The host name is replaced with a 420-character string that causes a buffer overflow.

```
GET /NULL.printer HTTP/1.0
Host: 420-character input to launch command shell
C:\WINNT\system32\>
```

The third line is the response from the webserver. The attack code executed when the request arrived has caused Windows to create a new command shell—what used to be called a DOS prompt. The attacker is now in a sensitive directory. In addition, the attacker has SYSTEM privileges, which means that he or she can do anything that he or she wishes to do in this directory and most other directories.

TEST YOUR UNDERSTANDING

2. a) What is a buffer? b) What is a buffer overflow attack? c) What impacts can buffer overflows have? d) In a stack overflow, what is overwritten by the overflow? e) To where does the overwritten return address point? f) In the IIS IPP buffer overflow attack, what buffer is overflowed?

Few Operating Systems, Many Applications

Although the mechanics of vulnerabilities, exploits, patches, and work-arounds are not fundamentally different for operating systems and applications, what is different is the small number of operating systems that most firms support versus the large number of applications they typically support.

For operating systems, most firms have to deal with only vulnerability reports, patches, and work-arounds from a handful of vendors. However, firms might run application programs from dozens of application software vendors. In most firms, the lion's share of all vulnerabilities and fixes relate to application programs.

Just finding information about vulnerabilities and fixes can be a maddening chore because each vendor releases information about its products' vulnerabilities and fixes in its own way. Although various bug tracking services (especially BugTraq at SecurityFocus.com) help, server administrators have to visit their application vendors' websites frequently.

Each vendor, furthermore, has different mechanisms for downloading patches.

TEST YOUR UNDERSTANDING

3. Why are patching applications more time consuming than patching operating systems?

Application Security Actions

How can companies harden applications so that they are difficult to attack? Firms can take several actions to accomplish this.

Understand the Server's Role and Threat Environment

The first task in security is to understand the environment to be protected. If a service such as e-mail runs on a single computer, for instance, then the systems administrator can rigorously cut out everything that does not deal directly with e-mail and perhaps with remote administration. However, if a server must support multiple applications, cutting out services will be a less viable option.

The threat environment is also important. If the threat environment is very dangerous, even remote administration might have to be cut off.

The Basics

As discussed in Chapter 2, servers and clients must be protected with physical security. As we saw in Chapter 6, they also need to be backed up properly, and their operating systems need to be hardened with patches and high-security configuration settings.

Minimize Applications

Minimize Main Applications As also noted in Chapter 6, firms should minimize the applications they run in the first place. The fewer applications a computer runs, the fewer opportunities an attacker has to take over the host by compromising an application.

Minimize Subsidiary Applications Hackers often attack obscure programs that are started automatically when the operating system is installed with default settings or when a complex application depends on subsidiary applications, as all webserver programs do.

For example, when users of many older versions of Windows 2000 start the IIS webserver, the operating system also starts the Gopher service automatically. Gopher was a service that showed great promise for information retrieval just before the World Wide Web tidal wave hit. Today, almost nobody uses it. Yet, until recently, IIS started Gopher automatically when IIS was installed with default settings. When attackers found a problem with the obscure Gopher program, they made almost every IIS implementation immediately vulnerable to attack.

Security Baselines Again, our old friend from Chapter 6, the security baseline, should guide us. The installer must know which optional helper programs to install for a given application and which are installed automatically that should be deleted after installation.

Delete Optional Learning Aids

Many programs come loaded with optional **learning aids**, such as example scripts to help programmers learn how to use the system. Example scripts are not necessary on production servers and they probably are of little use on development servers. Using a good security baseline, installers should delete anything that is not needed for a server to be a production server or a development server.

Install Patches and Updates

Most importantly, the installer should ensure that all application patches are installed. As noted earlier, this usually involves tracking vulnerability and fix reports from many application vendors.

In addition, the company should install a recent version of the software, updating the software if necessary. Newer versions of applications, once beyond the initial "teething period," usually are much safer than older versions.

Minimize the Permissions of Applications

As noted earlier, if attackers can take over an application, they can execute commands with the privileges of the program. Some programs must run with root privileges, but many can run with lower levels of privileges and should be run with the minimum privileges possible for them to do their job.

UNIX offers the **chroot** command, which allows a program to be run in a subdirectory although it thinks it is running in the root directory. If attackers take over a "chrooted" program, they can cause mischief only in that subdirectory and subsidiary subdirectories.

Unfortunately, it is possible for many attackers to break out of the "chroot jail" and attack other parts of the computer's file system. Most unfortunately, chroot jail-breaks are most common for programs that run at root privileges. Such programs are the very ones in greatest need of being contained.

Add Application-Level Authentication

One way to stymie attackers is to disregard input from anyone who has not been authenticated properly. To compromise a system, then, the attacker would have to have both an exploit and authenticated access to the system.

The operating system account password system provides some protection, but many applications also provide their own authentication. For sensitive applications, the application program could require its own password—one with strong complexity. Or, the application program might require a smart card or some other form of strong authentication.

However, adding rigorous authentication is not always possible. In consumer-oriented e-commerce, it is rarely possible to strongly authenticate residential customers. Even in business-to-business e-commerce, authentication might have to be limited.

Furthermore, if an attacker takes over a client computer whose authentication credentials (username and password, etc.) are stored on the computer, the attacker might be able to break into its authorized servers, posing as an account that has been compromised.

Although adding application-level authentication is difficult and sometimes impossible, it should be done wherever possible. This is especially true for highly sensitive applications, such as human resource databases and customer information databases.

Implement Cryptographic Systems

In Chapter 8, we saw the strong protection offered by cryptographic systems, such as SSL, PPTP, and IPsec. Cryptographic systems provide initial authentication and message-by-message authentication. They also provide cryptography and anti-replay protection. They, too, should be used whenever possible.

TEST YOUR UNDERSTANDING

4. a) Why must you know a server's role to know how to protect it? b) Why is it important to minimize both main applications and subsidiary applications? c) Why are security baselines needed? d) Why should optional learning aids be deleted? e) Why is it

important to minimize permissions? f) In UNIX, what does chroot do? g) Is chroot completely effective? h) Why is application-level authentication desirable? i) Why is it often not done?

WEBSERVICE AND E-COMMERCE SECURITY

The Importance of Webservice and E-Commerce Security

Companies now depend heavily on their websites and e-commerce sites. External parties and corporate employees often need information at corporate websites to do their work. In addition, many companies depend heavily on their e-commerce sites to generate sales.[1]

The Cost of Disruptions

The cost of disruptions when webservers are taken over or taken down by denial-of-service attacks can be very high in terms of both lost revenues and lost productivity. Now that webservers and e-commerce servers are so important, they must be available at all times or the company will lose a great deal of money.

The Cost of Loss of Reputation and Market Capitalization from Defaced Websites

In many cases, the biggest cost of defaced websites is loss of reputation. If consumers find that a major e-commerce site has been hacked or that customer credit card numbers have been revealed, they are not likely to remain customers.

Although loss of reputation may be viewed as a "soft" loss, it often leads directly to lost sales and can affect a firm's market capitalization (based on its stock price) if widely publicized.

Customer Fraud

In e-commerce, **customer fraud** is a serious matter. When customers do not pay for the goods they receive (for instance, if they ordered with a stolen credit card number), the merchant will be left with a loss. In addition, the credit card company usually tacks on sizeable charge-back fees.

Customer fraud, including fraud by credit card thieves, is rampant; it has put many weaker e-commerce sites out of business and has savaged the profits of many others. It is imperative that e-commerce companies use external services that check credit card numbers.

The Cost of Privacy Violations

Many websites contain sensitive customer information, including credit card numbers. Customers trust companies to keep private information safe. If attackers break in and steal sensitive private information, the company may suffer a major loss in reputation that will translate into lost business.

---

[1] A good source for information on World Wide Web security is Miles Tracy, Wayne Jansen, and Mark McLamon, *Guidelines for Securing Public Webservers*, Special Publication 800-44, National Institute for Standards and Technology, September 2002. csrc.nist.gov/publications/nistpubs/index.html.

IMPORTANCE OF WEBSERVICE AND E-COMMERCE SECURITY

Cost of disruptions

The cost of loss of reputation and market capitalization

Customer fraud (including credit card fraud)

   Loss of revenues when product is not paid for

   Credit card company charge-back fees

   Must use external firm to check credit card numbers

Cost of privacy violations

Links to internal corporate servers

WEBSERVERS VERSUS E-COMMERCE SERVERS (Figure 9-4)

Webservice provides basic user interactions

   Microsoft Internet Information Server (IIS)

   Apache on UNIX

   Other webserver programs

E-commerce servers add functionality: Order entry, shopping cart, payment, etc.

Custom programs written for special purposes

Links to internal corporate databases and external services (such as credit card checking)

SOME WEBSERVER ATTACKS

Website defacement

Numerous IIS buffer overflow attacks, many of which take over the computer

IIS directory traversal attacks

   Normally, paths start at the WWW root directory

   Adding ../ might take the attacker up a level, out of the WWW root box

   If traverse to command prompt directory in Windows 2000 or NT, can execute any command with system privileges

   Companies filter out / and \

   Attackers respond with hexadecimal and UNICODE representations for / and \

Apache has problems, too

PATCHING THE WEBSERVER AND E-COMMERCE SOFTWARE AND ITS COMPONENTS

Patching the webserver software is not enough

Also must patch e-commerce software

E-commerce software might use third-party component software that must be patched

CONTROLLING DYNAMIC WEBPAGE DEVELOPMENT

Static versus dynamic webpages

For static webpages: GET */path/filename.extension* HTTP */version*

CGI to pass parameters to a program

   GET */path/programname.exe?variable1="value"&variable2="value"* ...

   Inefficient. Starts new copy of program with each request

ASP is Microsoft's server-side scripting language

(continued)

Figure 9-3 Webserver and E-Commerce Security (Study Figure)

ISAPI from Microsoft starts a .dll program on the server
   Component continues to run; no need to start a new copy with each request
Controlling software development
   Programmer training in safe programming methods
   Auditing for security weaknesses
Deployment
   Development server: Developers have wide privileges
   Staging servers: Only testers and systems administrators have privileges
   Production servers: Only systems administrators have privileges

USER AUTHENTICATION

None: No burden on customer
Username and password provide some protection but may be given out without checking customer quality
IPsec and digital certificates: Expensive and difficult for customers
TLS with client digital certificates: Less expensive than IPsec but difficult for customers

BROWSER ATTACKS

Interesting information and can use browser to attack internal systems
Client-side scripting
   Java applets: Small Java programs
   Scripting languages (not full programming languages)
     JavaScript (not scripted form of Java)
     VBScript (Visual Basic scripting from Microsoft)
   Active-X from Microsoft; highly dangerous because it can do almost everything
Malicious links
   User must click on them to execute (but not always)
   Common extensions are hidden by default in windows
     attack.txt.exe seems to be attack.txt
Attacks
   File reading and executing a command
   Redirection to unwanted webpage
     Scripts might change the registry, home page
     Might Trojanize the program called when user mistypes a URL
     Pop-up windows behind main window so source is hard to find
   Choose domain names that are common misspellings of popular domain names
   Cookies and web bugs
     Cookies are placed on user computer; can be retrieved by website
     Can be used to track users at a website
     Web bugs—links that are nearly invisible—can do the same
   Opening two windows; transfer information from client window to webserver window, which can be read over the Internet
Enhancing Browser Security
   Patches and updates
   Set strong security options (Figure 9-5) for Microsoft Internet Explorer 6.0
   Remotely managing browsers on employee client PCs

Figure 9-3 (Continued)

Legal punishments also can result (see Chapter 12). In the United States, stringent privacy rules apply in the health care and financial services industries, and the Federal Trade Commission sues companies that violate their stated privacy policies. In Europe, sanctions for not protecting private information are strong.

Links to Internal Databases

As noted later, webservers often need to link to internal databases within the firm. This requires creating holes in the firewall that protects the internal corporate site. If holes must be punched through firewalls, the security of the webserver and of back-end internal servers must be strong.

TEST YOUR UNDERSTANDING

5. a) List the reasons why webserver and e-commerce server security are important. b) What monetary losses might come from website defacements? c) From customer fraud? d) From a failure to protect private data?

Webservers Versus E-Commerce Service

Some confusion occurs over the terms *webservice* and *e-commerce*. Figure 9-4 shows the distinction between them.

Webservice

We will use the term **webservice** for the basic functionality of HTTP webservers, including the retrieval of static files (fixed webpages) and the creation of dynamic webpages (webpages created for a specific query) using software on the webserver or client.

In Microsoft Windows, the native webserver program is **Internet Information Server (IIS)**. This software is free and dominates webserver use on Windows Server hosts. On LINUX and UNIX hosts, the dominant software is the freeware Apache webserver program. Many more webservers use Apache than IIS, although among commercial webservers, IIS probably has a much larger market share. Large UNIX vendors, such as SUN, offer their own webserver programs.

Webserver programs, as Figure 9-4 shows, often have components that come from different companies. For instance, the PHP application development software is

Figure 9-4   Webservice Versus E-Commerce Service

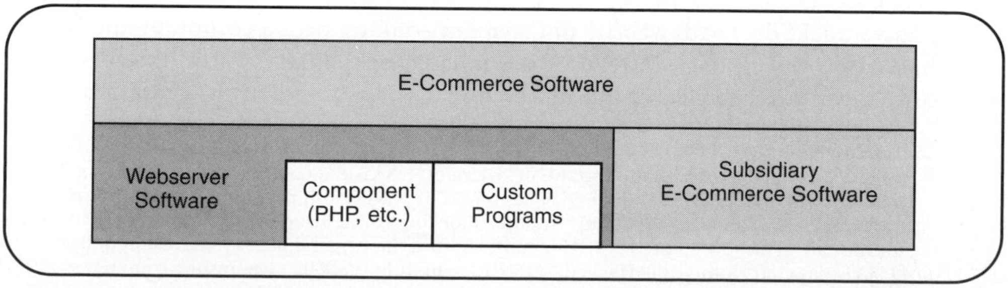

built into many webservers. In 2002, a serious vulnerability was found in the PHP programs on webservers from most webserver vendors.

Custom Programs

Most webservers can run software developed especially for them using CGI, ASP, JSP, and ISAPI, to name just a few of the ways to run custom programs within webservers. Although webserver programs and commercial add-in products such as PHP arguably were well tested before release, many firms do a poor job of overseeing the development of these custom programs. Consequently, attackers often can exploit vulnerabilities in custom programs or, even more insidiously, write their own custom programs that they can execute on the victim server to aid in their attacks.

E-Commerce Service

The term **e-commerce** will be used here to refer to the additional software needed for buying and selling, including online catalogs, shopping carts, checkout functions, connections to back-end databases within the firm, and links to outside organizations, such as banks.

External Access

In addition, we have noted that an e-commerce server needs to have online access to a number of systems external to itself, including servers within firms (for order entry, accounting, shipping, and so forth) and servers outside the firm in merchant banks and companies that check credit card numbers for validity. The webmaster or e-commerce master often has no control over the security of other systems.

TEST YOUR UNDERSTANDING

6. a) Distinguish between webservice and e-commerce service. b) Why are custom programs written? c) What kinds of external access are needed for e-commerce? d) Does the webmaster or e-commerce master have control over the security of other servers inside and outside the firm?

Some Webserver Attacks

How do attackers attack webservers? In this section, we will look at a number of **attack methods**. We will focus on attacks on Microsoft's IIS webserver software because these have been the most frequent attacks on webservers. However, the devastating virus and worm attacks of 2001 have resulted in improved patching for IIS webservers, and attackers increasingly have been turning much of their attention to Apache webservers and other webservers running on LINUX and other UNIX computers.

Website Defacement

Many attacks deal with **website defacement**—taking over a computer and putting up a hacker-produced page instead of the normal home page. Although this generally is only a nuisance,[2] it can be much worse. For instance, after a fatal crash, hackers

---

[2] To give an example of a nondestructive defacement, USAToday.com's home page and six other pages were defaced in July 2002. Several news items were replaced with prankish entries, such as, "Oops says the Pope/Christianity a Sham" and "Another shocking ruling from 9th Circuit Court–Pentagon unconstitutional?" The attack lasted only 15 minutes before the original pages were restored. Bob Sullivan, "USAToday.com Home Page Hacked," MSNBC.com, July 12, 2002. www.msnbc.com/news/779372.asp.

defaced the ValueJet website with the statement, "So we killed a few people." Even worse, hackers sometimes install "Out of Business" home pages to get customers to go away and stay away.

In many instances, ISPs cache the home pages of popular websites. Even after a defaced webserver is fixed, the defaced home page could still be in many ISP caching sites, sometimes for several days. Customers of these ISPs will continue to see the cached defaced homepage for some time after the problem is fixed.

The IIS IPP Buffer Overflow Attack to Launch a Command Shell

Earlier in this chapter, we discussed the IIS IPP buffer overflow vulnerability and the jill.c program used to exploit the vulnerability. We noted that the attacker gets a command shell and strong (SYSTEM) privileges. IIS has been subject to many other buffer overflow attacks with equally devastating impacts.

IIS Directory Traversal Attack

Sometimes, the attacker knows that a certain sensitive file, such as a password file, normally is stored in a particular directory under a particular name. The attacker would like to download many of these sensitive files.

When users send a request for a file to be downloaded, the "root" is really a particular directory owned by the webserver. We will call this directory the **WWW root**. If the user types the path */reports/somereport.html*, the request does not go to the server's root and then go one level down to a *reports* directory. It starts at the WWW root directory and goes one level down to the *reports* subdirectory.

However, IIS attackers learned that if they began with "../" in their path, some webserver programs would allow them to break out of the WWW root box and get to the directory above the WWW root. If attackers issued several ../ path entries, then appropriate trailing information, they could get to sensitive directories, including the command prompt directory (WINNT in Windows NT and Windows 2000). They could then download a sensitive file or, in some cases, execute any command. This was the basic IIS **directory traversal attack.**

The IIS Directory Traversal with Hexadecimal Character Escapes

As usually happens, the vendor (Microsoft) responded with a patch that rejected HTTP request messages containing slashes or backslashes. Next, as often happens, attackers soon found a variant of the basic attack that would succeed against this countermeasure. For instance, IIS allows hexadecimal input, in which % is followed by two symbols between 0 and F. Each symbol represents four bits, so the two symbols together represent a byte.

Soon, attackers were sending HTTP directory traversal messages with %2F (the hex code for /) in place of the slash. For a while, this **hexadecimal directory traversal attack** was successful. Then Microsoft issued a patch to stop it.

UNICODE Directory Traversal

This cat and mouse game has continued ever since. For instance, the UNICODE coding system was created to represent non-English languages. Each character in each language is assigned a code sequence. Some of these code strings in various languages represent slash or backslash. Soon, attackers used several UNICODE representations to get around the Microsoft hex patch. In turn, Microsoft created a patch for **UNICODE directory traversal attacks**. Attackers have continued with subsequent exploits to get around Microsoft patches, and Microsoft has responded with further patches.

Apache Problems

IIS webservers traditionally have been the favorite food of hackers due to their widespread use, the availability of nutritious vulnerabilities, and a poor IIS patching culture among corporations. However, the Great Worm Attacks of 2001 (Code Red, Code Red II, Nimda, etc.) forced companies with IIS to install patches, and the patching culture of IIS users has improved considerably. IIS is increasingly becoming difficult to attack.

Consequently, hackers have begun to turn their attention to LINUX computers, which predominantly run **Apache** as their webserver program. In 2002, attackers latched onto a number of LINUX and Apache vulnerabilities, most notably a flaw in the OpenSSL software that most LINUX distributions use to create SSL security for Apache. The Slapper worm, which exploited this vulnerability, created a peer-to-peer network of machines that could be used in distributed denial-of-service attacks.

TEST YOUR UNDERSTANDING

7. a) What is website defacement? b) Why is it damaging? c) Has IIS been subject to many buffer overflow take-over attacks? d) What are directory traversal attacks? e) How have attackers circumvented filtering designed to stop such attacks?

Patching the Webserver and E-Commerce Software and Its Components

E-Commerce Software Vulnerabilities

In 2000, the webhosting company MindSpring suffered an embarrassment when it was found that its servers exposed the passwords of some of the websites they hosted.[3] The problem was tracked to a single website that used a commercial e-commerce program and failed to register it. The website's owners were not notified of an important patch because of the failure to register the product. Two years later, the vulnerable software was discovered.

The website was one of several websites running on a single Sun Solaris (UNIX) server at the webhosting company. That server was configured incorrectly, and the vulnerability in the single website ended up opening access to password files on other websites hosted at the same machine.

This example underscores the importance of patching e-commerce server software (and of configuring shared machines properly). E-commerce software is complex and has many subsystems. It would be foolish to assume that vulnerabilities will never be found in a firm's e-commerce software, and much of this software runs as root, giving attackers open access to the entire server if they compromise the software.

[3] Ann Harrison, "MindSpring Site Exposes Password Files: E-Commerce Application Opens Floodgates," Computerworld.com, October 23, 2000. www.computerworld.com/industrytopics/retail/story/0,10801,52714,00.html.

Components of Web Software and E-Commerce Software

Even when a webserver or e-commerce server produces clean code, some subsystems often are left open to attack by their vendors. Many webserver programs, for instance, support PHP programming. A series of flaws in PHP discovered in January 2002 allowed attackers to take over a website, sometimes easily. More PHP vulnerabilities were found later in the year as bug hunters increasingly turned their attention to PHP after initial disclosures. To give another example, a flaw in the OpenSSL component rendered most Apache webservers open to attack later in 2002.

Other Website Protections

Website Vulnerability Assessment Tools

Several webserver-specific vulnerability assessment tools have been developed, most prominently Whisker. Running a vulnerability assessment tool against the website frequently should be viewed as normal maintenance.

Website Error Logs

In addition, websites usually log responses that contain error messages. Log reviews should be done frequently to look for signs of attacks. For instance, an excessive number of 500 error messages may indicate that an attacker is trying to send invalid data to the sender. In turn, an excessive number of 404 errors might indicate that an attacker is searching blindly for files on your website.

Webserver-Specific Application Firewalls

Some products are application firewalls for webserver programs. They check incoming request messages for signs of buffer overflow attacks and other problems. They also stop outgoing response messages that are inappropriate.

IIS Lockdown

A major problem of Microsoft's IIS is that it enables many things by default and does not do buffer overflow checking or implement other basic protections. In 2002, Microsoft developed a lockdown tool for earlier versions of IIS. This tool applied strong configuration options. IIS 6.0, which was released that year, had all of these lockdown protections plus buffer overflow filtering and other protections.

TEST YOUR UNDERSTANDING

8. a) What software must be patched on an e-commerce server? b) What three other webserver protections were mentioned in the text?

Controlling Dynamic Webpage Development

Static Versus Dynamic Webpages

Two types of webpages exist. **Static webpages** are written in HTML. Their content does not change until the webmaster replaces them with other static webpages. In contrast, **dynamic webpages** are generated only when a user sends in a request; they are tailored to that user's particular request. Many e-commerce functions require dynamic webpages.

Dynamic webpages are created with programming languages. We will focus now on languages designed to run on the webserver, although Java applets, Active X, and other programs can run on browsers.

Basic HTTP

When you request a static webpage, you type a URL into your browser or click on a link and have your browser enter the URL. Here is a typical URL. It asks for a specific file (*file.html*) in a specific directory (*/adirectory*) on a specific server (*www.target.html*).

```
http://www.target.com/adirectory/file.html
```

Server-Side Programming Approaches

CGI   The original **server-side programming** approach was the **Common Gateway Interface (CGI)**. CGI passes variables to a particular program. In the example that follows, that program is *scriptfile.exe* in the *scriptsdirectory* directory. The variables are *lastname* and *firstname*. Their values are *Lee* and *Pat*, respectively.

```
http://www.target.com/scriptsdirectory/scriptfile.exe?lastname=
Lee&firstname=Pat
```

CGI does not force you to use a particular programming language to create scripts. It is merely a method for starting a program, passing variables to that program, and for returning webpages created by the program to the user issuing the HTTP request. The program to which the data is passed can be written in any language.

One problem with CGI is that it is slow. Each time a request arrives, CGI invokes (starts) the program. This is much slower than passing variables to a running program. Consequently, CGI is used only in low-volume applications.

Another problem with CGI is that it has a terrible track record on security. For instance, CGI scripts often are stored in a predictable directory, cgi-bin, making them easy to find. In addition, many implementations have pre-installed learning scripts to do such things as learn the server's environmental variables. Attackers often can run these standard scripts and learn an unpleasant amount of information. In general, it is easy for poor programmers to accidentally create CGI scripts that attackers can exploit. Finally, if attackers can store their attack programs in the CGI directory, they can execute attacks using these scripts any time.

Active Server Pages (ASP)   Microsoft has created two approaches to server-side programming. The simpler of these approaches is **Active Server Pages (ASP)**. If a user calls an .asp page, scripts on the .asp file are executed on the server and the resultant page is sent to the user's browser.

Internet Server Application Programming Interface (ISAPI)   For intensive, high-volume work, Microsoft offers the **Internet Server Application Programming Interface (ISAPI)** standard. ISAPI programs run constantly once invoked, allowing rapid and efficient operation.

Controlling Software Creation

Even if the developers of webserver and e-commerce programs create clean code, many people are likely to develop vulnerable dynamic webpages. All server-side program developers need to be trained.

Training Developers   Often, active webpage developers are not trained programmers or are working in programming environments where security, documentation, and other values frequently are sacrificed to speed of development. They must be trained in secure development, and good practice must be enforced.

Auditing for Security Weaknesses   Companies must institute rigorous programs of auditing for both server-side and client-side application development. Code reviews by other developers trained in the recognition of security flaws must be part of the development process.

Controlling Deployment

It is also critical to control the **deployment** of new server-side applications. Firms with rigorous deployment policies use three types of servers: development servers, staging servers, and production servers.

Development Servers   Server-side programs should be created on **development servers** dedicated to that purpose. Developers need extensive permissions on these servers.

Staging Servers   After development, including peer testing, the program should be moved to a **staging server** for testing. Developers should have no access permissions on this server. Only testers should have access permissions to make changes so that developers do not slip in back doors and last minute changes. ("It's just a few lines of code.")

Production Servers   After a program has been tested fully on the staging server, it should be moved to the **production server** that will serve users. On the production servers, even testers should be given no change permissions. Only the systems administrators needed to run the production server should have any permissions beyond reading and execution.

TEST YOUR UNDERSTANDING

9. a) Distinguish between static and dynamic (active) webpages. b) Create a URL to retrieve the file dawgs.htm under the rainbow directory on the host www.pukanui.com. c) Does CGI require you to use a particular scripting language? d) Create a URL to pass the values 45 and $749 for the variables *number* and *total* to the *order.exe* program in the *escripts* directory under the */scripts* directory. e) Which vendor supports asp and ISAPI? f) What two steps should be taken to control software creation for server-side dynamic webpages? g) List the purposes of development, staging, and production webservers and who should have permissions on each.

User Authentication

One way to reduce fraud and other security problems is to authenticate users or customers. This can be done in several ways.

None or User Names and Passwords

Many website visitors are unwilling to create user names and passwords, and websites that require even this mild form of authentication might lose many visitors. In addition, few websites that do require user names and passwords check the quality of the customer before issuing them.

IPsec VPNs and Digital Certificates

For high-value customers, especially business customers, it might be necessary to establish full cryptographic system protection using the IPsec virtual private network technology discussed in the previous chapter. To use these VPNs, customers will need to establish digital certificates from a certificate authority. The merchant also needs a digital certificate.

Getting a digital certificate is easy if a company already has a D&B (formerly Dun and Bradstreet) D-U-N-S number. Most larger firms, including subsidiaries of other corporations, have these numbers. D-U-N-S numbers are used widely in business searches, and having a D-U-N-S number is strong proof of a corporation's existence. Smaller and start-up firms must provide proof of their existence in other ways, with incorporation papers and other proofs dictated by the certificate authority.

TLS with Certificates

Another option is to use Transport Layer Security (TLS), which was discussed in Chapters 2 and 8, instead of the more complex IPsec VPN technology. Customer browsers already can work with TLS, so customers do not need to add any software.

As discussed in the previous chapter, many firms do not require customers to use digital certificates with TLS. However, using digital certificates on the client side always is an option. Some firms will not do business with TLS customers unless the customers have digital certificates that the merchant trusts.

TEST YOUR UNDERSTANDING

> 10. Explain the benefits and drawbacks of using a) no authentication, b) user name/password authentication, c) IPsec authentication, and d) TLS with customer certificates.

Browser Attacks

Although many World Wide Web/e-commerce attacks focus on servers, browser clients are also popular targets. As many firms tighten their server security, browsers could become even more popular targets.

Dangers

Browser security in the World Wide Web and e-commerce security is important because, as noted in Chapter 6, attackers might want to have data stored on the client and because attackers can use a compromised client to attack other systems for which the client has access credentials.

Scripting

Taking over a client PC using a webserver or e-commerce server typically is done using scripts built into the webpage. These scripts execute active content. Although this can enhance the browser user's surfing experience, scripts can be used to poke large holes in the client's security.

Java Applets   Many languages are used in client-side scripting. **Java applets** (small Java programs[4]) probably are the safest because many attack-related actions are dis-

---

[4]   Java applets are not scripts per se but rather are called by scripts on webpages.

abled; however, this protection is far from perfect; therefore, Java generally should be turned off.

Scripting Languages: VBScript and JavaScript   Two other popular **scripting languages**, which are easier to use than full programming languages like Java, are **VBScript** and **JavaScript** (which is not a scripted version of Java despite its name). These scripting languages, although easier to use than Java, lack the protections of Java and should be turned off in the browser.

Active-X   Another major language for active website content is **Active-X**, a technology created by Microsoft. Active-X is powerful and can do almost anything on the client machine. This power, coupled with the fact that Active-X offers no protection against misuse, makes Active-X supremely dangerous. Always disable Active-X and doubt the security expertise and honesty of anyone who sends you an Active-X component.

Microsoft initially said that Active-X components are safe because they must be cryptographically signed by the developer, and if you can trust the developer, you should be able to trust its programs. However, users often do not know the developer, and even good developers can create products with vulnerabilities. Worse yet, once you tell Internet Explorer that you trust a particular developer, it might not ask you again for confirmation if another program comes in from that developer.

Danger: Malicious Links

Browsers typically are attacked by **malicious links** in webpages and in e-mail bodies. If the user clicks on a malicious link, an attack script in the downloaded page will be executed. Sometimes, the script will activate even if the user does not click on it, depending on how the browser or e-mail program is configured.

Sometimes, users look at a link to see if it seems to be trustworthy. However, the client Windows default is to turn off common extensions, so the attack program *attack.txt.exe* will appear as *attack.txt*, causing the user to think it is a harmless text file. In some cases, even if the user turns off the hiding of common extensions, the attacker can disguise the extension.

Client-Side Attacks

Many client-side attacks are possible. We will discuss just a few to give you a concept of the possibilities.

File Reading and Executing Arbitrary Commands   In 2000, a Java applet delivered primarily via e-mail essentially turned the user's client PC into an unwilling file server, making all of its files easily accessible to the attacker. Such file-reading attacks are common.

Worse yet, several common malicious script attacks allow attackers to execute any command they choose on the victim's computer. This gives the attackers carte blanche permission to do anything they want.

Getting Users to Visit Attacker Websites   How do attackers get users to go to websites that will deliver attack scripts? Sometimes they do so through social engineering. For instance, you may get an urgent message telling you that your computer is infected with a virus and that you should go immediately to a particular URL to learn how to get the virus out of your system. Sometimes, the social engineer tells you to go to a popular website, such as CNN.com. However, although the link says CNN.com on the screen, it may actually be a link to an attack website.

In addition, many attackers register domain names that are common misspellings for legitimate website domain names, for example, micosoft.com. In some cases, they merely find an .org nonprofit website and register the .com version of its name. For example, whitehouse.com is a pornography site. Users who find themselves at these sites often find themselves reading pages with malicious scripts.

Redirecting Users to Unwanted Webpages   A number of scripts permanently change your browser settings and even your computer registry. The next time you use your computer, you might find that your automatic home page has been changed to a pornography site or to another site with content you do not want to see.

More subtly, when you make errors typing URLs, you might find you are taken to one of several unauthorized sites because the script has Trojanized your DNS error-handling routine.

You also might see lurid **pop-behind ads** that appear behind your visible window. You do not see these ads until long after they are created, making their source difficult to find. Some people have to reinstall their browsers.

Cookies and Web Bugs   Some websites use **cookies**. A cookie is a small text string that the website owner can place on a client computer. The website owner can later retrieve cookies they have written (but not cookies written by other websites).

Cookies are valuable in transactions that require the exchange of several messages because they can keep track of where the user is in the process. Cookies also can remember your login name and password for easier access to websites that require authorization.

Unfortunately, cookies also can track where you have been at a website. Quite a few users turn off cookies to prevent tracking. To counter this protection, some websites and e-mail senders turn to **web bugs**—hyperlinks that are one pixel wide and tall and that are often in the same color as the background. Although the users cannot see them, the HTTP request messages that they send automatically tell the webserver owners what page they are reading.

Opening Two Windows   In another attack, a malicious script opens **two windows**—one is in the remote computer's domain. It is visible. The other is a local computer window. It is behind the visible window. It is possible to transfer information from the local window to the webserver window, allowing the transferring information from the local computer to the webserver.

TEST YOUR UNDERSTANDING

11.   a) Why do hackers attack browsers? b) How do HTML scripts aid hackers? c) What is a Java applet? d) How do scripting languages compare to full programming languages? e) Is JavaScript a scripted form of Java? f) Why is Active-X dangerous? g) Do users have to click on malicious links to actuate them? h) Using Windows defaults, what will malicious.txt.exe look like to a user? i) If a user has been involuntarily redi-

rected to an unwanted webpage, what effects might the user see? j) Why do attackers want to get domain names such as micosoft.com? k) How are cookies used to track users within a website? l) How do web bugs track users?

Enhancing Browser Security

Patching and Upgrading

All of the attacks just covered can be stopped by installing patches on Internet Explorer and other browsers. However, relatively few users patch their browsers, giving attackers long windows of opportunity. In fact, many users have versions that are so old that patches are not created for them when new vulnerabilities are found.

Settings

Stopping browser attacks also involves changing browser configuration settings to reduce the likelihood of damage. Unfortunately, different browsers do this differently, and even different versions of IE do it differently.

Internet Options   In IE 6.0, users begin to change their settings by selecting Internet Options under the Tools menu. This opens the **Internet Options dialog box** shown in Figure 9-5.

Security Tab   The dialog box is opened to its *Security tab*. From this tab, the user can select security settings for general Internet websites, intranet websites, trusted websites, and restricted websites. The defaults are not bad choices for security, but the user can select the *Custom Level* button to change the settings for the four types of websites to control content more finely.

For instance, in the general Internet zone, signed Active-X controls (Active-X controls with digital signatures) will be executed after a prompt that identifies the creator of the Active-X control. Employees might not have sufficient knowledge to understand the danger of using even signed Active-X controls. In addition, active scripting is enabled by default, including Java scripting. These are at least somewhat risky choices.

Privacy Tab   In addition to the Security tab, there is the *Privacy tab*. The Privacy tab allows the user to control what information is released to websites, including how cookies are used. IE 6.0 gives a sliding scale that the user can push up for greater privacy and down for reduced privacy. The default is medium privacy. An *Advanced* button allows more specific control over cookies.

Content Tab   Finally, under the *Content tab*, the user can cause IE to at least flag websites that appear to have offensive content. The default is to turn off this rather simplistic content checking. This tab also provides control over digital certificates.

Remotely Managing Browsers on Employee Clients

The big problem with users is that they do not download patches for the application software they use, including browsers. A number of firms are now remotely administering employee PCs that have access to the corporate network. This involves such tasks as the following.

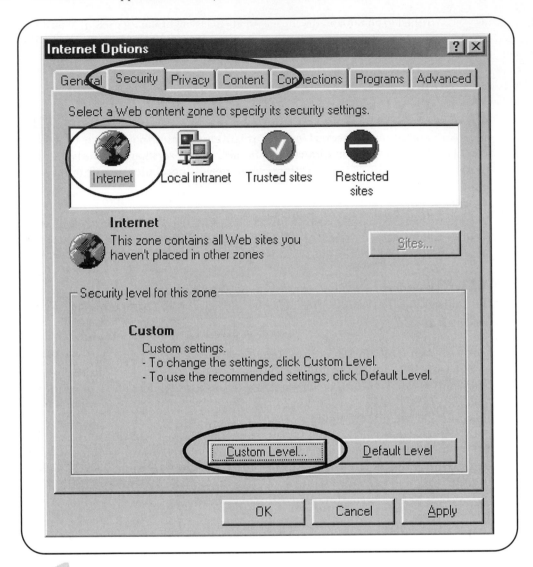

Figure 9-5   Internet Options Dialog Box in Internet Explorer 6.0

➤ Periodically checking browsers for versions and updates and in some cases down-
  loading updates directly.
➤ Checking browser settings to ensure that scripting has been deselected.
➤ Ensuring that antivirus software is being used and is being updated regularly.

This generally requires the placement of software on the client PC. If a firm has
many remote employee PCs, this can be expensive.

TEST YOUR UNDERSTANDING

12. a) What can users do to enhance browser security? b) Under Internet Options in IE6.0, what do the three security-related tabs control? c) Why is the remote management of browsers desirable?

E-MAIL

We have been looking at webservice/e-commerce security. The other big application on the Internet is **electronic mail (e-mail)**. In this section, we will look at e-mail security.[5]

E-Mail Technology

Client PCs and Mail Servers

Figure 9-7 illustrates the main standards in e-mail. Note that users generally work on client PCs. Each user has a mail server (possibly several).

Mail Server Software   For mail servers, **Sendmail** dominates on UNIX systems despite being a poster child for server software vulnerabilities. On corporate mail systems running on Windows computers, Microsoft **Exchange** and Lotus/IBM **Notes** are popular.

E-Mail Client Software   Microsoft Windows dominates client operating systems. Microsoft **Outlook Express** does not offer as many features as **Outlook**, but most attacks on Microsoft e-mail clients focus on Outlook because Outlook Express has limited ability to execute active content. Some Windows users use third-party e-mail clients, such as Eudora.

Sending Mail with the Simple Mail Transfer Protocol (SMTP)

To send outgoing messages, the sender's e-mail client uses the **Simple Mail Transfer Protocol (SMTP)** standard to send the message to the sender's mail host.

The sender's mail host then uses SMTP again, this time to send the message to the receiver's mail host. If the message is addressed to several parties, the sender's mail host will need to make SMTP connections to the mail hosts of all of the different receivers.

Downloading Mail with POP and IMAP

When the mail gets to the receiver's mail host, the mail host puts the mail in the receiver's online **mailbox**. Messages sit there until the receiver downloads them. This arrangement is necessary because receivers might not be online when mail arrives for them.

POP   The simplest and most widely used protocol for downloading mail to a client is the **Post Office Protocol (POP)**. It downloads some or all mail, and mail users manage messages *on their client PCs.*

---

[5] A good source for information on e-mail security is Scott Bisker, Miles Tracy, and Wayne Jansen, *Guidelines for E-Mail Security*, Special Publication 800-45, National Institute for Standards and Technology, March 2002. csrc.nist.gov/publications/nistpubs/index.html.

E-MAIL TECHNOLOGY

E-Mail Clients and Mail Servers (Figure 9-7)

    Mail server software: Sendmail on UNIX, Microsoft Exchange, and Lotus/IBM Notes dominate on Windows servers

    Microsoft Outlook Express is safer than full-featured Outlook because Outlook Express generally does not execute content

SMTP to send messages from client to mail server or from mail server to mail server

To download messages to client e-mail program from receiver's mail server

    POP: Simple and popular; manage mail on client PC

    IMAP: Can manage messages on mail server

E-mail bodies

    RFC 822 / RFC 2822: Plain English text (in ASCII code)

    HTML bodies: Graphics, fonts, etc.

    HTML bodies might contain scripts, which might execute automatically when user opens the message

Web-based e-mail needs only a browser on the client PC (Figure 9-8)

E-MAIL CONTENT FILTERING

Antivirus filtering and filtering for other executable code

    Especially dangerous because of scripts in HTML bodies

Spam: Unsolicited commercial e-mail

Volume is growing rapidly: Slowing and annoying users (porno and fraud)

Filtering for spam also rejects some legitimate messages

Sometimes employees attack spammers back; only hurts spoofed sender and the company could be sued

INAPPROPRIATE CONTENT

Companies often filter for sexually or racially harassing messages

Could be sued for not doing so

E-MAIL RETENTION

On hard disk and tape for some period of time

Benefit: Can find information

Drawback: Can be discovered in legal contests; could be embarrassing

Must retain some messages for legal purposes

Shredding on receiver's computer to take messages back

    Send key to decrypt

    Make key useless after retention period so cannot retrieve anymore

    Might be able to copy or print before retention limit date

    Not good for contracts because receiver must be able to keep a copy

Message authentication to prevent spoofed sender addresses

Employee training

    E-mail is not private; company has right to read

    Your messages may be forwarded without permission

    Never to put anything in a message they would not want to see in court, printed in the newspapers, or read by their boss

    Never forward messages without permission

(*continued*)

Figure 9-6 E-Mail Security (Study Figure)

E-MAIL ENCRYPTION (Figure 9-9)

Not widely used because of lack of clear standards

PGP and S/MIME for end-to-end encryption

How to get public keys of true parties?

PGP uses trust among circles of friends: If A trusts B, and B trusts C, A may trust C's list of public keys

Dangerous: Misplaced trust can spread bogus key/name pairs widely

S/MIME requires expensive and cumbersome PKI

Ease of Use

S/MIME usually built in if available at all

PGP usually a cumbersome add-on to e-mail

TLS

Between client and server

Figure 9-6   (Continued)

Figure 9-7   E-Mail Standards

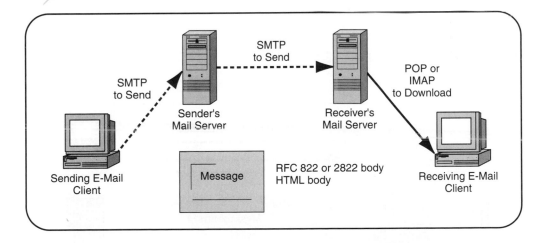

IMAP   The **Internet Message Access Protocol (IMAP)**, developed at Stanford University, is less widely used but is more sophisticated. The user can manage messages *on the mail server*, organize them in folders, delete them, and so forth. This is good if the user accesses mail from many locations.

Message Headers and Bodies

An e-mail message has two parts. The first is the **header**, which has fields for the date, sender's e-mail address, receiver's e-mail address, and so forth. The second is the **body**, which contains the information to be delivered.

RFC 822 and RFC 2822: Plain English Text   E-mail headers and bodies were first standardized in **RFC 822**. This standard, which was later updated in **RFC 2822**, specifies headers and trailers that are limited to English text. This is the e-mail we lived with for many years. It represents characters by the ASCII code.

HTML Bodies   More recently, we have seen the widespread use of **HTML bodies** that can include fancy fonts and even embedded graphics and other user interface advances. Unfortunately, HTML bodies also can contain scripts, including malicious scripts. Sometimes, scripts in HTML bodies execute automatically as soon as a message is opened.

Web-Based E-Mail

Figure 9-7 looks at normal e-mail technology. However, many users turn to **web-based e-mail**, which is illustrated in Figure 9-8. With only a browser, a user can access mail from anywhere, without the need for a specialized e-mail client. However, web-based e-mail tends to be maddeningly slow.

Web-based e-mail is not the same as having HTML bodies. Although web-based e-mail always supports HTML bodies, many traditional e-mail clients that use SMTP to send and POP or IMAP to receive also let their users view HTML bodies.

Figure 9-8   Web-Based E-Mail

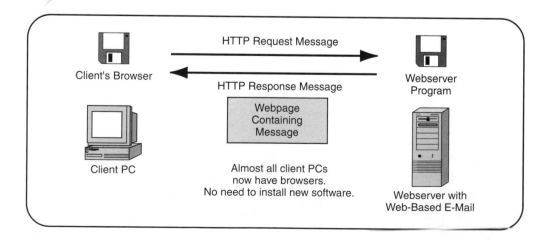

TEST YOUR UNDERSTANDING

13. a) In e-mail, list the computers the message goes through from the sender to the receiver. b) List the standard that governs each hop between computers. c) What e-mail software dominates on UNIX servers? d) What is Microsoft's main e-mail server product? e) Why is Microsoft's Outlook Express safer than Outlook? f) Describe the RFC 822 and RFC 2822 standards. g) Why are HTML bodies dangerous?

E-Mail Content Filtering

Many firms now filter incoming e-mail messages (and sometimes outgoing messages) for dangerous or inappropriate content.

Malicious Code in Attachments and HTML Bodies

As we saw in Chapter 4, e-mail attachments can contain viruses, worms, and other malicious code. That chapter also discussed the importance of doing antivirus filtering in depth, at individual computers, at corporate mail servers, at corporate HTML firewalls, and perhaps even at an outsourced antivirus filtering company that filters messages for viruses before they even reach the receiving corporation.

In addition, now that many e-mail systems can show messages with HTML bodies, scripts in the bodies may execute malicious code, as we saw earlier in this chapter. Microsoft Outlook, for instance, uses Internet Explorer to render HTML bodies, leaving Outlook vulnerable to IE vulnerabilities.

One particularly powerful use of e-mail tagging is to put in a script that sends a message to a website whenever a message is forwarded. This allows the attacker to map an organization. It also allows a sender to determine if his or her message has been forwarded, perhaps inappropriately.

Spam

A Growing Problem   One of the most annoying aspects of e-mail is that most users are deluged by **spam**[6]—unsolicited commercial e-mail. Spam clogs mailboxes, annoys users, and requires users to spend time deleting the unwanted messages. In many firms, more than half of all incoming mail is spam, and this fraction is rising rapidly.[7] If nothing is done, 90 percent or more of all mail could soon be spam. If the situation gets to this level, many people may stop using e-mail.

Pornography and Fraud   In addition, spam often deals with pornography and fraud. Many corporations fear that if they do not filter out pornographic spam, they may be sued by their employees for allowing a hostile work environment. However, spam filtering is time consuming and expensive.

Filtering Spam   Given the large volume of spam today, quite a few firms are beginning to filter incoming mail to discard spam. The IETF has even developed a standard way to write filtering rules, **Sieve**, which should allow firms to share filtering rules.

---

[6] Spam is a canned meat product (it is not an abbreviation for spongy pink animal matter). Hormel, which owns the name Spam, allows the use of the term *spam* in the e-mail context if it is spelled in lowercase except at the beginning of a sentence.

[7] One company put an e-mail address on a single page on a public webserver. Spam began arriving at the address within 8 hours. Justin Beech, "Spam and Web-Visible E-Mail Addresses," *Broadband Reports*, February 17, 2002. www.dslreports.com/shownews/15234.

Firms also tend to filter out image files because so many contain pornographic images for spam messages.

However, firms that filter incoming spam find that they often over-filter arriving mail. A growing number of legitimate messages are being rejected as spam, and few spam-filtering systems warn either the sender or the receiver if a message is rejected. Companies that filter spam should quarantine dropped messages to study them later and to address receiver and sender complaints about lost messages. Where this has been done, a fair number of false drops have been found. Legitimate newsletters in particular tend to get stopped by spam filters.

One nightmare is that some people try to retaliate by sending abusive messages to the spammer—or at least who they think the spammer is. However, almost all spammers hide their own e-mail address, so abusive messages almost always go to an innocent party whose e-mail address has been spoofed into the From field. Abusive messages sent by employees can result in ill will toward the organization. If employees engage in denial-of-service attacks to "punish the spammer," their company could and should be sued. It is important to educate employees about not retaliating against spam.

Inappropriate Content

In some cases, employees send sexually or racially harassing or abusive e-mail to fellow workers. If the company does nothing to attempt to prevent this, it will be liable for lawsuits. Consequently, a growing number of firms scan all e-mail for indications of sexual, racial, or abusive content. Many already have fired employees for sending inappropriate e-mail.

TEST YOUR UNDERSTANDING

14. a) Where should antivirus filtering be done? b) What is spam? c) Why is spam filtering dangerous? d) Why do companies filter sexually or racially harassing message content?

E-Mail Retention

Many mail servers store messages on their disk drives for some time, then **archive** messages onto tape. The coordinated use of online storage and backup storage for messages is referred to as **retention**.

The Benefit of Retention

On the positive side, retention allows users to go through their old mail to look for information. A great deal of a corporation's "organizational memory" and of an individual employee's working information is stored in online e-mail files and archives. Although most messages retrieved are recent ones, corporate projects can last a long time, and some retrievals must go back months or sometimes even years.

The Dangers of Retention

On the negative side, lawyers can use the legal **discovery process** in lawsuits to dredge up messages in which an employee has said something embarrassing or even obviously illegal. In the Federal Microsoft antitrust lawsuit, for instance, e-mail messages from

Bill Gates and other senior managers found during the discovery process were vivid and damaging to Microsoft.

Accidental Retention

Some firms have responded to the specter of discovery by refusing to archive e-mail at all or by keeping mail for only 30 days or some other short period of time. However, mail servers are backed up routinely using magnetic tape, and information can stay on those tapes for long periods of time. Oliver North, the central figure in the Iran Contra scandal during the Reagan administration, deleted his e-mail messages, but the prosecution was able to find them on routine backup tapes.

In some cases, the e-mail messages will be very difficult to retrieve, turning the backup files into a "write-only memory." However, courts have consistently ruled that if such archives exist, companies under discovery orders must use their own money to create programs to sort through the accidental archives.

Legal Archiving Requirements

In addition, in the financial services industry, companies are *required* to archive their communication, including e-mail. In 2002, the U.S. Securities and Exchange Commission fined six financial services firms a total of $10 million for failing to maintain good electronic mail archives. Many government agencies are also required to return e-mail messages as public documents, although transient communications usually are exempt from this rule.

All industries, in fact, are legally required to retain certain forms of communication, whether these are on e-mail or on paper. In such cases, deleting messages will not make a company immune from punishment. Examples include involuntary terminations, public information on job openings, and complaints about certain medical problems that might be caused by toxic chemicals. In one court case, Sprint was fined in a patent lawsuit for failing to keep good e-mail records relevant to the patent.[8]

Overall, corporations need to develop archiving plans for e-mail that reflect their legal environments. It is important to work with the firm's legal department in creating such archives. Yet in 2000, only 31% of all firms had archiving policies.[9]

Receiver-Side Shredding

Even if server information can be protected, recipients of e-mail messages might decide to store them on their own computers (or mail servers). However, new **shredding tools** are capable of deleting messages on the *receiver's* computer.

Actually, these tools do not delete messages on the receiver's machine. Rather, when a message is first sent, a key stored on the sender's server must be used to open the message. After a period of time, the key is no longer made available to the receiver, so the message cannot be read any longer.

---

[8] Michael Osterman, "E-Mail Archiving," *Network World Fusion Focus: Michael Osterman on Messaging,* Electronic newsletter, August 4, 2000.
[9] Michael Osterman, "Today's Focus: Archiving in Message Systems, Part 1," *Network World Fusion Focus: Michael Osterman on Messaging,* Electronic newsletter, August 8, 2000.

Shredding is a way to enforce maximum retention periods. Shredding is also a useful "oops" feature if the sender sends a message to the wrong person or, after reflection, wishes that he or she had not sent a message.

However, the receiver can display the message onscreen and copy it to a word processing document. The receiver also might be able to print it. And, of course, legal contracts cannot be sent this way because the receiver must be able to retain a copy.

Archiving and Message Authentication

It is embarrassingly easy to fabricate a message so that it appears to come from someone else. Networked e-mail was less than two years old when the first spoofed message was sent over the ARPANET. This message claimed to come from a DARPA official, announced an unpopular policy, and was broadcast widely to ARPANET users. (This also might have been the first case of spam.) Spoofed messages can be used to frame other employees, so a good archiving system—and indeed a good e-mail system—must have authentication protections built in.

User Training

Although technology may help companies, the key to avoiding problems in the discovery process is to train users in what not to put into e-mail messages.

Users tend to think of e-mail messages as personal. However, the law does not view them that way. Discovery can dredge them up, they might be sent to the wrong party accidentally, and they can be forwarded to unintended parties. In addition, employers generally have the right to inspect e-mail messages and restrict messages to company business. Employees must be taught never to put anything in a message that they would not want to see in court, printed in the newspapers, or read by their boss.

Employees must be taught never to put anything in a message that they would not want to see in court, printed in the newspapers, or read by their boss.

Users also need to be taught not to forward messages unless specifically authorized to do so. Once messages are forwarded, all control is lost. Even the list of original receivers can be damaging information.

TEST YOUR UNDERSTANDING

15. a) Why is retaining e-mail for a long period of time useful? b) Why is it dangerous? c) Comment on a corporate policy of deleting all e-mail after 30 days. d) What do shredding tools do? e) Are e-mail messages sent by employees private?

E-Mail Encryption

E-mail is a perfect candidate for cryptographic protection. However, relatively few corporations have their employees encrypt e-mail for confidentiality, authenticity, message integrity, or replay protection. In a 2002 survey,[10] only 41 percent of all organiza-

---

[10] Michael Osterman, "Secure Messaging Scarcely Used, Survey Says," *Network World Newsletter: Michael Osterman on Messaging,* July 23, 2002.

tions had any sort of e-mail encryption in place; among small firms, this percentage was only 27 percent. Furthermore, even this minority of firms did not encrypt all messages. Only 15 percent of all e-mail users felt that they should encrypt their mail frequently, another 22 percent felt they should do so occasionally, and 59 percent felt they seldom or never needed to encrypt messages.

IETF Indecisiveness

One problem has been that the Internet Engineering Task Force has not come up with a single definitive solution for e-mail cryptographic protection. As Figure 9-9 shows, three major cryptographic systems are in fairly widespread use: PGP, S/MIME, and TLS. Given this confusing situation, e-mail vendors have been slow to provide cryptographic protection natively, and organizations have been reluctant to standardize on a cryptographic method that might become obsolete.

Pretty Good Privacy (PGP)

A Checkered History   Pretty Good Privacy (PGP) was developed in 1991 by Phil Zimmerman as a way to get around government restrictions on strong encryption. However, it originally infringed on several copyrighted encryption methods. This problem eventually was solved, but Network Associates, which purchased PGP, was unable to make it a commercial success. Although PGP was purchased by another company in 2002, development has lagged. Many vendors have begun to turn to the similar **OpenPGP** standard, but although this new standard shows promise, it also has added to confusion about PGP.

Difficulty of Use   One problem with PGP is that it often is difficult to use. It is not built into many e-mail clients, so two users who want to communicate with PGP security usually have to invoke a separate PGP program to handle secure communication. This alone has kept it from widespread acceptance.

Figure 9-9   Cryptographic Protection for E-Mail

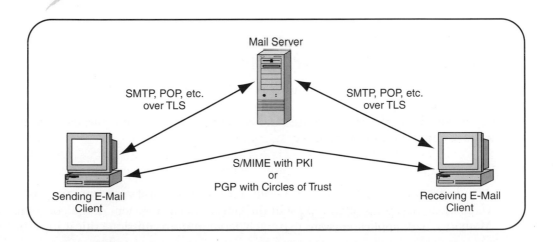

Circles of Trust PGP messages have digital signatures, which use public key encryption. As discussed in Chapter 7, public key authentication requires the receiver/verifier to get the sender's public key from a trusted third party.

Instead of using a centralized public key infrastructure, PGP tends to use **circles of trust**. If you trust Pat, and if Pat trusts Leo, then you can trust the public key/name pairs on Pat's **key ring**, even if a pair was first trusted by Leo and never checked by Pat. This is dangerous because if misplaced trust is present anywhere in the system, bogus public key/name pairs may circulate widely. PGP has had most success in person-to-person communication without corporate control.

S/MIME

Like PGP, **S/MIME (secure MIME)** offers end-to-end cryptographic protection. However, while PGP relies on circles of trust to pass around correct public key/name pairs, S/MIME requires a traditional public key infrastructure. This is much better from the viewpoint of corporate security management. However, PKIs are so difficult to create that the use of a PKI is both a blessing and a curse.

Transport Layer Security (TLS)

Transport Layer Security (TLS) was discussed in Chapter 2 and Chapter 8. This is an outgrowth of SSL. We saw that TLS provides cryptographic protection at the transport layer, protecting any application-layer program that is TLS-compatible. Furthermore, TLS does not require client-side certificates but can work with usernames and passwords.

Although TLS protection is strong, it provides only cryptographic protection between a client and a mail server. It provides end-to-end protection only if the sender and the receiver use TLS and the same mail server and if the mail server protects stored mail cryptographically.

TEST YOUR UNDERSTANDING

16. a) Is encryption widely used in e-mail? b) Compare PGP and S/MIME in terms of how verifiers learn the true party's public key. c) Describe the advantages and disadvantages of each approach. d) How does TLS differ from the other two common encryption methods?

SECURITY ISSUES IN OTHER APPLICATIONS

There are many other applications, each with its own problems. There is not enough room in this chapter to discuss security in all applications. However, we will look at two applications that are likely to raise serious security problems in firms: database applications and instant messaging.

Database

The Importance of Database Applications and Database Passwords

Database applications often represent the central nervous system of the corporation. Many database applications are extremely large and are mission-critical in terms of

OTHER APPLICATIONS

There are many other applications
Each has its own security issues

DATABASE

Often used in mission-critical applications
Application layer authentication: Many database applications have passwords beyond
    the computer login password
Relational databases: Tables with rows (entities) and columns (attributes)
Granularity of access control
    Restrict users to certain columns (attributes) in each row
        For instance, deny access to salary column to most users
    Limit access control to rows, for instance, only rows containing data about people in
        the user's own department
    Prevent access to individual data: Allow trend analysts to deal only with sums and
        averages for aggregates such as departments
Problems with commercial database servers
    Empty administrative password for Microsoft's SQL Server allowed break-ins
    New version of SQL Server will be more locked down

INSTANT MESSAGING (IM)

Allows instant text communication and voice if has "click to talk"
Retention problem: Not integrated into retention schedules
File transfer problem: File transfers are not checked by antivirus programs, although
    a few popular antivirus programs check file transmissions for a few popular IM
    programs.

Figure 9-10   Database and Instant Messaging Security Concerns (Study Figure)

an organization's continued functioning. It is not surprising, then, that many database applications add their own layer of security, for example, adding **application layer authentication** in the form of a separate password for the computer and for the application.

Relational Databases

Most databases are relational. They store their data in tables whose rows represent individual people, transactions, and other "entities." Columns, in turn, are attributes of the entity. For instance, in a table containing data on employees, one column may represent salary. A field is the cell at the intersection of a row and a column. To continue the last example, a cell might hold a particular employee's salary.

Granularity in Access Control

A key issue in database access is **granularity of access**, that is, how much detail a specific user is allowed to see.

Attribute Granularity   For example, only a few employees who have access to the database might be allowed to retrieve information in the salary column. Other employees could read other attributes but not salaries.

Entity Granularity   Moving from columns to rows, access control may limit a user's access to certain rows, for example, to the rows containing information for the employees in a particular user's department.

Forbidding Access to Individual Data   In addition, when a database is used for trend analysis and other functions, it may be desirable to reduce the granularity an analyst may use. For instance, in analyzing data for personnel, privacy concerns may restrict searches to being no smaller than a department sums and averages.

Problems in Database Software

Unfortunately, even commercial database security may be weak. In 2002, a worm attacked applications built on Microsoft SQL Server because a critical administrative password was left unset by default, allowing anyone to log in. This security gaffe allowed a worm, SQLSnake, to spread widely among SQL Server hosts in 2002. Fortunately, the next version of Microsoft SQL Server will not allow unset passwords. In addition, it will have many options disabled by default, for instance, not allowing public access to meta-information on the structure of the database.

Instant Messaging (IM)

Instant Communication

In **instant messaging (IM)**, two employees or an employee and an outsider may be able to carry on typed conversations in real time. They may even be able to use a *click-to-talk* feature to converse orally. If the other party is not in, a user can send short messages for later reading. Users can even share files while conversing.

IM Retention

Although instant messaging is attractive because it adds a new dimension to corporate communication, it raises some serious security issues. One is that IM messages are rarely recorded, so retention requirements in certain industries and government agencies (discussed earlier) cannot be met. Although a few security-focused IM products do allow retention, they are not the popular IM products that employees want to use.

IM File Transfer and Malware

The other serious concern is file transfer. It is easy for someone to mistakenly send an infected file to an IM "buddy." Few IM programs go through antivirus programs, so the technology that companies have put into place to stop viruses are bypassed and ineffective. In effect, IM opens file transfer back doors into the firm. Fortunately, a few popular antivirus vendors are beginning to filter IM file transfers, but they are doing so only for the most popular IM programs.

TEST YOUR UNDERSTANDING

17.   a) Why is it good for database applications and other applications to have their own passwords beyond the computer's login password? b) What is granularity in database access control? c) What are the security concerns raised by instant messaging?

CONCLUSION

In this chapter, we looked at why application security is important, at general principles for application security, at webserver/e-commerce security, at e-mail security, and briefly at database and IM security. However, there are many other user applications with security implications, for example database, Internet relay chat (IRC), Telnet, and FTP. Most have significant vulnerabilities.

In general, "classic" Internet user services such as Telnet and FTP are dangerous because they often fail even to encrypt passwords and generally offer little or no security of any type.

In addition, many "supervisory" protocols make the Internet and corporate networks function, including DNS, routing protocols to allow routers to exchange information (RIP, EIGRP, OSPF, BGP, etc.), and the Simple Network Management Protocol (SNMP). Many offer no user authentication, allowing attackers to attack them easily.[11] Although newer versions of supervisory protocols generally are safer, few require a public key infrastructure, which is the gold standard for authentication and should be used to protect the critical Internet and corporate infrastructures.

THOUGHT QUESTIONS

1. Applications run on hosts. Why do you think applications were not discussed immediately after host security in this book?
2. Why do you think it is difficult to get management to allocate money to pay for patching?
3. What can programmers do to avoid buffer overflows, which are epidemic today?
4. Why do you think most national governments have not moved to outlaw spam?
5. Do you think programmers should be allowed to develop server-side dynamic webpages, given the dangers that are involved in their doing so?
6. Client-side scripting attacks usually require the client to visit a webserver with malicious content. How do you think attackers get users to visit such webpages?

---

[11] For instance, most SNMP systems allow all devices with the same "community string" to communicate automatically. Many corporations do not even change the default community string, which often is "public". Any attacker guessing the community string will be able to send SNMP queries to any device on the network, using this information to plan attacks or even telling devices to change key parameters of their operation.

7. What three main topics would you select for a one-hour user training session on e-mail security? This question requires you to be selective. Do not create topics that are extremely broad to avoid being selective.

8. What three main topics would you select for a one-hour training session for senior managers on e-mail security? This question requires you to be selective. Do not create topics that are extremely broad to avoid being selective.

TROUBLESHOOTING QUESTIONS

1. An employee working at home complains that some of her messages to fellow employees at the firm's headquarters site are not getting through. What might be the problem?

2. A company is warned by its credit card companies that it will be classified as a high-risk firm unless it immediately reduces the number of fraudulent purchases made by its e-commerce clients. What should it do?

CHAPTER 10

INCIDENT AND DISASTER RESPONSE

Learning Objectives

By the end of this chapter, you should be able to discuss:

- The classification of incidents by severity.
- Backup.
- Intrusion detection system (IDS) technology.
- Intrusion response for major incidents.
- Business continuity planning.
- Disaster recovery.
- Vulnerability testing.

INTRODUCTION

Incidents Happen

In previous chapters, we have been discussing the protection phase in the plan-protect-respond cycle. Physical protection, firewalls, server hardening, and cryptographic systems can reduce the chances that a firm will be attacked successfully.

However, these protections, even when applied in depth, sometimes break down. According to the FBI, about 1 percent of all attacks are successful. So even companies with good security must be prepared to handle successful attacks, which are known as **security incidents** or **security breaches**. In this chapter, we will look at different types of security incidents and appropriate corporate responses.

TEST YOUR UNDERSTANDING

> 1. a) What is a security incident? b) What is a security breach? c) Can good protection eliminate security incidents?

Incident Severity

Not all incidents are equally severe. Incidents range from situations mild enough to ignore to threats against the very continuity of the business. We will use a four-category incident severity threat scale in this chapter: false alarms, minor incidents, major incidents, and disasters.

False Alarms

False alarms are situations that at first seem to be incidents (or at least potential incidents) but that turn out to be innocent activities. The actions that attackers take often are similar to those that systems administrators or network managers routinely take in their work. Intrusion detection systems are likely to flag many legitimate activities as suspicious. In fact, in almost all intrusion detection systems, a large majority of suspicious activities will not turn out to be real incidents.

False alarms waste a great deal of scarce and expensive security effort. More subtly, too many false alarms may dull security personnels' readiness to investigate each potential incident. This may allow real incidents to go unnoticed.

Minor Incidents

Minor incidents are breaches that affect only one or a few systems of modest importance. These include such things as cleaning out a dozen user PCs that were damaged in a successful antivirus attack or replacing a single defaced website. Minor incidents tend to be handled well within most firms by the on-duty staff and through informal mechanisms. In addition, response approaches tend to be breach-specific and so are difficult to talk about in general. For these two reasons, minor incidents will not be addressed in this chapter.

Major Incidents

More severe incidents, which we will call **major incidents**, affect multiple systems of moderate importance or one or a few systems of major importance. These represent substantial threats to revenue or expenses. IT and security departments must handle these incidents quickly, efficiently, and effectively in order to contain losses.

INCIDENTS HAPPEN

Protections sometimes break down

INCIDENT SEVERITY

False alarms
Minor incidents
Major incidents
Disasters

SPEED IS OF THE ESSENCE

The need for speed
The need for prior preparation for speed and correctness during incidents
Most important actions occur before the incident happens
Backup, training, rehearsals, etc.

Figure 10-1   Incident Response (Study Figure)

In addition, successful response requires the coordination of efforts in IT and non-IT departments. For instance, if customer privacy is breached, the corporate communication department and even senior management might have to be called in to make important decisions.

Heavy focus will be placed on responses to major incidents in this chapter because of the importance and complexity of this type of incident response.

Disasters

In the worst cases, a disaster is so bad that the business itself is at risk. **Disasters** capable of terminating a business or at least seriously damaging it include natural disasters (fires, floods, and so forth) and human-made disasters (sabotage, the destruction of the IT infrastructure by a hacker, and so forth).

TEST YOUR UNDERSTANDING

2. a) What are the four severity levels of incidents? b) Which two will we examine in this chapter?

Speed Is of the Essence

A critical characteristic of major security breaches and threats to business continuity is time pressure. Until attackers are stopped, they will continue to do damage. Attackers also will continue to take steps to make their actions more difficult to detect and analyze. Even after an attacker is stopped, the need for speed continues. In many cases, important corporate systems will have failed, and their failure can cost the company a great deal of money each hour they are down. Rapid recovery is critical to reducing corporate damages from an attack.

The only way to be able to respond rapidly is to prepare ahead of time. Paradoxically, the actions taken before an incident occurs usually are more critical than the actions taken after an incident is detected. Organizations have to plan and rehearse incident response and take prior actions such as backing up data and protecting log files.

Paradoxically, the actions taken before an incident occurs usually are more critical than the actions taken after an incident is detected.

TEST YOUR UNDERSTANDING

3. a) Why is speed important? b) How can good response speed be achieved?

BACKUP

An extremely crucial protection is **backup**. Servers often hold mission-critical corporate data or data for dozens or hundreds of users. In any major incident or disaster, it is likely that programs and data will be destroyed, will be altered, or at least will become suspect. Under these circumstances, a company might need to turn to its program and data backup files.

Backup Technology

As Figure 10-3 on page 364 illustrates, it is common to be able to back up multiple servers from a single **backup console** (workstation). This avoids the cost of installing backup systems on all servers. On the negative side, centralized backup increases network traffic and might not be available for restorations during an attack. It also creates a single point of failure if the backup workstation fails or if the backup operator uses an incorrect procedure.

TEST YOUR UNDERSTANDING

4. a) What are the elements of a centralized backup system? b) What is its advantage? c) What is its disadvantage?

Managing Backup

Although backup technology is important, the procedures used to manage backup are critical if corporate data are to be protected by the technology.

Frequency of Backup

Full Backups   Most firms fully back up each computer about once a week. This includes the backup of all programs and data files.

Partial Backups   Firms usually also conduct partial backups on a nightly basis. These partial backups only save program and data files that have been changed.

Restoration Order   If a computer's files are lost, the last full backup is restored first. Then, partial backups are restored in the order in which they were made, with the earliest partial backup being restored first.

BACKUP TECHNOLOGY

Centralized backup (Figure 10-3)
Centralized restoration is problematic during attacks
Can be a single point of failure

MANAGING BACKUP

Frequency of Backup
    Full backup about once per week
    Daily partial backups to record changes
    Restore tapes in order recorded (full first, then partials in original order)
Protecting Backup Media
    Storage off-site for safety (If stored on-site, disasters could destroy backup media)
    Store in fireproof containers until moved
Testing Restoration Is Mandatory
Retention Policies
    How long to retain backup tapes before reuse
    Need a policy that reflects importance of server and other factors
Journaling
    All data since last backup normally is lost in crashes
    Journaling: Store transactions as they occur on writeable CDs or DVDs
Real-Time Database Duplication
    Maintain duplicate database at remote site
    Transmit data changes in real time to maintain consistency
    Prevents almost all data loss
    Expensive in terms of hardware and data communications

Figure 10-2   Program and Data Backup (Study Figure)

Storing Backup Media Away from the Main Site

In cases of fires or floods, backup tapes stored in the computer room probably would be destroyed along with the computers. It is important to store backup tapes off-site so that if a data center is destroyed, the program files and data can be restored on another machine.

Although data should be moved out of the data center daily, they typically reside there for several hours at least. During that period, they should be kept in a fireproof safe.

Testing Restoration

It is important to test the backup system periodically by reinstalling some files or by installing all files on a new machine. When a massive data loss occurs, this is a poor time to learn that your backup system is not functioning well.

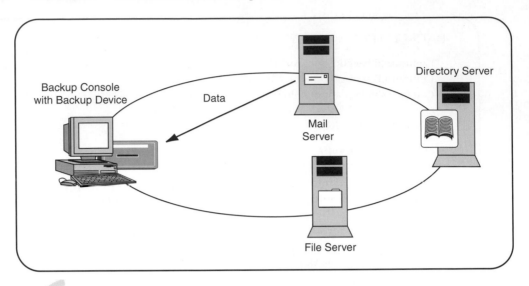

Figure 10-3 Backup Technology

Retention Policies

Sometimes, no one realizes for some time that a problem has existed in a system. In such cases, an earlier backup is needed. Most firms store all partial backups for the most current week or two. For earlier weeks, they might store only weekly full backups. Over the longer term, only quarterly backups might be stored. Companies need to have a **backup retention plan** to decide how long backup tapes will be stored before being reused. This will depend on such things as the importance of a particular server.

Journaling

Although full and partial backups at specific times are good, all new data will be lost between the time of the last backup and the time of file loss. When data is very important, say when orders are taken by an e-commerce system, a transaction log should be recorded frequently to writable CDs or DVDs. This is called **journaling** because this is the type of information written into accounting journals.

Real-Time Database Duplication

The best backup is the real-time duplication of entire databases at remote sites, so that if there is a disaster at the main site, almost no data will be lost. In addition to protecting all data, real-time backup databases make disaster recovery very rapid because the data is in the form needed by the backup production program. Of course, real-time data backup is extremely expensive in terms of both hardware and data transmission.

TEST YOUR UNDERSTANDING

5. a) Distinguish between full and partial backups. b) In what order are backup tapes restored? c) Where should backup media be stored? d) How should they be stored before they are moved? e) Why is it important to do restoration tests? f) Why are backup retention plans needed? g) What is journaling, and why is journaling better than periodic backup? h) Why is real-time database duplication even better? i) What is the disadvantage of real-time database duplication?

INTRUSION DETECTION SYSTEMS (IDSs)

When attacks occur, they proceed invisibly from the viewpoint of humans—merely changing magnetic patterns on disks or electronic patterns in memory. An **intrusion detection system (IDS)** is software and sometimes hardware that captures network and host activity data in event logs and provides automatic tools to generate alarms and query and reporting tools to help administrators analyze the data interactively during and after an incident.

An intrusion detection system (IDS) is software and sometimes hardware that captures network and host activity data in event logs and provides automatic tools to generate alarms and query and reporting tools to help administrators analyze the data interactively during and after an incident.

An IDS is like a security camera in a building. A security camera may provide real-time intrusion detection, and it provides tapes that can be examined after an incident, but security cameras in buildings do not replace door locks or safes. Similarly, an IDS is only an element in the security architecture. It does not eliminate the need for protections to prevent attacks.

TEST YOUR UNDERSTANDING

6. What is an IDS?

Elements of an IDS

Figure 10-5 on page 369 shows that an IDS has four important modules: logging, analysis, action, and management.

Logging (Data Collection)

The logging element captures discrete activities, such as the arrival of a packet or an attempt to log in. Each activity is time stamped and stored in a sequential file sorted initially by time. These are the raw data that IDSs administrators must analyze to allow intelligent intrusion detection response.

IDSs

Event logging in log files
Analysis of log file data
Alarms
    Too many false positives (false alarms)
    Too many false negatives (overlooked incidents)
Log files for retrospective analysis by humans

ELEMENTS OF AN IDS (Figure 10-5)

Event logging
Analysis method
Action
Management

DISTRIBUTED IDSs (Figure 10-6)

Managers
Agents
Distribution of functionality between agents and managers (analysis and action)
Batch Versus Real-Time Data Transfer
    Batch mode: Every few minutes or hours; efficient
    Real-time: As events occur or shortly afterward; little or no data loss if attacker
        eliminates log file on agent's computer
Secure manager–agent communication
Vendor's automatic updates with secure communication

NETWORK IDSs (NIDSs) (Figure 10-6)

Capture packets flowing through the NIDs
Stand-alone NIDS collects data for only its portion of the network
Switch or router NIDSs can collect data on all ports
NIDS placement (Figure 10-6)
    Between main firewall and internal or external network for relevant or all attacks
    At internal points to detect internal mischief
Weaknesses
    Blind spots in network where no NIDS data is collected
    Cannot filter encrypted packets

Figure 10-4 Intrusion Detection Systems (IDSs) (Study Figure)

HOST IDSs ON INDIVIDUAL HOSTS (Figure 10-6)

Protocol Stack Monitor (like NIDS)
    Collects the same type of information as a NIDS
    Collects data even if host is in NIDS blind spot
    Gives data specific to hosts; relevant for diagnosis
    Might see data after decryption
Operating System Monitors
    Collects data on operating system events
    Failed logins
    Attempts to change system executables
    Attempts to change system configuration (registry keys, etc.)
Application Monitors (Monitor Specific Applications)
    What users did in terms relevant to an application for easy interpretation
    Filtering input data for buffer overflows
    Signatures of application-specific attacks
Weaknesses of Host IDSs
    Limited Viewpoint; Only one host
    Host IDSs can be attacked and disabled
Other host-based tools
    File integrity checker programs
        Create baseline message digests for sensitive files
        After an attack, recomputed message digests
        This tells which files were changed; indicates Trojan horses, etc.
    Operating system lockdown tools
        Limits changes possible during attacks
        Limits who may make crucial changes
        May interfere with software functioning

LOG FILES

Flat files of time-stamped events
Individual logs
Integrated logs
    Aggregation of event logs from multiple IDS agents (Figure 10-6)
    Difficult to create because of format incompatibilities
    Time synchronization of IDS event logs is crucial (NTP)

EVENT CORRELATION (Figure 10-7)

Suspicious patterns in a series of events across multiple devices

(continued)

Figure 10-4   (Continued)

ANALYSIS METHODS

Static packet filtering

Stateful filtering

Full protocol decoding (filters based upon stage in dialog—login, etc.)

Statistical analysis (frequency thresholds for reporting)

Anomaly detection (compares normal and current operation)

    Creates many false positives

ACTIONS

Alarms

Interactive analysis

    Manual event inspection of raw log file

    Retrieval by pattern in the data

Reporting

Automated response

    Dangerous

    Special danger of attack-back (might be illegal; might hurt victim)

    Automation for clear attacks brings speed of response

MANAGING IDSs

Tuning for precision

    Too many false positives can overwhelm administrators, dull interest

    False negatives allow attacks to proceed unseen

    Tuning for false positives turns off unnecessary rules, reduces alarm levels of unlikely rules

    IDS might make tuning difficult

Updates

    Program, attack signatures must be updated periodically

Performance

    If processing speed cannot keep up with network traffic, some packets will not be examined

        This can make IDSs useless during DoS attacks

    If memory requirements are too large, system might crash

        Making logs smaller by saving them more frequently hurts longer-duration event correlation

Figure 10-4   (Continued)

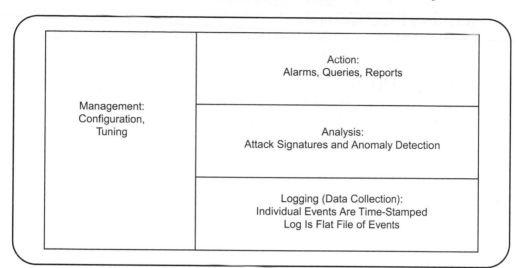

Figure 10-5   Elements of a Simple IDS

Analysis

Attack Signatures   Several general methods are available for finding patterns in the large amount of data collected by an IDS in its log files. The simplest IDS analysis method is like static packet filtering, which you saw in Chapter 5 for firewalls. It works on the basis of attack signatures.

Anomaly Detection (Heuristics)   The most sophisticated technique is anomaly detection, in which heuristic patterns try to detect variations from historically normal operation. Major IDS log file analysis methods will be examined later.

Action

Alarms   Merely collecting and analyzing data accomplishes nothing. IDSs must use results from analysis to interact with humans. Most obviously, they generate **alarms** if analysis indicates a dangerous condition.

Retrospective Interactive Data Analysis   In addition, IDSs help humans make sense of data collected by providing interactive query tools. This allows security administrators to drill down into log files to better understand an ongoing or completed attack.

Management

The final module is management. IDSs are not like toasters that are merely plugged in and work immediately. IDSs must be configured, updated, and actively managed in other general ways. An IDS with a poor management module will require excessive work and might even be useless if the required management work is too poorly supported.

7. a) What are the four functional modules in IDSs? b) What types of action were mentioned in this section?

Distributed IDSs

Figure 10-5 shows a simple IDS in which all four modules exist in a single device. Such all-in-one, stand-alone IDSs do exist, but they are of limited use. To understand a security incident, it normally is necessary to see the broader picture of which packets are flowing through the network and what is happening at multiple hosts. It is normal for a single host to reboot. If several hosts reboot in a short period of time, however, this should be a serious wake-up call. Figure 10-6 shows a distributed IDS that can collect data from many devices at a central manager console (client PC or UNIX workstation).

Agents

Each monitoring device has a software agent that collects event data and stores them in log files on the monitoring devices. Sometimes, agents also do some analysis and alarm reporting.

Manager

The manager is responsible for integrating the information from the multiple agents that run on multiple monitoring devices. To do this, the manager must collect log files from various devices and integrate them into a single log file (or at most a few log

Figure 10-6 Distributed IDS

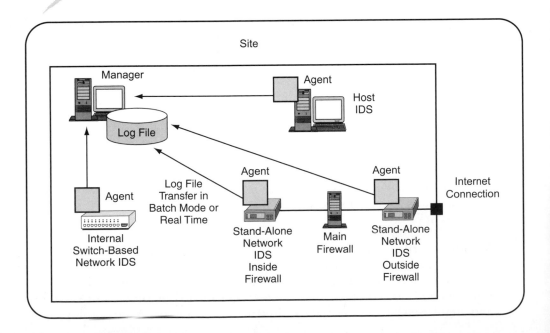

files). The manager must analyze the log file data, generate alarms, and allow humans to do interactive data queries.

Distribution of Functionality Between the Manager and Agent

A major issue in design is how much work the agents will do. In the simplest case, the agents merely collect data, as just noted. The manager must do all of the analysis and take all actions.

However, some agents also do at least limited analysis and alarm generation. These advanced capabilities might be helpful in periods of intense activity, when the manager is heavily loaded with work. During such periods, the manager might take too long to analyze the data and create alarms. On the other hand, because each agent sees only the data on its device, it will be less precise than a central manager and so might generate many false positives (false alarms).

Batch Versus Real-Time Data Transfer

Batch-Mode Transfers   The agent can transfer log files to the manager in two ways. The most common is **batch-mode** transfer, in which the agent waits until it has several minutes or several hours of data and then sends a block of log file data to the manager. Batch-mode transfers place the least load on the network because sending blocks of data can be done efficiently. It also minimizes the number of times the manager is interrupted by receiving data. (Every interruption on a host requires considerable CPU activity.)

Real-Time Transfers   In turn, in real-time transfers, each event's data is transferred to the manager immediately. This is desirable because one of the first things that many attackers do is delete or at least disable event logging. If they succeed, and if the last batch mode transfer was before they hacked into the system, then data for all of their activities will be lost. With real-time transfers, only the activities after the deletion or disabling of event logging will be lost.

Secure Manager-Agent Communication

Communication between the agents and the manager should be secure, with authentication, integrity checking, confidentiality, and anti-replay protection. If an attacker can hack a computer and spoof an agent or manager, the results would be chaos.

Vendor Communication

The vendor also has a role in this process. Vendors periodically create new filtering rules. These must be downloaded and propagated throughout the system, usually via the manager. Communication between the vendor and the manager also needs to be secure, with authentication, integrity checking, confidentiality, and anti-replay protection.

TEST YOUR UNDERSTANDING

   8. a) What is the advantage of a distributed IDS? b) Name the elements in a distributed IDS. c) Distinguish between the manager and agents. d) What functional modules may be found on agents? e) On the manager? f) Distinguish between batch and real-mode transfers. g) What is the advantage of each type? h) What types of communication should be secure?

Network IDSs

So far, we have spoken vaguely of "agents." Now we will look at the specific types of agents that are installed on devices. We will begin with **network IDSs (NIDSs)**, which capture packets as they travel through a network.

Stand-Alone NIDSs

As Figure 10-6 shows, **stand-alone NIDSs** are boxes that are plugged into the network. They operate in **promiscuous mode**, which means that they read and analyze all network frames that pass by them. They are corporate-owned sniffers.

Switch and Router NIDSs

In contrast, **switch NIDSs** and **router NIDSs** are built into switches and routers, respectively. Typically, these capture data on all ports.

In the past, it often has been said that network IDS does not work well in switched or routed networks because switched and routed networks segregate traffic. A NIDS attached to a switch or router port can only see traffic going to and from that port. However, now that switches and routers themselves can contain agents for each port, switched and routed networks do not create problems. On the negative side, an organization tends to get locked into whatever NIDS technology its switch and router vendors employ.

NIDS Placement

Where should NIDSs be placed? As Figure 10-6 shows, two popular locations for NIDSs are on the two sides of the border firewall that links the firm to the Internet.

Between the Border Firewall and the Internet   Placing a NIDS between the firewall and the Internet will allow the NIDS to see all traffic, so that the types of attacks the firm currently is facing can best be analyzed.

Between the Border Firewall and the Internal Network   However, most of these attacks are stopped by the firewall, so an NIDS placed between the firewall and the internal network will not be burdened by attacks that fail to get into the internal corporate network. It can concentrate on dangerous attacks that got through the firewall. Most importantly, administrators will experience less overload when they read through massive event logs.

Internal Placement   Placement next to a border firewall is good for monitoring Internet attacks but does nothing to monitor attacks coming from inside the network as a result of dishonest employees or compromised internal computers. Consequently, it is good to place internal NIDS monitors at strategic points in the network, such as near sensitive accounting servers.

Strengths of NIDSs

The strength of NIDSs is that they can see all packets passing through some locations in the network. Often, these packets are highly diagnostic of attacks.

Weaknesses of NIDSs

However, NIDSs have a number of weaknesses that cause problems unless supplemented by non-network IDSs.

Blind Spots   Although switch and router NIDSs offer the possibility of internal data collection, few firms can afford to install and manage agents on all internal switches and routers. Consequently, most firms have blind spots where NIDSs cannot see packets. If only border NIDSs are used, then the entire internal network is one large blind spot.

Encrypted Data   Just as firewalls cannot scan encrypted data, NIDSs cannot make sense of encrypted information. Although they can scan unencrypted parts of an encrypted packet (typically, an added IP header), this provides limited information. As encryption increases in popularity, the effectiveness of NIDSs will degrade proportionally.

TEST YOUR UNDERSTANDING

9.   a) At what information do NIDSs look? b) Distinguish between stand-alone NIDSs and switch-based NIDSs. c) What NIDS problems do there tend to be in switched networks? d) Name the three places NIDSs are typically placed and the advantages of each location. e) What are the two weaknesses of NIDSs?

Host IDSs

A firm has many host computers. The most critical hosts are the firm's servers. **Host IDSs** work on data collected on the host computer.

Although some client PCs can have stand-alone host IDSs—called **personal IDSs**—few of these can be integrated into centralized corporate IDS systems today.

Host IDSs: Protocol Stack Monitors

NIDSs examine packets flowing past their position in the network. In turn, some host IDSs are **protocol stack monitors**, which examine those packets arriving at or leaving a host. Protocol stack monitors work like NIDSs but only look at packets coming into or going out of a single host.

➤ Protocol stack monitors are attractive because even if the host is in a blind spot in the NIDS network, the protocol stack monitor can still collect the data relevant to that host.

➤ Also, only data that pertain to the particular host on which the host IDS is installed are collected. This simplifies analysis.

➤ Some protocol stack monitors see the data after decryption, so the problem that NIDSs normally have with decryption is eliminated.

Host IDSs: Operating System Monitors

Although protocol stack monitors are useful, most host IDSs are **operating system monitors**, which focus on operating system events. (In Chapter 6, we looked at Windows Event Viewer.) This is a good supplement to NIDS and protocol stack monitor data. Here are some data typically collected by operating system monitor IDSs.

➤ Multiple failed logins.

➤ Creating new accounts.

➤ Adding new executables (programs—may be attack programs).

➤ Modifying executables (installing Trojan horses does this).

➤ Adding registry keys (changes how system works).

➤ Changing or deleting system logs and audit files.

➤ Changing system audit policies.

➤ User accessing critical system files.

➤ User accessing unusual files.

➤ Changing the OS monitor itself.

Host IDS: Application Monitors

Application monitors are host IDSs that examine activities at the application level. Although fairly uncommon, application monitors can be powerful because application activities usually have obvious meanings and may reveal patterns that large numbers of log events at the operating system or protocol levels would be needed to reveal.

What Users Did   Most basically, application monitors record what users did—when they logged in and out, what files they accessed, what data they changed, and so forth. This information is highly diagnostic.

Filtering User Input Data   Buffer overflow attacks involve user inputs with unusually large data volumes and often include binary information. Such inputs should be logged and sometimes actively stopped.

Signatures of Application-Specific Attacks   More generally, popular application exploits tend to have well-defined signatures that can be detected with pattern matching.

Weaknesses of Host IDSs

Limited Viewpoint   Host IDSs have two major weaknesses. First, they have a limited view of what is happening on the network. The same myopic focus that allows them to be specific also means they cannot see the broader picture. Repeated login failures on one host are a cause for concern. Repeated login failures on multiple hosts within a short time period are a much greater cause for concern.

Host IDSs Can Be Attacked   In addition, host IDSs are subject to attack. They sit on the computer the attacker has just compromised, and their files can be deleted or changed. Although some operating systems create binary event logs that are written by the operating system kernel and cannot be deleted or changed, most host IDS log files can be attacked by hackers directly.

Other Host-Based Tools

Two other host-based tools should be mentioned. Although not precisely IDSs, they serve to supplement IDSs.

File Integrity Checkers   Chapter 7 explained that message digests can help users know if a message has been changed. **File integrity checkers** create message digests of all system files that are likely to be changed rarely or never. They can check this database periodically against newly generated message digests to determine whether any changes have been made. Unfortunately, quite a few system files do change occasionally for legitimate reasons, so the number of false alarms is high until such files are eliminated from checking.

Operating System Lockdown Tools   Some programs create **operating system lockdown**, which prevents changes from being made to registry settings, prevents Trojans from being installed, prevents log files from being changed, and does many other similar things.

Sometimes, changes are needed, but only certain users may be allowed to take certain actions in certain directories or on certain files.

Although operating system lockdown programs are powerful, some application programs cannot work with them. Also, if operating system lockdown is applied blindly, many proper user actions will be stopped.

TEST YOUR UNDERSTANDING

    10.   a) At what types of information do host protocol stack monitors look? b) List three reasons why is it better to collect packet information on a host than to collect it on a NIDS. c) List some things at which host-based operating system monitors look. d) Why are application monitors good? e) At what do application monitors look? f) What are the two weaknesses of host IDSs? g) How do file integrity checkers identify problems? h) What do operating system lockdown programs do?

Log Files

Time-Stamped Events

All log files have the same core format. Each is a flat file of log entries. Each **log entry** has a *time stamp* and an *event type*. Beyond that, log files may have other information to help diagnose the event. For instance, NIDS log files might contain basic packet field values. In turn, host IDS entries regarding suspicious file operations will name the file, the action performed on the file, and the user or program taking the action.[1]

Individual Logs

The trouble with log files from individual NIDSs or host IDSs is that each log file represents only a local view of activities at any moment. The slow scanning of many hosts on the network, for instance, is not likely to be noticed by any single host or network-monitoring agent.

Integrated Logs

As Figure 10-7 shows, distributed IDSs import log file data from multiple host IDSs and NIDSs.[2] In addition to storing all the log files on one computer, distributed IDSs attempt to aggregate all log entries from multiple sources into a single **integrated log**

---

[1] Some NIDS log files use the popular Tcpdump format. Tcpdump is a free packet-logging program that runs on UNIX. Another version, Windump, runs on Windows computers. Several freeware NIDSs, most notably Snort, add NIDS capabilities to Tcpdump.

[2] On UNIX systems, the Syslog program is a popular way to send log files to a central logging server. Compatible products are available for Windows servers.

Sample Log File
(Many Irrelevant Log Entries Not Shown)

1. 8:45:05. Packet from 1.15.3.6 to 60.3.4.5 (network IDS log entry)
2. 8:45:07. Host 60.3.4.5. Failed login attempt for account Lee (Host 60.3.4.5 log entry)
3. 8:45:08. Packet from 60.3.4.5 to 1.15.3.6 (network IDS log entry)
4. 8:49:10. Packet from 1.15.3.6 to 60.3.4.5 (network IDS log entry)
5. 8:49:12. Host 60.3.4.5. Failed login attempt for account Lee (Host 60.3.4.5 log entry)
6. 8:49:13. Packet from 60.3.4.5 to 1.15.3.6 (network IDS log entry)
7. 8:52:07. Packet from 1.15.3.6 to 60.3.4.5 (network IDS log entry)
8. 8:52:09. Host 60.3.4.5. Successful login attempt for account Lee (Host 60.3.4.5 log entry)
9. 8:52:10. Packet from 60.3.4.5 to 1.15.3.6 (network IDS log entry)
10. 8:56:12. Packet from 60.3.4.5 to 123.28.5.210. TFTP request (network IDS log entry)
11. (no corresponding host log entry)
12. 8:56:28. Series of packets from 123.28.5.210 to 60.3.4.5. TFTP response (network IDS)
13. (no more host log entries)
14. 9:03.17. Packet from 60.3.4.5 to 1.17.8.40. SMTP (network IDS)
15. 9:06:12. Packet from 60.3.4.5 to 1.40.22.8. SMTP (network IDS)
16. 9:10:12. Packet from 60.3.4.5 to 60.0.1.1. TCP SYN=1, Destination Port 80 (network IDS)
17. 9:10:13: Packet from 60.3.4.5 to 60.0.1.2. TCP SYN=1, Destination Port 80 (network IDS)

Figure 10-7 Event Correlation for an Integrated Log File

that contains data from many places around the network for any given moment. This is **aggregation**.

Difficult to Create   If a company has NIDSs and host IDSs from multiple vendors, each IDS is likely to use a different format for log file entries. If this is the case, it will be extremely difficult and perhaps impossible to create an integrated log. However, few firms are likely to standardize on one vendor simply to be able to create integrated logs. In addition, some vendors deal only with host logging, stand-alone network logging, or switch or router logging.

Time Synchronization   If the times on the various IDSs are off by even fractions of a second, it will be extremely difficult to see what is happening at a particular moment in time—especially if the attack is automated and occurs quickly. It is important to synchronize all system times.

The **Network Time Protocol (NTP)** allows this type of synchronization. It is sufficient, by the way, for all devices to be synchronized to a single internal NTP server. Although the internal NTP server's time might not be synchronized precisely to time servers in the outside world, relative time is the key to success when aggregating log entries from different sources. An external NTP server can be used to synchronize the internal NTP server, but this could open an avenue of attack against the internal NTP server.

Event Correlation

Often, single events are suspicious. If an application program tries to change a system executable, this is highly suggestive of an attack. In other cases, events are not suspicious individually because attackers tend to do many of the same things that ordinary users do. In such cases, only sequences of several events are likely to be suggestive of attacks. The analysis of multi-event patterns is called **event correlation**.

For instance, one manager noted with some interest that a server was having a large number of SMB authorization failings, indicating unsuccessful attempts to access files on another server.[3] However, when three other servers began to have large number of failed SMB authorizations, the investigation was kicked into high gear. The problem turned out to be the spread of a virus, Sircam, that spread partially by infecting network shares on other computers. This allowed the company to begin acting while the virus was just beginning to spread.

Figure 10-7 shows an integrated log file that contains information from network logs and a host operating system log. Only events pertaining to the attack are shown. In the thought questions, you will be asked to describe patterns of activities that are suspicious and whether they are suggestive of an attack or definitively prove an attack.

To get you started, note that the person logging in has two failed logins before succeeding. This could indicate password guessing. However, ordinary users sometimes mistype or forget their passwords, so the two failed logins are not collectively definitive. Also note that there is enough time between login attempts to indicate a human actor. If the attempts were only a few milliseconds apart, that would suggest an automated attack and would be fairly definitive proof that an attack is occurring.

TEST YOUR UNDERSTANDING

11.   a) Why are integrated log files good? b) Why are they difficult to create? c) Explain the synchronization issue for integrated log files. d) How is this issue addressed? e) What is event correlation? f) Distinguish between aggregation and event correlation.

Analysis Methods

Although it is possible for humans simply to read all log files looking for suspicious patterns, this usually is an activity of last resort and, in fact, usually is impossible because of the amount of time that would be needed to do so. During a major attack, there may be several thousand logged events per hour. Reading through this mass of data manually would take days at the least. Consequently, all IDSs use analysis methods to create indicators of problems.

---

[3]   NetForensics, "Case Study: Major New York Hospital System," undated. Accessed July 17, 2002. www.netforensics.com/healthcarecase.html.

Static Packet Filtering

In Chapter 5, we saw static packet filtering, which looks at IP, TCP, UDP, and ICMP headers in single packets in isolation. This method also is used in many network IDSs. However, although static packet filter firewalls compare packets with rule sets to create pass/deny decisions, static packet filter NIDSs merely flag certain packets as suspicious and add them to the log file.

Stateful Inspection

In Chapter 5, we saw that stateful inspection firewalls also keep track of the state of each connection (whether it is open or closed). Many NIDSs also use this information.

Full Protocol Decoding

In **full protocol decoding**, the NIDS keeps track of where an application is in its life cycle. For instance, during initial login, certain attack patterns will be compared against packets. These comparisons will not be done after login. Full protocol decoding reduces the number of rules that must be applied at any time and produces fewer false positives.

Statistical Analysis

Sometimes, a single instance of an event—for instance, a failed login attempt—is not a cause for concern, but many instances of this same event in a brief period of time may strongly indicate a threat. **Statistical analysis** examines frequency patterns in the data.

In some cases, alarms are set off if the frequency of events passes some pre-set **threshold** value. For instance, if more than five failed login attempts occur within a two-minute period, an alarm might be generated.

Anomaly Detection Analysis

A more difficult to discuss analysis method is **anomaly detection analysis**, in which current event patterns as a whole are compared to normal event patterns as a whole. Anomaly detection analysis is powerful because it can catch attacks that have never been seen before. However, it is difficult to tell what is normal or unusual because activity patterns vary widely in real systems. Anomaly detection consequently tends to generate many false positives.

TEST YOUR UNDERSTANDING

12. a) List the main IDS analysis methods. b) How does static packet inspection detect attacks? c) How does stateful inspection detect attacks? d) What is full protocol decoding? e) Why is full protocol decoding efficient? f) How does statistical analysis detect attacks? g) How does anomaly detection detect attacks? h) What kinds of attacks can anomaly detection identify that other analysis methods cannot? i) What is the main problem with anomaly detection?

Action

As noted earlier, IDSs can generate alarms automatically and allow interactive user analysis to help the security administrator see patterns in the log files. We will see that IDSs also can take a few other actions.

Alarms

To be effective, alarms should be generated only when a real problem occurs. (They should not be like hair-trigger car alarms.) When alarms are generated, they should be as specific as possible, giving the user a description of what the problem is and, preferably, how it can be tested for accuracy and what the security administrator should do.

IDSs should have flexible alarm delivery, because no single approach is perfect.

➤ Putting an alarm on the manager console screen is not effective at nights or on weekends if the console is not being observed.

➤ Pager warnings will reach the security administrator, but only high-probability attacks should be signaled this way or the security administrator will throw the pager away.

➤ E-mail also is not good for instant announcements. E-mail is good if the security administrator checks e-mail frequently, but during attacks, e-mail cannot be trusted because the e-mail system may have been compromised.

An IDS should offer a mixture of alarm methods and tools to decide which threats are sufficiently dangerous to justify immediate notification methods such as pagers.

Interactive Analysis

The big problem with log files is that they contain thousands or tens of thousands of entries. Some way must be found to locate patterns within this mass of data.

Manual Event Inspection   Full manual event inspection is impossible. However, if an attack is suspected of having begun at a particular time, manual inspection is possible by taking all events near that time and allowing the analyst to ignore irrelevant entries, leaving something like the entries shown in Figure 10-7.

Pattern Retrieval   In some cases, patterns that should be characteristic of certain attacks can be expressed in ways that allow only log entries relevant to that specific to be retrieved. For instance, if a password guessing attack in Telnet is suspected, the system can be told to show only failed logging attempts and packets that are Telnet packets (Port 23) and that contain a login request.

Reporting

IDSs also produce periodic reports that summarize trends in suspicious activity. These reports help security supervisors understand broad patterns in recent network and host activities.

Automated Action

Many IDSs can take limited automated action without human intervention based on certain event patterns. Most commonly, network IDSs use this ability to thwart denial-of-service attacks. In host IDSs, the IDS might stop users from taking certain actions.

The Danger of Automated Actions   However, automated action should be extremely limited because most IDS patterns merely indicate suspicious activity, not provably wrong action. In addition, IDSs do not understand the company's business situation. The decision to cut a public webserver's connection to the Internet should be made only by someone in authority who understands the implications of the action. In the worst cases, active defense will create an effective denial-of-service attack that is more devastating than the attack it was attempting to thwart.

Automated Attack-Back Responses   A few IDSs even attack the attacker. These attack-back practices are extremely dubious. In the worst case, they either are illegal or might attack an innocent party whose machine was compromised.

The Appropriate Use of Automated Action   Nevertheless, some patterns are so clear that automated action is perfectly reasonable. In such cases, the ability of IDSs to act immediately is extremely valuable. For example, during a denial-of-service attack from a single IP address, that address might be black-holed automatically.

TEST YOUR UNDERSTANDING

13.   a) What information should alarms contain? b) What are the advantages and disadvantages of different ways to deliver alarms? c) What is interactive analysis? d) What are the two common forms of interactive analysis? e) What is the purpose of reports? f) What is automated action? g) Why is automated action dangerous? h) Why is automated attack-back especially dangerous? i) When is automated action good?

Managing IDSs

IDSs cannot be plugged in and left to work. Perhaps more than any other security technologies today, IDSs require constant management attention. Companies without considerable security expertise and commitment to continuing outlays of time and money should not purchase IDSs.

Tuning for Precision

An important management concern is **precision**, meaning that the IDS should report all attack events and report no events that are not attack events.

False Positives   All too often, IDSs generate many false alarms, known technically as **false positives**. In many cases, false positives will outnumber true alarms ten-to-one or even more. In fact, the large number of false positives generated by IDSs is the major problem with IDSs today, causing many firms to stop using them after a trial period.[4]

False Negatives   IDSs also have many **false negatives**—failures to report attack activities. False negatives are even more important than false positives because they allow real attacks to continue undetected. However, because false negatives are not intrusive and often are undetected, their importance often is unappreciated.

---

[4]   Even with tuning, false positives will tend to dominate alerts. Counterpane, a managed security company, found that even after tuning, only 14 percent of alarms were actual attacks. Counterpane Internet Security, "Counterpane Internet Security's Customers Show Dramatic Improvement in Internet Security," April 11, 2002. www.counterpane.com/pr-500.html.

Tuning   The number of false positives can be reduced by **tuning** the IDS. Tuning is turning off unnecessary rules and reducing the severity level in the alarms generated by other rules.

First, rules that make no sense in a particular environment should be dropped. For instance, if an organization uses all UNIX servers, why should an IDS test for and create an alarm for an attack designed to compromise the IIS webserver program (which runs only on Windows servers)?

In fact, having vast numbers of attack signatures is a bad idea because too many false alarms will be generated by signatures of marginal value. Tuning reduces the number of false alarms. This is the opposite of the situation for antivirus protection.

However, reducing the number of attack signatures also might increase the number of false negatives. Security administrators might not be as overloaded, but they also might not realize that attacks are underway.

Tuning Problems   Tuning is so essential that one might assume that IDSs make it easy to do; however, most IDSs today make tuning extremely difficult. A high number of false positives coupled with the difficulty of tuning have caused many firms to avoid IDSs or to remove already-implemented IDSs.

Updates

Nearly all IDSs must be updated frequently. Often, new versions of the software are available every six months or so. Signatures and similar detection elements also need to be updated weekly or more often. Automatic updating from the vendor's site and automatic updating to agents can reduce this work.

Considering Performance

Precision is an important purchase criterion for IDSs, but IDS performance problems can make an IDS useless.

Processing Performance at Peak Network Loads   It takes a good number of CPU cycles to process each event. As network traffic grows, and as the number of attack signatures increases, the IDS may lack the **processing performance** needed to process packets at high network loads.

If this happens, the IDS will skip some packets and so may miss attacks. Performance problems are extremely problematic because many types of attacks, such as DoS attacks, increase network traffic dramatically. An IDS that functions well only when the system is not under attack is worthless.

Performance tests must be made using realistic data. Some vendors use only long packets in tests, so there will be fewer test packets for a given level of network traffic than there would be if packets of realistic size were used. Some aspects of packet processing time are proportional to the number of packets, so fewer long packets will require fewer processing cycles than packets of realistic size. If realistic packet sizes are not used in tests, the tests are likely to suggest that an IDS can handle high traffic levels when in fact it might not be able to do so.

Storage Performance   Log files can be very large. Yet many IDSs limit the sizes of log files. In the worst case, the system will run out of storage capacity and crash. Although this is poor program design, it is somewhat common.

To address this problem, some IDSs limit log files to certain maximum sizes. However, this means that the time period of each log file will be limited. Any event that spans log files is difficult to detect.

TEST YOUR UNDERSTANDING

14. a) What is precision in an IDS? b) What are false positives, and why are they bad? c) What are false negatives, and why are they bad? d) How can tuning reduce the number of false positives? e) Why is tuning dangerous? f) Why is it bad if tuning is difficult to do? g) Why must IDSs be updated? h) What processing problems may IDSs have? i) What does an IDS do if it cannot process all of the packets it receives? j) What may happen if a system runs out of storage space? k) Why is keeping log files relatively small undesirable?

THE INTRUSION RESPONSE PROCESS

Intrusion detection technology is only one element in successful intrusion response. Intrusion response is a process, not a set of hardware and software processes.

Organizational Preparation

As noted earlier in this chapter, when incidents occur, organizations are under enormous time pressure. If a company needs to organize its intrusion response processes after an incident occurs, severe damage will be done before the company can react, and intruders will be able to hide their tracks. In addition, when people are under time pressure, they tend to make bad decisions that ignore broader issues that would become apparent during proper planning processes. Hasty action can even take the company down paths that are fruitless and that further delay effective response. The most critical time period in intrusion response is before the incident happens.

Incident Escalation Procedures

Most incidents will turn out to be false alarms or minor incidents. So the initial response can be handled at a low level in the IT department, by the on-duty staff. However, if the initial responders find that the problem appears to be severe, clear **escalation** procedures must be in place to specify who has permission to call an escalation in threat severity, who will be called in to handle the problem, and what their responsibilities will be.

Computer Emergency Response Team (CERT)

For major incidents, many firms create **computer emergency response teams (CERTs)**. Creating a formal CERT clarifies responsibilities.

How large is a CERT? The answer will be different in every company. One financial services firm has a core incident response team of 12 full-time specialists.[5] Even this large group calls in members from human resources and the legal department when appropriate. Obviously, smaller firms cannot support this level of active expertise.

---

5   Jaikumar Vijayan, "Build a Response Team," *Computerworld*, July 15, 2002. computerworld.com/
securitytopics/security/story/0,10801,72637,00.html.

FOR MAJOR INCIDENTS

ORGANIZATIONAL PREPARATION

Incident response procedures
Formation of a Computer Emergency Response Team (CERT) for major incidents
Communication procedures
Rehearsals

INITIATION AND ANALYSIS

Initiation
  Report a potential incident
  Everyone must know how to report incidents
Analysis
  Confirm that the incident is real
  Determine its scope: Who is attacking; what are they doing
If deemed severe enough, escalate to a major incident

CONTAINMENT

Disconnection of the system from the site network or the site network from the
  internet (damaging)
  Harmful, so must be done only with proper authorization
Black-holing the attacker (only works for a short time)
Continue to collect data (allows harm to continue) to understand the situation

RECOVERY

Repair of running system (hard to do but keeps system operating with no data loss)
Restoration from backup tapes (loses data since last backup)
Reinstallation of operating system and applications from installation media
  Must have good configuration documentation before the incident

PUNISHMENT

Punishing employees is fairly easy
The decision to pursue prosecution
  Cost and effort
  Probable success if pursue (often attackers are minors)
  Loss of reputation
Collecting and managing evidence
  Call the authorities for help
  Preserving evidence (the computer's state changes rapidly)
    Information on disk: Do immediate backup
    Ephemeral information: stored in RAM (who is logged in, etc.)
  Protecting evidence and documenting the chain of custody
  Ask upstream ISPs for a trap and trace to identify the attacker

(*continued*)

Figure 10-8 Intrusion Detection Processes (Study Figure)

COMMUNICATION

Warn affected people: Other departments, customers
Might need to communicate with the media; Only do so via public relations

PROTECTING THE SYSTEM IN THE FUTURE

Hacked system must be hardened
Especially important because many hackers will attack it in following weeks or
months

Figure 10-8   (Continued)

Communication Procedures

During crises, it will be important to locate people quickly. Each person should have multiple contact methods, including e-mail, fax, and office, home, and cellular telephones. These numbers should be stored in a contact list.

During a network crisis, electronic communication through e-mail might be unavailable or compromised, so telephone contact is essential. For the same reason, although contact numbers can be stored online, paper copies must be printed.

It is important to update contact numbers frequently. During a crisis is not a good time to find out that a third of the CERT and other parties have changed telephone numbers since the contact list was created.

Rehearsals

Again because of time pressure, it is critical for the CERT to hold rehearsals for incident response processes. Simulating an incident as realistically as possible highlights weaknesses in plans and procedures. It also gives team members a better understanding of how to do specific procedures.

TEST YOUR UNDERSTANDING

15.   a) What is escalation? b) What is a CERT? c) Why may communication be difficult during an incident? d) Why is rehearsal important?

Initiation and Analysis

Two priorities will emerge at the beginning of an incident. The first is to recognize quickly that an incident has occurred. The second is to analyze it to be sure that it is a real event, to determine its damage potential, and to gather information needed to begin planning for containment and recovery.

Initiation

As noted earlier, intrusion detection systems might alert the firm to an attack, a security analyst might find suspicious event patterns while analyzing an IDS log file, or an employee might notice that a system has failed or appears to be malfunctioning. It is critical that however an apparent incident is discovered, the person discovering it knows how to report it to get the response process started immediately. This is **initiation**.

Analysis

Once an intrusion response is initiated, the security analyst must understand it before effective action can be taken. Initially, the security analyst will not even be sure whether the incident is a security problem, an equipment problem, a software glitch, or even normal operation.

Frequently, much of the **intrusion analysis** phase is done by reading through log files for the time period in which the incident probably began. As shown in Figure 10-7, this might reveal how the attack was done, who perpetrated the attack, and what has happened since the beginning of the incident. Armed with this information, the CERT can proceed effectively.

TEST YOUR UNDERSTANDING

16.   a) Distinguish between initiation and analysis. b) Why is good analysis important for the later stages of handling an attack?

Containment

The next step is **containment**, that is, preventing the situation from becoming worse.

Disconnection

One radical way to contain the situation is to disconnect the server from the local network or even to disconnect the site's Internet connection. Although **disconnection** stops intrusions, it also prevents the server from serving its legitimate users. In effect, it goes the attacker one better by making the server completely unavailable. The business impact can be severe if the server is an important one.

Black-Holing the Attacker

Another approach to containment is to cut off the attacker, say by **black-holing** the attacking IP address so that packets from that attack will no longer be accepted. However, attackers often can break in with a different IP address quickly if they have access to multiple attack systems. In addition, black-holing definitively notifies the hackers that they have been detected. If the attackers come back in again, their next approach might be stealthier and more difficult to detect.

Collecting Data

If the damage is not too severe, a company might allow the hackers to continue working on the server. During this time, the company can observe what the attackers do. This information may aid in analysis and may be needed to collect evidence for prosecution.

However, not kicking off attackers as soon as possible is dangerous. The longer attackers are in a system, the more invisible they become through the deletion of IDS logs, and the more backdoors and other damage the attackers can create.

TEST YOUR UNDERSTANDING

17. a) What is containment? b) Why is disconnection undesirable? c) What is black holing? d) Why is it only a temporary containment solution? e) Why might an attacker be allowed to continue working in the system? f) Why is this dangerous?

Recovery

Once the attack is contained, **recovery** is necessary. The attack undoubtedly left the server littered with backdoors and other problems. The system must be returned to proper operation. In fact, the system has to be better than before so that the attackers cannot come back in.

Repair During Continuing Server Operation

It might be possible to **repair** the damage by reinstalling the software on the computer. If the server is using good checksum software, it might be possible to identify Trojan horses that need to be removed. It also might be possible to find directories the attackers used to store their rootkits and to perform other mischief.

Unfortunately, it is very difficult to root out all of the Trojan horses, registry entries, and other unpleasant surprises planted by an attacker. For a virus or worm attack, there sometimes are programs that remove the specific artifacts created by the specific attack. For handcrafted break-ins, however, there is no general detection program, and there always is a strong concern that "we may have missed one."

Restoration from Backup Tapes

If the attack is known to have occurred at a particular time, then one option might be to restore files from the last trusted backup tape. However, data collected since the last backup is likely to be lost. Worse yet, if the attacker began the attack earlier than believed, the "trusted" backup tape might restore the attackers' Trojan horses and other artifacts.

Reinstallation of All Software

Without strong measures such as program checksum, many organizations believe that they must do a complete reinstallation of the operating system and programs. As noted earlier, this is an involved process and does not address the issue of data loss. It is important to document the software's configuration before an incident, so that the software can be properly configured after reinstallation.

TEST YOUR UNDERSTANDING

18. a) What are the three major recovery options? b) Why is repair good? c) Why may it not work? d) Why is restoration from backup tapes undesirable? e) What is lost when there is full software reinstallation?

Punishment

Some companies focus entirely on recovery, ignoring the possibility of punishing the intruder. However, some firms will choose to try to punish intruders under certain circumstances.

Punishing Employees

Prosecuting an outside attacker is very complex. It is considerably easier to punish an employee who is attacking internally or from home. Although the courts require strong evidence for prosecution, the justification for reprimanding or terminating an employee can be much weaker. Consequently, most companies are far more likely to punish an employee than to try to prosecute an external hacker.

The Decision to Pursue Prosecution

Pursuing the prosecution of an attacker is desirable for a number of reasons, but many firms are reluctant to do it.

Cost and Effort   One pair of reasons for not reporting incidents is the cost and effort that would be needed for prosecution. These are not trivial.

Probability of Success   In many cases, the intruder will turn out to be living in another country or to be a teenager who would get only a few months in a detention center.

Loss of Reputation   In addition, prosecution is a public process. The firm will be admitting publicly that it could not prevent an intrusion. This could hurt the firm's reputation, and this loss of reputation could cost the firm some of its customers. At the least, some customers will mentally put the firm on probation.

Bringing Lawsuits   Even if a firm decides to go after an attacker, it may not wish to pursue criminal prosecution. Instead, it might decide to sue the attacker in civil court, going after the attacker's assets and requiring the attacker to pay for at least his or her own legal fees.

Collecting and Managing Evidence

The courts have stringent rules for how evidence must be collected and handled after collection. If prosecution is contemplated, evidence handling must be done carefully.

Call the Authorities for Guidance and Help   The best solution is to call in the local police or the FBI. Although the FBI normally focuses on computers used in interstate commerce or when the attacker is in a different state than the victim, they sometimes get involved in purely intrastate matters. They will advise on evidence handling and might even do it themselves. For instance, they might come in with a kit to copy the hard disk on a server or client PC.

Preserving Evidence   Although the authorities should be called in as rapidly as possible, IT employees must understand the basic rules of evidence handling. For instance, it is critical to **preserve evidence**. The contents of a computer's disk change rapidly. An immediate backup will preserve the evidence if it is accompanied by documentation on who was online and other information. The specifics of the backup must be documented as well.

In addition, computers often contain ephemeral evidence, such as who is logged in at any given moment. This information, stored in RAM, must be collected separately from disk information.

Protecting Evidence and Documenting the Chain of Custody   Another important principle is documenting what happens to the evidence after collection. The **chain of custody** is the history of all transfers of the evidence between people and how the evidence is protected from tampering while in a person's possession. The chain of custody must be clear and well documented. Otherwise, a judge probably will disallow the evidence. Even if the evidence is admitted, the jury might not believe the evidence if significant custody problems were uncovered.

Contact Your ISP   Although some attackers do launch attacks from their own computers, it is good to contact upstream ISP providers to request a **trap and trace** to get information about an attack or at least to request that they preserve the information for law enforcement agencies. Most ISPs keep data on connections only for very brief periods of time.

TEST YOUR UNDERSTANDING

19.   a) Is it easier to punish employees or to prosecute outside attackers? b) Why do companies often not prosecute attackers? c) Why is preserving evidence difficult? d) What is the chain of custody, and why is it important?

Communication

Strong communication is needed throughout the process. Affected people inside the firm must be notified of a problem and also of the system's recovery. Customers should be warned if appropriate, and they should be kept appraised of recovery progress and completion. In major incidents, the media also might have to be continually apprised of the situation, and this should be done only by the public relations department—never by the IT or security staff.

Protecting the System in the Future

After the incident ends, steps will be needed to make the attacked system safe from future attacks. The specific vulnerability that led to the penetration must be fixed. In addition, other problems are likely to be identified during the incident response process. It is important to identify and implement security improvements in the affected servers and in other systems with similar weaknesses.

When hackers take over a computer, they often publicize their success and invite other attackers in by identifying the exploit they used or even giving directions to exploit a back door. Consequently, systems that have been hacked tend to be attacked frequently for the next few weeks or longer. Systems that have been attacked successfully must be especially hardened against further attack.

Postmortem Evaluation

During response, some things will inevitably not go well. It is important to do a postmortem evaluation of what went right or wrong after an attack and to implement any improvements needed in the response process.

TEST YOUR UNDERSTANDING

20. a) Who should be notified of problems? b) Who should communicate with the media? c) Why is it important to implement improvements in hosts that have been attacked? d) Why is evaluation undertaken after an attack?

BUSINESS CONTINUITY PLANNING

Natural disasters such as floods and hurricanes, major building fires, and massive security incidents such as cyberterror or cyberwar could place the company's basic operation in jeopardy and could even threaten the survival of the firm. Every company should have a strong **business continuity plan** that specifies how a company plans to restore core business operations after natural or human-made disasters. According to SunGard Availability Systems, only 20 percent of U.S. firms had such plans in late 2002.

A **business continuity plan** specifies how a company plans to restore core business operations when disasters occur.

Figure 10-9 Business Continuity Planning (Study Figure)

BUSINESS CONTINUITY PLANNING

A business continuity plan specifies how a company plans to restore core business operations when disasters occur

BUSINESS PROCESS AND ANALYSIS

Identification of business processes and their interrelationships
Prioritizations of business processes
    Downtime tolerance (in the extreme, mean time to belly-up)
Resource needs (must be shifted during crises)

COMMUNICATING, TESTING, AND UPDATING THE PLAN

Testing (usually through walkthroughs) needed to find weaknesses
Updated frequently because business conditions change and businesses reorganize
    constantly
    Telephone numbers and contact numbers must be updated even more frequently
        than the plan as a whole
Updating the plan

A business continuity planning team with broad representation from departments across the firm creates the plan. The plan specifies what business actions will be taken, not simply what technological actions need to be taken. The narrower matter of restoring the firm's technological base at a backup site is contained in the firm's more specific disaster recovery plan.

Interest in business continuity planning understandably increased after the September 11, 2001, catastrophe.[6] However, interest did not translate into widespread action. A year after the disaster, only 25 percent of all major firms had comprehensive business continuity/disaster recovery plans according to the Meta Group. Only 10 percent of the companies it studied had changed their plans since the September 2001 terrorist attacks.

Although the Meta Group forecasts that 35 percent of all major firms will have business continuity/disaster recovery plans in 2003, and that this will rise to 40 percent in 2004, even this growth means that most large firms will remain unprotected or poorly protected for some years to come.

TEST YOUR UNDERSTANDING

21. a) What do business continuity plans specify? b) Distinguish between business continuity plans and disaster recovery plans. c) Do most firms have business continuity plans?

Business Process Analysis

The first step in creating a plan is to identify a firm's major processes and to decide which ones need to be restored first during recovery. A firm is a web of interdependent business processes, such as accounting, sales, production, and marketing.

Identification of Business Processes and Their Interrelationships
The first step is to identify all relevant business processes and their interrelationships.

Prioritization of Business Processes
The next step is to prioritize business processes, so that the most important business processes can be restarted first. A key factor is how sensitive a function is to downtime. Order entry systems must be restarted quickly or sales will be lost. Billing can be down a little longer before it begins affecting the business.

Specify Resource Needs
In addition to prioritizing each process, planning should specify which resources the process needs. These resources might have to be shifted from lower-priority processes.

TEST YOUR UNDERSTANDING

22. What are the three steps in business process analysis?

Communicating, Testing, and Updating the Plan

Once a business continuity plan is developed, using input from a wide variety of departments and external business partners, the plan must be tested and updated.

---

[6] Tiffany Kary, "From Ground Zero Up: How 9/11 Changed Disaster Planning," ZDnet.com, September 10, 2002. techupdate.zdnet.com/techupdate/stories/main/0,14179,2879843,00.html.

Testing

Although plans will be created diligently, they almost certainly will overlook vital actions. The only way to refine the plan is to test it. Live testing generally is impossible, but it is common to have **walkthroughs**, in which managers and other key personnel involved get together and go sequentially through the steps everybody will take. Business continuity plan walkthroughs are major undertakings because they involve people from many departments, not simply the IT staff.

Updating the Plan

The plan must be updated frequently because business conditions change constantly and because businesses reorganize constantly. During a crisis is a bad time to wonder who must take over responsibilities assigned to a department that no longer exists. It is an even worse time to discover that your plan does not cover new business activities. Telephone numbers and other contact information changes even more rapidly and should have more frequent update schedules.

TEST YOUR UNDERSTANDING

23. a) Why are business continuity plans more difficult to test than incident response plans? b) Why is frequent plan updating important? c) Why should contact information be updated even more frequently?

DISASTER RECOVERY

Business continuity planning lays out a general strategy for getting the company working again. In turn, **disaster recovery** looks specifically at the technical aspects of how a company can get IT back into operation using backup facilities.[7]

Disaster recovery looks specifically at the technical aspects of how a company can get IT back into operation using backup facilities.

Disaster recovery planning is critical to rapid and successful business continuity recovery. In the attack on the World Trade Center, two law firms near the center were badly damaged when the two towers collapsed.[8] One had a good disaster recovery program and was back to normal business operations in 2 days. The other did not and lost all of its computerized data. A year later, the second firm was still in the process of going through printed papers in warehouses to reconstruct its records. To partially replicate its data, it had to go to clients and even competitors.

Although disaster recovery is sometimes viewed as "a concern for the techies," top management has to have a good understanding of disaster recovery realities. In one insurance company, for instance, executives thought that they could be back to

---

7   Elizabeth Lennon's "Contingency Planning Guide for Information Technology Systems" is a comprehensive guide to disaster recovery planning. It is published by the Information Technology Laboratory of the National Institute of Standards and Technology, csrc.nist.gov/publications/nistpubs/index.html.

8   Tiffany Kary, "From Ground Zero Up: How 9/11 Changed Disaster Planning," ZDnet.com, September 10, 2002. techupdate.zdnet.com/techupdate/stories/main/0,14179,2879843,00.html.

DISASTER RECOVERY

Disaster recovery looks specifically at the technical aspects of how a company can get back into operation using backup facilities

TYPES OF BACKUP FACILITIES

Hot sites
- Ready to run (power, HVAC, computers): Just add data
- Considerations: Rapid readiness versus high cost

Cold sites
- Building facilities, power, HVAC, communication to outside world only
- No computer equipment
- Might require too long to gct operating

Site sharing
- Site sharing among a firm's sites (problem of equipment compatibility and data synchronization)
- Site sharing across firms (potential problem of prioritization, sensitive actions)

Hosting
- Hosting company runs production server at its site
- Will continue production server operation if user firm's site fails
- If hosting site goes down, there have to be contingencies

RESTORATION OF DATA AND PROGRAMS

Restoration from backup tapes: Need backup tapes at the remote recovery site
Real-time journaling (copying each transaction in real time)
Database replication

TESTING THE DISASTER RECOVERY PLAN

The importance of testing: Find problems in the plan, work faster

Walkthroughs
- Go through steps in real time as group but do not take technical actions
- Fairly realistic
- Unable to catch subtle problems

Live testing
- Full process is followed, including technical steps (data restoration, etc.)
- High cost
- Realistic and can catch subtle errors

Figure 10-10   Disaster Recovery (Study Figure)

full operation in 48 hours.[9] However, the IT executive knew that even the model called for 6 days of recovery, and the model had never even been run through to determine if it was feasible.

TEST YOUR UNDERSTANDING

24.   What is disaster recovery?

Types of Backup Facilities

When a major computer facility becomes inoperable, the work has to be shifted to a **backup facility**, usually one at another location. Several types of backup facilities exist. Each type has strengths and weaknesses.

Hot Sites

An attractive backup facility is a **hot site** that is ready to go in an emergency.

Capabilities   This is a physical facility with power, HVAC (heating, ventilation, and air conditioning), hardware, installed software, and up-to-date data. As soon as people can be moved in, the hot site can take over the full operation of the damaged site. With a skeleton crew, basic operation can begin even earlier.

Considerations   Hot sites are attractive when processes have little downtime tolerance. They can be back in operation rapidly, and there rarely are the major delays that can occur when software is difficult to install on the computers used in other types of backup facilities.

However, hot sites also are extremely expensive. Consequently, they are not as widely used as they should be.

Cold Sites

Cold sites offer physical facilities, electrical power, and HVAC, but they basically offer empty rooms plus connections to the outside world. To use a cold site, the company usually has to procure, bring in, and set up hardware; install software; and mount data. By the time all of this happens, the company could be bankrupt. Cold sites are inexpensive, but companies must assess realistically how useful they would be in practice.

Site Sharing

During natural disasters, people who are not affected often take in victims who have lost their homes or who have been forced to evacuate. **Site sharing** is the same thing but with technology.

Site Sharing Within a Firm   Companies that have multiple data centers can shift the work of a damaged center to another center in the firm. This can rarely be done automatically, however. A way must be devised of installing programs and data files on

---

[9]   Sandra Gittlen, "Today's Focus: Data Prioritization: Not as Easy as You Think," *Network World Newsletter: Sandra Gittlen on IT Education and Training*, May 22, 2002. E-mail newsletter.

machines in other sites. In addition, if sites are too close together, a natural disaster could take down backup sites, as well.

As an example of site sharing within a firm, UAL Loyalty Services has two data centers that do site sharing in the Chicago area.[10] To keep data at the two sites synchronized in real time, the company uses a gigabit per second metropolitan area network. In addition to providing disaster recovery, real-time data synchronization provides the ultimate in general backup.

Site Sharing Across Firms   Sometimes firms enter into site-sharing agreements with other firms. Partners agree to shift some of their resources to victim firms in emergencies. This spreads the risk of site outages across multiple firms. However, operational difficulties can arise. Firms might be reluctant to install programs from other firms on their machines. Firms also might place excessive limits on the resources the victim firm is allowed to use—especially if the firms are close geographically and may both suffer from a natural or humanly made disaster.

Hosted Sites

Many companies now have some of their servers located in **hosting companies** that run computers, maintain them, and troubleshoot them at their own sites. This is particularly popular for webservers. Hosting companies are likely to be able to continue operation for hosted production servers even if a company's own site goes down. If the hosting site goes down, in turn, most firms have staging (testing) servers that maintain an image of the production server at the firm's own site. It may be possible to use the staging server to clone a production server at a new hosted site quickly. However, it is safer if a firm maintains duplicate hosting sites.

TEST YOUR UNDERSTANDING

25.   a) What are the four main alternatives for backup sites? b) What is the strength of each? c) What are the problems of each?

Restoration of Data and Programs

Earlier in this chapter, we looked at the archival backup of program and data files. **Restoration** of these files is needed at the backup computer site.

Restoration from Backup Tapes

Restoration from backup tapes is one way to move files to the backup site. If this is the goal, then the backup site must have the proper equipment to do the restoration. In addition, backup tapes need to be delivered to the backup site rapidly. This can be difficult to do during natural disasters or if the backup site is far from the storage site for backup tapes.

Real-Time Journaling

Journaling, in which transactions are logged as they occur, are better than periodic backups. In case of an emergency, the backup site would need only a fairly recent

---

[10]   James Cope, "Put Your IT Eggs in Different Baskets," *Computerworld*, July 15, 2002. www.computerworld.com/securitytopics/security/story/0,10801,72638,00.html.

backup tape. After restoring data on the tape, the backup site personnel can apply the journaled transactions to the database fairly rapidly.

Database Replication
With real-time database replication, there actually is no recovery necessary. The backup system is immediately ready to go.

TEST YOUR UNDERSTANDING

26. a) What is the process of restoring data from backup tapes? What is lost? b) What is the process of restoring data if journaling is done? c) What is the process of restoring data if real-time database synchronization is done?

Testing the Disaster Recovery Plan

The Importance of Testing
Refining the Plan   Plans on paper sound good but might not work well in practice. A key step might be left out, or a key piece of equipment might be forgotten. It is important to test disaster recovery plans after developing them in order to refine them.

Experience Brings Speed   In addition, practice may not make perfect, but it does make speed. Testing makes personnel familiar with the processes of disaster recovery and builds communication between members of the disaster recovery team. This familiarity facilitates the rapid work speed needed in disaster recovery.

Walkthroughs
In walkthroughs, as noted earlier in this chapter, the project team members go sequentially through the steps of the plan without doing anything hands-on. For instance, if the plan calls for the public relations department to be notified at a particular time, the disaster recovery team member responsible for that step makes a call. At the backup site (or simulated backup site), team members read out the steps they must take without doing them.

Although walkthroughs are fairly realistic, they are likely to miss subtle problems, such as incompatibilities between operating system configurations that prevent an important program from being installed.

Live Testing
In **live testing**, all employees go through their procedures for disaster recovery step by step. At the backup site, equipment is brought in and programs are loaded if needed. Data are fully restored. Sample transactions are fed into the system to see whether it is working.

Live testing is expensive, but only live testing will reveal the subtle but critical weaknesses in the plan that result from technology problems or the omission of a critical step in a procedure. For example, during one live test, it was discovered that an important piece of information was sitting on a Post-it note at the original site. A walkthrough would not have caught this.

TEST YOUR UNDERSTANDING

27. a) Why is it important to test the disaster recovery plan? b) Why are walkthroughs attractive compared to live testing? c) Why is live testing attractive compared to walkthroughs?

CONCLUSION

Incidents happen. Minor incidents can be handled informally, but for larger problems, careful planning is needed, and complex technical and personnel processes must be managed during emergencies.

Backup

At the heart of all intrusion handling is the backup of program and data files. If a company does not protect these files, it will not be able to resume full operation rapidly or at all. For major incidents and disasters, backup must be effective and well tested.

Intrusion Detection Technology

Intrusion detection technology has two purposes. One is to alert security administrators to apparent problems. The other is to provide a searchable log file of events plus event correlation functions to help security administrators look through these log files after an incident already has begun.

Unfortunately, intrusion detection technology is still embryonic. Alarm functions produce far too many false alarms. Event correlation functions are rudimentary and require excessive labor. Security analysts, who should read log files daily to look for suspicious patterns, often face extreme information overload.

Intrusion Response Processes

Major incidents are too large to handle informally but do not create extreme risks for the firm. Companies typically create computer emergency response teams (CERTs) to manage major incidents.

In handling major incidents, a number of steps should be followed. Actions must be taken quickly in order to reduce the ultimate level of damages, and yet speed has a tendency to result in poor decisions. Tension also exists between the desire to begin containing an intrusion and the desire to obtain more data to facilitate recovery plus punishment, or prosecution.

Business Continuity and Disaster Recovery Planning

Business continuity planning and disaster recovery planning work together when a major disaster occurs at one or more sites.

Business continuity planning identifies business (not IT) processes that must be restored first to get the business's operations restarted with minimum damage to the firm and specifies what actions must be taken and by whom to restore operations. Order taking is a typical process that must be started as soon as possible.

Disaster planning focuses more narrowly on computers and networking. The focus of disaster planning is how to shift technology to a backup site and how to transfer computer operations to the backup site.

THOUGHT QUESTIONS

1. Examine the integrated log file shown in Figure 10-7. a) Identify the stages in this apparent attack. b) For each stage, describe what the attacker seems to be doing. c) Decide whether the actions in this stage work at human speed or at a

higher speed, indicating an automated attack. d) Decide whether the evidence in each stage is suggestive of an attack or conclusive evidence. e) Overall, do you have conclusive evidence of an attack? f) Do you have conclusive evidence of who committed the attack?

2. You are a fairly small company. a) Should you use a firewall? b) Should you use antivirus systems? c) Should you use an intrusion-detection system? Explain your decisions, especially in the last part of the question.

3. You do a full backup each Sunday night. You do partial backups each night. a) Your partial backups are incremental backups that only record file changes in the previous day. Your system fails on Wednesday, at noon. Which backups will you restore and in what order? b) Repeat for nightly differential partial backups, which back up all changes since the *last full backup*. c) Based on your answer, what is the advantage of differential backups? d) Why do many firms do incremental backups anyway?

TROUBLESHOOTING QUESTION

1. After you restore files following an incident, users complain that some of their data files are missing. What might have happened?

C H A P T E R

MANAGING THE SECURITY FUNCTION

Learning Objectives

By the end of this chapter, you should be able to discuss:

- Organizational issues, especially where to place the IT security department in the corporate hierarchy.
- Risk analysis.
- Creating a technical security architecture.
- Principles for controlling security-related processes.
- Managing operations securely.
- Training users and mobilizing them to be security assets.
- Vulnerability testing.

INTRODUCTION

We have been saying since Chapter 1 that security is more about process than technology. However, until we had discussed the technology of security, any discussion of security management would have been confusing and abstract. Now, however, you have the knowledge of security technology needed to understand the practical issues in security management.

Many aspects of security management already have been covered in previous chapters.

➤ Chapter 1 laid out basic management principles, including the plan-protect-respond cycle.

➤ In addition, when we discussed firewalls and other security technologies, we discussed key aspects of their management.

➤ Chapter 10 dealt primarily with the management aspects of intrusion detection, business continuity planning, and disaster recovery.

ORGANIZATION

A first step for a corporation in managing security is to consider where the security function will sit on the firm's organization chart. There are no magic answers for the question of to whom the **chief security officer (CSO)** and his or her security department staff should report.

Top Management Support

Few firms have the CSO report directly to the firm's chief executive officer (CEO) or to another top manager. However, top management support is crucial to the success of any security program. Few things as pervasive as security programs succeed unless top management gives strong and consistent support.

Top-Management Security Awareness Briefing

Generally, top management will need to be convinced that expensive and inconvenient security measures are necessary. To create top management security awareness, the security function, wherever it is located initially, should create a **top management security awareness briefing** that gives case examples of what has happened to other firms plus an assessment of vulnerabilities in the firm. This needs to be a short briefing because the time that top managers can spend on any one business function is limited.

Corporate Security Policy Statement

What does top management support entail? First, it is good if top management releases a strong **corporate security policy statement** addressing the importance of security to the organization and giving a broad vision of how security will be implemented. Although the CSO probably will write or at least draft the corporate security policy statement, top management needs to release it and later support it.

TOP MANAGEMENT SUPPORT

Top-Management Security Awareness Briefing (emphasis on brief)
Corporate Security Policy Statement: Vision, not details
Follow-through when security must be upheld in conflicts
Business champions to give support and business advice

SHOULD YOU PLACE SECURITY WITHIN IT?

Locating Security Within IT
  Compatible technical skills
  Making the CIO responsible for security breaches gives accountability
  Placing security within IT is not a panacea
    Difficult to blow the whistle on the IT staff
    Vendor preference differences with networking staff
Locating Security Outside IT
  Can blow the whistle on IT actions
  If a staff group, can only give advice

SECURITY AND AUDITING

IT Auditing has the skills to determine whether IT rules are enforced, but IT auditing does not set policy
Internal Auditing also can audit IT-related *procedures*, but it does not make policy

MANAGED SECURITY SERVICE PROVIDERS (Figure 11-2)

On-Site Logging, Off-Site Analysis
Practice-Based Expertise
  Get plenty of experience on a daily basis—like fire departments
Separation of Responsibilities: Can blow whistle on IT, even the CIO
What to Outsource?
  Typically, intrusion detection and vulnerability assessment
  Rarely policy and other control practices
  Not commonly antivirus protection and other aspects of security, but MSSPs are expanding
Evaluating the MSSP
  Diligence: Is it really reading the logs? (Contracts often are vague)
  Skills and background of testers

(continued)

Figure 11-1   Organizational Issues (Study Figure)

SECURITY AND BUSINESS STAFFS: CANNOT JUST LOB POLICIES OVER THE WALL

SECURITY AND BUSINESS PARTNERS: YOUR BUSINESS PARTNER'S SECURITY AFFECTS YOU

UNIFORMED SECURITY PERSONNEL

They often are called first by suspicious users
They support investigations

STAFFING AND TRAINING

Hiring Staff: Expertise
Training is necessary because few people on the market are security experts
Certifications are good but vary in what they require
Background checks should be done on the security staff
All workers involved in IT should have background checks, including the maintenance staff, consultants, and contractors
Should You Hire a Hacker?
They are likely to have the knowledge you need
But would you be afraid to fire or lay off one?

Figure 11-1 (Continued)

Follow-Through

The proof of top management support, however, comes in subsequent actions.

➤ If top management will not ensure that security has an adequate budget, the policy statement will be only lip service.

➤ Top management also has to support security when there are conflicts between the needs of security and the needs of other business functions—for instance, when a new system is being rushed into place with inadequate security.

➤ Subtly, but importantly, top managers have to follow security procedures themselves, for instance, when they work from home and remotely access corporate resources. Everything that senior management does is symbolically important.

Business Champion

In addition to supporting the security function, it is highly desirable for one or more senior managers to become **business champions**, who not only support security actively but who also provide direction to the CSO on how to focus on business issues and corporate directions.

TEST YOUR UNDERSTANDING

1. a) What is the manager of the security department called? b) Why is top management support important? c) What should a top management security awareness briefing cover? d) What should a corporate security policy statement contain? e) For what three reasons is top management follow-up important? f) Why is having a business champion good?

Should You Place Security Within IT?

Locating Security Within IT

Compatible Technical Skills   One possible location for the **security department** is within the information technology (IT) department. This is reasonable because security and IT have many of the same technological skills. Other managers might not understand technology skills well enough to manage the security function.

Making the CIO Responsible for Security Breaches   Another benefit is that if security and other IT functions report to the firm's chief information officer (CIO), it is likely to be much easier for security to get other IT groups to implement security. If security is under the CIO, then the CIO will be accountable for security breaches. The CIO is likely to back the security department in its efforts to create a safe IT infrastructure.

In contrast, when security is outside IT, there are inevitable difficulties in getting the IT function, including the CIO, to accept the "mere advice" of the security department. Even if security reports to a senior executive, it will be difficult for that executive to marshal support for security, especially if IT's reporting line goes through a different senior executive.

A fundamental problem in separating IT security from IT is that separation reduces accountability, perhaps to a fatal degree. If security is a staff department, it cannot tell IT what to do. No single person becomes accountable for corporate security except the firm's top executives, who have a broad range of concerns. To twist Harry Truman's classic statement, "The buck stops nowhere."

Placing Security Within IT Is Not a Panacea   Even if security is placed within IT, however, conflicts are likely. In addition to the ordinary conflicts caused because other parts of IT will resent the restrictions created by security, subtle cultural conflicts often occur based on vendor selection. For instance, the networking staff is likely to want to stay with the security products of their traditional networking vendors, such as Cisco— even if these products are not "best of breed." In turn, security is likely to support the top security vendors, such as Check Point, even if this means that integration with networking products is difficult or incomplete.

Independence from IT: The Ability to Monitor IT

Although placing security within IT has several benefits, it also has one serious negative consequence. Security loses its **independence** from IT. As discussed in Chapters 1 and 1a, a large fraction of all corporate security attacks come from the IT staff itself— sometimes from senior IT managers. If security reports to the CIO, how can it enforce security over the CIO's actions? Turning in your boss to a higher manager for breaching corporate security policies, standards, or procedures is career suicide.

TEST YOUR UNDERSTANDING

    2.   What are the pros and cons of placing security within IT?

Security and Auditing

Another organizational issue is how security should relate to a firm's existing auditing departments. Auditing departments ensure that a firm's policies are being implemented properly by individual departments.

IT Auditing

Most firms already have an **IT auditing** function that looks at whether the IT department is functioning as it should. Traditionally, the IT auditing function has looked at security as well as other aspects of IT functioning. Placing at least the security technology auditing function explicitly within IT auditing is attractive in terms of organizational independence.

However, auditors do not make policies. They merely certify or fail to certify that good practices are being followed. Placing security auditing under IT auditing does not create independence in the *creation* of security policies.

In addition, auditors can only make suggestions, which audited departments are not required to accept unless compelled to do so by the line of authority above them.

Internal Auditing

Firms usually also have **internal auditing** departments that are not IT-focused but that are responsible for auditing all departments to ensure that their business processes are consistent with corporate policies and best practices. Placing security auditing explicitly within the internal auditing department's responsibilities has the benefits of giving oversight responsibilities to a department that already examines how departments function in the firm.

TEST YOUR UNDERSTANDING

    3.   a) What are the two types of traditional auditing departments in firms? b) How do they differ? c) What are the pros and cons of placing the security auditing function in these departments?

Managed Security Service Providers (MSSPs)

On-site Logging, Off-site Analysis

One possibility is not to locate most security functions within the firm at all but to outsource much of the security function to an outside firm called a **managed security service provider (MSSP)**.

As Figure 11-2 shows, an MSSP watches over your firm. It places a central logging system on your network. This system compresses and uploads the firm's integrated log data to the MSSP site. There, scanning programs and security experts look through the log data, classifying events by severity level and throwing out false positives, such as attacks designed to hack the IIS webserver application if the server runs UNIX.

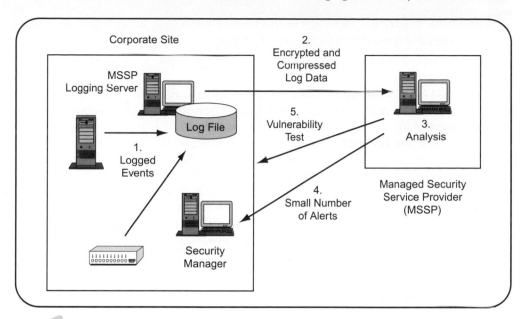

Figure 11-2 Managed Security Service Provider (MSSP)

Benefit

If the MSSP is doing its job, it will have to examine several hundred suspicious events each day. It will quickly identify many as obvious false positives. It will do more analysis to classify other events as nonthreats. Still others will be classified as threats but negligible ones, such as minor scanning attacks. On a typical day, only one or two threats will be brought to the attention of the client via pager or e-mail alerts, depending on their possible severity. By distilling the flood of suspicious incidents into a handful of important events requiring client action each day, MSSPs free the security staff to work on other matters.

Practice-Based Expertise

Why should a company use an MSSP? As Bruce Schneier, the head of MSSP Counterpane Internet Security, has said on multiple occasions, outsourcing security is done for the same reasons that companies outsource fire fighting and police work to the government. Internal fire and police forces would be idle nearly all the time. In addition, when they would be called upon, they would be inexperienced because they would not have had the daily fire fighting and police work experience that municipal fire and police workers have.

Separation of Responsibilities

A more subtle advantage of using an MSSP is the **separation of responsibilities**. If MSSP employees see even the client firm's chief information officer doing something that is not part of the client firm's policy, the MSSP will notify a higher-level official in the firm. Therefore, members of the IT staff cannot do harm under the assumption that they are trusted and so will not be stopped.

What to Outsource?

In Figure 11-2, the MSSP does vulnerability testing and intrusion detection. This makes sense because intrusion detection and vulnerability assessment require similar technical skills and a similarly detailed knowledge of the internal network.

Typically, firms do not outsource everything to MSSPs. Most fundamentally, policy and planning rarely are outsourced to the MSSP, although the MSSP must be well aware of policies and procedures created by the firm.

In addition, firms typically handle virus scanning in-house or outsource it to an antivirus outsourcing company. Most MSSPs focus on IDS and vulnerability testing services, and antivirus expertise tends to be different from expertise in these areas. However, MSSPs and antivirus outsourcing firms are beginning to merge.

Evaluating the MSSP

Although MSSPs can be a great help, they sometimes do a poor job. If a contract specifies that the firm will look at logs but is not more specific, the outsourcing firm might simply scan log files in a cursory way every week or so. One firm reported that in the first six months of service, not a single alert was sent to it. The company believed that this indicated total neglect on the part of the outsourcing firm.

TEST YOUR UNDERSTANDING

4. a) What is an MSSP? b) What is the main benefit of using an MSSP? c) Why are MSSPs likely to do a better job than security department employees? d) What security functions should and should not be outsourced? e) What should a firm look for when selecting an MSSP?

Security and Business Staffs

However it is organized, the security department needs to have good relationships with other business functions. It cannot merely "lob policies over the wall" and expect them to be followed.

It is important for the security staff to establish reasonable relationships with general business functions. Security is almost always mistrusted by other departments because of its potential to make life harder (and often its potential to stop existing practices that violate security policies). As one security staff member put it, "When I come into an office, people put wreaths of garlic around their necks and chant warding spells."

Although security personnel cannot always be buddies with personnel in other departments, they do have to learn to speak their language. Security policies should be accompanied by return on investment (ROI) analysis and realistic business impact statements. Security personnel also need to understand the workings of and terminology used in individual departments. Security is indeed about management more than technology, and knowledge of business and management often is more important than technological knowledge.

TEST YOUR UNDERSTANDING

    5.   What can the security staff do to get along better with other departments in the firm?

Security and Business Partners

Firewalls and a number of other security tools assume that a border exists between the corporation and the outside world. However, one of the biggest trends in recent years has been close but wary integration between firms and their business partners, including buyer organizations, customer organizations, service organizations, and even competitors.

        For close cooperation, it often is necessary for external firms to access internal systems. This means poking holes through firewalls, giving access permissions on internal hosts, and taking other dubious security actions. Things are especially difficult if systems such as virtual private networks require cooperation between the security devices of different firms. Things are at their worst when **interorganizational systems** are created to automate communication and data exchange between the firms.

        It is highly desirable to audit the security of close business partners for whom security issues exist. For instance, one energy firm found that a firm that audits energy transfers between energy firms had terrible security—not even a firewall. Yet the energy firm had to send the auditing firm highly sensitive competitive information that was vulnerable to espionage on the auditing firm's host computers.

        Sometimes, firms rush into business partnerships. However, it is important for them to exercise **due diligence** in doing so, meaning that they should investigate the implications of these partnerships closely before beginning them. This includes security implications.

TEST YOUR UNDERSTANDING

    6.   a) What are business partners? b) Why are they dangerous? c) What is due diligence?

Uniformed Personnel

Security staff members do have to deal with the police, and in larger companies, they have to deal with a company's uniformed security staff.

        Security incursions are likely to be reported first by employees to the uniformed security staff because employees are taught to call the security office if problems arise. In fact, the security staff often has a telephone number like 6911 for memorability. The reporting of IT security incursions to the uniformed security staff should be formalized, and the uniformed security staff should be trained in how to hand off reports.

        Second, the IT security staff sometimes will be needed for enforcement. If an employee is suspected of wrong doing, the uniformed security staff should escort the IT security staff to the suspect's computer and should oversee any IT staff members taking evidence from the suspect's computer.

        Serious cases can involve the local police or FBI. It is good for IT security personnel to meet with the police or FBI before an actual incident to clarify what should be done.

TEST YOUR UNDERSTANDING

    7.   What relationships can the IT security have to the corporation's uniformed security staff?

Staffing and Training

Hiring security staff is difficult because so few trained security professionals are on the market. Part of the reason for the lack of trained personnel is long-standing neglect on the part of universities. Historically, few computer science programs taught security, and when they did, they tended to focus on topics such as encryption methodologies, which are useful in vendor firms rather than in corporations that face security threats. In business schools, textbooks oriented toward corporate security were not even available until late in 2002.

Hiring Staff: Expertise

In hiring staff members, it is highly desirable for new employees to have at least some security expertise. However, this is not always possible. The best solution might be to hire some highly seasoned security professionals to form a core for the security department, then train other members of the staff.

Training

A number of national training programs have been designed for security professionals, and local programs probably can be found as well. Some of these programs are short and superficial; others provide much more depth, although few offer the intensiveness found in university security degrees.

Surprisingly few programs offer hands-on training, although this often is available in vendor-oriented security courses, which teach such things as how to harden a router or how to use an IDS.

Certifications

One measure of expertise is an applicant's possession of a security **certification**, such as the CISSP and CSSP certifications of the International Information Systems Security Certification Consortium (www.isc2.org), the extensive GIAC certification of SANS (www.sans.org), and the Security+ certification from CompTIA (www.comptia.org).

However, these certifications vary widely in required depth of knowledge. Most of them guarantee that someone has basic theoretical expertise, but advanced knowledge and practical skills often are not part of the program.

Surprisingly few certifications involve hands-on training. Several even proclaim vendor neutrality. This means that they are entirely theoretical and ignore the reality that certain vendors are dominant in the business.

Vendor-specific programs do offer hands-on training, but this is vendor specific, of course. Still, such training is broadly beneficial because many theoretical concepts are not really understood until they are applied.

Background Checks

Given the sensitivity of the work done in security, it is advisable to do background checks on all security applicants. In fact, it probably is good practice to require background checks on all workers in sensitive positions outside the security department.

The Screening of All Workers Involved in IT

IT workers in general should be carefully screened before hiring. These include programmers, systems analysts, systems administrators, operators, and other IT specialists. However, this category also includes the cleaning and maintenance staffs, temporary workers, contractors, and consultants. Anyone who has not been screened must not be allowed to even touch sensitive computers.

Should You Hire Hackers?

One issue is whether you should hire someone who has hacked systems without permission in the past. Some companies do so because such people have the expertise to do deep vulnerability testing and because reformed hackers can see things from the hacker's point of view.

However, hiring a hacker is extremely dangerous because many of them continue to hack almost as if they are addicted to it. In addition, can you trust hackers enough to be confident that if you fire them for cause or have to let them go in an economic layoff, they will not retaliate?

TEST YOUR UNDERSTANDING

8. a) How can a firm obtain a good IT security staff? b) What are the pros and cons of hiring reformed hackers? c) What are the advantages and limitations of security training certifications? d) Who should be subjected to background checks when they are hired?

RISK ANALYSIS

Financially Sensible Protections

Chapter 1 discussed the reality that security countermeasures can never eliminate risk. Rather, security plans must limit risks to a level that makes sense in terms of the value of assets being protected, the likelihood of compromise, and the cost of compromises. It makes no sense to spend a million dollars a year to protect an asset whose loss would cost only a few thousand dollars.

To ensure that their security programs make sense economically, companies must engage in risk analysis before they begin thinking about adding protections. **Risk analysis** compares the probable cost of threats with those of protections.

Risk analysis compares the probable cost of threats with those of protections.

TEST YOUR UNDERSTANDING

9. What does risk analysis do?

Enumeration of Assets

Asset

An **asset** is anything a firm must protect, including such things as computers, networks, application programs, and databases.

FINANCIALLY SENSIBLE PROTECTIONS

Risk Analysis: Balance risks and countermeasure costs

ENUMERATION OF ASSETS

Assets: Things to be protected (hosts, data, etc.)
Up-to-date asset lists must be created first (can be very difficult)
Asset Responsibilities: Each asset should have someone accountable for it

ASSET CLASSIFICATION

Business continuity asset classifications
    Scope and percent of disruption: How many things, how bad the damage
    Financial impacts of a slowdown or shutdown
Cost of repairs asset classification

THREAT ASSESSMENT

Threat Likelihood
Difficulty of Estimation

RESPONDING TO RISK

Risk Reduction: Implement countermeasures
Risk Acceptance: Do nothing; suitable for low-threat risks and expensive
    countermeasures
Risk Transference: Get insurance. Good for low-probability risks

RISK ANALYSIS CALCULATIONS

Threat Severity Analysis (Expected Loss)
    Cost of attack if it succeeds times the probability that the attack will succeed
    Expressed in terms of some time period, such as a year
Value of Protection
    Reduction in threat severity (benefit) minus the cost of the countermeasure
    Invest in a countermeasure only if the value of protection is positive
Priority
    Invest in countermeasures with the greatest value of protection first
Return on Investment (ROI) Analysis
    For a single-year countermeasure, value of protection divided by the cost of the
        countermeasure
    For multiple-year investments, discounted cash flow analysis of multi-year values of
        protection and countermeasure investments
        IRR allows investments of different sizes to be compared directly
        There usually is a hurdle rate of 15% to 25%, and investments that fall below the
            hurdle rate will not be accepted

QUALITATIVE RISK ANALYSIS

Danger of business termination: Can't be put entirely into dollar terms
Loss of reputation: Difficult to quantify but very important

Figure 11-3 Risk Analysis (Study Figure)

Up-to-Date Asset Lists

The first step in risk analysis is to enumerate the assets you are protecting. During the Year 2000 (Y2K) crisis of the late 1990s, most larger firms created a comprehensive list of IT assets in order to assess their exposure to Y2K bugs. It was an extremely large task, although a relatively small number of assets usually accounted for most of the risk exposure. Hopefully, firms have kept their asset analyses up to date. If not, **asset enumeration** will be a large chore.

Asset Responsibility

In asset enumeration, each asset should be described in some detail, including who is **responsible** for it. Any asset that does not have a clearly responsible person or role is a serious concern.

TEST YOUR UNDERSTANDING

   10.   a) What is an asset? b) Why is asset enumeration the first step in security planning? c) Why is asset responsibility important?

Asset Classification

Because not all assets are equally important, a way must be devised to classify the importance of individual assets after identifying them.

Business Continuity Classifications

Scope and Degree of Disruption   Some assets directly affect business continuity— the ability to continue business operations if the asset is compromised. Assets that can put large parts of the company out of business for several days or even weeks must be given top priority. Other assets might have a negligible impact on business continuity if compromised. Yet others might reduce productivity in a small part of the company's operations. **Scope** (number of functions affected) and **percent of disruption** are important.

Financial Impacts of a Slowdown or Shutdown   Another issue is the cost of a business slowdown or partial shutdown. The impacts of a disruption can be enormous, as discussed in the previous chapter. However, unless these impacts are placed in dollar terms, shutdown disruption threats are difficult to assess.

Cost of Repairs Classification

Another way to classify objects is by their **cost of repair**—how much it would cost to restore an asset to its previous secure state. The last chapter discussed these costs in some depth. It noted that repair costs can be considerable, even for relatively simple assets.

TEST YOUR UNDERSTANDING

   11.   a) Why does security planning categorize assets? b) Explain classification by scope and percent of disruption. c) Explain cost of repairs classification.

Threat Assessment

Once assets are understood, the next step is to assess threats. Many assets will face multiple threats, including the risk of information exposure, denial-of-service attacks, and machine takeovers. These threats must be enumerated and described for each asset.

Threat Likelihood

It is important to estimate the **likelihood** of threats, that is, the probability that various threats will occur and how often they are likely to occur.

Difficulty of Estimation

Unfortunately, it is difficult to estimate the likelihood that threats will succeed because past experience tends to be misleading.

➤ First, threats have been doubling annually in recent years, so past experience will tend to underestimate threat likelihood for the future.

➤ In addition, some attacks rise rapidly, peak, and then level out, but others continue to grow; so it is important not to focus too heavily on last year's big attacks.

➤ New security technology might make the risks of certain threats lower than they have been in the past.

TEST YOUR UNDERSTANDING

12.   a) What is threat likelihood? b) Why is it difficult to estimate?

Responding to Risk

In general, there are three main ways to respond to risk.

Risk Reduction

The most obvious way to respond to risk is **risk reduction**—taking active countermeasures, such as installing firewalls and hardening hosts.

Risk Acceptance

However, if the impact of a compromise would be small, and if the cost of risk reduction would exceed the probable impact of a breach, then it makes sense to choose **risk acceptance**—implementing no countermeasures and absorbing any damages that occur.

Risk Transference

The third alternative is **risk transference**—having someone else absorb the risk. The most common example of risk transference is **insurance**, in which an insurance company charges an annual premium, in return for which it will pay for damages if a threat materializes. Risk transference is especially good for rare but enormously damaging attacks. This is why homeowners purchase fire and flood insurance.

Insurance companies often require companies to install reasonable countermeasures before they will provide coverage, so insurance can never be used totally as a way to avoid risk reduction. Also, insurance may have high deductibles.

One concern is what threats insurance policies cover or do not cover. Damages resulting from natural disasters, cyberterror, and cyberwar attacks are often specifically excluded from coverage.

TEST YOUR UNDERSTANDING

13. a) What are the three ways of responding to risk? b) Which involves insurance? c) Which involves doing nothing?

Risk Analysis Calculations

Chapter 1 showed one way to do a risk assessment calculation. We will recap the methodology here.

Threat Severity (Expected Loss)

The **threat severity** is the cost of an attack if it succeeds times the probability that it will succeed. Probabilities depend on the time period under consideration. Annual threat severities use a single year as the period of analysis. In essence, **annual threat severity** is the expected annual cost of attacks.

Value of Protection

The **value of protection** compares the threat severity with the cost of countermeasures. If the **annual cost of protection** is less than the cost of the annual loss (threat severity) it will prevent, the value of protection is positive, so the countermeasure is economically worthwhile.

Often, the threat will not completely be stopped but will instead be reduced. In such cases, the dollar value of the reduction in threat severity should be compared with the cost of the countermeasure.

In either case, if the countermeasure costs less than the probable damage it removes, then the countermeasure is worthwhile economically. If not, the countermeasure is too expensive for the probable benefit it will create.

Priority

Typically, a company will not be able to afford to apply all worthwhile countermeasures. Consequently, it usually is good to prioritize the installation of countermeasures in terms of their value of protection dollar amounts, beginning with the countermeasure that will produce the greatest value of protection.

Return on Investment (ROI)

Single-Year ROI   Another way to determine which countermeasure to implement is to use a **return on investment (ROI)** calculation. Using only a 1-year horizon, one can simply divide the value of protection by the cost of the countermeasure. This will give a percentage value that is similar to an interest rate on a savings investment.

Multi-Year ROI and Discounted Cash Flows   Many countermeasure investments provide protection benefits for multiple years. Typically, countermeasure investments also spread over multiple years, often with a large investment in the first year. In multi-year situations, ROI requires **discounted cash flow analysis**. If you have taken a finance or managerial accounting course, you probably learned how to do a discounted cash flow analysis to compute ROIs.

Why Use ROI?   ROI computed as **internal rate of return (IRR)** attractive because it does not depend on the size of the countermeasure cost. It basically shows how good the countermeasure is as an investment. The IRRs of competing investments of different sizes can be compared directly, even if they are of different sizes.

Many companies have a **hurdle rate**, which is the minimum IRR they will accept in an investment given their other opportunities to invest money. This typically ranges from 10 percent to 20 percent. Even if the value of a countermeasure is positive, companies will not implement it if its expected IRR falls below the hurdle rate because competing investments will make more sense.

TEST YOUR UNDERSTANDING

14.   a) How is the threat severity calculated? b) How can you compute the value of a countermeasure? c) Using countermeasure value, how could you prioritize investments in countermeasures? d) How do you compute ROI for a single year? e) What method must be used to compute ROI if investments in the countermeasure and threat reductions will take place over multiple years? f) Why is IRR a good way to compare competing investments? g) What is a hurdle rate, and how is it used?

Qualitative Risk Analysis

Although quantitative risk analysis is good, some risks are more **qualitative** in nature.

Business Termination

One consideration is that attacks that would cause a business to terminate its existence are not acceptable under any circumstances. Such **mission-critical** threats must be addressed if they are even slightly likely, even if the value of safeguards exceeds probable losses.

Loss of Reputation

Although many companies try to keep major security incidents secret, they often fail to do so. If the trust that other companies place in a company is a major part of its competitive advantage (as in the case of a bank), then countermeasures that do not make strict sense economically might be advisable. (It can be argued that the cost of loss of reputation should be computed, but this often is not possible.)

TEST YOUR UNDERSTANDING

15.   How does risk analysis change for mission-critical threats?

SECURITY ARCHITECTURE

Security Architectures

Technical Security Architectures

A company's technical **security architecture** includes all of the technical countermeasures a company has in place—including firewalls, hardened hosts, IDSs, and other tools—and how these countermeasures are organized into a complete system of protection.

A firm's security architecture includes all of the technical countermeasures a company has in place—including firewalls, hardened hosts, IDSs, and other tools—and how these countermeasures are organized into a complete system of protection.

Architectural Decisions

The term *architecture* indicates that a firm's security systems should not simply evolve through an uncoordinated series of individual security investment decisions. Rather, a coherent architectural plan should be in place that allows a company to know that technical security protections are well matched to corporate asset protection needs

Figure 11-4   Corporate Security Architecture (Study Figure)

SECURITY ARCHITECTURES

   Technical security architecture: Countermeasures and their organization into a system
   Architectural decisions: Plan broadly before installing specific systems
   Start in the design phase if possible: The earlier the better
   Deal with legacy security technologies

FIVE PRINCIPLES

   Defense in Depth
   Single Points of Vulnerability
      The dangers of single points of vulnerability
      The need for central security management consoles
   Diversity of Vendors
      Security Effectiveness: Each product will miss some things; jointly will miss less
      Product Vulnerabilities: Each will have some; jointly will have fewer
      Vendor Survival: If one vendor fails, others will continue
   Minimizing Security Burdens on Functional Departments
   Planning, Protecting, and Responding Phases

ELEMENTS OF A SECURITY ARCHITECTURE

   Border management: Border firewalls, etc.
   Internal site management: To protect against internal threats
   Management of remote connections: Remote users and outsiders are difficult
   Interorganizational systems: Linking the computer systems of two organizations
   Centralized management: Control from a single place where information is gathered

and external threats. A major goal is to create a security umbrella with no holes for attackers to walk through.

Start in the Design Phase

Ideally, such an architecture should begin in the design stage, before a company has committed any money to security. However, except in start-up companies, this is impossible.

Dealing with Legacy Security Technology

Security architectures, then, usually must build upon **legacy security technology**. In some cases, legacy security technology that does not measure up should be discarded and replaced. However, as in legacy networking technology and legacy applications, companies often have to work around legacy security technology, adding strengths in other areas to compensate for the limits of the legacy security technology.

TEST YOUR UNDERSTANDING

16. a) What is a firm's security architecture? b) Why is a security architecture needed? c) When is the best time to create one? d) Why don't firms simply replace their legacy security technologies?

Principles

Although creating a security architecture requires that many decisions be made on the basis of complex situational information, some general principles should guide the security architecture's design.

Defense in Depth

The first principle is our old friend, defense in depth. Any attacker should have to be able to break through at least two defensive countermeasures, preferably more. For instance, to attack a server, an attacker might have to break through a border firewall, through an internal VPN, and finally through a hardened application on the server.

The reason for defense in depth is simple. Vulnerability reporters find problems in nearly every security countermeasure once or more per year. While a vulnerability in one defensive element is being fixed, others in the line of attack will remain strong, thwarting the attacker.

Single Points of Vulnerability

A subtle point is that **single points of vulnerability**—elements of the architecture where an attacker can do a great deal of damage by compromising a specific system—should not exist or must be strongly protected.

After the terrorist attacks of September 11, 2001, for instance, it was discovered that many telecommunications carriers brought their transmission lines together under the World Trade Center. This maximized damage to telecommunications in the area. To give another example, in 1998, a single Galaxy IV satellite failed, knocking out pager service in most of the United States.

The Dangers of Single Points of Security Vulnerability   Attackers are happy to find single points of vulnerability in security architectures.

➤ For example, attackers often look for potential vulnerabilities in DNS hosts because causing DNS hosts to crash will shut down most browser users; and taking over DNS servers can allow the attacker to redirect many people in the firm to pornographic websites or other undesired websites.

➤ Network and security management consoles are other highly vulnerable choke points in security operation. Taking over a central network or security management console would allow the attacker to do an enormous amount of damage because such consoles can tell managed devices to shut down, reconfigure themselves, or even create attacks.

➤ Firewalls and download servers for vulnerability patches and antivirus databases are other prime targets to attack because of their centrality.

The Need for Central Security Management Consoles   However, the growing trend to centralize the management of many security devices is creating a dilemma for security architects. Any security architecture whose devices are not controlled centrally might implement inconsistent policies, and many actions taken to thwart an ongoing attack require a systemic response that can work only through a central point of control. As central management of security resources grows, it will become ever more important to secure **central security management consoles** and their communication with a firm's security devices.

Diversity of Vendors

Although it is most convenient to work with a single vendor, it often is wise to use a mix of products from different vendors.

Security Effectiveness   In the case of antivirus products, different vendors will find and miss particular viruses, worms, and Trojan horses. If two antivirus systems are used in sequence, one is likely to catch problems the other one misses.

Product Vulnerabilities   In addition, if one vendor's products become vulnerable, **vendor diversity** will keep a firm safe because other vendors are not likely to have the same vulnerability.

Vendor Survival   In the worst case, a vendor will fail as a business, leaving its customers unprotected or protected only by non-upgraded product versions. As a result, vulnerabilities discovered after the failure will not be patched. In such cases, vendor diversity will keep protection in place while the components of the failed vendor are being replaced.

Minimizing Security Burdens

Another core principle is **minimizing security burdens** on functional departments. To some extent, security inevitably reduces productivity and may slow down the pace of innovation by requiring that security issues are addressed before innovations are rolled out. It is important to choose security architectures and elements that minimize lost productivity and slowed innovation.

In fact, in firms that are highly innovative, security might be the only factor retarding growth. The common complaint of functional managers, "You don't get it," often is correct. The value of growth compared to the value of security protection must be weighed carefully.

However, many actions can greatly reduce user burdens, such as moving to Kerberos single sign-on service so that each individual will have to remember only one password.

Realistic Goals

Although it would be nice to be able to remove all vulnerabilities overnight, it is important to have realistic goals for improvements. For instance, in 1999, NASA developed a list of the most serious vulnerabilities—a list that it has continued to update.[1] Beginning in 2000, all network-connected systems were tested for these flaws. NASA created a goal of decreasing the ratio of vulnerabilities to computers from 1-to-1 to 1-to-4. In 2002, the ratio fell to 1-to-10. By creating a spirit of competition, NASA was able to achieve strong gains while spending only $2 million to $3 million per year ($30 per computer).

TEST YOUR UNDERSTANDING

17.   a) Why is defense in depth important? b) Why are central security management consoles dangerous? c) Why are they desirable? d) Why is having a diversity of vendors good? e) Why is it important to minimize the burdens that security places on functional units in the firm? f) Why do you think it is important to have realistic goals for reducing vulnerabilities?

Elements of a Security Architecture

Because most of the elements of a security architecture were covered in earlier chapters, we will just list them here.

Border Management

Traditionally, companies have maintained a border between their internal networks and untrusted external networks, most commonly the Internet. Firewalls and DMZs have been the staples of border management and should continue to remain so.

Internal Management

Internal management of the trusted internal network is also crucial. For prevention, internal firewalls, hardened clients and servers, IDS data collection facilities, and the other tools that have been discussed in previous chapters should be used.

Management of Remote Connections

Beyond the border, remote connections are needed between corporate sites, to individual remote employees, and to business partners, as we saw in Chapter 8. Virtual private network technologies have been central to the management of communication between trusted users and sites across untrusted networks, such as the Internet.

Individual employees working from their homes and hotel rooms represent a special problem, especially when employees put personal software on their remote

---

[1]   Megan Lisagor, "NASA Cyber Program Bears Fruit," *Federal Computer Week*, October 14, 2002. www.fcw.com/fcw/articles/2002/1014/mgt-nasa-10-14-02.asp.

access computers. In fact, they often use their own home computers to access corporate sites. The general lack of security discipline among home users can be mitigated by technology, but training and the enforcement of rules are crucial.

Interorganizational Systems

Interorganizational systems, in which two companies link some of their IT assets, are especially troublesome because neither organization can directly enforce security in the other and because their security technologies may not be highly compatible.

Centralized Management

An important goal in security architectures is centralized management—being able to manage security technologies from a single security management console or at least from a relatively few security management consoles that each manages a cluster of security technologies. Although the latter approach will require security administrators to run back and forth between consoles (which are hopefully in the same room), it is at least a good start.

TEST YOUR UNDERSTANDING

18. a) Why is border management important? b) Why isn't it a complete security solution? c) Why are remote connections from home especially dangerous? d) Why are interorganizational systems dangerous?

CONTROL PRINCIPLES

Having good technology and a good plan are important, but it is important to implement controls to ensure that plans and the technological infrastructure will be implemented.

Policies

Policies are the highest level of control. **Policies** are broad statements of vision that express a company's commitment to security and that lay out key values and principles that will guide corporate security activities. Policies usually are extremely concise—usually a paragraph or two.

Although policies are limited in what they say, they are intended to guide lower-level security activities. When a decision is made at a lower layer, a key question to ask is which alternatives are consistent with corporate policies.

Standards

Standards are more specific directives that are *mandatory*, meaning that employees subject to them—including managers—do not have the option of not following them. They are also fairly specific, although they do not lay out in detail how specific actions should be carried out. For instance, a company might have a standard that each employee who accesses the network from home must install an antivirus program whose virus definitions database is updated daily.

It is important to audit adherence to standards. Thanks to the specificity and mandatory nature of standards, it should be relatively straightforward for auditors to decide whether or not a standard is being followed in a particular situation.

POLICIES

Brief visions statements
Cannot give details because the environment and technology keep changing

STANDARDS

Mandatory actions that MUST be followed

BASELINES

The application of standards to specific products
For example, steps to harden a Red Hat 7.2 LINUX server

GUIDELINES

Voluntary recommended action
Although voluntary, must *consider* in making decisions
Good when the situation is too complex or uncertain for standards
Unfortunately, sometimes should be standards but lack of political power prevents this

PROCEDURES

Sets of actions taken by people
Steps to do background checks on employees
Steps to add user on a server

EMPLOYEE BEHAVIOR POLICIES

For general corporate employees
Theft, sexual harassment, racial harassment, pornography, personal use of office
equipment, revealing of trade secrets, etc.

BEST PRACTICES AND RECOMMENDED PRACTICES

Best practices are descriptive of what the best firms do
Recommended practices are prescriptions for what the firm *should* do
Both allow a firm to know, at a broad level, if it is doing what it should be doing

Figure 11-5   Control Principles (Study Figure)

Baselines

Baselines are a bit more specific than standards. For instance, a standard might specify that strong security options should be chosen during operating system installations. Although it is possible to audit whether or not the installer has made some effort to set security options, this is not enough to guide installers and auditors.

Baselines go into detail about how a specific standard should be implemented with a specific technology. For instance, baselines should be established for setting security options for Windows 1000 Server, Windows NT Server, Red Hat LINUX, and so forth.

Guidelines

In contrast to standards, which are mandatory, **guidelines** are discretionary. For instance, a company might have a guideline that each new employee should have a background check.

Although it is mandatory for a decision maker to *consider* guidelines, it is not mandatory to *follow* guidelines if good reasons can be given not to. For instance, in an emergency hiring situation, the department head of the new employee might be allowed to hire the person before a background check is completed.

Guidelines are needed in complex and uncertain situations for which rigid standards cannot be specified.

Unfortunately, guidelines also tend to be issued instead of standards when the security department lacks the political clout to require an action that really should be a standard.

Procedures

At the most detailed level, **procedures** specify the actual steps that must be taken by an employee. Procedures go beyond technology to include the actions that humans must take.

For instance, in a movie theater, one employee sells tickets and another takes the ticket to let the customer into the theater. If the ticket seller also allowed the customer in, the ticket seller might take the money and let the customer in without ringing up the sale, then pocket the money. Only if the sale is recorded is the ticket printed. Unless there is collusion between the ticket seller and the ticket taker, this security procedure is fairly effective.

Employee Behavior Policies

In addition to IT security policies, a company often has general employee behavior policies and standards. These address such activities as theft, sexual and racial harassment, and the revealing of trade secrets. Although these are not IT security matters, IT is increasingly involved in enforcing them. For instance, the first clue that sexual harassment is taking place might come from the content scanning of e-mail messages. In addition, the corporation's uniformed security group might need the IT security staff's help in searching the suspected employee's computer for evidence.

Best Practices and Recommended Practices

Best Practices

Although companies work hard on their policies, standards, guidelines, and procedures, they often want to compare what they are doing with what other companies are doing. **Best practices** are descriptions of what the best firms in the industry are doing about security. Best practices usually are put together by consulting firms, but trade associations and even governments are beginning to develop them.

Recommended Practices

Best practices are different than recommended practices, which are prescriptive statements about what companies *should* do. Recommended practices usually are put together by trade associations and government agencies. Perhaps the most widely known general statement on recommended practices is the British BS 7799 standard, *A Code of Practice for Information Security Management.*

TEST YOUR UNDERSTANDING

19. a) Distinguish between policies and standards. b) Distinguish between standards and baselines. c) Distinguish between standards and guidelines. d) When are guidelines issued instead of standards? e) Distinguish between standards and procedures. f) Distinguish between best practices and recommended practices.

MANAGING OPERATIONS

Operations are the day-to-day activities that take place within IT functions, including backing up servers, running production servers, developing new applications, and updating applications.

Principles

A number of important general principles have been established for managing operations. These principles should be kept in mind whenever designing or auditing operations for good security.

Clear Roles

The first principle is that there should be clear roles for doing things in the operation. Individual people are assigned to **roles**, but procedures are assigned to roles instead of to individuals.

In a procedure's description, each action in each sequence should be assigned to a particular role. Only one role should be assigned to each action.

Separation of Duties

Another general principle is the **separation of duties**. Earlier, we saw how movie theaters separate ticket selling from ticket taking so that collusion is needed for an employee to pocket money paid for tickets. Similarly, separate people normally are assigned to the roles of application developer and production server systems administrator. To make an unauthorized change to a production system, the application developer would have to collude with the systems administrator.

OPERATIONS

The day-to-day work of the IT department and other departments
Systems administration (server administration) especially
Entering data, upgrading programs, adding users, assigning access permissions, etc.

PRINCIPLES

Clear roles
   Who should do what in each step
   Assign tasks to roles, then assign individuals to roles as needed
Separation of duties
Rotation of duties and mandatory vacations to prevent people from maintaining
   deceptions
Prospects for collusion: Reduce them
   Check family and personal relationships assigning people to duties

ACCOUNTABILITY

Accountability and roles
   Owner: Responsible for the asset
   Custodian: Delegated responsibility
Auditable protections and controls for specific assets
Exception handling

MANAGING DEVELOPMENT AND CHANGE FOR PRODUCTION SERVERS

Tiers of Servers
   Development Server: Server on which software is developed and changed
      Developers need extensive permissions
   Staging (Testing) Server: Server on which changes are tested and vetted for security
      Testers should have access permissions; developers should not
   Production Server: Server that runs high-volume production operations
      Neither developers nor testers should have access permissions
Change Management Control
   Limit who can request changes
   Implement procedures for controlling changes
   Have security examine all candidate changes for potential problems (bad encryp-
   tion, lack of authentication, etc.)
Auditing Development for individual programs
   Do detailed line-by-line code inspection for security issues

Figure 11-6 Operations Security (Study Figure)

Rotation of Duties and Mandatory Vacations

If the same people are permitted to perform the same roles for long periods of time, they can take unauthorized actions that go undetected for long periods of time. Typically, they will have to maintain their illicit practices actively to keep their deception going, so if they are kept away from their role, their misbehavior will be detected.

One remedy is to require the **rotation of duties**, with each person acting in a particular role only for a limited period of time. This also breaks down collusion partnerships based on relative roles. The rotation of duties also ensures that individual employees cannot blackmail a firm because they are the only ones who know how to do important tasks. On the negative side, the training required for the rotation of duties is expensive.

Mandatory vacations also will make the maintenance of illegal activities impossible. While the employee is on vacation, the deception is likely to break down.

Prospects for Collusion

Collusion is dangerous because it tends to circumvent other procedural protections. Companies often analyze the dossiers of their employees to see whether employees are relatives, close friends, have worked together in another company, or are dating. Employees who are potential colluders should not work together if possible, although employee rights and various practical matters might outweigh the dangers of collusion.

TEST YOUR UNDERSTANDING

20.   a) What are operations? b) What are the major principles for protecting operations? c) Which can be defeated by collusion? Explain. d) Which are designed to reduce the probability of collusion?

Accountability

Accountability means that if misbehavior happens, it will be clear who is responsible. If people are accountable for the management of assets they are responsible for, they are more likely to be diligent in implementing necessary protections.

Accountability and Roles

Owner   Every asset should have a clear **owner** who is responsible for it. The owner is responsible for applying the correct standards, guidelines, and procedures to the asset.

Custodian   Some assets have **custodians** to whom the owner delegates responsibility for the asset. Although the owner still is responsible if things go wrong, the owner depends on the technological skills of the custodian.

Auditable Protections and Controls for Specific Assets

The owner is responsible for applying specific protections and controls for each asset to ensure that the asset is protected. These protections should be auditable so that if they are broken, an audit trace of the misbehavior will be possible.

Exception Handling

Although standards, baselines, and procedures are mandatory, the world is a complex place. Inevitably, some situations will arise in which blind adherence to standards, baselines, and procedures will be counterproductive.

In such situations, it is important to allow exceptions to be made. However, exceptions are dangerous, and rules must be in place for **exception handling**. Each exception must be clearly documented, and a responsible party must sign off on it. A straightforward audit of all exceptions should be possible simply by looking in a single document file.

TEST YOUR UNDERSTANDING

21. a) What is accountability? b) Why is it important? c) Distinguish between owners and custodians. d) Why is auditing important for accountability? e) Why is exception handling needed? f) How can it be controlled?

Managing Development and Change for Production Servers

A company's production servers are those that directly serve internal and external users. The compromise of production servers is a serious threat because of their importance.

Tiers of Servers

As discussed in Chapter 9, there usually are three tiers of servers.

➤ Development servers are used to create new software and to make changes to production software. As discussed in Chapter 9, developers should be given broad permissions on development servers.

➤ Staging servers, also known as **testing servers**, are used to test changes created by developers on the development servers, including security testing. Testers should have extensive permissions on staging servers, but developers should have no permissions on these servers.

➤ Production servers run only tested software. The specific systems administrators assigned to each production server need extensive permissions on their assigned production servers, although backup operators and other employees with limited roles should have limited permissions. However, developers, testers, and even systems administrators for other production servers should have no access permissions.

Change Management Control

Of course, production server software must be changed, sometimes frequently. In addition to placing controls on servers, an overall **change management process** is necessary for making updates to production server application software.

To begin with, a limited number of programmers should be allowed to make **change requests**. If every programmer is allowed to make changes, every programmer will be a security risk. Only a few programmers are legitimately involved in program design, so a restriction on who can initiate changes is not unrealistic.

Second, security should be required to approve all changes after reviewing the change for security implications. No nasty surprises should surface later.

Finally, there should be an audit trail for all changes. This should include who initiated the change, who approved the change, who made the change, and who posted the change. If there is an incident, audit files are critical in identifying possible wrong-doers.

Auditing Development for Individual Programs

Finally, the initial software development and the development of software changes should be fully audited. Change request auditing merely looks at changes from a broad security point of view. Development auditing should be much more detailed. It should involve the **code inspection** of every line of code by someone who is an accomplished programmer and who is trained in the development of software to avoid security weaknesses.

TEST YOUR UNDERSTANDING

22.   a) Explain the roles of the three tiers of servers for production services. b) Who should have access permissions on each? c) What is change control management for production servers? d) How should it be implemented? e) When should programs and program changes be audited for security problems? Why?

MOBILIZING USERS

Users are the first line of defense for IT security. Security personnel sometimes believe that users are their worst problem, but it is important to mobilize users to be full partners in security.

User Training

The key element in mobilizing users is user training. The issue is what kinds of training to provide to users.

Security Awareness

The first step has to be **security awareness** training. The goal of this training is to help users understand that serious threats exist. This training should include data on attack patterns and case studies (some of this information is discussed in Chapters 1 and 1a). Hopefully, this training will provide motivation.

Accountability Training

Second, users have to be trained in **accountability**. They will need to understand that they have duties to perform and activities they need to refrain from doing. They also need to understand the specific rules that involve them.

Self-Defense Training

The next step is to provide **self-defense training**. In the martial arts, self-defense training prepares an individual to take appropriate action if attacked, including knowing which actions are permissible. In IT self-defense training, the user is taught how to respond during an attack.

A major part of self-defense training should focus on social engineering because these are the types of attacks that users are most likely to encounter, and proper user

USER TRAINING

> Security Awareness
> Accountability Training
> Self-Defense Training
>> Social engineering threats and correct responses
>> Make users early warning scouts who know whom to inform if breach suspected
>> In general, mobilize as partners

AUTHENTICATION

> Nontechnical Problems in Providing Access Permissions
>> Who may submit people for usernames and passwords? Limit it
>> Human resources know when people are hired and fired
>> But on specific servers, many people might submit needs to sys admin
>>> Project managers for projects on the server
>>> For many people: Individual employees, contractors, consultants, temporary hires
> Terminating Authentication Credentials
>> People often do not have their permissions terminated when they no longer need them
>> Person who requests their permissions should have to periodically review them for continuation

Figure 11-7   Mobilizing Users (Study Figure)

responses to social engineering attacks are crucial. Users must be given specific scenarios and informed of the appropriate ways to deal with them and why these ways are appropriate. Group scenario discussions are useful for helping users internalize self-defense training.

The second major aspect of self-defense training is enlisting users as early warning scouts. Often, users are the first people to detect problems when attacks occur. In addition, in cases of improper user behavior, such as people being in restricted areas without badges, other users are likely to observe the improper behavior. In both situations, users need to report problems to uniformed security for investigation. In the case of IT-based attacks, the uniformed corporate security staff will pass the information on to IT security. In the case of misbehavior, uniformed security should investigate the situation directly. During this training, each user should be given telephone stickers with the extension number of uniformed security.

TEST YOUR UNDERSTANDING

23. a) Distinguish among user security awareness training, accountability training, and self-defense training. b) What should self-defense training cover?

Authentication

Another critical issue involving users is authentication, as discussed in previous chapters, especially Chapters 2 and 8.

Nontechnical Problems in Providing Access Permissions

As discussed in Chapter 8, personal key infrastructures (PKIs) are critical in implementing authentication. However, PKI technology is far from mature. In addition, as discussed in Chapter 2, biometric technology promises to do away with passwords, but current biometric products have not stood up well to impersonation tests and have had unacceptable accuracy problems in the real world.

Although these technical problems are severe, they pale beside nontechnical problems with authentication. For example, who is allowed to submit someone's name for a username and password? In most businesses, many people can initiate applications. Because human relations department personnel know when people are hired, they can submit employee names for **authentication credentials** such as user names and passwords.

However, few companies have a full, single sign-on system. Consequently, usernames and passwords typically are assigned on individual servers. In such cases, applications to add someone to a server's list of authorized users may come from many people, including project leaders who depend on one of the programs on the server for their projects and who wish to add someone to the project. In other cases, temporary workers, consultants, employees of contractors, and others must be given permissions for specific programs on specific servers. Under these chaotic conditions, social engineering attacks are likely to succeed regardless of how good the technology is. All of the September 11, 2001, hijackers had real identification cards or good fakes.

Even if single sign-on technologies could be created, they might make the pattern worse, given the number of potential initiators of authentication credentials. If attackers get permissions on any server, they might be able to extend those permissions to other servers.

Terminating Authentication Credentials

Although permitting the issuance of credentials is problematic, terminating authentication credentials is even more problematic from a procedural point of view. Various sources suggest that 30 percent to 50 percent of all access permission profiles on a typical server should not exist because the subject has left the firm or has changed to a role that does not require the degree of access provided. The problem is simply that nobody has reviewed the access permissions.

One potential remedy is to audit authorizations and record who initiated requests for permissions. The organization could have that person periodically reassert the need for the named people to have their permissions confirmed.

TEST YOUR UNDERSTANDING

24. a) Describe nontechnical problems for giving authentication credentials to employees and others. b) Describe nontechnical problems for terminating authentication credentials.

VULNERABILITY TESTING

Although plans, standards, baselines, and procedures can be effective in implementing security, they mean nothing unless they are enforced and tested. Earlier, we discussed auditing. In this section, we will look at **vulnerability testing**, in which vulnerability assessment tools are turned on the corporate network by authorized testers to find vulnerabilities.

Figure 11-8   Vulnerability Testing (Study Figure)

VULNERABILITY TESTING TECHNOLOGY

Using Attacker Technology
Using Commercial Vulnerability Testing Tools
  Not as up-to-date as attacker tools
  Less likely to do damage as side effect
  Focus on reporting
Reporting and Follow-Up Tools
  Reports should clearly list vulnerabilities and suggested fixes
  Follow-up report should document which vulnerabilities fixed, not fixed

VULNERABILITY TESTING CONTRACTS

Need a contract before the testing begins to cover everyone involved
What Will Be Tested: Specifics
How It Will Be Tested: Specifics
Hold Blameless for Side Effects

LIMITING FALSE POSITIVES WITH TUNING

Avoid meaningless tests, for instance, Apache threat on Microsoft Windows server

WHO SHOULD DO VULNERABILITY TESTING?

Outside Firms
  Expertise
  Use of reformed hackers?
The IT or Security Department
  Has good knowledge of internal systems
  If IT staff is the attacker, can hide wrongdoing
IT Auditing Departments
  Trained to audit whether standards and procedures are being followed
  Have to upgrade their specific vulnerability testing skills

    25.   What is vulnerability testing?

Vulnerability Testing Technology

Using Attacker Technology

Chapter 4 examined the **hacker vulnerability testing tools** that attackers use to gather information about target networks and target hosts, including the fingerprints of operating systems, the mapping of available ports, and other matters. In addition, these tools can identify unpatched vulnerabilities.

Using Commercial Vulnerability Testing Tools

Vulnerability testing generally uses the same tools. However, some **commercial vulnerability testing tools** are specifically designed for vulnerability testing instead of attacking. Hackers tend to deprecate these tools because they often are not as up to date as hacker tools are.

    Commercial vulnerability testing attacks are not designed to do damage if they find a vulnerability but rather to take some innocuous action to demonstrate that the vulnerability exists. However, sometimes they accidentally do some damage. This damage is referred to as a **side effect**, and it is similar to the side effects of medicines in the sense of being an unwanted consequence that sometimes occurs.

Reporting

An important outcome of vulnerability testing is the creation of a **vulnerability and recommended remedies report** that, as its name suggests, documents vulnerabilities in a way that allows the company to understand its vulnerabilities and that specifies remedial actions that need to be taken to reduce the discovered vulnerabilities.

Follow-Up

Ideally, a **follow-up report** will be presented several months later, in order to document which of the actions listed in the needed remedies report have been implemented or not implemented.

    26.   a) What are side effects? b) Describe reporting needs. c) Describe the need for follow-up.

Vulnerability Testing Contracts

If the vulnerability testing is done by an outside firm, it is important to develop a detailed **vulnerability testing contract** that specifies exactly which vulnerability tests will be performed. Any unauthorized tests could result in contract termination and perhaps even lawsuits and criminal prosecution against the testing firm.

    At the same time, unexpected side effects are inevitable, and they must be viewed as a risk of testing. The testing firm must be held blameless if side effects occur, even serious ones. This must be laid out clearly in the contract.

    If an internal department does the testing, a contract is just as necessary as it is if an external testing service is used. Under no circumstances should anyone in the firm do vulnerability testing without a written agreement signed by his or her superior. This written agreement, like an external contract, should specify which tests will be run against which systems and clearly state that side effects are possible.

TEST YOUR UNDERSTANDING

    27.   What should be in a vulnerability testing contract?

Limiting False Positives with Tuning

One problem with hacker and commercial vulnerability testing tools is that both tend to generate large numbers of false positives—reported vulnerabilities that do not exist. As in the case of the intrusion detection systems (IDSs) discussed in Chapter 10, it is possible to tune vulnerability testing tools to reduce the number of false positives. Tuning works in the same way for IDSs and vulnerability testing tools. The process involves turning off vulnerability reports that do not make sense, say by eliminating reported Apache vulnerabilities for Windows 2000 servers that use IIS.

    For tuning to be successful, good knowledge of the system being tested is necessary. This allows unneeded tests to be skipped. However, depending on one's knowledge of the network, skipping tests should be done somewhat warily because few firms have completely up-to-date asset management databases of all of their network, host, application, and data assets.

TEST YOUR UNDERSTANDING

    28.   How can tuning reduce the number of false positives in vulnerability testing?

Who Should Do Vulnerability Testing?

Outside Firms

Who should do vulnerability testing? The advantage of having an outside firm do the vulnerability testing is the objectivity that comes from having a disinterested party do the analysis. However, it is important that the vulnerability assessment firm not be so dependent upon any corporate department that its objectivity is compromised. The Arthur Anderson disaster in financial auditing illustrates the dangers of having functions that are being audited selecting and paying the auditing firm.

    One issue in using an outside firm, however, is how the firm's vulnerability testing staff obtained its knowledge. If they are "reformed" hackers, this is a serious concern. Although former hackers are likely to have the advanced skills to do an effective vulnerability test, whoever does vulnerability testing learns enough about the firm to be extremely dangerous. On the other hand, if the testers merely have learned the mechanics of how to use a commercial vulnerability testing program, they will be able to do only extremely superficial testing.

The IT or Security Department

The IT department and the security department are logical choices for doing vulnerability testing. They have the internal knowledge of the corporate network needed to do the work, and they either know how or can learn to use the tools.

However, if someone well placed in the department that conducts the test is attacking the firm, it is relatively easy to modify the results so that crucial vulnerabilities are hidden. This approach violates the separation-of-duties principle but is pragmatically the easiest to implement.

IT Auditing Department

Another possibility is to use the firm's IT auditing department to do vulnerability testing. Using the IT auditing department satisfies the separation-of-duties principle, and members of the IT auditing department are likely to be able to develop the technical skills needed to do vulnerability testing.

TEST YOUR UNDERSTANDING

29. a) Why is using an outside firm to do vulnerability testing good? b) Why is understanding the skills and backgrounds of outside vulnerability testers important? c) Why is using the IT or security department to do vulnerability testing good and bad? d) Why is having the auditing department to do vulnerability testing good?

CONCLUSION

Although security management has been discussed in earlier chapters, this chapter has looked at security management in more depth, focusing on the actions of the firm's IT security department and other departments.

THOUGHT QUESTIONS

1. Is the rule to stop when a traffic light turns red a policy, a standard, a baseline, or a procedure? Explain. Is this still true in New York City?
2. Create a corporate policy statement.
3. Create three corporate security standards.
4. Create three corporate security guidelines.
5. Should the following countermeasure investment be made, given the value it will produce? Do NOT use discounted cash flow.

	Year 1	Year 2	Year 3	Year 4
Threat Severity Reduction	$ 50,000	$50,000	$50,000	$50,000
Countermeasure Investment	$100,000	$25,000	$25,000	$25,000

6. If you have the required background, redo the previous question with discounted cash flow analysis to get the IRR. The company has a hurdle rate of 15 percent. Should the investment be made?

CHAPTER 12

THE BROADER PERSPECTIVE

Learning Objectives:

By the end of this chapter, you should be able to discuss:

- Laws governing hacking and other computer crimes.
- Consumer privacy.
- Employee workplace monitoring.
- Government surveillance.
- Cyberwar and cyberterror.
- Hardening the Internet against attack.

INTRODUCTION

So far, this book has focused primarily on security concerns *within* corporations. However, IT security staff members also need to have an understanding of broader issues in the world outside the firm.

Laws Governing Hacking

We will look first at the laws governing hacking and related activities. This is material that every security professional needs to understand.

Privacy

Next, we will look at the large, complex, and contentious topic of privacy. This includes protecting the personal privacy of customers, employee workplace monitoring, and government surveillance.

Cyberwar and Cyberterror

Finally, we will look at the nightmare scenario for corporate security: massive attacks by cyberterrorists or by a foreign government executing cyberwar.

LAWS GOVERNING COMPUTER CRIMES

Computers and networks are relatively new, at least compared to the glacial pace of change in law. Although governments around the world are working to develop laws to deal with computer and network attacks, the legal situation today is far from satisfactory. In recent years, the virus writer who created and released the highly malicious CIH virus was not prosecuted in Hong Kong because of poorly written laws, and the suspected creator of the Love Bug virus, which did billions of dollars in damage, was not prosecuted in the Philippines for lack of relevant legal statutes.

TEST YOUR UNDERSTANDING

  1.   What is the general status of computer abuse laws around the world?

U.S. National Laws

Although the United States is a sovereign country, even its name emphasizes that it is, in many ways, a confederation of individual states. Although federal laws cover some things, many intrastate attacks are covered only by state laws.

Computer Hacking, Denial-of-Service Attacks, and Other Attacks

In the United States, the main federal law regarding hacking is **Section 1030** of United States Code Title 18, Part I (Crimes). Although this section does not specifically use the terms *hacking, viruses,* and *denial of service attacks,* these are its main focuses. This section is the result of a series of acts, including the **Computer Fraud and Abuse Act of 1986**, the **National Information Infrastructure Protection Act of 1996**, and the **Homeland Security Act of 2002**.

U.S. NATIONAL LAWS

Title 18, Section 1030
 Enabling Legislation
  Computer Fraud and Abuse Act of 1986
  National Information Infrastructure Protection Act of 1996
  Homeland Security Act of 2002
 Prohibitions
  Criminalizes intentional access of protected computers without authorization or in excess of authorization (Hacking)
  Criminalizes the transmission of a program, information, code, or command that intentionally causes damage without authorization of a protected computer (Denial-of-Service and Viruses)
 Punishment
  For first offenses, usually 1–5 years; usually 10 years for second offenses
  For theft of sensitive government information, 10 years, with 20 years for repeat offense
  For attacks that harm or kill people, up to life in prison
Title 47
  Electronic Communications Privacy Act of 1986 (ECMA)
  Prohibits the reading of information in transit and in storage after receipt
Other federal laws for fraud, etc.

U.S. STATE LAWS

Federal laws only protect some computers
State laws for purely intrastate crimes vary widely

LAWS AROUND THE WORLD VARY

The general situation: lack of solid laws in many countries
Cybercrime Treaty of 2001
Signatories must agree to create computer abuse laws and copyright protection
Nations must agree to work together to prosecute attackers

Figure 12-1 Laws Governing Hacking

Hacking   Section 1030 of Title 18 section prohibits the intentional access of certain protected computers without authorization or exceeding authorization.[1] Roughly, these **protected computers** are financial computers, medical computers, government computers (or computers used by the government), and computers used in interstate or international commerce. Computers other than protected computers are not covered by federal law, making state and local laws regarding hacking important.

Denial-of-Service and Virus Attacks   Section 1030 also prohibits the transmission of "a program, information, code, or command that intentionally causes damage without authorization to a protected computer." This paragraph essentially prohibits denial-of-service attacks, virus attacks, and various other types of automated attacks.

Punishment   Punishment in Section 1030 of Title 18 varies according to the seriousness of the offense.

➤ For first offenses, maximum punishments usually vary from 1 to 5 years depending on the type of offense and the amount of damage done. For repeat offenses, punishments usually vary from 5 to 10 years.

➤ The maximum penalty is 10 years for the theft of sensitive government information, and this is doubled for repeat offenses.

➤ For computerized terrorist attacks that attempt to harm or that actually harm or kill people, to the maximum penalty is life in prison without possibility of parole.

Confidentiality in Message Transmission

Title 18 of the U.S. Code deals with multiple types of computer crimes. **Title 47** specifically covers crimes dealing with electronic communications from telegraphy to networking. Title 47 broadly prohibits the interception of messages both en route and after the message is received and stored. The most important recent act defining Title 47 offenses was the **Electronic Communications Privacy Act of 1986 (ECMA)**.

Other Federal Laws

Of course, the federal government has many other laws involving extortion, the theft of trade secrets, and many other matters. If computer intrusions involve these other laws, the penalties in these other laws—which usually are substantially higher—will apply.

TEST YOUR UNDERSTANDING

2. a) What does Title 18 Section 1030 of the U.S. Code prohibit? b) Does it apply to all computers? c) What are typical punishments for first-time offenders? d) What Title governs the security of electronic communication? e) Does it protect communication during transmission, after reception, or both? f) Which acts have defined Title 18 Section 1030 and Title 47 crimes and punishments?

---

[1]   In the *United States vs. Sablan* (1996), the U.S. District Court for the District of Guam ruled that although access has to be intentional, damage does not have to be intentional for a crime to be committed.

U.S. State Laws

Although federal laws govern many computer intrusions, purely intrastate attacks often are not covered. Unfortunately, there are wide variations in computer intrusion laws from state to state within the United States.

Laws Around the World

Laws around the world vary tremendously. Two recent studies have surveyed computer crime legislation around the world. In 2001, Schjolberg[2] surveyed penal legislation in 42 countries. In 2000, McConnell International[3] also examined international computer crime legislation. Both found a pattern of increasingly effective legislation in some countries but little progress in other countries. McConnell estimated that in 2000, 10 countries had substantially or fully updated laws, another 9 had partially updated laws, and 33 had no updated laws.

In general, computer crime is being clarified, and penalties are getting tougher.[4] The most important global development has been the **Cybercrime Treaty of 2001,** created by the Council of Europe.[5] Signatories of this treaty (which was heavily influenced by the United States) agree to create computer abuse laws, as well as laws in copyright protection. The treaty also makes it easier for countries to work together to prosecute attackers in other countries.

TEST YOUR UNDERSTANDING

> 3.   a) What is the state of computer crime statutes around the world? b) What does the Cybercrime Treaty of 2001 require?

The Limitation of Laws

A subtle but important point about laws is that preventing attacks is not their goal, except indirectly through the deterrence created by the prospect of punishment. Rather, their goal is to punish misbehavior after the fact. Good laws are crucial for punishment, but they do not relieve companies of the need to create good technical and procedural protections against attacks.

CONSUMER PRIVACY

Introduction

"You have zero privacy now. Get over it!"[6] When SUN Microsystems CEO Scott McNealy made this comment in January 1999, he was implicitly emphasizing two

---

2   Schjolberg, Stein, "The Legal Framework—Unauthorized Access to Computer Systems: Penal Legislation in 42 Countries," November 27, 2001. www.mossbyrett.of.no/info/legal.html.

3   McConnell International, LLC. "Cyber Crime . . . and Punishment? Archaic Laws Threaten Global Information," December 2000. www.mcconnellinternational.com/services/cybercrime.htm.

4   The United Kingdom has strong anti-hacking and antivirus legislation through the Computer Misuse Act of 1990. In Australia, the Cybercrime Act protects government computers and attacks using the telephone. Within Australia, Victoria has passed strong local laws that call for penalties of up to 10 years. In Hungary, all hacking, including attempted hacking, is illegal, regardless of the amount of damage.

5   The Council of Europe is not the European Union. However, the E.U. is developing specific rules for implementing the Cybercrime Treaty.

6   Andrew D. Wright, "The Big Picture: Life in the 21st Century, Chapter 1: A Penny for Your Thoughts," undated. Accessed December 2, 2002. www.chebucto.ns.ca/Newsletter/Beacon/Back/A9908/bigpic2.htm.

INTRODUCTION

Scott McNealy of SUN Microsystems: "You have zero privacy now. Get over it!"
But privacy is strong in European Union countries and some other countries

CREDIT CARD FRAUD AND IDENTITY THEFT

Widespread concern (Gartner)
   One in 20 consumers had suffered credit card number theft in 2002
   One in 50 consumers had suffered identity theft in 2002
   Only about a fifth of this is online, but online theft is growing the most rapidly
Carders steal credit card numbers
Many merchants fail to protect credit card numbers
Carders test and sell credit card numbers
Merchants also suffer fraud from consumers and carders
Identity theft: Set up accounts in person's name
   Victim may not discover identity theft until long afterward

TRACKING CUSTOMER BEHAVIOR

Within a website and sometimes across websites
Some information is especially sensitive (health, political leanings, etc.)
Access to data and analysis tools are revolutionizing the ability to learn about people
What consumers wish for
   Disclosure of policies
      What information will be collected?
      How the information will be used by the firm collecting customer data?
      Whether and with whom the information will be shared
   Ability of consumer to see and correct inaccurate personal information
   Limiting collection and analysis to operational business needs
      Limiting these needs
   Opt in: No use unless customer explicitly agrees

CORPORATE RESPONSES

Privacy disclosure statements
TrustE certifies corporate privacy behavior
Platform for Privacy Preferences (P3P); Standard format for privacy questions
Federal Trade Commission
   Enforces privacy statements
   Imposes fines and required long-term auditing
   Does not specify what should be in the privacy statement
Opt out: Customer must take action to stop data collection and sharing
No opt: No way to stop data collection and sharing
Passport and Liberty Alliance

(*continued*)

Figure 12-2: Consumer Privacy

CONSUMER REACTIONS

Checking privacy disclosure statements (rare)
Not accepting cookies (rarer)
Anonymous websurfing services (extremely rare)

U.S PRIVACY LAWS

No general law
Health Information Portability and Accountability Act (HIPAA) of 1996
    Protects privacy in hospitals and health organizations
    Focuses on protected information that identifies a patient
Gramm-Leach-Bliley Act (GLBA) of 1999
    Protects financial data
    Allows considerable information sharing
    Opt out can stop some information sharing
Children's Online Privacy Protection Act of 1998
    Protects the collection of personal data from children under 13
    Applies in child-oriented sites and any site that suspects a user is under 13
    No protection for older children
Registration for Kids.US domain is controlled
State privacy laws vary widely

INTERNATIONAL LAWS

European Union Charter of Fundamental Rights
    Right to protection of personal information
    Personal information must be processed for specific legitimate purposes
    Right to see and correct data
    Compliance overseen by independent authority
E.U. Data Protection Directive of 1995
    Opt out with opt in for sensitive information
    Access for review and rectification
    Independent oversight agency
    Data out of country only to countries with "adequate" protections
Safe harbor
    Rules that U.S. firms must agree to follow to get personal data out of Europe
    Are GLBA rules to be considered in financial industries? E.U. is resisting.

Figure 12-2:   (Continued)

things. The first was that modern technology already has made huge inroads into the traditional privacy enjoyed by ordinary citizens. The second was the general attitude that American businesses in general have had toward privacy—dismissing it except when pressed to pay attention by public opinion or by the government.

In this section, we will focus especially on the U.S. situation. However, we also will look at privacy in the rest of the world, especially in Europe, where McNealy's statement has been read with puzzlement. Privacy is very much alive in Europe, and U.S. multinational firms that do business in Europe have to take privacy very seriously.

While businesses and governments are sparring back and forth, with the government generally unwilling to impose rules on companies, ordinary consumers have hardly been listened to at all. Although strongly disturbed by the loss of privacy on the Internet—which actually is worse than they fear—consumers have had little impact on the privacy debate until now.

Privacy has some technical issues, but privacy is largely about business and regulation. Our discussion will focus on this reality.

TEST YOUR UNDERSTANDING

    4.   Compare privacy laws in the United States with those in the European Union.

Credit Card Fraud and Identity Theft

The two strongest fears of consumers are **credit card number theft** and **identity theft**.

Widespread Concern

Surveys have shown consistently that people are widely concerned with credit card number theft, identity theft, and other privacy dangers (including the ability of others to find where they live). These surveys also have found that these concerns cause many people to avoid e-commerce or to use it as rarely as possible.

These concerns are not misplaced. The Gartner Group estimated in 2002 that 1 in 20 consumers had experienced credit card fraud in the previous year, and 1 in 50 had suffered identity theft.[7] Only a few percent of these thefts were committed online, but online card and identity theft are growing more rapidly than other forms of these crimes.[8]

At the same time, the law protects consumers in the United States and many other countries. In the United States, the maximum risk exposure is $50 per unauthorized use under the **Fair Credit Billing Act**. Leading credit card companies often waive even this liability. In practice, however, it can take months of intensive work to clear a person's credit record.

---

[7]   Bob Sullivan, "Credit Card Fraud Hit 1 in 20 Users," msnbc.com, March 4, 2002. www.msnbc.com/news/718115.asp.

[8]   Dan Verton, "Identity Thefts Increase, but Few Occur Online," *Computerworld*, February 13, 2001. www.cnn.com/2001/TECH/industry/02/13/identity.thefts.idg/index.html.

A Dismal History of Protection

How can **carders** (credit card number thieves) and identity thieves get their information? The main way to steal credit card numbers today is to break into the poorly protected databases of e-commerce companies. CD Universe lost 300,000 credit card numbers in one attack.[9] Egghead.com reportedly lost 3.5 million credit card numbers.[10] In 2001, crime syndicates in Russia and the Ukraine stole as many as one million credit card numbers, according to the FBI's National Infrastructure Protection Center.[11]

After the Theft

After thieves steal credit cards, they often test them by making small purchases that their owners are not likely to notice and that might slip under the radar of the e-commerce sites at which these purchases are made. In September 2002, one e-commerce company received 140,000 fake charges for $5.07 each.[12] About half of the credit cards were accepted, indicating that they were valid numbers. Several other firms were hit with similar probes that night.

Next, carders sell their stolen credit card numbers. Typically, they market them through Internet Relay Chat discussions. In May 2002, credit card numbers typically sold for between $0.40 and $5.00 each, depending on how well the card numbers had been tested for validity.[13] In bulk, sellers often charged $100 for 250 numbers to $1,000 for 5,000 numbers.

Credit Card Fraud Problems of Merchants

Fraud using stolen credit card numbers is a major problem for merchants, as well. A 2000 survey by Celent Communications found that 0.25% of all online MasterCard sales were fraudulent, compared to only 0.09% of face-to-face transactions.[14] This is, however, much lower than the 20% rates found in some early studies of e-commerce sites.

To reduce problems, Visa, MasterCard, and American Express have created programs that both assist merchants and require merchants to implement certain protections that reduce the frequency of fraud, most notably by verifying the validity of each credit card submitted with an external verification company.

Credit card theft usually is difficult to prosecute. First, finding carders usually is difficult. Second, the thief might live in another country, and international cooperation is fairly poor, although the U.S. Federal Trade Commission is pooling its complaint data with similar agencies in several other countries. Third, even when evidence is strong and when the thief can be conclusively identified, law enforcement agencies are not likely to pursue prosecution unless the theft is many thousands of dollars.

---

[9]   Mike Brunker and Bob Sullivan, "CD Universe Evidence Compromised," msnbc.com, June 7, 2001. zdnet.com.com/2100–11–502482.html.

[10]   Bob Sullivan, "Massive Credit Heist, Fraud Reported," msnbc.com, December 22, 2001.

[11]   Dan Verton, "FBI Investigating Eastern European Hacker Break-Ins," *Computerworld*, March 12, 2001. www.computerworld.com/cwi/stories/0,1199,NAV47–68–84–88–93_STO58492.html.

[12]   Bob Sullivan, "Massive Credit Card Heist Suspected," msnbc.com, September 13, 2002. www.msnbc.com/news/807675.asp.

[13]   Matt Richtel, "Rampant Trade of Stolen Credit-Card Numbers Shows Lack of Security," *The Mercury News*, May 12, 2002. www.siliconvalley.com/mld/siliconvalley/news/editorial/3252532.htm.

[14]   Matt Richtel, "Rampant Trade of Stolen Credit-Card Numbers Shows Lack of Security," *The Mercury News*, May 12, 2002. Op cit.

Identity Theft

Even more devastating than credit card number theft is **identity theft**, in which the thief collects extensive information about the victim. Using this information, the thief creates fake corporations, opens lines of credit, and engages in other actions to exploit the victim's credit. The victim often does not even realize that his or her identity has been stolen because bills and warnings typically go to a fake addresses created by the identity thief. By the time the victim realizes that his or her identity has been stolen, the damage may take weeks or months to undo.[15]

TEST YOUR UNDERSTANDING

5. a) Distinguish between credit card number theft and identity theft. b) How widespread are these threats? c) What protection does the U.S. Fair Credit Billing Act provide to consumers? d) What is a carder? e) What do carders do with card numbers after stealing them? f) Is consumer fraud a problem for merchants? g) Why can identity theft go on for some time before the victim realizes it?

Knowing Too Much: Customer Tracking by Commercial Companies

Beyond concerns about financial theft, consumers also are concerned that businesses simply know too much about them.

Tracking Shopping

Although financial losses are disturbing to consumers, Internet users also are concerned with the amount of data that websites and other IT innovations can collect about them.

For example, even if a user is not required to log into a website, cookies will allow the website to track the user's path through the website's pages. Mathematical analysis can be used to tailor the customer's websurfing experience. To businesses, this analysis means profits through incremental revenues. To consumers, it is like walking around stores with salespeople following them and taking notes on everything they do.

Sensitive Information

Customers also are concerned that **sensitive personal information** about them is kept in corporate databases, including medical information, television viewing habits, reading habits, and political activities. Consumers do not want this type of data recorded, much less analyzed, shared among firms, and perhaps stolen by hackers because of poor security.

The Access and Analysis Revolution

Although sensitive information has been stored about people for years, public database access used to be difficult. Essentially, the information was stored in "write-only memory." With Internet access, however, a great deal of publicly available information

---

[15] It is good to check one's credit rating about every 6 months. There are three major credit rating services in the United States: Equifax (www.equifax.com), TransUnion (www.transunion.com), and Experian (www.experian.com). All can offer reports that cover data contained in all three services.

is now readily available for the first time, and it is becoming easy to capture sensitive information about shopping and websurfing behavior.

In addition, powerful computers now make it possible to correlate information from multiple sources. Fuzzy logic programming can be used to identify relationships within the data patterns that would help a thief or a government agency. (We will discuss government surveillance later in this chapter.)

TEST YOUR UNDERSTANDING

6.   a) Why do consumers object to having their viewing and purchasing information analyzed? b) Why are improved access and analysis tools reducing privacy?

Issues in Privacy for Sensitive and Shopping Information
What privacy limitations do customers wish to impose on businesses? The following is a reasonable list of expectations.

Disclosure of Policies   First, websites should disclose their privacy policies, especially:

➤   What information they collect about their consumers.

➤   How they will use this information within the firm.

➤   Whether and with whom they will share any of this information.

Seeing and Correcting Personal Information   Consumers should be able to see any information collected about them and to have any incorrect information changed.

Limiting Collection and Analysis to Operational Needs   The website should limit data collection to information needed strictly for its own operational needs.

Limiting Operational Needs   These operational needs should be very limited, for instance, not using information to track users and analyze their activities.

Opt In   For any information the website needs to collect beyond limited operational needs, the website may ask for the information, but this should be strictly on an **opt-in** basis, meaning that the user must explicitly agree to its collection with full knowledge of how the information will be used.

TEST YOUR UNDERSTANDING

7.   a) What five privacy limitations do consumers wish to place on businesses? b) What three things should privacy policy disclosure statements describe? c) What is opt in?

Corporate Responses
Privacy Disclosure Statements   How have corporations responded to consumer unease about data collection? On the whole, they have done comparatively little. Basically, most sites in the United States now have **privacy disclosure statements**, but these often are convoluted legal statements that are difficult to understand.

TrustE   The TrustE Corporation has standards for what should be in these statements and gives its seal of approval to companies that have statements meeting its disclosure guidelines. However, this only deals with disclosure, not privacy in general. In addition, although there has been some misbehavior on the part of companies with TrustE seals, TrustE has not forced any organization to stop using its seal at the time of this writing.

P3P   One promising trend is **P3P**, the **Platform for Privacy Preferences**. P3P provides a set of rigidly defined questions for a website to answer and put in a database. Consumers with P3P-compliant browsers can query the website to see if its policies fit a profile with which they are comfortable. However, P3P has not become popular on websites. Microsoft introduced P3P in Version 6.0 of Internet Explorer, although in limited form. Most importantly, few consumers, although concerned about privacy, will take even the actions needed to use P3P.

Federal Trade Commission's Enforcement of Privacy Policies   In one positive legal step, the U.S. **Federal Trade Commission (FTC)** has been holding companies to their privacy disclosure statements with fines and other measures if these policies are violated. For instance, the FTC reached a settlement with Eli Lilly in 2001 when that company accidentally released 700 customer addresses collected at the firm's Prozac.com website; the settlement requires independent audits in the future.[16]

Howard Beales, the FTC's consumer privacy chief, said that the FTC asks two questions, "Did you have a system in place that was appropriate for the sensitivity of the information, and did you follow your procedures?"[17]

Even companies that change their privacy policies have been taken to court by the FTC. Still, the FTC generally merely requires companies to do what they say they will do. It does not require them to have consumer-friendly policies.

Opt Out and No Opt   Relatively few U.S. websites are opt-in sites that ask a customer for permission to collect and use private information. Some of these opt-in sites refuse service if the customer will not opt in, and some will allow opt in only for some information.

More sites offer only **opt-out** service, in which customers must take specific actions to not have their data used. Most offer **no-opt** service, in which consumers have no choice about how their information will be used.

Passport and Liberty Alliance   One concern is electronic wallet or **identity management** services, which store information about consumers centrally and allow the consumer to release information selectively to merchants. Microsoft was the first major company to offer such a service, called Passport. Microsoft achieved a large user base for Passport by requiring people buying Microsoft software to enter information into Passport as a requirement to use the software. Microsoft then did a poor job of securing this sensitive private information. It was sued by the Federal Trade Commission and is currently under close supervision by the U.S. government.[18] (For instance, an

---

[16]   Patrick Thibodeau, "FTC, Eli Lilly Settle Privacy Case," *Computerworld*, January 18, 2002. www.computerworld.com/securitytopics/security/story/0,10801,67517,00.html.

[17]   Patrick Thibodeau, "Privacy Issues a Growing Concern for Business," *Computerworld*, January 31, 2002. www.computerworld.com/databasetopics/data/story/0,10801,67883,00.html.

[18]   Todd R. Weiss, "Update: FTC, Microsoft Reach Settlement on Passport Probe," *Computerworld*, August 8, 2002. www.computerworld.com/securitytopics/security/story/0,10801,73300,00.html.

independent audit of Passport must be performed every 2 years for the next 20 years.) Passport also is currently under investigation by the European Union.[19] Microsoft has moved to make Passport less consumer unfriendly, for instance by allowing opt-out through a website (a call to customer service had been required initially). Several Microsoft competitors have formed the Liberty Alliance to offer competing identity management services.

TEST YOUR UNDERSTANDING

8. a) What are privacy disclosure statements? b) Why is P3P important? c) When does the FTC take action? d) What actions can the FTC take? e) Does the FTC specify what should be in a privacy policy? f) Distinguish among opt in, opt out, and no opt. g) What is Microsoft Passport? h) What is the Liberty Alliance?

Consumer Reactions

Checking Privacy Disclosure Statements   Although consumers have expressed broad concern over privacy on the Internet, few of them bother to check privacy disclosure statements, much less use this information to decide where to shop or not shop.

Not Accepting Cookies   Some consumers do not permit cookies to be placed on their machines. However, it is difficult to use many websites if you do not accept their cookies; in some cases, it is impossible.

Anonymous Websurfing   A few consumers even use **anonymous websurfing services** that hide a surfer's identity. The surfer first goes to one of the service's hosts, then to general websites on the Internet. In many of these services, it is not even possible for the service to track which of its customers sent a particular message to a website. Although a number of anonymous surfing services exist, for instance Anonymizer.com, the number is getting smaller because of poor user demand. In addition, some websites will not deal with anonymous users.

However, anonymous websurfing is receiving a boost from the Chinese government's crackdown on websurfing. A number of human rights activists smuggled anonymous websurfing software into the country for Chinese citizens to use.[20] This software also is going into Middle East countries with restrictive websurfing laws.

One caveat is that some anonymous surfing services are not truly anonymous because they keep identification data that can be used in disclosure processes during lawsuits to determine the identity of someone who defames someone or who sends threatening and other illegal messages.

TEST YOUR UNDERSTANDING

9. a) How do some consumers attempt to protect their privacy? b) How anonymous is anonymous websurfing?

---

[19]   Paul Meller, "Microsoft Faces EU Privacy Probe," *Computerworld*, May 28, 2002. www.computerworld.com/ databasetopics/data/story/0,10801,71500,00.html.

[20]   Reuters, "Hackers Challenge Internet Monitoring," ZDNET.com, July 15, 2002. zdnet.com.com/ 2102–1105–943797.html.

U.S. Privacy Laws

In general, the United States has not passed laws that affect privacy in most industries. The sentiment in the U.S. Congress has been to depend on voluntary restrictions by industry. However, in some industries, Congress has passed significant legislation affecting privacy.

Health Information Portability and Accountability Act (HIPAA)   For health care institutions, the **Health Information Portability and Accountability Act (HIPAA) of 1996** requires hospitals and other health care organizations to protect patient data fairly stringently. Specifically, HIPAA safeguards **protected information**, which is information in any form (paper, electronic, or audio) that identifies a patient or customer of health care services.

For protected information, health care institutions must have procedural access control over who may see patient data; they must encrypt data and provide other technical security protections; they must have good physical-level access controls; and they must have audit trails. Failures to protect data adequately can result in fines and criminal penalties.

In addition, health care institutions must educate patients on their rights, ensure patients access to their data, obtain uncoerced consent before releasing information, and allow recourse if privacy rules are violated.

Gramm-Leach-Bliley Act (GLBA)   In financial institutions (including insurance companies), if a disclosure of sensitive information due to hacking can cause serious harm, the **Gramm-Leach-Bliley Act (GLBA) of 1999** requires putting stringent protections in place. Typically, data must be given security protections including encryption, limitations on who can access data, and data auditing. The goal is to protect data from attackers, and fines for lack of compliance are substantial. For financial institutions, GLBA is requiring the extensive retooling of corporate information infrastructures. This is good news for consumer privacy.

Unfortunately, GLBA does little to control deliberate information sharing by financial institutions. It allows broad information sharing with unaffiliated firms, although it requires an opt-out capability. No limitations apply to information sharing among affiliated institutions.

Children's Online Privacy Protection Act   In turn, the **Children's Online Privacy Protection Act (COPPA) of 1998** prohibits certain actions by websites and similar services that are directed at children and by any sites that have reason to believe a site visitor is younger than 13. COPPA prohibits them from collecting and using identifying information from children under 13 unless they get verifiable parental consent. Personal information includes such things as first and last names, postal addresses, e-mail addresses, and social security numbers. In addition, registration requiring personal information is prohibited as a requirement for playing games, applying for prizes, and other activities.

Although the act provides some strong protections, children older than 13 are not protected. In addition, the act preempted state laws, so the tougher children's privacy regulations in some states were thrown out by the act.

The Federal Trade Commission is primarily responsible for enforcing the act. However, state attorneys general are permitted to sue in federal district court under the act.

Kids.US   In another step, the U.S. government supervises the **kids.us** top-level domain.[21] By definition, firms that obtain second-level domains under kids.us are focusing on children and must agree to strong privacy procedures.

State Privacy Laws   A number of states have established privacy requirements for Internet-based information, and some have privacy rights built into their constitutions. This state-by-state regulation has caused a great deal of confusion for vendors, but Congress is so divided on Internet privacy that it has taken only limited steps to create general national Internet privacy laws. However, firms are placing pressure on Congress to create weak privacy laws that will preempt stronger state privacy regulations.

TEST YOUR UNDERSTANDING

10. a) Does the United States have a general privacy law? b) What does HIPAA protect? c) What protections does it require? d) What does GBLA protect? e) What protections does it require? f) What privacy protections are required for children? g) What protections are not required for children? h) Why is Kids.US important?

International Laws

Laws on personal privacy vary around the world. We will focus on Europe because the European Union has the most comprehensive system of data privacy laws.

European Union Charter of Fundamental Rights   The European Union has a **Charter of Fundamental Rights** to which all member countries must subscribe. Unlike the U.S. Constitution, the charter lists privacy as a fundamental freedom. Chapter II, Article 8 specifically requires the protection of personal data. Three protections are specifically listed in the article.

➤ Everyone has the right to the protection of personal data concerning him or her.

➤ Such data must be processed fairly for specific purposes and on the basis of the consent of the person concerned or some other legitimate basis laid down by law. Everyone has the right of access to data that has been collected concerning him or her, and the right to have it rectified.

➤ Compliance with these rules shall be subject to control by an independent authority.

This statement on privacy rights is strong and specific in its guarantees. The requirement for an independent privacy authority provides protection even against the government.

---

[21] By a quirk of naming, kids and us are both considered to be top-level domains, and so is the kids.us combination.

Data Protection Directive   This fundamental declaration of information privacy rights led to the 1995 **Data Protection Directive**,[22] which specified what personal information could be collected and how it could be used. This directive took effect in October 1998. It specified a large number of protections, including the following:

➤ The ability to opt out of many uses of personal data and opt-in protection for sensitive personal data such as medical conditions.

➤ Data subjects must be given access to their data for review and rectification.

➤ There must be recourse to an independent authority to enforce these protections.

Safe Harbor Protection for U.S. Companies   The Data Protection Directive specified that personal data could be transferred to countries outside the European Union only if those countries provide "adequate" protection for personal data. U.S. data privacy laws clearly are inadequate, raising the specter of U.S. firms not being able to work well with European companies. This could severely harm the more than $100 billion in annual trade between the United States and the European Union countries.

Fortunately, the E.U. and the U.S. Department of Commerce were able to negotiate a **safe harbor** agreement in 2000. This agreement specifies a stringent set of rules for data protection. These rules include such things as not transferring personal data to a third party without the explicit agreement of the subject (opt in) and giving subjects access to their data for review and correction. These rules also mandate the maintenance of security to protect stored data from illegitimate access. The Federal Trade Commission was given power to regulate fidelity to safe harbor provisions.

U.S. companies agreeing to these rules for processing personal data from the E.U. would be allowed to take data out of the E.U. For financial firms, however, the United States has argued that the Gramm-Leach-Bliley Act (GBLA) discussed earlier in this chapter should satisfy the adequacy requirement without the need to resort to the safe harbor protections. The E.U. has rejected this interpretation because GBLA does not provide all of the protections of the directive; for example, GBLA allows data sharing among firms in ways that are specifically protected by the E.U. directive.

Spreading Commercial Privacy Protections   Although the E.U. Data Protection Directive is the most important international privacy rule, many other nations with which U.S. firms do business also are developing strong commercial data privacy laws. Canada, for instance, has implemented the Personal Information Protection and Electronic Documents Act, which creates similar prohibitions against cross-border transfers of personal data to countries without similar privacy protections.

In this increasingly protective international environment, a number of multinational firms are creating global privacy protections consistent with those of the E.U. Data Privacy Directive, rather than creating different privacy protections in different countries.

---

[22] Directive 95/46/EC, on the protection of individuals with regard to the processing of personal data and on the free movement of such data.

TEST YOUR UNDERSTANDING

11. a) What data privacy protections are provided in the E.U. Charter of Fundamental Rights? b) What protections does the E.U. Data Privacy Directive provide? c) Why are safe harbor provisions important for U.S. firms? d) What is the conflict over U.S. banking privacy laws? e) Why are some U.S. firms creating global privacy protections consistent with the E.U. Data Privacy Directive?

EMPLOYEE WORKPLACE MONITORING

Another individual privacy concern is **employee workplace monitoring**—the monitoring of employee websurfing, e-mail, and other communications, as well as the examination of files on an employee's office PC.

Monitoring Trends

The American Management Association (AMA) (www.amanet.org) has been surveying employee workplace monitoring among U.S. firms since 1997. During that time, it has seen a strong increase in monitoring. In 1997, for instance, only 15% of all firms monitored e-mail messages. In 2001, this had risen to 46%. During that same period, the monitoring of files on computers rose from 14% to 36%. In addition, 63% of all companies monitored Internet connections in 2001. (This category was added in 2000, so trend data is not available.)

The American Management Association survey counts both systematic (regular) monitoring and spot checks. A survey by the Privacy Foundation in 2001 looked only at the more intrusive practice of systematic monitoring. It found that 35% of all firms were conducting systematic monitoring in 2001.

In addition, firms are taking action when they see violations of their policies. In the 2001 American Management Association survey, 76% of the firms reported that they had disciplined workers, and 31% reported dismissing employees. Still, companies only intensively investigate about 1% of their employees in any given year.[23]

Why Monitor?

Why are companies engaging in monitoring? One answer is simply that technology makes it increasingly possible. However, companies do have serious concerns pushing them to monitor employee computer behavior at work.

Loss of Productivity

One concern of companies is that employees will waste excessive amounts of time at work on personal e-mail and personal websurfing. In 2001, 60% of workers surveyed said that they send personal e-mail and surf the Internet at work.[24] Furthermore, 90% of the respondents said that they spend at least 30 minutes a day surfing the World

---

[23] Declan McCullagh, "Employers Hold Off On Monitoring," ZDNET.com, October 29, 2002. zdnet.com.com/2102–1105–963677.html.

[24] Scarlet Pruitt, "Is E-Mail Putting Your Company at Risk?" *PC World*, September 12, 2001. www.pcworld.com/news/article/0,aid,61623,tk,dn091201X,00.asp.

MONITORING TRENDS

American Management Information survey

E-mail monitoring use from 15% to 46% between 1997 and 2001

Internet connections in 2001: 63% monitored

In 2001, 76% had disciplined an employee; 31% had terminated an employee

WHY MONITOR?

Loss of productivity because of personal Internet and e-mail use

Significant personal Internet and e-mail use is occurring

Employees and companies generally agree that a small amount of personal use is acceptable

Biggest concern is abnormally heavy personal use

Some employees are addicted to personal use

Harassment

Title VII of the Civil Rights Act of 1964: sexual and racial harassment

Pornography, other adult content are fairly common

Monitoring for keywords can reduce pornography and harassment and provide a legal defense

Viruses and other malware due to unauthorized software

Trade secrets: Both sending and receiving must be stopped

Commercially damaging communication behavior: Can harm reputation, generate lawsuits, and run afoul of stock manipulation laws

THE LEGAL BASIS FOR MONITORING

Electronic Privacy Communications Act of 1986

Allows reading of communications by service provider (firm)

Allows reading if subject agrees (make condition of employment)

Employee has no right to privacy when using corporate computers

In United States, at-will employees can be disciplined, dismissed easily

Must not discriminate by selective monitoring

Unions often limit disciplining, agreement to be monitored

In multinational firms, stronger privacy and employment rules might exist

SHOULD A FIRM MONITOR? (DANGER OF BACKLASH)

COMPUTER AND INTERNET USE POLICY SHOULD SPECIFY THE FOLLOWING

No expectation of privacy

Business use only

No unauthorized software

No pornography and harassment

Damaging communication behavior

Punishment for violating the policy

EMPLOYEE TRAINING

Figure 12-3   Employee Workplace Monitoring

Wide Web. In 2001, the Pew Internet & American Life Project found that a quarter of those who made gift purchases online did so from their office.[25]

Although webserving appears to be a serious concern, personal e-mail use at work appears to be fairly moderate. A 2002 study on e-mail at work by the Pew Internet & American Life Project (www.pewinternet.org) surveyed more than 1,000 employees who use e-mail at work. Of these employees, 74% said that they send only a little e-mail at work or none at all. This was especially true in larger firms, which are much more likely to have policies against personal e-mail at work. However, some employees reportedly sent and received a good deal of personal e-mail at work.

Interestingly, a 2000 survey of both employees and companies by Vault.com found that most individuals and corporations are tolerant of modest amounts of personal Internet use at work. Seventy-five percent of employees reported doing an hour or less of websurfing per day, and 52% reported sending five or fewer personal messages per day. Fifty percent of employers, in turn, felt that up to 30 minutes per day of websurfing would be acceptable per day, and another quarter would permit up to an hour. Fifty-three percent of employers felt that up to five personal e-mails would be acceptable each day.

What *is* of a concern for employers is the heavy personal user. In the Vault.com survey, a quarter of the employees admitted to spending more than an hour per day online, and 13% reported spending more than 2 hours per day online for personal matters. In some cases, employees seem addicted to personal Internet use.

To address concerns over lack of productivity, some firms monitor the length of time employees spend on the Internet each day and also monitor e-mail sent into and out of the corporation.

Harassment
Title VII of the **Civil Rights Act of 1964** prohibits sexual and racial harassment. Damages in harassment cases can be large. For example, a petroleum company paid more than $2 million to four women offended by messages they received on the firm's e-mail system.[26] Although the U.S. Supreme Court has ruled that a single instance of potentially harassing behavior is not actionable in court,[27] a repeated pattern of unwanted e-mail or the repeated display of pornography on work PC screens can easily lead to lawsuits. Obviously, firms wish to avoid these lawsuits and, more positively, to protect their employees. Under some circumstances, in fact, the very act of attempting to monitor and stop harassing material can act as a defense in legal cases.[28]

Harassing content appears to be all too common at work. In 1999, a survey by Elron Software found that 64% of adults who send or receive personal e-mail at work

25   Mike Koller, "Workers Shopping on Customer Time," *InternetWeek*, December 28, 2001. www.internetweek.com/story/INW20011228S001.
26   Michael Osterman, "Today's Focus: E-Mail Policies Can Cut Liabilities," *Network World Newsletter: Michael Osterman on Messaging*, April 17, 2001.
27   *Computerworld*, "Court Says Isolated Crude Remark Not Harassment," April 23, 2001. www.cnn.com/2001/LAW/04/23/scotus.workplace.speech.ap/index=html.
28   Specifically, sexual harassment by a fellow employee can result in penalties against the firm if the company was not diligent in looking for harassment. However, diligence gives no protection against sexual harassment by a supervisor. Raymond R. Panko and Hazel Glenn Beh, "Monitoring for Pornography and Sexual Harassment," *Communications of the ACM*, 45(1), January 2002, pp. 84–87.

said that they sent or received adult-oriented personal e-mail. In 2002, Jupiter Media Metrix, Inc. found that 37% of all Internet users surf adult sites, and SexTracker found that 70% of porn surfing is done at work. A 2001 survey by the Center for Online Addiction in 2001 found that 55% of all workers sent potentially offensive messages at least once a month.

To cope with harassment concerns, many firms scan the content of downloaded webpages and e-mail messages. Typically, this scanning searches for keywords that indicate sexual or racial content, such as the word "sex," the string "XXX," and racial epithets. Repeated scanning hits suggest a pattern of behavior that needs to be investigated. Some firms then examine the files on the employee's disk drives to see if the pattern seen in scanning is real or apparent.

Viruses and Other Damaging Content

In 2001, a third of the employees in one survey admitted that they had sent or received virus-infected e-mail more than once.[29] Companies are concerned that personal use is more likely to lead to viruses than company use, and firms are concerned that sending messages from company e-mail addresses will make it easier for spammers to find the firm.

In addition, employees have a tendency to bring in personal software on disks or to download software from websites or FTP sites. This software could contain Trojan horses or might violate company policy, for instance in the cases of prohibited instant messaging software or pirated software.

To reduce the number of virus attacks and other malware attacks, many firms prohibit the downloading of executable files through HTTP, FTP, and instant messaging. They also may scan traffic for unauthorized instant messaging and other unauthorized programs. Some firms periodically monitor the software on employee PCs to identify unauthorized software.

Trade Secrets and Commercially Damaging Behavior

Other dangers are that employees might do something to harm the company legally or do something to harm the company's reputation. In 2001, in a survey of 498 employees, 40% of the respondents admitted receiving confidential information about other companies.[30] This was a 356% increase over 1999. Receiving trade secrets can result in legal penalties against the company. If employees send trade secrets out of the firm, this can be even more damaging.

Disparaging remarks against the firm or against competitors made by employees in chat rooms or newsgroups also can be harmful, and any remarks made that might affect stock prices can result in prosecution under stock manipulation laws.

Some firms prohibit the uploading of files outside the firm without specific permission in order to prevent employees from uploading files with proprietary information. They also might scan e-mail for the addresses of competitors and for keywords linked to ongoing and proposed projects.

---

[29] Scarlet Pruitt, "Is E-Mail Putting Your Company at Risk?" *PC World*, September 12, 2001. www.pcworld.com/news/article/0,aid,61623,tk,dn091201X,00.asp.

[30] Scarlet Pruitt, "Is E-Mail Putting Your Company at Risk?" *PC World*, September 12, 2001. www.pcworld.com/news/article/0,aid,61623,tk,dn091201X,00.asp.

The Legal Basis for Monitoring

Is it legal for companies to read employee e-mail in the United States? The answer is yes, although this statement is a somewhat guarded one.

Electronic Communications Privacy Act

The Electronic Communications Privacy Act of 1986 (ECPA) broadly prohibits the interception of electronic communication both when it is occurring and after it is received and stored. Obviously, ECPA was created to prevent most monitoring.

However, ECPA provides two exceptions to its prohibition against reading traffic.[31] The first is that service providers may read messages. For internal mail systems and internal networks to carry HTTP and FTP traffic, the company is the service provider.

The second exception is that reading traffic is not prohibited if the user consents. Many firms now make consenting to having computer traffic monitored a condition of employment. Firms that do not specifically get employee consent may still be legally justified in employee monitoring, but the simple act of getting prior approval would reduce many possible legal hurdles if cases go to court.

Rights to Privacy

Many employees believe that they have a right to privacy when they use their e-mail or desktop PC. However, federal law in the United States does not create any **expectation of privacy**. E-mail and desktop PCs are the property of the employer. Sometimes, however, individual state laws may create some expectations of privacy, so blanket statements are dangerous.

It is good to cover this lack of privacy in employee training because of widespread beliefs to the contrary. In fact, in *Restuccia v. Burk Technologies, Incorporated*,[32] a Massachusetts court refused to give the firm a summary judgment against the employee because a failure to notify the employee that e-mail, backup tapes, and desktop computer files were not private. The judge required that this issue to be considered in the trial. In contrast, in *U.S. v. Simmons*,[33] the employer had an explicit policy that computers and e-mail were not private, and the courts upheld a search of the employee's computer.

Disciplining Employees

In general, companies have the right to discipline their **"at-will"** employees appropriately, and companies usually have widespread rights to punish or dismiss employees without long legal processes. As noted earlier, many companies already have disciplined employees for Internet-related actions, and the courts generally have upheld them. Again, however, varying state laws complicate matters somewhat.

---

[31]   Raymond R. Panko and Hazel Glenn Beh, "Monitoring for Pornography and Sexual Harassment," *Communications of the ACM,* 45(1), January 2002, pp. 84–87.
[32]   *Restuccia v. Burk Technologies, Inc.*, WL 1329386 (Mass. Super.).
[33]   *United States v. Mark L. Simmons*, 206 F.3d 392 (4th Cir. 2000).

Nondiscrimination

In investigations, it is important not to single out an employee for unrelated reasons before doing an investigation. It is imperative to cast the net widely and pursue investigations that result. Otherwise, employees might claim that they were singled out on the basis of age or some other factor irrelevant to the monitored behavior and so suffered discrimination. It is always unwise to single out a general problem employee and to look for ways to discipline that person.

Union Rules

Things are somewhat different if a firm is unionized. Contracts normally specify detailed processes for punishment and grievances. In addition, requiring existing employees to sign a statement agreeing to be monitored will require negotiation with the union, although it might be possible to put this agreement into hiring contracts as an initial condition of employment.

Multinational Firms

Multinational firms will find the monitoring climate different in different countries. Europe, as noted earlier in this chapter, has strong privacy laws. Countries also vary in their permissiveness for firms intercepting internal electronic communication. Unionization also varies widely among countries, as do laws for disciplining employees.

TEST YOUR UNDERSTANDING

12. a) According to the AMA, what fraction of all U.S. firms monitored Internet use in 2001? b) What percent say that they have dismissed employees for violations? c) For what reasons is monitoring done? d) Do most employers feel that a small amount of personal Internet use is acceptable? e) Why can monitoring Internet and e-mail use reduce harassment suits? f) Why can companies monitor employee communications despite ECPA? g) Should employees have an expectation of privacy for information in corporate e-mail and for information on their PCs? h) Do U.S.–based firms generally have wide latitude in dismissing employees under the law? i) How do unions limit this freedom? j) Do multinational firms generally have wide latitude in dismissing employees under the law?

Should a Firm Monitor?

Although monitoring is increasing and is generally legal, a question remains whether a firm *should* monitor its employees. The danger always exists that monitoring can create a backlash in employee morale and anger that can be damaging to the firm. This is especially likely if the introduction of monitoring is handled poorly.

For example, when the federal judicial system decided to monitor its own employees, including judges, some judges rebelled. A council of senior judges in the Ninth Circuit ordered their IT staff to disable the monitoring software on 10,000 computers used by judges and other employees. At the time of this writing, the U.S. Judicial Conference, which is a panel that sets policies for the Federal Court, is reviewing the matter. In such a highly charged environment, fully re-imposing monitoring would be difficult.

Computer and Internet Use Policy

Any firm that is considering employee workplace monitoring should have a strong **computer and Internet use policy** that lays out what employees may do, what they may not do, and how they may be monitored and disciplined.

No Expectation of Privacy

The policy needs to have a strong statement that e-mail, the employee's desktop computer, and corporate servers are not private and that the company has the right to inspect them at any time.

Business Use Only

The policy also needs to state that all company resources are to be used for business purposes only, although allowing a small, specified amount of personal use might be permitted explicitly.

No Unauthorized Software

The policy should state that no unauthorized software may be installed on the user's desktop computer.

No Pornography and Harassment

A strong statement should make clear that neither sexual nor racial harassment will be tolerated and that pornography is explicitly prohibited.

Proper Commercial Behavior

A strong statement should address the fact that in dealing with the outside world, the employee is the firm's representative, so no "personal" comment that affects the firm is really personal. Sending and receiving trade secrets also should be strongly prohibited.

Punishment

The policy should state potential punishments for violating these policies as well as who should administer the punishment and what evidence will be considered.

Employee Training

Employees need to be trained in this computer and Internet use policy. Many employees have incorrect beliefs about the privacy of their computers and other usage issues. Even in seemingly clear areas such as pornography, confusion often arises. For example, one employee accused of downloading pornography admitted surfing porn sites but argued that he had visited only free sites and had not paid for them, so his actions should be acceptable.[34]

TEST YOUR UNDERSTANDING

13. a) Why might firms not wish to monitor their employees? b) What should be in a computer and Internet use policy? c) Why is employee training necessary?

---

[34] Vince Tuesday, "The Naked Truth about Porn Surfers," *Computerworld*, June 24, 2002. computerworld.com/securitytopics/security/story/0,10801,72166,00.html.

GOVERNMENT SURVEILLANCE

Although there is a trend toward greater commercial data privacy around the world, we have seen that the opposite is true for employee workplace monitoring. Government surveillance also is increasing, especially in the wake of the September 11, 2001, terrorist attacks.

U.S. Tradition of Protection from Improper Searches

The U.S. Constitution does not include explicit privacy protection, but American experiences with British rule prompted the framers of the Constitution to add protection against unreasonable search and seizure as the Fourth Amendment, which states, "The right of the people to be secure in their persons, houses, papers, and effects, against unreasonable searches and seizures, shall not be violated, and no warrants shall issue, but upon probable cause, supported by oath or affirmation, and particularly describing the place to be searched, and the persons or things to be seized."

Strict Limitations

The Fourth Amendment provides a number of limitations on searches. First, searches must be limited in what will be searched and seized so that law enforcement agencies cannot go on fishing expeditions and search houses indiscriminately.

Probable Cause

Another crucial term is **probable cause**, which means that the law enforcement agency must have good reason to suspect that a crime has occurred or is about to occur. This is a fairly high standard of proof. In practice, probable cause normally must be presented to a judge, who will issue a highly specific search warrant. In extreme cases, however, warrantless searches are possible if the officer has probable cause and if the delay will cause serious problems.

The Hoover Backlash

More recently, J. Edgar Hoover ran the U.S. Federal Bureau of Investigation (FBI) for many years. During that period, he accomplished many things. However, during the 1960s, Hoover had the FBI conduct surveillance on many individuals and domestic groups who were merely protesting government actions regarding civil rights and the Vietnam War. When the extent of this illegal domestic surveillance was revealed, the FBI was widely viewed with suspicion for many years.

TEST YOUR UNDERSTANDING

14. a) Does the U.S. Constitution specify a privacy right? b) What protections does the Fourth Amendment provide? c) What is probable cause? d) What are warrants? e) Why have many people distrusted the FBI?

Telephone Surveillance

Wiretapping

Two laws have long given U.S. enforcement agencies the ability to gather data on the telephone conversations of suspects. The **Federal Wiretap Act of 1968** did this for

U.S TRADITION OF PROTECTION FROM IMPROPER SEARCHES

No privacy protection in Constitution
Fourth Amendment: No unreasonable searches and seizures
    Can search only with probable cause
    Can only search specific things
FBI misuse of data collection during Hoover's leadership

TELEPHONE SURVEILLANCE

Wiretapping
    Federal Wiretap Act of 1968 for domestic crimes
    Foreign Intelligence Surveillance Act of 1978 (FISA) for international terrorists and
        agents of foreign governments
    Need warrant with probable cause and inability to get information by other means
Pen registers and trap and trace orders
    Pen registers: List of outgoing telephone numbers called
    Trap and trace: List of incoming telephone numbers
    Not as intrusive as wiretap because content is not captured
    Electronic Communications Privacy Act of 1986 allows
    Must be based on information to be collected being likely to be relevant to ongoing
        investigation (weak)
    Judge cannot turn down warrant
Communications Assistance for Law Enforcement Act of 1994
    Requires communication providers to install the technology needed to be able to
        provide data in response to warrants
Patriot Act of 2001
    Extends roving wiretaps to FISA
    Get billing information from telecommunications providers

INTERNET SURVEILLANCE

Extends pen register and trap and trace to Internet traffic
Same weak justification as for telephone traffic
But much more intrusive: e-mail addresses, URLs (which can be visited), etc.

CARNIVORE

Monitoring computer placed at ISP
FBI installs Carnivore computer, collects information
Can limit filtering to restrictions of warrant
No accountability through audit trails

(continued)

Figure 12-4   Government Surveillance

THE POSSIBLE FUTURE OF GOVERNMENT SURVEILLANCE

Intrusive airport security through face scanning
Possible national ID cards
New ability to gather and analyze information from many databases

Figure 12-4   (Continued)

domestic crimes. The **Foreign Intelligence Surveillance Act (FISA) of 1978** extended this to the surveillance of foreign terrorist groups and agents of foreign powers.

To conduct wiretaps, an agency needs a **wiretap warrant**, and this requires a finding of probable cause and a finding that normal investigative procedures have been tried and failed. These are strong requirements. A special court has been set up for FISA wiretaps.

Pen Registers and Trap and Trace Orders

Law enforcement agencies also are able to get less intrusive information from telephone conversations through techniques called pen registers and trap and trace orders. With **pen registers**, the telephone company receives a warrant to record the telephone numbers *dialed by a subject's telephone*. In a **trap and trace** order, the telephone company receives a warrant to record the numbers of telephones *calling the subject.*

Pen registers and trap and traces are less intrusive than wiretaps because nobody listens to the actual conversations. Consequently, warrants can be issued with a lesser degree of certainty. The legal standard set forth in the Electronic Communications Privacy Act of 1986 for issuing pen register and trap and trace warrants is that law enforcement officials must state that "the information likely to be obtained is relevant to an ongoing criminal investigation" (18 USC 3121 et seq.). If the government makes that assertion, the judge *must* grant the warrant.

Communications Assistance for Law Enforcement Act

The **Communications Assistance for Law Enforcement Act of 1994** required telecommunications providers to provide the technology needed to collect information for law enforcement agencies when issued warrants.

The Patriot Act of 2001

The **Patriot Act of 2001** extended FISA by allowing **roving wiretaps**. Traditional wiretaps are only issued for a single telephone line. However, criminals can move from one communication system to another. ECPA previously provided this for domestic crimes; the Patriot Act of 2001 extended roving wiretaps to the surveillance of foreign terrorists and agents of foreign governments.

The Patriot Act also expanded on the information that law enforcement could get from telecommunications providers to include billing financial information.

Internet Surveillance

The Patriot Act also extended pen register and trap and trace principles to the Internet. The act extends pen registry and trap and trace information to be collected to "dialing, routing, and signaling information." The act did not specify what these terms meant, but it is likely that they include e-mail addresses, URLs, and other information that is much more revealing than the telephone numbers that were previously the only data provided. A URL, for example, may allow a law enforcement officer to see the precise information the subject saw.

The Patriot Act also allows ISPs to cooperate voluntarily (without a warrant) in investigations of hacking, where delay might cause serious problems. Law enforcement must be involved in a lawful investigation, must have reasonable grounds to believe that the information will be relevant to an investigation, and must ensure that only the suspect's communications will be intercepted.

Carnivore

Although the Patriot Act only clarified the collection of Internet surveillance information in 2001, the FBI had been using an Internet surveillance system for a few years. This is **Carnivore**, which was renamed DCS1000 after bad publicity in 2000. Carnivore places a computer at an ISP. This computer captures all packets, but its filters only save information from some packets and then only selected information. Filtering in Carnivore is highly adaptable so that the requirements of different warrants can be fulfilled.

TEST YOUR UNDERSTANDING

15. a) What is necessary for a wiretap warrant to be issued? b) Distinguish between pen registers and trap and trace orders. c) Why are pen registers and trap and trace orders less invasive than wiretaps? d) What is needed for a pen register or a trap and trace order? e) Can a judge turn down a request for a pen register or a trap and trace order? f) What are roving wiretaps? g) How did the Patriot Act extend pen registers and trap and trace orders? h) Why do these extensions reduce privacy? i) What voluntary cooperation between law enforcement and ISPs does the Patriot Act allow? j) What data does Carnivore collect?

The Future of Government Surveillance

Although government surveillance still is limited in the United States and other democracies, disturbing possibilities loom on the horizon.

Airport Security

For the near term, a number of airports already conduct face recognition scans of people in public areas. Although the purpose is to look for terrorists and criminals, the technology also could be used for the renewed Hooverian surveillance of mere protesters and other innocent groups.

In airports and other public areas, no one can have a legal expectation of privacy. However, limits on technology still gave a reasonable degree of privacy even in such areas. If face recognition technology improves, the real loss of privacy from face scanning in public areas will be substantial.

Prospects for National ID Cards and Database Data Mining

One concern of civil libertarians is the prospect of national identification cards that could be used to trace people anywhere they go in their countries. Japan already has created a national ID card system, but the exposure of sensitive data and other difficulties initially created a large number of problems. Some provincial governments even balked at implementing the system.

In fact, however, credit card databases and other databases already contain a great deal information that could be tracked to reveal a great deal about individuals. Data mining, including fuzzy logic approaches that can find nonobvious relationships in the data, allows an unprecedented level of information finding if credit card databases and other databases can be combined for analysis.

In one development, the Defense Advanced Research Projects Agency in the U.S. Department of Defense established the **Information Awareness Office** in 2002.[35] The job of this office is to develop ways to analyze data across multiple public and commercial databases for government surveillance. This office is headed by John Poindexter, President Regan's national security advisor who was convicted of lying to Congress in the Iran-Contra scandal but whose conviction was overturned on appeal because of his immunized testimony given to Congress. The office's main project is Total Information Awareness.

TEST YOUR UNDERSTANDING

16. a) Describe potential future trends in government surveillance b) Why is each dangerous?

CYBERWAR AND CYBERTERROR

Individual attackers already have done billions of dollars in damage through viruses and worms. However, concentrated attacks by groups of terrorists or national governments could do tens of billions of dollars to hundreds of billions of dollars in damage and might even result in the loss of life.

Threats

Attacking the IT Infrastructure

Both cyberterrorism and cyberwar involve two related threats. The first is to attack a country's **IT infrastructure**. Attackers might attempt to bring down the Internet within a country by targeting its ISPs or even bring down the Internet worldwide. Attackers also might target a country's economic system by attacking critical banking systems or the country's stock market.

Attacking the Physical Infrastructure

Second, attackers could use the Internet and IT in general to attack a country's **physical infrastructure** by disrupting a country's electrical system, transportation system, water system, or other physical infrastructure. Many of these systems are highly dependent on computers and networks. In the worst cases, attackers could take over IT control

---

[35] Gary H. Anthes, "Global Surveillance: The Government's Plan," *Computerworld*, November 25, 2002. www.computerworld.com/securitytopics/security/privacy/story/0,10801,76117,00.html.

THREATS

Attacking the IT infrastructure
Using computers to attack the physical infrastructure (electrical power, sewage, etc.)
Using the Internet to coordinate attacks

CYBERWAR

Conducted by governments
Direct damage
Disrupting command and control
Intelligence gathering
Propaganda
Industrial espionage
Integrating cyberwar into war-fighting doctrines

CYBERTERRORISM

By semi-organized or organized groups
Psychological focus
    Indirect economic impacts (for example, losses because of reduced travel after
        September 11, 2001, terrorist attacks)
    Goals are publicity and recruitment
Indiscriminate damage
Hacktivism—politically motivated attacks by unorganized or loosely
    organized groups
Who is a terrorist? Spectrum from activism to full cyberterror

BUILDING A NATIONAL AND INTERNATIONAL
RESPONSE STRATEGY

National governments
    Coordinated responses
    Intelligence gathering
    Research and training
    Economic incentives
Private enterprise
    Importance of hardening individual firms
    Requiring hardening to meet responsibilities
Hardening the telecommunications infrastructure with decentralization and
    other methods
International cooperation is needed because of worldwide attackers

(continued)

Figure 12-5   Cyberwar and Cyberterror

HARDENING THE INTERNET

Hardening the underlying telecommunications system

Adding security to dialogs with VPNs

Hardening Internet protocols

 IETF is making progress by adding confidentiality, authentication, and other protections to core Internet protocols

 Generally not using digital certificates in a public key infrastructure for strong security

Making the Internet forensic

 ISPs might be forced to collect and retain data for long periods of time

 ISPs might be forced to do egress filtering to stop attacks at the source

 The cost to ISPs would be high

Figure 12-5   (Continued)

systems for power plants or other critical resources. Even if attackers can simply bring down critical control systems for extended periods of time, service to customers could be seriously affected.

Using the Internet to Coordinate Attackers

In addition, attackers can use the Internet to coordinate cyberattacks and physical attacks. It is nearly impossible to trace communication through the Internet, particularly if attackers use tools to make themselves anonymous. Strong encryption, in turn, can make their communication impossible to decipher even if the attackers are identified.

TEST YOUR UNDERSTANDING

 17. What two threats do cyberwar and cyberterror present?

Cyberwar

Direct Damage

In **cyberwar**, a country's military makes a concerted attack upon another country's IT infrastructure, physical infrastructure, or both. A major goal of cyberwar is to do a massive amount of damage in a brief period of time, often in conjunction with a traditional physical military attack.

Disrupting Command and Control

One of the first goals of any physical military attack is to bring down a country's **command and control system** so that leaders cannot direct their troops effectively. This typically is done by bombing communication facilities. However, it might be possible to do this more rapidly and safely by staging a cyberattack on a country's telecommunications infrastructure.

Intelligence

Another goal of the military is surveillance—gathering **intelligence** about enemy intentions and troop dispositions. The United States and several other countries have implemented the **Echelon** system to intercept communications worldwide. Echelon and systems like it can capture military planning information if it is not properly encrypted. Even if messages cannot be decrypted, data from these systems can even be used in traffic analysis to analyze changes in communication patterns that could indicate troop movement or other activities.

Propaganda

During war, countries often use **propaganda** to attempt to weaken the morale of the enemy's government, troops, and population. During the Kosovo war, the United States sent repeated e-mail over the Internet to supporters of the Yugoslavian leadership telling them that their economic assets would be targeted if they continued to support President Milosevic.

Sometimes, it is desirable for propaganda purposes *not* to attack the Internet within a country. During the Kosovo war, the United States reportedly refrained from attacking the Internet in Yugoslavia so that unfiltered news from the outside world could reach citizens directly.

Industrial Espionage

Even in times of peace, potential enemies traditionally have collected intelligence information about one another. After the end of the cold war, many national spy groups reportedly turned increasing attention to industrial espionage, in which they focused on stealing technological or business information to assist their country's firms.

Integrating Cyberwar into War-Fighting Doctrine

It is difficult to know the capabilities of nations for waging cyberwar because countries understandably keep this information top secret. However, the United States and many other countries are believed to have active cyberwar programs.

A major challenge in any case will be to integrate cyberwar technologies into overall **war-fighting doctrines**. It often takes a long time after a weapon is developed to learn how to integrate it into general war-fighting techniques. For example, when airplanes first appeared, they were viewed primarily as scouting tools. Only later were the offensive capabilities of airplanes to attack ground forces realized, and even then, it took many years to integrate air power into air-land battle strategies that combined aircraft with land battles.

TEST YOUR UNDERSTANDING

18. a) What actions can be taken in cyberwar? b) Why is integrating cyberwar capabilities with general war-fighting doctrines important?

Cyberterrorism

In **cyberterrorism**, the attackers are not national governments but rather groups of terrorists. However, national governments sometimes support terrorists, so the distinction between cyberwar and cyberterror is not entirely clean.

A Psychological Focus

Indirect Economic Impacts   Although cyberwar usually is intense for a prolonged period, terrorist attacks tend to be sporadic and limited. The actual damage done often is far less important than the spreading of terror or at least uncertainty. For example, the direct economic damage of the September 11, 2001, terrorist attacks on the World Trade Center and Pentagon was far smaller than the economic losses caused by subsequent reduced travel by worried Americans and foreign tourists.

Publicity and Recruitment   Terrorists are also concerned with bringing publicity to their causes. Even attacks that are universally reviled can be effective by focusing attention on the terrorist's causes and as a tool for recruiting new members.

Indiscriminate Damage

One concern of national cyberwar efforts is how to disrupt the Internet and other communications within a target country without doing wider damage to international communications. Terrorists do not face that concern. Terrorists do not belong to nations, and Internet use is concentrated in rich countries, so damage caused by a broad attack would be asymmetrically high in developed countries. Bringing down the entire worldwide Internet is an attractive goal, as is launching a devastating global worm or virus.

Hacktivism

Although one usually thinks of cyberterror attacks by established terrorist groups, a strong recent trend has been **hacktivism**—politically motivated attacks by unorganized or loosely organized groups.

During the Kosovo war, for instance, the United States bombed the Chinese embassy in Yugoslavia. A barrage of cyberattacks from China on U.S. websites and other targets immediately followed this. U.S. hackers quickly retaliated. Another round of U.S.–China hacktivism followed the downing of a U.S. spy plane off Chinese waters and the death of a Chinese pilot. After the September 11, 2001, attacks, attacks on Arab websites and other Internet resources were widespread. Arabs and Israeli hackers have been attacking one another's computers for several years.

So far, hacktivists seem to have engaged in spontaneous attacks that were not co-ordinated beyond the informal communication that has long existed among hackers. However, given the technical capabilities of hackers, it would not be difficult to foresee groups of hackers banding together to produce coordinated attacks that go far beyond the simple website defacement and other vandalism attacks that have characterized hacktivism attacks to date.

Who Is a Terrorist?

Given the growing use of hacktivism, who is a terrorist? Many groups that hack for polit-ical reasons have been admired by their sides, so blanket attacks on hacktivists might not be popular. In addition, the dividing line between acceptable activism and terrorist hacktivism often is not clear in practice. When do protests and civil disobedience rise to a level that could be called terrorism? The answer is more political than legal.

In addition, what about an individual virus releaser who does millions or even billions of dollars in damage? One could argue that such large-scale attacks on the Internet should be viewed as terrorism. Certainly, the short jail terms under most current laws for widespread virus releases do not seem to fit the magnitude of the damage done. Although a growing number of countries, including the United States, now impose up to life sentences for attacks that cause or threaten to cause the loss of life, perhaps wide economic damage also should lead to long sentences.

TEST YOUR UNDERSTANDING

19. a) Why does cyberterrorism focus on psychological impacts? b) Why will terrorists do things that national governments will not? c) What is hacktivism? d) Why might individual virus releasers be considered terrorists?

Building a National and International Response Strategy

What would happen if the United States or another country were subjected to a large-scale cyberwar or cyberterror attack? Today, the answer is that national responses would be almost universally inadequate. Quite simply, nations are not ready for massive cyberattacks.

National Governments

Coordinated Responses National governments must lead during times of crisis. This includes having an action plan in advance and preparing to implement the plan. However, countries have not yet developed these plans, which would require the massive coordination of many agencies. Consequently, if major attacks occurred, government responses would be chaotic.

Intelligence Gathering The best way to foil an attack is to learn about it in advance and stop it before it occurs or at least prepare for it. As noted earlier in this chapter, the Echelon system created by the United States and other governments does massive snooping on international communication. However, encryption and simpler ploys can make this type of information collection relatively ineffective.

Another approach is to infiltrate hacker groups. To do this, government agents can break into protected systems and post their successes on major hacking sites. After a reputation is built this way, agents can communicate directly with hackers and perhaps even learn of future planned attacks. It would be especially important to penetrate hacktivist groups in order to know what they are planning and perhaps even to point them at a target in a deniable way.

Research and Training National governments also could become more heavily involved with security research and training. Although security companies already conduct a great deal of research, national programs to improve security technology in general through research may be needed to ward off massive attacks. In addition, one problem facing corporations that wish to increase their security is that so few IT professionals are trained in security, especially the information systems majors that tend to work within end-user corporations. In 2002, the United States created a multibillion-dollar program to improve security research and security training.

Economic Incentives Corporations have been reluctant to harden their systems heavily due to high costs and the operational unpleasantness that living with hardened systems inevitably brings. Their efforts to date are roughly sufficient for the level of hacking we see today. Getting firms to spend vast amounts of money for a remote cyberwar threat, however, will be difficult. Governments might have to provide financial incentives such as tax credits or even direct investment.

Private Enterprise
The Importance of Hardening Individual Firms   Individual companies also will have to be involved in protection against cyberterror and cyberwar. To date, most firms have done a poor job of hardening their corporate IT infrastructures. Even patching all existing corporate systems across many firms would go a long way toward making the national infrastructure difficult to attack. If individual firms are not hardened, there is no hope of hardening the national infrastructure. Conversely, if individual firms were well hardened, cyberterror and cyberwar would be extremely difficult.

Requiring the Hardening of Individual Firms: Lawsuits   In general, companies will have to take more responsibility for their systems. Today, denial-of-service attacks often involve the taking over of systems in one firm and using them to attack other firms. Companies whose computers are taken over and turned into zombie attackers today usually are considered victims. However, their negligence in protecting their systems contributes to the harm done to other firms. In addition, poor antivirus policies and practices cause viruses and worms to spread widely. Lawsuits against negligent firms and perhaps even laws to require good security practice might be needed to get firms to act responsibly.

Requiring the Hardening of Individual Firms: ISP Requirements   A small but growing number of Internet service providers require their customers to apply reasonable security protections to their network. The motivations for doing so are the costs of dealing with problems created by customers and the danger of the entire ISP being blacklisted by other ISPs and corporations. Other ISPs and individual corporations may refuse to carry the packets of blacklisted ISPs.

The Communications Infrastructure
Internet communication and other communication tend to run over a country's basic telephone infrastructure. Often, this infrastructure is highly vulnerable to cyberattack and physical attack. For instance, the World Trade Center was a major nexus for communications facilities, and disruptions were widespread and prolonged after the attack for many services. Although the Internet continued to function, this was hardly surprising because the Internet itself was not attacked directly.

One problem with national telecommunications infrastructures is that *many* key points linking major trunk lines and carrier interconnections are highly concentrated. A relatively few physical attacks could bring down a great deal of a country's telecommunications infrastructure, perhaps for a prolonged period of time. We need to consider what would be needed to redistribute functionality to make our telecommunications infrastructure more secure.

International Cooperation
Countries cannot stand alone in their planning. Attacks often come from hackers in other countries. Countries are beginning to develop joint plans to track down hackers and extradite them if attacks occur. This cooperation is just beginning, however.

U.S. Plans

In 2002, the U.S. federal government announced a broad program to increase Internet safety. Unfortunately, the program relies primarily on voluntary cooperation by companies and ISPs. As just noted, there is little evidence of willingness on their parts to increase security.

More controversially, the plan calls for measures to centralize Internet traffic data analysis to identify widespread attacks more quickly. There is some concern that the collected information could be used for surveillance instead of merely for early warning purposes.

TEST YOUR UNDERSTANDING

20.   a) Who must provide leadership in cyberattacks? b) What actions should governments take to reduce cyberattack dangers? c) Why is it important to harden individual firms? d) Why should firms be viewed as responsible for hardening their systems? e) Why must the telecommunications infrastructure be hardened? f) Why is international cooperation crucial?

Hardening the Internet

The Internet itself needs to be hardened, as well. Although it is sometimes said that the Internet was designed to withstand nuclear war, this was never true, and even if it were, hacking attacks might be far more damaging.

Hardening the Telecommunications System

As just noted, the telecommunications systems over which Internet traffic runs often are vulnerable to attack because of concentrated nexuses of communication lines. Furthermore, the Internet itself depends on access points to connect ISPs with one another and with backbone carriers. Relatively few major **access points** exist, and a handful of extremely large access points handle a great deal of traffic.

Adding Security to Dialogs

In Chapter 8, we saw virtual private networks, which essentially add security to dialogs despite the poor security of the Internet in general. However, although VPNs help individual companies, they do nothing to harden the Internet in general. In addition, if the Internet fails, VPNs will be useless.

Hardening Internet Protocols

One possibility is to harden Internet protocols by adding authentication, confidentiality, message integrity, and anti-replay protection. In fact, the IETF is already doing this broadly, although few updated protocols require the strong authentication that comes from public key infrastructures.

If IPsec were used widely, this alone would greatly strengthen the Internet. However, IPsec only works well on a large scale if a strong system exists for creating and managing digital certificates. This does not exist today, and it would be difficult to build a system that strongly authenticated digital certificate applicants so that certificates would not be issued to impostors.

More generally, the Internet has a number of supervisory protocols whose breakdown would cripple the Internet. For example, the Domain Name System (DNS) is needed for clients to find server hosts. Yet in 2002, a simple denial-of-service attack came close to crippling the 13 root DNS hosts. Even a moderately more sophisticated attack carried on over days might have caused widespread disruption.

The Internet has many other supervisory protocols. For instance, routing protocols are used by routers to exchange information about available routes. If a router can be taken over in order to feed false routing information to other routers, disruptions could be widespread. The Internet Engineering Task Force has been upgrading authentication and other elements of security for routing protocols and many other key supervisory protocols.

However, even these improvements generally lead to only moderately strong security. Worse yet, until they are widely and perhaps almost universally implemented, they will not provide protection.

Making the Internet Forensic

When the Internet was created, no anonymity existed. All hosts were large computers serving terminals, and every host had a fixed IP address. It was not difficult to trace attacks back to machines and to correlate attack times with login times for users of the computer.

Difficulty of Tracing IP Addresses   Today, however, the Internet has become fairly anonymous. IP addresses are given out to clients in ways that are difficult to trace, and IP address spoofing tends to be extremely easy to do. Attackers also can take over chains of computers, making trace-back to the source client difficult.

If we are to be able to combat terrorism, we need ways to make the Internet more forensic; that is, to make the Internet capable of tracing attacks.

Requiring ISPs to Retain Traffic Data   One way to do this is to require ISPs to maintain data on IP traffic for long periods of time. Today, ISPs either fail to collect this information or store it for only brief periods of time for billing purposes. Storage of traffic data for weeks or even months might be necessary to trace attackers. ISPs are extremely reluctant to do this, both to protect their customers and because of the costs that would be added by this storage.

As noted earlier, we have seen a long-term trend toward making ISPs data sources in investigations.

➤ The Communications Assistance for Law Enforcement Act of 1994 later required telecommunications providers to install the technology needed to collect information for law enforcement agencies when issued warrants.

➤ The Electronic Communication Privacy Act of 1986 traditionally required ISPs to keep their data secret except when required to reveal it through warrants. The Patriot Act of 2001 reversed the ECPA tradition of ISP secrecy and allowed ISPs to reveal information voluntarily in response to some investigations of hacking.

➤ The Homeland Security Act of 2002 broadened pen register and trap and trace orders to include information beyond telephone numbers, such as e-mail addresses and URLs. Although these acts require warrants, judges are required to issue these warrants when presented with law enforcement assertions of possible relevance to an ongoing investigation.

Requiring ISPs to do Ingress Filtering   In addition, ISPs should block attack traffic at the source. If an account is sending packets with spoofed IP addresses or is sending packets that clearly are probes or attack packets, the source ISP is a logical place to stop these attacks. Yet hackers today often can send massive barrages of attack packets from their homes with no adverse consequences. Again, however, cost is a major problem. Adding egress firewalls would cost a great deal of money, and ISPs would have to bear the cost burden.

In either the cases of traffic data storage or ISP customer data filtering, strong legal protections would be needed. Traffic data is extremely sensitive and should require probable cause and a warrant for analysis. Customer data filtering and even the dropping of customers who hack would require strong legal protection for ISPs and customers in order to prevent abuse.

Fines for Illegal Traffic   One possibility is to take the onus of responding to customer misbehavior off of ISPs by making the sending of attack packets a misdemeanor punishable by a significant fine and by taking the decision to drop customers out of the hands of ISPs and giving it to local authorities.

TEST YOUR UNDERSTANDING

21. a) What steps can be taken to harden the Internet? b) What actions might be forced upon ISPs?

CONCLUSION

In previous chapters, we looked inside the firm. In this final chapter, we looked at the legal and political environment outside the firm. Security professionals in firms need to understand this legal and political environment, and they need to be aware of the constant changes that are occurring in these areas.

The nightmare scenarios for IT security are cyberwar and cyberterror. These two threats can create damages that are one or two orders of magnitude greater than those we are experiencing today. If companies merely protect themselves from normal attacks, a cyberwar or major cyberterror attack could cut through the economy like butter. National security planning must be based on cyberwar and cyberterror, not ordinary cyberattacks. This might require burdening ISPs and corporations with costs that make only moderate sense for ordinary attacks.

THOUGHT QUESTIONS

1. Why do you think the United States has weak consumer privacy protection compared to Europe?
2. a) Argue for opt-in privacy. b) Argue for opt-out privacy.
3. Argue that firms should monitor their employee e-mail and Internet usage. Argue that they should not.
4. Suggest one thing not listed in the text that countries can do to protect themselves from massive cyberterror or cyberwar attacks.
5. Do you think a major cyberwar or cyberterror attack is likely in the next year?

Glossary

3DES (Triple DES). Extension to DES in which each block is encrypted three times. If three keys are used, can give an effective 168–bit key length.

802.1x. Authentication method for wired and wireless LANs.

802.11. Family of wireless LAN standards.

802.11i. Standard for the use of the 802.1x authentication method to 802.11 wireless LANs.

Access card. Card that contains information for access to buildings, doors, computers, or other resources.

Access control. The body of strategies and practices that a company uses to prevent improper access. The policy-driven limitation of access to systems, data, and dialogs.

Access control lists (ACLs). Ordered lists of firewall filtering rules that specify which packets should be allowed or denied.

Access control policy. Policy specifying access permissions (authorization) rules for a resource.

Access permissions (authorizations). Define whether a role or individual should have any access at all and, if so, exactly what the role or individual should be allowed to do to the resource.

Access point. 1. In wireless LANs, controls wireless devices and is a bridge between the main wired LAN and the wireless LAN. 2. On the Internet, location where ISPs interconnect to exchange traffic.

Accountability. Ensuring that if misbehavior happens, it will be clear who is responsible.

ACK (Acknowledgement). Message that acknowledges a correctly received message sent by the other party.

Acknowledgement (ACK). Message that acknowledges a correctly received message sent by the other party.

Acknowledgement number. Field that indicates which previous message is being acknowledged.

ACLs (Access control lists). Ordered lists of firewall filtering rules that specify which packets should be allowed or denied.

Active content. Program or script on a webpage or e-mail message with an HTML body.

Active Directory Users and Computers. On a Microsoft Windows server, an Microsoft Management Console (MMC) that manages resources across a domain.

Active Directory. Microsoft's directory server product.

Active fingerprinting. Sending messages whose responses will identify the manufacturer and version number of a program running on a prospective victim host.

Active Server Pages. Server-side programming language widely used on Microsoft Windows Server webservers.

Active-X. A programming language from Microsoft. Dangerous when used to create active content because it places no limits on program actions.

Address field. Field in a header that specifies the source or destination address.

Address spoofing. Replacing the sender's source address with another address. Usually used in IP addressing.

Administrative Tools. In recent Microsoft Windows Server, program group that contains most systems administration tools.

Administrator. Superuser account in Windows.

Advanced Encryption Standard (AES). New symmetric key encryption standard that is efficient in terms of processing power and memory and that can use key lengths of 128, 192, or 256 bits.

Adversary. An opponent; someone who attacks you.

AES. *See* Advanced Encryption Standard.

Aggregation. In IDSs, the collection of log event data from many individual log files around the network in a central integrated log.

AH (Authentication Header). IPsec header that offers authentication and message integrity but not confidentiality. May be used where confidentiality is illegal.

Air gap. Extreme protection technique in which a network is not connected to other networks. Especially useful in military security.

Alarm. Notification when an attack appears to be occurring. May only be issued for apparent incidents above a certain severity level.

Annual cost of protection. Annual threat severity minus annual cost of counter-measures.

Annual threat severity. Expected cost of an attack per year.

Anomaly detection analysis. IDS detection method in which current event patterns as a whole are compared to normal event patterns as a whole.

Anonymous websurfing services. Websurfing services that hide the websurfer's identity.

Anti-replay protection. Assurance that if an attacker captures a message and transmits it again later, the receiver will not accept the message.

Antivirus programs. Software designed to prevent viruses from spreading onto user computers and servers by filtering out viruses (and usually worms, Trojan horses, and other attack content).

Apache. Widely used webserver application on UNIX (including LINUX) computers.

Applicant. In authentication, the side that tries to prove its identity to the other party.

Application firewall. A firewall that screens packets based upon application layer content and behavior.

Application layer. For standards to allow the two application programs to work together.

Application layer authentication. Providing authentication at the application layer, usually as an additional line of defense in depth.

Application monitors. Type of host IDS that examines activities at the application level.

Archive. In e-mail, to store e-mail on tape for later retrieval.

ARPANET. The first packet-switched wide area network; precursor to the Internet.

ASCII. Code for representing simple English letters, digits, and other keyboard characters, plus a few control codes. Each character is represented by a seven-bit string, which is stored in a byte.

Asset. Anything a firm must protect, including such things as computers, networks, application programs, databases, and people.

Asset enumeration. Listing all assets that must be protected.

Asymmetrical warfare. The company has to close all security holes; the attacker has to find only one that is not closed.

Attachment. File delivered with an e-mail message. May be executable or contain a macro virus.

Attack automation. The use of a program that can carry out attacks without human intervention.

Attack software. Victimization software that allows an attacker to use a compromised computer to attack other computers.

Attacker-in-the-middle attack. Attack in which the attacker intercepts messages going between two parties. May read, delete, or modify messages after interception.

Audit. 1. When an attack team hired by the firm attempts to penetrate the system in order to identify security weaknesses. 2. When an auditor seeks to find problems in the way an organization is implementing security.

Audit logs. Log files that record who took what actions and when these actions were taken.

Authenticate. Prove the identity of someone claiming to be a particular person.

Authentication credentials. Things such as user names and passwords used in authentication.

Authentication Header (AH). IPsec header that offers authentication and message integrity but not confidentiality. May be used where confidentiality is illegal.

Authenticator. In Kerberos, information presented with a ticket that only the true party could send. Tested with information encrypted within the ticket that only the verifier can decrypt.

Authorizations (access permissions). Define whether a role or individual should have any access at all and, if so, exactly what the role or individual should be allowed to do to the resource.

Automated action. In IDSs, when an IDS takes preventive action without human intervention.

Autonomous. Capable of acting on its own.

Availability. Means that authorized users can get access to IT resources.

Backdoor. A way of getting back into a system easily.

Backdoor account. Account with full privileges that allows an attacker back in easily.

Backdoor Trojan. Trojan horse program that allows an attacker back in easily. Typically, a system file is replaced by a Trojan of the same name to make detection difficult.

Background checks. Investigation of a potential employee's past.

Backup. Periodic archival copying of program and data files to a storage medium.

Backup console. Computer from which multiple other computers can be backed up. No hardware is needed on computers that are being backed up.

Backup facility. A remote site a firm can use as a temporary IT site.

Backup retention plan. Policy for how long different types of backup media will be saved.

Banner. Login response that frequently divulges an operating system's or application program's manufacturer and version number.

Baselines. Prescriptions that go into detail about how a specific standard should be implemented with a specific technology.

Bastion host. Specially hardened server in a DMZ.

Batch mode. In a distributed IDS, mode of operation in which the agent sends log entries to the manager only periodically, in batches. Produces less load on computers than real-time transfer, but attacker can delete IDS files after the break-in but before transfer to hide all of their activities.

Batch scripts. Contain a series of individual commands to be executed. When a batch script name is given, the commands are executed in order.

Behavioral scanning. Antivirus identification by looking for suspicious activities in programs as they run.

Benign payload. Virus or worm payload that it not designed to do damage (but may do damage accidentally or that may be viewed by the victim as damaging).

Best practices. Descriptions of what the best firms in the industry are doing about security.

Biometric authentication. Authentication based on human physical and motion (bio) measurements (metrics).

BIOS password. Password you must type when your PC boots up. Can be defeated by removing battery from computer.

Black. Secret; used especially in military security.

Black hat hackers. Break into corporate networks for their own benefit.

Black hole. (verb) To deny all packets from an IP address or IP address range.

Blended threats. Automated attacks that combine the features of viruses, worms, and nonmobile malware; spread in multiple ways.

Block encryption. When the message to be encrypted is broken into blocks of fixed size and each block is encrypted.

Body. In e-mail, one of two main parts of an e-mail message. Contains narrative, graphical, or multimedia information to be conveyed to the user.

Border firewalls. Firewalls that screen packets passing between their private networks and external untrusted networks, especially the Internet.

Bourne Shell and Bourne Again Shell (BASH). Popular CLI shell programs in UNIX.

Breach. Successful attack.

Bridge. Device that connects two LANs of different technology; for instance, 802.3 and 802.11 technologies.

Brute-force guessing. Trying all possible passwords or keys in order to determine the correct one.

Buffer. Section of RAM programs use to store information temporarily.

Buffer overflow. If the attacker sends a message with more bytes than the programmer had allocated for a buffer, the attacker's information will spill over into other areas of RAM. This is a buffer overflow.

Bulk encryption. Encrypting messages and files of normal (long) lengths. Uses symmetric key encryption.

Business champions. Senior managers who not only support security actively but who also provide direction to the CSO on business issues and corporate directions.

Business continuity plan. Specifies how a company plans to restore core business operations when natural or human-made disasters occur. Broader than IT-oriented disaster recovery.

Business process analysis.   Identifying, describing, and prioritizing a firm's major business processes.

CA.   *See* certificate authority.

Carder.   Someone who steals credit card numbers.

Carnivore.   U.S. Internet law enforcement surveillance tool to capture selected information going through an ISP. Renamed DCS1000.

CBC.   *See* cipher block chaining.

Central security management console.   Computer from which multiple security systems can be managed.

Cert.   Another name for digital certificate (not mentioned in the text).

CERTs (Computer emergency response teams).   Teams created to handle security incidents above a certain level.

Certificate authority (CA).   An independent and trusted source of information about the public keys of true parties. Provides this information in a digital certificate.

Certificate revocation list (CRL).   List of the serial numbers of digital certificates revoked by a certificate authority.

Certification.   External evaluation of an employee's expertise.

CGI (Common Gateway Interface).   Popular but inefficient server-side programming language.

Chain of evidence.   Unbroken record of who had custody of evidence and how it was handled.

Challenge message.   In challenge-response authentication, the message sent by the verifier.

Challenge-Handshake Authentication Protocol (CHAP).   PPP authentication protocol in which the response message is created by adding a shared secret to the challenge message and then hashing the combination.

Challenge-response authentication.   An authentication in which the verifier sends a challenge message and the applicant sends a response message that proves its identity.

Change management process.   Process to follow when it is necessary to make updates to production server application software.

Change request.   A request to make a change in a production system. Only some employees should be allowed to make change requests.

CHAP (Challenge-Handshake Authentication Protocol).   PPP authentication protocol in which the response message is created by adding a shared secret to the challenge message and then hashing the combination.

Charter of Fundamental Rights.   European Union guarantees of basic rights and freedom, including privacy.

Chief security officer (CSO).   Director of the security function.

Children's Online Privacy Protection Act.   U.S. law that protects the privacy of children under 13 at websites.

Chmod.   In UNIX, the (change mode) command changes the owner, group, or world permissions.

Chown.   In UNIX, the chown command is used by the file owner or systems administrator to transfer ownership of the file to another user account.

Chroot.   UNIX command that allows a program to be run in a subdirectory although it thinks it is running in the root directory. Attackers who take over the program may be restricted to the chroot directory and its subdirectories.

CIA.   An acronym for confidentiality, integrity, and availability.

Cipher Block Chaining (CBC).   Block encryption method in which the ciphertext depends not only on the key and the plaintext but also on the previous block of ciphertext, or, in the case of the first block, on an initiation vector.

Ciphertext.   The result of encrypting plaintext. Can be sent with confidentiality.

Circles of trust.   In PGP, authentication based on a list of people you trust and sometimes on people trusted by people you trust. Dangerous because if one party misplaces trust, others may automatically trust an attacker.

Circuit firewall.   General-purpose proxy that can handle any type of application.

Civil Rights Act.   U.S. law protecting (among other things) employees from sexual or racial harassment. Displaying pornography in the workplace can be sexual harassment.

Class A.   IP addresses lie between 0.0.0.1 and 127.255.255.254. Traditionally assigned in blocks of 16,777,214 contiguous IP addresses. Now usually assigned to ISPs, who assign smaller blocks to customers.

Class B.   IP addresses that lie between 128.0.0.1 and 191.255.255.254. Traditionally assigned in blocks of 65,535 addresses.

Class C.   IP addresses that lie between 192.0.0.1 and 223.255.255.254. Traditionally assigned in blocks of 256 addresses, 254 of which may be assigned to hosts.

Classful addressing.   System of IP address allocation in which allocation sizes fall into three classes. Superceded by classful addressing.

Classified.   Military security system in which documents are rated for sensitivity. Different procedures are in place for using documents of different sensitivity.

Classless InterDomain Routing (CIDR).   System for assigning IP addresses to firms in blocks of flexible size.

Client firewall.   Firewall software on a client PC. Provides the last or only line of defense against attack packets.

CLIs (command-line interfaces).   Interfaces in which the user types commands at prompts.

Closed-circuit television (CCTV).   Technology used to monitor business premises.

Code inspection.   Examining a program's code, line by line. Traditionally done to find errors. In security, done to find security errors or malpractice.

Cold sites.   Backup sites that offer empty rooms; electrical power; heating, ventilation, and air conditioning; and connections to the outside world. To use a cold site, the company has to procure, bring in, and set up hardware; install software; and mount data.

Collusion.   When two or more people work together to commit a crime.

Command and control system.   Communication facilities by which a country controls its military.

Command-line interface (CLI).   User interface in which the user types commands at prompts.

Commercial vulnerability testing tools.   Tools that are specifically designed for vulnerability testing instead of attacking.

Common Gateway Interface (CGI).   Popular but inefficient server-side programming language.

Common word passwords.   Passwords that are ordinary words found in a dictionary, or passwords that are combinations of common words.

Communications Assistance for Law Enforcement Act.   U.S. law that requires telecommunications providers to install the technology needed to collect information for law enforcement agencies when issued warrants.

Comprehensive security.   The effort to close *all* avenues of attack.

Compromise.   To take over a computer.

Compulsory tunneling.   When tunneling is done whether or not the remote user wishes to have it done.

Computer and Internet use policy.   Policy statement that lays out what employees may do, what they may not do, and how they may be monitored and disciplined.

Computer Emergency Response Team/ Coordination Center (CERT/CC).   Center at Carnegie-Mellon University that provides information for corporate computer emergency response teams.

Computer emergency response teams (CERTs).   Teams created to handle security incidents above a certain level.

Computer Fraud and Abuse Act of 1986.   Act that first defined computer crimes under Section 1030 of Title 18 of the U.S. Code.

Computer Management.   A Windows 2000 MMC for many administrative tools to manage the local computer.

Computer-based firewall.   Firewall software added to a general-purpose computer.

Conduit.   Pipe through which wires run. Provides physical protection against wiretapping.

Confidentiality.   Freedom from the fear that messages are being read by eavesdroppers who should not be able to do so.

Configuration.   Most programs and devices have optional settings. Configuration is the choosing of specific optional settings.

Connectionless.   Service in which there is no formal opening or close and no management of messages in between. Each message is sent separately.

Connection-oriented. Service in which there is a formal opening, a formal close, and the management of messages in between.

Containment. In incident response, preventing the situation from becoming worse.

Content Vectoring Protocol (CVP). Check Point FireWall-1 standard for sending packets to another server for application filtering.

Cookie. A small text string that the website owner can place on the client computer and retrieve later.

Corporate security policy statement. Statement from top management that is a broad vision of how security will be implemented.

Cost of repair. How much it would cost to restore an asset to its previous secure state.

Countermeasure. Technical or procedural measure taken to stop a threat.

Cracking. If hacking is viewed as simply innovative computer use, cracking is what the book defines as hacking. The term *cracking* also is used in the specific context of guessing passwords.

Crafted. Packets that are hand-built by an attacker or by an attack program.

Credentials. Things such as user names and passwords used in authentication.

Credit card number theft. The theft of credit card numbers in order to place orders fraudulently.

CRL (Certificate revocation list). List of the serial numbers of digital certificates revoked by a certificate authority.

Cryptanalyst. Professional who breaks encryption.

Cryptographic system. Product that automatically implements confidentiality, authentication, integrity, and other safeguards as a package; software processes that implement cryptographic security automatically, often without the awareness of the communicating parties; protocols that automatically provide confidentiality, authentication, message integrity, key exchange, and (usually) protection from replay attacks. These cryptographic systems work with little or no user intervention.

Cryptography. Originally "secret writing." A way of manipulating a message for confidentiality or for authentication and message integrity; the use of encryption to achieve security goals.

CSIRTs. Computer security incident response teams. Another name for computer emergency response teams.

CSO. *See* chief security officer.

Custodian. Someone to whom the owner delegates responsibility for the asset.

Customer fraud. In e-commerce, when attackers order goods and do not pay for them.

Customer premises. The land and buildings owned by an organization.

Cybercrime Treaty of 2001. Signatories of this Council of Europe treaty (which was heavily influenced by the United States) agree to create computer abuse laws and laws for copyright protection. The treaty also makes it easier for countries to work together to prosecute attackers in other countries.

Cyberterror. Attacks by nongovernmental groups that focus on a country's IT infrastructure and its physical infrastructure; in the latter case, attackers may use computers to assist in the physical attack.

Cyberwar. Attack in which a country's military makes a concerted attack upon another country's IT infrastructure, physical infrastructure, or both. A major goal of cyberwar is to do a massive amount of damage in a brief period of time, often in conjunction with a traditional physical military attack.

Daemon. In UNIX, program that runs autonomously.

Data Encryption Standard (DES). Widely used symmetric encryption method. Key length is 56 bits.

Data link. The path a frame takes from the source station to the destination station across zero or more switches within a single network.

Data link layer. Standards that govern the switching of a frame from the source station to the destination station across zero or more switches within a single network. Bits are organized into messages called frames.

Data Protection Directive. In the European Union, directive requiring member nations to create laws to protect personal privacy.

Database replication. When copies of critical databases are maintained in real time at a main facility and a backup site. The best form of site backup.

DCS1000. *See* Carnivore.

DDoS (Distributed DoS).   Denial-of-service attack that hits a victim with streams of messages from many compromised computers.

Decapsulation.   Removing a message from the data field of another message.

Decision criterion.   In biometrics, a minimum acceptable value for a match index.

Decryption.   Descrambling an encrypted message to make it readable. More formally, a mathematical process applied to ciphertext that produces plaintext for secure transmission.

Decryption key.   A bit string used with a decryption method to convert ciphertext into plaintext.

Decryption method.   A mathematical algorithm used in decryption.

Default.   A value provided automatically if the user or manager does not select a different one.

Defense Advanced Research Projects Agency (DARPA).   U.S. agency that created the Internet. Contrary to popular belief, Al Gore did not claim to have invented the Internet; he claimed to have been instrumental in its creation, which he certainly was through spearheading government funding for the Internet.

Defense in depth.   Exists when the attacker has to break through multiple countermeasures to succeed.

Demilitarized zone (DMZ).   An IP subnet that contains hosts and firewalls that must be accessed by external hosts.

Denial-of-service (DoS).   Attack in which the adversary renders a system unavailable to its users.

Deny.   Action by a firewall to prevent an arriving packet from continuing.

Deny All.   Last rule in most access control lists; drops any packet not explicitly passed by earlier rules.

Deployment.   Putting a program or host into service. In application software deployment, this is best done on development, staging, and production servers.

DES.   *See* data encryption standard.

Destination unreachable.   *See* ICMP destination unreachable.

Development server.   Server on which new applications are developed or existing applications are extended.

Dialog.   Bidirectional message exchanges between two parties.

Dictionary attacks.   Compare passwords to dictionary lists of common words.

Differential backup.   Archiving all files created or changed since the last full backup. Allows faster restoration than incremental backup, but each backup is slower.

Diffie-Hellman key agreement.   Method for having two sides agreeing securely on the symmetric session key they will use for confidentiality.

Digital certificate.   Document that gives the public key of the true party and other information.

Digital signature.   Small bit string added to a message to prove that the sender knows the true party's private key and therefore must be the true party.

Digital watermarking.   Adding information steganographically to identify an image.

Directory traversal attack.   Attack in which the attacker can retrieve files outside of the WWW root directory and its subdirectories.

Disaster.   A natural disaster or security incident so bad that business continuity itself is at risk.

Disaster recovery.   The technical and procedural aspects of how a company can get IT back into operation using backup facilities. More specific than business continuity planning.

Disconnection.   In incident response, breaking a server's connection to the local network or even disconnecting the site's Internet connection. Radical containment mechanism requiring authorization.

Discounted cash flow analysis.   Way of computing current value or internal rate of return of benefits and costs taking place over multiple future years.

Discovery process.   In e-mail, legal requirement during a lawsuit or governmental investigation to provide copies of all messages relevant to proceedings.

Distributed DoS (DDoS).   Denial-of-service attack that hits a victim with streams of messages from many compromised computers.

Distributed firewall architecture.   Firewall architecture for a firm with multiple sites; allows central management.

Distributed IDS.   Intrusion detection system that can collect data from many devices at a central manager console (client PC or UNIX workstation).

Distribution. In LINUX, the LINUX kernel plus other programs taken primarily from the GNU project.

DMZ (demilitarized zone). An IP subnet that contains hosts and firewalls that must be accessed by external hosts.

Document format standards. At the application layer, standards that govern the formatting of documents so that the two parties can communicate meaningfully. *See* Document transfer standards.

Document transfer standards. At the application layer, standards that move documents from one application program on one computer to another application program on another computer. *See* Document format standards.

Domain controller. In Microsoft Windows Server, a server that administers computers and other resources within a domain. Other servers in the domain are member servers.

Domain. In directory services, a cluster of resources.

DoS (denial-of-service). Attack in which the adversary renders a system unavailable to its users.

Drive-by hacking. Hacking a wireless LAN from outside the customer premises.

Drop. Action, by a firewall, to prevent an arriving packet from continuing.

Due diligence. Investigating the implications of interorganizational systems closely before agreeing to them.

Dumpster diving. Digging through dry trash bins to find recording media that contain valuable information.

Dynamic port numbers. Another name for ephemeral port numbers.

Dynamic webpages. Webpages that change when they are retrieved, either in the client or the webserver.

EAP. *See* Extensible Authentication Protocol.

Eavesdropping. Listening to a conversation surreptitiously.

ECC (Elliptic Curve Cryptosystem). Public key encryption method that is particularly efficient for a public key encryption method.

Echelon. System to intercept communications worldwide; developed by the United States and other countries.

Echo. ICMP message that asks another host to reply.

Echo reply. Reply to a host that receives ICMP echo message.

E-commerce. Buying and selling on the Internet.

Edgar. Database of information about U.S. industries. Provided by the Securities and Exchange Commission.

EFS. *See* Encrypting File System.

Egress filtering. Stopping attack packets from going out of a site by filtering them out at a border firewall.

Electronic Communications Privacy Act of 1986 (ECPA). A broad act that prohibits, under Title 47, the interception of messages en route and after the message is received and stored.

Elevating privileges. Being able to do things that should be possible only if a user has higher access permissions than their account was assigned.

Elliptic Curve Cryptosystem (ECC). Public key encryption method that is particularly efficient for a public key encryption method.

Employee workplace monitoring. The monitoring of employee websurfing, e-mail, and other communications, as well as the examination of files on a person's office PC.

Encapsulating Security Payload (ESP). IPsec header that offers confidentiality, authentication, and message integrity.

Encapsulation. Placing a message in the data field of another message.

Encrypting File System (EFS). Windows system for encrypting files and working with encrypted files.

Encryption Control Protocol. PPP phase in which the details of how encryption will be performed are negotiated.

Encryption key. A bit string used with an encryption method to convert plaintext into ciphertext.

Encryption method. A mathematical algorithm used in encryption.

Encryption. Effectively "scrambles" messages so that the message looks like random strings of bits to eavesdroppers. More formally, a mathematical process applied to plaintext that produces ciphertext for secure transmission; the process of converting plaintext into ciphertext.

Enhanced Generic Routing Encapsulation (GRE). General method for encapsulating a message in an IP packet.

Enrollment. In biometrics, entering a user's biometric information in a database.

Entangled bits. Q-bits that will both decohere to the same value if acted upon by a random process.

Ephemeral port numbers. Random port numbers generated by a client to indicate a specific connection.

Error advisement. Type of message that tells a sender that an error has occurred. This is not followed by a retransmission, so no error correction takes place.

Escalation. The act of declaring an incident or apparent incident to be more severe than previously thought; may trigger certain actions.

ESP (Encapsulating Security Payload). IPsec header that offers confidentiality, authentication, and message integrity.

Espionage. Penetrating a company to learn information useful to the spy's employer.

Ethical hacking. Hacking according to a hacker code of ethics. Still illegal unless authorized by the target.

Event correlation. The analysis of simultaneous and sequential events from many IDSs across the network.

Event Viewer. Systems event logging program in Windows 2000.

Exception handling. Sometimes, exceptions to security practices are needed. These must be carefully documented with clear accountability assigned for the exception.

Exchange. Popular mail server software from Microsoft.

Executable files. Program files, such as those with the .exe extension.

Execute. In UNIX, the ability to execute a program file.

Exhaustive search. Process in which interceptors try all possible keys to see which one will decrypt the ciphertext.

Exploit. Noun: Attacker tool (usually a program) for exploiting a known weakness. Verb: To take advantage of a known vulnerability to attack a system.

Extensible Authentication Protocol (EAP). Open-ended PPP authentication protocol that allows users to select a specific authentication protocol from a list of options. Used in 802.1x authentication.

External auditing tools. Auditing tools that run on a different machine than the machine being audited.

External DNS server. DNS server in a DMZ that only provides information about hosts in the DMZ.

Extortion. Threatening to divulge sensitive information or do damage if a company does not pay the extortionist.

Face scanning. Biometric access method that compares information from a scanned image of a face with that of a stored photograph. Can be used for surreptitious scanning.

Fair Credit Billing Act of 1974 (amended 1986). Among other things, governs credit card services; specifically limits consumer liability to $50 in case of fraud.

False acceptance rate (FAR). The percentage of applicants who should be rejected but who are accepted.

False alarm. Apparent security incident that turns out to be innocent activity.

False negative. When an event takes place that is not detected; dangerous.

False positive. Another name for false alarm.

False rejection rate (FRR). The percentage of applicants who should be admitted but who are rejected.

FAR (false acceptance rate). The percentage of applicants who should be rejected but who are accepted.

Federal Trade Commission (FTC). U.S. regulatory agency that enforces adherence to privacy disclosure statements.

Federal Wiretap Act. U.S. law that permits domestic telephone wiretaps under specified circumstances.

Field. Subpart of a header or trailer; or, the data field.

File integrity checkers. Programs that create message digests of all system files that are likely to be changed rarely or never. They can check this database periodically against newly generated message digests after an attack to determine whether any changes have been made.

File-infector viruses. Viruses that attach themselves to program files as additional instructions and to data files as macros.

FIN. In TCP, a message that requests the closing of a connection; the FIN bit is set.

Fingerprint recognition. Biometric access technology based on patterns on one or more fingers. Inexpensive but least secure form of biometric analysis.

Fingerprinting. Identifying the manufacturer and version number of a program running on a prospective victim host. Done because most exploits are product specific.

Firewall. Device that examines every packet that arrives or leaves, permitting the packet to pass or dropping it (and storing it in a log file).

Firewall appliances. Closed boxes that you simply plug into your router at one end and into your network at the other end.

Firewall architecture. A firm's plan for selecting and organizing its firewalls.

FireWall-1. Main firewall product of Check Point.

FISA (Foreign Intelligence Surveillance Act). U.S. law that permits domestic telephone wiretaps for agents of foreign governments and terrorist groups.

Fix. A way to protect against vulnerability. Includes patches, work-arounds, and updates.

Flag. One-bit field that is either set (1) or not set (0).

Flash viruses. Viruses that spread so rapidly that antivirus firms cannot update their antivirus protections before widespread infection has occurred.

Flooding DoS attacks. Denial-of-service attacks that overwhelm the victim computer with a stream of messages.

Flow control. Asking a host to transmit more slowly or pause its transmission.

Follow-up report. Report presented several months after an audit, in order to document which of the actions listed in the needed remedies report have been implemented or not implemented.

Foreign Intelligence Surveillance Act (FISA). U.S. law that permits domestic telephone wiretaps for agents of foreign governments and terrorist groups.

Forensics. The application of science to legal problems.

Fourth Amendment. Part of the U.S. Constitution that protects people against unreasonable searches and seizures and that requires probable cause to undertake searches and the limiting of searches.

Four-way close. The normal connection closing in TCP; usually requires an exchange of four messages.

Fragment offset. IP header values used in the reassembly of fragmented IP packets. Fragments are placed in order in increasing value of the fragment offset field.

Fragmentation. Dividing an IP packet into smaller packets if necessary to pass through a subnet.

Frame. Message at the data link layer.

FreeBSD. Free version of UNIX.

FRR (false rejection rate). The percentage of applicants who should be admitted but who are rejected.

FTC (Federal Trade Commission). U.S. regulatory agency that enforces adherence to privacy disclosure statements.

Full backup. Archiving all files on a computer.

Full protocol decoding. Analysis method in which the NIDS keeps track of where an application is in its life cycle. Only attacks appropriate for that phase are considered.

GCOS. In UNIX, a field in the password file that contains humanly readable information about an account owner.

GET. In HTTP and FTP, a command that requests a file download.

GLBA (Gramm-Leach-Bliley Act). U.S. law that protects the privacy of customer information in financial institutions.

GNU. Project to develop open-source software for UNIX.

GPO. *See* group policy object.

Gramm-Leach-Bliley Act (GLBA). U.S. law that protects the privacy of customer information in financial institutions.

Granularity of access. In databases, how much detail a user is allowed to see. May only be able to see information for certain entities and then only certain records and only certain fields (attributes) within these records. May only be able to see summaries instead of actual data.

Grey hat hackers.   Do both white hat and black hat hacking at different times.

Group ID (GID).   In UNIX, a numerical value in the password file that specifies a specific group.

Group policy object (GPO).   In Microsoft Active Directory, a set of rules for managing a certain type of resource within a domain.

Guest.   Windows account that can be used before logging in. Should be disabled.

Guidelines.   Discretionary prescriptions that must be considered but do not have to be followed if there is a valid reason not to follow them.

Hacker code of ethics.   Statement by hackers about how they will limit damage. Ethical hacking is still illegal.

Hacker vulnerability testing tools.   Tools that attackers use to gather information about target networks and target hosts and to identify unpatched vulnerabilities.

Hacking.   Intentionally accessing (using) a computer without authorization or beyond authorized permission.

Hacking root.   Hacking the root account in UNIX; sometimes hacking the super account in any operating system.

Hacktivism.   Politically motivated hacking attacks by unorganized or loosely organized groups.

Hand geometry scanning.   Biometric access method based on finger lengths, finger widths, palm widths, and similar characteristics.

Handler.   In a distributed denial-of-service attack, one of several compromised computers that relay attack commands to zombie computers.

Hand-shaking stages.   In cryptographic system, initial stages that involve the negotiation of security methods and options, authentication, and key exchange.

Harden.   Taking a series of actions that make a client PC or a server more difficult to exploit.

Hardening.   A series of actions corporations should take to make their hosts more difficult to attack.

Hash.   The output of a hashing operation.

Hashed Message Authentication Code.   *See* Key-Hashed Message Authentication Code.

Hashing.   A mathematical process that, when applied to a bit string of any length, produces a value of a fixed length called the *hash*. Hashes are one-way functions.

Header.   In e-mail, one of two main parts of an e-mail message. Contains a number of searchable fields, including To: and From:; the part of a message that comes before the data field.

Header checksum.   IP header field that contains a value that allows the receiving process to check for errors in the header.

Header destruction.   Application firewall protection; deletion of all information in lower-layer message headers; prevents attacks using these headers.

Header length.   A header field that tells the length of the header (not of the total message).

Health Information Portability and Accountability Act (HIPAA).   U.S. law that protects the privacy of customers of medical services.

Hexadecimal directory traversal attack.   Directory traversal attack in which the data are presented in hexadecimal (base 16) format to avoid directory traversal attack data screening.

Hierarchical.   1. In addressing, having an address that consists of successively smaller location indicators, such as country, city, zone, street, and number in postal delivery. 2. In switching, having a root switch and successive lower-layer switches with child switches.

HIPAA (Health Information Portability and Accountability Act).   U.S. law that protects the privacy of customers of medical services.

HMAC.   *See* Key-Hashed Message Authentication Code.

Home page.   Initial page when you go to a website; most likely target of hacker defacement.

Homeland Security Act of 2002.   Act that further defined illegal actions under Section 1030 of Title 18 of the U.S. Code, focusing on terrorist computer attacks.

Host assessment tools.   Auditing tools that run on the machine being audited.

Host firewall. Firewall software installed on a client or server host to protect that particular host.

Host IDS. Intrusion detection system that works on data collected on a host computer. The three types of host IDS are protocol stack monitors, operating system monitors, and application monitors.

Host part. Part of an IP address that designates a specific host on a specific subnet within a single network on the Internet.

Hosting companies. Firms that run computers, maintain them, and troubleshoot them at their own sites. This type of outsourcing will still work if the firm using the hosting facility is hit by natural disaster. Hosting companies also need disaster plans.

Hot site. Backup facility that can be switched to rapidly.

HTML (Hypertext Markup Language). Language for creating webpages on the World Wide Web.

HTML body parts. E-mail body formatted in HTML. Can contain tags for text fonts, graphics, and general multimedia elements. Can also contain malicious executable code and links to unwanted sites.

HTTP (Hypertext Transfer Protocol). Standard for requesting file transfers on the World Wide Web.

HTTP proxy server. Application server that filters HTTP traffic.

Https. Keyword in URL when using SSL/TLS.

Hybrid attacks. Password-guessing attacks that try simple modifications of common word passwords, such as placing a digit at the end (hello2).

Hybrid TCP/IP-OSI architecture. De facto standards architecture using OSI at the physical and data link layers and TCP/IP standards at the internet, transport, and (usually) application layers.

Hypertext Markup Language (HTML). Language for creating webpages on the World Wide Web.

Hypertext Transfer Protocol (HTTP). Standard for requesting file transfers on the World Wide Web.

ICMP (Internet Control Message Protocol). TCP/IP standard for internet layer supervisory information.

ICMP code. ICMP header field that identifies the specific kind of ICMP message being sent within an ICMP type.

ICMP control messages. ICMP messages that control the operation of a host or router.

ICMP destination unreachable. ICMP error advisement message, usually sent by a router, to tell the sender of an IP packet that the packet could not be delivered to the destination IP address in the packet.

ICMP echo. *See* Echo.

ICMP redirect. ICMP message that tells a host or router to send packets to a particular destination IP address to a different router in the future.

ICMP source quench. ICMP control message that asks a host to transmit more slowly.

ICMP time exceeded. ICMP error advisement message, usually sent by a router, to tell the sender of an IP packet that the packet could not be delivered because its time-to-live field had been decremented to zero and so had been discarded.

ICMP type. ICMP header field that identifies the general kind of ICMP message being sent.

IDEA. Symmetric encryption method that uses 128–bit keys.

Identification. 1. In authentication, used to determine the identity of a person by comparing their credentials against all users in an authentication database. *See* Verification. 2. IP header value used in the reassembly of fragmented IP packets. All fragments from the same original have the same identification field value.

Identity badge. Badge that contains identifying information for its user.

Identity card. Card that contains identifying information for its user.

Identity management. Services that store information about consumers centrally and allow the consumer to release information selectively to merchants.

Identity theft. The thief collects extensive information about the victim. Using this information, the thief creates fake corporations, opens lines of credit, buys a car, or engages in other actions to exploit the victim's credit.

IDS. *See* intrusion detection system.

IETF (Internet Engineering Task Force). The standards-making body for the Internet.

IIS. *See* Internet Information Server.

IKE. *See* Internet Key Exchange.

IM. *See* instant messaging.

IMAP. *See* Internet Message Access Protocol.

Imposter. Someone who claims to be someone else.

In the clear. Sent without encryption for confidentiality.

Incident. An event in which security is breached successfully by an attacker.

Incident analysis. After a potential security incident has been reported, determining if it is real and how severe it is.

Incident severity. How damaging a security incident is.

Incremental backup. Archiving all files created or changed since the full or incremental backup (whichever came last). Allows faster backup than differential backup, but restores are slower because they involve more tapes.

Inetd. UNIX daemon for starting program when client requests are received.

Inetd.config. Configuration file for inetd.

Information warfare. Another name for cyberwar. Attacks by governments that focus on a country's IT infrastructure and its physical infrastructure; in the latter case, attackers may use computers to assist in the physical attack.

Ingress filtering. Stopping attack packets from coming into a site by filtering them out at a border firewall.

Initial authentication stage. In cryptographic system, initial stage in which one side is authenticated or both sides are authenticated.

Initial negotiation. In cryptographic system, initial stage that involves the negotiation of security methods and options.

Initiation. In incident response, the initial reporting of a security incident.

Installation. The process of getting a device or program ready to use. Includes physical installation and configuration.

Instant messaging (IM). Communication application that alerts users when certain people are online and are open to chat. People can type messages back and forth and even exchange files. Dangerous because messages may not be retained as required by law and because may contain message content that is forbidden. File transfer usually takes place outside of ordinary antivirus protection systems.

Insurance. Arrangement in which an insurance company charges an annual premium, in return for which it will pay for damages if a threat materializes.

Integrated log. Log that aggregates data from many logs around the network for any given moment.

Intellectual property. Proprietary corporate information that should not be divulged outside the firm. Increasingly used for copyrighted material.

Intelligence. Information about enemy intentions and troop dispositions.

Interior doors. Doors inside a building. Access through these doors may be controlled.

Internal auditing. Corporate function that is not specifically IT-focused but that is responsible for auditing all departments to ensure that their business processes are consistent with corporate policies and best practices. Can be used to audit security processes.

Internal firewall. Firewall within a site that filters traffic traveling between different IP subnets within a site.

International Organization for Standardization (ISO). One of the two standards agencies for OSI.

International Standards Organization. The correct name is the International Organization for Standardization.

International Telecommunications Union–Telecommunications Standards Sector (ITU-T). One of the two standards agencies for OSI.

Internet Control Message Protocol (ICMP). TCP/IP standard for internet layer supervisory information.

Internet Engineering Task Force (IETF). The standards-making body for the Internet.

Internet Information Server (IIS). The webserver application program that comes with Microsoft Windows Server.

Internet Key Exchange (IKE). Although its name suggests that IKE does only key exchange, it is a general method to handle all of the steps needed to establish a secure dialogue. IPsec creates security associations within IKE-protected dialogues.

Internet layer. Standards that govern the routing of a packet from the source host to the destination host within an internet, across multiple networks connected by routers.

Internet Message Access Protocol (IMAP). Sophisticated protocol for clients to download incoming messages from their mail servers.

Internet Official Protocol Standards. List of IETF RFCs that are approved standards.

Internet Protocol (IP). TCP/IP protocol for delivering packets at the Internet layer.

Internet Server Application Programming Interface (ISAPI). Server-side programming language widely used on Microsoft Windows Server webservers for high-volume applications.

Internet use policy. *See* Computer and Internet use policy.

Internet. The global internetwork.

Internets. Several individual networks connected by routers. *Internet* is capitalized to refer to the worldwide Internet.

Internetwork Operating System (IOS). Operating system for Cisco routers and some switches.

Interorganizational systems. Systems created to automate communication and data exchange between different firms.

Intranet. Private internet within a corporation—uses TCP/IP standards.

Intrusion detection system (IDS). A device that warns administrators if it detects a possible attack underway. Also collects data on suspicious packets for subsequent analysis. Sometimes takes action on its own to stop an attack; software and sometimes hardware that captures network and host activity data in event logs and provides automatic tools to generate alarms, and query and reporting tools to help administrators analyze the data interactively during and after an incident.

IOS (Internetwork Operating System). Operating system for Cisco routers and some switches.

IP (Internet Protocol). TCP/IP protocol for delivering packets at the Internet layer.

IP address hiding. In NAT and application firewalls, the ability to hide internal IP addresses from sniffers on the external network.

IP address spoofing. Replacing the sender's source IP address with another IP address.

IP security (IPsec). Internet-layer VPN protocol that offers transparent protection to internet-layer and higher-layer protocols.

IPsec (IP security). Internet-layer VPN protocol that offers transparent protection to internet-layer and higher-layer protocols.

IPsec gatekeeper. Server at site that creates tunnel mode connections to IPsec gatekeepers at other sites.

IPsec header. Header inserted after the main IP header to give protection to the packet.

Iris scanning. Biometric access method based on patterns in the iris in the front of the eye. Most expensive but most secure form of biometric analysis.

ISAPI. *See* Internet Server Application Programming Interface.

ISO. *See* International Organization for Standardization.

IT auditing. Corporate function that looks at whether the IT department is functioning as it should. Can be used to implement security audits.

IT infrastructure. A firm's or country's networks, computers, databases, and other IT resources.

ITU–T (International Telecommunications Union–Telecommunications Standards Sector). One of the two standards agencies for OSI.

Java. Popular programming language for creating small programs, called applets, that can be executed on a webpage.

Javascript. Popular scripting language. Javascript is not Java.

Journaling. Backing up each transaction as it occurs into a journal file.

Kerberos. Authentication system based on symmetric key encryption.

Kerberos authentication service. Kerberos service provided to computer when the computer first authenticates itself to the Kerberos server.

Kerberos server. A server that authenticates users and provides keys and tickets for service.

Key distribution center.   In Kerberos, a server that authenticates users and provides keys and tickets for service.

Key escrow.   Process in which a copy of the decryption key is stored on the computer of a trusted party so that files still can be decrypted if the encryption key is lost.

Key exchange.   The secure exchange of secret symmetric keys.

Key features.   In biometrics, a small amount of data derived from a scan.

Key length.   Number of bits in the key. Each additional bit doubles the time needed for exhaustive search.

Key ring.   In PGP, a group of public keys for people you trust.

Key-Hashed Message Authentication Code (HMAC).   Message-by-message authentication method that uses a shared secret (key) and hashing to create the HMAC to be added to each outgoing message. No encryption is done to create the HMAC.

Keystroke capture program.   Program that captures users' keystrokes as they type in order to get encryption keys, passwords, and other information; victimization software that allows the attacker to record encryption keys and other important information.

Keystroke recognition.   Biometric access method based on distinctive rhythms in the timing between keystrokes for certain pairs of characters.

Kiddie script.   Attack script written for use by nonskilled hackers.

Kill.   Command to stop a running process in UNIX.

Known vulnerability.   Software security weakness that has been widely reported.

L2TP.   *See* Layer 2 Tunneling Protocol.

Lamer.   Term of derision used by hackers to refer to hackers with poor skills.

LAN (Local Area Network).   Customer premises network limited to computers in an office, a building, or a campus.

LAN Manager.   Early Microsoft network operating system; had poor password security.

LAND attack.   Single message denial-of-service attack in which the attacker sends a packet with the target host's IP address in *both* the source and destination IP address fields. The source and destination port number are also those of the victim.

LANMAN.   Microsoft LAN Manager network operating system.

Latent fingerprint.   Fingerprint left on a glass or other surface.

Layer 2 Tunneling Protocol (L2TP).   PPP tunneling protocol that delivers PPP frames across an Internet (tunneling). Unlike PPTP, does not provide security in addition to tunneling.

Learning aids.   Tutorials and examples that come with a program. Can be used by attackers so they should be deleted unless needed.

Legacy security technology.   Security technology already in place. May be less than optimal.

Liberty Alliance.   Industry group that is creating identity management services.

Likelihood of a threat.   The probability that a threat will occur and how often it is likely to occur.

Link Control Protocol.   In PPP, the stage in which the data link operation is negotiated.

LINUX distribution.   The LINUX kernel plus other programs taken primarily from the GNU project.

LINUX.   Family of UNIX operating systems for personal computers.

Live testing.   Process testing in which all employees go through their procedures for disaster recovery step by step, using actual equipment.

Local Area Network (LAN).   Customer premises network limited to computers in an office, a building, or a campus.

Local Users and Groups.   In Windows, snap-in for managing user accounts and group membership.

Lock down.   Mode in which changes cannot be made easily.

Log entry.   Event entry in a log file. Each event has a *time stamp* and an *event type*. Beyond that, log files may have other information to help diagnose the event.

Logging.   The recording of essential information about events.

Logic bomb.   Program that does damage when a certain event occurs.

Login password.   A password you type when you log in. In consumer versions of Windows, can be bypassed with Escape; offers no security. In professional and server versions of Windows, the login password does offer security. Also offers security in UNIX.

Ls. In UNIX, the ls command lists the files and subdirectories in a directory.

MAC (Media Access Control). Data link layer sublayer in 802 standards that controls when stations may transmit.

Macros. Set of operations embedded in a document; executed by the document's program when some action is taken, such as loading the file.

Magnetic stripe card. Access card that contains information on a magnetic stripe on the back of the card.

Mail host. Server that provides mail service to users. Accepts mail from client for delivery; stores messages until client can retrieve them.

Mail server antivirus program. Program that does antivirus filtering on the mail server, before e-mail reaches users.

Mail server. Server that provides mail service to users. Accepts mail from client for delivery; stores messages until client can retrieve them.

Mailbox. Folder on a mail host that stores messages until the client retrieves them. Sometimes also stores them afterward.

Main firewall. At a site with multiple firewalls, the firewall that does the main filtering for arriving and leaving packets.

Major incidents. Security incidents that affect multiple systems of moderate importance or one or a few systems of major importance.

Malicious links. Link on a webpage that downloads malicious code to execute or that takes the user to a malicious website.

Malicious payload. Virus or worm payload that is designed to do damage.

Malicious software (Malware). A general term for a variety of programs, including viruses, worms, remote-administration Trojans, and other forms of attack software that act autonomously or semiautonomously.

Malware (malicious software). A general term for a variety of programs, including viruses, worms, remote-administration Trojans, and other forms of attack software that act autonomously or semiautonomously. (*Mal* means "bad" in Latin.)

MAN (Metropolitan Area Network). Wide area network spanning a metropolitan area.

Managed security service provider (MSSP). Outsourcer that handles some or all of a firm's security functions.

Mandatory default algorithms. Security algorithms that must be available to communicating partners and that will be used if the partners do not specify another algorithm.

Mandatory vacations. Requiring people to take vacations so that misconduct can be revealed during their absence.

Man-in-the-middle attack. *See* attacker-in-the-middle attack.

Mask. In routing tables, bit string whose number of initial ones specifies the length of either the network part of an IP address or the network plus subnet parts.

Master key. In Kerberos, reusable key that the computer shares with the Kerberos server. Used in the Kerberos authentication service.

Match index. In biometrics, a computed value that determines the goodness of fit between key feature data from an access scan and the information stored in a template in a database.

MBSA. *See* Microsoft Baseline Security Analyzer.

MD5 CHAP. Challenge-response authentication method using MD-5 hashing.

MD5. Hashing algorithm that always produces a hash of 128 bits.

Media Access Control (MAC). Data link layer sublayer in 802 standards that controls when stations may transmit.

Member server. In a domain, a server that is not a domain controller.

Message digest. The output from hashing a long bit string.

Message integrity. The ability to tell if a message has been modified en route; the assurance that the receiver will be able to detect any changes made en route.

Metamorphic viruses. Viruses that try to radically change the way they appear— including by placing their code at several places within the body of the infected program.

Metropolitan Area Network (MAN). Wide area network spanning a metropolitan area.

Microsoft Baseline Security Analyzer (MBSA). MBSA scans one or more systems for a wide range of security weaknesses, including patches that need to be installed, insecure configuration practices, the running of unnecessary services, accounts without passwords or with extremely weak passwords (such as *password*), and many other weaknesses.

Microsoft Challenge-Handshake Authentication Protocol (MS-CHAP). PPP authentication protocol in which the response message is created by adding a shared password to the challenge message and then hashing the combination.

Microsoft Management Console (MMC). A specific Windows administrative tool or cluster of tools; MMCs have a standardized user interface.

Microsoft Point-to-Point Encryption (MPPE). Nonstandard encryption protocol widely used in PPP encryption for confidentiality.

MIME filtering. Filtering based on the MIME type of an application message. MIME is a general standard for describing file formats.

Minimizing security burdens. Minimizing the burdens of security on functional departments.

Minor incidents. Security breaches that affect only one or a few systems of modest importance.

Mission-critical. Capable of stopping the firm's operations, either temporarily or permanently.

MMC (Microsoft Management Console). A specific Windows administrative tool or cluster of tools; MMCs have a standardized user interface.

Mobile content. *See* active content.

More fragments. IP header values used in the reassembly of fragmented IP packets. All fragments except the last have the more fragments field set to one. The last has the value of zero.

MPPE. *See* Microsoft Point-to-Point Encryption.

Multilevel security. Military security system in which documents are classified by sensitivity. Different procedures are established for using documents of different sensitivity.

Multi-pronged attacks. The simultaneous implementation of multiple IT attacks, each using a different attack method, to maximize destruction and to confuse defenders.

NAT (network address translation). Firewall protection that prevents a site's internal IP addresses and port numbers from appearing in packets traveling over the Internet.

National Information Infrastructure Protection Act of 1996. Act that expanded on the definitions of computer crimes under Section 1030 of Title 18 of the U.S. Code.

NetBIOS. Mechanism used in early versions of Windows for peer-to-peer file sharing.

Netstat. Command that lists current user connections, including the two hosts that are communicating and the service they are using.

Network address translation (NAT). Firewall protection that prevents a site's internal IP addresses and port numbers from appearing in packets traveling over the Internet.

Network IDSs (NIDSs). IDSs that capture packets as they travel through a network for an analysis of attack signatures.

Network login key. In Kerberos, key that a station receives during the Kerberos authentication service. Station will use this key to communicate with the Kerberos server during this login session.

Network mask. In routing tables, a bit string whose number of initial ones specifies the size of the network part of an IP address.

Network monitoring tools. Tools that look outward from the host being studied, at arriving packets, for indications of external attacks.

Network part. Part of an IP address that specifies the host's network on the Internet. All hosts on a network have the same network part.

Network Time Protocol (NTP). Protocol for ensuring that the times of various computers are synchronized. Necessary to analyze integrated log files.

NIDS. Network (based) intrusion detection system.

Nimda. Sophisticated and rapidly spreading blended threat released in 2001.

No opt. Service in which consumers have no choice about how their information will be used.

Nonce. Randomly generated number created for a particular message; nonce is included in reply to prevent replay attacks. Only the first message with a nonce should be accepted.

Nonrepudiation. Means that senders cannot plausibly deny that they sent a message. Digital signatures provide nonrepudiation.

Notes. Popular mail server from IBM.

NT LAN Manager (NTLM). Password system in Windows NT; has stronger passwords than LAN manager.

NTLM (NT LAN Manager). Password system in Windows NT; has stronger passwords than LAN manager.

One-time password. Password that is used only once, in contrast to more common reusable passwords.

One-way function. A mathematical function that cannot be reversed to produce the input if you know the output. Hashing is an example.

Ongoing communication. In a cryptographic system, final stage after initial handshaking stages. Messages are exchanged with confidentiality and usually with message-by-message authentication and integrity.

OpenBSD. Free version of UNIX.

OpenPGP. Nonproprietary form of Pretty Good Privacy (PGP).

Operating system lockdown. Tool that prevents changes from being made to registry settings, prevents Trojans from being installed, prevents log files from being changed, and does many other similar things.

Operating system monitor. Type of host IDS that focuses on operating system events.

Opt in. When the user must agree explicitly to its collection with full knowledge of how the information will be used.

Opt out. Service in which customers must take specific actions to not have their data collected or used.

Options. In a header, fields beyond those normally used.

OSI (Reference Model of Open Systems Interconnection). Standards architecture managed by the ITU-T and ISO; dominates network standards at the physical and data link layers.

Outlook Express. Simple e-mail client from Microsoft. Has fewer vulnerabilities than Outlook.

Outlook. E-mail client from Microsoft; famous for its many vulnerabilities.

Outsourced antivirus protection. Antivirus filtering is done by an external company before e-mail ever reaches the target firm.

Owner. In UNIX, the creator or current owner of a file; person responsible for an asset.

P3P. *See* Platform for Privacy Preferences.

Packet inspection. Firewall filtering focuses on the contents of IP, TCP, UDP, and ICMP headers. The two types of packet inspection are static packet inspection and stateful inspection.

Packet. Message at the internet layer.

Palladium. Security chip and related software being developed by Microsoft.

PAP. *See* Password Authentication Protocol.

Pass phrase. A memorable phrase that is converted into a key.

Pass. Action by a firewall to allow an arriving packet to continue.

Passive fingerprinting. Identifying the manufacturer and version number of a program running on a prospective victim host by listening to traffic from that host.

Passport. Identity management service from Microsoft.

Passwd. In UNIX, file in the /etc directory that holds information about individual accounts.

Password Authentication Protocol (PAP). Form of PPP authentication in which user names and passwords are sent in the clear, without encryption for confidentiality.

Password reset. Changing an account's password to a new password if the user forgets the current password.

Password-cracking software. A program that automates the discovery of passwords.

PAT. *See* Port address translation.

Patch test system. Server used to test patches before deploying these patches to production servers.

Patch. Piece of software to fix a vulnerability.

Patriot Act of 2001. U.S. law that extended the Foreign Intelligence Surveillance Act by allowing roving wiretaps. Also extended trap and trace and pen register warrants to cover data traffic, and permitted ISPs to provide certain information without warrants.

Payload. Section of code that is executed some time after a virus or worm infects a new system. Takes actions on the victim system.

Pen registers.   When the telephone company receives a warrant to record the telephone numbers dialed by a subject's telephone or when a data carrier receives a warrant to record outgoing IP addresses, e-mail addresses, URLs, and other descriptive information. Actual communication content beyond this is not recorded, so legal requirements for pen register warrants are minimal.

Percent of disruption.   How completely an asset is disrupted by an attack.

Performance.   In firewalls, the ability to handle the volume of traffic likely to be generated.

Permissions.   Define what the user or group can do to files and subdirectories, if they can do anything at all.

Permit All.   Last statement in a screening firewall access control list, as opposed to Deny All on most firewall ACLs. Passes all packets not explicitly denied by earlier rules.

Personal Identification Number (PIN).   Short series of digits that must be pressed in the correct order for access.

Personal IDS.   Intrusion detection system that works on data collected on a user's client PC.

PGP (Pretty Good Privacy).   Popular cryptographic system for e-mail. Weak authentication through circles of trust paradigm.

Physical layer.   Standards layer that governs each connection between pairs of devices—a station and a switch, two switches, a switch and a router, or a station and a router. Governs media, connectors, and signaling.

Physical link.   A connection between pairs of devices—a station and a switch, two switches, a switch and a router, or a station and a router.

PID (Process ID).   Each running process in UNIX has a PID.

Piggybacking.   Following a legitimate person through a security door without being authenticated.

PIN.   *See* Personal Identification Number.

Ping (Packet INternet Groper).   Widely used program to send ICMP echo messages.

Ping scanning.   Sending ICMP echo messages to a range of IP addresses in order to identify possible victim hosts.

Ping-of-Death.   Single message denial-of-service attack that used a ping packet whose length was greater than 65,535 bytes.

PIX.   Main firewall product of Cisco.

PKI (Public key infrastructure).   The technology and management needed for a certificate authority to create public key/private key pairs, distribute private keys, issue digital certificates, and maintain certificate revocation lists.

Plaintext.   In confidentiality, a message to be protected by encryption.

Plan-protect-respond (PPR).   Security life cycle in which the firm first plans for security, then institutes protections, and then responds when protections break down. The cycle is endless.

Platform for Privacy Preferences (P3P).   Standardizes a set of rigidly defined questions for a website to answer and put in a database. Consumers with P3P-compliant browsers can query the website to see if its policies fit a profile with which they are comfortable.

Point-to-Point Protocol (PPP).   Data link layer protocol designed to operate over a point-to-point data link, such as a telephone circuit or a leased line.

Point-to-Point Tunneling Protocol (PPTP).   Protocol for carrying a PPP frame across an internet with multiple data links, with added security.

Policies.   Broad statements of vision that express a company's commitment to security and that lay out key values and principles that will guide corporate security activities.

Policy-based audits.   Audits based on policies designed to specify protections; ensure that the specific required protections are being provided.

POP (Post Office Protocol).   Most common standard for clients to download incoming messages from their mail host to their mail client.

Pop-behind ads.   Web advertisements that open a window behind the current window. This makes their source difficult to detect.

Port address translation (PAT).   The port-changing portion of NAT.

Port numbers.   In TCP and UDP, 16–bit header fields that specify the source and destination processes at the application layer.

Port scanning. Scanning a range of TCP port numbers, UDP port numbers, or both for a single host IP address in order to identify services running on the host.

Port spoofing. When an application uses a well-known or registered port number despite not being the service that normally uses that port number.

Port-switching application. Application that switches its TCP or UDP port during a connection or that creates a new connection with a different TCP or UDP port.

Post Office Protocol (POP). Most common standard for clients to download incoming messages from their mail host to their mail client.

POST. In HTTP, a command that requests a file upload. May be filtered out.

Postmortem analysis. Analysis conducted after an incident to determine what went right, what went wrong, and what should be done differently.

Power users. In Windows, a group is assigned greater permissions by default than the Administrators group but far more permissions than the Everyone group.

PPP (Point-to-Point Protocol). Data link layer protocol designed to operate over a point-to-point data link, such as a telephone circuit or a leased line.

PPS. Packets per second.

PPTP (Point-to-Point Tunneling Protocol). Protocol for carrying a PPP frame across an internet with multiple data links, with added security.

PPTP access concentrator. Server that remote access user dials into at his or her ISP access point. This access concentrator creates a secure connection to the RAS at the remote site.

Precision. When an IDS should report all attack events and reports no events that are not attack events.

Preserving evidence. Safeguarding of evidence needed to punish attackers.

Pretty Good Privacy (PGP). Popular cryptographic system for e-mail. Weak authentication through circles of trust paradigm.

Prime authentication problem. The problem of what proof a certificate authority should require before issuing a digital

certificate. This often is the weak link in the authentication process.

Principle of least permissions. States that each user should be given the minimum possible permissions to be able to do their work.

Privacy disclosure statements. Corporate statements about how they will use private information collected from online customers. Often available through the corporate website.

Private IP addresses. Ranges of IP addresses that should be used only within firms: 10.x.x.x, 192.168.x.x, and 172.16.x.x to 172.131.x.x.

Private key. In public key encryption, a key that only its owner should know.

Private network. A company's internal network.

Private port numbers. Another name for ephemeral port numbers.

Probable cause. Law enforcement agency must have good reason to suspect that a crime has occurred, is occurring, or is about to occur. Necessary for a search.

Probes. Messages sent to a target system to elicit responses for surveillance purposes.

Procedures. Prescriptions that specify the actual steps that must be taken by an employee. Procedures go beyond technology to include the actions that humans must take.

Process ID (PID). Each running process in UNIX has a PID.

Processing performance. The processing power needed to process packets at high network loads. An IDS without sufficient processing power will not examine all packets during peak periods.

Production server. Server on which an application is made available to users. Only production systems administration personnel should have access to this server.

Promiscuous mode. Mode of operation in which a NIDS reads all traffic passing through it.

Propaganda. The attempt to use messages to weaken the morale of the enemy's government, troops, and population.

Propagation vector. Mechanism that a virus or worm uses to travel from host to host.

Prosecution. Seeking criminal legal sanctions against an attacker.

Protected information. In HIPAA, information in any form (paper, electronic, or audio) that identifies a patient or customer of health care services.

Protocol enforcement. Application firewall protection; ensures that an application using a well-known port number actually is the application that should be using the port number.

Protocol field. In an IP header, the field that specifies the contents of the data field.

Protocol stack monitors. Type of host IDS that examine packets arriving at or leaving a host. Protocol stack monitors work like NIDSs but only look at packets coming into or going out of a single host.

Proxy. On an application firewall, a program that screens a particular application.

Proxy firewall. Another name for application firewall.

Ps. UNIX command to list running processes.

Public key encryption. Family of encryption methods in which each party has a public key that is not secret and a private key known only to the party.

Public key infrastructure (PKI). The technology and management needed for a certificate authority to create public key/private key pairs, distribute private keys, issue digital certificates, and maintain certificate revocation lists.

Public key. In public key encryption, a key that is given to other people without secrecy.

PUT. In FTP, command that transmits a file to an external device. Often blocked by application firewalls.

Q-bit (quantum bit). In quantum computing, a bit that is a zero and a one simultaneously.

QKD (quantum key distribution). Method of key distribution that can securely distribute keys and that can tell if the bits have been intercepted en route.

Qualitative threat analysis. Aspects of threat damage that are important but difficult or impossible to quantify.

Quantum bit (Q-bit). In quantum computing, a bit that is a zero and a one simultaneously.

Quantum computing. Computing in which each bit can represent a one and a zero simultaneously. These are called Q-bits.

Quantum key cracking. The ability to test many keys simultaneously by representing the key with Q-bits.

Quantum key distribution (QKD). Method of key distribution that can securely distribute keys and that can tell if the bits have been intercepted en route.

R Services. Set of dangerous UNIX services that allow access without logging in (r services).

RADIUS (Remote Authentication Dial-In User Service) Server. Central authentication server that remote access servers query to authenticate a remote user.

RAS (remote access server). Server that remote users connect to in order to be admitted to a site.

RAT. *See* remote administration Trojan.

Rc Scripts. In UNIX, rc scripts are executable scripts for starting and stopping programs when certain conditions (called run modes) appear.

RC4. Symmetric encryption method that uses 40–bit keys.

Read. In UNIX, the ability to read but not change files.

Realm. In Kerberos, a group of computers controlled by the same Kerberos server. In Disneyland, one of several theme areas.

Real-time backup. Backing up each transaction as it occurs onto another computer for immediate takeover if the main computer fails.

Real-time. In a distributed IDS, mode of operation in which the agent sends log entries immediately to the manager. Produces greater load on computers than batch-mode transfers, but attacker cannot only delete early IDS log file entries during an attack.

Re-authentication. In a cryptographic system, repeating the initial authentication stage occasionally during the ongoing communication stage.

Recommended practices. Prescriptive statements about what companies *should* do.

Recovery. In incident response, returning a system to proper operation.

Recovery agent. Key escrow agent in Windows.

Redirect. *See* ICMP redirect.

Reference Model of Open Systems Interconnection (OSI). Standards architecture managed by the ITU-T and ISO; dominates network standards at the physical and data link layers.

Registered port numbers. Port numbers that normally are used by applications less important than those to which well-known port numbers are assigned.

Rehearsal. Simulating a security process as realistically as possible to highlight weaknesses in plans and procedures.

Re-keying. In a cryptographic system, repeating the initial key exchange stage occasionally during the ongoing communication stage.

Reliable. A protocol that does error correction.

Remote access server (RAS). Server that remote users connect to in order to be admitted to a site.

Remote access VPNs. VPN created for giving a remote PC access to a network or to a particular server.

Remote access. Giving a remote PC access to a network or to a particular server.

Remote administration Trojans (RATs). Programs that allow the attacker to control all aspects of the victim computer remotely, almost as if the attacker were sitting at the keyboard.

Remote Authentication Dial-In User Service (RADIUS) Server. Central authentication server that remote access servers query to authenticate a remote user.

Repair. Undoing the damage caused by a successful virus attack or some other type of attack.

Replay attack. Attack in which an adversary intercepts an encrypted message and transmits it again later.

Repudiation. Means that senders deny that they sent a message. Feasible with HMAC message-by-message authentication because the receiver also could create the HMAC.

Request for comment (RFC). Document of the Internet Engineering Task Force.

Reset (RST). In TCP, a message that indicates the abrupt closing of a connection; the RST bit is set.

Response message. In challenge-response authentication, the message sent by the applicant in response to the challenge message.

Restore. Copying files from archival storage back onto the original computer.

Retention. In e-mail, policy-based practice for how long to keep archives of various types of messages. Retention may be required by law.

Retinal scanning. Biometric access method based on patterns in the retina in the back of the eye.

Return address. In a stack entry, the return address lists the RAM location of the next command to be executed after the stack entry is retrieved.

Return on investment (ROI). Method for calculating the value of security investments.

Reusable password. Password that the account user can use for weeks or months at a time. Most passwords are reusable passwords.

Revocation. The process of a certificate authority declaring a digital certificate invalid before the end of its valid period.

RFC (request for comment). Document of the Internet Engineering Task Force.

RFC 2822. Extended Internet standard for all-text (ASCII) e-mail messages.

RFC 822. Original Internet standard for all-text (ASCII) e-mail messages.

Risk acceptance. Implementing no countermeasures and absorbing any damages that result if a threat occurs.

Risk analysis. Comparing the probable cost of threats with those of protections; process by which firms weigh the costs of threats against the costs of defenses.

Risk reduction. Taking active countermeasures, such as installing firewalls and hardening hosts.

Risk transference. Having someone else absorb the risk, typically through insurance.

Rlogin. UNIX r service to log into a remote host without logging in.

ROI. *See* Return on investment.

Roles. Job positions responsible for carrying out specific activities. People are assigned to roles.

Rootkit. A set of programs designed for post-hack activities. Attackers download the rootkit to the target computer from their personal site (dangerous), from another computer they have compromised, or from a public site.

Rotation of duties. Having a person act in a particular role only for a limited period of time.

Route. The path a packet takes from the source host to the destination host within an internet, across multiple networks connected by routers.

Router NIDS. Network IDS built into a router. Can read all traffic passing through all ports on the router.

Roving wiretaps. Wiretaps that follow a subject across multiple communication connections. Not limited to a single telephone line, a single cellular telephone, and so forth.

RPM. Program widely used in LINUX to download patches and other programs.

RSA. Popular public key encryption method created by Rivest, Shamir, and Adleman.

Rsh. UNIX r service to start a shell on a remote host without logging in.

RST (Reset). In TCP, a message that indicates the abrupt closing of a connection; the RST bit is set.

Run mode. In UNIX, a group of numbers (or the letter s) that specify conditions such as start-up and shut-down.

RunAs. In Windows, this command will allow the systems administrator logged in as another account to give a single command with superuser privileges. Must give the administrator password.

RWX. The three permissions in UNIX—read, write, and execute.

S/MIME. *See* Secure MIME.

SA. *See* Security association.

Sabotage. Damaging a system to keep it from working.

Safe harbor. Set of privacy protections U.S. firms must agree to and uphold in order to be able to export private data from the European Union.

Scanning attacks. Obtaining information about a target system by sending messages and observing elicited responses.

Scanning. In biometrics, collecting user biometric authentication.

Scope of an asset. Number of functions affected by an asset.

Screen saver password. Password you must type to get rid of a screen saver.

Screening firewall. Border firewall with lightweight firewall filtering software.

Screening router. A router that screens out high-volume, simple attack packets. This reduces the work that must be done by the site's main firewall.

Script kiddie. Someone who uses an attack script created by someone else and who does not have the skills to hack independently.

Scripting language. Language in which a series of commands are written down to be executed in order. Simpler to use than full programming languages.

Scripts. Programs created for hackers to use to automate some aspects of hacking.

SEC. *See* Security and Exchange Commission.

Section 1030. Part of Title 18 of the U.S. Code that makes hacking, malware attacks, and denial-of-service attacks illegal.

Secure MIME (S/MIME). Cryptographic system primarily used in e-mail; generally requires a public key cryptosystem.

Secure Shell (SSH). Standard for remote login with security.

Secure Sockets Layer (SSL). Transport layer cryptographic system often used to protect HTTP traffic and sometimes used to protect SMTP traffic. Renamed Transport Layer Security by the IETF.

Securities and Exchange Commission (SEC). U.S. Agency that oversees financial services firms.

Security architecture. All of the technical countermeasures a company has in place—including firewalls, hardened hosts, IDSs, and other tools—and how these countermeasures are organized into a complete system of protection.

Security association (SA). Agreement about how two hosts or two IPsec gateways will provide security.

Security audits. When an attack team hired by the firm attempts to penetrate the system in order to identify security weaknesses.

Security awareness. Employee understanding of security needs and their roles.

Security baseline. Specific set of actions for making a program or computer secure.

Security breach. Successful attack.

Security center. Guard station for uniformed security personnel; contains TV monitors and feeds from other surveillance devices.

Security department. Department in a firm responsible for IT security. There may be a separate uniformed security department of physical security and employee dishonesty.

Security incident. An event in which security is breached successfully by an attacker.

Security patches. Pieces of code added to a program to remove a known vulnerability.

Security policies. Statements that specify at a broad level what should be done in terms of security.

Security through obscurity. The false belief that you are safe if you are not well known or have a poorly documented security system.

Security-Enhanced LINUX. Version of LINUX with strong security.

Self-defense training. Training in which the user is taught how to respond during an attack.

Sendmail. Popular mail server program on UNIX computers.

Sensitive personal information. Information that could harm an individual if revealed, such as credit card numbers, general financial information, medical information, television viewing habits, and political activity.

Separation of duties. Having different employees do different tasks so that collusion is necessary for misbehavior.

Separation of responsibilities. Having separate people who are responsible for implementing security and looking for security violations.

Sequence number. Field containing a value indicating the order in which a message was sent in a sequence of messages. Messages with duplicate sequence numbers should be rejected to thwart replay attacks.

Sequential processing. In access control lists, the processing of rules one at a time, in order, until a pass/deny decision is made.

Server room. Room where many servers are stored. Access to these rooms must be controlled.

Server-side programming. Program executed on the webserver; creates a page on the fly to be delivered to the browser.

Service Set Identifier (SSID). All wireless devices that work with an access point must know the access point's SSID value. Usually, the access point broadcasts its SSID periodically, and SSIDs usually are sent in the clear. Overall, SSIDs provide little protection.

Service ticket. In Kerberos, ticket that gives an applicant station access to a verifier station.

Services and Applications. Windows server snap-in for managing services and applications running on the server.

Session hijacking. Taking over an existing communication session (usually a TCP session) between two parties, so that the attacker can impersonate one of the parties.

Session key. Symmetric key used only during a single communication session. This limits the amount of input sent in encrypted form, making it difficult for cryptanalysts to break the key by analyzing the traffic.

Set. In flag fields, a value of 1.

SHA-1. Hashing algorithm that always produces a hash of 160 bits. Newer versions of SHA allow even longer hashes. SHA-192 and SHA-256 are named after their hash lengths.

Shadow password file. In UNIX, file in the /etc directory that holds encrypted password values from the passwd file.

Shared password. Single password that is used by several people for access; makes accountability meaningless.

Shared secret. A secret value shared by two communicating parties, for example an encryption key, a password, or a bit string to be added to plaintext before encryption or hashing.

Shell. In UNIX, a program that provides a user interface to the operating system. Sometimes used this way in Windows; user interface, especially in UNIX.

Shoulder surfing. Watching someone type passwords in order to get the password or part of it.

Shredding tools. Tools that delete e-mail messages *after* receipt.

Side effect. When a vulnerability assessment tool accidentally does damage.

Sieve. An IETF standard for the format spam-filtering rules; allows rules to be exchanged among users and vendors.

Signature. A pattern that identifies something or someone. In viruses, a pattern of bits that antivirus programs use to identify a virus.

Signature recognition. Biometric access method based on the timing and pressure of the signature writing process, as well as character shapes.

Signing. To encrypt with one's private key.

Simple Mail Transfer Protocol (SMTP). Main e-mail standard for sending messages from a client to the client's mail host and between two mail hosts.

Single points of vulnerability. Elements of the architecture where an attacker can do a great deal of damage by compromising a single system.

Single sign-on (SSO). An authentication system that allows a station to log in once and then get access to multiple servers in a system without further logins. Kerberos provides this.

Single-message break-in. Being able to hack a computer by sending a single message.

Site sharing. When two sites in a firm or different firms agree to act as backup facilities for each other.

Site-to-site VPNs. VPNs created to carry the protected traffic of many pairs of computers between two sites.

SMTP (Simple Mail Transfer Protocol). Main e-mail standard for sending messages from a client to the client's mail host and between two mail hosts.

SMTP relay proxy server. Application server that filters SMTP traffic and passes it on to a mail server.

Smurf. Flooding DoS attack that relies on routers that send broadcast messages to the computers they serve.

Snap-in. A specific tool added to a Microsoft Management Console.

Sniffer. Device placed in a portion of a network through which traffic passes; reads and saves important information from passing traffic.

Social engineering. Tricking an employee into giving out information or taking an action that reduces security or harms a system.

Socket. Notation consisting of an IP address, a colon, and a port number. Indicates a specific application process on a specific host. Example: 128.171.17.13:80.

SOCKS. Popular circuit firewall standard.

SOHO. Small office or home office.

Solaris. UNIX version for SUN workstations and workstation servers.

Source quench. *See* ICMP source quench.

Spam filtering. Filtering incoming e-mail messages to detect which are spam. Either deletes messages judged to be spam or places them in a special folder.

Spam. Unsolicited commercial e-mail. Spelled with all lowercase letters when used this way. If capitalized as Spam, refers to a Hormel meat product.

Special permissions. In Windows, a set of 13 detailed permissions that collectively give the six standard permissions.

Spy. Someone who penetrates a company to learn information useful to the spy's employer.

Spyware. Victimization programs that communicate with the attacker, sending back information from the compromised computer, including social security numbers, passwords, and other sensitive information.

SSH (Secure Shell). Standard for remote login with security.

SSID. *See* Service Set Identifier.

SSL (Secure Sockets Layer). Transport layer cryptographic system often used to protect HTTP traffic and sometimes used to protect SMTP traffic. Renamed Transport Layer Security by the IETF.

SSO (single sign-on). An authentication system that allows a station to log in once and then get access to multiple servers in a system without further logins. Kerberos provides this.

Stack entry. When a program must put one subprogram on hold to run another, it writes information about the suspended program in a stack entry.

Staging server. Server on which an application is tested before production deployment. Only testing personnel should have access to this server.

Stand-alone NIDS. Network IDS in a dedicated hardware box.

Standard permissions. In Windows, a set of six basic permissions.

Standards architecture. Layered framework for creating standards.

Standards. Prescriptions that are *mandatory*, meaning that employees subject to them—including managers—do not have the option of not following them.

State table. In a stateful inspection firewall, the table that maintains state information for existing connections.

State. The status of a connection; in the simplest case, whether the connection is open or closed.

Stateful firewall. Firewall that bases pass/deny decisions primarily on the state of the connection to which the packet belongs.

Stateful inspection. Firewall packet inspection technique that bases pass/deny decisions primarily on the state of the connection to which the packet belongs.

Static packet filtering. Firewall filtering method that looks only at values in selected fields of IP, TCP, UDP, and ICMP headers and only looks at individual packets in isolation.

Static webpages. Webpages that do not change when they are retrieved.

Statistical analysis. Examining frequency patterns in IDS data to detect attack patterns.

Steganography. Literally, hidden writing. Confidentiality message that hides information in images and other documents so that an eavesdropper will not even realize that information has been hidden.

Stream encryption. When a message is encrypted without first breaking it into blocks of fixed size.

Strong keys. Keys that are long enough for safety. For symmetric key encryption, strong keys are more than 100 bits. For RSA, a strong key is more than about 1,000 bits.

Su (switch user). In UNIX, the su command will allow the systems administrator logged in as an account other than root to give a single command with superuser privileges. Must give the root password.

Subject. In a digital certificate, the field that contains the name of the true party.

Subnet. Part of a larger network. In internets, a single network connected to other subnets by routers. All hosts on the same subnet have the same network and subnet parts for their IP addresses.

Subnet mask. In routing tables, bit string whose number of initial ones specifies the size of the network plus subnet parts of an IP address.

Subnet part. Part of an IP address that specifies the host's subnet on its network. All hosts on a subnet have the same network and subnet part.

Super account. Account that has the access privileges to do anything its owner wishes in any directory on the server.

Supplicant. In authentication, the side that tries to prove its identity to the other party. Also called the applicant.

Surreptitious scanning. Identifying someone without their knowledge.

Surveillance. Obtaining information about a target system by observing traffic, including elicited responses.

Switch NIDS. Network IDS built into a switch. Can read all traffic passing through all ports on the switch.

Symmetric key encryption. Family of encryption methods in which both sides encrypt and decrypt with the same key.

SYN Flooding DoS attacks. Denial-of-service attacks that overwhelm the victim computer with a stream of SYN TCP segments.

SYN. In TCP, a message that requests the opening of a connection; the SYN bit is set.

SYN/ACK. TCP segment in which the SYN and ACK bits are set. Indicates a positive response to a SYN message. If not sent in response to a previous SYN message, this is a probing attack designed to elicit a response indicating that the target's IP address is that of a live host.

Sys admin. Short for systems administrator.

Syslog. In UNIX, a program that sends log entries to various directories or even to other computers running the syslog program.

System. Another name for host.

Systematic monitoring. Sustained monitoring, in contrast to occasional monitoring.

Systems administration. Another name for host administration.

Systems administrator. Someone who manages a server.

Systems penetration. Another name for hacking.

Tar. In UNIX, the tar (tape archive) command creates an archive file for individual files, groups of files, or entire trees of directories and subdirectories.

Targeted attacks. Attacks that aim at a specific organization.

Target-of-opportunity attacks. Attacks that hit firms randomly, such as most virus attacks.

TCP (Transmission Control Protocol). Reliable transport layer protocol in TCP/IP.

TCP port scanning. Scanning a range of TCP port numbers for a single host IP address to identify services running on the host.

TCP segment. TCP message at the transport layer.

TCP/IP standards. Standards created for the Internet; now widely used in business above the data link layer.

TCP/IP-OSI architecture. De facto standards architecture using OSI at the physical and data link layers and TCP/IP standards at the internet, transport, and (usually) application layers.

Teardrop.   Single-message denial-of-service attack that created a series of packets that had the form of fragments; their lengths and fragment offset values were not consistent.

Telecommunications closet.   Room on each floor from which wiring emerges; typically has switches and other devices of interest to attackers.

Template.   In biometrics, information about an individual stored in a biometric database.

Temporal Key Integrity Protocol (TKIP).   Interim wireless security algorithm that changes encryption keys frequently.

Testing server.   Another name for staging server.

TFTP (Trivial File Transfer Protocol).   File transfer standard that is simpler than FTP and does not require a user name or password.

TGT.   *See* ticket granting ticket.

Threat enumeration.   The identification of all threats.

Threat severity.   The estimated cost of an attack—the cost of a successful attack times the probability of a successful attack.

Three-way open.   The normal connection opening in TCP; requires an exchange of three messages.

Threshold.   Frequency of events above which an alarm will be generated in an IDS.

Ticket granting ticket (TGT).   In Kerberos, a bit string that the Kerberos server sends to the station during the authentication service. The station must send the ticket-granting ticket to the Kerberos server in future requests.

Ticket-Granting Service.   In Kerberos, a service that allows a station to ask for an authenticated connection to a verifier station.

Time bomb.   Program that does damage at a preset time.

Time exceeded.   *See* ICMP time exceeded.

Time stamp.   Field containing the time when a message was sent. To prevent replay attacks, old messages should not be accepted.

Time-to-live (TTL).   In an IP header, the field that specifies how many more router hops a packet has before it should be discarded.

Title 18.   Section of the U.S. Code that defines multiple types of federal crimes, including computer hacking, denial-of-service attacks, and malware attacks.

Title 47.   Part of the U.S. Code that covers crimes dealing with electronic communications from telegraphy to networking.

TKIP.   *See* Temporal Key Integrity Protocol.

TLS (Transport Layer Security).   Cryptographic system at the transport layer. Formerly called secure sockets layer (SSL) security; transport layer cryptographic system often used to protect HTTP traffic and sometimes used to protect SMTP traffic. Formerly called SSL.

Token.   An access card or other small device that has a number that changes frequently and is visible on its screen.

Total length.   A header field that tells the length of the entire message.

Traceroute.   UNIX program that identifies the routers along the way to a destination host.

Tracert.   Windows program that identifies the routers along the way to a destination host. (*See* Traceroute for UNIX systems.)

Trade secrets.   Proprietary corporate information that should not be divulged outside the firm.

Trailer.   The part of a message that comes before the data field.

Translation table.   In NAT, a table that lists internal IP addresses and port numbers and stand-in IP addresses and port numbers.

Transmission Control Protocol (TCP).   Reliable transport layer protocol in TCP/IP.

Transparent protection.   Form of protection in which the process protected by a cryptographic system does not need to be changed from its normal way of operating.

Transport Layer Security (TLS).   Cryptographic system at the transport layer. Formerly called secure sockets layer (SSL) security; transport layer cryptographic system often used to protect HTTP traffic and sometimes used to protect SMTP traffic. Formerly called SSL.

Transport layer.   Standards layer that governs communication exchanges between the source and destination hosts.

Transport mode.   In IPsec, mode of operation that offers end-to-end security between the source and destination hosts.

Trap and trace.   Asking an ISP to collect and preserve information about an attacker's IP address; when the telephone company receives a warrant to record the telephone numbers that dial a subject's telephone or when a data carrier receives a warrant to record incoming IP addresses, e-mail addresses, and other descriptive information. Actual communication content beyond this is not recorded, so legal requirements for trap and trace warrants are minimal.

Tri-homed.   Router that connects to and passes packets between three subnets—an untrusted external network, a trusted internal network, and a demilitarized zone.

Triple DES (3DES).   Extension to DES in which each block is encrypted three times. If three keys are used, can give an effective 168–bit key length.

Tripwire.   In UNIX, a popular file integrity checker.

Trivial File Transfer Protocol (TFTP).   File transfer standard that is simpler than FTP and does not require a user name or password.

Trojan horse backdoor program.   Program that allows an attacker back in easily; disguised as a program with a different purpose. Often, a Trojanized system program, that is, a system program replaced with a Trojan of the same name and extension.

True party.   The person a message appears to be from.

TTL (time-to-live).   In an IP header, the field that specifies how many more router hops a packet has before it should be discarded.

TTLS.   *See* Tunneled TLS.

Tuning.   In an IDS, turning off unnecessary rules and reducing the severity level in the alarms generated by other rules.

Tunnel mode.   In IPsec, mode of operation that offers protection only between IPsec gateways at the two sites.

Tunneled TLS (TTLS).   Version of TLS used in the extensible authentication protocol; allows clients to use passwords for authentication.

Tunneling.   Carrying one message in the data field of another. In PPP, used in delivering a PPP frame across multiple data links in an internet, usually by encapsulating it in an end-to-end packet.

TV monitor.   Display for viewing closed-circuit television camera feeds.

Two windows attack.   Web attack that opens two windows on a browser and copies information from a window showing content on the computer to a window accessible to the outside world.

Two-factor authentication.   Using two methods to authenticate a person; one method usually is a password or PIN.

UDP datagram.   UDP message.

UDP port scanning.   Scanning a range of UDP port numbers for a single host IP address to identify services running on the host.

UID (User ID).   In UNIX, a numerical value in the passwd file that specifies an individual account.

Umask.   In UNIX, the umask command sets up default permissions for subsequent files.

UNICODE directory traversal attack.   Directory traversal attack in which the data are presented in UNICODE format to avoid directory traversal attack data screening.

Uniformed security personnel.   A firm's general (not IT) security personnel.

UNIX.   Family of operating systems used primarily on workstation servers but increasingly on PCs (primarily under the name LINUX).

Unnecessary services.   Programs that do not need to be running; may contain vulnerabilities so should be turned off.

Unreliable.   A protocol that does not do error correction. Unreliability is good for switches and routers because error correction is so expensive that doing error correction at each hop between switches or routers would greatly increase transmission cost.

Untrusted network.   Network whose traffic must be inspected carefully; for instance, the Internet.

Update.   Install a newer version of a piece of software; often fixes vulnerabilities in older versions.

Upgrade.   Install a newer version of a piece of software; often fixes vulnerabilities in older versions.

URL filtering. Application filtering based on the host name and perhaps other information in a URL.

Use policy. *See* computer and Internet use policy.

User Datagram Protocol (UDP). Unreliable transport layer protocol in TCP/IP.

User ID (UID). In UNIX, a numerical value in the passwd file that specifies an individual account.

Valid period. Time period before and after which the digital certificate is valid.

Value of protection. The cost of the threat severity minus the countermeasure cost.

VBscript. Popular scripting language based on Visual Basic.

Vendor diversity. Using multiple vendors to keep a firm safe because multiple vendors are not likely to have the same vulnerability and using a single dominant vendor is dangerous because of potential vendor failure.

Verification. In authentication, used when a user claims to be a specific person; there is a one-to-one comparison between the applicant and a single profile in the authentication database. *See* Identification.

Verifier. In authentication, the side that tries to authenticate the identity to the other party.

Victimization software. Program or programs installed by an attacker to continue taking action after an attack concludes.

Video recorder. Device used to record closed-circuit television images for later playback if questions arise or for evidence in legal prosecution or employee disciplining.

Virtual private network (VPN). Communication that uses the Internet for transmission but that adds security to the dialogues that take place over the nonsecure Internet; the use of the Internet with added security for protected dialogues.

Virus. A piece of code that attaches itself to a file (file-infector) or, infrequently, to a sensitive system sector of the victim computer's hard disk; malware that infects files and spreads when the file executes or is executed by another program.

Voice recognition. Biometric access method based on speaking.

Voluntary tunneling. When the remote user has the option whether or not to use tunneling.

VPN (virtual private network). Communication that uses the Internet for transmission but that adds security to the dialogues that take place over the nonsecure Internet.

Vulnerability assessment tools. Programs that attempt to find weaknesses in a firm's protection suite, giving the systems administrator an understanding of what work still needs to be done.

Vulnerability reporters. People who report vulnerabilities.

Vulnerability testing contract. Contract that specifies exactly which vulnerability tests will be performed by a tester. Any unauthorized tests could result in contract termination and perhaps even lawsuits and criminal prosecution against the testing firm.

Vulnerability testing. Testing in which vulnerability assessment tools are turned on the corporate network by authorized testers to find vulnerabilities.

Walkthroughs. Type of process testing in which people involved talk through each step in a process sequentially but do not take actual actions.

WAN (Wide Area Network). Network that links remote sites. Supplied by a carrier.

War driving. Driving through a city identifying wireless LANs with weak security.

War-fighting doctrine. Military methods of operation.

Warrant. Judicial permission to a law enforcement agency to make an arrest, conduct a search, or do other things.

Weak keys. Keys that are too short for safety. For symmetric key encryption, weak keys are less than 100 bits. For RSA, a weak key is one less than about 1,000 bits.

Web bug. Hyperlinks that are one pixel wide and tall and that are often in the same color as the background. Although the users cannot see them, the HTTP request message that they send automatically tells the webserver owners what page the user is reading.

Web service. A uniform way of accessing program objects on other computers.

Web-based e-mail. E-mail that uses HTTP for all communication with the webserver mail host, instead of SMTP and POP or IMAP. Can be accessed from any computer with a browser and Internet connection.

Webservice. The retrieval of files from a webserver.

Website defacement. Taking over a webserver and putting up a hacker-produced page instead of the normal homepage.

Well-known port numbers. Port numbers between 0 and 1023 that normally are used by well-known applications, such as HTTP and SMTP.

WEP (Wired equivalent privacy). Weak and vulnerable security standard for wireless LANs.

White hat hackers. 1. Hackers who break into corporate networks but tell network administrators or the vendor of the security system they compromised how they broke into the network and, preferably, how to prevent this attack in the future. Still illegal unless the hacked firm has given prior permission. 2. Hackers who attack only as part of approved auditing efforts.

Whois. Internet database containing information about owners of second-level domain names, such as pukanui.com.

Wide Area Network (WAN). Network that links remote sites. Supplied by a carrier.

Wi-Fi. Industry certification of 802.11 WLAN technology. Guarantees interoperability and a certain level of features.

Wired equivalent privacy (WEP). Weak and vulnerable security standard for wireless LANs.

Wireless Fidelity Alliance. Industry group responsible for certifying 802.11 WLAN equipment as Wi-Fi compliant, which guarantees interoperability and a certain level of features.

Wireless LAN (WLAN). Local area network that uses wireless transmission.

Wireless NIC. Network interface card that uses radio transmission instead of wire connections.

Wireless Protected Access (WPA). Protections required in future 802.11 WLANs by the Wireless Fidelity Alliance for Wi-Fi certification. Will require the phased implementation of TKIP, selected parts of 802.11i, and having security turned on as a default during installation.

Wiretap warrant. Judicial warrant to allow a wiretap. Requires a finding of probable cause and a finding that normal investigative procedures have been tried and failed. These are strong requirements.

WLAN (Wireless LAN). Local area network that uses wireless transmission.

Work-around. Series of manual steps to fix a vulnerability.

World Wide Web (WWW). The worldwide collection of HTTP servers on the Internet.

Worms. Autonomous attack programs that spread themselves to other computers without human intervention; these automated attack programs propagate on their own.

WPA. *See* Wireless Protected Access.

Write. In UNIX, the ability to create, change, and delete files.

WWW. *See* World Wide Web.

WWW root. Directory holding the top level of the webservice directory structure. Only files below this directory normally can be retrieved.

X. In UNIX, the abbreviation for the execute permission.

X.509. Standard for digital certificates. Version 3 is the most widely used.

Zombie. In distributed denial-of-service attacks, one of many compromised computers that attacks a victim.

Index